Foreign Direct Investment in Russia

Also by Paul Fischer

THE COMMONWEALTH OF INDEPENDENT STATES AND THE EUROPEAN UNION: Facts and Figures

OPTIMIZING RUSSIAN STATISTICS DURING TRANSITION, 1993–1997: Strategic Orientations for the Russian Government and Statistical Services

PROTECTION OF MINORITIES AND HUMAN RIGHTS: A Prerequisite for Peace and Stability in Post-Communist Europe

RETAILING IN THE SINGLE EUROPEAN MARKET

AUF SICHEREN WEGEN DEN US-MARKT ERSCHLIEßEN

Foreign Direct Investment in Russia

A Strategy for Industrial Recovery

Paul Fischer

First published in Great Britain 2000 by
MACMILLAN PRESS LTD
Houndmills, Basingstoke, Hampshire RG21 6XS and London
Companies and representatives throughout the world

A catalogue record for this book is available from the British Library.

ISBN 0–333–77483–3

First published in the United States of America 2000 by
ST. MARTIN'S PRESS, INC.,
Scholarly and Reference Division,
175 Fifth Avenue, New York, N.Y. 10010

ISBN 0–312–23055–9

Library of Congress Cataloging-in-Publication Data
Fischer, Paul.
Foreign direct investment in Russia : a strategy for industrial recovery / Paul Fischer
p. cm.
Includes bibliographical references and index.
ISBN 0–312–23055–9 (cloth)
1. Investments, Foreign—Russia (Federation) 2. Russia (Federation)—Economic conditions—1991– I. Title.

HG5580.2.A3 F574 2000
332.67'3'0947—dc21

99–049536

This book is printed on paper suitable for recycling and made from fully managed and sustained forest sources.

10 9 8 7 6 5 4 3 2 1
09 08 07 06 05 04 03 02 01 00

Printed and bound in Great Britain by
Antony Rowe Ltd, Chippenham, Wiltshire

To the people of Russia

Contents

List of Figures

List of Tables

List of Boxes

List of Maps

Foreword

The opening of Russia's economy has brought in new businesses, products and services; but most importantly, it has introduced new ideas and new management practices. It is this intercultural enrichment through an exchange of ideas that will have a lasting impact, as it will shape the human potential that will be the motor for socioeconomic development in our country.

We are convinced that Russia should, and can, take its destiny in its own hands. One positive effect of the crisis is that it has checked immoderate dependence on imports and given a chance to local industry. Interenterprise cooperation with foreign investors will accelerate the progress of Russian companies. Already, in what appears to be a win–win situation, those investors with a long-term commitment to Russia are gradually seeing the benefits of local production over exports.

I am proud that the Moscow State University of Economics, Statistics and Informatics (MESI) was given the opportunity to participate in the realization of this seminal work on foreign direct investment (FDI). I particularly thank the German government, whose financial and technical support enabled the establishment and development of ICA, the first investment-oriented consulting agency established by ministerial regulation in a Russian university.

Over the past three years, ICA has enhanced its human and technical capabilities, guided by the bilateral cooperative programme. Today, the ICA team conducts studies and advisory projects for the Ministry, national and foreign organizations, and potential investors. In return, these consultancy assignments yield useful material and ideas for the training programmes at MESI and, increasingly, other universities. All concerned – students, teaching staff, officials, young entrepreneurs and managers of companies and banks – learn and grow in the process.

The success of this pilot agency shows its relevance. I would welcome the idea of creating similar centers of excellence in other universities in Moscow and the regions. The network could then effectively serve as a think-tank for Russia's policy-makers and as a valuable support to a federal FDI agency for initiating and implementing investment-related projects.

I congratulate the author – who is the Strategic Advisor for the cooperative programme between Germany and Russia – for his commitment and contribution to the Russian effort and trust that the publication will receive the acceptance that it deserves.

Professor Alexander F. Kiselev
First Deputy Minister of Education
Russian Federation

Preface

In an increasingly interdependent world, when a country like Russia faces a crisis, its immense potential is lost to the global economy. The world needs Russia as much as Russia needs the world. Paradoxically, the current crisis has shown its own solution: revive the industrial sector to create a strong foundation for the real economy. Industry is the pillar for all other economic activities, and it makes the country less vulnerable to the whims of financial markets.

Germany has supported Russia's reforms by promoting concrete projects in the manufacturing, infrastructure, and energy sectors through its TRANSFORM programme. During his last two visits, Chancellor Schröder reiterated that targeted investments, rather than general financial assistance, would have a positive impact. It is along these lines that Germany will defend Russia's case with the European Union, the international funding agencies, and the WTO.

Official bodies such as KfW, CIM, GTZ, DEG, as well as the German Federation of Industry (BDI) and the Association of German Chambers of Industry and Commerce (DIHT) have played a pivotal role in promoting cooperation and foreign direct investment (FDI) in manufacturing. Today, Germany is Russia's first creditor and trading partner. It is also one of the largest investors in Russia, with a total accumulated FDI of about DM1.8 billion, which, however, accounts for only 0.3 per cent of German stock worldwide.

Russia's share in global FDI inflows hardly matches the potential that the country offers. Germany's *Mittelstand,* with its tens of thousands of companies, represents an immense untapped potential in capital, know-how, and technology. Many of these companies as well as those from other countries are waiting to expand their business to Russia. However, they need adequate assurance that their investments are safeguarded and that the Russian government is serious about integrating FDI. A far-sighted FDI policy, buttressed by strong institutions and accompanied by a clear commitment to the rule of law, would improve investors' confidence.

I am pleased to present this publication on FDI as a serious option for industrial revival in Russia. It is the result of years of study and analysis by the author in the framework of a bilateral programme sponsored by the German Ministry of International Cooperation (CIM–GTZ facility) and implemented in close cooperation with the Russian Ministry of Education (MESI–ICA).

I sincerely hope that it will be successful in its endeavour to inform and guide Russian policy-makers, scholars and businessmen in their efforts to ultimately create confidence in Russia as a promising investment destination.

Dr Ernst-Jörg von Studnitz
Ambassador of the Federal Republic of Germany to Russia

A Word from the Author

The decision to write this book was taken in 1995 when I was sent as advisor for enhancing investment and interenterprise cooperation as part of the TRANSFORM Programme[1] between Germany and Russia. I had observed during earlier missions (1993–95) on behalf of the European Commission (TACIS Programme) that foreign direct investment (FDI) could be a realistic option for reviving Russia's economy.

At that time, technical assistance by multilateral donors, although generous, was already showing little impact. General institution building and training programmes were useful in the early years of reforms; what is needed now is a strategy that involves foreign enterprises as suppliers of equity capital, processing technologies and know-how. Such a strategy would supplement current efforts towards macro-level structural adjustment based on neokeynesian and monetarist theories developed in a free-market context.

Policy-makers, academics and donors are slowly understanding that the only sustainable solution for overcoming Russia's persistent crisis hinges on industrial recovery. For this, Russia's manufacturing sector needs substantial capital and investments. But the state budget is insufficient and other sources of finance are not available. FDI could make the difference as seen by the success stories of China, India and Mexico. In these countries, pragmatic reforms at micro level led to an improvement of macroeconomic and financial indicators. By adopting an investor-friendly, strategic approach, the Russian government could acquire a much larger share of global FDI flows. Annually, transnational corporations (TNCs) invested close to US$450 billion worldwide during 1995–98 (US$650 in 1998). Russia received on average only US$2–3 billion – not even 1 per cent of global flows. Given Russia's potential, FDI inflows could easily be increased four to five times by 2005.

For the TNCs, an investor-friendly Russia offers a promising market, qualified professionals and a diversified raw materials base. There have been many success stories of TNCs in Russia, but they have not been publicized. There are opportunities for many more foreign companies. To succeed, new entrants will have to change their management attitudes. Like other large emerging markets (LEMs), Russia requires a long-term approach rather than strict adherence to the rule of immediate returns dictated by the 'shareholder value' imperative. Russian consumers, like those of other countries, will reward companies that have a long-term strategy and commitment, and are good corporate citizens.

It is in the interest of Germany and other creditor governments to cooperate with Russian authorities for promoting FDI. This will also help their own companies, both big and medium-sized, gain access to a practically undiscovered market. Contrary to common perceptions, outward investment to Russia helps expand business and therefore employment in the home country. Supporting Russia will be a positive-sum game where all parties will become winners. Prosperity in Russia will mean stability on the Eurasian continent. Reengineered factories and the introduction of less polluting technologies will reduce environmental risks that would have global repercussions. On their part, the Russian authorities will need to step up their efforts to gain investor confidence by rapidly improving framework conditions, opening joint stock companies to foreign investors and defining a clear FDI strategy.

Success in this endeavour will gradually reduce Russia's dependence on foreign loans and help its people regain confidence in themselves, their leaders and their country. Russia has all the assets – human and natural – to take its destiny in its own hands and achieve a Russian *chudo*.[2]

I would like to express my particular thanks to the German government for this unique opportunity to participate in its TRANSFORM Programme during this interesting period of change in Russia. I would also like to thank all my Russian colleagues at MESI and other specialists, who enabled me to gain an understanding of Russia's hidden potential. I am particularly grateful to Mira Shah for her indefatigable support with the English typescript.

Paul Fischer

Notes

1. The bilateral programme promotes private sector development and aims to facilitate Russia's transition to a market economy.
2. Russian word for 'miracle'.

List of Acronyms

APEC	Asia-Pacific Economic Cooperation
ASEAN	Association of Southeast Asian Nations
ASSOCHAM	All-India Association of Chambers of Commerce
BDI	Bundesverband der Deutschen Industrie, Germany
CCFI	Cabinet Committee on Foreign Investment, India
CII	Confederation of Indian Industry
CIM	Centrum für Internationale Migration, Germany
CIS	Commonwealth of Independent States
COMECON	Council of Mutual Economic Assistance
DEG	Deutsche Entwicklungsgesellschaft, Germany
DETDZ	Dalian Economic and Technological Development Zone, China
DIHT	Deutscher Industrie- und Handelstag, Germany
EBRD	European Bank for Reconstruction and Development
EMR	exclusive marketing rights, India
EOU	export-oriented units, India
EPZ	export processing zones, India
EU	European Union
FDI	foreign direct investment
FIC	Foreign Investment Commission, Mexico
FICCI	Federation of Indian Chambers of Commerce and Industry
FIG	financial–industrial groups, Russia
FIL	Foreign Investment Law, Russia
FIPB	Foreign Investment Promotion Board, India
FIPC	Foreign Investment Promotion Council, India
GATT	General Agreement on Tariffs and Trade
GEA	greater economic areas, Russia
GTZ	Gesellschaft für Technische Zusammenarbeit, Germany
HCI	Hellenic Centre for Investment, Greece
ICA	International Consultancy Agency, MESI, Russia
ICT	information and communication technology
IDA	Investment Development Agency, Ireland
IDP	investment development path
IFC	International Finance Corporation
IIC	India Investment Centre
IIM	Indian Institute of Management
IIT	Indian Institute of Technology
IMF	International Monetary Fund

INEGI	Instituto Nacional de Estadística, Geografía e Informática, Mexico
IPC	international product cycle
ISIC	International Standard Industrial Classification
KfW	Kreditanstalt für Wiederaufbau, Germany
LEM	large emerging market
MAI	Multilateral Agreement on Investment
MERCOSUR	Mercado Común del Sur
MESI	Moscow State University of Economics, Statistics and Informatics, Russia
MIBA	Moscow International Business Association, Russia
MIGA	Multilateral Investment Guarantee Agency
MITI	Ministry of International Trade and Industry, Japan
MOFTEC	Ministry of Foreign Trade and Economic Cooperation, China
NAFTA	North American Free Trade Association
NCAER	National Council for Applied Economic Research, India
NIC	newly industrialized country
NIP	New Industrial Policy, India
NOI	net outward investment
NRI	nonresident Indian
OCB	overseas corporate body, India
OECD	Organisation for Economic Co-operation and Development
OEM	original equipment manufacturer
OSCE	Organization for Security and Cooperation in Europe
PPP	purchasing power parity
PSU	public sector unit, India
RBI	Reserve Bank of India
SAARC	South Asian Association for Regional Cooperation
SBI	State Bank of India
SDZ	special development zone
SECOFI	Secretaria de Comercio y Fomento Industrial, Mexico
SEZ	special economic zones, China
SIA	Secretariat for Industrial Assistance, India
SME	small and medium-sized enterprises
SOE	state-owned enterprise, China
SPC	State Planning Commission, China
TNC	transnational corporation
TRIM	trade-related investment measure
TRIP	trade-related intellectual property
UN	United Nations
UNCTAD	United Nations Conference on Trade and Development
UNIDO	United Nations Industrial Development Organization
VTE	village and township enterprises, China
WTO	World Trade Organization

Introduction

Introduction: Background and Rationale of the Study

I FDI: a new challenge for Russia

The 1990s will be remembered as crucial years in the history of Russia and the world. They mark the first decade of peaceful coexistence between East and West after being separated by the Iron Curtain for almost one century. Following the events of 1990–91 which brought about German reunification, the opening of central European economies and, almost concomitantly, the demise of the Soviet Union and its communist regime, Russia has emerged as the central player of the newly formed Commonwealth of Independent States (CIS).

Russia remains, even after the disintegration of the Soviet empire, the largest territorial power and an industrial and military heavyweight in the world. Its land mass spreads over 17 million sq km, from central Europe across northern Asia up to the Bering Strait, which separates it from Alaska. It is the only country that is geostrategically located between the main industrialized economies of Europe, Asia and North America – the Triad economies. Russia has diverse and abundant natural resources, and long scientific, industrial and cultural traditions. It is the world's largest supplier of natural gas, minerals, precious metals and forest products and a major supplier of oil, coal, fertilizers and other raw materials. It has the potential to also become a major producer of food products, consumer goods, chemicals and plastics, and machinery, if increased investment leads to renovation and innovations in its industry.

Following the introduction of a free market system, Russia offers foreign operators access to a huge market of 150 million consumers, with another 140 million in the adjacent CIS countries. For European companies faced with saturated home markets, Russia offers an excellent opportunity to expand and gain leadership. The significance of Russia's rising potential as a business destination is reflected in the growing interest of western transnational corporations (TNCs).

But Russia also faces tremendous challenges, which, if not addressed effectively, could cause serious social and ethnic frictions across the entire territory. Russia's economic well-being and status as an industrial power will largely depend on the government's ability to alleviate the burden that the country's enterprises and population have inherited after 70 years of planned economy and closed borders. The abrupt freeing of the economy and disengagement of the State have made Russian industry lose its competitive edge in many sectors. Despite competent local management, most Russian enterprises have underperformed because they lack capital and still need to adapt to economic transition and international competition. The government must urgently address critical problem areas, which tend to fuse into a vicious spiral: record losses in industrial production due to changes in the economic system, new enterprise structures and disruption of intrasectoral ties; credit crunch, inflation, and lack of capital for new investments; low income levels and increasing unemployment; industrial pollution and environmental problems; regional tensions and separatist tendencies in border areas.

To overcome these difficulties, Russia's policy-makers will need to create a stable macroeconomic environment by checking inflation, supporting private sector development and generating financial resources. They should focus on raising the competitiveness of the country's factories, especially by fostering alliances between Russian and foreign companies. The success of policies oriented towards the industrial sector will determine whether the country will eventually regain its position in the top league of nations or lose the historical opportunity offered by global economic integration and be reduced to a peripheral player and raw materials supplier.

Revitalization of the real economy in modern Russia can be achieved through industrial restructuring, acquisition of state-of-the-art skills and technologies, and effective conversion of the military–industrial complex. These measures require farsighted macroeconomic and financial state guidance including the creation of solid banking structures,[1] but also massive domestic and foreign investment and capital generation programmes both at federal and regional levels. Industrial competitiveness requires capital generation through the country's own resources (owner equity financing, bank consortiums, leasing companies, venture capital from private entrepreneurs and financial organizations, state budget), international donor capital (EBRD, IMF, IFC–World Bank), and FDI by TNCs.

FDI can supplement and activate other forms of finance and offers a range of advantages over local capital and international donor funding:[2]

- FDI combines capital infusion with skill transfer, managerial input and mutually beneficial exchange of know-how (including ways to access world markets).

- Its multiplier effect can set a virtuous investment cycle in motion, which will produce a positive impact in manufacturing but also in other economic sectors (pull effect on agriculture, push effect on services).
- FDI could bring more competition[3] and help develop small and medium-sized enterprises (SMEs).
- If properly channelled, promoted and organized,[4] FDI can accelerate simultaneous development in key industries and the major regions.
- It contributes to overall socioeconomic stability and a reduction of economic crime by promoting productive investments in tangible assets (machinery, equipment, process technologies) as opposed to speculative and volatile portfolio investments in the financial markets, which can be withdrawn suddenly with disastrous effects on the entire economy.[5]
- FDI will further the reform process as it will raise the asset value of domestic enterprises and improve their financial capabilities, which was overlooked by the earlier schemes of mass privatizations through vouchers. This will have a positive impact on the banking system, which could provide project finance for investment operations.[6]
- Capital and know-how inflows through FDI benefit the real economy, stabilize employment and raise general income levels and tax revenues; they thus reduce dependence on international funding agencies by increasing the domestic savings capacity.[7]
- By building production capacity locally, FDI reduces barter, the 'dollarization' of the Russian economy, and chronic balance of payments problems which Russia is increasingly facing because of excessive imports of essential consumer and industrial goods.[8]
- Flight capital (about US$140 billion are apparently held by Russian citizens abroad in bank accounts or cash) and domestic savings[9] can be ploughed back into the Russian economy once confidence is reestablished.

Cooperation with leading western companies could give the necessary impetus for developing value-added exports, innovative product and process technologies, human resources, total quality and time management, customer orientation, and R&D. FDI-related cooperation based on know-how and technology for concrete industrial projects would be much more effective than general expert advice under international public assistance programmes. The establishment of modern industries would galvanize Russia's human, scientific and intellectual potential. FDI projects should be channelled into critical sectors, and their socioeconomic and environmental impact should be carefully monitored.

The governments of leading OECD countries should support Russia's efforts by establishing special bilateral investment agencies and offering fiscal incentives to TNCs for investments into Russia.[10] Western governments share a common responsibility for industrial modernization and enterprise restructuring in Russia. In a context of global interdependence, stability in Russia is of interest to all. Countries across the world, including industrialized and developing countries, have been affected by the loss of the Russian market following the breakup of the Soviet Union. They would all benefit from positive developments in Russia. The pull effect on CIS and Eastern European economies, which still have supplier and user links with Russia, would bring political stabilization to this troubled region. The environmental threat posed by Russia's polluting factories is an equally important reason for industrialized countries to assist Russia.

The opening of economies worldwide and the growing interest of TNCs in emerging markets are favourable to the restructuring of industry and raising of living standards in Russia. The former socialist economies of Central Europe have been comparatively swift in adapting to the changes; most countries have applied for full membership in the European Union (EU). China has opened up its economy to Russia, which has already led to increased cross-border trade and investment. India, Russia's traditional partner, has liberalized its economy and is developing new investment and trade relations with Russia. International organizations continue to press for worldwide liberalization of trade and financial markets; they are learning from the recent financial crises to institute tighter control on volatile capital and to fund more long-term projects in industry while promoting foreign investment protection and the rule of law. Russia should take advantage of all these factors to revitalize its economy and reengineer major industries.

II Need for a national programme for investments in industry

The manufacturing or industrial complex plays a crucial role in the economy of every nation. Social stability and technological progress are directly related to the performance of industry, and governments of industrialized nations undertake all possible efforts to stay in the vanguard of technological progress by enhancing the global competitiveness of their industries and enterprises. In developing and transition countries, public authorities also promote industrial diversification to reduce dependence on raw material exports and labour-intensive industries. International organizations have long been promoting programmes to support the industrial sector. Reports from the United Nations Industrial Development Organization (UNIDO) provide evidence of a statistical relationship between industrial development and both GDP and productivity growth.[11] There is a similar link between manufacturing output and exports, which in turn generate the necessary revenue and know-how for further strengthening the industrial sector. Sustained economic growth and technological advancement depend on investment in human capital, renewal of process know-how and the steady accumulation of physical capital in industry.

State structures are not able to ensure indispensable investments across the entire economy,[12] but governments remain important investment facilitators as they can offer fiscal and financial incentives. In open market economies, global competition compels each national government to formulate appropriate policies to optimize investments. Favourable framework conditions (e.g. reliable legislation, effective administration, tax incentives) reduce uncertainties and encourage entrepreneurs to undertake the necessary investments in the real economy. Political and legal uncertainty is the most serious constraint to manufacturing, where sunk costs of entry and exit are generally high. In unstable environments, companies are likely to wait and opt for more liquid assets (e.g. portfolio investments) instead of irreversible fixed investment, trapping the economy in a perpetually low investment and income situation.

The Russian government needs to develop a set of coherent policy mechanisms, including a strong FDI institution for directing capital and know-how into factories, and thus ensure higher industrial output and income generation through more stable employment and possibly exports. Policies for investment generation, industrial development and trade promotion should be coordinated; they form priority policy areas aimed at systematically raising national wealth and competitiveness (Figure I.1). Investment generation policies should optimize all possible domestic and international sources of finance, including FDI, which should form an integral part of any national investment strategy as it could become a significant catalyst for industrial growth in Russia.[13]

Until August 1998, efforts of successive governments in Russia were directed at monetary and financial stability, mainly through anti-inflation programmes, tight control of money supply and budget deficits, and large-scale privatization. The initial reform years saw the formation of private banking and insurance institutions, stock exchanges, and the introduction of modern financial services and instruments. The reforms met with wide support from international donor organizations, but now need to be underpinned by measures focused on strengthening the real economy, including enterprises and infrastructure. It is these measures that will bring about macroeconomic stabilization.

The consecutive financial crises, which shook the Russian economy during 1998 and led to a 300 per cent devaluation of the national currency and a sharp depreciation of the assets of a large part of the population, highlighted the risk of one-sided dependence on short-term capital generation. The financial system should function as a lubricant, but it also needs to be kept in check by a healthy and dynamic manufacturing sector. A competitive industrial sector can buffer the economy against similar international crises in the future.[14] So far, no comprehensive government programme has been specifically designed to modernize national industries through FDI.[15] The Russian Ministry of the Economy, which is responsible for conducting

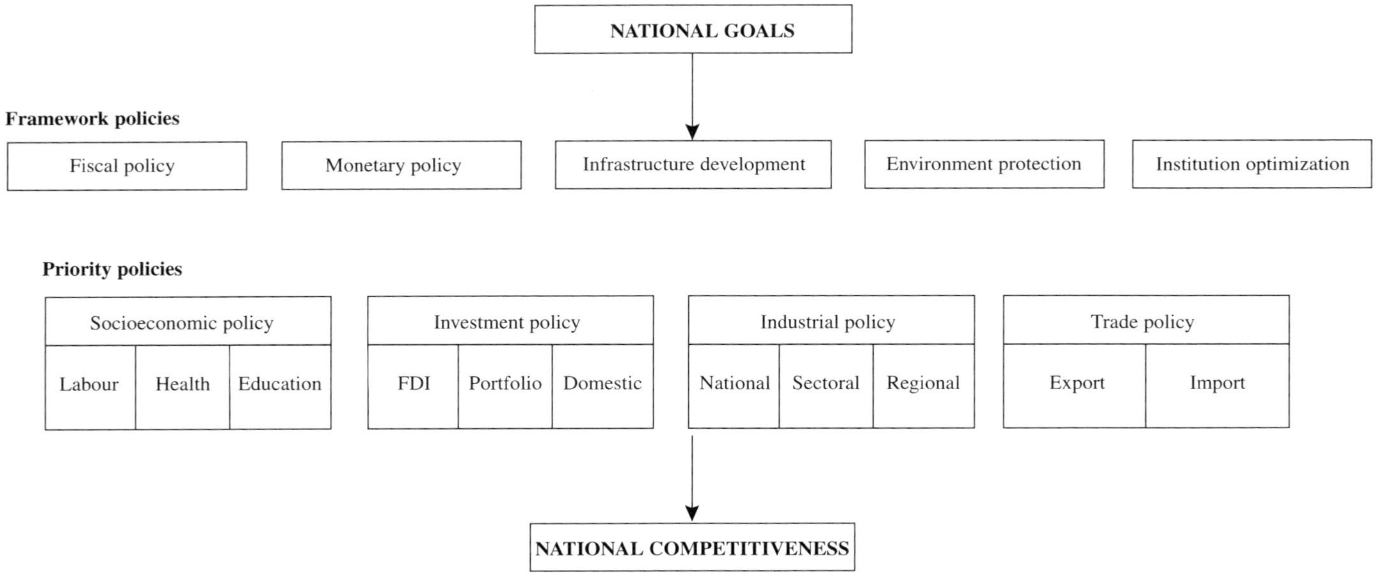

Figure I.1 Polices for stimulating national competitiveness.

the country's investment policy, is concerned with the defining of overall investment targets. FDI is considered an addendum to the national investment policy package, and not an independent policy area with a strategic link to policy measures aimed at industrial modernization.

Overall targets have not yet been attained because of budgetary restrictions and financial difficulties. Foreign investors could have filled the gap, but they have not been numerous because of unsatisfactory framework conditions and inadequate information and promotion efforts by the Russian authorities.[16] Russia as a promising new market and investment destination is losing valuable FDI potential to its major competitors: China, India, Mexico and the European transition economies. These countries have launched programmes to attract multinational companies through incentives and other locational advantages (e.g. fast-track approval, transparent and liberal policies, guarantees and protection mechanisms, and the possibility to own land).[17]

Russia should project its advantages compared with its main competitors, which also offer similar assets (large consumer base, pent-up demand and virgin markets, low production costs, skilled labour and qualified professionals). It should highlight its cultural affinity with western industrialized countries, the status it holds at G8 meetings as a former superpower, its central location on the Eurasian continent, and its vast reserves of raw materials. These assets and many others give it a competitive edge which it should reinforce through appropriate policies, incentives and guarantees.

III FDI in current international debate

There is hardly any subject in current economic and political debate that is more controversial than FDI. Advocates of higher economic integration through free trade and FDI face fierce opposition from politicians wishing to protect domestic industry by limiting the influence and encroachment of multinational companies.

Although representatives of international organizations, net FDI-exporting countries (which are also the main FDI recipients) and export-oriented emerging economies favour further FDI liberalization, significant opposition still prevails in certain developing and transition countries which have only recently switched to more open regimes. Brazil, India, Indonesia, Mexico and even Russia are examples of countries where multinational companies are perceived by many people as symbols of exploitation and foreign domination. The fear of 'selling out the crown jewels' or 'being taken over by the rest of the world' reigns among politicians independently of party ideology.[18]

In FDI-exporting countries, trade unions hold outbound FDI responsible for high unemployment and the loss of industrial competitiveness. But this view has been refuted by several studies, which demonstrate the stabilizing effect of outward FDI on overall business activity, exports, economic growth and employment.[19] Advanced economies have achieved supremacy in a number of high-tech and defence-related sectors, and governments therefore tend to regulate or limit inbound FDI that challenges this leadership. France, Japan, the United Kingdom and the United States provide ample examples of mutual restrictions of FDI in strategic industries: aerospace, automobiles, computers, nuclear power, banking, insurance, air transport.

Large emerging economies such as China and India apply similar policies, but additionally tend to restrict FDI in food and consumer goods industries where domestic enterprises have gained a competitive edge. In 1997, the former Director General of the Confederation of Indian Industry (CII) issued a note listing a number of undesirable features of TNC operations in India:[20]

- they have a 'sales approach' as distinct from manufacturing;
- they focus on the short term rather than on the long term;
- they bring in outdated technology and their investments are limited to second-hand machinery;
- they enter on a 50:50 basis and then quickly seek majority control;[21]
- despite having a joint venture with a local partner, diversified TNCs often set up a 100 per cent subsidiary to cover another industry;
- TNCs tend to use expatriate managers and CEOs rather than Indian managers;
- they have a 'cowboy approach' whereby a single TNC may be tied up with different Indian companies for different product lines;
- they tend to relocate industries that use environment-polluting technologies;
- through their enormous financial clout, they manage to influence decision-makers and get favourable terms by playing out one region against the other.

Russian authorities will have to closely watch the activities of important investors to minimize such practices, but without restricting FDI in general.

Divergent views may run across party lines in industrialized countries. Conservative administrations, which normally advocate liberal ideas in national economic policy, can become fiercer opponents of FDI than 'interventionist' opposition parties or even socialist governments. Republicans in the United States during the Reagan administration showed strong anti-Japanese sentiments when Japanese FDI had reached unprecedented levels. Similar anti-Korean and anti-Japanese sentiments were observed during successive conservative governments in France.

Significant differences can also exist within the same country. An interesting example is India, where certain regional governments such as Andhra Pradesh, Karnataka and West Bengal have developed more investor-friendly environments than other states (e.g. Bihar, Orissa). Traditionally a communist state, West Bengal has realized that its past policies did not help its industry, and it is now actively amending its approach. Such examples can also be found in Russia, where foreign investors enjoy nondiscriminatory treatment in regions run by liberal administrations (e.g. Bashkortostan, Moscow, Nizhny Novgorod, St Petersburg, Tatarstan), but are discriminated in others (e.g. Northern Caucasus).

There seems to be no general rule worldwide about the influence of culture and religious values on the long-term approach to FDI.[22] Paradoxically, countries with orthodox religious traditions, such as Dubai (Islam), Malaysia (Islam), Indonesia (Islam and Hinduism), Saudi Arabia (Islam), and Thailand (Buddhism) have been more open to FDI than countries with more liberal traditions (e.g. Morocco, Turkey, Venezuela). A comparison of FDI-hostile Japan and South Korea, and FDI-friendly China and Singapore provides other examples of differences between countries belonging to the same geocultural context.

The attitude towards FDI is mostly determined by the level of economic development. Generally, in a rich and stable economy the government is less concerned about protecting domestic industries and more disposed to opening the economy to foreign investors. Japan and South Korea are exceptions since they achieved high standards of living without encouraging inbound FDI. Resistance to FDI is higher in countries that are secluded from international trade and investment for political, cultural and historical reasons: for example Cuba, Iran, Iraq, Laos, Myanmar and Nicaragua. Similarly, India's autarkic approach made it FDI-averse until 1991, when it opened and deregulated its economy under pressure from the IMF following a foreign currency reserve crisis.

Motivations for opting for higher inward FDI may also differ: job creation and social stability (France, United Kingdom), industrial restructuring and raw materials exploitation (Brazil, Chile, Venezuela), export development and skill transfer (China), development of a strong agricultural and mining sector (Argentina, Australia), pressure from international donors such as the IMF (India, Philippines), and the immediate need for capital infusions (Mexico, Thailand, Indonesia). Often, government decisions to promote FDI are driven by a combination of factors and reasons.

In spite of prevailing differences and constraints, liberal movements worldwide are gaining ground; they defend the need to import fresh capital, know-how and technologies, especially during economic transition. Progressive countries generally favour open FDI policies, but with clear rules (e.g. reinvestment without immediate profit repatriation during a certain time period) and incentives for TNCs to contribute to the national economy. TNCs are increasingly trying to act as 'good corporate citizens' in their host countries and have understood that this attitude will ensure long-term success in the market. Even countries that had no clear FDI policies in the past have begun to think about more proactive ways of attracting foreign TNCs. Germany, for example, where FDI has dropped to the lowest level ever in postwar history, now makes considerable efforts both at federal and *Länder* levels to improve locational conditions for TNCs. It is expected that overdue tax and labour market reforms will be put in place by the newly elected Socialist–Green coalition; FDI enhancement intentions are motivating the government to move in this direction.

Similarly, the emerging economies in Asia and Latin America have understood how to integrate FDI into dynamic economic policies directed at high economic growth, development of advanced industries, and regional integration (ASEAN, MERCOSUR). In the early 1990s, Central and Eastern European economies moved towards a free market system. These countries now aim at closer regional integration, either by applying for membership in an enlarged European Union (Central European Visegrad countries) or by forming their own free-trade area (CIS countries).

In retrospect, countries open to FDI have gained in economic terms over those that continued restricting TNC operations.[23] China, which received an average of around US$25 billion annually during 1990–97, has provided the world with the best example of how quickly a backward economy can be reoriented and modernized with the help of FDI. Mexico provides another case, especially after it joined NAFTA in 1994. Among emerging economies, Brazil, India, Indonesia, Malaysia and Thailand have also been quite successful in attracting foreign companies and their managerial and technological know-how.

Practically all important economies have started competing for capital and technologies provided by the leading TNCs. However, few countries have adopted targeted and investigative FDI policies. In most cases, medium-sized enterprises, who can be significant aggregate investors, have been overlooked. Together, these companies could generate at least as much FDI-induced economic growth as the totality of larger TNCs. Medium-sized enterprises form the industrial backbone of most industrialized nations as they represent millions of jobs and a higher total turnover than all the large ones put together.[24] Central and local governments have understood the importance of providing assistance mechanisms that enable SMEs to grow, especially through exports and worldwide participation in fairs. But, so far, no effective concept has been designed to link these operators with similarly structured industries in the leading emerging economies.

IV Study contents and methodology

This study aims to provide decision support tools to Russian specialists in charge of designing, implementing and monitoring the country's future industrial and investment policy. Its objectives are:

1. To contribute to general socioeconomic progress in Russia by reestablishing industrial competitiveness through targeted FDI.

2. To provide an analysis of global FDI facts, trends and prospects as a basis for formulating a clear FDI strategy for the country.
3. To inform policy-makers at federal and regional levels of the significance of FDI for industrial modernization.
4. To make Russia's leadership aware of the importance of strategic action for enhancing FDI.
5. To incite policy-makers and legislators to pursue an integrated, long-term policy approach, involving continuous improvement of the general investment climate for foreign firms in Russia.
6. To sensitize executives of western TNCs to the business potential in Russia and public authorities to attract foreign investors.
7. To provide major international and bilateral donor agencies with first-hand information so that they encourage, formulate and promote technical assistance programmes for inter-enterprise cooperation with Russia.

On the basis of experience in other countries, the study aims to highlight appropriate strategies for FDI enhancement in Russia. The analysis focuses on the significance of FDI for socioeconomic planning aimed at industrial and social transformation in Russia's transition economy.

The study attempts to provide Russia's policy-makers with strategically relevant information and ideas for enhancing direct investment in domestic industries. The concepts could be used to stimulate FDI in services, which – although not covered specifically – constitute an important support sector for industrial development in any modern economy.[25] Portfolio operations, which form an essential part of international capital transfers, are not analyzed in-depth because they cannot directly contribute to industrial modernization and the transfer of 'real' technologies and know-how. The technicalities of FDI transactions (risk analysis, investment calculations and feasibility studies)[26] are not covered in this study, which focuses more on the socioeconomic aspects of the issue.

Various theories have been put forward to explain FDI. They are summarized in Part I as they are useful for understanding global FDI developments and TNC behaviour, and for comparing possible FDI policy implications. In Part II, FDI flows and prospects are examined so that Russian policy-makers can foresee the opportunities and threats linked to the inflow of foreign capital and know-how. The role of TNCs is explained, particularly their motivations for investing in foreign countries, and the growing significance of medium-sized enterprises is highlighted. These findings evidently need to be updated regularly through economic and business intelligence, which is a prerequisite for formulating any well-informed strategy.

The study aims to be both informative and strategic, in that it recommends policy directions based on a detailed analysis of Russia's present FDI policy and industrial assets. In Part IV, the overview of Russia's industry (Chapter 8) is intended to remind Russian policy-makers of persisting weaknesses of domestic manufacturers while indicating areas of competitiveness that could be developed quickly through FDI. The description of major industries, FDI trends, and laws (Chapter 9) is also meant to provide western investors with essential information to take strategic FDI decisions.

Policy instruments employed by selected emerging economies (China, India and Mexico) are evaluated in Part III as examples of successful FDI policies. These economies are similar to Russia's in terms of size and market prospects, availability of natural and human resources, and low costs; they are also Russia's main competitors for FDI. Useful lessons can be drawn from their approaches to FDI, including legislation, incentives and the organization and functioning of national FDI agencies. Developments in competing and other economies should be monitored so that Russia's FDI policy can be regularly adjusted and opportunities detected more quickly.

Policy considerations in Part V focus on the need to ensure strategic state guidance for FDI activities. Basic concepts of strategic management can be usefully applied to FDI to optimize procedures and ensure efficient interaction between public authorities and the private sector. Through strategic state guidance, FDI policy can be harmonized with industrial, commercial and fiscal objectives. On the other hand, FDI can only thrive in an accommodating environment of predictable taxation, labour laws, land property rights, and transparent interministerial cooperation and coordination. They need to be included as macro components in the government's FDI enhancement package (Chapter 15).

The FDI policy recommendations at the end of the study are concrete measures for a long-term impact on Russia's industrial capabilities (Chapter 16). Emphasis is placed on vital supports, especially information, promotion and image-building campaigns, and the development of strategic advisory services for potential investors. A special chapter is dedicated to the importance of providing finance, either through leasing or national bank consortiums, for large-scale projects such as construction, infrastructure projects to modernize transport and energy supply, involving local and regional governments. Precise policy requirements can be specified once concrete FDI targets are defined in close coöperation with regional authorities (Chapter 14).

The creation of an independent FDI agency is essential for a systematic implementation of the FDI policy agenda (Chapter 17). This one-stop alternative would have clear advantages compared with the present system in which various agencies are in charge of FDI issues and a department of the Ministry of the Economy serves as a partial coordinating body. Most competing economies already operate strong agencies with a clear political mandate to increase FDI inflows. To be effective, the agency will have to examine and approve all important FDI projects, provide strategic intelligence, coordinate activities with regional bodies, and undertake the required canvassing and information efforts in FDI source countries.

Various sources were contacted and fact-finding missions were carried out in many countries to obtain information on current FDI policy issues and plans for further liberalization and general improvement:

- Books, reports, statistical publications and articles in international journals published by specialists, national bodies, and international organizations in different countries including Russia (desk research).
- FDI promotion offices of major emerging countries; particularly interesting were the on-site discussions held with FDI specialists in China and India.
- Trade commissions and FDI officers at various embassies in Europe (especially from the United Kingdom, Ireland, Mexico, Poland and the leading US states).
- FDI specialists, policy-makers and university professors in Europe and Russia.
- Innumerable interviews with western companies (potential investors) across sectors highlighted the main problem areas that need to be addressed before major investment decisions can be taken.[27]

With some adaptation, certain fundamentals of the strategic FDI enhancement concept may also be applied to improve related policy areas (e.g. domestic state investment policy, trade policy, research and development policy), which could set in motion a virtuous circle of general economic improvement. The concept could also serve as a model for other transition and industrialized countries searching for ways to cooperate with Russia in the area of foreign investment.

Notes

1. The Russian government's commitment to reforming the banking system was reiterated in a speech of former Prime Minister Primakov on the occasion of the APEC summit in Malaysia on 17 November 1998. In addition, a public bank for industrial reconstruction and development could be established from the next IMF tranche.
2. See also Appendix: Definitions and Explanatory Notes.
3. Lack of domestic capital and low overall investment levels have led to the formation of powerful financial–industrial groups (FIG). While these oligopolistic structures offer both capital and managerial experience (often in the form of a holding structure), they can also artificially maintain higher-than-average price levels for essential products and services.
4. For example, by creating special investment zones around important city agglomerations. See Chapter 16.2.

5. As in the recent financial crises in Southeast Asia, Russia and Brazil.
6. V. Popov, 'Konstruktor delo finansista' [Model for a financial system], *Expert*, 11 October 1999, pp. 17–21.
7. See Chinese, Indian and Mexican examples, Chapters 5–7.
8. M. Sarafanov, 'Mogila ispravit' [Hopeless situation], *Expert*, 5 July 1999, pp. 15–19.
9. According to 'modest' estimates, at least US$50 billion are held by Russian citizens outside the national banking system (compared with only US$7 billion kept in bank accounts). See also A. Birman, 'Tikhii azhiotazh vkladchikov' [Discreet rush of depositors], *Kompaniya*, 8 March 1999, p. 14.
10. Such agencies could be part of a network covering Russia and other large emerging markets, which will be important FDI destinations for medium-sized TNCs in the coming century. See Chapter 17.
11. UNIDO. *Industrial Development Report 1997*.
12. According to UNIDO, direct public sector investment accounts for only about one-fifth of total investment. See *Industrial Development Report 1997*.
13. In fast-growing economies such as the United Kingdom, Canada, Mexico, China or Chile, FDI can account for up to 15% of GDP and one-quarter of domestic investment (Chapter 3.1.3). FDI can accelerate integration with the global economy during the initial phases of transition.
14. In the coming years, it will also be important to monitor capital movements of a speculative character. China, for example, managed to protect itself from speculative attacks on its currency, the renminbi, following the Asian crisis by maintaining tight control on foreign currency transactions and purchases of shares by foreigners. See (a) D. Heribert, *Die Asienkrise* [The Asian crisis], 1998, pp. 154–8. (b) P. Seidlitz, 'Peking will Terminmärkte nicht liberaliseren [Beijing does not want to liberalize securities trading], *Handelsblatt*, 1 December 1998.
15. The government's anti-crisis programme formulated during September–October 1998 specifies the importance of FDI as a motor for developing the real sector of the national economy. See 'On measures by the Russian Government and Central Bank to stabilize the socio-economic situation in the country', *Rossiiskaya Gazeta*, 17 November 1998, pt. 3.4.
16. Russian representations abroad (embassies, trade attachés, investment officers, bilateral chambers of commerce) have an important role to play as catalysts, by persuading foreign investors to consider Russia as an investment destination.
17. See country chapters in Part III.
18. N. Gusakov *et al.*, *Nationalnye interesy i vneshneekonomitcheskaya bezopasnost Rossii* [Russia's national interests and external economic security], 1998, p. 101.
19. The positive effects of FDI were already analyzed in the late 1980s. See also A. M. Rugman *et al.*, 'Canada's Reversal from Importer to Exporter of FDI', *MIR*, March 1987, vol. 27, pp. 23–4. Recent studies of inward and outward FDI in France and the United States show how FDI can activate foreign trade both in the home and the recipient country. CEPII, *Compétitivité des nations* [Competitiveness of nations], 1998, pp. 193, 201–20.
20. Indira Gandhi Institute of Development Research; *India Development Report 1997*, pp. 132–3.
21. For many years, approval of 50:50 joint ventures was faster than for wholly-owned subsidiaries in India.
22. Chapters 15.4.1 and 15.4.2.
23. UNIDO. *Industrial Development Report 1997*.

24. In Germany and Italy, the share of SMEs in total industrial turnover is about 70%.
25. In most developed economies, services already account for a larger share in GDP than industry and agriculture put together. However, the economic history of industrialized nations demonstrates that services (including banking and insurance) develop around strong industries and not vice versa.
26. There are numerous interesting publications available in English and Russian to assist decision-makers in conducting FDI-related evaluations and feasibility studies. An important reference is the *UNIDO Manual for the Preparation of Industrial Feasibility Studies.*
27. P. Fischer, *Enterprise Survey Evaluation and Conclusions for the Strategic Orientations and Launch of an International Consultancy Agency,* internal report, MESI, 1996.

Part I

FDI Theories and Policy Implications

1
Overview of Main FDI Theories

1.1 FDI theories from a historical perspective

In the nineteenth century, classical economic theories (e.g. those of Adam Smith, David Ricardo) regarded international trade as a motor of economic internationalization and integration. Internationalization through trade was considered an essential catalyst for generating domestic wealth, especially when a country sought specialization in those economic activities where it had comparative advantages. Private companies had become the principal economic agents of the capitalist system in place, and leading scholars in countries with open economies like England favoured deregulation and liberalization in all possible spheres of economic life so that trade relations could be expanded with other countries. Unlike the 'interventionists' in France, the liberal 'free traders' in England and the United States emphasized the importance of a 'natural order of things' pushing for a lean State that would interfere as little as possible in the 'invisible' hand of the market, which would always find its own equilibrium.[1]

International trade was initially promoted by mainly Dutch, English and French companies in overseas colonies, where they controlled sales outlets, and warehousing and assembly facilities. These companies had also established some manufacturing capabilities in distant markets, but it took almost a century – towards the mid-1950s – before transnational corporations (TNCs) in the modern sense started appearing in the United States, with full-fledged production networks spanning the globe. The position of uncontested leadership acquired by some of these corporations enabled them to commit part of their human and financial resources to productive investments in the growing markets of Latin America and Europe, where they benefited from postwar reconstruction efforts. These extensive internationalization activities of US corporations like Coca-Cola, Dupont, General Electric, General Motors, IBM and Xerox provided academicians and analysts in the United States and Europe with the empirical basis for identifying explanatory variables of FDI decisions and behaviour patterns.

It was at that time that western scholars began to devise comprehensive theories for explaining the origin and causes of FDI, as well as its impact on the economies of host and home countries.

Theories and concepts of foreign investment have been adjusted and constantly refined since the 1960s, but they have not yet been able to provide foolproof analytical tools to governments seeking to anticipate FDI company behaviour *ex-ante* and to effectively influence international movements of capital, technology and know-how. Certain paradigms, however, contain interesting findings, which can be of assistance in formulating and implementing strategic FDI policies for economic growth and industrial development. Broad empirical research also offers valuable insights into shifts of global FDI patterns and motivations of foreign investors in response to economic policies and incentives in host countries.

For several decades, scholars and policy-makers in transition countries were practically excluded from the public debate on global business integration and the role of FDI in national economies. Systemic and ideological differences did not permit free research and policy suggestions on this issue. The theories described in this chapter aim to help readers from Russia and other transition economies understand the historical stages of business transnationalization through FDI in western and developing countries, and its impact on national economies and world trade. They serve as a basis for further analysis of inbound and outbound FDI and to understand why certain nations and sectors remain more competitive than others.

Future research and observation will need to be focused on companies from western countries, which are major capital generators for global investment.[2] In the coming years, decision-makers in transition countries will need to draw on international findings to build their political and legal frameworks for attracting FDI, which is becoming a scarce but indispensable factor for economic development and technology transfer. Strategic FDI policies should one day enable local manufacturers to gain ownership-specific advantages[3] and become themselves foreign investors, thus pushing transition countries further up the investment development path.[4] Transition countries like Poland, Hungary and the Czech Republic are already reaping the fruit of carefully designed FDI policies, which are also the result of in-depth analysis of prevailing theories and experiences made in other FDI recipient countries (e.g. China, Spain, United Kingdom).

A number of disciplines have attempted to provide a theoretical framework for explaining the transnationalization of business and foreign investment behaviour of corporations: economics, international business strategy, marketing, and even political science and sociology. Each of these subject areas offers an understanding of the nature and conditions of overseas investment and capital commitment, from their specific disciplinary angle. For example, 'product policy' within the functional business area of marketing provides the basis for the international product cycle paradigm.[5]

Political science came up with its 'bargaining power' theory, which emphasizes the relationship between TNCs and host governments.[6]

This Part focuses on FDI concepts developed by leading scholars of international economics and – to a lesser extent – international business. The latter provides valuable insights into industrial competitiveness and key factors of success of companies and nations.[7] International economics offers a vast literature on the subject, and many books and articles have been published in a number of countries over the past 20 years. Most contributions are extensions or syntheses of previous findings, but a few novel concepts have been developed contributing to a deeper understanding of FDI for the world economy. The leading theories that influenced government policy in a number of countries are reviewed in the sections that follow (Table 1.1). The paradigms surveyed provide a theoretical base for analyzing transnational corporate behaviour from a historical perspective (international product cycle) and the economic advancement of nations as shaped by in- and outbound FDI (investment development path).

The findings also provide the theoretical basis for proposing proactive FDI strategies to Russian policy-makers.[8] To attract foreign companies (including medium-sized ones) with advanced technologies and know-how, national authorities need to enhance the country's location-specific (L) advantages and the ownership-specific (O) advantages of domestic enterprises.[9] It is also interesting to position Russia and other competing economies (e.g. China, India) on the investment development path (IDP), as has been attempted in the country chapters. Certain theories can guide national FDI experts to pursue a systematic sector- and country-oriented approach to attract suitable investors.[10] Special databases could be established within a specialized investment promotion agency[11] containing details on foreign investors who could be classified, for example, according to their country of origin, size, industrial priority and motivations to invest.

1.2 International product cycle paradigm

The international product cycle (IPC) paradigm, which was elaborated in 1966 by the French scholar R. Vernon,[12] describes the dynamic interaction between international trade and foreign investment. Its empirical setting was the growing trade and investments by US corporations during postwar reconstruction in Europe. The originality of the concept resides in the combination of elements of international economics (trade patterns between countries and reasons for relocation of industries) with those of marketing theory (product life-cycle curve).

According to the theory, the natural life-cycle of products and the accompanying cost considerations prompt three types of decisions by corporate leaders: to produce at home, to export or to transfer production to

Table 1.1 Historical overview of main FDI theories, 1960–94

Theory/paradigm	Author(s)	Unit of analysis	Functional base/discipline	Key issues
International product cycle	Vernon (1996)	American TNCs	Economics, marketing	FDI and trade flows, impact of technology and product life-cycle on international business development
TNCs and market imperfections (monopolistic competition)	Hymer (1960) Kindleberger (1969)	American TNCs	Economics, international business	Reasons for TNC competitiveness and internationalization strategies
Oligopolies and FDI	Knickerbocker (1973) Vernon (1974) Graham (1978)	American and European TNCs	Economics, international business	Oligopolistic market structures and FDI strategies
Internalization	Buckley and Casson (1976, 1981) Rugman (1985)	TNCs	International business	Transnationalization, vertical and horizontal integration
Flying geese paradigm	Kojima (1978) Ozawa (1995)	Japanese TNCs	International economics	Economic development through inbound FDI
Competitive advantage of nations	Porter (1990)	TNCs in industrialized countries	International business, economics	Competitiveness of countries and industries
Eclectic paradigm	Dunning (1981)	TNCs in industrialized countries	International economics	Company- and country-specific determinants for FDI
Investment development path	Dunning (1981, 1986, 1993) Dunning and Narula (1994)	Industrialized and emerging economies	International economics	Classification of countries according to their net outward investment position
Bargaining power theory	Gilpin (1975) Rothgeb (1989, 1991)	TNCs and governments	Political science	Government–TNC interactions, investment dependence and political conflict

foreign markets. The life of a product consists of three distinct phases: innovation, maturity and standardization. Innovating companies can enjoy temporary monopoly in their home markets during new product launches, enabling them to recover part of the initial R&D and marketing investment. When the products pass on to phases two and three of the cycle, the company has to adopt an internationalization strategy if it wants to survive *vis-à-vis* its competitors. Companies usually seek export markets when their products lose part of their novelty appeal on reaching maturity. At this stage, competition becomes fiercer, resulting in higher unit production costs and lower profit margins. Eventually, during standardization, low-cost production sites have to be identified in other countries, preferably those that also constitute large markets. During product standardization, companies undertake foreign investments to defend their position as leaders, with a view to later reexport the products to the home country, where the innovation originated.

When it was formulated, the theory provided a useful explanation for decisions by US companies to shift their production overseas. Since then, the international economic situation has changed dramatically. Competition has spread from the home to the global market as corporations and their competitors move to overseas production sites. In the rush for new markets, corporate leaders form strategic alliances or acquire companies abroad to maintain and expand their leadership by gaining access to new markets and technologies. Their decisions are guided more by strategic imperatives than by products reaching certain stages of maturity in their respective life-cycles. Government intervention and incentive mechanisms (e.g. UK FDI promotion strategy to attract Japanese investors in the late 1980s) can also have a significant influence on investors' decisions. Today, a typical TNC adopts trading and investment strategies simultaneously in various countries, which all form links in a complex network of inter-company transactions and cross-shareholdings.

In the 1970s and 1980s, powerful TNCs started emerging outside the United States, especially in Europe; recently, companies in emerging economies of Southeast Asia and Latin America have also joined the league. US TNCs face stiff global competition and in many industries their leadership has vanished. The earlier hierarchical order between countries and national economies suggested by the theory is now blurred. However, the theory incites FDI-oriented governments to observe life-cycles at a global level, if not of individual products (this would add to the complexity of the task), then at least of larger product families, industries and technologies.[13]

The establishment of a research and intelligence unit within a competent FDI authority would serve a useful purpose in this respect as it could study and monitor global life-cycle stages of leading industries (e.g. machinery and equipment, pharmaceuticals, high-tech chemicals, heavy commercial vehicles, aerospace) and state-of-the-art technologies (e.g. microelectronics, new materials, biotechnologies). Such a unit could, through its research work, easily guide national policy-makers in identifying those TNCs that offer innovative technologies and seek markets and production sites abroad to expand their operations and/or to avoid high factor costs at home.[14]

1.3 Monopolistic competition and market imperfections

The reasons for the growth of (US) multinationals and their decisions to produce abroad were analyzed by S. H. Hymer in 1960.[15] His thesis is based on the following assumption: foreign investors need to exploit market imperfections since investments in overseas manufacturing facilities involve higher risks and costs than productive investments in the home country. Additional investments are required to cover operational and organizational costs of managing foreign subsidiaries from a distance and higher marketing and business development expenses due to language and cultural barriers, and the possibility of discrimination. Therefore, the investing firm must have a specific, in fact a monopolistic advantage, which is derived from market imperfections.

C. P. Kindleberger (1969)[16] expanded Hymer's concept by defining, on the basis of market imperfections, four key factors that underline the success of TNCs wherever they operate, with or without government intervention, and which may alter cost and benefit structures:

- Product-induced imperfections: marketing techniques, brand image, product differentiation.
- Imperfections related to factors of production: exclusive control over manufacturing, proprietory technologies, skills of staff, privileged access to capital markets.
- Possibilities of exploiting internal and external economies of scale.
- Government policies and interference.

The application of the theory of monopolistic competition specifically to TNCs led to an exploration of elements such as multi-country access to factors of production and to consumers, as well as economies of scale in international production, distribution and purchasing. This type of analysis has been used to study the factors contributing to the enormous success of TNC operations, both in home and overseas markets. Monopolistic or oligopolistic[17] aspects of TNC activities abroad have provoked specific government policies, although these may not differ greatly from policies towards domestic enterprises.

Subsequent theories, which were based on broader and more up-to-date empirical samples, found out that in most cases a specific advantage was a necessary, but not a sufficient, condition for firms to invest and produce abroad. A company may well exploit its specific advantage in the home country and export or simply sell a license, thus avoiding high costs of relocation.

While Hymer emphasized technology- and innovation-related advantages, other authors after him (Horst,[18] 1972; Lall,[19] 1980) identified other company-specific advantages as explanatory variables for investing abroad: size of the company, vertical integration, product differentiation (measured as advertising expenses over turnover). For certain authors (e.g. Kimura[20] 1975, 1989), however, the company's size and competitive position in the home market reflect other advantages (superior technologies, corporate strategy, and so on) and are not explanatory variables for FDI. The veracity of this argument is demonstrated by the internationalization of an increasing number of medium-sized TNCs, which incidentally have become a central target of FDI promotion strategies of certain governments such as Singapore, China and Chile. In these cases, state-of-the art technologies and know-how controlled by these firms have been crucial elements for global presence. Nevertheless, a critical size is also a decisive factor for investing abroad. This critical size is determined by the number of employees, annual turnover and profit levels.

A number of conclusions can be drawn from this theory for economic and industrial development in a transition country like Russia:

- Foreign investors should be analyzed carefully, particularly their corporate assets and possible contribution to the transfer of superior technologies and know-how; their company-specific advantages determine their readiness to invest and the possible form of investment (e.g. joint ventures vs wholly-owned subsidiary).
- The success rate for placing an investing company in the right sectoral and regional context increases with the amount of information collected by public bodies (for example by careful evaluation of annual reports and financial accounts, study of press releases and historical developments, and so on).
- It is crucial to match the key factors of success of a foreign company with the development strategy of the host country.

These advantage- or imperfection-based theories were later complemented by scholars like Dunning and Porter, whose integrated concepts supply additional elements for targeting potential investors.[21]

1.4 FDI and defensive oligopolistic behaviour

In competitive industries, market structures and the behaviour of the market leader can determine the process and speed of transnationalization of competitors. On the basis of an empirical study of the international activities of 187 US multinationals during 1948–67, F. T. Knickerbocker[22]

(1973) discovered that in oligopolistic industries, market leaders who had ventured abroad were automatically followed by rival companies from the home country. In 45 per cent of the cases, this 'follow the leader' strategy was observed within three years after the initial investment, and in 75 per cent of the cases, within seven years.

In sectors with extremely high rates of concentration (e.g. energy, steel), such an FDI strategy is less common as the leaders prefer market sharing to head-on competition, which would lead to drastic price cuts and losses for all oligopolists. Similar attitudes were observed among certain European investors in the United States and Japanese investors in Europe and the United States (e.g. in automobiles and consumer electronics sectors).

E. M. Graham[23] (1978) slightly adjusted the model, mainly to explain the investment behaviour of European TNCs in the United States, whose aim was to counter the strategies of their US rivals in Europe rather than outmanoeuvre their 'home' competitors. The Europeans intensified their internationalization efforts on perceiving the US threat in their home markets. Thus, FDI is not always determined by tangible reasons of economic benefit – at least not in the initial stages – but by countermeasures aimed at checking major competitors at home and abroad. This modified version of the model has remained valid until today and can be observed especially among financially strong TNCs originating from countries with a similar level of economic development, especially in the Triad markets (Europe, Japan, United States).

The oligopoly model does not explain the motivation for the initial investment by the market leader. But economic planners and industrial policy-makers in Russia could still use it to target the competitors (globally and in the market of origin) of industry leaders who have already entered the Russian market, especially in sectors with oligopolistic structures. Besides, a broad base of participants in public tenders enhances the government's bargaining power. Needless to say, the policy-makers should exercise extreme caution and tact during their search to avoid en masse negative reactions from oligopolistic giants. Their selection should be based on careful analysis of targeted companies and their key factors of success (leadership skills, financial accounts, global behaviour, size and so on), and the sectoral structure in the home countries. A database with company and sector-specific information would assist policy-makers in their decision-making.[24]

The oligopoly paradigm is based on empirical research conducted in oligopolistic structures; it therefore neglects the role of medium-sized TNCs in modernizing industries in transition countries. These medium-sized TNCs can, depending on the country, belong to sectors that are not oligopolistic, but are nevertheless crucial for economic development (e.g. services, food, consumer goods industries).[25]

1.5 Internalization theory

The internalization concept establishes a link between FDI by large corporations and their internal organization reflected by the hierarchic integration of business functions. It assumes a situation of market imperfections and was formulated in the second half of the 1970s by P. J. Buckley and M. Casson,[26] two economists of Reading University in the United Kingdom. According to them, large firms are able to expand because of their integrative capacity and the exclusion of competitors from their know-how. The authors reproached previous theories (such as those of Hymer and Kindleberger) for focusing on the production function and neglecting other unique advantages (leadership skills, international organization, marketing and sourcing capacities, human resource development and sound financial management) that enable companies to maintain their leadership and to expand into other markets and business areas. True international operators derive their competitive advantage not from one specific asset in one determined functional area, but from their capacity to internalize their know-how instead of allowing it to be transferred to other (external) organizations.

Internalization is particularly common in manufacturing businesses with high R&D costs and capital intensity (e.g. chemicals, automobile), and large-scale flows of intermediary products in the form of components and semi-manufactured goods (e.g. consumer electronics, pharmaceuticals). Progressive FDI agencies (e.g. Taiwanese and Singaporean investment development boards) have started establishing a link between high R&D expenditure and transnationalization (FDI) potential: when faced with alternatives, they privilege TNCs that can demonstrate high R&D expenses as a percentage of their turnover. This ratio is also used to canvass new TNCs for the development of specific industrial sectors. The theory may also help understand the internationalization strategies of companies in raw materials and agricultural sectors, and even in services (Buckley and Casson, 1985).

Taxation and other restrictive policies of certain host governments in the form of high import duties, local component content, and non-tariff barriers can also favour the internalization of functions 'under one roof'. Exports thus become less lucrative than direct investment, especially if the target market is large and of strategic importance (e.g. Brazil, China, India, Indonesia).

According to A. M. Rugman (1981),[27] the internalization theory is basic to other paradigms on direct investment. Former theories of multinationalization, in particular those developed on the basis of market imperfections, product life-cycle and defensive oligopolistic behaviour, can be grouped under the general paradigm of internalization. The internal organization of a TNC can itself be considered as an alternative market (e.g. sales between affiliates and headquarters) whereby transfer costs can be reduced through economies of scale. A company can preserve the competitive advantage acquired in its home market by integrating its foreign subsidiaries globally into a network of 'internal' markets.[28]

The internalization theory provided a strong intellectual base for subsequent studies (e.g. Dunning, Porter), which attempted to integrate it into broader concepts that linked FDI to interactions between competitive advantages, internalization attempts and host country attractiveness. Recent studies on TNCs have shown that endeavours to internalize all activities can be counter-productive and that companies increasingly revert to downsizing and international sourcing – 'make or buy' decisions – to reduce costs and raise profitability levels.

1.6 The 'flying geese' paradigm of economic development

The 'flying geese' paradigm was originally conceived in the late 1930s as a general theory of economic development by the Japanese scholar K. Akamatsu. According to Akamatsu's original work, an industry develops in three phases:

Phase 1: products are introduced into an economy through imports from overseas manufacturers;
Phase 2: local production facilities are set up to serve growing domestic demand;
Phase 3: excess capacities are exported to new markets abroad.

Akamatsu based his paradigm on observations of the textile industry in Japan (then a developing country) and its trajectory of development over a period of 40–50 years, starting from the late nineteenth century. He discovered that, graphically, the sequential appearance of imports (M), domestic production (P), and exports (X) produced a pattern analogous to a flying formation of wild geese (Figure 1.1). These patterns were found for textile raw products (cotton yarn, cotton fabrics) and, later, also in upstream capital goods industries (cotton textile machinery). By examining the full development cycle of these products and industries over long life spans, Akamatsu could demonstrate restructuring processes and changing competitiveness in the Japanese manufacturing sector.

Later, Japanese scholars built on the model to describe the situation in newly-industrialized (e.g. South Korea, Taiwan) and developing (e.g. Thailand, Malaysia) countries, where many capital-intensive industries had developed through FDI-induced transfer of know-how and product introductions. According to K. Kojima (1978),[29] Akamatsu's 'catching-up cycle' paradigm is constructed from a latecomer's point of view. It presupposes interaction and dynamic changes in economic relations between

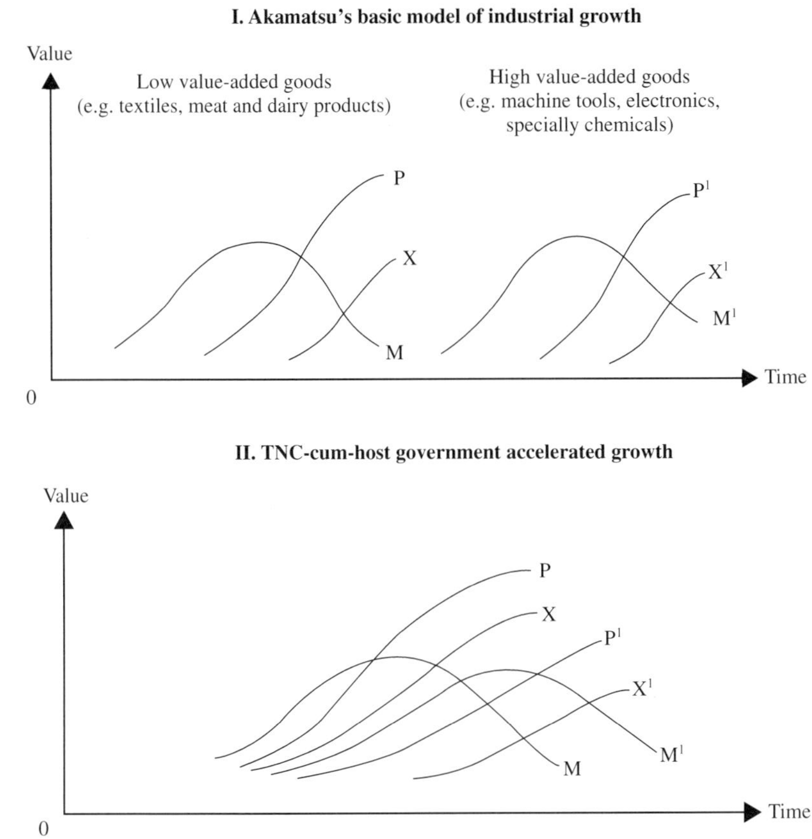

P: domestic production, X: exports, M: imports

Source: Ozawa *in* UNCTAD, *World Investment Report 1995*.

Figure 1.1 The 'flying geese' paradigm

advanced (leading) and developing (catching-up) countries, whereby the latter develop their economies by emulating the leaders.

This theory is confirmed by the successful catching-up process of many developing countries, especially in Asia, in a number of (low value-added) consumer goods industries. Although trade relations are still hampered sometimes by protectionist measures in the more industrialized countries (for example the Multifibre Agreement for textiles, and US and EU agricultural policies for protecting their food industries), emerging economies have seized opportunities to catch up and eventually to develop their own industrial base. The same phenomenon can be observed to a certain extent in the transition countries of Central and Eastern Europe, which also face obstacles when exporting certain goods to the European Union (e.g. agricultural goods, steel products, aluminium). But competitive labour costs and availability of raw materials, especially in CIS countries, represent important assets that can qualify these countries as major new recipients of FDI. For the catching-up process to work, trade barriers have to be removed and foreign TNCs put in a position to transfer their technology and know-how on a large scale.

The importance of government policy has not been explicitly studied by Akamatsu as a prerequisite for a country's success in its catching-up cycle. However, the paradigm broadly inspired the Japanese government to simultaneously pursue policies of strategic trade and protection of its infant industries during the post-Second World War period. The dual policies carried out under the supervision of the powerful Ministry of International Trade and Industry (MITI) paid off and led to a rapid upgrading of the country's industry and conferred leadership in many high-tech sectors (e.g. consumer electronics, cars, motorcycles, optical instruments). The role of foreign TNCs and FDI is also not covered by Akamatsu's original work, probably because economic and financial integration between countries was quite low in those days.

Forty years later, K. Kojima and T. Ozawa[30] added the FDI dimension to the paradigm and thus demonstrated how economic development in developing countries could be accelerated by technological and capital contributions of foreign TNCs. They had before them the example of Japanese companies that had transferred their manufacturing and plant management skills to neighbouring China and Southeast Asia. Although these investments were motivated exclusively by strict cost and market access considerations, they had an 'altruistic' beneficial effect on host economies. Japanese involvement substantially helped to build a number of highly competitive industries, such as textiles and automotive components in Thailand, consumer electronics in Malaysia and Hong Kong, and microcomputers in Taiwan.

Today, with the appearance of an increasing number of transnational operators, including medium-sized ones,[31] the export stage (X-curve) of the paradigm is frequently skipped, or at least accelerated. Through targeted FDI, a catching-up country can in fact develop its consumer and capital goods industries simultaneously, without much time lag between the two phases. In this way, TNCs can help compress the time needed to build up first the competitive consumer goods sector, followed by the capital goods sector and, later, the high-tech industries (e.g. telecommunication devices, computers, biotechnologies, new materials). TNCs thus become the 'inter-stage agents of economic development' (Kojima and Ozawa, 1985; Ozawa 1990, 1992 and 1993).

Besides demonstrating the role of FDI as a facilitator of industrial transformation, Kojima (1973) also made the distinction between pro-trade and anti-trade FDI. While pro-trade FDI (through its export effect) tends to move from a home country's comparatively disadvantaged industry to a host country's comparatively advantaged industry, anti-trade flows are observed when TNCs belonging to a home country's comparatively advantaged industry invest in a host country's disadvantaged sector. When a country practises import substitution policies, it usually attracts anti-trade FDI into its highly protected industries. In recent years, however, most developing countries have embarked on outward-looking, export-oriented policies with the aim of canvassing investments in trade- and export-oriented production facilities.

The flying geese paradigm provides three interesting findings for decision-makers and analysts in Russia, who should bear them in mind when designing future economic development and FDI policy measures:

- The paradigm demonstrates that international economic integration allows a transition economy to catch up and even overtake more advanced economies. The country should remain open to the outside world and, in particular, to FDI from foreign TNCs, which is an indispensable supplement to public aid.
- The FDI dimension, which was introduced into the paradigm by Kojima and Ozawa, stresses the importance of formulating appropriate FDI policies to accelerate this process.[32]
- Interestingly, FDI-induced economic development in a lead country can cascade into neighbouring countries, especially if policies are coordinated. Positive results in Russia, for example, would enhance the economic potential of the entire CIS, and trigger off a virtuous economic cycle in the region, similar to the positive effects of Japanese FDI in ASEAN countries.

1.7 FDI and the competitive advantage of nations

In *The Competitive Advantage of Nations* (1990), M. Porter presented the results of his extensive field research conducted in 10 industrialized economies. Porter studied the competitiveness of more than 100 industries that accounted for a significant share of total exports in their respective home countries, and his analysis attempted to explain:

- why corporations belonging to selected industries had been successful in penetrating certain foreign markets but not others;
- why some countries were able to attract FDI in certain value-added activities but not in others; and
- why investments by TNCs in particular countries and sectors successfully increased the technological and organizational efficiency of local companies, and why in other cases industrial upgrading was inhibited.

Porter's findings illustrate the dynamic interplay between TNC strategies and competitive advantages of recipient countries. Although the theory of comparative advantage was criticized by certain scholars including Dunning,[33] it certainly contributed to the advancement of research on transnational activities of companies by emphasizing four determining factors of competitive advantage that together form the 'diamond of competitive advantage' (Figure 1.2):

Factor 1 *Corporate strategy, structure and rivalry*: management and leadership practices, company goals, new business formation and entrepreneurship, availability of venture capital, and so on.

Factor 2 *Factor conditions*, in particular human and physical resources, knowledge, capital, infrastructure.

Factor 3 *Demand conditions*, such as the size of domestic demand, growth rate, consumer segmentation, characteristics of buyers (demanding, sophisticated, with high or medium purchasing power, internationally mobile consumers, and so on.)

Factor 4 Existence of *related and supporting industries*.

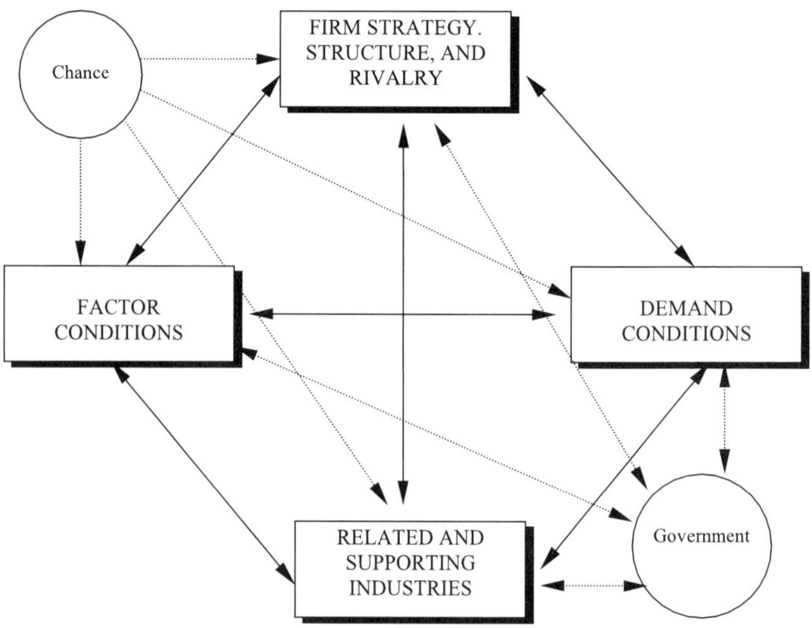

Source: M. Porter, *Competitive Advantage of Nations*, 1990.

Figure 1.2 Porter's diamond of competitive advantages

The existence of strong support industries is an important determining factor for FDI. When designing strategic FDI policies, transition countries must aim at developing interdependent clusters of core and supporting industries. The establishment of a modern food industry, for example, will depend on the existence of suppliers of agricultural raw materials (milk, meat, spices, preservatives, etc.), adequate filling and packaging equipment, and a modern retail system; car and vehicle manufacturers will need the support of automotive component manufacturers (plastic parts, engine heads, batteries, wiper systems, etc.) to thrive. Sustainable industrial competitiveness and medium-term economic growth can therefore be achieved only through such an integrated approach.

In Russia, for example, McDonald's could take definitive investment decisions only after it had studied the local supplier structures (potato, meat, sauce and drinks manufacturers). For foreign investors, local supplies usually mean lower costs than imports, although critical components or ingredients may need to be imported in the beginning until a strong local supplier structure is put into place. Innovative suppliers also allow TNCs to fulfill local component content requirements or avoid high import tariffs that might suddenly be imposed by certain governments. Gradually, TNCs also integrate local suppliers in joint problem solving activities which may concern practically all functional areas essential for quality improvement (purchasing, manufacturing, just-in-time logistics, finance, and sometimes even R&D).

A strategic FDI policy should aim at the promotion of sectoral clusters; that is, at the development of strategic subsectors in relation to their respective lead sectors.[34] Domestic supply and demand patterns must therefore be accurately analyzed for the main industrial sectors that the country's authorities have decided to develop through policy intervention. In this case, it is useful to implement the FDI policy in combination with industrial, SME, tax, labour and other related policies. A one-stop agency for FDI enhancement would be most appropriate to inform the respective ministries about sectors and subsectors to be developed through coordinated policy measures.[35]

The industrial competitiveness of Japanese industry can be largely explained by detailed studies of structures and value chains of western competitors. Japanese car, van and motorcycle producers, for example, can draw on world-class local suppliers of electrical devices, brakes, tyres and other components. The same phenomenon can in fact be observed in all other industrialized countries that have a strong automobile industry. Similarly, Swedish and German leadership in fabricated steel products (e.g. ball bearings, cutting tools) stems from the existence of reliable suppliers of specialty steels in both countries. Italian textile and apparel manufacturers have become world leaders thanks to close links with domestic companies supplying high-quality processed materials (cotton, wool, leather) and customized spinning, weaving and knitting machinery. Internationally competitive supplier industries underpin the success and competitiveness of leading economies in world markets.

At a later stage, Porter added two other elements to his diamond of competitive advantages:

- The role of chance or corporate 'destiny' reflected by significant shifts in world financial markets or exchange rates, sudden surges in world or regional demand, as well as wars.
- The impact of government intervention (liberal as opposed to restrictive policies).

Governments are considered only as an attribute to the diamond (expressed as circles in Figure 1.2), but they can determine its proper functioning and overall efficiency. Through their intervention, governments can directly influence the supply and demand conditions for domestic and international resources. They are the ultimate decision-makers who shape economic systems and set the rules of the game for fiscal, monetary and FDI-related policies. A far-sighted government's FDI policy is important to enhance the locational (L) advantages of a country, which is a prerequisite for raising confidence levels among potential investors and for attracting the required capital, expertise and technologies.[36]

1.8 The eclectic paradigm

The eclectic paradigm theory was formulated for the first time in 1981 by J. H. Dunning,[37] another well-known economist from the University of Reading, United Kingdom. The attribute 'eclectic' was chosen because, according to the definition of the term, the paradigm (a) aims to select what appears to be best in various methods, doctrines or styles, and (b) is composed of elements drawn from various sources. Dunning has published a number of articles and reference books on the subject[38] and, together with Narula, conceptualized the investment development path paradigm, which situates the eclectic paradigm into a more global context of economic development through FDI.[39]

The paradigm sets out a generalized framework for explaining levels and patterns of FDI activities of companies. It postulates that, at any given point in time, the stock of foreign assets owned and controlled by multinational firms is determined by three conditional elements:

- The extent and nature of ownership-specific or competitive advantages of foreign investors, especially compared with national operators (O-advantages).
- The extent and nature of location-bound endowments and markets offered by certain countries to investing firms (L-advantages) that would add further value to their already existing competitive advantages.

- The extent to which companies internalize (I-advantages), or control their competitive advantages, rather than transfer and market them directly to foreign firms, for example through exports or licensing.

The configuration of ownership, location and internalization (OLI) advantages contains objective and subjective components, as it varies with the nature of activity, company-specific characteristics, and expected and real benefits the host country may offer to the foreign investor. The propensity for corporations to invest in foreign locations increases with their comparative (O) advantages, which are to be measured in relation to competition, as well as the profits or value accrued to corporations from foreign location (L) advantages. Some of the important OLI variables are summarized in Table 1.2.

The eclectic paradigm is a comprehensive theory that can help explain all types of internationalization according to the existing advantages for a foreign investor. A company having both comparative (O) and internalization (I) advantages will decide to invest abroad, if the location-specific (L) advantages are situated outside its home territory. Conversely, a company with the same O and I advantages will prefer to export its products and services, if the foreign location offers only low L advantages. In case company-specific advantages cannot be defended, the company may decide to sell licences to foreign enterprises so that production levels can be maintained at home.

Dunning's eclectic paradigm represents an extension of the internalization theory (through its I-advantages); additionally, it draws on essential elements of business and strategic management theory (through its O-advantages). In this respect, the competitive advantages stressed by business scholars like Porter as determinants of internationalization do not differ very much from the O-advantages expounded by Dunning. Both aim to offer a comprehensive and integrated theory for the understanding of FDI.

Policy-makers in transition countries and their foreign advisors should study and carefully develop essential L-variables so that capital and know-how can be attracted systematically for improving industrial competitiveness and the employment situation. These advantages or disadvantages, depending on the country, have been confirmed by several econometric studies as major determinants for inward investment. FDI flows tend to concentrate on those countries that offer comparative advantages not only in terms of natural resources and low factor costs, but also sound economic management, a reliable legal system, and promising perspectives for sustainable growth and development.

Dunning's theory has been adapted by other authors to explain FDI flows from a different perspective. For example, R. Mucchielli[40] from France designed a synthetic analysis (1985) by relating the internationalizatio strategy of companies to the comparative advantages of their home countries. In this case, FDI decisions by TNCs are mainly determined by factor or market insufficiencies in home markets (Table 1.3).

Table 1.2 OLI variables according to Dunning

A. **Ownership-specific advantages (O-advantages)**
(represent assets *vis-à-vis* major competitors)
- Size of company and established position in domestic and international markets
- Management and leadership skills
- Product know-how
- Process technologies, engineering skills, R&D capacity
- Monopoly/oligopoly power, allowing exclusive or favoured access to inputs, e.g. labour, natural resources
- Trade marks
- Organizational, marketing systems

B. **Internalization-specific advantages (I-advantages)**
(protect against market failure and enable control of assets)

I-advantages can be developed:
- where there is buyer uncertainty about the nature and value of products and technologies being sold
- where the market does not permit price discrimination
- where there is a need for the seller to protect product quality

I-advantages enable:
- a reduction in costs related to market research, negotiations and monitoring
- the capture of economies of scale and interdependent activities
- compensation for absence of future market
- the avoidance or exploitation of government-related barriers (e.g. quotas, tariffs, price controls, tax differences)
- the control of supplies and conditions of sale of inputs (including technology)
- the control of market outlets (including those that might be used by competitors)
- engagement in cross-subsidization and internal pricing strategies so that profits are shifted to low-tax environments

C. **Location-specific advantages (L-advantages)**
(may favour home or host countries)
- Spatial distribution of inputs and markets
- Competitive input prices: labour, energy, raw materials, components, transport and communications
- Political stability, balance of power
- Liberal policies: low tariffs, favourable tax rates, FDI incentives, good climate for investment
- Reliable legal system
- Developed physical infrastructure: roads, railways, airports, ports, telecommunications
- Sociocultural proximity: language, history, mentality, business practices
- Long-term market potential and size (possible economies of scale)

Source: Adapted from Dunning (1981, 1992).

Table 1.3 Competitive advantage and internationalization

Competitive advantages of home country		Chosen internationalization strategy
Factor supply	Product demand (market)	
+	+	Production and sale in home country
–	–	Outward FDI
–	+	Outward FDI and reimport
+	–	Export

A similar decision matrix on the basis of Dunning's OLI concept was established by Stehn (1989).[41] It tries to standardize the type of internationalization decision (licence, export, FDI) according to existing advantages (O, L, I). In this case, FDI is undertaken only if all three advantages are combined (Table 1.4). The existence of company-specific ownership advantages are a prerequisite for all three strategies of internationalization.

Table 1.4 OLI advantages and internationalization

Strategies	Internationalization		
	Licence	Export	FDI
Ownership-specific advantages	x	x	x
Internalization	0	x	x
Location-specific advantages	0	0	x

x: required; 0: not required.

The eclectic paradigm also helps understand how countries move ahead on the investment development path from their initial position as exclusive recipients to their subsequent position as originators of FDI.

1.9 The investment development path of nations

The notion of the investment development path (IDP) implies that the outward and inward FDI position of a country is directly related to the level of its economic development in relation to the rest of the world. The basic elements of the theory were formulated by Dunning in 1981; they were further refined and extended in cooperation with Narula from Limburg University, the Netherlands (1994). The IDP paradigm suggests that countries pass through five main stages of development (Table 1.5), and they can be classified according to their propensity to be inward and/or

Table 1.5 Main features of the five stages in a country's NOI position

Stage	O-advantages	L-advantages	I-advantages	Industry characteristics	Government intervention
Stage 1					
Low inbound FDI Nonexistent outbound FDI Decreasing NOI curve	Low competitive advantages of domestic firms Little indigenous technology accumulation Few firm-created assets	Insufficient country-specific assets to attract FDI: low domestic demand levels; inappropriate economic systems or government policies; inadequate infrastructure such as transportation and communication facilities Low level of education and training of workers	Very low compared with foreign competitors	Labour intensive low skill manufacturing Primary sector processing	Protection of infant industry Import controls Local content policies Upgrading of human resources through education and training Import substitution and anti-FDI policies
Stage 2					
Rising inbound FDI Negligible out-bound FDI Worsening NOI position	Increasing competitiveness of domestic firms, especially in traditional sectors and through growing export activities	Rising country-specific advantages (e.g. growing domestic markets)	Increasing I-advantages of domestic firms	Semiskilled and moderately knowledge-intensive	Tariff and nontariff barriers Less protectionist FDI policy

continued …

Table 1.5 (*continued*)

Stage	O-advantages	L-advantages	I-advantages	Industry characteristics	Government intervention
Stage 3					
Slower growth of inbound FDI Faster growth of outbound FDI Upward NOI curve	Increased competitiveness of local firms	Increase in per capita income, demand for high-quality goods	Existing I-advantages of domestic firms	Deteriorating advantages in labour-intensive activities Domestic wage increases	Liberal FDI and export-oriented policies
Stage 4					
Outward FDI stock is equal to or exceeds inward FDI stock Rate of growth of outward FDI is still higher than for inward FDI	High competitiveness of domestic firms both at home and abroad due to modern production processes and innovative products	Fairly high per capita income	Increasing I-advantages of domestic companies	Expansion of capital-intensive industries World leadership in a number of industries	Liberal FDI policies
Stage 5					
NOI position falls slightly and fluctuates around zero Both inward and outward FDI continue increasing	High competitiveness of domestic TNCs	Very high levels of average per capita income (on average above US$20 000 p.a.)	High I-advantages of domestic companies	World leadership in capital-intensive and high-tech industries	Continuation of liberal FDI policies Promotion of outward FDI

outward direct investors. The paradigm illustrates the net outward investment (NOI) position of a country, which is defined as the difference between inward and outward FDI stock. A positive NOI position means that the country has become a net outward investor, and vice versa in the case of a negative NOI position. In line with Dunning's eclectic paradigm, a country's propensity to attract or not to attract FDI rests on three types of advantages related to ownership, location and internalization.

The IDP suggests that companies tend to invest in markets with lower per capita GDP than their home countries, at least until they reach the fifth stage (Figure 1.3). A positive net outward FDI position offers a measure of the transfer of created assets to lower-income countries; it is compatible with the technological advantage in the home country of the investing TNC. This measure must be confronted with other types of FDI such as market-seeking FDI or strategic asset-acquiring FDI (mergers and acquisitions). There is, however, no absolute tendency to always invest downstream in lower-cost countries. Besides, a wide variation of net ownership

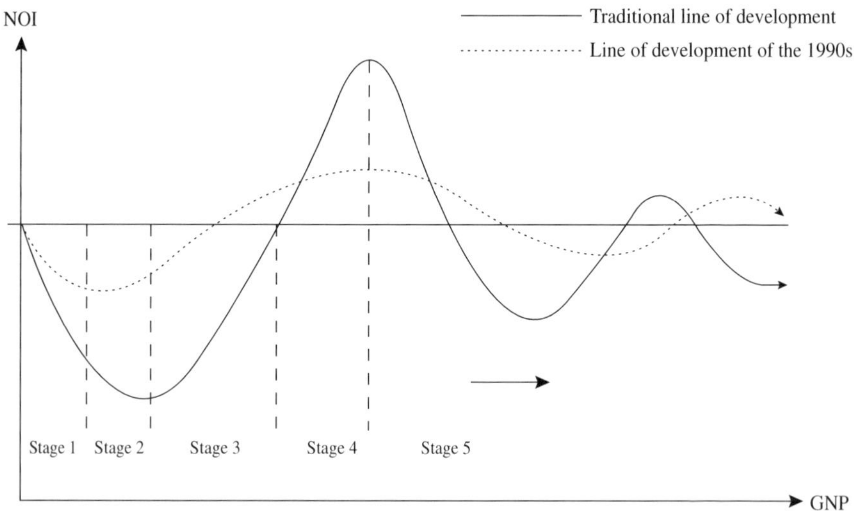

Examples:
Stage 1: Bulgaria, Russia, Vietnam
Stage 2: Hungary, India, Indonesia, Poland
Stage 3: Brazil, China, Mexico
Stage 4: France, Germany, Italy, Spain, United Kingdom, United States
Stage 5: Canada

Source: Adapted from J. H. Dunning 'The Investment Development Path Revisited', in *Foreign Direct Investment and Governments. Catalysts for Economic Restructuring*, 1996, p. 2.

Figure 1.3 Investment development path

advantages can exist across industries leading to investments in countries with higher per capita GDP by TNCs from countries in stages 2 and 3 (e.g. Tata from India in the United States, United Kingdom, and Singapore; Salim from Indonesia in the United States, Europe and Japan; Hyundai from South Korea in Canada). Per capita GDP is not the only determinant of a country's FDI position. Net outward investment per capita is likely to be higher in countries that depend on 'created' assets (e.g. know-how, technologies, management) for their prosperity than in countries where natural resources abound (e.g. China vs Singapore, Russia vs Hungary). Government measures may also stimulate or restrict the level of either inward or outward investment and can significantly alter a country's net outward FDI position.

The FDI position of a country is also conditioned by its general economic performance, particularly the stage of development of its industries, which reflects its endowment of labour, capital and other resources. Countries where labour-intensive, low-skill manufacturing or natural resource extraction prevails are mostly net FDI importers. As they move on to capital-intensive industrial activities, domestic companies gain financial strength and start undertaking investments abroad (stages 2 and 3 on the IDP). The Chinese and Indian economies reached that stage on the IDP during the early 1990s.[42] The net FDI position starts improving further with the expansion of more advanced high-tech and knowledge-intensive goods and services, especially if there is a clear policy of TNC-facilitated industrial upgrading that allows a country to move on to stage 4 of the IDP (e.g. France, Germany).

Russia is in a somewhat paradoxical situation. Since economic transformation started many years ago, the country has not been able to attract volumes of FDI commensurate with its size and potential resources. On the other hand, if official statistics can be taken at face value, Russia has built up the strongest outward FDI position among European transition countries. Outward FDI corresponds to about one-third of inbound FDI and is growing, while inbound FDI is still stagnating.[43] This fact places the country at stage 3 of the IDP. Although low inbound volumes mainly reflect the lack of a coherent FDI policy and the still unclear legal conditions for foreign investors, the Russian case shows that intermediary positions and even jumps on the IDP are possible, and that the theory cannot claim to be a foolproof recipe for economic development with the support of FDI.

However, the theory postulates that countries at stages 2 and 3 first experience increases in inward and then in outward FDI, which is hardly the case for Russia in 1999. If Russian authorities will make all the necessary efforts in the coming years to attract more FDI, then much higher inbound than outbound flows are to be expected. The theory would thus regain its full validity, placing Russia at the very beginning of stage 2 of the IDP, which would be in line with the country's overall level of current economic and industrial development. In fact, if abstraction is made of current outbound flows, Russia would currently be somewhere at stage 1 of the IDP, i.e. at the beginning of a long process of massive inbound FDI. It should be the aim of the Russian government to fuel industrial development through an adequate FDI policy so that stage 3 can be reached during 2005–10. This would demonstrate a certain ability of Russian enterprises to compete in world markets.

1.10 Policy implications of major FDI theories

FDI theories elaborated by leading scholars attempt to find plausible explanations for the motivations of cross-border investment activities of TNCs and ways of economic advancement of countries through FDI. They include findings that can offer policy-makers valuable tools for increasing FDI by anticipating TNC behaviour, acting on fundamental decision-making variables at corporate level, and monitoring the FDI position of a national economy with respect to competitor nations. Some of the policy implications of the different theories are summarized in Table 1.6. FDI theories can provide significant guidelines for policy-making at the highest level, provided the assumptions underlying a specific theory are adapted to the local Russian context. The findings of a few selected theories can assist policy-makers in optimizing the entire FDI enhancement process, from strategic planning to the analysis phase and implementation, including the use of appropriate policy instruments and efficiency control. FDI specialists can thus be motivated to positively influence potential investors so that the desired investment can be solicited.

The theories presented in this chapter already demonstrate the complex nature of the 'FDI issue', which demands state-of-the-art intelligence, information and promotion mechanisms. To approach foreign investors effectively, the authorities will need to bestow an independent body or agency with the needed executive and advisory powers in the field of FDI.[44] The agency needs to become credible quickly and therefore must enjoy the highest possible political legitimation by liaising with the top level of the Russian executive and legislative. In a transition economy, it would be ineffective to split FDI-related issues among several ministerial departments. Strong coordinating powers are required to rectify Russia's foreign investment situation and to achieve speedy industrial upgrading.

Independently of the definitive FDI strategy adopted by the Russian leadership, regular monitoring and intelligence operations are indispensable in a dynamic world marked by intense competition and growing economic integration among nations. Major FDI theories provide a valuable incentive so that political decisions are based on actual facts and realistic projections with respect to global opportunities and competition.

Table 1.6 Policy implications of major FDI theories

Major FDI theories	FDI parameters affected	Policy implications and intelligence efforts
International product cycle	Industrial sectors (low, medium, high-tech), process technologies (traditional, innovative)	• To encourage policy-makers to conduct systematic intelligence operations on the development of promising economic sectors and industries • To observe closely which sectors are moving from a pattern focused on foreign trade towards a pattern focused on FDI
Monopolistic competition, defensive oligopolistic behaviour	TNCs	• To monitor global activities of market leaders and their key factors of success (corporate resources, motivations, type of technologies and know-how, R&D budgets, type of preferred investment, etc.) by screening annual reports (mainly for public limited companies) and press releases in specialized and other journals. The organization in charge of FDI monitoring in Russia should subscribe to these information sources from major FDI-exporting countries. These journals also include valuable information on medium-sized TNCs • To study, each year, the international ranking of the world's leading oligopolist TNCs. The analysis could focus on a number of essential variables: type of activity, turnover, assets abroad and employment. Monitoring should cover the top 500 or, at least, the top 200 companies. A separate intelligence activity should cover the largest TNCs from emerging countries (Brazil, China, India, Indonesia, Malaysia, Mexico, South Korea) and their global FDI activities
Internalization theory	TNCs, international firm competition	• To incorporate in Russia's FDI intelligence efforts observation of company-specific know-how, both for large and medium-sized TNCs • To focus on technologies and know-how offered by medium-sized operators in selected countries and sectors on the basis of Russia's industrial potential and the government's priority sectors to be developed in the coming 10–15 years • To build intelligence resources and skills that general research operations cannot generate

continued ...

Table 1.6 (*continued*)

Major FDI theories	FDI parameters affected	Policy implications and intelligence efforts
Flying geese paradigm	Competitor LEMs and other emerging economies	• To observe macroeconomic indicators, particularly foreign trade patterns of technology-exporting countries • To monitor evolution of industrial competitiveness in competitor countries • To study the positive effects of industrial upgrading through FDI in Russia for neighbouring CIS economies • To speed up the catching-up process through international economic integration
Competitive advantage of nations	Industrial competitiveness criteria, national policy agenda	• To understand the importance of strategy and planning • To consider the impact of government policy on national well-being • To monitor industrial competitiveness and factors of success • To determine the correlation between the FDI situation and economic/industrial performance
Eclectic paradigm	TNCs, competition among nations	• To monitor domestic company-specific factors for raising competitiveness • To improve location-specific advantages in the economic, political and legal spheres
Investment development path	Competition among nations	• To measure national competitiveness by monitoring a country's net outward investment position • To achieve higher sector competitiveness through targeted FDI

Notes

1. A. Smith, *Wealth of Nations*, 1776.
2. Part II.
3. Chapter 1.8.
4. Chapter 1.9.
5. Chapter 1.2.
6. This theory is not covered in this publication because of its political rather than economic emphasis.
7. Chapter 1.7.
8. Part V.
9. Chapter 1.8.

10. Chapter 13.2.
11. Chapter 17.1.
12. R. Vernon, 'International Investment and International Trade in the Product Cycle', *Quarterly Journal of Economics*, 1996, 80:190–207.
13. Chapter 12.2
14. Chapter 17.1.2.
15. S. H. Hymer, *The International Operations of National Firms: A Study of Direct Investment*, 1960.
16. C. P. Kindleberger, *American Business Abroad*, 1969.
17. Chapters 1.3. and 1.4.
18. T. Horst, 'The Industrial Composition of US Exports and Subsidiary Sales to the Canadian Market', *American Economic Review*, 1972, 62:37–45.
19. S. Lall, *Monopolistic Advantages and Foreign Investment by US Manufacturing Industry*, 1980, pp. 102–22.
20. Y. Kimura, 'Firm-specific Strategic Advantages and Foreign Direct Investment Behaviour of Firms: The Case of Japanese Semi-conductor Firms', *Journal of International Business Studies*, 1989, 20:296–314.
21. Chapters 1.7 and 1.8.
22. F. T. Knickerbocker, *Oligopolistic Reaction and the Multinational Enterprise*, 1973.
23. E. M. Graham, 'Transatlantic Investment by Multinational Firms: A Rivalistic Phenomenon', *Journal of Post-Keynesian Economics*, no. 1, 1978.
24. Chapter 16.3.
25. Chapter 4.2.
26. P. J. Buckley and M. Casson, *The Future of the Multinational Enterprise*, 1976.
27. A. M. Rugman, *Inside the Multinationals, the Economics of Internal Markets*, 1981.
28. Chapter 2.5.
29. K. Kojima, *Direct Foreign Investment: A Japanese Model of Business Operations*, 1978.
30. K. Kojima and T. Ozawa, 'Micro- and Macro-Economic Models of Direct Foreign Investment: Toward a Synthesis', *Hitotsubashi Journal of Economics*, no. 25, 1984.
31. Chapter 4.
32. See Part VI for policy options.
33. Chapter 1.8.
34. Chapter 12.3.
35. Chapter 17.1.
36. Chapter 1.8.
37. J. H. Dunning, *International Production and the Multinational Enterprise*, 1981.
38. J. H. Dunning, *Multinational Enterprises and the Global Economy*, 1992.
39. Chapter 1.9.
40. R. Mucchielli, *Les firmes multinationales : mutation et nouvelles perspectives* [Multinational corporations: evolution and new developments], 1985.
41. J. Stehn, *Determinanten differenzierter Internationalisierungsstrategien* [Determining factors of differentiated internationalization strategies], 1989.
42. Chapters 5 and 6.
43. Chapters 3.3.3 and 9.3.
44. Chapter 17.

Part II

Global FDI Potential and Opportunities for the Russian Economy

Introduction

Part II presents an overview of the current investment situation in the world. For the most important countries and regions, outward and inward flows are studied from a historical perspective to highlight the economic significance of FDI. The analysis of global FDI trends[1] and their relevance to Russia's economy is preceded by a description of the main determining factors for FDI. One of the most significant external factors, the increasing globalization and integration of world economies, is driven by transnational corporations (TNCs) as they gain market shares through their control of worldwide manufacturing and R&D networks. International operations by TNCs have surged to a level that enables them to directly influence the volume and type of FDI through greenfield investments, acquisitions and strategic alliances.[2]

The global importance of FDI in terms of its share in GDP and gross capital formation or domestic investment of recipient countries has risen considerably during the past decade. The employment, income and export effects of inbound FDI have contributed appreciably to the double-digit growth rates reported by China and several other emerging economies (e.g. Chile, Malaysia, Thailand) during the early and mid-1990s. FDI-induced industrial restructuring operations in Central Europe (e.g. Czech Republic, Hungary, Poland) during 1991–98 have been equally successful, and these trends have benefited the world economy as a whole.

The G5 economies – France, Germany, Japan, the United Kingdom and the United States – have accumulated substantial stocks of FDI in all the major world regions. TNCs residing in these countries represent the most important source of global FDI, accounting for roughly two-thirds of outward FDI stock in the world. Western and Japanese TNCs are also the main potential providers of capital, know-how and product innovations for CIS countries, including Russia. Their strategies and FDI motivations therefore require special analysis.

The geographic and sectoral distribution of global FDI has shifted over time. While OECD economies continue representing the most important source of capital and technologies, certain emerging economies have set out on their investment development path[3] by reducing their external dependence and by becoming themselves countries of origin for certain types of investment. Outward FDI flows and stocks of countries like Taiwan, South Korea, Malaysia and even China have risen considerably since the late 1980s. They offer an alternative FDI source for European transition economies.

South Korean automobile TNCs, for example, have recently invested in production facilities in Hungary, Russia and Uzbekistan. In late 1997, a Chinese state-owned enterprise decided to invest US$50 million to produce 42 000 motorcycles annually in Brazil.[4]

So far, CIS countries have not been able to attract adequate annual flows of FDI.[5] Their FDI stock was about US$20–21 billion in 1997, more than half of which was in Russia.[6] This is lower than the stock in Austria (US$22 billion in 1997) and represents only 0.6 per cent of global FDI stock. The reason is simple: TNCs pursue objectives of profitability and efficiency and are therefore prepared to undertake major investments abroad only if political and economic risks are sufficiently low so that the invested capital is paid back within a predefined period.

Confidence levels in the Russian economy and the country's political stability are quite low, although tight FDI legislation is already partially in place providing western investors with fair treatment and adequate guarantees.[7] Russia, however, has a chance of becoming an interesting destination for FDI only if it manages to convert current obstacles, especially the still unclear legal and fiscal situation, into visible advantages for foreign investors. Property rights have to be granted to foreign companies and frequent changes in taxation avoided (e.g. corporate, value-added and many other taxes for companies; income tax for expatriates). The remaining CIS countries are in a similar situation of flux and continuous change.

Russian industry would benefit greatly from foreign capital and know-how, tapped from the G5 and other industrialized (OECD) countries and selected emerging economies. However, efforts of the Russian authorities will be challenged by aggressive FDI policies of other large emerging economies, which are also massively restructuring and privatizing their economies (e.g. Brazil, Mexico, Poland) or have recently abandoned their import-substitution model for a more pragmatic export-oriented approach based on FDI (e.g. China, India, Indonesia). Russia will also have to compete with an array of medium-sized countries in Asia, Latin America and Central Europe now that FDI is widely recognized as a potential catalyst for better social welfare and living standards. As an example, the combined inward stock of six ASEAN countries – Indonesia, Malaysia, Philippines, Singapore, Thailand, Vietnam – already exceeded US$225 billion in 1997 (US$202 billion in 1996 and US$110 billion in 1995); only the United States and the United Kingdom have so far accumulated higher stocks, as individual countries. In 1996, ASEAN absorbed about US$31 billion (US$21 billion in 1995) of FDI, placing the region third after the United States and China, but before France, the United Kingdom, Belgium and Spain.[8] Although cultural differences persist within ASEAN, the region is considered as a growing and fairly homogeneous market where a manufacturing presence can be of strategic significance for TNCs.[9]

To design, promote and implement an efficient FDI policy,[10] Russian specialists need to first construct an efficient FDI intelligence system that will allow them to trace the origin of required technologies (countries, sectors, types of investment), to comprehend why certain markets have become preferred targets (motivations of TNC executives), and to study how national authorities in other countries actively influence FDI decision-making and attract high volumes of foreign investment through incentives packages, and information and promotion missions to canvass potential TNCs directly in their home countries. Compared with other leading emerging markets,[11] the attractiveness of Russia as a destination country will be determined by a combination of factors such as good economic prospects, possibilities to function as a platform for neighbouring markets, favourable FDI legislation and investor-friendly FDI policies.

Notes

1. Chapter 3.
2. Chapter 4.
3. Chapter 1.9.
4. *Euro-Brazil*, no. 27, 28 August–3 September 1997.
5. Chapter 3.3.3.
6. UN Economic Commission for Europe. *Statistical Survey of Recent Trends in Foreign Investment in East European Countries*, 23 November 1995. UNCTAD, *World Investment Report 1998*.
7. Chapter 9.4.
8. In 1997 and 1998, FDI inflows to ASEAN dropped to US$25 billion and US$22 billion, respectively, as a result of the financial crisis that hit the entire region. UNCTAD, *World Investment Reports 1995, 1996, 1997, 1998*.
9. Following the financial crash that occurred in the region at the end of 1997, TNCs are expected to strengthen their position further now that local currencies have been devalued.
10. Part VI.
11. Part III.

2
Determinants of Global FDI

Foreign investment is conditioned by the global context of economic and technological change and overall industrial competitiveness of countries and their industries. The prevailing macroeconomic (e.g. per capita income, growth rates, inflation, currency exchange rate, industrial output, trade surplus, balance of payments situation) and microeconomic conditions (e.g. competitive position and financial strength of local enterprises, sectoral conditions and concentration rates, corporate strategies) that determine volume and pattern of FDI flows can in turn be transformed by these flows.

FDI is a facilitator of industrial development and export growth through its contribution to economic transformation, modernization and job creation in both recipient and home countries. Political risk factors such as internal conflicts or external instabilities are heavily weighted variables in the decision-making process of foreign investors. The upsurge in FDI activities during the past 15 years can be attributed to the improved business performance and profit situation of TNCs. But the dynamics of FDI are also linked to a combination of other more structural factors, which increasingly affect national economies and the readiness of companies to invest abroad. Successful implementation of liberal economic policies, economic integration at a regional and global level, deregulation of international capital movements, availability of new technologies, and the peaceful resolution of internal and external conflicts have all given impetus to FDI (Figure 2.1).

To enhance FDI inflows, Russia needs to send positive signals to the international community by participating in all international endeavours aimed at removing current barriers for global FDI. It should

- deepen economic integration within the CIS;
- cooperate closely with the EU, Japan and NAFTA;
- liaise regularly with large emerging markets (LEMs),[1] especially China and India;

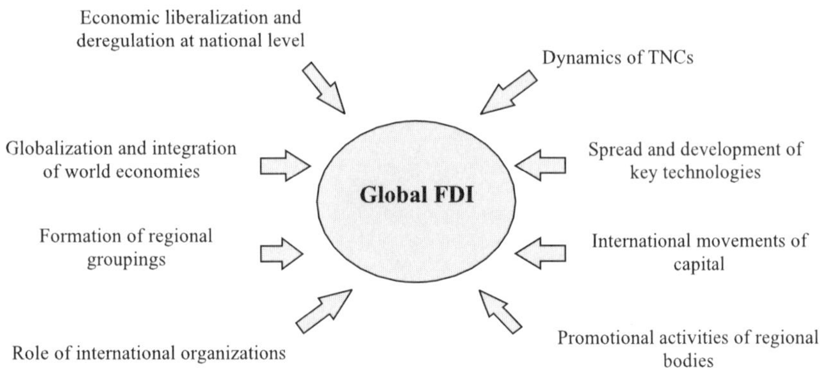

Figure 2.1 Global determinants for increased FDI

- join the World Trade Organization (WTO); and
- consult with the Organisation for Economic Co-operation and Development (OECD).

Internally, the government should intensify market reforms and economic liberalization, and integration with the world economy (endogenous variables). Long-term investment decisions by TNCs in Russia will largely depend on the existence of modern infrastructure (roads, communications and energy supply) and a comprehensive, investor-friendly FDI policy.

2.1 Economic liberalization and deregulation at national level

At the beginning of the 1980s, most industralized countries in western Europe and North America were caught in a general economic recession, obliging governments to look for additional revenue and to cut public spending. Among the first countries to deregulate their economies and privatize state assets were the United States and the United Kingdom, followed later by Germany, France, Italy, Spain and other EU member states. Labour, tax and foreign trade laws were simplified and many state monopolies in sectors like telecommunications, energy, air transport, insurance and banking were dissolved. National and foreign investors were invited to participate in public tenders, to bring in their capital and to engage in local production or the acquisition of local companies.

In 1989, the United States attracted US$68 billion in FDI,[2] more than any other country in the world. The United Kingdom ranked second with inbound flows of US$30 billion that year. Four years later, in 1993, France reported record inflows of US$21 billion. In the following years, the government embarked on a massive sale of its participation in aerospace (Aérospatiale), automobile (Renault), electrical engineering (Bull), banking and insurance (BNP, Crédit Lyonnais, Assurances de Paris), chemicals (Rhône-Poulenc), and public utilities (Générale des Eaux) state-owned enterprises. The French government's objective was to raise annual revenues of US$10–12 billion during 1994–97 only through the sale of state assets, while limiting non-EU participations to one-fifth of the privatization value.[3]

Following the French example, Italy started privatizing its state conglomerates, especially in the utilities, oil and telecommunications sectors. Germany's large-scale privatization programme, undertaken in 1990 in the eastern *Länder*, was engineered by the *Treuhand* agency, but it boosted inbound investment only in the first two years. Foreign investors were soon deterred by a number of locational disadvantages including rising labour costs, the rigid tax structure and stringent environmental control regulations which were applicable to both the western and eastern *Länder*. Currently, government efforts in Germany to reform the tax and social welfare system are aimed at removing such obstacles and to attract more FDI into the country.

It did not take long before numerous developing countries followed suit and began to open up their protected economies to international investors. Economic stagnation at home imposed a radical shift from inward-looking, import substituting (IL–IS) trade and investment concepts towards outward-looking, export oriented (OL–EO) regimes. The change in policy came about as domestic industries were reorganized and oriented towards foreign markets.

Outward-looking policies were also encouraged by GATT (today WTO) and international organizations like the World Bank and the IMF, which offered special loan facilities only on condition that governments liberalize and privatize their economies, cut their budget deficits and allow entry of foreign investors. The global FDI situation improved after larger emerging countries like Brazil, China, India, Indonesia and Mexico, where protectionist measures hindered market penetration by foreign investors, eventually started opening their economies and removing important obstacles to foreign trade and investment in the late 1980s and early 1990s.

Finally, liberal ideas and economic concepts made their way into countries with a socialist past such as Poland, Hungary, Russia, Ukraine and Vietnam. Governments in these countries introduced free market systems starting from 1990–91, and now widely recognize the significance of consistent policies aimed at price stabilization, careful public spending, and foreign trade and investment liberalization for enhancing domestic economic performance and industrial competitiveness. Economic liberalization and waves of privatization of former state enterprises observed in transition countries in the first half of the 1990s have given a new impetus to global integration.

The adherence to free market systems around the globe paved the way to broad economic restructuring and industrial diversification through FDI. In 1995, privatizations accounted for about 55 per cent of inward FDI into the transition economies of Central and Eastern Europe.[4] Russia's reform programme led to the privatization of 40–50 per cent of its industrial enterprises, but the annual contribution by foreign investors during 1993–97 was insignificant (US$2.6 billion on average).[5] As a comparison, China managed to attract FDI worth US$44 billion during 1996–98, mainly through joint ventures and greenfield investments and, to a lesser extent, through foreign participation in domestic enterprises as part of a large-scale privatization programme.[6]

Governments usually decide to sell state assets in periods of overall recession and budgetary pressure. Today, deregulation combined with privatization has been declared an economic policy objective that will also help unleash the innovation potential and vitality of the private sector. Entrepreneurs and private enterprises, goaded by efficiency motivations, are expected to spot the best business opportunities instantly so that shareholder value can be enhanced and employment generated through higher sales. Deregulation of the national economy is usually accompanied by important concessions and guarantees to foreign investors: protection from expropriation, unhindered repatriation of profits, possibility of majority stakes in local companies, and wide-ranging incentives such as tax holidays and short-term depreciation of assets.

Restrictive trade and FDI policies are widely considered as counterproductive as they lead to economic isolation and stagnation. Empirical evidence suggests that countries with deregulated economies and a strong private sector are more likely to attract FDI and are more successful in raising their citizens' living standards and generating sustainable economic growth than countries with overregulated economies (Figure 2.2). In 1998–99, deregulated economies are expected to grow between 2 per cent (Russia) and 7.5 per cent (China). However, to be truly effective, economic liberalization measures must be combined with a targeted industrial and FDI policy that will actively promote and channel the transfer of capital and vital manufacturing technologies. Such a policy must be embedded in a set of interlinked socioeconomic institutions, which strengthen the multiplier effect of TNC operations in the host country.

2.2 Globalization and integration of world economies

The current globalization trend is the logical consequence of a long process of internationalization that began centuries ago when traders looked for new opportunities to exchange surpluses for goods they needed from other parts of the world. Arab traders travelled as far as central Africa and the Indian subcontinent to offer their commodities as early as the seventh century. Another example is the famous *Hanse* league, an association of merchants which formed the first-free trade area stretching from Brugge in Belgium to Novgorod in Russia, between the thirteenth and fourteenth centuries. Trade

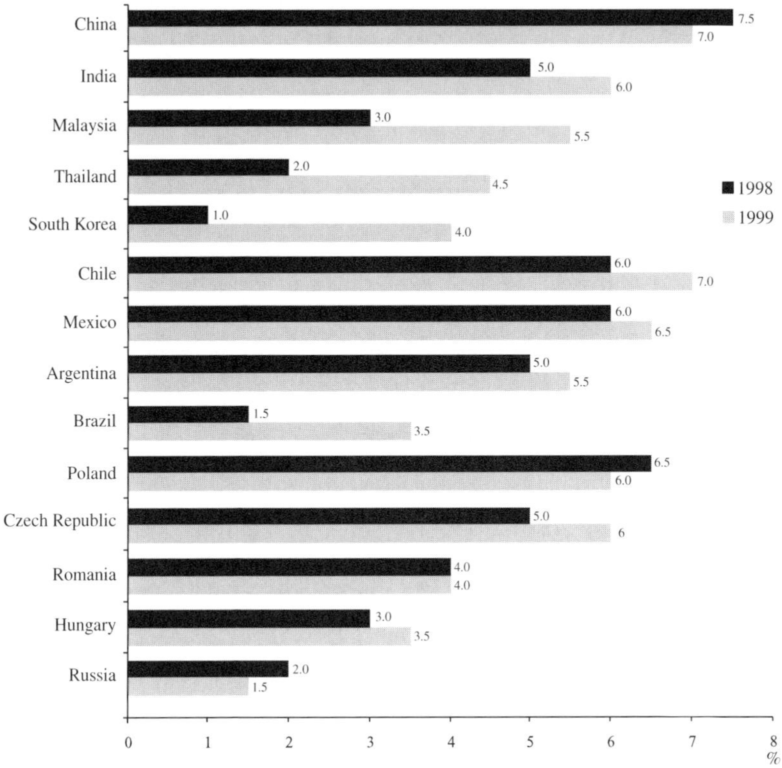

Source: OECD; *The Economist* 'Indicators', several issues, 1998, 1999.

Figure 2.2 GDP growth in emerging countries, 1998–99

relations also led to the transfer of cultural values and religious beliefs. During the nineteenth and twentieth centuries, the European colonial powers opened trading posts practically all over the world, which also spread their cultural, administrative and legal systems.

Today's national economies have moved even closer. National borders no longer represent major obstacles to TNCs, which besides trading products and services are also transferring capital, process and product technologies, management skills, knowledge and information, and their brands. In the 1960s, western TNCs started investing heavily abroad by establishing international production and distribution networks enabling them to become insiders in the most important consumer markets. In the 1980s, leading TNCs engaged in strategic FDI by controlling sophisticated technology and information networks that allowed them to pick up equal or majority stakes in local enterprises, or set up joint ventures and wholly-owned subsidiaries in charge of local production, product adaptation and distribution facilities.

In spite of the controversies raised by FDI exports (e.g. plant closures, lay-offs, brain drain, capital outflows, labour unrest), the process of globalization will continue. Analysts expect that the world's economies will become even more interdependent through a combination of foreign trade, cross-border alliances and investment operations by multinational companies. However, globalization requires technology-exporting countries to constantly develop new skills to stay ahead of global competition and to maintain a certain level of employment by anticipating relocation (foreign production) to less-developed countries in certain industries (e.g. electronics, automobiles, textiles machinery, apparel).

International economic integration affects highly populated and resource-rich countries as much as smaller countries. No economy – mature, emerging or in transition – can be self-sufficient any more in terms of available factors of production, manufacturing technologies and capital needs. The process of globalization has gained momentum with the sudden end of the Cold War, which allowed the return of former socialist countries into the world community. In Eastern Europe, China and Vietnam, people had been isolated for many decades for ideological reasons. They now have the freedom to travel and to expand their horizons by engaging in international business activities. The other side of the coin is that Russia and its CIS neighbours were abruptly pushed into a fast-moving international environment without possessing the competitive industrial infrastructure to assert themselves on world markets. A prime objective in the years to come will therefore be to raise industrial output, economic growth and living standards through the exchange of products, technologies and know-how with other countries through FDI.

Globalization has already generated higher FDI and trade flows than in former times. Modern communication, transport and financial links are rapidly making the 'global village' a reality, but globalization can also reduce the manoeuvring capacity of governments. They will have to join forces to supervise cross-border activities, and information and capital networks of TNCs. As businesses increase their information advantages, policy-makers will need to change their neglectful attitudes to the global challenge.

The globalization of world economies and the foreign investment operations by TNCs have definitely benefited consumers, as international competition gives them the possibility to choose and put downward pressure on final prices (Box 2.1). Global media networks (e.g. CNN, Euronews, BBC) also keep the growing middle class well-informed about world events and new possibilities of consumption. Consumers are also voters: governments therefore have no real choice but to give due consideration to their demand for better and cost-effective goods and services.

Countries must therefore join the race of globalization and compete by developing strong domestic industries. Russia is no exception.

Box 2.1 Realities of globalization

- Intermediary products and semimanufactures have a growing share in world trade and intra-company transfers.
- FDI rises more quickly than foreign trade and production at a global level.
- Fierce competition has spread beyond the economy and business to penetrate all spheres of life (e.g. research, science, education, media, culture).
- Importance of human capital and knowledge as a determinant of national competitiveness.
- Powerful oligopolistic enterprises occupy dominant positions in global production in a number of industrial and service sectors.
- Industrialized countries attempt to remain competitive by developing high-tech sectors with a high R&D component and by moving away from mass production.
- International division of labour enables TNCs to relocate manufacturing operations to countries presenting the best locational advantages.
- Information and communication technologies are integrated into the planning and manufacturing processes of TNCs.
- International financial centres (banks, stock exchanges, currency markets) are interlinked and lead to high capital flows, which are not necessarily related to trade in goods and services.
- English is generally accepted as the *lingua franca*, which facilitates intercultural communication, learning and understanding.

2.3 The formation of regional groupings

Regional groupings like the European Union (EU), the North American Free Trade Association (NAFTA), the Association of South-East Asian Nations (ASEAN), the South Asian Association of Regional Cooperation (SAARC), the Commonwealth of Independent States (CIS), and MERCOSUR in South America were formed to further integrate national economies and to strengthen the bargaining power of member countries *vis-à-vis* third countries (Map 2.1). The aim is to generate economic growth and to create employment by improving trade and investment relations between member countries, and by attracting more FDI from third countries.

The EU, launched in 1957 under the name of the European Economic Community, is one of the first associations of countries. It is the only

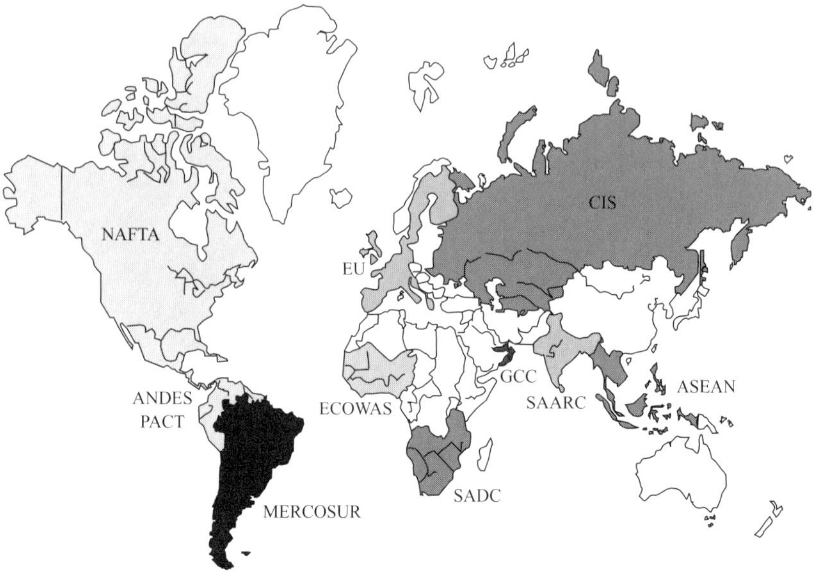

Andes Pact: Bolivia, Ecuador, Colombia, Peru, Venezuela
Association of Southeast Asian Nations (ASEAN): Brunei, Cambodia, Indonesia, Laos, Malaysia, Myanmar, Philippines, Singapore, Thailand, Vietnam
Commonwealth of Independent States (CIS): Armenia, Azerbaijan, Belarus, Georgia, Kazakhstan, Kirgizistan, Moldova, Russia, Tadjikistan, Turkmenistan, Ukraine, Uzbekistan
Economic Community of West African States (ECOWAS): Benin, Burkina Faso, Côte d'Ivoire, Gambia, Ghana, Guinea, Guinea-Bissau, Cabo Verda, Liberia, Mali, Mauritania, Niger, Nigeria, Senegal, Sierra Leone, Togo
European Union (EU): Austria, Belgium, Denmark, Finland, France, Germany, Greece, Ireland, Italy, Luxembourg, Netherlands, Portugal, Spain, Sweden, United Kingdom
Gulf Cooperation Council (GCC): Bahrein, Kuwait, Oman, Qatar, United Arab Emirates
Mercado Comun del Sur (MERCOSUR): Argentina, Brazil, Bolivia, Chile, Paraguay, Uruguay
North American Free Trade Area (NAFTA): Canada, Mexico, United States
South Asian Association for Regional Cooperation (SAARC): Bangladesh, Bhutan, India, Maldives, Nepal, Pakistan, Sri Lanka
Southern African Development Area (SADC): Angola, Botswana, Lesotho, Malawi, Mauritius, Mozambique, Namibia, Republic of South Africa, Swaziland, Tanzania, Zambia, Zimbabwe

Figure 2.3 The world's main regional groupings

grouping that has a parliament with representatives elected by the people of the member states. It is unique in so far as its institutions – Council of Ministers, Commission, Parliament, Court of Justice, Court of Auditors and European Investment Bank – have increasing autonomy and for certain aspects supranational powers. It has been criticized for its cumbersome decision-making procedures (unanimity, simple and qualified majority voting) and complicated regulatory mechanisms (regulations, directives, decisions, recommendations).

For a long time, leading EU member states (e.g. France and Italy) were accused of setting up a fortress against imports and investments from third countries.[7] This led to massive inflows of capital and other forms of investments in the more liberal EU countries (e.g. United Kingdom, Germany, the Netherlands, Denmark, Belgium), especially by US, Japanese, South Korean and ASEAN companies. Transplants, greenfield operations and acquisitions were launched especially in the United Kingdom, the 'Trojan horse' that would help them conquer the European mainland. Other destination countries were Belgium (machinery, pharmaceuticals, automotive components, food), Ireland (computers and software), Italy (processed food, chemicals, machinery), the Netherlands (chemicals, machinery, consumer products) and Spain (transport equipment, consumer electronics).

But third-country FDI into the EU is not yet commensurate with the region's economic size and future potential. High taxes and strict labour laws (e.g. regulation to install EU-wide labour councils in enterprises with over 1000 employees and over 150 employees in at least two member states) are major deterrents. In 1997, third-country investments into the 15 countries that now form the EU amounted to US$36 billion, only one-third of what the United States was able to absorb that year and much less than the volume of intra-EU investments (US$110 billion).[8]

The integration process has, however, increased intra-EU trade and investment leading to a high degree of economic and financial interdependence among the member states. Germany, for example, the second largest exporting country in the world, concentrates 60 per cent of its foreign trade and 45–50 per cent of its FDI within the EU.[9] The big challenge for the EU in the coming years will be to design coherent policies for employment generation, environment protection and efficient public spending. The burden on enterprises will have to be reduced so that investors within and outside the EU regain confidence in the region as a profitable location for investment. These measures will be decisive factors for a successful shift to the euro, the common currency adopted by 11 member states on 1 January 1999.

Depending on the degree of economic integration (Table 2.1), member countries can enjoy free trade regimes, have a common customs area *vis-à-vis* third countries, offer citizens freedom of travel and establishment in other member states, and adopt common commercial policies in case

Table 2.1 Degrees of economic integration

		A Free trade between members	B Common external customs tariffs	C Free movement of major economic factors (labour, goods, services)	D Harmonization of economic policies	E Free movement of capital, common institutions, common currency	F Common foreign and security policies
I	Free trade area	X					
II	Customs union	X	X				
III	Common market	X	X	X			
IV	Economic union	X	X	X	X		
V	Economic and monetary union	X	X	X	X	X	
VI	Political union	X	X	X	X	X	X

Source: Adapted from A. C. Hornero, *Integración economica y regionalismo* [Economic integration and regionalism], 1994.

of disputes with third countries, especially for foreign trade and investment. The EU is the world's most integrated grouping; it is now preparing for the ultimate step of integration, the realization of a monetary and political union between certain core countries, which need to fulfill established convergence criteria (low inflation rate, budget deficit below 3 per cent of GDP, public debt of up to 60 per cent of GDP) by the turn of this century.[10]

Integrated groupings like the EU adopt common standards and policies *vis-à-vis* third countries and a common stand in international organizations like the WTO, UN, OECD and the World Bank. The statutes of regional groupings increasingly include special provisions for regulating and protecting FDI. Intensification of global FDI activities is thus correlated to progress in regional economic cooperation and integration. Regulatory practices for FDI also increase with the degree of integration, and the EU has progressed farthest in this respect. A supranational competition policy empowers the EU Commission (Directorate-General IV) to block inter-company agreements as well as possible abuses of a dominant position by enterprises and of state aid, if the provisions of the Union Treaty are violated (Union Treaty, Articles 85–6, 90–4). Additionally, the EU Merger Control Regulation[11] obliges companies engaging in a merger or acquisition to notify the Commission for its approval (Box 2.2). A special Merger Task Force in DG IV looks into the matter, drafts a decision and sends it to the member state authorities for consultation.[12] Other less integrated groupings such as free trade areas (e.g. CIS, ASEAN) or common markets (e.g. MERCOSUR) also tend to include special provisions in their founding agreements to foster and protect foreign investments from both member and third countries.

Box 2.2 Notification criteria for the EU Merger Control Regulation

- Merging companies must have a combined (world) turnover of €5 billion or more.
- At least two of the companies concerned must realize sales of €250 million within the EU.
- No notification is necessary, if each company achieves two-thirds of its turnover within one member state (mergers whose impact is primarily national are excluded).

The CIS – established in 1991 – today comprises Russia and 11 other countries, which gained their independence following the dissolution of the Soviet Union. The three Baltic States rejected the offer to join the CIS and opted for closer economic ties with the EU with a prospect of full membership by 2000–05; they have followed the Visegrad countries Czech Republic, Hungary, Poland, Slovakia and Slovenia. For Russia, by far the largest member of the

CIS, followed by Kazakhstan (in area) and Ukraine (in population), good neighbourly relations with other member countries are crucial to promote trade and investment. Open borders and complete abolition of trade barriers within the CIS will increase the locational advantages of the entire region. Third-country TNCs contemplating investment in Russia are bound to plan expansion of their operations to neighbouring markets. These changes are urgently needed as intra-CIS trade, which was based on traditional links between enterprises in the former Soviet republics, has dropped dramatically since the newly independent states introduced their own national currency and decided to leave the rouble zone during 1991–93. A common investment policy under the aegis of the CIS Interstate Committee of the Economic Union,[13] a permanent executive and coordinating body established in 1994, aims to foster economic integration. In addition, Russia needs a consistent policy to improve trade relations with its neighbours.

A recent example of a successful grouping with a positive economic fallout for its members is MERCOSUR, which was launched the same year as the CIS (1991). Its current membership includes Argentina, Brazil, Paraguay, Uruguay and subsequent members Bolivia and Chile, which both joined in 1996. Unlike in the CIS, however, intra-regional trade in MERCOSUR increased almost fourfold, from US$3.4 billion in 1991 to almost US$15 billion in 1995.[14] Intra-MERCOSUR investments rose by over 20 per cent during that period, and substantial FDI has flowed in from the United States and the EU, the main trading and investment partners. MERCOSUR has become the world's fourth largest economic grouping (200 million inhabitants) with a combined GDP of US$800 billion and exports worth US$63 billion. Some 95 per cent of intra-MERCOSUR trade is already duty-free, with remaining tariffs expected to be removed before 2000.

Before MERCOSUR, there were fewer than 20 Brazilian companies with offices, plants and subsidiaries in Argentina. In 1995, there were more than 400, with total investments of US$1 billion. Also by 1995, an estimated 80 Argentinian companies had set up operations in Brazil, investing about US$250 million. MERCOSUR has succeeded in attracting considerable flows of FDI since 1995; Brazil alone received a record US$29 billion in foreign investment in 1998, Argentina and Chile about US$5–6 billion each.[15] There were more than 200 acquisitions of MERCOSUR companies by western (mainly US and European, but also Japanese and South Korean) TNCs. The most common sectors for FDI operations are automobiles, chemicals, pharmaceuticals, computers, consumer electronics, food and sports goods. MERCOSUR's FDI stock will exceed US$200 billion during 1999; it could soon challenge ASEAN as a second major destination.

The EU signed a cooperation agreement with MERCOSUR in 1992 and since then has actively supported the integration process by providing financial and technical assistance. This success is mainly related to a mix of tariff reductions, internal economic reforms and privatizations, macro-economic policy coordination between the member states, specialization in internationally competitive sectors; and a clear commitment to attract foreign know-how through liberal FDI policies.

NAFTA[16] and ASEAN provide other examples of groupings that have successfully increased economic and industrial relations between their members. Russia and its CIS partners should draw lessons from these developments by studying the integration efforts of such regional groupings. They should also seek to ensure close ties with established groupings – represented by their institutions as in the case of the EU – as well as directly with main member countries.

Another grouping, which could become of major importance to Russia as a transcontinental power, is the Asia-Pacific Economic Cooperation (APEC) forum, which unites all the Pacific Rim countries. Towards 1998–99, Russia is expected to join APEC, together with Peru and Vietnam. Under an agreement reached in Indonesia in 1994, APEC aims at free trade and investment in the region, by 2010 for industralized members and by 2020 for developing economies. Unlike the EU, APEC has no supranational institutions with fixed procedures and is only represented by a small secretariat based in Singapore. The grouping is poised to become a major vehicle for intensifying trade and investment across the Pacific in the twenty-first century.[17]

2.4 The role of international organizations for global investment standards

Economic globalization, interdependence and integration between countries and regions is promoted by specialized agencies that aim to facilitate foreign trade and, increasingly, to protect foreign investment. They have a difficult task because of their global scope. These agencies have to ensure, among many countries at different stages of economic development, the acceptance, respect and enforcement of multilateral rules. Although multilateral rules governing FDI are still weak, international organizations like the WTO and OECD are pondering over ways to reduce discrimination against foreign investment, which distorts international trade in much the same way as tariffs and import quotas.[18]

International investment operations were earlier undertaken outside the control and supervision of international bodies and often exposed to discriminatory practices by national governments. Such practices are still quite common. Private companies can now seek protection for individual projects that are carried out and insured under the aegis of the World Bank (MIGA facility) or covered by bilateral investment protection agreements between the two countries. Russia, for example, has signed such agreements with a number of countries such as Austria, Canada, France, Germany, Italy and the United States. In 1994, Russia also signed a cooperation and partnership treaty with the EU which, however, does not include firm provisions for foreign investment.

The increase in global FDI during the early 1990s can be attributed to the growing commitment of the international community to open and fair trade. For almost 50 years, GATT provisions had outlawed discrimination among members and between imported and domestically-produced goods. Since the establishment of GATT in 1947, average tariff levels have fallen progressively, from almost 40 per cent to under 5 per cent, over its seven trade rounds. The Uruguay Round, which lasted from 1986 to 1993, led to additional tariff reductions and established new trade rules for agriculture, services, intellectual property rights and dispute settlement. The World Trade Organization (WTO), which succeeded GATT as a full-fledged institution on 1 January 1995, is the legal guarantor of the multilateral trading system. It aims to 'provide investors, employers, employees and consumers with a business environment encouraging trade, investment, and job creation as well as choice and low prices in the market place'.[19]

Recently, the WTO began to study the issue of foreign investment promotion and protection. At the first WTO Ministerial Conference, which took place during 9–13 December 1996 in Singapore, scope and contents of possible multilateral investment rules were discussed and a decision taken to establish a work programme on FDI. Global investment regulations become necessary as only very few provisions of selected WTO agreements, such as those on services, trade-related investment measures (TRIMs) and intellectual property rights (TRIPs), touch upon foreign investment issues. In the relevant provisions (e.g. Services Agreement, Articles I and XXVIII), the term 'investment' had to be replaced by other terms such as 'commercial presence',[20] mainly out of consideration for certain member countries that did not want FDI to be mentioned specifically in a multilateral legal document.[21]

A multilateral agreement under the supervision of the WTO would have several advantages: a close link between freer trade and freer investment; existing agreements on goods, service and intellectual property rights; endorsement by over 130 countries including all major FDI recipients (except China, but it has announced its readiness to join); and the possibility of establishing a global dispute settlement system. Russia is not yet a member of the WTO, but participates in sessions as an observer. Currently, the EU is pressing for the formulation and rapid ratification of a separate agreement covering all essential aspects of FDI under the aegis of the OECD. The United States and certain developing countries, however, see no urgency to conclude such an agreement and would first like to see the remaining agreements fully implemented.

Another earlier initiative chaired by the OECD, the feasibility and viability of investment rules, was discussed by member countries, and a cycle of multilateral negotiations was launched in May 1995 and continued until June 1997.[22] The OECD had already adopted several codes to liberalize capital movements and FDI in transport, communication and financial services (banks, insurance), which used to be strictly regulated. Member countries agreed to notify the OECD about restrictive measures and in 1998 signed a declaration enshrining the principle of status quo that would prevent the introduction of new measures, whereby foreign companies would be treated differently from domestic enterprises. TNCs in turn are expected to respect a code of good conduct by informing and consulting with national authorities about their investment intentions so that they are in line with the long-term social and economic objectives of the host country. OECD countries have yet to reach a formal agreement on FDI liberalization as some countries make this dependent on the approval of an international competition strategy.[23]

In 1998, negotiations on the Multilateral Agreement on Investment (MAI) by the 29 OECD member countries, which account for 85 per cent of outward FDI and 60 per cent of inward FDI, were formally discontinued at the instance of certain member states (e.g. France). The key idea was to put an end to restrictive practices, to oblige all signatory countries to create clear and harmonious rules for foreign investors (according to the most favoured nation principle) and not to treat FDI less favourably than domestic investments (including the hiring of foreign experts, capital, and real estate acquired by foreigners). International cooperation currently relies on 1600 or so bilateral investment treaties and regional agreements. MAI would have covered all forms of FDI and portfolio investments, and aimed at liberalizing, nurturing and protecting FDI. It would have been binding for all signatory countries and open to non-OECD members as well. As the treaty would have enabled companies to sue governments for compensation, several governments had submitted requests for country-specific exceptions, exclusion of certain sectors (e.g. books, films and television, by France and Canada), special environmental provisions, and concessions in case of general measures related to national security and public order.[24]

A new investment codex for TNCs to be enforced by a special joint WTO and UN supervisory body was still under discussion in 1999. The codex would contain special protection provisions for foreign investors but also a series of obligations for TNCs. Following the wave of international acquisitions and strategic alliances in the 1980s, proposals were submitted to formulate an international competition policy, which would limit concentration of companies if these have a negative impact on a country's economy, and impose a uniform social and environmental codex for cross-border operations. So far, these efforts have not resulted in any concrete measures. The EU remains the only regional grouping with its own supranational competition policy (Articles 85–94, Union Treaty).

International organizations like the WTO and OECD are slated to play an important role in further liberalizing FDI flows. Their aim is to standardize FDI rules and to promote a set of liberal ideas and common principles for adoption by the international community (Box 2.3). Once these basic principles are accepted, each participating country is expected to develop its own adaptations depending on its economic structures and the competitive situation in strategic domestic industries.

Box 2.3 The six leading principles guiding an international investment agreement[25]

- Right of establishment: markets should be generally open to foreigners through FDI.
- Nondiscrimination: foreign firms should not be confronted with discriminating regulations that change over time and according to political circumstances.
- National treatment: foreign-owned firms should be dealt with in the same way as companies owed by locals.
- Most-favoured nation: all foreigners should be treated alike.
- Supportive state intervention: government efforts, either in form of onerous conditions on FDI or distortionary incentives, should be kept to a minimum.
- Dispute settlement: the system should be open to TNCs and other investors who should be allowed to bring cases against host governments.

Another international organization that is also active on the subject of foreign investment is the United Nations Industrial Development Organization (UNIDO) with headquarters in Vienna. UNIDO's mission is to promote industrial development in developing and, increasingly, transition economies of Eastern Europe. It has organized a number of investment promotion conferences including some in major regions of the Russian Federation. It also established Investment Promotion Services (IPS) in selected countries, which are supposed to act as intermediaries between potential investors in the advanced economies and developing and transition countries. IPSs are connected on-line with the UNIDO representative offices in the main industralized countries. UNIDO also has an investment promotion unit in Moscow and its managerial staff is keen to cooperate with FDI authorities in Russia and major potential investor countries.

A number of multilateral agencies such as the European Bank for Reconstruction and Development (EBRD), based in London, and the International Finance Corporation (IFC), which is part of the World Bank group and based in Washington, DC, provide venture capital and project finance for viable companies located in emerging markets.[26] In 1995, IFC approved a total of US$2.4 billion for private investment projects in developing and transition economies, four times the volume that had been allocated 10 years ago.[27] In Poland, EBRD became the largest single investor, with capital outlays of US$1.5 billion directed at the banking sector and a number of promising industries.

Even more politically motivated organizations like the Organisation for Security and Cooperation in Europe (OSCE) have started fostering FDI as a major element of regional cooperation and economic development. At a high-level seminar held in Minsk, Russia, during 25–26 September 1996, a package of measures was put together to promote FDI: private-sector partnerships, reform of the administrative system, an assistance programme for SMEs, involvement of national associations of industrialists to enhance cross-border industrial cooperation, and elaboration of transparent guidelines defining rights and duties for TNCs.

An important guarantee organization is the Multilateral Investment Guarantee Agency (MIGA), which was created in 1988 under the auspices of the World Bank. MIGA serves as an insurer of FDI against political risks in host countries and provides policy guidance and development assistance to transition economies. Political risks covered are: inability to transfer FDI proceeds out of the host country, expropriation without due compensation, as well as wars, provided that the corporation has been wrongfully denied access to the host country's legal system, in particular the initial dispute resolution mechanisms. Thus MIGA mainly insures against the denial of justice by a host government to the company insured under MIGA.

2.5 Dynamics of transnational corporations

'Stateless' transnational corporations (TNCs) have become indispensable agents of global economic growth and technological transformation.[28] They are the chief initiators of cross-border movements of finance, technology and management skills and directly influence the international division of labour through global product, distribution and purchasing strategies. As true global players, TNCs open foreign affiliates to adapt products and services to new markets and to acquire foreign companies to benefit from their local brand equity (in case of an acquisition, local brands are usually integrated into global corporate brand concepts), assembly and manufacturing operations, and distribution infrastructure. They launch international joint ventures and strategic cooperation alliances to exploit common synergies in R&D, manufacturing and marketing. Today, TNCs control about 80 per cent of private worldwide technological capacity and account for a similar impressive share in global trade.[29] The foreign share of total turnover and production of certain corporations can be substantial.

Global strategies through foreign trade and investment are considered as the only alternatives for profit maximization, international growth and market leadership. TNCs can pursue different strategies to internationalize their operations.[30] Individual aims of companies, however, may clash with priorities set by national governments (protection of local industry, pollution control, labour laws). Especially, large oligopolists (e.g. chemicals, automobile, oil and gas multinationals, international banks) can muster the necessary financial and technological clout to obtain important concessions such as grants and long-term tax holidays from local authorities in desperate need of FDI. This has led to a number of investments with negative social (unemployment, class differences) and environmental effects, especially in developing and transition countries. These highly publicized instances have overshadowed the useful contribution of FDI to economic development.

To maintain a high level of bargaining power, national FDI experts therefore need to understand the investor's motivations, real strengths and weaknesses, and the competitive situation in the industry, preferably from a global perspective. International intelligence, data analysis and investor surveys by specialized government agencies or departments are therefore a prerequisite for formulating and implementing strategic FDI policies.

Growth and expansion of TNCs are warranted by long-term profitability and shareholder value. Countries with high political risk ratings are therefore outflanked by locations with higher political stability and investor-friendly FDI laws and incentives. Size and natural resources do not automatically guarantee a high level of inbound FDI. Smaller countries can compensate for their low market and resource potential through economic and political stability and nonambiguous laws. Singapore, for example, enjoys worldwide confidence among corporate executives; as a city-state with a very small area of 633 sq km, it managed to attract about US$10 billion worth of foreign investment in 1997,[31] and political predictability drew substantial Japanese investments to the United Kingdom in the 1980s. US companies turned increasingly to Mexico after the country joined NAFTA in 1994, obliging it to improve conditions for foreign investors.

TNCs select investment locations mainly on the basis of their strategic intentions in relation to their global competitors and customers. As a selection criterion, political risk overrides expected market potential, level of education and technical skills and availability of natural resources. In a survey carried out among executives of leading TNCs from Germany and published in 1996, political stability received the highest rating. Crucial for investment decisions were the risk of dramatic shifts in political power, expropriation, restrictions in capital transfers, and border conflicts. Investment and fiscal incentives in the recipient country are increasingly considered an asset as more countries compete for globally limited capital resources.[32] A correlation is observed between economic and industrial upgrading and the number of TNCs operating in the country. Foresighted governments usually orient TNCs with considerable FDI volumes towards those sectors and regions that need to be developed in line with domestic policy objectives. The global structure of the investing organization and its affiliate's contribution to the overall strategic goals of the corporation also determine the impact on technology and human capital.

Although TNCs are usually quite diversified, especially the larger ones, there seems to be a common trend worldwide for internationally-oriented companies to concentrate on core activities by reducing the number of product areas through divestment. These consolidation efforts are generally accompanied by reorganization (reengineering) and rationalization (cost-cutting) measures, leading to substantial downsizing of operations and a general reduction of the workforce. Owing to labour cost differentials, staffing levels are often reduced at home while employment is expanded abroad. The 1990s have also seen a large number of medium-sized TNCs increasingly take part in the global process of economic integration.[33]

Basically, four main types of TNCs can be distinguished, depending on the degree of autonomy of foreign affiliates and the relationship between production units located in various countries: multidomestic, multiregional, global and transregional (Box 2.4).

Box 2.4 Types of TNCs

- *Multidomestic TNCs*: The foreign affiliates have broad autonomy and their responsibility covers assembly, production and distribution of products in their markets. There is no strong central coordination from headquarters.
- *Multiregional TNCs*: Regional affiliates play a certain coordinating role, whereas national affiliates tend to specialize in products and services where their country markets possess distinct comparative advantages. Only regional affiliates enjoy a high degree of autonomy.
- *Global TNCs*: Economies of scale and scope are generated by organizing product families and functional areas (R&D, production, assembly, warehousing, distribution) according to the most profitable location. Strategic functions such as global investment decisions, cooperation with international partners, employment of top management and factory automation are decided at headquarters. Global integration of production sites can take three forms: network (by function), cluster (by industry) or total interrelation.
- *Transregional TNCs*: This model has become popular since the late 1980s; it attempts to combine the advantages of total integration (coordination of strategic activities that concern the entire group) and market adaptation and flexibility (highest possible degree of autonomy of affiliates for decisions concerning their markets).

Source: Adapted from M. Dicken, *Global Shift: The Internationalization of Economic Activity*, 1992.

2.6 Promotional activities of regional bodies

In federally-organized countries such as Belgium, Canada, Germany, India, Italy, Russia, Switzerland and the United States, regional and local governments have become important partners in the long-term political and economic decision-making process. While national governments have a special interest in territorial and security-related issues and macroeconomic stabilization (overall employment, inflation), regional authorities demand a greater say in FDI-related policies with a regional impact.

Large TNCs interested in carrying out an FDI operation in a specific regional market have to directly negotiate with the local authorities to clarify the conditions under which the investment is mutually acceptable: restructuring of local enterprises, project-related taxation, environmental and labour regulations, and possible incentives (direct contributions, tax concessions, etc.). Depending on the strategic importance of the investment for the country, preliminary talks are conducted with the central government. Regional authorities in industrialized countries vet investment projects from TNCs very carefully and then put forward the prerequisites for the investment and possible incentive components, depending on the size and impact of the project on the local economy and surrounding areas.

The federal–regional dichotomy is a common feature of large economies like Brazil, China, India, Indonesia, Mexico, Russia and the United States. The economic weight and strategic significance of each region (e.g. population, raw materials, geographic location) determine the power wielded by the respective regional authorities. In the United States and Germany, individual State and *Land* authorities enjoy a high degree of autonomy and dispose of substantial financial resources. Decision-making is also decentralized for certain provinces of northern Italy (Piemont, Liguria, Lombardy, Veneto, Emilia-Romagna) and Spain (Madrid, Catalunia, Galicia, Cantabria, Basque Country). Even regions in traditionally centralist France (Languedoc-Roussillon) and Japan (Shutoken, Kansai) are claiming greater autonomy. Greater FDI flows are also correlated to higher degrees of independence of regional authorities (e.g. Liaoning and Shanghai in China, Gujarat and Andhra Pradesh in India). Capital and other major cities that also constitute large markets have their own local administration dealing with FDI (e.g. Bangalore, Beijing, Los Angeles, Mexico City, Moscow, Mumbai, New Delhi, New York, Sao Paulo, Shanghai, St Petersburg).

The most important US federal states – California, Illinois, New York, Texas – are particularly independent and proactive. They run their own FDI promotion bureaus in western Europe and Japan, which are remarkably successful at winning new foreign investors. The United States has attracted the highest volumes of FDI not only because it has the world's largest consumer market, but also owing to efficient management, organization and international presence of dynamic FDI promotion offices in the major Triad countries. These offices are connected with investment promotion boards at home and are very well informed about prevailing tax legislation, rights of foreign investors and potential partner companies for strategic alliances. Regional representatives of the federal states initially operated from US embassies in industrialized countries. Independent offices were opened once these states became wealthier and gained FDI-related experience. Cooperation with selected US federal offices and promotion authorities in Europe and Japan would indeed be useful for identifying appropriate partners for Russian enterprises.

In Russia, important regional 'subjects' (e.g. cities of Moscow and St Petersburg; *oblasts* of Leningrad, Moscow, Vladimir, Nizhny Novgorod, Novosibirsk and Tyumen; republics of Bashkortostan, Tatarstan and Tuva) participate in the formulation of regional economic policies through the Federation Council in Moscow. So far, regional involvement in FDI-oriented measures including legislation has been minimal, possibly because Russia still does not have a targeted FDI policy at national level. Larger or semiautonomous regions like Tatarstan have therefore gone ahead and enacted their own investment laws.[34] It is difficult to judge, however, how far these efforts have resulted in attracting higher volumes of FDI. Certain regions of the Russian Federation recently opened their own information and FDI promotion offices in leading western countries, notably in Germany.[35] Together with embassies, consulates and chambers of commerce, these offices could become a focal point for inter-agency cooperation and exchange of information.

Involving regional authorities is certainly positive as they know local industry best; they are also more committed because the welfare and industrial future of their regions is at stake. Fundamental aspects of an overall FDI policy should, however, be entrusted to a central authority because they involve policy decisions and the support of national structures for representing the country abroad (e.g. embassies, chambers of commerce).[36]

2.7 The spread and development of key technologies

Technological progress, particularly in information, communication and transport, has been instrumental in accelerating business exchange as it enables the free movement of people and global transfer of goods, services, capital and know-how. Information highways and satellite links have reduced the costs of voice, data, text and image transfers as well as international payments. Internet is revolutionizing commerce and information dissemination, and its full potential and impact have yet to be discovered. Together with the liberalization of economies and financial markets, new technologies are responsible for the growing competition among countries and companies and for the speed at which they must respond to new challenges. Information and communication technologies (ICT) ensure a fast exchange of knowledge and information. Both FDI and portfolio investments benefit strongly from these developments as they facilitate – and necessitate – the organization and coordination of global assembly, production and distribution networks.

Developments in key technologies (microelectronics, new materials, biotechnology and communications) supplement and reinforce one another. Progress in microelectronics and chip processing technology largely depends on fundamental research and findings on new materials (e.g. high-performance metals, plastics and ceramics alloys). Inversely, computers and software provide researchers with the necessary tools to develop materials to sophisticated specifications. Western and Japanese TNCs, under pressure to innovate, improve and change, have spearheaded the development of advanced technologies through their worldwide R&D and production networks. In Triad countries they are supported by their governments, which may cosponsor private sector R&D projects. Although public funds have recently been cut drastically in most industrialized countries due to budgetary constraints, the significance of investments in R&D is widely recognized (Table 2.2). While in Russia, public sources account for almost the total of national R&D expenses, they represent only one-third of the volume in other industrialized countries, the rest being covered by semiprivate and private structures.[37]

Table 2.2 R&D expenses by major economies, 1996

	Total R&D expenses (US$ bn)	Per capita R&D expenses (US$)	Share in GDP (%)	Number of scientists per 10 000 inhabitants	Number of students per 10 000 inhabitants
United States	149.2	593	2.77	76	258
Japan	67.0	542	3.07	91	155
Germany	32.3	511	2.81	59	147
Russia	9.6	64	0.78	93	186
Switzerland	3.8	567	2.86	40	99

Source: OECD; *Ost–West Contact*, June 1997.

Efforts are also undertaken to avoid duplication by tightly coordinating R&D projects of the private and public sectors. In most cases, core R&D activities are carried out in the home country and only rarely in an FDI recipient country, although final production may take place there. A US multinational, for example, which invests in a manufacturing operation in western Europe, would transfer all major functions to the new production site while leaving its strategic R&D department at headquarters in the United States.

While advanced technologies are themselves a decisive factor for the recent increase in global FDI, more and more countries try to develop their own industrial base in specific high-tech sectors in an effort to tap the considerable global sales potential (Table 2.3). ASEAN countries and China have been targeting electronics multinationals from Japan and the United States since the late 1980s, and the success of the focused FDI policy of these and other countries is reflected in the spread of technology parks[38] where many TNCs have started producing key components such as memory chips, wafers

Table 2.3 Market potential of selected advanced technologies, 1990–2000

a. New materials	World consumption (US$ bn)		
	1990	1995	2000
Metals	12.8	22.0	34.0
Ceramics	25.0	38.1	59.8
Polymers	27.0	41.5	63.0
Composites	8.3	10.5	12.8

b Microelectronics	Regional shares (%)	Consumption (%)	
		1994	2000
North America	41	32.9	32.0
Japan	41	28.8	25.0
Europe	9	19.5	23.0
Rest of the world	9	18.8	20.0
Market volume (US$ bn)		115	210

c. Biotechnologies	Sales potential by main application (US$ bn)	
	1992	2000
Pharmaceuticals	1.2	23.9
Agriculture and food	2.4	40.0
Chemicals	0.1	14.6
Environment protection	0.4	2.0
Military-industrial complex	1.0	5.8
Total	5.1	86.3

d. Environmental technologies	Market volume (US$ bn)		Annual growth (%)
	1990	2000	
Equipment	152	220	5.0
Water treatment	60	83	4.0
Waste management	40	63	6.4
Air purification	30	42	4.4
Services	52	74	3.2
Total	**334**	**482**	**4.4**

Source: Stiftung Entwicklung und Frieden, *Globale Trends* [Global trends], 1996.

and circuits. Russia, too, is trying to capitalize on the opportunities offered by the new international division of labour by developing its aerospace and satellite technologies. The telecommunications sector also has enormous potential for development in collaboration with foreign partners. Several strategic alliances have been formed between Russian organizations and AT&T, Bell Atlantic, Bell Canada, Deutsche Telekom, Telecom Italia, France Télécom, Nokia and US Sprint.

Among the emerging economies, India and Singapore have been particularly successful in promoting themselves as software centres, while Brazil and Malaysia excel as production sites for computers and peripherals. Although most FDI in advanced technologies originates in Triad economies, other emerging and transition countries also have the potential to attract a wide range of western technologies by consolidating their strengths, especially in basic research. For Russia, a three-pronged effort could be launched to exploit its technological potential and to become a leading player in high-tech industries:

- To dismantle or convert the military-industrial complex, which still absorbs a large share of R&D expenses, in favour of modern industries manufacturing high-tech products, using state-of-the-art manufacturing technologies and processes.
- To attract R&D capacity from leading TNCs in high-tech industries: specialty chemicals, aerospace, transport equipment, telecommunications, biotechnologies, environmental technologies, new materials.
- To stem the brain drain by offering better opportunities to specialists and researchers who are attracted to and sought after by the G5 countries, especially Germany, the United Kingdom and the United States.

Russian FDI specialists must work closely with R&D authorities including the Ministry of Science and Technology and leading research institutes; they must share information so that FDI specialists can match potential domestic firms with appropriate foreign partners.[39]

2.8 International movements of capital

Finance is the linchpin in FDI decisions by TNCs. A country's financial rating and the performance of its industries (technology levels, share prices, know-how transfer potential) determine its long-term suitability for FDI. Easy convertibility of currencies and free movement of capital have a direct impact on the process of global economic integration through FDI. International capital flows generated by the world's stock exchanges together with the financial liquidity created by international banks are rising faster than world trade and production; they also account for much higher business volumes. By 1998, annual turnover on the foreign exchange market will be about 90 times higher than the value of world trade; daily turnover on this market has increased from US$15 billion in

1973 and US$200 billion in the mid-1980s to over US$1.6 trillion (or US$1600 billion) by 2000.[40]

Deregulation of national financial markets and the removal of capital restrictions in many countries such as France, Italy and Sweden in the early 1990s had intensified cross-border capital flows. Progress in information technology allows trading around the clock and around the globe through interconnected financial and currency markets. TNCs can now issue and sell securities and borrow funds worldwide at the most profitable rate, and certain large manufacturing TNCs generate more turnover through financial transactions than by selling their own products (e.g. Toyota, Siemens).

Having attained a high degree of autonomy, capital movements on international financial markets determine exchange and interest rates and influence – very often independently of actual economic developments – investments and competition in national economies. Although international monetary institutions like the IMF and the World Bank may set the overall direction of conditional financial assistance and worldwide policy rules for basic macroeconomic stabilization, they exert little influence on currency movements, interest rates and international financial transfers. Following the 1997–98 financial crises in Asia and Russia, G7 governments announced the need to monitor and even regulate global capital flows. But so far no viable mechanism is in place to avert speculative behaviour and mass sales of debentures by large investment houses and private tycoons leading to financial instability especially in emerging and transition economies.

In 1996, private transnational bank loans and securities emissions amounted to almost US$6000 billion against US$500 billion for public international loans by national authorities in OECD countries and international organizations.[41] Private banks and other financial institutions (securities houses, investment brokers, insurance operators) provide the indispensable credit infrastructure that allows TNCs to take strategic FDI decisions for globalizing their manufacturing operations.[42] Active financial markets with strong credit institutions and stock exchanges are therefore a prerequisite for transnational business activities. The development of viable financial institutions has always been a priority of technical and financial assistance aimed at kickstarting the reform process in Russia (EU TACIS programme, IMF loan facility, World Bank and EBRD assistance, etc.)

Transnational banks are themselves acting as TNCs by extending their presence through an international network of subsidiaries. They support industrial TNCs by providing start-up or venture capital and by offering up-to-date financial products and instruments (derivatives such as options, futures and swaps) at prevailing market conditions. Since the late 1980s, the markets for such derivatives have been expanding rapidly and today represent financial volumes far exceeding the GDP of the world's most advanced economies (Table 2.4).

Table 2.4 Markets for main derivative instruments (US$ trillion)

Derivative	1990	1992	1994	1996	2000*
Traded in stock exchanges (traded contracts):					
Interest futures	1.5	2.9	5.8	7.9	10.5
Interest options	0.6	1.4	2.6	4.1	6.5
Currency futures	0.01	0.03	0.04	0.05	0.07
Currency options	0.06	0.08	0.09	0.15	0.25
Share index futures	0.07	0.08	0.13	0.16	0.2
Share index options	0.1	0.2	0.3	0.4	0.5
Traded outside stock exchanges (new contracts):					
Interest swaps	1.3	4.1	6.2	8.4	11.2
Currency swaps	0.2	0.3	0.9	1.2	1.5
Other swap derivatives	0.3	1.1	1.4	1.6	1.8

* Estimates.
Source: Stiftung Entwicklung und Frieden, *Globale Trends* [Global trends], 1996.

Private banks are also key players in debt-repayment negotiations such as debt for equity swaps with developing and other debtor countries. Up to 70–75 per cent of Russia's foreign debt of US$140 billion in 1999, for example, is owed to about 600 private western banks (London Club).[43] This amount is mainly owed by the central government, which had to take over earlier debts of the Soviet Union (about US$65 billion) and now has to increasingly support privatized companies with financial problems. Internationally, third-world debt amounted to about US$1.6 trillion in 1997, most of which was owed to western and Japanese credit institutions, the IMF and other international donors.

General commercial banks and specialized securities and investment houses are increasingly taking part in recipient countries' economic development by investing in local stock exchanges and providing direct loans to domestic enterprises with good credit ratings. Despite persistent fears that foreign financial institutions (FFI) take money out in difficult times, they have also become major investors. India's policies, for example, are aimed at attracting foreign capital through both FFI and FDI routes. In 1997, capital flows generated by FFI in India amounted to US$12 billion, about six times the volume generated by FDI. In Russia, too, portfolio investments are about 2–2.5 times higher than FDI inflows.[44]

Notes

1. The following countries can be defined as large emerging markets or LEMs: Brazil, China, India, Indonesia, Mexico, Nigeria and Russia. LEMs have populations around or exceeding 100 million people. They have a large landmass with abundant resources of raw materials.

2. This record level was broken only in 1996, when inward FDI rose to US$85 billion. See Chapter 3.3.1.
3. D. Tersen and J.-L. Bricout, *L'investissement international* [International investments], 1996.
4. World Bank. *World Development Report 1996.*
5. Russia has been much more successful at attracting portfolio investment (US$4.5 billion in 1996), which is, however, volatile and far less conducive to industrial restructuring than FDI. Following the 1998 crisis, portfolio investments are expected to diminish considerably for at least 1–2 years. See also Goskomstat, *Investment trends 1995–1996, 1996–1997* (in Russian); *Russia in Figures 1997, 1998.*
6. Chapters 5.2, 5.3.
7. France and Italy did not abandon the last of their restrictions on cross-border investment until the early 1990s. One of the last strongholds was the automobile industry in these two countries, which had to be specially protected from Japanese imports and investments. EU restrictions on Japanese car imports will be abolished at the end of 1999. See also *Handelsblatt*, 'Japan darf mehr Autos nach Europa verkaufen' [Japan is allowed to sell more cars to Europe], 25 March 1998.
8. *World Investment Report 1999*, pp. 38–42; Eurostat, *News Release*, no. 49, 1999.
9. Deutsche Bundesbank, *Zahlungsbilanzstatistik* [Balance of payments statistics], August 1996.
10. For more details, see Union Treaty, *Title VI: Economic and Monetary Policy* (Articles 102–109), 1993.
11. European Commission, DG IV, *Merger Control Regulation no. 4064/89*; it entered into force in September 1990.
12. Other industrialized countries also apply strict merger control regulations to ensure fair competition. See UNCTAD, *World Investment Report 1997*, pp. 291–293.
13. See also Chapter 17.1.2.
14. Bundesstelle für Auslandsinformationen, *Mercosur—ein Markt mit Zukunft* [Mercosur – a market with future potential], 1995. *Time Magazine*, 'Keep it in the Neighborhood', 26 August 1996.
15. UNCTAD, *World Investment Report 1999.*
16. For details on NAFTA, see also Chapter 7 on Mexico.
17. *Moscow Times*, 'Russia Prepares to Join APEC Club by Fall '98', 19 February 1998.
18. *The Economist*, 'Free Trade, Fettered Investment', 14 September 1996, p. 92.
19. WTO, *Trading into the Future*, 1995.
20. GATT Secretariat, *The Results of the Uruguay Round of Multilateral Trade Negotiations*, 1995.
21. Unofficial reason given by a WTO source (July 1997).
22. Organisation for Economic Co-operation and Development (OECD), *Progress Report by the MAI Negotiating Group*, 1996.
23. CEPII, *Compétitivité des nations* [Competitiveness of nations], 1998, pp. 198–9.
24. Reuters, *OECD Investment Treaty – What's at Stake*, 18 February 1998; *World Investment Report 1999*, pp. 128–37.
25. Adapted from E. Graham, *Global Corporations and National Governments*, 1996.
26. While IFC provides equity capital for industrial ventures worldwide, EBRD focuses on participations in investment projects in European transition countries.
27. *Business India*, 'A Private Affair', 8–21 April 1996.

28. Chapter 4.
29. J. Dunning, 'International Investment Patterns' *in* L. Oxelheim, *The Global Race for FDI*, 1993, pp. 108–109. UNCTAD, *World Investment Reports 1995, 1996, 1997, 1998.*
30. Chapter 4.3.1.
31. UNCTAD, *World Investment Report 1998.*
32. Chr. Maisch, *Beurteilungskriterien für Auslandsinvestitionen deutscher Unternehmen – Ergebnisse einer empirischen Studie* [Evaluation criteria for foreign investment operations of German companies], 1996.
33. Chapter 4.2.
34. Chapter 9.4.
35. *Ost-West Contacter*, January 1999, p. 38.
36. Chapter 17.
37. See also *The Economist*, 'Science in Russia. The Diamonds in the Rubble', 8 November 1997, and publications of the Centre for Science Research and Statistics (Russian Ministry of Science and Technology).
38. Chapter 16.2.
39. Chapter 16.3.
40. *The Economist*, 'Capital Goes Global', 25 October 1997, pp. 99–100.
41. Stiftung Entwicklung und Frieden, *Globale Trends* [Global trends], 1996, p. 191; A. Gamblin, *Images économiques du monde 2000* [World economic trends 2000], 1999, pp. 390–1.
42. Chapter 16.6.
43. After almost 10 years of transition, about 80 per cent of Russia's enterprises have been privatized. It is rather surprising that enterprise assets have so far only to a very small degree been offered directly and systematically to western investors, for example as part of a debt-for-equity scheme monitored closely by the Russian and western governments. Such a scheme would have contributed significantly to overall reduction of Russia's debt while opening the way for transfer of technology and managerial know-how into industry.
44. Portfolio investments by transnational banks (TNBs) and insurance companies are not included in international statistics on FDI. They are not analyzed further in the framework of this study, although they represent essential capital flows for most emerging economies.

3
Global FDI Trends

FDI involving overseas manufacturing and cross-border exchange of know-how and technology has experienced an unprecedented growth since the beginning of the 1990s. Earlier, global economic integration was mainly spurred by intensified trade relations[1] and, partially, through public aid transfers from advanced economies to developing countries. FDI has turned out to be an essential catalyst for integrating national economies into a globally interdependent production and services network. In the new division of labour, which now embraces the transition economies of Central and Eastern Europe as well, FDI is poised to become the lubricant for economic development, industrial modernization and fair trade relations across the Eurasian continent.

Russia is a relative newcomer on the global FDI scene, but far-sighted policies should enable it to garner a sizeable share of the available international FDI potential.

3.1 Significance of FDI for the world economy

3.1.1 Main FDI indicators

Internationally, the economic importance of foreign investment, measured as the ratio of outward FDI stock to world production or GDP, has more than trebled, from 4.4 per cent in 1960 to almost 14 per cent in 1998 (about 15–17 per cent by 2000).[2] Following the economic recovery in the industrialized countries in the mid-1980s, international investment intensified and its growth outpaced that of world production, gross fixed capital formation (a proxy indicator for domestic investment) and international trade. Between 1986 and 1990, FDI outflows increased by over 28 per cent, compared with 10 per cent for domestic investment, 11 per cent for world production (GDP) and 14 per cent for overall exports of goods and services (Table 3.1). Outward FDI stock and sales of foreign TNC affiliates – two proxy indicators of international production – also grew considerably, by 20 per cent and 17 per cent, respectively, during the same period. During 1991–96, growth rates for FDI outflows (12 per cent) and outward stock (11 per cent) slowed down, but were still around twice as high as the increase in world production, domestic investments and exports.

Table 3.1 Selected world FDI and economic indicators, 1981–98

Indicator		Average annual growth rates (%)				
	1998 (US$ bn)	1981–85	1986–90	1991–96	1997	1998
FDI outflows	649	1	28	12	27	37
FDI outward stock	4 117	5	20	11	14	20
Sales of foreign affiliates of TNCs	11 427	1	17	4	7	18
GDP (factor costs)	30 550*	2	11	6	1	1
Gross fixed capital formation[a]	5 900*	1	10	5	–2.5	–
Exports of goods and services	6 710[b]	0.5	14	7	3	–2

Notes: * Estimates; [a] Proxy for domestic investment; [b] Merchandise: US$5035 bn; commercial services: US$1675 bn.
Sources: Adapted from UNCTAD, IMF, OECD and WTO; *The Economist*.[3]

In absolute terms, average annual FDI outflows, which stood at US$94 billion during 1983–88, more than doubled to US$216 billion during 1989–94. Worldwide outflows peaked in 1990 (US$244 billion) and 1994 (US$222 billion). 1995 saw a further surge of global FDI, by 35 per cent over 1994, to an unprecedented level of US$339 billion. By 1998, annual FDI outflows already stood at US$649 billion.[4] 1997 and 1998 were record years for FDI-related indicators, but the financial crises in Southeast Asia, Brazil and Russia intensified flows between the United States and the European Union. If the 1994–98 trend persists, global annual outflows could hit the US$1000 billion mark at the turn of the century (towards 2001–02), assuming minimum growth rates of 10–15 per cent per annum. This volume, which would bring FDI to almost 15 per cent of world merchandise exports, is quite realistic now that an increasing number of recipient countries are attracting more flows and even becoming outward investors (e.g. China, Hong Kong, Malaysia, Singapore, Taiwan). In 1998, global FDI stock (both outward and inward) exceeded US$4100 billion representing a more than 19- and 6-fold increase – in actual prices – over 1973 (US$211 billion) and 1985 (US$619 billion), respectively.

3.1.2 FDI and public aid

For most emerging economies, FDI already has a much greater and more direct economic impact than global aid packages and technical assistance programmes, not only through its higher monetary flows, but because it combines capital input, transfer of essential manufacturing technologies, managerial know-how and access to foreign markets. FDI helps upgrade the host country's industries, boost employment and generate tax revenue. Direct investments are undertaken by private corporations, which, unlike public aid schemes, must maintain operational efficiency to shorten the pay back period and to optimize profitability.

FDI also reduces dependence on international donor bureaucracies such as the EU, IMF, World Bank and UN (through its UNIDO programme), which provide loans or grants according to strict financial and accounting standards.[5] Against the background of diminishing bilateral aid (Figure 3.1), governments of most developing countries have understood the advantage of FDI versus aid and provide the necessary legal and fiscal conditions to encourage private capital inflows from the main investing nations. In 1997, outgoing FDI from G5 countries was on average 5–7 times higher in absolute terms than public aid, and the gap between the two sources of capital is expected to widen as most governments struggle with economic stagnation and lower tax revenue at home. With a certain time lag, reduced financial possibilities of major donor countries eventually result in budgetary cuts for the leading international organizations, which depend on these countries to maintain or raise capital levels.[6]

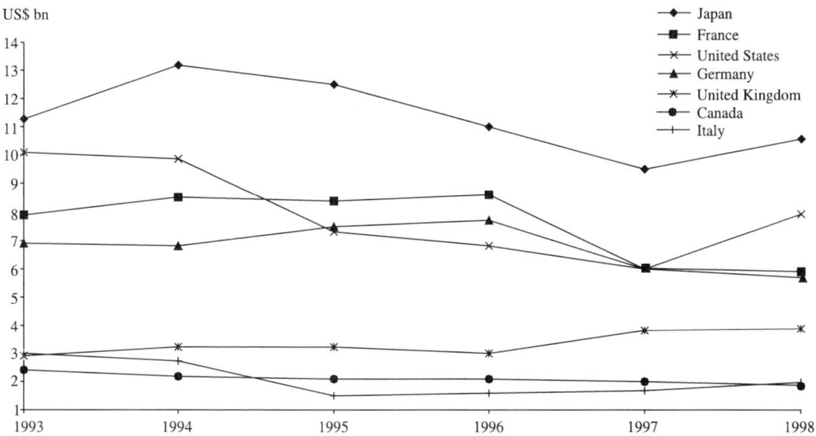

Source: OECD, *The Economist*, various publications and issues.

Figure 3.1 Development aid, G7 countries, 1993–98

For example, the German government was forced to cut its public aid to developing and transition countries for the third consecutive year. In 1997, it was reduced by 1.2 per cent to DM12 billion. Germany's public aid package for Russia now stands at only DM40 million (1999) or about 0.5 per cent of Germany's technical assistance package worldwide. At the same time, FDI outflows by German TNCs have skyrocketed since 1993 and touched DM65 billion in 1997 (DM60 billion in 1996). Outflows are expected to rise further during 1998–2002 as German companies continue to relocate their factories to low-cost and high-growth countries. Similar trends can also be observed in the other G7 countries[7] and most OECD economies.

Although the commonly accepted target for public aid funds (technical assistance, loans and grants) is 0.7 per cent of GDP, in reality they represent only 0.1–0.4 per cent for most industrialized countries, with a trend towards further reduction in the coming years. Only few countries such as Sweden and the Netherlands have been able to attain the target so far. In comparison, the share of outgoing FDI (flows) in GDP has been on average between 1.2 per cent (United States) and 4.2 per cent (United Kingdom) for the G5 countries in the first half of the 1990s (Figure 3.2). Japan's FDI outflows/GDP ratio was exceptionally low during 1994–97 – 0.8 per cent – but nevertheless considerable in absolute terms.

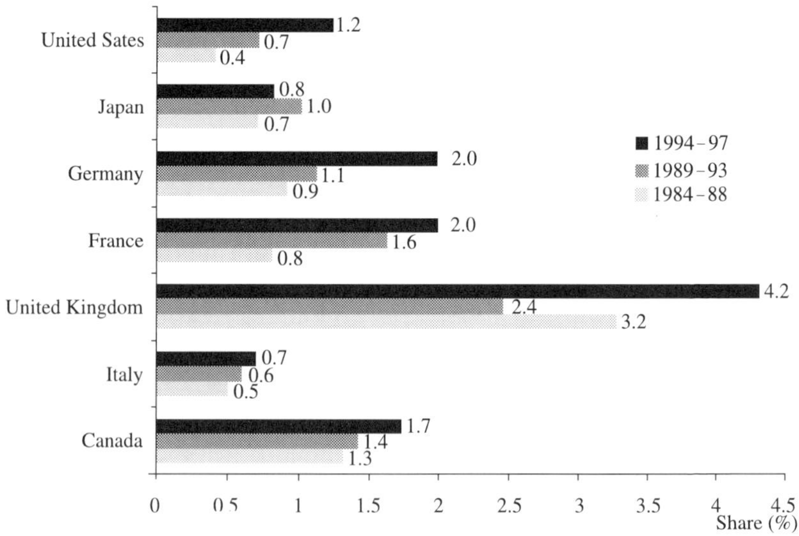

Source: Author's calculations based on OECD and UNCTAD data.

Figure 3.2 Outward FDI flows/GDP, G7 countries, 1984–97

On the recipient side, the share of public aid in total capital inflows into developing countries dropped considerably, from 60 per cent in the early 1980s to only 24 per cent in 1995.[8] The balance is increasingly financed through private bank loans, portfolio investments and FDI. Foreign investment has become not only the single largest item in net capital flows to developing countries (54 per cent of the total in 1996), but is also responsible for the continued upward trend of these flows. The halving of portfolio equity inflows from the 1993 peak of US$46 billion to US$22 billion in 1996 was more than offset by large and sustained increases in FDI inflows. The exception was Latin America, where the growth of FDI inflows could not compensate the sizeable decline in portfolio equity flows into the region.[9]

FDI is often the only source of international private capital to countries that have not received the necessary ratings required for borrowing abroad or tapping international capital markets (portfolio investment). It has a visible advantage over other types of finance (public assistance, portfolio investment) in that it is not only determined by sound macroeconomic management of governments, but also by other pull factors such as size of the market, availability of resources not found elsewhere and the pressure of international competition. Large and resource-rich countries like Brazil, China, India, Mexico and Russia will benefit from these pull factors in the future. Together with Indonesia, these large emerging markets (LEMs) account for almost 40 per cent of the combined debt of developing and transition economies (Figure 3.3). FDI is increasingly considered the only viable option for reducing third world debt, which in 1998 reached US$2500 billion.

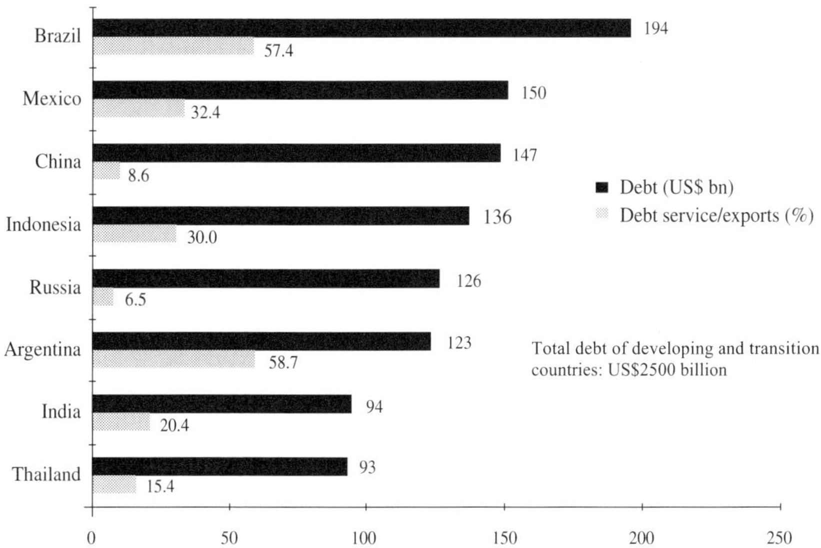

Source: World Bank, *Global Development Finance 1999*.

Figure 3.3 External debt of leading emerging economies, 1997

Today, governments of most emerging economies in Asia, Latin America and Eastern Europe actively promote FDI to modernize their manufacturing and technological base and to enhance the international competitiveness of crucial domestic industries. Since the transition countries joined the international division of labour, more nations have to compete for limited know-how and capital, which largely originates from industrialized countries, with support from public funds (expected to stagnate and even decline) and private investment (expected to rise).

3.1.3 Global economic integration through FDI

FDI plays a fundamental role in the economic well-being and industrial development of nations. In a large number of countries, foreign investors have become insider-players enjoying the same rights as domestic companies. Traditional free traders like the United Kingdom, United States and Germany were the first to open their markets to foreign TNCs. The economic performance of these countries and the worldwide encouragement of free trade regimes incited many other governments to take the necessary measures for increasing FDI. With the opening of the markets of Central and Eastern Europe, the last barrier has fallen to total economic integration around the globe.

FDI is a major driving force for global economic integration and improvement of economic conditions in developing economies. About 80 per cent of the world's FDI still circulates between developed (OECD) economies, but other economies (e.g. China, Malaysia, Mexico) could strengthen their position as both recipients and exporters of capital and know-how. In the coming 20–30 years, FDI movements towards and from developing and transition countries of Latin America, Asia and Eastern Europe will be intensified.

Four fundamental variables (or ratios) explain the degree of economic integration and industrial competitiveness of countries:

- Outward stock/GDP, mainly for advanced economies (measure for global integration).
- Outward flows/gross fixed capital formation (domestic investment), mainly for advanced economies (measure for outward orientation and insider position in host countries).
- Inward stock/GDP, for developing and advanced economies (measure for global integration, locational advantages and consistent liberal policies).
- Inward flows/gross fixed capital formation, for developing and advanced economies (measure of contribution of foreign TNCs to industrial development).

As a rule, countries with small populations (e.g. Australia, Belgium, Canada, the Netherlands, Sweden, Singapore, Malaysia) tend to be more integrated than larger ones (Figure 3.4). Larger economies with long overseas traditions (e.g. United Kingdom, United States) have also built an effective trading and production network around the globe. They seem to be better positioned to face the global challenges of the coming century than economies focusing mainly on export activities (e.g. Germany, Italy). Nevertheless, the pull effect of global FDI on economic development in less advanced countries has been significant on all the continents.

Newcomers on the world economic scene such as Hungary, Poland, Russia and Ukraine are now compelled to participate in the process so as not to be

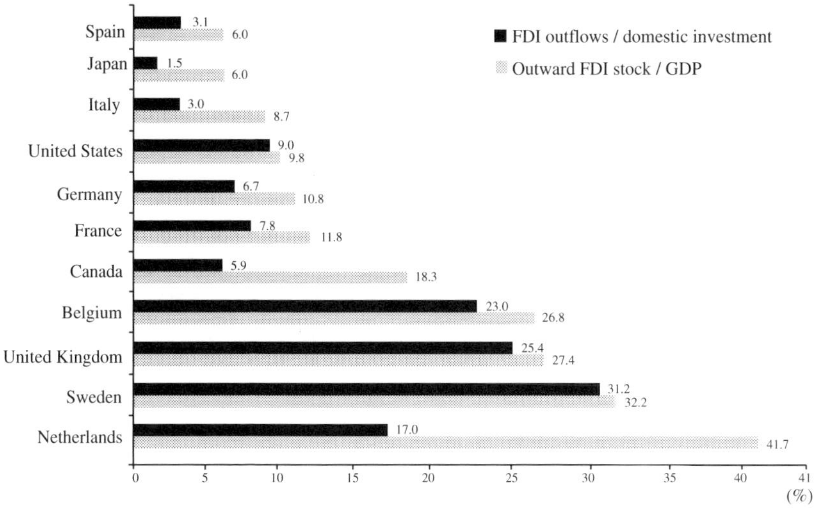

Source: Adapted from UNCTAD, *World Investment Reports 1996, 1997*.

Figure 3.4 Economic importance of FDI, main source countries, 1996

left behind. European transition economies will face an extremely complex task: to open up their domestic economies further while ensuring free trade and channelling inbound FDI into those activities that help generate employment and income, and promote overall industrial competitiveness. While Central European economies can rely on the guiding hand of their western European neighbours (through the EU), Russia, Ukraine and the other CIS economies will have to cooperate closely and devise new strategies to compete in the world markets.[10] Although progress has been made in trading and finance, these countries are still at the beginning of global economic integration through FDI. Considering the dire state of domestic factories and the extremely high level of imports of finished products, there will be few alternatives for these countries' governments but to direct foreign technologies to important industries.

Most developing and emerging (non-OECD) countries saw the volume of inbound investment flows relative to gross fixed capital formation (domestic investment) increase significantly between 1986 and 1996.[11] The inward FDI/domestic investment ratio was generally lower for industrialized countries, where it ranged from 2 per cent (Germany) to 13 per cent (United Kingdom) in 1996. These averages dissimulate much higher inbound FDI/domestic investment ratios for countries with attractive home markets, a strongly developed services sector and investor-friendly FDI policies. These countries include LEMs like Brazil, China and Mexico where FDI has led to a significant rise in industrial production and employment.[12]

Smaller economies belonging to economic groupings such as the EU (e.g. Belgium, Ireland), MERCOSUR (e.g. Argentina, Chile, Venezuela) and ASEAN (e.g. Malaysia, Singapore) tend to be quite dependent on FDI financing for their national investment activities. This also applies to countries that have decided to open widely their economies to outside investors, such as China, Hungary and Poland. In 1996, Hungary (60 per cent), Bolivia (48 per cent) and Sweden (43 per cent) were by far the most dependent countries on foreign investment, which became almost as important as domestic investment for their economic progress. Russia's ratio that year was only 1 per cent (Figure 3.5).

Increased economic integration through FDI appears to have been beneficial to both recipient and major source countries. Although certain union leaders in advanced economies have imputed higher unemployment at home to outgoing FDI, the main socioeconomic indicators of leading FDI exporting

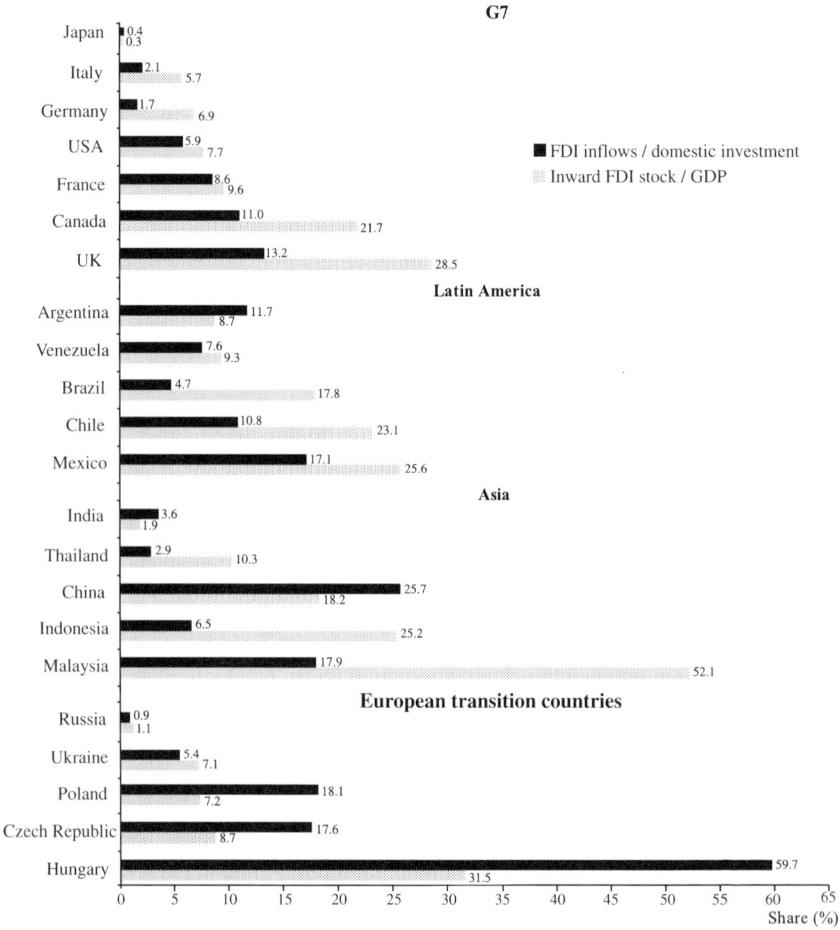

Source: Adapted from UNCTAD, *World Investment Reports 1996, 1997.*

Figure 3.5 Role of FDI in domestic economies, main recipient countries, 1996

countries suggest that the contrary is probably true. Thus, during 1993–96 the United States, the United Kingdom, the Netherlands, Belgium, Switzerland and many other OECD countries experienced a significant increase in GDP, employment and domestic investment activity, while simultaneously reporting record FDI outflows. In the United States, FDI from EU countries exceeded US$500 billion by 1996, accounting for a job increase of 3 million during 1992–96, with another 3 million envisaged during 1997–2000.[13] It is true that in countries like France, Germany and Spain unemployment rose dramatically during 1993–97, coinciding with an increase in FDI outflows, but this appears to be related more to structural problems such as inflexible labour regulations and a high tax environment, which hamper entrepreneurship and deter both domestic investment and inward FDI.

3.1.4 The Triad and its cluster regions

Most emerging economies have benefited from the proximity of powerful Triad neighbours: Central European and Maghreb (North African) countries from France, Germany, the United Kingdom and other member states of the EU; central and Latin American countries from the United States; and East (especially China) and Southeast Asia from Japan and, increasingly, also South Korea, Taiwan and Hong Kong. The United States is the only true global FDI player, which is strongly represented in all important clusters.

Countries tend to prosper within 'cluster' regions under the sphere of influence of locomotive economies, which generate the necessary FDI flows for regional economic development. Taken together, the Triad countries and their clusters combine almost all the existing FDI stock in the world. Due to its territorial extent and central location, Russia is in a unique geographic position to benefit from the three main Triad regions simultaneously: the EU, East Asia (Japan, South Korea, China), and North America (Canada, United States).

Whereas the three Triad regions of western Europe, North America and East Asia (Japan, Taiwan and South Korea) have maintained their net outward investment (NOI) position, the remaining world regions are still net importers of FDI (Figure 3.6). The difference between inward and outward stock was highest for Latin America (US$339 billion) and Asia as a whole (US$305 billion). These two continents are expected to draw more FDI in the coming years as they comprise many fast growing economies that will build up stock. At the same time, leading local TNCs of selected countries (e.g. Japan, South Korea, Taiwan, Singapore, China, and India in Asia; Argentina, Brazil, Chile, and Mexico in Latin America) are well positioned to become important outward investors.[14] In 1997, the ratio for European transition countries was 9:1 (18:1 in 1996). In the years to come, Central and Eastern European countries including Russia are expected to attract additional FDI flows, which may contribute to a deterioration of their NOI position before stronger domestic industries are able to use their increased competitiveness to export and invest abroad and thus improve the investment position.

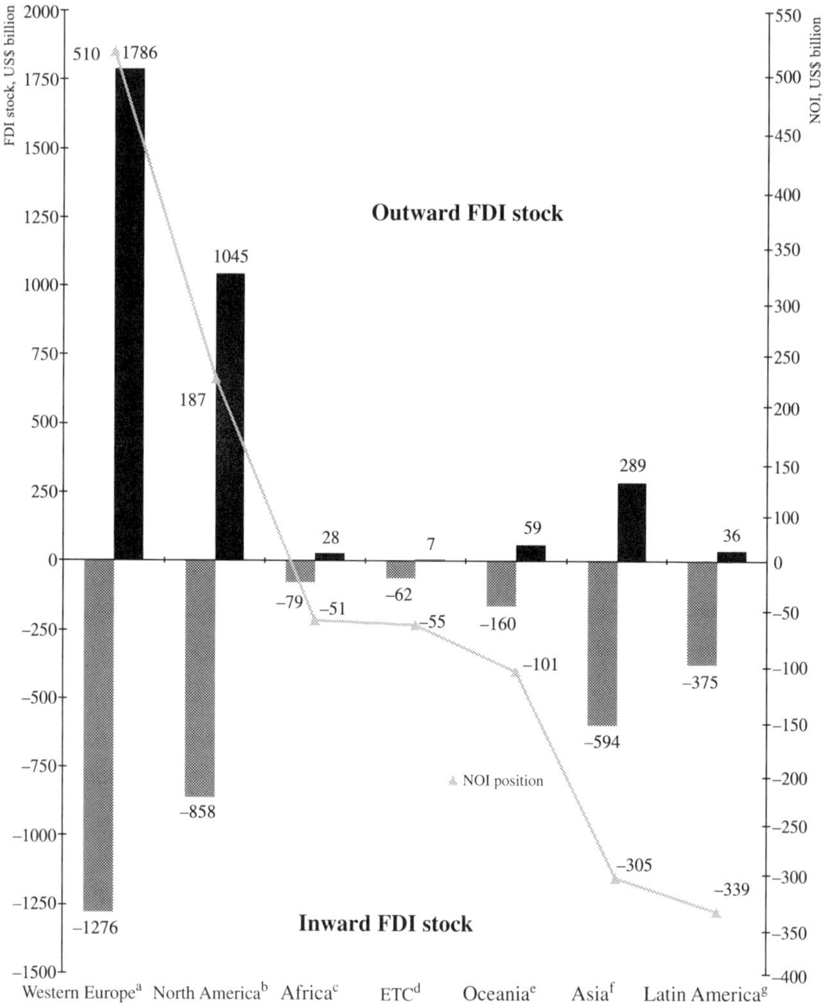

[a]EU, Switzerland and Norway
[b]United States and Canada
[c]Including South Africa
[d]European transition countries
[e]Australia and New Zealand
[f]West, South, Southeast, East Asia
[g]Central and South America including Mexico

Source: Adapted from UNCTAD, *World Investment Report 1998*.

Figure 3.6 NOI position of main world regions, 1997

3.2 Main investing nations

3.2.1 Historical shifts in outward FDI

Contrary to general belief, international investment is not a recent phenomenon. At the beginning of this century, it already played a significant role for the international transfer of capital and technical skills. In 1914, just before the First World War, outward FDI stock was estimated at US$15 billion; by 1938 it had risen to US$26 billion. At that time, very few countries – basically the three colonial powers (United Kingdom, France, Germany until 1918) and the United States – controlled almost the entire FDI stock abroad.

The United Kingdom held about 40–45 per cent of the world's FDI stock until the Second World War (Table 3.2). A number of determining factors explain the country's dominant position during this period: technological and industrial leadership, sales outlets for UK products in the Commonwealth, the City of London as the world's financial centre, an efficient banking network, and the pound sterling as the leading international reserve currency. After the Second World War, the supremacy of the United Kingdom diminished to give way to a new power, the United States, as major provider of FDI. Stimulated by the Marshall Plan, which allocated a total of US$14 billion[15] in public aid for Europe's reconstruction during 1946–52, US companies invested substantially on the European continent. US assets abroad reached a peak in the 1960s and early 1970s, accounting for almost 50 per cent of global outward stock. Resentment began to rise, especially in France. It was the time of the best-seller *Le défi américain* (The American challenge) written by the French politician and journalist Jean-Jacques Servan Schreiber in 1969.

Table 3.2 Outward FDI stock by region (%), 1914–97

	1914	1938	1969	1973	1985	1994	1997
G5 economies	86.9	81.2	72.8	75.7	71.6	65.4	63.0
• United States	18.5	27.7	48.3	48.1	36.9	25.7	25.6
• United Kingdom	45.5	39.8	16.3	12.8	14.8	11.7	11.7
• Japan	0.1	2.9	0.8	4.9	6.5	11.7	10.1
• Germany	10.6	1.3	1.2	5.7	8.8	8.6	9.2
• France	12.2	9.5	6.2	4.2	4.6	7.7	6.4
OECD economies	10.8	15.0	18.4	14.8	17.2	21.8	19.5
• Netherlands	–	–	10.3	7.5	7.0	6.1	6.0
• Switzerland	–	–	3.4	3.4	3.7	4.0	4.4
Developing and transition economies	2.3	3.8	8.8	9.5	11.2	12.8	17.5
Global FDI stock (US$ billion)	100 (14.5)	100 (26.3)	100 (66.1)	100 (210.5)	100 (618.6)	100 (2378)	100 (3541)

Source: Adapted from J. H. Dunning, *Multinational Enterprises and the Global Economy*, 1992; UNCTAD, *World Investment Reports 1995, 1996, 1997, 1998.*

Notwithstanding open criticism and the public outcry in Europe and increasingly also in Latin America, US outward stock continued to grow in absolute terms throughout the 1980s and 1990s. But the country's overall share has practically halved since the 1970s, to approximately one-quarter of the world's outward stock today. US TNCs remain, however, the foremost providers of foreign investment and capital in the world. The United Kingdom ranks second, but it is being challenged by Japan, which has rapidly consolidated its international investment position since the mid-1970s. Starting from the 1980s, Germany was able to regain its role as one of the leading investing nations with around 9 per cent of global outward stock during 1985–97; this roughly corresponds to its position before the First World War, when its share in global FDI stock was 10–11 per cent.

3.2.2 FDI from G5 countries

Today, the largest part of global FDI stock is controlled by the five leading industrialized (G5) countries (Figure 3.7; for per capita values see Figure 3.8):[16] the United States (US$907 billion in 1997), the United Kingdom (US$413 billion), Japan (US$356 billion), Germany (US$326 billion) and France (US$227 billion). However, the overall share of these countries as global FDI providers has been steadily declining, from 87 per cent of global outward stock in 1914 to 65 per cent in 1994 and 63 per cent in 1997. TNCs from other industrialized (OECD) countries such as the Netherlands, Switzerland, Sweden, Canada, Belgium and Australia started investing heavily

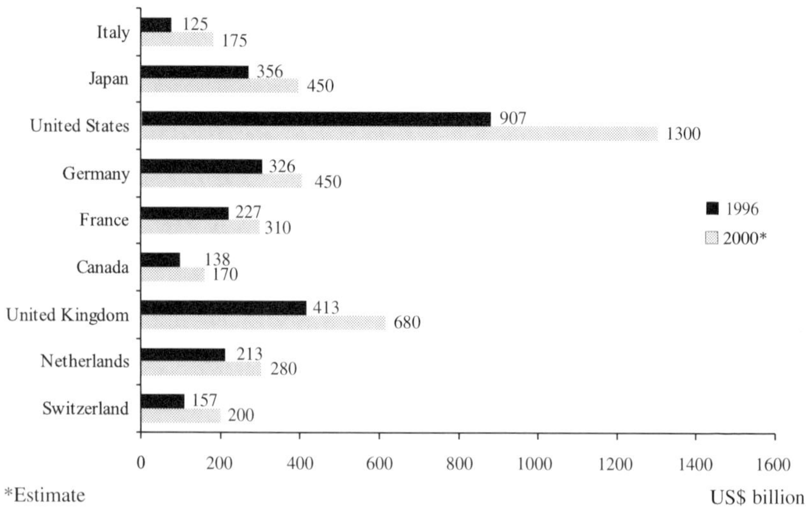

Source: Adapted from UNCTAD, *World Investment Reports, 1996, 1997, 1998.*

Figure 3.7 The world's leading investors, outward FDI stock, 1997–2000

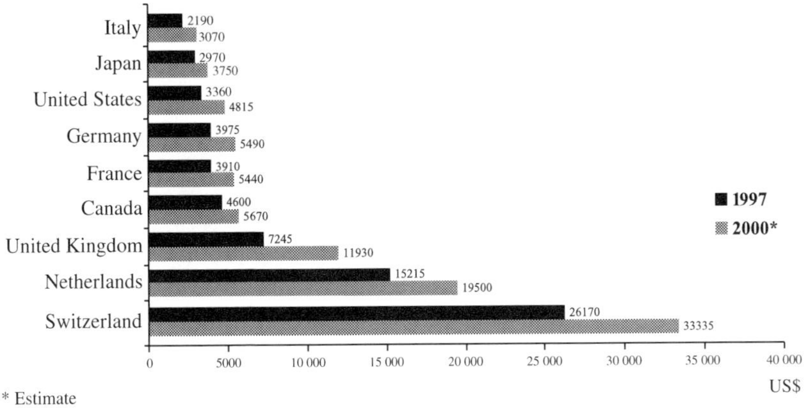

Source: Adapted from UNCTAD, *World Investment Reports 1996, 1997, 1998.*

Figure 3.8 The world's leading investors, per capita outward FDI stock, 1997

abroad after the Second World War, leading to an overall increase in their share by 10 percentage points during 1914–97.

Besides controlling the largest FDI stocks abroad, G5 countries also account for the highest annual outflows (Figure 3.9; for per capita values see Figure 3.10). During 1989–94, the United States ranked first among investing nations (average annual outflows US$40 billion), followed by Japan (US$29 billion), France (US$25.5 billion), the United Kingdom (US$23 billion) and Germany (US$21 billion). 1995 was a record year for the G5 countries except France. FDI outflows from the United States and the United Kingdom more than doubled during 1995–97. Even higher average outflows are expected during 1998–2000, especially from Germany, Italy and France, as medium-sized TNCs are pressing into international markets to become insiders and secure leadership positions.

Whereas US companies invested record amounts abroad (US$95.5 billion in 1995; US$85 billion in 1996; US$114 billion in 1997), Japan recorded the sharpest drop among the G5 countries during 1989–94 (2.5 times). Although FDI picked up again during 1995–97, Japanese TNCs had made the bulk of their FDI during 1989–91 to counter trade restrictions in the United States (voluntary quota on imports of cars and electronics from Japan) and in anticipation of the EU single market (nontariff barriers such as local content rules, self-restraint agreements). In the early 1990s, Japanese TNCs reoriented their FDI strategies towards neighbouring markets in Asia, particularly ASEAN, Australia and China, where investment was also more convenient owing to the favourable yen/local currency exchange rate.

Since 1992 economic relations have also been intensified with Russia, especially its eastern territories. However, a closer look at inbound FDI patterns

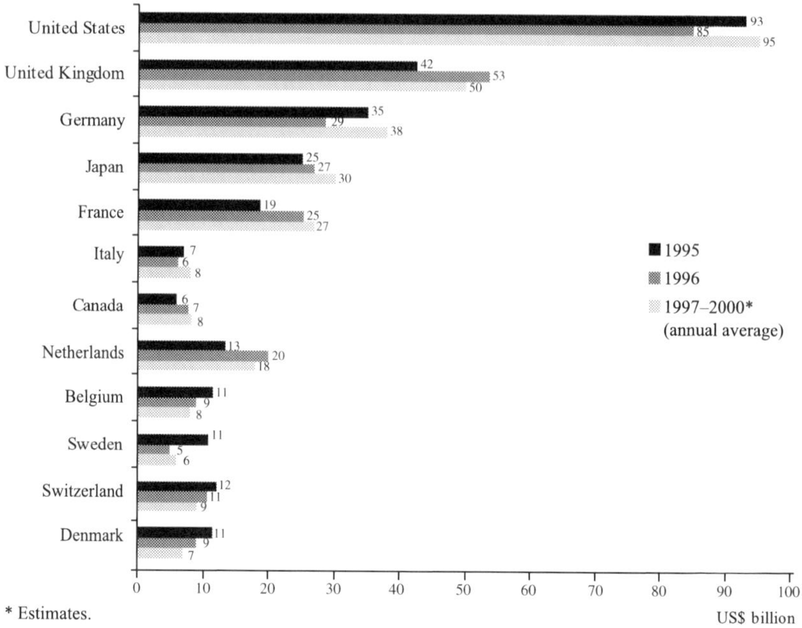

* Estimates.

Source: UNCTAD, *World Investment Reports 1997, 1998.*

Figure 3.9 The world's leading investors, FDI outflows, 1995–2000

for Russia shows that Japanese investment is still low and could be expanded further, especially to develop industries in western Siberia and the Far East. Sectors that could be revamped are wood processing, mining, steel, shipbuilding, automobiles, consumer electronics, instruments, machinery and medical equipment. Until now, the unsettled dispute over the Kuril islands, and lack of trust and high-risk evaluation among major Japanese policymakers, industrialists and associations have restrained major investments from Japan in Russia. Special confidence-building measures should therefore be directed at potential Japanese investors.[17]

Companies in Germany have also stepped up foreign investment. Hampered by excessive labour costs and tax rates at home, German TNCs are looking for new locations for more profitable manufacturing operations. Besides, the general recession in EU markets is obliging them to look for new outlets in the high-growth markets of Central Europe, Asia and Latin America. In 1995, German TNCs invested a record US$35 billion abroad, almost drawing level with the United Kingdom. Outflows remained high in 1996 (US$29 billion) and 1997 (US$34 billion). Germany could thus retain its position as the third largest investing nation in the world, before Japan[18] and France. In terms of per capita FDI, Germany was still behind France in 1997 (US$415 against US$432).

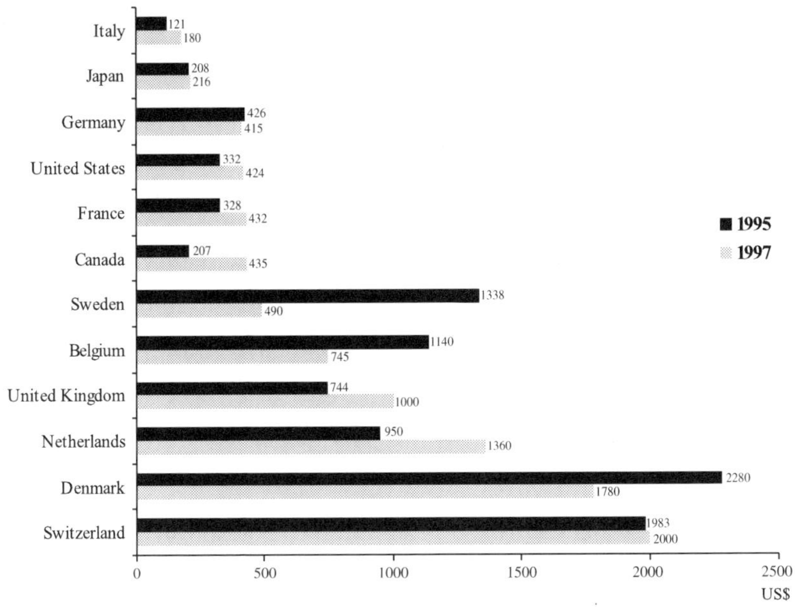

Source: UNCTAD, *World Investment Reports 1996, 1998.*

Figure 3.10 The world's leading investors, per capita FDI outflows, 1995–97

German investments are concentrated in the EU and North America, but increasingly also in Eastern Europe, Asia and Latin America. Central and Eastern European countries have recorded the highest increase in FDI from Germany; their share rose from only 3.7 per cent in 1991 to 13 per cent in 1994. The significance of these countries for German TNCs went down to about 10–11 per cent during 1995–97, but is expected to rise again in the coming years, especially if confidence is reestablished in the Russian and major CIS (Belarus, Kazakhstan, Ukraine, Uzbekistan) economies.

3.2.3 FDI from other industrialized and emerging economies

The outward stock held by newly industrialized and emerging Asian economies (e.g. Hong Kong, Singapore, Taiwan, South Korea, China) is also rising. TNCs from these countries generally invest in nearby markets around the Asia–Pacific rim, including Australia and North America (United States, Canada). In Europe, their attention is mainly directed at the United Kingdom, Spain and Germany. The growing share of outward stock held by TNCs from East and Southeast Asia has raised the share of emerging markets in global FDI from 2 per cent to 18 per cent during 1914–97.[19]

The following countries in this group are also worth mentioning for their accumulated stock abroad until 1997: Canada and Hong Kong (US$137 billion each), Australia (US$52 billion), Singapore (US$43 billion), Taiwan (US$34 billion), China (US$20 billion), South Korea (US$18 billion), South Africa and New Zealand (US$12 billion each), Kuwait (US$10 billion), and Brazil (US$9 billion).

Several non-G5 European and Asian countries have recorded significant annual outflows since 1989: the Netherlands (US$20 billion in 1997), Switzerland (US$12 billion), Italy and Spain (US$10 billion each), Belgium (US$7 billion), Australia (US$6 billion), Taiwan (US$5 billion). Most of these countries are members of the EU or the OECD.

Major reasons for the considerable increase in FDI outflows are economic growth and privatizations in industrialized countries accompanied by economic liberalization and transformation in China, India, Southeast Asia and, lately, Central Europe.

Hong Kong reported extremely high capital outflows of above US$22 billion annually during 1993–97. From average outflows of only US$1.5 billion during the 1980s, its outward FDI position started improving substantially when overseas Chinese businessmen and TNCs from third countries (Japan, United States, EU, Taiwan, Singapore) started using Hong Kong as a platform for their investments in China.

All the countries listed in Annex 3.1 represent important sources of FDI and should be included in any future Russian strategy aimed at enhancing inbound private sector flows.[20] Interestingly, Russia's outward stock has increased to almost US$4 billion in 1997, which corresponded to about one-third of the volume of FDI that had entered the country. It is expected that in future years the inbound potential and needs will exceed the outbound FDI capabilities of Russian enterprises.[21]

3.3 Major destination countries for global FDI

The volume of FDI inflows reflects the liberal FDI and general economic policy framework of recipient countries and, to a large extent, the confidence investors have in purchasing national assets in host economies. These must have superior locational advantages over other potential destinations.[22] Since the beginning of the century, there has been a major shift in the destination of FDI from developing countries (former colonies) towards advanced economies of western Europe, North America and, recently, Asia (Table 3.3). Starting from the 1970s, western Europe has been able to strengthen its position as the region with the highest accumulated inward stock (US$1276 billion in 1997 or 36.9 per cent of the world total). North America (United States, Canada) became an important region of destination after the Second World War and reached its peak during the 1980s. In 1997, North America's stock was 24.8 per cent (US$858 billion) of the world total. Asia climbed rapidly during the 1980s and 1990s (US$59 billion or 17.2 per cent of inward stock in 1997); its share has doubled since 1980 and is gradually moving towards the share it held at the beginning of this century. In 1997, increases in stock were also recorded for other regions: Latin America (US$375 billion, share of 10.9 per cent), Oceania mainly Australia and New Zealand (US$160 billion, 4.6 per cent), and Central and Eastern Europe (US$62 billion, 1.8 per cent).

Table 3.3 Inward FDI stock by region (%), 1914–97

	1914	1938	1969	1973	1985	1995	1997
Advanced economies	27.3	32.6	67.3	72.9	72.1	74.0	67.7
• North America	10.3	7.4	13.9	10.4	33.4	23.8	24.8
• Western Europe	7.8	7.4	22.9	36.5	32.9	41.6	36.9
• Other OECD economies	9.2	17.8	30.5	26.0	5.8	5.8	6.0
Developing economies	72.7	67.4	32.7	27.1	27.7	27.6	32.3
• Latin America	32.7	30.8	15.6	12.5	10.3	9.7	10.9
• Africa	6.4	7.4	5.5	2.9	2.9	1.9	1.9
• Middle East	2.8	2.6	2.8	–	5.8	1.9	0.5
• Asia	20.9	25.0	7.9	4.8	8.6	15.8	17.2
European transition economies	9.9	1.6	0.9	–	0.1	1.2	1.8
Global FDI stock	100	100	100	100	100	100	100
(in US$ billion)	(14)	(24)	(55)	(167)	(745)	(2866)	(3455)

Source: Adapted from J. H. Dunning, *Multinational Enterprises and the Global Economy*, 1992; UNCTAD, *World Investment Reports 1996, 1997, 1998.*

During the second half of the twentieth century, advanced economies attracted most FDI, but the number of recipient countries is increasing. Newcomers are Argentina, Brazil, Chile, China, Czech Republic, Hungary, India, Indonesia, Malaysia, Mexico, Poland and Thailand. Their domestic industries have developed a considerable capacity to absorb know-how and capital from foreign TNCs, and they therefore represent major competitors of Russia for FDI flows.

3.3.1 FDI in the industrialized Triad economies

In 1997, the Triad regions – North America (United States, Canada), the 15 EU member countries and Japan – received about 55 per cent of global FDI inflows (US$220 billion), 29 percentage points less than in 1980.[23] The declining importance of these regions is evidenced by the insignificant average inflows of not even US$1 billion per year to Japan since 1989, and the decreasing attractiveness of Germany as a major destination for global FDI. During 1993–97, average annual inflows to Germany amounted to only US$3.8 billion, compared with US$9 billion during the unification years (1989–91). After a slump in successive years, inflows into Germany rose slightly again during 1994–96, but are in no relation to the country's economic weight.

Germany's cost-intensive social system and its repercussions on corporate taxes and labour costs adversely affect inbound FDI. The over-regulated economy, including strict antipollution laws, increasingly deters non-EU companies and often obliges them to explore other options in France, the Netherlands or the United Kingdom. In a recent survey, a large majority of US corporate executives admitted to looking at FDI options in the United Kingdom and France as their German operations were increasingly hampered by the strong position of unions, which impose a 35-hour working week and six weeks of paid holidays. Besides, they criticized the excessive corporate tax of 47.1 per cent which is much higher than either in France (39.7 per cent) or the United Kingdom (28.4 per cent).[24] Should Germany's locational advantages not improve in the coming years through more flexible legislation, FDI inflows will remain low. Even medium-sized German companies nowadays seek investment options outside their home country because of these reasons and the need to conquer new markets, particularly in Eastern Europe, Asia and Latin America.

During the first half of the 1990s, the United States was the largest FDI recipient worldwide. In 1997, the country reported record inflows of US$91 billion. The only other main contenders in the Triad have been the United Kingdom and France (both recorded higher inflows than the United States in 1992), and China outside the Triad (Figure 3.11). The United Kingdom has benefited from massive investments from Japan, South Korea and Germany. The three Triad countries – the United States, France and the United Kingdom – together with China accounted for 48 per cent of global FDI inflows in 1997 (51 per cent in 1996). The highest per capita inflows were recorded for Singapore, Belgium, the Netherlands and Sweden (Figure 3.12).

The United States held the largest inward stock in 1997, US$721 billion or 21 per cent of the world total (Figure 3.13). The United Kingdom ranked second (US$274 billion), followed by China (US$217 billion), France (US$174 billion) and Belgium (US$143 billion). The other countries with considerable FDI accumulation (stocks) were: Germany and Canada (US$137 billion each); Australia, the Netherlands and Brazil (US$127 billion each); and Spain (US$111 billion). After joining the EU in 1986, Spain received large investments especially from Germany, France, United States and Japan. On a per capita basis, the smaller OECD countries of Europe (Belgium, Denmark, Netherlands) and Asia–Pacific (New Zealand, Singapore, Taiwan) have outperformed their larger rivals (Figure 3.14). Over the years they have developed attractive port, warehousing and logistics facilities for inward FDI. Smaller countries usually also offer favourable tax conditions for

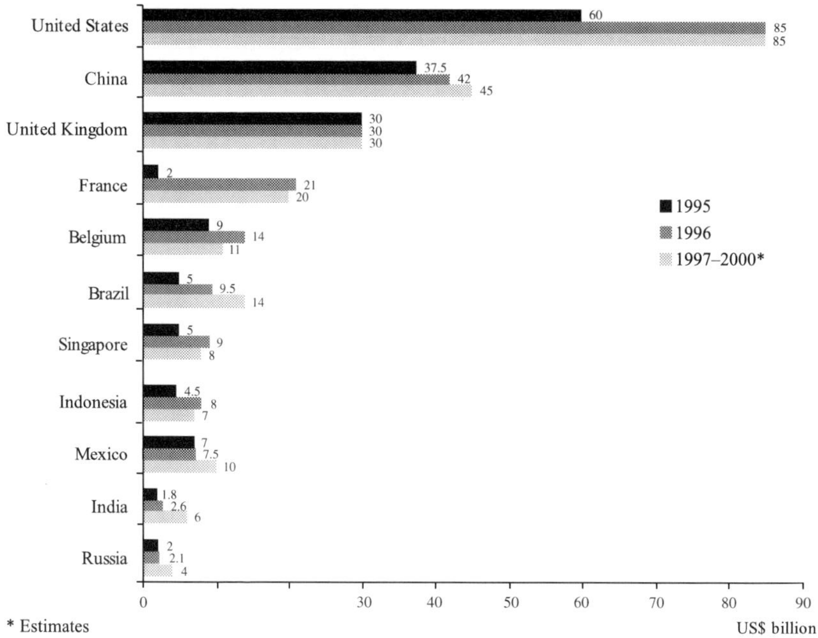

Source: UNCTAD, *World Investment Reports 1996, 1997, 1998.*

Figure 3.11 The world's leading recipients, FDI inflows, 1995–2000

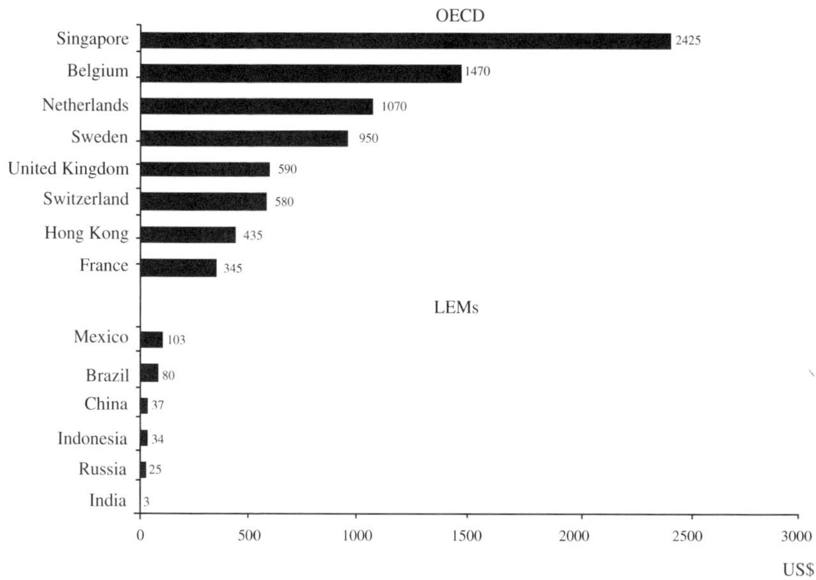

Source: UNCTAD, *World Investment Reports 1996, 1997, 1998.*

Figure 3.12 The world's leading recipients, per capita FDI inflows, 1996–97 (annual average)

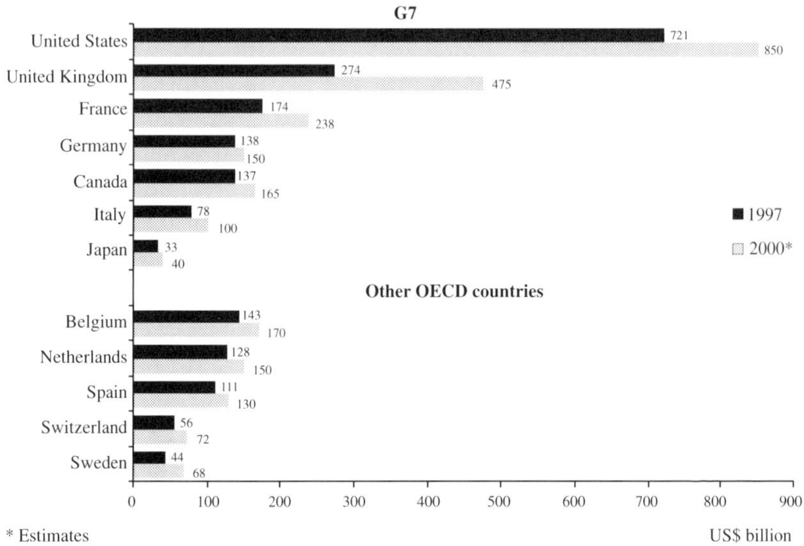

Source: UNCTAD, *World Investment Reports 1996, 1997, 1998.*

Figure 3.13 Leading OECD recipients, FDI stock, 1997, 2000

foreign TNCs, who can thus set up their regional headquarters for expanding trade into neighbouring markets.

Japan, a major outward investor, has attracted negligible volumes of FDI so far, which are hardly commensurate with its economic weight and industrial potential. The main reasons are excessively high land prices, fierce domestic competition and a preference for locally produced products. To a lesser extent, this also applies to South Korea and Taiwan. In 1997, the combined outward stock of the three countries (Japan, Taiwan and South Korea) was six times higher than inward stock.

3.3.2 FDI in the emerging economies of Asia and Latin America

The fast-growing emerging economies of Asia, South America and recently also of Central Europe (Czech Republic, Hungary, Poland) have become attractive markets. Asia is by far the fastest growing region and a serious challenger to the leading traditional recipients. In 1996, FDI flows into Asian economies (US$84 billion) accounted for 24 per cent of world inflows, a substantial jump from previous years (17 per cent in 1992; 15 per cent in 1991). Inward FDI stock in Asia more than trebled during 1991–96, an increase that has so far remained unrivalled by any other world region.

A case in point is China, which attracted flows of US$45 billion in 1997 (11 per cent of global inflows), a tenfold increase over 1989–90. With

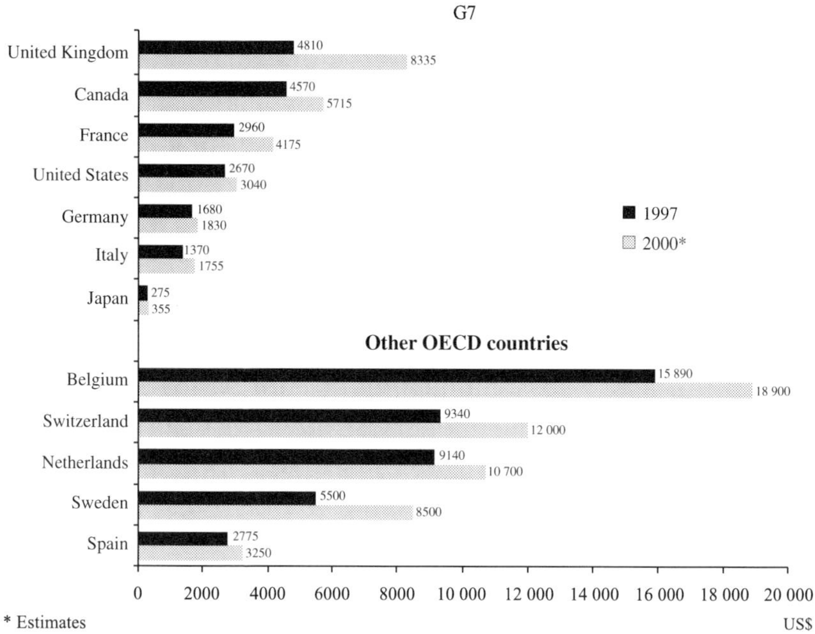

Source: UNCTAD, *World Investment Reports 1996, 1997, 1998.*

Figure 3.14 Leading OECD recipients, per capita FDI stock, 1997, 2000

US$217 billion in 1997, the accumulated inward FDI stock of China has overtaken that of major industrialized countries (Figures 3.15). Today, Chinese inward stock is seven times higher than that of Japan and has contributed to the rise in the country's foreign reserves, from US$11 billion in 1990 to US$125 billion at the end of 1998. China's success is directly determined by its locational (L) advantages, especially its huge population (1.2 billion), healthy economic growth (8–11 per cent annually during 1990–97) and free market policies. The Chinese government understood how to market its L-advantages abroad and attract a large number of leading western and Japanese TNCs through investor-friendly FDI policies,[25] and the Chinese authorities anticipate further increases. The 1998–2000 inflows for China are estimated at US$50–55 billion, with a prospect of exceeding US$70 billion by 2000–02.

Since the early 1990s, inward FDI has gained considerable momentum in Mexico, India and the ASEAN countries, especially Singapore, Malaysia, Thailand and lately Indonesia. ASEAN has been transformed into one of the most dynamic regions in the world.[26] Indonesia, for example, almost trebled its inflows in only three years, from US$2 billion in 1993 to

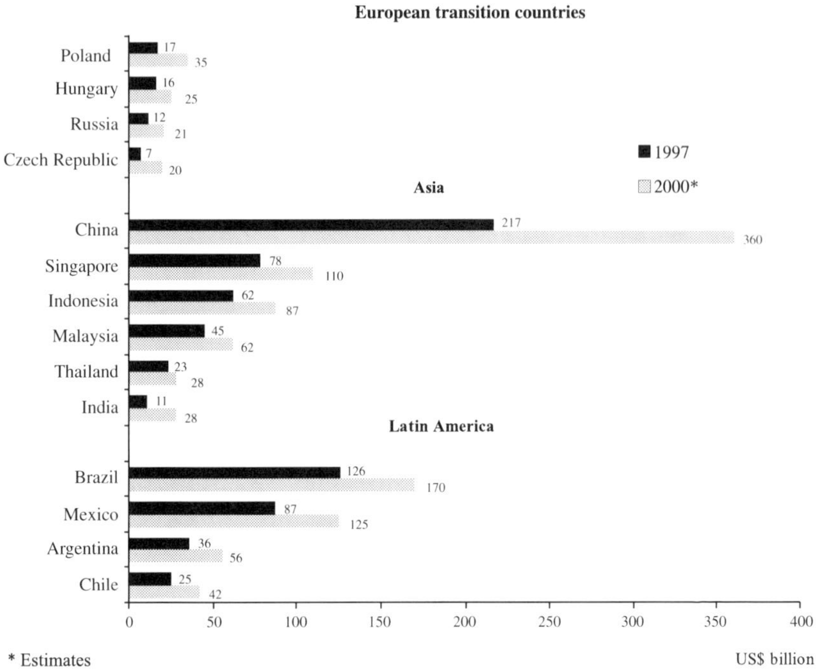

Source: UNCTAD, *World Investment Report 1998.*

Figure 3.15 Leading non-OECD recipients, FDI stock, 1997, 2000

US$6 billion in 1996 and 1997. ASEAN countries, as well as NAFTA member Mexico (US$12 billion in 1997) and MERCOSUR members Brazil (US$16 billion) and Argentina (US$6 billion), have embarked on more liberal FDI policies as part of a comprehensive strategy to accelerate economic development and industrial transformation. With US$126 billion, Brazil has accumulated the largest inward stock in Latin America.

In the coming century, the large emerging markets (LEMs)[27] will become serious challengers of major OECD recipient countries, which are suffering from slow economic growth, rigid structures and saturated markets in most industrial sectors. Economic growth has already started shifting to the leading emerging economies, and, together with liberal policies, it is an important factor for their attractiveness as new important recipients of FDI.

3.3.3 FDI in European transition countries

Until the collapse of the Soviet empire, the socialist countries of Central and Eastern Europe were closed to foreign investment from the West. Industrial production was organized and coordinated through central planning agencies, which allocated resources and determined production targets. Sectoral ministries supervised whether these targets were met. Public enterprises were usually highly diversified manufacturing conglomerates producing an extremely wide range of products and services. Output quantities and prices were fixed in advance and not determined by the free interplay of supply and demand.

Eastern European economies were grouped under the Council of Mutual Economic Assistance (COMECON), a special economic area in which members benefitted from special trading and clearing facilities for inter-enterprise supplies and purchases. Export and import operations were mostly based on compensation and barter deals to avoid payment in foreign currency. Depending on the availability of know-how and raw materials, countries specialized in a few predefined industries, for which they had the responsibility of supplying other member countries. 'Mono-enterprise' industrial structures were quite common leading to high dependency ratios (imports over local production) among COMECON countries. For example, buses were produced mainly in Hungary, tramway cars in Czechoslovakia, passenger cars, chemicals and instruments in the German Democratic Republic. The Soviet Union was the exclusive supplier of defence-related equipment, planes, large harvesting machines and raw materials. Intraregional FDI did not develop as it was not necessary as long as enterprises were state-owned, and central planning agencies were responsible for production targets. Compensation mechanisms reduced the need for capital. FDI from western economies was practically forbidden.

It was only in the late 1970s that small countries starting with Romania and former Czechoslovakia began to open their doors to western companies by authorizing the formation of minority joint ventures. Such joint ventures were allowed in Russia only after 1987. Inward FDI of the entire former COMECON region was an insignificant US$200 million stock until 1989 (total world stock that year amounted to US$1300 billion).[28] FDI inflows into COMECON member countries were far too low to support the transfer of necessary managerial know-how, modern technologies and skilled jobs for industrial upgrading and economic development. Regular exchange of information and R&D results with western enterprises was therefore impossible. The lack of external inputs contributed to the economic difficulties Russia and other COMECON countries faced starting from the mid-1980s, resulting in the demise of the old system.

The FDI situation began to change dramatically with the fall of the Berlin wall in 1989. Democratically elected governments launched broad economic transformation programmes and opened their economies to foreign capital and know-how. In the Czech Republic, Hungary, Poland, Slovenia and the three Baltic States in particular, FDI was seen as an essential component of structural reforms and industrial upgrading. Authorities in these countries were convinced of the benefits of FDI for re-establishing competitive structures in formerly isolated markets to ensure a successful transition to a market economy. In terms of FDI per capita stock, Central European transition countries have almost drawn level with leading recipients in Asia and Latin America (Figure 3.16).

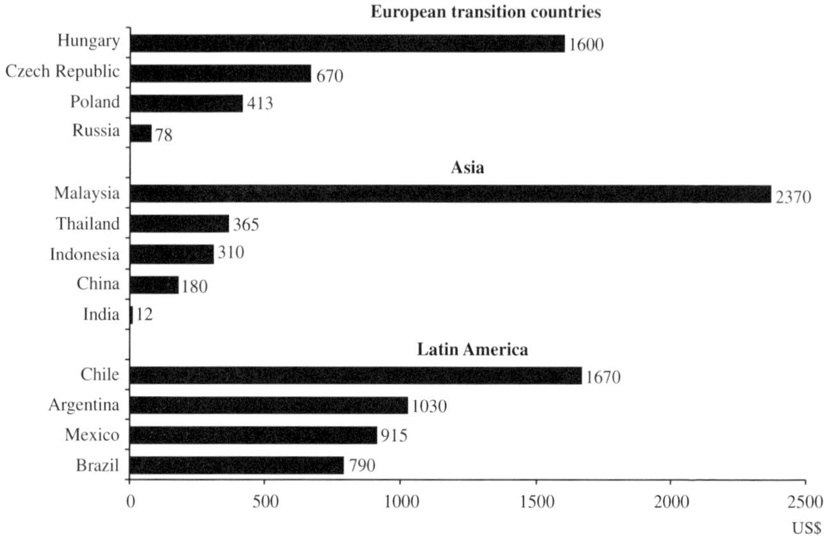

Source: Adapted from UNCTAD, *World Investment Report 1998.*

Figure 3.16 Leading non-OECD recipients, FDI per capita stock, 1997

Owing to more serious problems of economic adjustment and the greater distance to the markets of western Europe, governments in Russia and the other CIS countries had to adopt a slower pace and could not take all the necessary steps to attract foreign private capital. FDI has not been assigned so far the role it deserves in socioeconomic transformation. The legal system including its broad investment protection guarantees (national treatment, nondiscrimination), although in place, is not yet transparent to western businessmen, who therefore remain reticent to make the necessary commitments and confine their operations to the opening of small representative offices or – still rare – the establishment of small assembly units.

The FDI stock of former socialist economies of Central and Eastern Europe including CIS countries represents just about 2 per cent of the world total (US$69 billion in 1997), although inflows more than doubled during 1994–95. Inward stock has risen, especially in the Visegrad countries (Poland, Hungary, Czech Republic, Slovakia) since the opening of these economies to foreign investors in 1989 (Table 3.4). However, liberal FDI policies must be pursued in the coming years, if European transition countries are to catch up with other world regions. By comparison, the African continent held a combined stock of US$79 billion (including South Africa) in 1997, more than all transition countries of Central and Eastern Europe (including CIS) put together.

Table 3.4 FDI in Central and Eastern Europe, 1997

	FDI inflows 1997 (US$ bn)	FDI inward stock 1997 (US$ bn)	Per capita inward FDI stock 1997 (US$)	FDI outward stock 1997 (US$ bn)
CIS				
• Russia	5.3	11.5	82	3.7
• Ukraine	0.6	2.1	42	0.2
• Azerbaijan	0.6	1.8	225	–
• Belarus	0.2	0.5	50	–
• Kazakhstan	1.3	3.8	224	–
• Uzbekistan	0.1	0.4	18	–
• Turkmenistan	0.1	0.2	40	–
Central Europe				
• Hungary	2.1	15.9	1600	1.0
• Poland	5.0	16.5	425	0.8
• Czech Republic	1.3	6.7	670	0.4
• Slovakia	0.6	1.3	236	–
• Bulgaria	0.5	1.0	110	–
• Romania	1.0	2.6	180	0.1
• Slovenia	0.6	2.0	1000	0.4
• Baltic States	1.0	2.8	437	–
ETC total[a]	20.3	69.1		6.6
World total		3 455		

[a] ETC: European transition countries.

Sources: Adapted from UN ECE Secretariat; UNCTAD, *World Investment Report 1998*; Goskomstat, *Statistical Yearbooks* and annual publications, 1996, 1997, 1998 (for data on Russia).

In terms of FDI, Russia lags behind the countries of Eastern Europe, which can offer more attractive macroeconomic conditions and transparent legislation. Poland, for example, recorded five times higher per capita stocks in 1997. In the Czech Republic they were eight times higher than in Russia, and in Hungary 19 times. During 1996–97, Russia's average per capita stock was about three times lower than in Kazakhstan and Azerbaijan. However, these countries represent much smaller markets than Russia, which holds the highest economic and industrial potential in the region. In absolute terms, annual inflows to Russia increased from US$700 million in 1992/93 to US$2.1 billion in 1996 and US$5.3 billion in 1997. In 1997, Russia's inflows for the first time exceeded those of the leading recipient economies of Central Europe (Hungary, Poland). Russia's inward stock has grown gradually to almost US$12 billion in 1997. Today, Russia represents about 17 per cent of total inward stock in the European transition countries, less than Poland (US$16.5 billion, 24 per cent) and Hungary (US$16 billion, 23 per cent). As smaller and medium-sized Central European markets will soon have reached their maximum absorptive capacity, Russia stands a good chance to take the lead if the government succeeds in implementing a viable FDI policy to attract foreign TNCs.[29]

Russia's position as an outward investor is much better. In 1997, the country represented 56 per cent of the combined outward stock of European transition countries (US$3.7 billion), its outward stock – mainly in financial services and raw materials[30] – roughly corresponding to one-third of its inward stock in that year. But the inflow situation should improve considering the high demand for FDI by Russia's industry, provided that national authorities succeed in creating the right conditions for attracting FDI. The outbound/inbound FDI stock ratio is expected to be 1:4 or 1:5 within the next 5–7 years.

In 1997, major investors in Russia were the United States, the United Kingdom, Switzerland and Germany.[31] Interestingly, Japan, France, the Netherlands and Canada, which occupy leading positions for global FDI, have not been big investors in Russia. FDI is concentrated in a few major regions (Greater Moscow, Volga region, West Siberia, Greater St Petersburg) and sectors (finance, retailing, banking, oil and gas, construction). Stakes were bought in promising Russian enterprises as part of the ongoing privatization programme. Greenfield operations are still rare — they are mainly undertaken by large multinationals — because of the absence of a single authority with a clear policy. Individual government departments consider FDI as their responsibility for their respective areas and negotiate incentives on a case-by-case basis. A central agency with broad regulatory and coordinating powers is not in place.[32] Moreover, tax laws are frequently modified and the issue of property rights has not yet been clarified.[33] A certain reticence can therefore be observed among western investors to commit large equity contributions. In 1996, total assets in hard currency declared by foreign investors as their contribution to the equity in the authorized capital of joint ventures amounted to less than US$60 000 per venture.[34]

FDI into Central and Eastern Europe tends to follow trade patterns although with a certain time lag. Owing to geographic proximity, European companies have become major traders and investors in the Central and Eastern European region. Countries like Poland, Russia and Ukraine represent promising markets in terms of population and raw materials availability. Labour costs are also 10–15 times lower than in high-cost countries like Denmark, Finland, Germany, the Netherlands or

Sweden. Central and Eastern Europe, including all CIS countries, is therefore expected to emerge as one of the last frontiers for international investment and business.

3.4 Sectoral distribution of foreign investment

3.4.1 The growing role of services

In the first half of the twentieth century, access to natural resources was the main motivation for foreign investment, and it was mainly food, mining and oil multinationals that invested in the former colonies and developing countries of Africa, Asia and Latin America. The sectoral structure of FDI began to change towards the late 1950s and early 1960s, when the focus on value-added goods led to a shift from simple raw material processing to production of finished products: automotive components, chemicals, pharmaceuticals, furniture, textiles and apparel, leather goods, processed foods and beverages.

Starting from the late 1970s and early 1980s, the high-tech revolution and fierce competition compelled IT companies such as IBM, Intel, AT&T, Siemens, Toshiba and Alcatel to look for low-cost manufacturing sites for the assembly and production of computers, telecommunications and other information technology products (computer components and peripherals such as printers and disk drives, office automation equipment). To overcome trade restrictions, multinationals like General Motors, Volkswagen, Fiat and Ford began to produce cars in new markets such as Brazil and Mexico, which also offered labour cost advantages.

The early 1990s witnessed the rise of service TNCs: banks, insurance companies, transport agents, hotel chains, engineering firms, advertising agencies, management and legal consultants, and, more recently, real estate and retail companies. Their global expansion is linked to the growing importance of services for national economies. In the United States, France and the United Kingdom, the service sector already accounts for 65–70 per cent of GDP. According to the 1998 UNCTAD estimates, service TNCs accounted for about 55–60 per cent of global FDI stock, against 30–35 per cent in the early 1970s. Service TNCs were almost inexistent in the 1950s and 1960s, when almost one-third of the world FDI stock was still in natural resource extraction and processing.

In G5 countries, the share of services in total FDI stock ranged from 45 per cent (United Kingdom) to 67 per cent (Japan) during 1993–95 (Table 3.5). Interestingly, above-average shares for FDI in services were recorded by Germany and Japan, whose economies are based on strong secondary (industrial) sectors, and where services have grown less rapidly than in the other three G5 countries. Medium-sized service TNCs, like those in industry, are still very risk-averse and prefer to trade with but not invest in non-Triad countries where economic and political stability cannot be

Table 3.5 Sectoral breakdown of FDI stock held by G5 countries, 1975–95

Country	Year	Sectors (%)		
		Agriculture	Industry	Services
France	1975	22	38	40
	1987	4	50	46
	1995	9	41	50
Germany	1976	5	48	47
	1985	4	43	53
	1995	2	39	59
Japan	1976	28	32	40
	1985	17	30	53
	1995	5	28	67
United Kingdom	1984	33	32	35
	1995	17	38	45
United States	1975	26	45	29
	1985	15	44	41
	1995	11	36	53

Sources: Adapted from UNCTAD, *World Investment Reports 1992, 1994*; OECD, *International Direct Investment Statistics Yearbook*, 1996, 1997.

fully assessed. It will be a major challenge to win medium-sized TNCs (both in services and manufacturing) as investors and providers of advanced technologies to Russia in the coming years.[35]

For service TNCs, it is also easier to follow their industrial clients who relocate part of their production or to move closer to the final users in new markets. These companies can generally react more quickly than industrial TNCs to market changes. They require lower investments because they are less equipment-intensive and rely almost entirely on human resources.

The need for local presence to deliver services is another major reason underlying the shift towards services in the past 10 years. The situation is, however, beginning to change with growing cross-border trading and transportability of services due to advances in information and telecommunications technologies. This may reduce the need for FDI to deliver such services to foreign markets (e.g. insurance, management consulting). Still, FDI in services is expected to grow faster than that in the secondary (manufacturing) and certainly primary (agriculture, raw materials) sectors in the future. Strategic FDI decisions in services can be implemented very quickly, as these investments are less capital-intensive and face fewer FDI restrictions, as in the case of industrial and sensitive high-tech sectors (e.g. defence-related or protected industries, sectors governed by strict pollution-control regulations such as oil extraction and chemical plants). For this reason, service TNCs also diversify into other service areas. Retail chains, for example, move into financial and banking operations, as well as tourism.

The growing role of services in FDI also reflects the increased involvement of industrial TNCs in nonmanufacturing activities. Many automotive, electronics, IT and engineering TNCs from G5 countries, for example, offer leasing, insurance and advisory services to their clients. Japan's highly diversified and financially powerful industrial conglomerates (e.g. Matsushita, Mitsui) control their own banking operations and offer special loan facilities, trading and other services (e.g. market research, consulting, training) to other Japanese companies abroad.

Besides their role as providers of state-of-the-art manufacturing technologies, leading TNCs from western economies (e.g. oil and gas multinationals) also contribute to the rapid modernization of the services sector in developing and transition countries where they are needed to ensure the proper functioning of the free market economy. Policy-makers in Russia need to take this aspect into account when approaching potential investors from western countries, who may often represent diversified corporations possessing valuable know-how in both engineering/manufacturing and market services.

The increasing role of services should, however, not hide the fact that manufacturing companies will remain important foreign investors both in OECD and emerging and transition markets. Manufacturing enterprises, especially from non-G5 countries, are solicited by governments of emerging economies in Asia, Latin America and, increasingly, Eastern Europe to help upgrade important manufacturing sectors. They play a vital role in transferring modern technologies and know-how to raise overall living standards of the population. FDI in services is concentrated in OECD countries, where these sectors are already very developed. Transition economies have certainly made a quantum jump as far as the role of services in national economies is concerned, but they are still far behind the level of industrialized nations. Except for banking, trading and transport where considerable FDI has already taken place, a significant share of future investments in Russia and the neighbouring CIS countries will still focus on the manufacturing sector, which needs revamping and an injection of foreign technologies to meet the needs of more demanding consumers.[36]

3.4.2 Sectoral distribution of FDI in Central and Eastern Europe

The sectoral distribution of inbound FDI in Central Europe (including the Baltic states) is gradually approximating that observed in the emerging Asian economies. Shares of manufacturing and services FDI are increasing as these countries prepare to join the EU. Agriculture has remained important only in Romania (6 per cent of inward FDI stock in 1997); in all the other leading economies its share has dropped to 2–3 per cent (Table 3.6). This pattern reflects the evolution of domestic demand and increased domestic investment in manufacturing. The Polish, Hungarian and Czech economies already enjoy a free-trade agreement with the EU, and their industrial structures are approaching those of their EU neighbours. Services

Table 3.6 Sectoral distribution (%) of inward FDI stock, leading European transition economies, 1997

Sector/industry	Central Europe					CIS	
	Czech Republic	Hungary	Poland	Romania	Slovenia	Russia	Ukraine
Primary sector	**2**	**4**	**4**	**9**	**3**	**16**	**5**
• Agriculture, forestry, fishing	2	3	2	6	2	2	3
• Mining, quarrying, oil and gas	–	1	2	3	1	14	2
Secondary sector	**48**	**39**	**61**	**53**	**36**	**29**	**54**
• Food, beverages	16	9	21	12	3	9	20
• Machinery and equipment	1	12	17	17	5	4	9
• Basic metals and metal products	3	2	1	1	2	3	3
• Automotive	13	–	–	3	1	1	1
• Chemicals	8	8	5	5	6	3	7
• Building materials	3	3	6	6	2	2	7
• Wood processing, paper and printing	1	3	5	2	7	4	3
• Textiles, leather, apparel	2	2	3	4	2	1	2
• Other industries	1	–	3	3	8	2	2
Tertiary sector	**50**	**57**	**35**	**38**	**61**	**55**	**41**
• Banking and insurance	9	9	21	5	17	32	9
• Distributive trades	9	12	6	16	11	11	19
• Public catering and tourism	1	2	2	4	2	5	2
• Transport and telecommunications	18	8	5	4	2	2	5
• Real estate	3	8	1	4	13	2	2
• Other services	10	18	–	5	16	3	4
Total FDI stock (US$ bn)	**6.7**	**15.9**	**16.5**	**2.6**	**2.0**	**11.5**	**2.1**

Sources: Adapted from UNCTAD, *World Investment Report, 1998;* data from national statistical offices, 1997, 1998.

were most important in Hungary (57 per cent of inbound FDI in 1997) and Slovenia (61 per cent).

In the CIS countries, the situation is somewhat different. Economic reforms and industrial restructuring efforts have yet to produce a diversified industrial structure that would satisfy more sophisticated consumer demand. Owing to a lack of information and absence of effective industrial policies in the recipient countries, foreign manufacturers of finished goods have so far stayed out. In the CIS countries, especially Russia and the Central Asian CIS republics, they focus on primary activities: mining (including precious metals), oil exploration and extraction, engineering and metal processing and agribusiness (including dairy farming and livestock production). Twenty per cent of Ukraine's inbound FDI was directed to food processing and beverages. Across the CIS, FDI in light industries (e.g. food, apparel, sports goods, stationery, consumer electronics, white goods) and high-tech sectors (e.g. computers, telecommunication equipment) are still the exception rather than the rule although the development of such activities would be crucial for the long-term progress of industrial adjustment.

In Russia, industrial FDI represented only 29 per cent of inward FDI stock by 1997. Finance (32 per cent), trading and public catering (16 per cent) and mining and oil industries (14 per cent) have so far attracted the bulk of FDI, mostly in Moscow and St Petersburg. Service sectors are considered less risky by foreign TNCs than manufacturing, which is more exposed to political pressure and sudden changes in property laws.[37] FDI in manufacturing has remained very low despite the potential and the need for local industries to cooperate with western partners. Exceptions are engineering and metal processing, wood and paper, construction and construction materials; these have seen a certain rise in FDI, but the potential is far from being fully exploited.[38] The implementation of the 'large' privatization of former state conglomerates and the adoption of investor-friendly laws and regulations should improve the situation. A strategic approach including canvassing of individual TNCs should enable Russia to effectively balance FDI inflows in favour of the secondary sector.

Annex 3.1 The world's leading FDI source countries, 1983–97

Countries	Annual FDI outflows (US$ bn)											Outward FDI stock (US$ bn) 1997
	1983–88 (average)	1989	1990	1991	1992	1993	1994	1989–94 (average)	1995	1996	1997	
World total	**93.7**	**217.9**	**243.2**	**199.3**	**190.6**	**222.2**	**222.3**	**215.9**	**338.7**	**346.8**	**423.7**	**3541.2**
Western Europe	**51.9**	**124.1**	**143.5**	**113.5**	**110.5**	**103.7**	**113.9**	**118.2**	**163.8**	**176.2**	**195.6**	**1786.8**
European Union	**47.9**	**115.1**	**135.7**	**105.2**	**104.4**	**94.7**	**105.5**	**110.1**	**149.1**	**160.4**	**179.8**	**1597.6**
• United Kingdom	18.8	35.2	18.6	16.0	19.1	25.7	25.1	23.3	42.4	53.5	58.1	413.2
• Germany	7.9	18.3	28.7	22.8	16.1	17.4	20.6	20.7	34.9	28.6	34.3	326.0
• France	5.9	19.5	34.8	23.9	31.3	20.6	22.9	25.5	18.7	25.2	24.6	226.8
• Netherlands	5.2	14.8	15.4	13.5	14.5	10.0	11.4	13.3	13.3	20.0	20.4	213.2
• Italy	2.8	2.2	7.6	7.2	5.9	7.4	5.1	5.9	6.9	5.9	10.2	125.1
• Belgium[a]	1.5	6.8	6.3	6.2	11.3	4.0	0.0	5.8	11.4	8.9	6.7	94.4*
• Sweden	3.5	10.2	14.6	7.3	0.3	1.4	6.1	6.7	10.7	4.9	3.9	74.8*
• Spain	0.5	1.5	2.9	3.6	1.3	2.6	4.2	2.7	3.6	4.6	10.0	48.8
• Denmark	0.5	2.1	1.5	1.8	2.2	1.4	4.0	1.9	11.4	8.9	5.5	27.9
• Finland	0.9	3.0	2.7	–0.1	–0.8	1.7	3.8	1.7	1.7	3.5	2.5	20.8
• Austria	0.2	1.2	1.9	1.8	2.1	1.7	1.5	1.7	1.1	1.4	1.4	15.0
Non-EU												
• Switzerland	2.9	7.9	6.4	6.5	5.7	8.1	6.8	6.9	11.9	10.5	12.0	156.7
European transition countries[b]	–	–	–	–	–	**0.9**	**1.1**	–	–	–	–	**6.6**
• Russia	–	–	–	–	0.3	0.3	0.4	–	0.2	0.4	2.5	3.7

continued …

Annex 3.1 ***(continued)***

Countries	Annual FDI outflows (US$ bn)											Outward FDI stock (US$ bn) 1997
	1983–88 (average)	1989	1990	1991	1992	1993	1994	1989–94 (average)	1995	1996	1997	
NAFTA	**6.2**	**30.4**	**32.1**	**39.4**	**43.2**	**74.8**	**50.6**	**45.1**	**99.3**	**93.0**	**128.5**	**1048.5**
• United States	14.2	25.7	27.2	33.5	39.0	69.0	45.6	40.0	92.9	84.9	114.5	907.5
• Canada	4.3	4.6	4.7	5.7	3.7	5.8	4.8	4.9	5.8	7.5	13.0	137.7*
• Mexico	0.1	0.1	0.2	0.2	0.5	0.0	0.2	0.2	0.6	0.6	1.0	3.3
Oceania												
• Australia	3.4	3.3	0.3	3.0	0.0	1.1	6.0	2.3	4.1	1.3	6.4	52.4
Asia												
• Japan	14.0	44.1	48.0	30.7	17.2	13.7	17.9	28.6	22.5	23.4	26.0	356.2*
• Hong Kong	1.5	2.9	2.4	3.1	7.4	17.5	21.0	9.0	25.0	27.0	26.0	137.5
• Singapore	0.1	0.9	1.6	0.4	0.7	0.8	0.7	0.9	3.9	4.8	5.9	43.4*
• Taiwan	0.8	7.0	5.2	1.9	1.7	2.4	2.0	3.4	2.7	3.1	5.2	34.2
• China	0.5	0.8	0.8	0.9	4.0	4.4	2.0	2.2	2.0	2.2	2.5	20.4
• South Korea	0.1	0.3	0.8	1.4	1.0	1.1	2.1	1.1	3.5	4.2	4.3	18.0
• Malaysia	0.2	0.3	0.5	0.4	0.5	1.4	1.8	0.8	2.6	1.9	3.1	15.7
South America												
• Brazil	0.1	0.5	0.7	1.0	0.1	1.1	0.8	0.7	1.4	1.0	1.6	8.7
• Chile	0.0	0.0	0.0	0.1	0.4	0.4	0.9	0.3	0.7	1.0	1.9	5.8
• Venezuela	0.1	0.1	0.4	0.1	0.2	0.4	0.3	0.3	0.3	0.6	0.6	3.4

[a]Including Luxembourg. [b]Estimates; including CIS countries *Data differ significantly in *World Investment Reports 1997* and *1998*.

Source: Adapted from UNCTAD, *World Investment Reports 1995, 1996, 1997, 1998;* Goskomstat for data on Russia (1998).

Annex 3.2 The world's leading FDI recipient countries, 1983–97

Countries	Annual FDI inflows (US$ bn)											Inward FDI stock (US$ bn) 1997
	1983–88 (average)	1989	1990	1991	1992	1993	1994	1989–94 (average)	1995	1996	1997	
World total	**91.6**	**200.6**	**211.4**	**158.4**	**170.4**	**208.4**	**225.7**	**195.8**	**314.9**	**349.2**	**400.5**	**3455.2**
Western Europe	**28.9**	**88.6**	**110.6**	**82.6**	**80.1**	**76.4**	**73.7**	**85.3**	**115.6**	**105.4**	**114.9**	**1276.5**
European Union	**27.4**	**84.2**	**104.4**	**79.4**	**78.0**	**74.0**	**71.2**	**81.9**	**111.9**	**99.4**	**108.2**	**1196.2**
• United Kingdom	9.3	30.4	33.0	16.0	15.0	14.5	10.2	19.9	29.9	30.1	36.9	274.4*
• France	3.9	10.3	13.2	15.1	21.8	20.8	16.9	16.4	20.1	20.8	18.3	174.1
• Belgium[a]	1.8	7.1	8.1	9.4	11.3	10.7	6.0	8.8	9.1	13.9	12.5	143.1*
• Germany	1.5	10.8	9.2	7.9	5.5	1.8	4.4	6.6	9.0	3.8	–0.2	137.7*
• Netherlands	2.6	8.3	12.3	6.3	7.7	5.7	3.1	7.2	9.9	6.3	8.7	127.9
• Spain	3.4	8.4	13.8	10.5	8.1	6.8	8.2	9.3	8.3	6.4	5.6	110.6*
• Italy	2.4	2.2	6.4	2.4	3.1	3.7	3.6	3.6	4.3	3.7	3.5	78.5
European transition countries												
• Poland	–	–	–	0.3	0.7	1.7	1.9	–	2.5	5.2	5.0	16.5
• Hungary	–	–	–	1.5	1.5	2.3	1.1	–	3.5	2.0	2.1	15.9
• Russia	–	–	–	–	0.7	0.7	0.9	–	2.0	2.1	5.3	11.5
• Czech Republic	–	–	–	–	–	0.7	0.9	–	2.5	2.6	1.3	6.7
NAFTA												
• United States	34.4	67.7	47.9	22.0	17.6	41.1	49.5	41.0	60.2	84.6	90.7	720.8
• Canada	4.2	5.0	7.8	2.7	4.4	5.0	6.0	5.2	11.2	6.7	8.2	137.1*
• Mexico	2.3	3.2	2.6	4.8	4.9	4.9	4.4	4.1	7.0	7.5	12.1	86.8
Oceania												
• Australia	3.5	7.8	6.5	4.4	4.7	3.4	2.8	4.9	13.1	6.0	9.6	126.3
• New Zealand	0.3	1.4	1.7	1.7	1.1	2.6	1.8	1.7	2.5	2.9	1.3	29.5*

continued ...

Annex 3.2 (*continued*)

Countries	Annual FDI inflows (US$ bn)											Inward FDI stock (US$ bn) 1997
	1983–88 (average)	1989	1990	1991	1992	1993	1994	1989–94 (average)	1995	1996	1997	
ASEAN												
• Singapore	1.9	2.9	5.6	4.9	6.7	6.8	7.9	5.8	5.3	9.4	10.0	78.1
• Indonesia	0.3	0.7	1.1	1.5	1.8	2.0	3.0	1.7	4.5	8.0	5.4	62.1
• Malaysia	0.7	1.6	2.3	4.0	5.2	5.2	4.5	3.8	5.8	5.3	3.8	45.2
• Thailand	0.4	1.8	2.4	2.0	2.1	1.7	2.7	2.1	2.3	2.4	3.6	23.1
• Philippines	0.2	0.6	0.5	0.5	0.2	0.8	1.5	0.7	1.5	1.4	1.3	9.9
• Vietnam				0.2	0.4	0.5	0.7	0.5	2.0	2.2	1.2	7.5
East and South Asia												
• China	1.8	3.4	3.5	4.4	11.2	27.5	33.8	14.0	37.5	42.3	45.3	217.3
• Hong Kong	1.3	1.1	1.7	0.5	2.1	1.7	2.0	1.5	2.1	2.5	2.6	26.9
• Japan	0.3	1.0	1.8	1.4	2.7	0.1	0.9	1.3	0.1	0.2	3.2	33.2*
• Taiwan	0.4	1.6	1.3	1.3	0.9	0.9	1.4	1.2	1.5	1.4	2.2	19.9
• S. Korea	0.4	0.8	0.7	1.1	0.6	0.5	0.8	0.8	1.5	2.3	2.3	14.8
• India	0.1	0.3	0.2	0.2	0.3	0.6	0.9	0.4	1.8	2.6	3.3	11.2
South America												
• Brazil	1.5	1.3	0.9	1.0	1.6	0.8	2.2	1.3	4.9	9.5	16.3	126.3
• Argentina	0.5	1.0	1.8	2.4	4.2	6.3	1.2	2.8	3.9	4.3	6.3	36.1
• Chile	0.4	1.3	0.6	0.6	0.7	0.9	2.5	1.1	3.0	3.1	5.4	25.1

[a]Including Luxembourg. *Data differ significantly in *World Investment Reports* 1997 and 1998.

Source: Adapted from UNCTAD, *World Investment Reports 1995, 1996, 1997, 1998.*

Notes

1. International organizations such as GATT and OECD contributed significantly to liberalizing trade and reducing tariff and nontariff barriers. Today, these bodies increasingly concentrate on liberalizing FDI by establishing viable rules for foreign investors in recipient countries. See Chapter 2.4.
2. Most data in this chapter are derived from UNCTAD, *World Investment Reports 1996, 1997, 1998.*
3. *The Economist*, 'Trade Winds', 8 November 1997, pp. 99–100.
4. UNCTAD, *World Investment Report 1999.*
5. The IMF, for example, imposes strict policy rules including drastic cuts in spending and efforts to raise tax revenue. It is therefore often difficult for recipient countries to pursue long-term goals for reviving their industries.
6. *The Economist*, 'The Right to Fund the Fund', 21 February 1998, pp. 51–52.
7. G7 countries: Canada, France, Germany, Italy, Japan, United Kingdom and United States.
8. By 2000, this ratio is expected to drop below the 20 per cent mark.
9. World Bank, *World Development Report 1997.*
10. Parts V and VI.
11. This trend will be reinforced by increased globalization in coming decades.
12. Chapters 5–7.
13. Eurostat, *Foreign Investment Yearbook*, 1996.
14. Chapter 4.1.
15. US$100 billion, in today's prices. See also Société de Banque Suisse, 'Plan Marshall: des devises pour la paix' [Marshall Plan: its contribution to peace], *Le Mois*, November 1997, pp. 20–23.
16. For historical time series since the early 1980s, see also Annex 3.1.
17. Chapter 13.4.2.
18. Japan went through a phase of active internationalization during 1985–93, when major investments were made in North America, the EU and Asia.
19. See Table 3.2.
20. Chapter 13.
21. See also Chapter 1.9.
22. Chapters 1.7 and 1.8.
23. For historical time series since the early 1980s, see also Annex 3.2.
24. *Handelsblatt*, 20 October 1997.
25. Chapter 5.2.
26. This trend will not be affected by the financial crisis in Southeast and East Asia (especially South Korea, Indonesia and Thailand) at the end of 1997.
27. LEMs: Brazil, China, India, Indonesia, Mexico, Nigeria and Russia. See also Figures 3.11–3.16.
28. UN Economic Commission for Europe, *Statistical Survey of Recent Trends in Foreign Investment in East European Countries*, 1995.
29. Under favourable global economic circumstances, Russia could garner 25–30 per cent of FDI stock directed to Central and Eastern Europe by 2002–03, despite the 1998 financial crisis.
30. According to Goskomstat, Russia's FDI outflows amounted to US$1.1 billion in 1998, of which 90 per cent in financial services and the remainder mostly in gas and oil.
31. For more details concerning FDI in Russia, see Chapter 9.3.
32. Chapter 17.1

33. Chapter 9.4.
34. Goskomstat, *Statistical Yearbook 1997*.
35. Chapters 4.2 and 14.5.
36. This study will focus on industrial FDI, because the first priority for Russia consists in developing its manufacturing sector.
37. Chapter 9.4.
38. Chapters 8.2.2 and 9.3.

4
TNCs as Global Investors

Whereas inbound FDI volumes can be explained by existing locational advantages (L-advantages) of recipient countries, FDI outflows reflect ownership advantages (O-advantages) of investing companies. O-advantages refer mainly to financial capacity and intangible assets (technological, management and marketing know-how; intellectual property; brand equity; trade and customer links; etc.) of TNCs in host countries.[1]

TNCs have firmly established themselves as the key agents of international investment and transfer of know-how. Concentrating on technology-intensive activities, TNCs constitute the main medium for creating and disseminating technologies. TNCs belong to a wide range of sectors of activity, represent companies of different size categories (large-scale, medium-sized and, rarely, small) and operate through various forms of organization (e.g. sales subsidiary, joint venture, production affiliates).

The world's leading TNCs are true multinationals with diversified activities in manufacturing and, increasingly, services. In manufacturing, most industries have seen a trend towards 'transnationalization' over the past 30 years. Since the 1980s, service TNCs have also actively invested in foreign markets. Banking, insurance, telecommunications, media, retailing, transport, tourism and accounting–consulting have been recording the fastest expansion rates.

4.1 The world's leading TNCs and their FDI impact

According to UNCTAD's 1999 annual investment survey of leading multinationals, some 60 000 parent TNCs were operating through 500 000 foreign affiliates (up from only 7000 in 1970 and 24 000 in 1990), in practically all countries of the world. The largest 100 industrial and services TNCs (excluding banks) – ranked according to foreign assets – were all headquartered in industrialized (OECD) countries: Unites States (30 companies),

Japan (18), France (11), United Kingdom, (11), Germany (9), Switzerland (5), Canada (3), Sweden (3), Italy (3), the Netherlands (2), Belgium (1) and Australia (1). About 75 per cent of the top 100 TNCs were headquartered in G5 countries, with the 10 largest accounting for almost 30 per cent of foreign turnover and 34 per cent of foreign assets of the top 100.

In 1995, these corporations – just 0.3 per cent of the TNC universe – controlled an estimated US$1.8 trillion worth of global assets and held about one-third of global FDI stock. The combined stockmarket capitalization of the world's top 100 companies is now an enormous US$5.5 trillion, slightly below the GDP of the United States. In the 1970s, their share in global FDI stock had exceeded 50 per cent. The fall in share by about 12–15 percentage points indicates the growing importance of medium-sized TNCs in global asset creation and value-added activities abroad.[2]

In 1998, TNCs sold about US$11.4 trillion[3] worth of goods and services through their foreign affiliates, almost double the value of worldwide exports of merchandise and services (US$6.7 trillion), for which they are to a large extent also responsible.[4] An estimated one-third of world exports are in fact intrafirm deliveries between TNCs and their affiliates. If nonequity arrangements (licensing, subcontracting and franchising) are included, the size and scope of international trade generated by these TNCs would rise to a global sales volume of US$10–10.5 trillion. According to a survey conducted by the Washington-based Institute for Policy Studies (IPS),[5] the 200 largest TNCs generate sales amounting to almost 30 per cent of the world's GDP. Their combined sales exceed the GDP of all nations, excluding the nine largest economies.

The high job-creation potential of TNCs makes them even more attractive to host country governments and regional authorities. In 1997, the world's top 100 TNCs employed about 6 million people, corresponding to 8 per cent of the estimated 73 million employed by all TNCs worldwide, and just less than half (45 per cent) of the jobs created by the top 100 TNCs were in host countries.[6] The world's largest TNCs mainly operate in five industries: electronics and electrical engineering (17 firms); chemicals and pharmaceuticals (16); petroleum and other energy sources (14); automobile manufacturing, assembly and parts (14), and food and beverages (12). Electronics and electrical engineering TNCs control most foreign assets (Table 4.1); the combined turnover of their foreign affiliates represents about 80 per cent of global sales of electronics products (consumer and industrial electronics, telecommunications, electrical engineering).

Traditionally, TNCs are ranked according to their foreign assets, but increasingly other factors such as employment and turnover abroad are also taken into consideration to determine a company's degree of internalization. Foreign assets alone would understate the importance of transnational labour-intensive operations by some TNCs. Similarly, companies in extracting industries (e.g. petroleum refining, mining) usually

Table 4.1 Top 15 TNCs by foreign assets, sales and employment, 1997

Company	Industry	Foreign assets (% of total assets)	Foreign sales (% of total sales)	Foreign employment (% of total employment)	Trans-nationality Index
Bayer	Chemicals	89.8	63.3	54.6	82.7
Nestlé	Food	86.9	98.2	97.0	93.2
Volkswagen	Automotive	84.8	60.8	44.4	56.8
ABB	Electrical equipment	84.7	87.2	93.9	95.7
Exxon	Energy	73.1	79.6	53.7	65.9
Royal Dutch/Shell	Energy	67.8	73.3	77.9	58.9
Mobil	Energy	61.8	65.9	52.2	59.7
Elf Aquitaine	Energy	54.5	65.4	47.5	57.6
IBM	Computers	51.9	62.7	50.1	53.7
Nissan	Automotive	42.7	44.2	43.5	51.1
Daimler-Benz	Automotive	39.2	63.2	22.2	44.1
Toyota	Automotive	30.5	45.1	23.0	40.0
General Electric	Electronics	30.4	24.4	32.4	33.1
Ford	Automotive	29.0	30.6	29.8	35.2
General Motors	Automotive	24.9	29.2	33.9	29.3

Source: UNCTAD, *World Investment Reports 1998, 1999.*

employ little local labour in their overseas operations. For a more comprehensive evaluation of transnational activities for recipient countries, UNCTAD specialists calculate each year, for the top 100 TNCs, a new index of transnationality. It is a composite measure (average) of the shares of foreign to total assets, sales and employment. The weight of each indicator is set to 1, according to the following formula:

$$\text{Transnationality index} = \left(\frac{\text{foreign assets}}{\text{total assets}} + \frac{\text{foreign sales}}{\text{total sales}} + \frac{\text{foreign employment}}{\text{total employment}}\right)\Big/3$$

This index results in a different ranking of the top 100 TNCs and reveals the importance of certain sectors. The highest scorers are chemical (index of 61 per cent) and food (53 per cent) TNCs and not electronics firms (43 per cent), although they rank highest in terms of foreign assets. Trading companies ranked lowest (30 per cent) in 1993–94. According to the composite transnationality index, TNCs from smaller OECD countries (e.g. Belgium, Netherlands, Sweden, Switzerland, Finland) carry out a much larger proportion of their activities abroad than in home markets, particularly in France, Germany, Japan and the United States. Limited possibilities of market expansion at home compels them to look for opportunities abroad. This clearly demonstrates the necessity to include not only larger investing nations but also smaller OECD countries in any future effort towards enhancing inward FDI into Russia.[7]

Not surprisingly, the world's top 100 TNCs have attained considerable economic and even political influence. General Motors, Royal Dutch/Shell,

Exxon, AT&T, Wal-Mart, Coca-Cola, IBM, Siemens, Alcatel, Philips, McDonald's, Microsoft, Lufthansa, to name a few, are familiar names to policy-makers, economists and business scholars in developing and industrialized countries alike. These corporations fully use their financial clout during negotiations with recipient countries, particularly for establishing operations in any location of their choice.

To avoid one-sided dependence, national authorities should simultaneously consider competing applications, including those from medium-sized TNCs. Smaller TNCs, which increasingly have to follow the big players, can collectively represent a significant group. They are often more open to cooperation with local companies than megacorporations, which prefer to acquire controlling stakes and total control of the manufacturing operation or to opt for a greenfield investment. The drawback of smaller TNCs is their relatively limited financial and managerial capacity.

Concentration and internationalization increases with the size of the company. The largest TNCs control the bulk of FDI stock abroad and account for the most significant outflows (which is a prerequisite for building up stock). In all important FDI source countries, the top 50 TNCs control well over half of the outward stock (Figure 4.1). Whereas medium-sized TNCs can be covered through general canvassing among opinion leaders such as industry associations and chambers of commerce, the top TNCs in each country need to be approached directly by FDI specialists.[8]

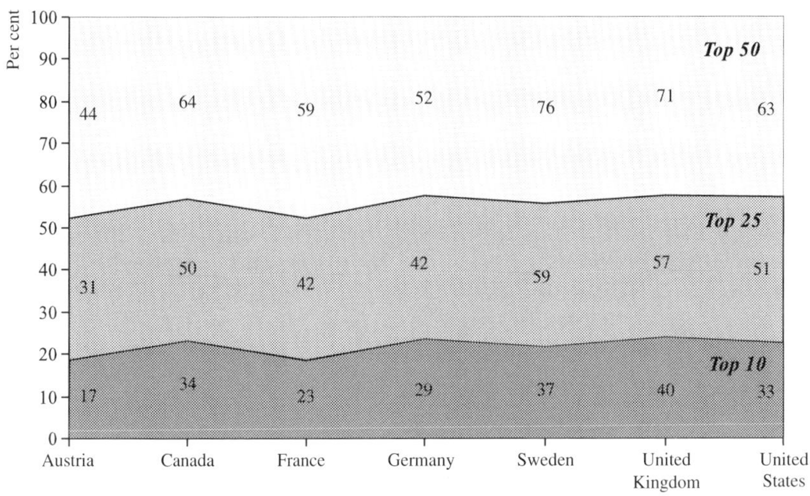

Source: Adapted from UNCTAD, *World Investment Report 1997*. Based on data provided by national central banks and statistical offices, 1998, 1999.

Figure 4.1 Concentration of outward FDI stock among top TNCs, 1997 (ranking by value of foreign assets)

Over the past 10 years, several home-grown TNCs have also made their appearance in emerging economies. Stimulated by high growth rates on the domestic front, these companies managed to grow substantially through investments in product development and exports. They include fairly large TNCs, which already compete aggressively against their OECD rivals. Examples of well-known TNCs from emerging economies that have started making inroads into OECD and European transition countries including Russia are:[9]

- Samsung, Hyundai, Daewoo and Lucky Goldstar from South Korea for electronics, information technologies and automobiles;
- Acer from Taiwan for computer hardware;
- China Resources, China Everbright and CITIC from China;
- Siam Cement and Thai Airways from Thailand;
- Astra and Salim from Indonesia;
- Proton Saga from Malaysia;
- San Miguel from the Philippines;
- Tata, Birla, Bajai Auto, Wipro, Reliance and NIIT from India;
- Petrobras (oil) and Embraer (aircraft) from Brazil;
- Cemex and Vitro from Mexico.

Russia, too, is gradually producing its own large-scale TNCs which are looking at opportunities to sell, cooperate and invest abroad (e.g. Ilyushin for aircraft; Lukoil for petroleum products, Gasprom for natural gas). Medium-sized companies from Russia are not yet in a position to compete effectively in foreign markets; the transnationalization of their activities will take many years, but could be accelerated by targeted cooperation with foreign TNCs.

4.2 The 'hidden champions': the growing importance of medium-sized TNCs

Although FDI by the top 100 TNCs produces a direct and immediate impact on the economy of recipient countries, the combined effect of medium-sized TNCs, whose share of FDI is growing, is far from negligible. These companies contribute significantly to the international division of labour, especially in niche industries and essential services. As an additional source of FDI and nonequity asset transfer to recipient countries they should not be overlooked. More risk-averse than their larger counterparts, medium-sized TNCs avoid capital-intensive greenfield investments or outright acquisitions of local firms to gain purely strategic advantages or market share. As limited finances usually impose fairly short pay-back periods, their tenet is fast earnings in niche areas with special technology requirements. They work closely with local companies or open small representation offices. They may also buy stakes in existing local operations, especially in familiar environments with low risk ratings. As a rule, medium-sized TNCs start out with low capital investment, which is gradually increased as business develops.

Smaller TNCs usually originate and invest in developed (Triad, OECD) countries, where low political risk, modern infrastructure, established customer–supplier links and niche potential allow them the rapid returns they need. After expanding their technological leadership in specialized market segments at home and in developed economies in the 1980s, some medium-sized market leaders now seek to gain additional market shares in nearby 'cluster' markets.[10] European medium-sized TNCs look at opportunities in other EU countries, and increasingly in Central and Eastern Europe. Medium-sized TNCs from the United States have expanded their market position in Latin America, but also in Hungary, Poland, Russia and Ukraine. Medium-sized TNCs from Japan prefer to invest in nearby Asian countries (Taiwan, China, ASEAN) and the Pacific Rim countries including Australia, Canada, New Zealand, Mexico and the United States.

The early 1990s saw a growing number of medium-sized TNCs seek investment opportunities in developing and transition countries, mainly to explore new sales outlets but also to benefit from low-cost labour. High saturation levels and fierce competition across all sectors in OECD economies practically force owners of smaller companies to follow their larger clients to distant markets (e.g. China, India, Mexico, Brazil), despite additional financial commitment and commercial risk. Their objective has been resource- and market-seeking FDI. The current volume of outward FDI by smaller TNCs does not correspond to their economic weight in the home countries. A considerable FDI potential therefore remains untapped, particularly in G5 and other countries such as Austria, Italy, the Netherlands and Switzerland which have a relatively high number of technologically advanced small and medium-sized enterprises (SMEs).

Certain governments even provide technical and financial assistance through specialized federal agencies and banks to support the transnationalization efforts of SMEs. In Germany, for example, the specialized development bank Deutsche Entwicklungsgesellschaft (DEG) offers venture capital and underwrites, for a predefined period, the capital of companies in the recipient countries. Another public agency, Kreditanstalt für Wiederaufbau (KfW), offers a special loan facility of up to DM1–1.5 million for investments in transition economies covering the preliminary phase of information-gathering and market research. Such government agencies are also a valuable source of information on cooperation potential and financial resources for potential foreign investors.

Executives of medium-sized TNCs have grown more attentive to promotional efforts by recipient countries. The UK and Irish investment promotion boards, for example, say they daily receive requests from SMEs in the EU and the United States. Even medium-sized TNCs from Japan and South Korea have started investing in the United Kingdom and Ireland. Medium-sized TNCs from Japan, the United States and Europe have become an important target of

FDI promotion efforts by Malaysia, Singapore, Taiwan and Thailand. The United States, Canada and Mexico have quite successfully targeted medium-sized TNCs from Europe through an efficient information policy on the FDI potential and incentives of their locations.

It is often difficult to distinguish larger medium-sized TNCs from smaller large TNCs as definitions can differ widely in different countries. According to UNCTAD, small and medium-sized TNCs are those with less than 500 employees in the home country; their average annual turnover is about US$350 million. Each year, UNCTAD updates its sample of 50 nonlarge TNCs from OECD countries, but it hardly covers the real potential offered by the hundreds of thousands of existing companies. In Germany, a qualitative definition supersedes the quantitative approach based exclusively on turnover figures. According to the qualitative definition, a medium-sized player is characterized by a controlling stake of the founding family and the legal form of personal or private limited company. Once the company's legal form is changed to a public-limited company and shares are owned by many individual and institutional shareholders, the company is no longer classified as a medium-sized firm although some of the original family traditions may still prevail (e.g. the Bertelsmann publishing group).

In Germany, for example, thousands of medium-sized companies are still run by owner-families who are proudly preserving their corporate traditions. About one-third of these companies were founded at the turn of the twentieth century (Figure 4.2). Their names stand for quality and efficiency. Companies like Hochland (cheese), Südmilch (yoghurts), Ritter Sport (chocolate), Schöller (ice cream), Staedtler (stationery), Uhu (glues),

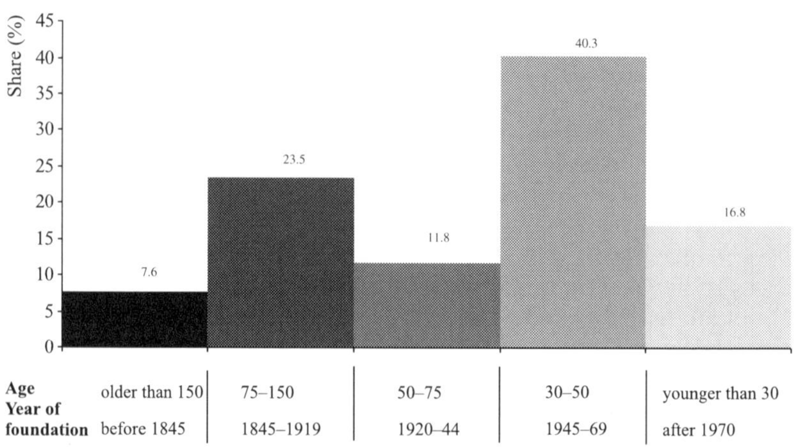

Source: H. Simon, *Hidden Champions*, 1996.

Figure 4.2 Age structure of German hidden champions

Beiersdorf (cosmetics) Stihl (chainsaws) and Plettac (scaffoldings), to name a few, have grown continuously.[11] Today, they have several thousand employees and are technology leaders in their respective industries. Similarly, Italy has hundreds of family-owned companies that have acquired worldwide fame, for example Benetton (apparel), Chicco (toys), Ferrero (chocolates), Fila (sports wear), Merloni (white goods), Marzotto (textiles, apparel) and Parmalat (milk products). Many of the leading medium-sized TNCs have been taken over by a new generation of business leaders, often the children or grandchildren of the founders. The new generation has usually acquired broad international experience, is fluent in foreign languages and willing to make financial commitments in large emerging markets like Russia.

Attracting leading medium-sized investors from important source countries would strengthen the support for local SMEs, which have multiplied across Russia since the reform process started. SMEs usually lack a broad capital base to carry out outright acquisitions or build new plants. They therefore represent a mutually beneficial option for interenterprise cooperation in a number of important sectors related to consumer goods, food processing and light engineering.

4.3 Global FDI strategies of TNCs

Internationalization strategies of TNCs are based on global competition and demand forecasts. These strategies are adjusted to local market conditions and general expectations of authorities in the recipient countries. Long-term success in a foreign market is determined by a healthy mix of consistent strategic behaviour and operational speed and competitiveness in the main functional areas. Successful global players combine technological (R&D) superiority and excellence in product differentiation and innovation with clear customer segmentation, continual promotion of brand image, and reliable after-sales service. The type of market entry selected can be crucial for further business development and is therefore an integral part of management strategy.

4.3.1 Options for market entry

Corporate strategy has changed from mere trading (export–import) to foreign investment through sales subsidiaries (most services sectors), greenfield operations, and strategic acquisitions and joint ventures[12] (Figure 4.3). When western companies began to globalize their manufacturing operations in the 1960s, they preferred to set up completely new factories through greenfield investments, and innovation policies were based on the resources and technological capabilities available in-house. Recipient countries still encourage greenfield investments in certain sectors

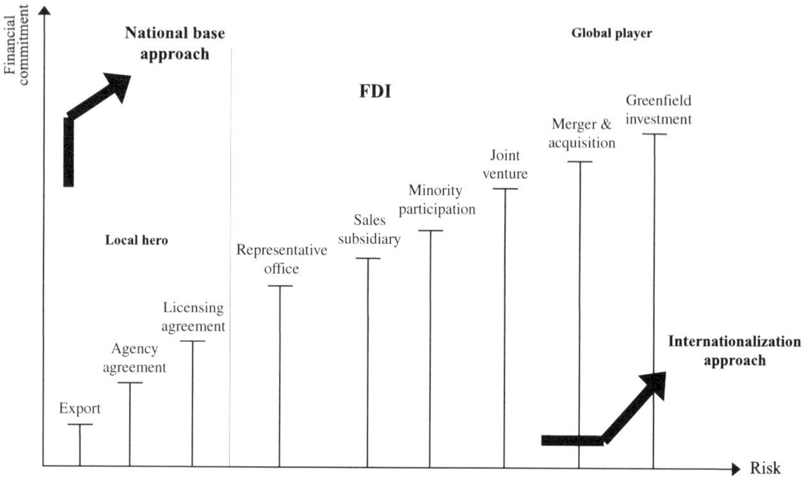

Figure 4.3 How to become a global player

or regions because of the beneficial effect on technological upgrading and employment.

Today, TNCs have a number of options for market entry. They frequently tie up with firms outside their production systems for transferring technology. Such collaborative arrangements include strategic alliances in the form of joint ventures or cooperation in the functional areas (R&D, production and marketing). Larger TNCs may also acquire minority or majority stakes, or total control of foreign companies, depending on equity participation rules in recipient countries. Initially, majority stakes or total control were not allowed in many host economies. But such stipulations are being relaxed in most countries following economic liberalization.[13] Strategic alliances, and mergers and acquisitions remained the main FDI strategies throughout the 1990s.

Accurate statistical information about developments of global FDI by type or entry strategy is still scarce and not easy to compare because of divergent national definitions and methodologies.[14] International organizations like UNCTAD, OECD or the IMF do not carry out regular and representative surveys on global FDI trends by form of investment. If carried out, these surveys are not comprehensive and cover only certain types of FDI. To get a broad overview, various national and international sources have to be consulted and the data compared, but the surveys often concern different years which makes it difficult to establish exact patterns by type of FDI for the major recipient regions, especially in anticipation of certain developments. However, depending on the available information, major trends can be observed and projected for the main regions of origin and destination.

Strategic alliances are increasingly popular, particularly in technology-intensive sectors and among medium-sized TNCs. Strategic alliances can take the form of financial participations in existing companies, the establishment of separate companies (joint ventures) or loose cooperation arrangements between key players. For the hidden champions, they are an interesting option for penetrating difficult markets with long-established or specific business structures and mentalities (e.g. most Asian countries). According to UNCTAD, the combined number of technology alliances in the high-tech areas of new materials, information and communication technology and biotechnology increased ninefold between 1980 (526) and 1995 (4512).[15] In the United States, Japan and the United Kingdom, joint ventures between domestic companies and foreign partners grew three times as fast as investments in greenfield operations and wholly-owned subsidiaries abroad during 1990–95 (although the share of wholly-owned subsidiaries in consolidated TNC turnover has also increased). Joint ventures represent an interesting form of FDI between oligopolistic TNCs in Triad markets, and such strategic alliances can cover all imaginable business functions, particularly manufacturing, distribution and increasingly R&D. In sectors where market penetration is difficult (consumer electronics, automobiles) or in high-tech industries (computers, aerospace), the objective of the partners is to carve up the global market and to circumvent head-on competition, especially if investment in R&D becomes too cost-intensive for a single TNC.

Examples of such alliances are controlling stakes of US automobile manufacturers in South Korean companies (Ford and Daewoo, Chrysler and Hyundai) and cooperation between Siemens, IBM and Toshiba to develop 16-gigabyte megachips for mainframe computer applications. National antitrust legislation may thwart the intentions of TNCs to form strategic alliances if there is an obvious danger of monopoly formation and price distortion for the final consumer.

Joint ventures with equal equity are common in major Asian markets: ASEAN countries, China, India, Japan, South Korea, Vietnam. Equity participation laws, local customs and complex demand structures oblige western TNCs to cooperate with competent local partners having widespread distribution networks and connections. Local partners can handle government approvals and often organize locally available government incentives, tax allowances and bank finance. In most transition countries of Central and Eastern Europe, language barriers and fast changing legislative patterns also warrant the association of informed local partners. Russia also has a huge potential for interenterprise cooperation between domestic and foreign companies. For joint ventures to work, both the local and foreign partners must share a similar philosophy, the same objectives in terms of business focus and expansion and contribute to the success of the venture.[16]

4.3.2 Cross-border mergers and acquisitions

Mergers and acquisitions (M&A), a fairly recent type of FDI, has so far met with mixed success. It represents a relatively risky and expensive form of market entry, but enables TNCs to gain market shares rapidly in highly competitive markets by acquiring existing plants, brands, supplier networks and distribution channels. The prerequisite is careful selection and smooth integration of the company to be acquired, given the cultural differences. M&A is most common among large TNCs, which have the necessary capital. In recent years, however, medium-sized TNCs have also started engaging in cross-border M&A transactions, particularly in electronics, business services, healthcare, construction and transport.

North American and western European markets have become frequent destinations for this type of investment since the 1980s. In 1995, global M&A transactions (purchases or sales) were valued at US$230 billion (Figure 4.4), twice the 1988 level, and represented four-fifths of new capital investments abroad (excluding reinvested earnings). In 1996, trans-border acquisitions rose by 69 per cent to US$275 billion, in 1997 again by 24 per cent to US$342 billion; in 1998, they rose further by 60 per cent to US$544 billion (75 per cent of the M&As resulted in the acquisition of a majority stake). In 1998, UNCTAD recorded 89 mega transactions exceeding a value of US$1 billion each. The mega deals accounted for about 60 per cent of the total value of all crossborder M&As; they mainly took place in the United States and the European Union (especially in the United Kingdom).

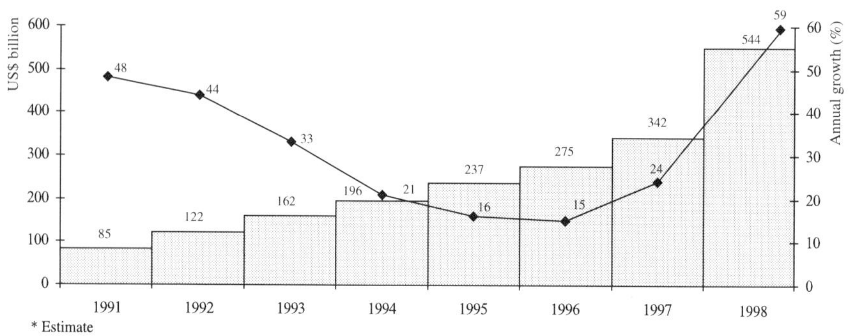

Source: Adapted from KPMG.

Figure 4.4 Global M&A transactions, 1991–98

In emerging economies (e.g. Brazil), the trend towards increased M&A has been driven mainly by the privatization of state monopolies (particularly in telecommunications and air transport), deregulation of national economies and growing cross-border FDI.[17] It is expected that the number and value of M&A deals will rise to well over US$1000 billion by 2001–02 as firms seek to rapidly increase market share in saturated markets.[18] In 1997, western Europe and North America were the main destinations for M&A, with inward flows of about US$138 billion and US$88 billion, respectively (Figure 4.5). Almost 60 per cent of international M&A operations involve companies in these two economic regions. Most acquisitions took place in the United States (US$65 billion, including minority participations), the United Kingdom (US$55 billion), Germany (US$19 billion), France (US$14 billion), Australia and Brazil (US$13 billion each) and China (US$11 billion).

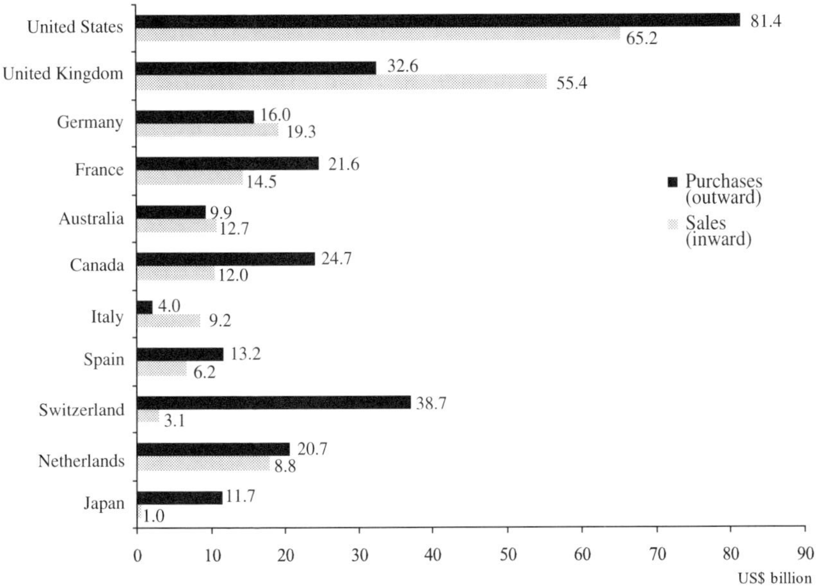

Source: KPMG cited in UNCTAD, *World Investment Report 1998.*

Figure 4.5 M&A transactions involving major OECD countries, 1997

M&A operations in China have grown fourfold since 1991 when their value stood at US$3 billion, but majority participations are still the exception. At the same time, western European companies spent US$168 billion for M&A abroad, of which 76 per cent alone involved EU companies. In 1997, US TNCs were the most dynamic investors through worldwide M&A operations, with total outflows of US$81 billion. Other M&A (including majority and minority M&A) players were TNCs from the United Kingdom (US$33 billion), Canada (US$25 billion), France and the Netherlands (US$21 billion each), Germany (US$16 billion), Spain (US$13 billion) and Japan (US$12 billion).

Developing countries account for only 30 per cent of international M&A sales (inbound flows). Before wide-ranging reforms in most countries, such transactions were mostly linked to the privatization of domestic companies in Latin America. Companies in Brazil and Mexico have become attractive M&A targets (Figure 4.6), and since 1992 Asian and Central and Eastern European companies have become major targets outside the OECD, at times even surpassing Latin America. This demonstrates a growing availability and attractiveness of companies in Asia and the positive results of the privatization programmes in Central and Eastern Europe. In Russia, where a comprehensive reform process was commenced in the early 1990s, western TNCs have also bought majority stakes in local companies and former state monopolies. In 1997, Russia's inbound M&A amounted to US$4 billion, the highest in Central and Eastern Europe.

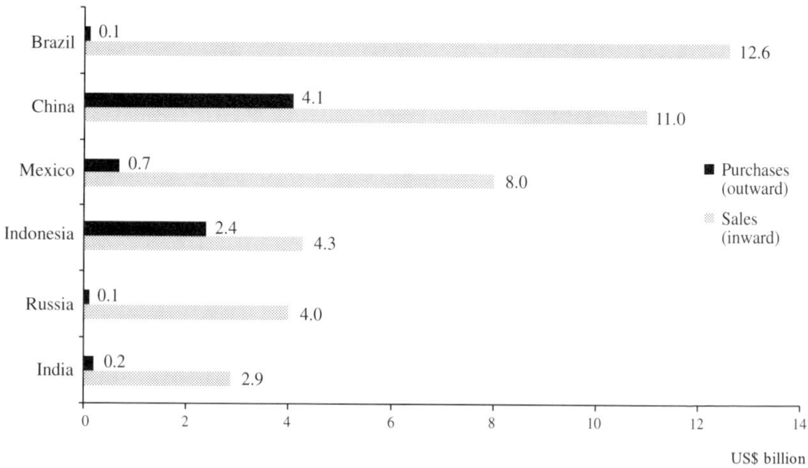

Source: KPMG cited in UNCTAD, *World Investment Report 1998*.

Figure 4.6 M&A transactions involving LEMs, 1997

In Europe, most M&A deals have been transacted in the oil and gas sector, followed by the chemicals, pharmaceuticals, telecommunications and banking sectors. Such projects usually involve large amounts of capital, and are long-term and research-intensive. The value of service-related M&A increased by almost 150 per cent between 1995 and 1997. Anglo-Saxon pension and investment funds increasingly own controlling stakes in some of the world's leading TNCs; they are thus involved in major investment and restructuring decisions. They can also be decisive in initiating or countering hostile takeover bids.[19]

In OECD countries, majority foreign participation is allowed in an increasing number of economic sectors. With economic liberalization, barriers to foreign investment are gradually being removed in most recipient countries. National FDI legislations in larger recipient countries (e.g. India, Brazil) have maintained some restrictions in certain strategic sectors (e.g. hydrocarbon exploration, mining, infrastructure, telecommunications, drugs and pharmaceuticals, insurance, banking). Certain countries like China, India and Mexico have opened up parts of their telecommunications sectors (equipment, basic services, value-added services such as Internet services) even before France and Germany. Recently, these countries have removed certain sensitive areas from their negative lists by allowing minority and sometimes majority stakes to accelerate development of the sectors (e.g. energy, infrastructure and insurance in India). Such investments may also benefit from faster approval procedures.

Authorities in smaller countries with less-diversified industries tend to impose fewer restrictions (e.g. ASEAN countries), but are equally cautious about distortions that certain types of investments may cause in the domestic economies. In certain cases, joint ventures with local business partners are therefore preferred to total control of domestic firms (majority stakes or total acquisition) by foreign companies. Usually, national legislation contains provisions describing those activities where foreign investment is forbidden, restricted to a minority stake (up to 49 per cent) or allowed for a majority stake in local operations. The share of majority participations in M&A purchases also reflects corporate traditions and preferences in different countries. Most Anglo-American and Dutch TNCs prefer to acquire majority stakes abroad. They are generally more aggressive than their German, Italian or Japanese counterparts, who mostly engage in licensing agreements, 50:50 joint ventures or greenfield investments (Figure 4.7).

In most developed and emerging economies, anti-monopoly agencies monitor large M&A transactions and their effect on concentration levels on a case-by-case basis. All foreign investments have to be vetted and approved, although these procedures are being simplified (single-window clearance). Automatic approvals and fast track projects are common in high-priority areas. In addition, they must conform with other local legislation (environmental and labour laws) in the same way as domestic industries.

Strategic cooperations and technology alliances are the least restricted type of entry. However, concentrative joint ventures are often treated like outright acquisitions and need to be notified owing to possible distortions of competitive structures (the EU Merger Regulation[20]).

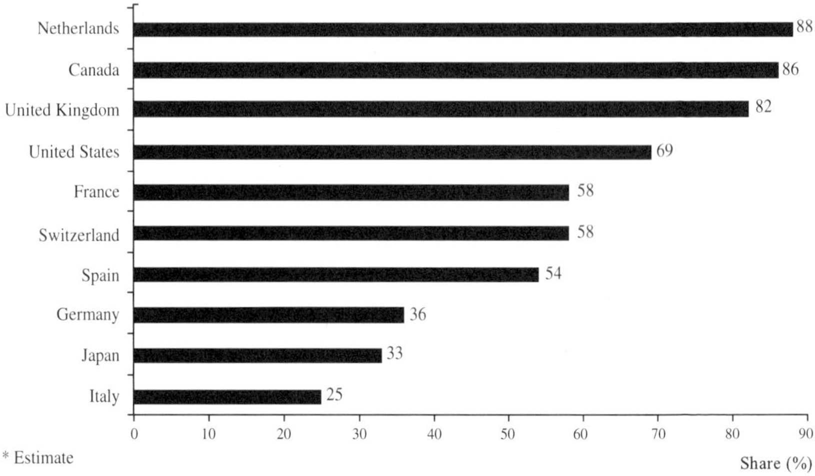

* Estimate

Source: KPMG cited in UNCTAD, *World Investment Report 1998*.

Figure 4.7 Majority participation in M&A deals (purchases), leading OECD investors, 1997

Notes

1. Chapter 1.8.
2. Chapter 4.2.
3. UNCTAD, *World Investment Report 1999*.
4. Chapter 3.1, Table 3.1.
5. Based on study by J. Cavanagh and S. Anderson, Institute for Policy Studies, Washington, DC, 1996.
6. In 1998, Germany's FDI outflows surged to US$86.6 billion following a number of mega mergers and acquisitions such as the acquisition of Bankers Trust by Deutsche Bank (US$9.1 billion) and the Daimler–Chrysler deal (US$40.5 billion). UNCTAD, *World Investment Report 1999*.
7. Chapters 13 and 14.4.
8. Chapter 16.4.
9. For more information on TNCs from emerging economies, see also Annex 4.2; derived from UNCTAD, *World Investment Report 1998*, pp. 48–9.
10. Chapters 3.1.4, 3.3.2 and 3.3.3.
11. Some of these companies have been converted into public limited companies to broaden their access to private share capital.
12. See Definitions and Explanatory Notes, 2. Types of FDI.
13. See also Chapters 5 (China) and 6 (India).
14. Institut für Wirtschaftsforschung, *Ifo Schnellbericht* no. 15, 1997.
15. UNCTAD, *World Investment Report 1996*.
16. M. B. Rao, *Joint Ventures. International Business with Developing Countries*, 1999, pp. 17–28.

17. *Handelsblatt*, 'Die Direktinvestitionen erreichen neue Rekorde. Fusionen and Übernahmen als Motor' [FDI attains new records. Mergers and acquisitions as new motor], 12 July 1997.
18. G. Marcial, 'The Whisper Stocks of 1996', *Business Week*, 25 December 1995.
19. A study conducted in 1999 revealed that such funds hold significant equity in a number of the world's leading companies: Philips (43 per cent), Royal Dutch (41 per cent), Mannesmann (40 per cent), Elf Aquitaine (39 per cent), Lafarge (32.5 per cent), Daimler–Chrysler (30 per cent), Deutsche Telekom (27.5 per cent). See also 'Fonds kapitalisieren Europas Firmenelite [Funds capitalize Europe's elite firms],' *Handelsblatt*, 8 November 1999.
20. Chapter 2.3.

Annex 4.1 The world's top 100 TNCs ranked by foreign assets, 1996

Ranking by				
Foreign assets	TR index[a]	Corporation	Country	Industry[b]
1	83	General Electric	United States	Electronics
2	32	Shell, Royal Dutch	United Kingdom/ Netherlands	Petroleum expl./ref./dist.[c]
3	75	Ford Motor Company	United States	Automotive
4	22	Exxon	United States	Petroleum expl./ref./dist
5	85	General Motors	United States	Automotive
6	52	IBM	United States	Computers
7	79	Toyota	Japan	Automotive
8	49	Volkswagen Group	Germany	Automotive
9	71	Mitsubishi	Japan	Diversified
10	38	Mobil	United States	Petroleum expl./ref./dist.
11	3	Nestlé	Switzerland	Food
12	2	Asea Brown Boveri	Switzerland/Sweden	Electrical equipment
13	47	Elf Aquitaine	France	Petroleum expl./ref./dist.
14	14	Bayer	Germany	Chemicals
15	34	Hoechst	Germany	Chemicals
16	57	Nissan Motor	Japan	Automotive
17	74	Fiat	Italy	Automotive
18	8	Unilever	Netherlands/ United Kingdom	Food
19	70	Daimler-Benz	Germany	Automotive
20	11	Philips Electronics	Netherlands	Electronics
21	9	Roche Holding	Switzerland	Pharmaceuticals
22	56	Siemens	Germany	Electronics
23	36	Alcatel Alsthom	France	Electronics
24	40	Sony Corporation	Japan	Electronics
25	19	Total	France	Petroleum expl./ ref./dist.
26	20	Novartis	Switzerland	Pharmaceuticals/ chemicals
27	35	British Petroleum	United Kingdom	Petroleum expl./ ref./dist.
28	62	Philip Morris	United States	Food/tobacco
29	81	ENI Group	Italy	Petroleum expl./ ref./dist.
30	69	Renault	France	Automotive
31	31	B.A.T. Industries	United Kingdom	Food/tobacco
32	68	Du Pont (E.I.)	United States	Chemicals
33	30	Rhône-Poulenc	France	Chemicals/ pharmaceuticals
34	1	Seagram	Canada	Beverages
35	42	BASF	Germany	Chemicals
36	46	Honda	Japan	Automotive
37	43	BMW	Germany	Automotive
38	77	Mitsui	Japan	Diversified
39	82	Nissho lwai	Japan	Trading
40	93	llochu	Japan	Trading
41	58	Hewlett-Packard	United States	Electronics
42	28	Ferruzzi/Montedison	Italy	Chemicals/ agribusiness
43	51	Daewoo	South Korea	Diversified

Assets		Sales		Employment		TR Index (%)
Foreign	Total	Foreign	Total	Foreign	Total	
82.8	272.4	21.1	79.2	84 000	239 000	30.7
82.1	124.1	71.1	128.3	79 000	101 000	66.6
79.1	258.0	65.8	147.0	–	371 702	37.7
55.6	95.5	102.0	117.0	–	79 000	72.7
55.4	222.1	50.0	158.0	221 313	647 000	30.3
41.4	81.1	46.6	75.9	121 655	240 615	54.3
39.2	113.4	51.7	109.3	34 837	150 736	35.0
–	60.8	41.0	64.4	123 042	260 811	55.3
–	77.9	50.2	127.4	3 819	8 794	41.4
31.3	46.4	53.1	80.4	22 900	43 000	62.3
30.9	34.0	42.0	42.8	206 125	212 687	95.3
–	30.9	32.9	33.8	203 541	214 894	96.1
29.3	47.5	26.6	44.8	41 600	85 400	56.6
29.1	32.0	25.8	31.4	94 375	142 200	79.9
28.0	35.5	18.4	33.8	93 708	147 862	65.6
27.0	58.1	29.2	53.8	–	135 331	50.4
26.9	70.6	19.8	51.3	90 390	237 865	38.2
26.4	31.0	45.0	52.2	273 000	304 000	87.1
–	65.7	44.4	70.6	67 208	290 029	41.9
24.5	31.7	38.9	40.9	216 000	262 500	84.9
24.5	29.5	12.6	12.9	39 074	48 972	87.0
24.4	56.3	38.4	62.6	176 000	379 000	50.4
23.5	48.4	24.6	31.6	118 820	190 600	62.9
23.5	45.8	32.8	45.7	95 000	163 000	60.5
–	30.3	25.8	34.0	–	57 555	75.8
21.4	43.4	28.6	29.2	91 192	116 178	75.2
20.7	31.8	39.2	69.8	37 750	53 700	63.8
20.6	54.9	30.7	69.2	94 659	154 000	47.8
–	59.5	13.2	39.3	–	83 424	33.5
19.0	42.2	19.4	36.0	43 381	140 905	43.2
18.9	63.5	30.8	38.2	149 217	163 854	67.2
18.4	38.0	20.8	43.8	34 000	97 000	43.7
–	27.1	13.3	16.8	41 818	75 250	67.4
18.2	18.6	12.2	12.6	–	31 000	97.3
17.9	28.2	23.8	32.4	42 339	103 406	59.2
17.8	33.5	26.4	42.3	–	101 100	56.6
–	29.1	25.5	34.8	51 900	116 112	59.1
17.1	61.2	56.6	132.0	–	11 250	35.4
–	47.2	28.8	89.1	1 997	6 684	32.4
15.2	66.1	40.2	153.5	2 584	9 766	25.2
15.2	27.7	21.4	38.4	48 200	122 000	50.0
–	21.6	11.8	15.5	17 570	29 564	68.3
14.9	32.5	10.2	26.4	37 501	47 609	54.5

continued ...

Annex 4.1 (*continued*)

Ranking by		Corporation	Country	Industry[b]
Foreign assets	TR index[a]			
44	27	News Corporation	Australia	Media
45	78	Chevron Corporation	United States	Petroleum expl./ ref./dist.
46	48	Dow Chemicals	United States	Chemicals
47	37	Robert Bosch	Germany	Automotive
48	86	Marubeni	Japan	Trading
49	15	Cable & Wireless	United Kingdom	Telecommunication
50	4	Thomson	Canada	Printing and publishing
51	66	Texaco	United States	Petroleum expl./ref./dist.
52	10	Michelin	France	Rubber and plastics
53	88	Matsushita Electric	Japan	Electronics
54	61	Xerox	United States	Photo equipment
55	23	Ericsson	Sweden	Electronics
56	6	Holderbank Financière	Switzerland	Construction materials
57	64	ANA	Canada	Telecommunication
58	39	Saint-Gobain	France	Industrial material
59	76	Broken Hill	Australia	Metal
60	97	Hitachi	Japan	Electronics
61	87	Sumitomo	Japan	Trading/machinery
62	7	Electrolux	Sweden	Electrical appliances
63	98	AT&T	United States	Telecomm./electronics
64	67	Procter & Gamble	United States	Chemicals/cosmetics
65	80	International Paper	United States	Paper
66	91	Amoco	United States	Petroleum expl./ref./dist.
67	45	Volvo	Sweden	Automotive
68	44	McDonald's	United States	Restaurants
69	18	Grand Metropolitan	United Kingdom	Food/beverages
70	16	Glaxo Wellcome	United Kingdom	Pharmaceuticals
71	26	BTR	United Kingdom	Plastics and foam
72	59	Johnson & Johnson	United States	Chemicals/ pharmaceuticals
73	65	Petroleos de Venezuela	Venezuela	Diversified/trading
74	89	Fujitsu	Japan	Electronics
75	25	Hanson	United Kingdom	Building materials
76	63	Motorola	United States	Electronics
77	92	Générale des Eaux	France	Diversified/utility
78	96	Nippon Steel	Japan	Metals
79	21	Akzo Nobel	Netherlands	Chemicals
80	99	Chrysler	United States	Automotive
81	55	Canon Electronics	Japan	Electronics
82	29	Coca-Cola	United States	Beverages
83	5	Solvay	Belgium	Chemicals/ pharmaceuticals
84	90	Mitsubishi Motors	Japan	Automotive
85	13	Northern Telecom	Canada	Telecommunication
86	24	Petrolina	Belgium	Petroleum expl./ref./dist.
87	53	Bridgestone	Japan	Rubber and plastics
88	84	Pepsico	United States	Beverages/food
89	50	Danone Groupe	France	Food/beverages
90	41	Crown Cork & Seal	United States	Packaging
91	94	Toshiba	Japan	Electronics

Assets		Sales		Employment		TR Index (%)
Foreign	Total	Foreign	Total	Foreign	Total	
14.5	24.2	8.6	9.9	17 212	26 513	70.6
14.4	34.9	14.9	42.8	12 095	40 820	35.32
14.4	24.7	11.3	20.1	21 039	4 0300	55.6
–	21.3	16.7	26.7	–	172 359	62.4
13.1	60.8	43.9	113.0	–	9 282	30.1
13.0	15.5	7.0	9.7	29 613	37 448	78.1
12.8	13.2	7.3	7.7	47 200	50 500	94.9
12.7	27.0	21.2	44.6	11 323	28 957	44.6
–	14.7	11.7	13.7	–	119 780	84.9
12.3	67.8	23.8	62.0	–	270 651	28.3
12.1	26.8	8.8	17.4	–	86 700	47.8
–	16.9	17.4	18.7	50 053	93 949	72.5
11.7	12.7	6.9	8.0	39 122	42 970	89.8
11.5	30.1	13.3	20.6	46 000	121 000	46.9
11.5	21.6	10.2	15.7	74 467	111 701	61.6
11.4	28.1	5.6	15.3	20 400	60 100	37.1
11.4	80.4	19.8	68.7	56 400	330 100	20.0
11.4	43.5	29.9	108.4	2 873	9 129	28.4
10.7	12.5	15.2	16.4	98 220	112 140	88.7
–	55.6	8.8	52.2	–	130 400	18.1
10.7	27.5	17.5	35.8	–	106 000	43.7
10.4	28.3	6.0	20.1	31 000	87 000	34.2
10.3	32.1	8.0	36.1	9 290	41 723	25.5
10.2	20.5	20.7	23.3	26 435	71 905	58.5
9.6	17.4	6.1	10.7	153 000	237 000	58.9
–	17.5	12.7	14.0	55 000	65 699	76.2
9.4	14.2	12.0	13.0	40 209	53 460	77.9
9.4	14.1	10.9	14.4	–	115 805	70.9
9.2	20.0	10.7	21.6	47 600	89 300	49.5
8.9	45.4	31.7	33.9	12 756	59 318	44.9
8.9	38.1	10.8	36.3	53 000	167 000	28.3
8.6	14.9	18.4	19.5	35 000	56 000	71.6
8.6	24.1	16.9	28.0	63 738	139 000	47.3
8.5	45.9	10.0	32.4	57 433	217 300	25.3
–	36.3	5.8	24.7	–	24 527	23.4
8.3	11.7	9.8	13.3	52 900	70 700	73.2
8.3	56.2	8.2	61.4	26 000	126 000	16.3
8.3	22.6	14.9	22.1	38 197	75 628	51.6
8.2	12.0	12.6	18.7	20 000	30 000	67.5
–	8.8	8.4	8.8	31 413	35400	92.2
8.0	26.1	8.5	29.6	18 900	74 700	28.3
7.9	10.9	11.4	12.8	–	67 584	80.6
7.8	11.6	15.9	19.8	9 217	13 588	71.8
7.8	15.2	10.0	18.0	–	92 458	53.5
7.8	24.5	9.2	31.6	–	486 000	30.4
7.8	19.4	9.2	16.4	55 987	81 579	54.9
7.6	12.6	5.0	8.3	–	44 611	60.2
7.6	46.8	14.0	44.0	–	186 000	24.0

continued ...

Annex 4.1 (*continued*)

Ranking by				
Foreign assets	TR index[a]	Corporation	Country	Industry[b]
92	12	Kvaerner	Norway	Shipbuilding/engineering
93	95	Atlantic Richfield	United States	Petroleum expl./ref/dist.
94	54	RTZ CRA9	United Kingdom/ Australia	Mining
95	73	Mannesmann	Germany	Engineering/ telecommunication
96	33	Pharmacia & Upjohn	United States	Pharmaceuticals
97	100	GTE Corporation	United States	Telecommunication
98	72	American Home Products	United States	Pharmaceuticals
99	17	Eridania Beghin-Say	France	Food
100	60	Société Au Bon Marché	France	Luxury products

Notes:
[a] The index of transnationality (TR) is calculated as the average of three ratios: foreign assets to total assets, foreign sales to total sales and foreign employment to total employment.
[b] Industry classification of companies follows the United States Standard Industrial Classification as used by the United States Securities and Exchange Commission (SEC)
[c] Petroleum exploration, refining, distribution

Source: UNCTAD–Erasmus University database.

Assets		Sales		Employment		TR Index (%)
Foreign	Total	Foreign	Total	Foreign	Total	
–	9.1	7.0	9.1	69 303	80 199	81.7
7.4	25.7	3.4	18.6	–	22 800	23.4
7.3	15.8	4.7	9.3	31 616	51 492	52.5
7.3	15.5	8.2	23.0	41 689	119 703	39.1
7.3	11.2	4.9	7.2	–	31 700	66.4
7.1	38.4	2.8	21.3	–	102 000	15.8
7.1	20.8	5.8	14.1	28 300	59 746	40.7
6.9	9.2	8.0	10.2	14 617	19 340	76.4
6.8	21.9	4.2.	–	22 862	47.9	

Annex 4.2 Top 50 TNCs of emerging economies, 1996

Ranking by				
Foreign assets	TR index[a]	Corporation	Country	Industry[b]
1	9	Daewoo	South Korea	Diversified/trading
2	15	Petroleos de Venezuela	Venezuela	Petroleum exp./ref./dist.[c]
3	11	Cemex	Mexico	Construction
4	4	First Pacific	Hong Kong, China	Electronic parts
5	5	Sappi	South Africa	Paper
6	22	Acer Group	Taiwan	Electronics
7	6	Jardine Matheson	Bermuda	Conglomerate/diversified
8	21	China National Chemicals	China	Diversified/trading
9	17	China State Construction Engineering	China	Diversified/construction
10	7	Compania de Telecomuni-caciones de Chile	Chile	Utilities
11	45	Sunkyong Group	South Korea	Energy/trading/chemicals
12	36	YPF	Argentina	Petroleum exp./ref./dist.
13	50	Petrobras	Brazil	Petroleum exp./ref./dist.
14	23	Cathay Pacific Airways	Hong Kong, China	Transportation
15	39	Samsung Electronics	South Korea	Electronics
16	20	New World Development	Hong Kong, China	Hotel/construction
17	19	Hyundai Engineering & Construction	South Korea	Engineering/construction
18	32	LG Electronics	South Korea	Electronics
19	31	Petroliam Nasional	Malaysia	Petroleum exp./ref./dist.
20	13	Citic Pacific	Hong Kong, China	Trading/distribution
21	47	Companhia Vale do Rio Doce	Brazil	Mining
22	43	China Shougang Group	China	Diversified/metals
23	18	Singapore Airlines	Singapore	Transportation
24	28	Hutchinson Whampoa	Hong Kong, China	Diversified
25	2	Panamerican Beverages	Mexico/Panama	Beverages
26	3	Guangdong Investment	Hong Kong, China	Miscellaneous
27	8	Fraser & Neave	Singapore	Beverages
28	1	Orient Overseas International	Hong Kong, China	Transportation
29	14	Dairy Farm International	Hong Kong, China	Retail
30	46	Comp. Cervejaria Brahma	Brazil	Beverages
31	40	South African Breweries	South Africa	Beverages/hotels
32	29	Tatung	Taiwan	Electrical equipment
33	42	San Miguel	Philippines	Beverages
34	38	Keppel	Singapore	Diversified

Assets		Sales		Employment		TR Index (%)
Foreign	Total	Foreign	Total	Foreign	Total	
14 933.0	32 504.0	10 238.0	26 370.0	37 501	4 7609	54.5
8 912.0	45 402.0	31 659.0	33 854.5	12 756	5 9318	44.9
5 259.0	9 941.0	2 027.0	3 365.0	9 783	2 0527	53.6
4 645.7	8 491.8	6 317.5	7 025.7	37 393	5 2880	71.8
3 760.3	4 846.1	2 248.6	3 438.2	8 744	2 1055	61.5
–	16 076.0	–	6 100.0	–	4 4000	36.1
3 380.2	7 788.0	8 187.4	11 605.0	140 000	200 000	61.3
3 201.6	6 166.8	7 965.6	17 955.0	828	6 466	36.4
2 810.0	5 730.0	1 590.0	5 080.0	2 500	–	40.2
2 735.6	4 406.3	768.8	1 274.0	4 997	8 982	59.4
2 693.0	30 793.0	10 302.0	42 094.0	2 500	33 299	13.6
2 650.0	12 084.0	8 64.0	5 937.0	2 139	9 762	19.5
2 583.1	33 736.3	1 508.0	26 758.7	22	43 468	4.4
2 555.0	7 968.0	2 023.0	4 151.0	4 038	15 757	35.5
–	25 837.0	–	23 456.0	–	59 086	16.3
2 321.2	12 413.5	471.6	2 162.4	31 440	45 000	36.8
2 287.0	8 404.0	1 461.0	5 116.0	15 950	28 000	37.6
2 083.2	1 6662.1	2 429.2	14 070.0	30 889	65 284	25.7
1 876.6	2 3219.9	6 134.1	8 901.4	72	13 640	25.8
1 678.6	6456.3	890.8	1 648.9	8 100	11 750	49.7
1 599.0	1 7891.0	1 342.0	4 938.0	86	15483	12.2
1 582.6	6 630.0	1 032.7	4 385.3	1 623	221 961	16.1
1 574.0	8 584.4	3 978.9	5 122.4	2 818	12 966	39.2
–	8 174.0	1 400.0	4 743.0	10 500	27 733	28.6
1 436.0	1 705.0	1 567.0	1 993.0	–	31 400	81.4
1 392.9	2 316.4	628.8	836.5	12 122	13 531	75.0
1 357.0	4 532.0	1 178.0	2 008.0	10 213	11 955	58.0
1 255.8	1 306.1	1 718.4	1 882.3	3 396	4 030	90.6
–	3 124.0	–	6 967.0	–	49 900	46.5
985.6	3 699.8	124.6	2 468.7	573	8 769	12.7
959.0	5 271.0	1 327.0	8002.0	15 006	106 900	16.3
–	3652.0	–	3 010.0	–	27 250	28.1
903.1	3761.6	329.9	3 241.8	3 9 94	28 544	16.1
887.8	1 3478.5	329.2	2 061.2	4 057	14 320	17.0

continued ...

Annex 4.2 (*continued*)

Ranking by				
Foreign assets	TR index[a]	Corporation	Country	Industry[b]
35	33	China National Metals Minerals Import & Export	China	Diversified/ trading
36	30	Sime Darby	Malaysia	Diversified
37	24	Dong-Ah Construction	South Korea	Construction
38	25	Wing On	Hong Kong, China	Retail
39	49	Reliance Industries	India	Chemicals
40	41	Sadia Concordia	Brazil	Food
41	26	Hongkong and Shanghai Hotels	Hong Kong, China	Hotel/property
42	34	Souza Cruz	Brazil	Diversified
43	48	Compania de Petroleos de Chile	Chile	Petroleum exp./ref./dist.
44	12	Malaysian Airlines	Malaysia	Transportation
45	16	Gruma	Mexico	Food
46	27	Barlow	South Africa	Diversified
47	44	Vitro	Mexico	Miscellaneous
48	37	Bavaria	Colombia	Beverages
49	35	Empresas CMPC	Chile	Pulp and paper
50	10	Plate Glass & Shatterprule	South Africa	Building, automotive, furniture

Notes:
[a] The index of transnationality (TR) is calculated as the average of the three ratios: foreign assets to total assets, foreign sales to total sales and foreign employment to total employment.
[b] Industry classification for companies follows the United States Standard Industrial Classification which is used by the United States Securities and Exchange Commission (SEC).
[c] Petroleum exploration, refining, distribution

Source: UNCTAD–Erasmus University database.

Assets		Sales		Employment		TR Index (%)
Foreign	Total	Foreign	Total	Foreign	Total	
884.6	2 388.1	1 282.4	4 950.4	182	1 288	25.7
833.0	1 0611.0	2 072.2	4 312.0	8 132	36 421	26.1
–	5 120.0	–	3 086.0	–	6 583	34.8
804.0	1 591.5	47.6	392.6	1 449	4 083	32.7
801.7	5 440.0	18.5	2 431.0	1 300	16 778	7.7
626.0	2 123.0	554.0	2 997.0	140	29 975	16.1
625.0	3 523.0	64.0	343.0	3 126	5 957	29.6
609.4	2 198.8	560.1	1 766.8	109	9 876	20.2
602.0	5 705.0	79.4	2 958.0	891	8 389	8.0
559.0	5 294.3	1 045.9	1 386.5	–	13 788	51.2
552.0	1 557.0	726.0	1 607.0	6 222	12 160	43.9
522.2	2 136.8	1 449.2	3 937.9	7 932	30 740	29.0
477.0	3 386.0	451.0	2 128.0	4 274	33 428	16.0
472.0	6 746.0	421.0	1 752.0	2 972	13 031	17.9
390.9	2 891.0	311.2	1 174.3	2 002	10 294	19.8
372.0	758.5	773.1	1 328.3	1 0533	19 300	53.9

Part III

FDI as the Catalyst for Industrial Transformation in Selected Large Emerging Markets

Introduction

This Part analyzes FDI patterns and policies in three important competitor countries: China, India and Mexico. During the first half of the 1990s, these countries carried out wide-ranging economic reforms and industrial restructuring operations including privatization and modernization of state enterprises. The process generated additional tax revenues, alleviated state budgets and promoted entrepreneurship. Significant elements of the economic strategy of the three countries were the opening of domestic capital markets to foreign companies (portfolio investment) and the possibility to invest directly in local enterprises (direct investment). FDI was integrated into a national industrial policy (China, India) or carried out as an independent instrument, but always in accordance with other policies to strengthen the overall impact (Mexico).

These measures have encouraged TNCs to invest in local manufacturing companies and to ultimately impact positively on national economies. Targeted FDI not only increased industrial production but also improved export performance as a consequence of sectoral diversification and technological upgrading. Similar policy changes in other countries also increased FDI flows with attendant beneficial effects.[1] These positive changes can be observed in important economies like Argentina, Brazil, Chile, Indonesia, Malaysia and Poland, and in a number of OECD countries (Ireland, Spain, United Kingdom).

A detailed look at FDI patterns and policies in China, India and Mexico shows interesting parallels with the present economic situation in Russia. The four countries represent large emerging markets (LEMs)[2] in terms of area, population and resources. A diversified industrial structure and improving economic indicators (low inflation, stable exchange rates, rising purchasing power) make LEMs promising destinations for investments outside the OECD area by TNCs in the twenty-first century. After long spells of import-substitution policies, LEM governments have realized the benefits of integration in the international economy; to this end they have embarked on liberalization programmes by opening national industries to foreign participation. This was in line with the general move from a planned to a free market economy.

All three LEMs studied in this Part offer interesting models for Russia. They are also significant contenders for foreign capital and know-how in the coming years. An analysis of the factors contributing to the success of their FDI policies will inspire new ideas for formulating and implementing viable industrial and FDI strategies in Russia. Since the beginning of the 1990s, China, India and Mexico have increased their FDI inflows considerably while Russia's FDI performance has hardly improved. China reported the highest FDI inflows among all LEMs in absolute terms, far more than the remaining two countries and Russia put together. On a per capita basis, Mexico has so far attracted the highest inflows and stocks among LEMs. A realistic target for Russia in the immediate future – considering its human resources, raw materials and market potential – would be to attain FDI levels similar to those envisaged by India and Poland for 2000 and to attain Mexico's level by 2005.[3]

Like Russia today, China, India and Mexico used to export a narrow range of products, mainly raw materials and low value-added goods, while essential finished products had to be imported from industrialized countries. Cautious economic policies aimed at export promotion and sectoral diversification have resulted in the establishment of competitive, knowledge-intensive industries. Although LEMs still depend on key technologies from advanced economies (mainframe computers, high-power telecommunications equipment, numerically-controlled machine tools, aeronautic equipment, high-power transport and agricultural equipment), they have by and large become serious competitors in a number of consumer goods and medium-tech sectors.

A detailed analysis of FDI developments and policy patterns in the three countries will yield decision-making tools for developing a reengineered FDI concept (policy) that could be implemented by the Russian authorities over 2000–05.[4] The three countries were selected as case studies because they share common features with Russia, and lessons drawn from their longer experience would be useful for it:

- They have become accessible to outside investors after decades of restrictive policies.
- They are leading FDI recipients where the state is actively involved in industrial planning and promotes foreign investment targeted at selected regions and sectors.[5]
- They are major competitors of Russia for FDI in all key industries.
- FDI is coordinated by specialized agencies (India's FIPB, China's MOFTEC, Mexico's SECOFI), which have designed incentive mechanisms to attract foreign investors.
- They have large populations and expanding domestic markets.
- Consumers in these countries have pent-up demand for consumer goods and aspirations for better living conditions.

- They all have equally qualified professionals and a skilled workforce.
- They have a wide diversity of natural resources (raw materials, energy, forestry resources and agricultural produce).
- Labour and energy costs for setting up domestic production facilities are still lower than in industrialized countries.
- They are prepared to cooperate with important international organizations (WTO, OECD) and groupings (Mexico and NAFTA, India and SAARC, China and APEC), but at the same time are cautious about losing their autonomy.
- All three LEMs have diversified industrial structures due to initial protection of national industries (industrial policy) and targeted FDI.
- They have the potential to develop bilateral and trilateral FDI with Russia based on existing trade links (especially China and India).

In the three countries, industrial transformation and economic adjustment through FDI is still not completed; it is more or less an ongoing process with evident parallels to the situation in Russia. But, having started earlier, China, India and Mexico have a slight lead for FDI. Russia has a realistic chance of figuring among the most prominent markets for global trade and FDI during the twenty-first century. But this will depend on how fast it succeeds in reshaping its industries because TNCs that seek market and sourcing opportunities require a competitive industrial structure. For this it needs to draw lessons from those LEMs that have advanced further on the investment development path.[6]

Notes

1. Chapters 2.1 and 2.6.
2. The other two LEMs, Brazil and Indonesia, are not covered by this analysis, but they also show similar trends: implementation of new economic policies and measures to enhance FDI.
3. Chapter 14.2.
4. Part VI.
5. The three LEMs regulate FDI inflows on the basis of industrial priorities and sector listings (see annexes at the end of each country chapter).
6. Chapter 1.9.

5
FDI Policies and Prospects in China

Map 5.1 China

5.1 Competitive advantages and lessons for Russia

China provides one of the most striking examples of economic recovery through targeted FDI. It illustrates how a large emerging economy can be steered to a high-growth course by sound macroeconomic management coupled with a long-term FDI policy. A closer analysis of Chinese FDI patterns and policies over the past 15 years shows a strong correlation between the country's high economic performance and appropriate instruments and incentives to systematically attract TNCs. FDI-induced industrial modernization and enterprise competitiveness were achieved through farsighted policy measures which helped increase locational advantages and the effective use of available resources.

China's experience is unique as its Communist leadership introduced far-flung economic reforms many years ago while maintaining established political structures and command mechanisms;[1] however, the mechanisms have come under strain as the country has intensified its commercial and cultural ties with other nations. In the future, China's authorities will find it more difficult to insulate the current political system from innovative free market mechanisms and FDI stimulation measures. Besides, only political openness and predictability[2] will gain the confidence of the international business community.

Starting from the early 1990s, China emerged as the second most significant FDI recipient country after the United States. The leadership's 'open door' policy and astute promotion of 'business prospects in the largest market in the world' triggered off an FDI rush among western[3] and Asian enterprises determined to benefit from China's economic growth and accumulation of wealth. With almost 1.3 billion people, China is the world's most populated country and will offer a huge potential market to businesses of all kinds for many decades to come.[4] At current growth rates, Chinese inbound FDI could even overtake that of the United States by the beginning of the twenty-first century. As one of the first emerging markets, China has gained a long experience in dealing with western TNCs, in promoting direct transfer of know-how to domestic enterprises – mainly through contractual and equity joint ventures[5] – and in channelling advanced western technologies and managerial expertise into specific regions and industries. Most consumer and capital goods sectors have been systematically developed and modernized through targeted FDI policies, which lay emphasis less on money or capital transfers than on a durable learning effect on local managers and engineers. During the 1980s, hundreds of new plants were built or revamped with the support of foreign companies; a large part of the output of these plants is already exported.

For its FDI policy, China followed the example of other East Asian economies (Japan, South Korea and Taiwan) that succeeded in developing domestic manufacturing capabilities through focused joint ventures, so that national enterprises could benefit and themselves become capital exporters. Other large emerging countries such as Brazil, India and Indonesia also seek to develop local industry in a similar way, but they opened a decade later and still have to acquire more experience in dealing with TNCs before the impact of FDI on their national economies can be fully assessed.[6]

China is now in a much stronger economic position than a few years ago. The country continues acquiring foreign managerial know-how and capital that enhance its industries' competitiveness, so that it can now export capital abroad. Many leading Chinese enterprises have won open tenders in nearby Asia (e.g. Philippines, Vietnam) and in distant Africa and South America. The country steadily proceeds on the investment development path as outbound FDI increases. In 1995, outbound flows reached a record level of US$3.5 billion, bringing it on par with industrialized countries like Italy and Spain. Today, outbound FDI flows represent almost 10 per cent of inbound flows and are expected to surge following the integration of Hong Kong on 1 July 1997.[7]

The Chinese government has continuously improved conditions for foreign investors, even if it recently started reducing certain incentives for foreign companies (e.g. reducing and even abolishing tax holidays) in an effort to put them at equal level with domestic enterprises, especially in the booming coastal regions and in nonpriority industries. Otherwise, a wide range of incentives has been kept in place enabling foreign companies to generate sufficient business and grow in China. TNCs are allowed to repatriate part of their profits and to wind down their operation if necessary. The government has also adjusted related policies (for customs duties, taxes, labor) to create an overall favorable climate for TNCs.[8]

This chapter will focus on China's reform process, how it helped improve the country's economic and industrial performance and the measures taken to increase FDI flows and channel them into predetermined industrial sectors.

The Chinese example offers Russian policy-makers six major lessons:

- How to integrate a coherent FDI policy into a detailed five-year master plan for economic development.
- How to offer wide-ranging incentives and legal protection mechanisms for foreign investors.
- How to strategically orient foreign technologies and know-how into specific sectors with global growth potential.
- How to promote the country's locational (L) advantages worldwide.
- How to target the world's leading TNCs and systematically attract them as foreign investors into specially designed industrial parks.
- How to provide support to powerful 'national champions' with an international focus.

5.2 Inward FDI policies and economic reforms, 1978–98

5.2.1 FDI policy adjustment since the late 1970s

Traditionally inward-looking and mainly agriculture-based, China embarked on a new economic course in 1978–79, when the economy was finally opened to the outside world after decades of isolation and economic stagnation. Party Chairman Deng Xiaoping,[9] a pragmatist and like Chairman Mao Zedong one of the symbolic father figures of contemporary China, led the way for widespread economic reforms promulgating the 'four modernizations' in agriculture, industry, science and technology, and national defence. In 1979, the Chinese government officially ended the prohibition of inward FDI by enacting special legislation permitting and protecting joint venture operations with foreign equity participation. In 1980, four special economic zones (SEZs) were created in two coastal provinces, which immediately started attracting significant FDI from nearby Hong Kong, Singapore and the United States.

The geographic proximity of the financial and commercial platform of Hong Kong was a locational advantage for the foreign companies in the SEZ, which established labour-intensive assembly operations for exports 'across the border'. China's labour costs were much lower than those in Hong Kong or other Southeast Asian countries. Most of the early investors belonged to the diaspora of about 55 million overseas Chinese whose personal connections with regional governors and other leaders, and knowledge of the language could influence decision-making and approval mechanisms within local bureaucracies. Many overseas Chinese investors from Hong Kong and Taiwan still have close family ties in their original homeland.

In the early days of political uncertainty, contractual joint ventures[10] were the preferred mode of entry representing over half of total FDI. Joint ventures with foreign equity were still rare and the few that were signed concentrated on oil exploration projects. A few others were established in the textile and similar light industries and were characterized mostly by their small size, strict ownership-control mechanisms and short-term duration.[11] Throughout the 1980s, the Chinese government increased its commitment to the reform process, which brought in FDI windfalls that spread from the coastal areas to major cities and selected regions in the interior. By 1984, 14 coastal cities and their hinterlands were opened to FDI, thus providing foreign companies with access to larger geographic and densely populated areas, a strong labour force, highly trained technicians, larger cities with a tradition in foreign trade, good transportation and communication facilities and the presence of small-scale suppliers. In 1985–86, these 14 coastal cities accounted for 23 per cent of China's industrial production and almost 40 per cent of its exports.[12]

Several FDI enhancement measures were introduced in cities and provinces. They coincided with decentralization of economic management and a loosening of the state planning system, particularly the abolition of centralized allocations of material supplies and production quotas for national enterprises. Simultaneously, tax and price reforms were introduced and the banking system was streamlined. Decentralization reduced the share of FDI contracted directly by sectoral ministries and other central government organizations (MOFTEC, Ministry of Finance), from 59 per cent to only 12 per cent during 1983–86. As a result of improved business conditions, overall inward FDI rose by 50 per cent in 1984 and 120 per cent in 1985.

In 1985, the three river deltas – Pearl, Yangtse, Fujian – were opened to foreign investors, who benefited from low-cost local sourcing in a number of labour-intensive, raw materials-oriented and subcontracting industries. Relocation of complete plants and modern production processes by foreign TNCs improved technology and capacities of local enterprises. As the motivation for FDI shifted from cost-advantage considerations to a more market-oriented approach, the proportion of equity joint ventures in the total value of contracted capital rose from 3 per cent during 1979–82 to 30 per cent during 1983–85 and about 50 per cent in 1999.[13]

Contractual and equity joint ventures were viewed by foreign investors as a way of gradually acquiring market experience, strategic information and access to central and regional bodies. The Chinese were interested in receiving advanced know-how and technology through their foreign partners, and the authorities also preferred joint ventures as they were suspicious of business operations totally controlled by foreign TNCs through wholly-owned subsidiaries. During the late 1980s foreign investment intermittently suffered from the consequences of severe exchange controls imposed by the central government to limit deficits in the balance of payments. With increased trading and production activities, several Sino–foreign joint ventures faced difficulties in obtaining foreign currency needed to import equipment and strategic raw materials. Foreign reserves at that time were still low and funding of large infrastructure projects depended mainly on direct contributions from international donors like the World Bank or the Asian Development Bank. Moreover, local authorities shielded their markets from outside competitors through special trade and nontrade barriers. Despite these initial obstacles, FDI rose and managed to stay at fairly high levels.

In 1986, the Chinese government issued a list of 22 provisions to encourage FDI and to improve the overall business climate in the country. Authorities opened special swap centres for foreign companies, which could henceforth redress their foreign exchange imbalances, import essential inputs and repatriate part of their profits. The autonomy of ventures with foreign equity participation was guaranteed without external bureaucratic interference, although authorities became more selective about the type and quality of FDI. Specific conditions were imposed on joint ventures such as priority sectors, technology and know-how transfer and export requirements. New corporate and copyright policies were enacted in 1986 and 1990, and, following their introduction, FDI from Japan, the United States and the EU increased significantly. Most of the world's top 500 TNCs and many medium-sized companies located in the surrounding Pacific Rim countries began to route increasing volumes of FDI into China, often via Hong Kong and Singapore.

During 1992–95, FDI incentives were extended to 18 capital cities of interior provinces, 5 cities along the Yangtse river, and 13 border cities in the remote northeastern, southwestern and northwestern regions. Previously prohibited sectors such as real estate, transportation, telecommunications, highway construction, airport infrastructure, port development, retailing, insurance, accounting and pollution control were gradually opened to foreign investors as a result of the government's efforts to liberalize services, a condition put forward by the international community for joining the World Trade Organization.

TNCs tried to gain access to new regional markets in the interior. Factories were moved further inland to benefit from lower labour costs and proximity to final customers. The combined share of the western and central regions in the total value of FDI rose from 6 per cent during 1989–91 to 11 per cent during 1992–93 and about 14 per cent in 1999.[14]

5.2.2 Main features of Chinese macro management

In 1992, the National Congress of the People's Communist Party, the country's supreme legislative authority, officially declared the 'socialist[15] market economy with Chinese characteristics' the only viable economic model to be followed by central and regional administrations in the country. This new line of thought ushered in the definitive abjuration of central planning and a shift towards a more decentralized economic system based on indicative state guidance for strategic industries and almost entirely free market mechanisms in other sectors.

The adherence to the market economy was reconfirmed during the fourth session of the Eighth National Congress in March 1996. The Chinese government is determined to pursue its open door and economic liberalization policy even after Party Chairman Deng Xiaoping's demise in February 1997. In September 1997, two months after the integration of Hong Kong, President Jiang Zemin recommended strict implementation of liberal economic policies including the privatization of state-owned enterprises (SOEs). Government and party officials are being removed from top positions in the enterprises to function more as macro planners in charge of setting the overall direction for industrial and FDI development. State authorities, however, are still closely involved in shaping the country's macroeconomic framework. Powerful central bodies such as the State Planning Commission or the State Economy and Trade Commission are responsible for the establishment of five-year plans defining targets and priorities for the country's economic and industrial advancement. Since the reform process was launched 15 years ago, each five-year plan identified priority sectors that had to be upgraded through direct state support, combined with foreign technologies and know-how.

Initial plans emphasized agricultural reform and modernization of food and consumer goods factories. Subsequent plans focused on industrial diversification and upgrading of key industries such as machinery, construction materials, chemicals and the automotive sector. Lately, the Chinese government has begun to promote high-tech sectors such as chips and wafer production, PCs and peripheral devices, telecommunication components, and new materials. Leading international corporations have been invited to invest in new plants across China, and investments have already been undertaken by the world's leading TNCs.

The latest five-year plan (1996–2000) aims to strengthen the country's export base for high-tech goods: electronics, computers, motorcycles, machinery and chemicals. Other objectives are to modernize transport infrastructure, to develop tourism and other services, to introduce technologies for protecting the environment and conserving energy, to raise the economic performance of interior regions, and to increase overall industrial competitiveness in order to improve the foreign exchange reserves situation.

China has upgraded its industrial sector through systematic technology transfers and a strong emphasis on export-oriented manufacturing. Both consumer and capital goods industries have been transformed with the help of foreign know-how, managerial input and capital injections. Many of the country's traditional industries such as textiles and apparel, chinaware, kitchen appliances, tools, sports goods, electrical devices and consumer electronics are now major challengers in emerging and industrialized markets. China did not follow a single comprehensive policy blueprint,[16] probably because it could not draw from any existing example at the time. When the country started opening its economy to western investors, there was no comparable case of a large country that was adopting a liberal FDI regime to rebuild its economy; countries like Brazil, India, Mexico and Indonesia had not yet opened their economies. FDI in large emerging countries was controlled by restrictive laws which had to be consistent with the prevailing ideology of import substitution over export promotion, unlike in the smaller 'tiger' economies of East and Southeast Asia (e.g. Taiwan, Malaysia, Singapore).

Partly owing to the farsightedness of its leadership, partly by lucky coincidence, China preempted other countries and had no major competitor when it started. It managed to attract high flows of FDI right from the first year of its opening of the market. On their part, China's FDI authorities were prepared to constantly improve the country's locational advantages, to adjust their policies and to take into account foreign investors' motivations and expectations. The most recent move is a gradual opening of the services and financial sectors. With certain exceptions, this process of continuous learning and adjusting has persisted to the present day, and is considered one of the main reasons for FDI growth in China. So far, local factor endowments such as technological and managerial capabilities, business standards, availability of inputs and service quality are constantly upgraded through forward and backward linkages between local and foreign firms.

China's unrelenting drive towards economic improvement is inspired by a series of fundamental policies which are similar to the principles underlying Russia's reform process. China's reforms are not yet completed, but they have been commended by the World Bank and UNCTAD.[17] On the whole, there has been rapid growth of private enterprises, increased competition, improvements in enterprise performance, and a steady rise in international confidence reflected by record levels of FDI. Over the past 15 years, the country as a whole has seen a period of rapid growth and overall prosperity, although a polarization of incomes is observed, especially in the cities. China has also maintained its tradition of establishing economic plans every five years. Using this approach, the authorities channelled FDI into priority industries for which national resources were combined with foreign technology. Unlike other socialist countries of Central and Eastern Europe (including Russia) where national plans were completely abandoned, Chinese authorities managed to pursue consistent strategies of industrial restructuring and upgrading.

However, the positive publicity China currently enjoys overlooks problem areas that may in the long term endanger its position as the world's second largest FDI recipient country. Although the economic reforms have been under way for almost two decades, the Communist Party still controls the political system and major industries. This distinction between economic reforms and preservation of political control (e.g. press censorship, one-party system, centralized decision-making, human rights abuses, increased nationalism and militarization in fringe areas) has survived, unlike the positive political changes and the irreversible democratization process in Central Europe, CIS countries and Mongolia. But the government's military intervention against student activists in June 1989 showed how quickly international confidence in a country's stability could be wiped out overnight. That year, FDI fell steeply from the 1985–88 high. FDI from the EU and United States remained extremely low in the following years and swung back after Party Chairman Deng Xiaoping's famous speech in 1992 in Shenzen calling for overall social and economic reform.

In the long term, a smooth transition to a more open political system is widely considered a prerequisite for sustainable economic development through FDI in China. Without it, confidence levels among TNCs could decline abruptly, leading to a spate of withdrawals. So far, FDI has had a positive effect on economic reforms, which in turn have been constantly adjusted to attract more flows. However, China's leaders will need to show greater foresight and avoid renewed public uprising or ethnic tensions in the border regions of Tibet and Xingjiang, which seek greater autonomy. The new political elite under Prime Minister Zhu Rongji is aware that gradual political opening is also needed for economic growth and stability (Box 5.1).

Box 5.1 China's policy objectives in the 1990s

- To diversify ownership structure by introducing private ownership, and to promote the private sector.
- To deregulate the economy along the principles of a free market economy.
- To reform the supply and distribution networks for final products.
- To relax state control on prices, to encourage competition by dissolving state monopolies and to reduce government interference in micromanagement of enterprises.
- To restructure enterprises by introducing new management techniques and accountability.
- To reform the financial sector and fiscal system.
- To establish an efficient infrastructure (transportation, telecommunications, public utilities, etc.).
- To provide more autonomy to the provinces and to decentralize decision-making.
- To integrate China into the world economy through trade liberalization and FDI promotion.

5.2.3 Formation of 'national champions' for industrial development

Already in the early phases of market reform and the 'open door' policy *vis-à-vis* foreign investors, the Chinese government pooled available resources and promoted the formation of powerful domestic industrial groupings. These enterprises were encouraged to develop strong domestic industries and trading subsidiaries, mostly in Hong Kong, which soon played the role of China's door to international markets and finance. Business-oriented 'national champions' were also meant to serve as an effective counterweight to a possible domination by large foreign multinationals. Their mandate was 'to sign contracts in a commercial manner and to bring in profits and foreign exchange for the sake of building a better socialism and improving the living conditions of the people'.[18]

While in most cases the initial capital injection came from the respective sector ministries, leading Chinese industrial corporations were requested to rapidly assume their own responsibility for managing funds and building up their own independent asset base.[19] Over the years, many of these red chip companies have become successful international players with strong expertise in key manufacturing technologies. Today, there are 12 famous state-level enterprises with diversified interests in key sectors of the Chinese economy:[20]

- China Resources
- China Everbright Group
- China International Trust and Investment Corporations
- China Automobile Industry Corporation
- China Construction Engineering Corporation
- China National Petrochemicals Corporation
- China Rural Development Trust and Investment Corporation
- China Overseas
- COSCO Pacific
- State Machinery, Electric Light Industry and Textile Investment Corporation
- State Raw Materials Investment Corporation
- Qingling Motors

Some of these corporations have their own in-house banking, insurance and consultancy subsidiaries; their management and staff are recruited from the best colleges in China and overseas, and are expected to have the requisite language skills and international experience.

The top 50 Chinese corporations, including trusts, banks and trading conglomerates,[21] are listed on the Hong Kong, Shenzen and Shanghai stock exchanges; their combined market capitalization exceeds US$60 billion.[22] Their business practices now serve as an example for restructuring nationally-oriented state enterprises, which have been depending on state subsidies and losing competitiveness because of a purely domestic outlook.[23]

Three companies stand out. First, the China International Trust and Investment Corporation (CITIC), established in 1979, developed rapidly, with the government's approval, into a diversified conglomerate with wide business interests in many continents. Its 48 subsidiaries are heavily involved in diverse industries such as chemicals, iron and steel, machine building, transport equipment and electronics. The company owns pulp mills in Canada and mining activities in Australia, and its trading arm is represented in the major Triad markets (Europe, North America, Japan). Its consulting subsidiary has carried out over 3500 assignments for domestic and foreign clients, and the company's market capitalization was about US$7 billion in 1997.

China Resources is another interesting case. Originally established as a private company in 1948 – just one year before the Communist takeover – it was restructured and put under the aegis of the Ministry of Foreign Trade as a group corporation in July 1983. Three years later, the central office was set up in Beijing. By 1985, the company had more than 200 subsidiaries, including joint ventures for industrial plants, shipping fleets, oil warehousing facilities, exhibition centres and department stores. Market capitalization of China Resources exceeded US$3 billion in 1997.

Finally, there is the Everbright Industrial Corporation, established in Beijing in April 1983 as a 'people's' company, meaning it represented neither Communist Party nor individual interests in public administration. The company was to participate in commercial and industrial investments in Hong Kong and overseas. Using Hong Kong as a major hub for its operations, the company received instructions from Chinese government bureaus and ministries to import high technology from around the globe and to bring overseas investments into China through joint ventures as well as foreign-owned enterprises. China Everbright recorded a market capitalization of almost US$1 billion in 1997.

The main mandate of these industrial and trading conglomerates was to serve as the Chinese government's window to the outside world, mainly through Hong Kong, and nowadays increasingly through Beijing and Shanghai; China's takeover of the former British colony is expected to stimulate their business. As these companies also pursue clear socio-economic aims, they benefit from the strong support of the Chinese authorities. China's top enterprises have become so powerful financially and technologically that they could spearhead a wave of Chinese FDI into Russia.

5.3 Foreign investment patterns in the 1990s: origins and destinations

FDI has been a major catalyst for changing ownership structures in domestic industry, promoting competition and improving economic efficiency, and facilitating enterprise reform and China's integration into the world economy. The positive impact of foreign investment on economic growth and industrial diversification has warranted the continuation of a market-oriented economic policy. Reciprocally, the reforms have maintained a favourable environment for FDI.

5.3.1 FDI inflows and stock

By 1992, FDI became the most important source of external capital for China. It exceeded the total of loans from foreign commercial banks, foreign aid, export credits and bond issues in international financial markets.[24] Although China ranks second after the United States among FDI recipients, the volume of FDI has fluctuated over the years, reflecting both changes in the global economic environment and the government's macro-economic adjustment policies. It fell, for example, during 1985–88, when the Chinese authorities imposed austerity measures, and tightened control on credit, foreign exchange and project screening. The Tiananmen event led to further reductions.

During 1991–92, the Chinese economy grew rapidly as foreign TNCs began to relocate their manufacturing facilities to countries that offered low-cost production sites and a large domestic market. Capital inflows were further encouraged by removing restrictions on FDI in services (transportation, retailing, banking) and by extending the status of special economic zones to additional locations in the interior. By 2000, FDI will be systematically encouraged in 28 cities along the Yangtse river, 13 border cities in the northeastern, southwestern and northwestern provinces, and 11 new tourist locations across the country.

By the end of 1997, cumulative FDI amounted to almost US$220 billion, exceeding that of most industrialized countries.[25] In terms of inward stock, China is today the world's third largest recipient country after the United States (US$721 billion) and the United Kingdom (US$274 billion).[26] On a per capita basis, China's FDI performance is less striking owing to the country's high population; in 1998, per capita stock was estimated at about US$170–175 (including Hong Kong), about four times higher than Russia's, although the FDI-induced impact on domestic industry has been substantially higher.

Average annual inflows since 1990 have amounted to US$14–15 billion, which place China in the same recipient group as the United States, the United Kingdom and France. Each year after 1992, China succeeded in increasing the volume of FDI in a steady upward trend. During 1995–97, FDI inflows increased by 20 per cent to reach US$45 billion, of which over 50 per cent were invested in equity joint ventures, 27 per cent in wholly-owned subsidiaries, and 20 per cent in contractual joint ventures.[27] Annual FDI inflows are expected to rise to a record level of about US$50 billion by 1999–2000. In the three-year period 1998–2000, Chinese authorities expect accumulated inflows of US$181 billion, averaging about US$60 billion annually (Figure 5.1). This would raise the country's FDI stock to US$ 400 billion (Figure 5.2) and practically double the annual per capita FDI in the country.[28]

A large part of the inflows are actually domestic capital, recycled via Hong Kong, Singapore and Taiwan (82 per cent of total FDI in 1992–95), mostly through companies controlled by overseas Chinese who are well-informed about new investment regulations and incentives. Since the start of economic reforms, these companies have invested massive sums in rebuilding and modernizing the Chinese economy and have always been the first to exploit business opportunities offered by the opening of the country to foreign investors.

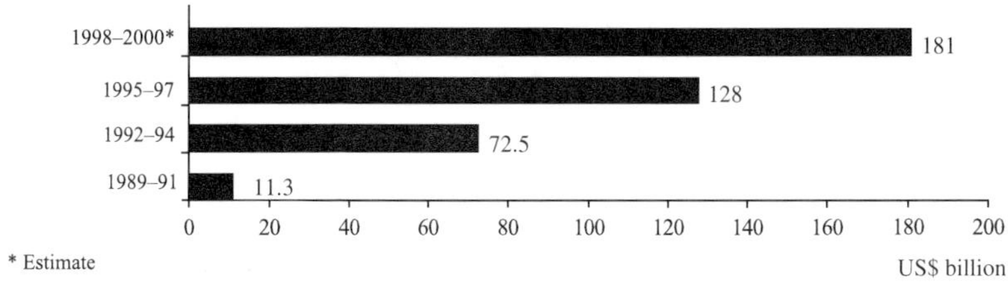

Source: UNCTAD, *World Investment Reports 1996, 1998.*

Figure 5.1 Cumulative inward FDI flows, China, 1989–2000

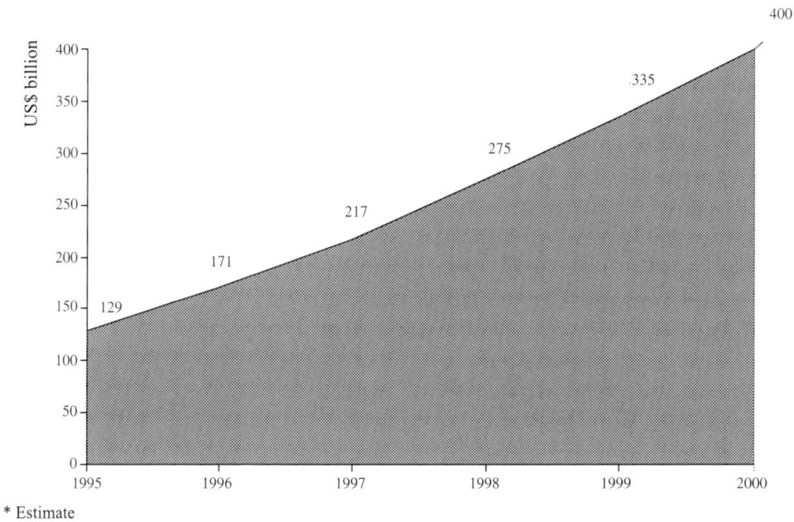

Source: UNCTAD, *World Investment Reports 1996, 1998.*

Figure 5.2 Inward FDI stock, China, 1995–2000

Hong Kong has been the main source of FDI for China (Figure 5.3). Before integration on 1 July 1997, the island state directed about 80 per cent of its outward FDI (US$53 billion during 1996–97) towards China and held an uncontested lead as an export and FDI platform for third-country TNCs. Statistically, these flows will no longer be considered as foreign transfers once Hong Kong becomes part of China in 1997, but overseas TNCs will continue to use Hong Kong as a major entry point to the mainland. There are, however, signs that Dalian, Shenyang, Shanghai and Tianjin will eventually challenge Hong Kong as FDI platforms, as economic activity is stepped up in the central

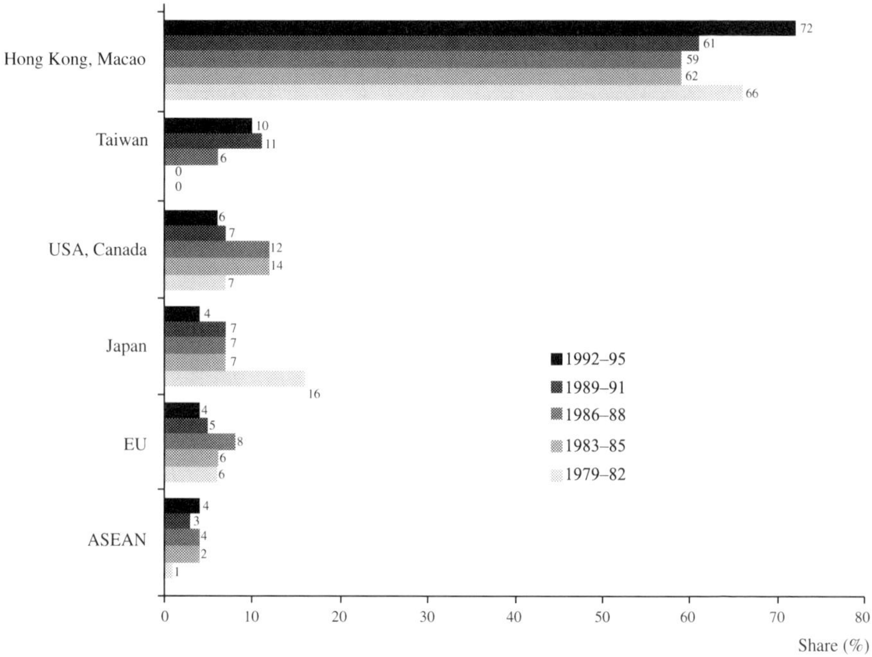

Source: MOFTEC, 1984–96.

Figure 5.3 Inward FDI by countries of origin, China, 1979–95

and northeastern regions. TNCs from Taiwan, Japan, the United States, Singapore and South Korea are expected to intensify their direct investments into China although the combined outflows of these countries into China are still much lower than those entering via Hong Kong. The largest European investors in 1997 were the United Kingdom (about 2 per cent of total Chinese inward FDI) and Germany (1 per cent).

5.3.2 Regional and sectoral distribution of FDI

For many years, FDI was directed to the southern province of Guangdong and the southeastern coastal regions of Fujian, Hainan, Jiangsu, Shanghai and Xiamen. Although most investment activities (domestic and foreign) still take place in these regions, since the late 1980s the focus has shifted to industrial locations further inland (Chengdu, Kunmin, Harbin, Wuhan) and in the northeast (Dalian, Qingdao, Shenyang, Changchun). The capital Beijing still commands a high share (Figure 5.4).

The first foreign investors focused on offshore oil drilling and refining, coal mining and property development (particularly for hotels and resorts). Subsequently, foreign TNCs turned to labour-intensive sectors such as textiles, apparel, footwear, toys, houseware and food processing. While

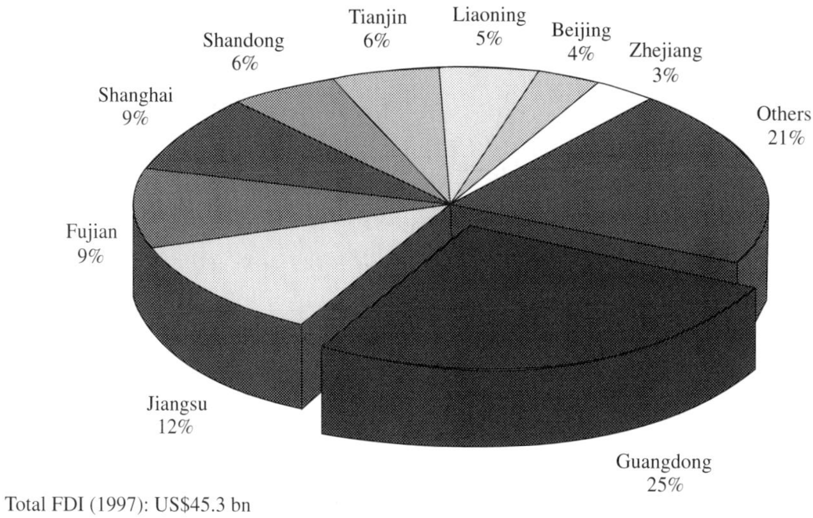

Source: State Statistical Bureau of the PRC *Statistical Survey of China*, 1998.

Figure 5.4 Regional distribution of FDI, China, 1997

processing and assembly of labour-intensive industrial products is still very common, a significant sectoral diversification has taken place (Figure 5.5). Today, Chinese authorities encourage FDI in capital-intensive sectors, where the country still lacks the necessary technologies and expertise: machine tools, automotive components, agricultural and construction

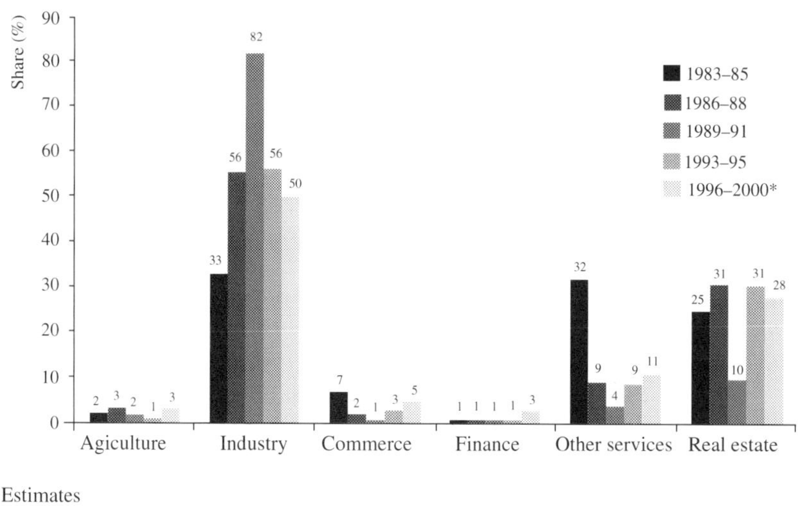

Source: MOFTEC, 1984–96.

Figure 5.5 Sectoral distribution of inward FDI, China, 1983–2000

machinery. The new policies also favour high-tech industries with a fairly large technology component such as telecommunications, computers, medical and printing equipment, laboratory instruments, specialty chemicals and pharmaceuticals. Since 1983, the share of manufacturing in total inward FDI rose from 33 per cent to 56 per cent. There was a peak in 1989–90 when it accounted for 82 per cent of total FDI.

5.3.3 Leading TNC investors in China

Most of the world's leading TNCs, from a variety of sectors, are present in China. They can be divided into three categories: western affiliates, Japanese affiliates and overseas Chinese companies. Large EU, US,[29] and Japanese TNCs mostly account for large-scale investments in the Chinese economy. In 1997, the top 100 investors generated almost US$40 billion in sales, or the equivalent of 7 per cent of China's GDP and 5 per cent of its total output.[30]

Many TNCs entered into equity joint ventures with local partners, mostly large state-owned enterprises (SOEs). Among the top 30 foreign investors in China are leading European automobile manufacturers (Volkswagen, Citroën), Japanese and US electronics companies (Sony, Matsushita, Hitachi, Motorola, Compaq, Microsoft), and German and US chemicals giants (Dupont, Bayer, Hoechst, BASF). Overseas Chinese affiliates top other foreign enterprises in terms of exports (63 per cent), number of enterprises (58 per cent), sales (48 per cent) and total assets (47 per cent); they also account for about 37 per cent of sales of the top 100 foreign TNCs in China and 43 per cent of their exports (Figure 5.6). EU and US TNCs performed better only in profits (44 per cent). With exports accounting for almost one-third of sales, Japanese TNCs were the most export-oriented. Western TNCs mainly supply the domestic market; their exports account for only 8 per cent of total sales. The one-sided export orientation of Japanese TNCs has recently come under attack by Chinese policy-makers, who consider these factories mere 'transplants' without much beneficial effect for technology transfer and local skill development.[31]

While overseas Chinese affiliates mainly invest in food, textiles, metalworking and small electrical equipment, western companies have become indispensable providers of technologies for chemicals, automobiles, specialized machinery, and turnkey and infrastructure projects (e.g. motorways, airports, ports, bridges, high-rise buildings, subway systems). Japanese companies are strong in their traditional sectors: automobiles, consumer electronics, electrical machinery and trading, including retail trade. Because of favourable legislation,[32] the establishment of a joint venture with a Chinese partner is the most common form of foreign investment in China (Figure 5.7). Joint ventures of all types represent about three-quarters of inward FDI. Whereas the share of equity joint ventures increased to about 50 per

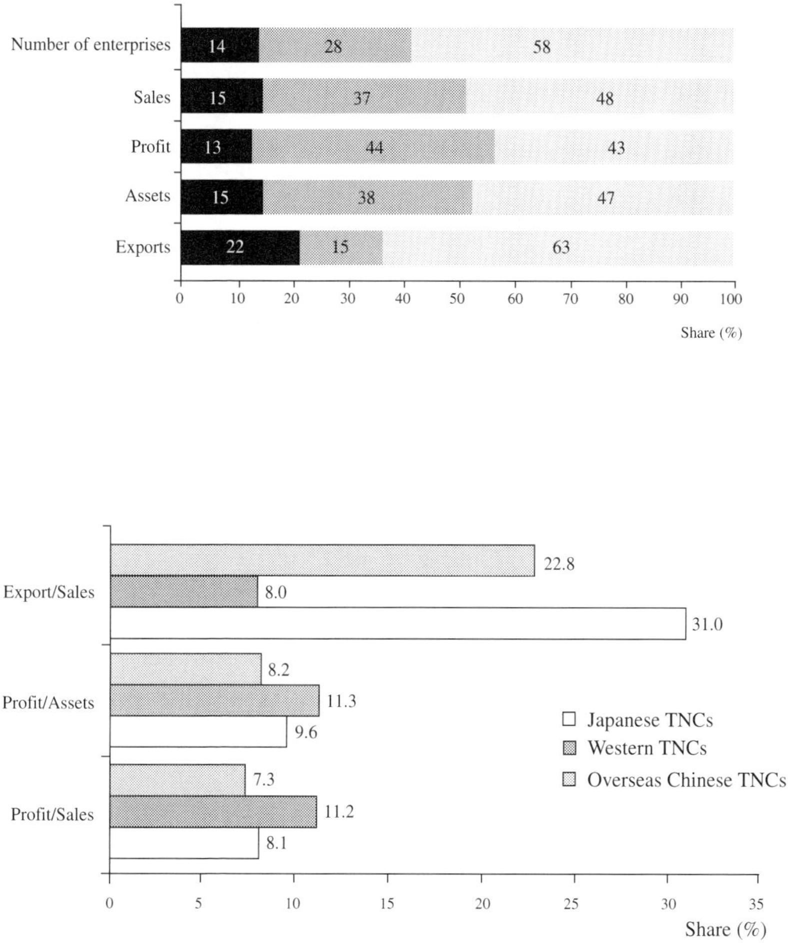

Source: Adapted from Guoji Shangbao, *International Commercial News*, 1996.

Figure 5.6 Performance of the top 100 TNCs by origin, China, 1996

cent during 1993–94, that of contractual joint ventures declined from 55 per cent (1979–82) to 7 per cent in 1999.

For both medium-sized and large TNCs, joint ventures represented the only form of market entry until 1986, when a new law permitted the establishment of wholly-owned subsidiaries. Over the past five years, investments for establishing wholly-owned subsidiaries have increased, as

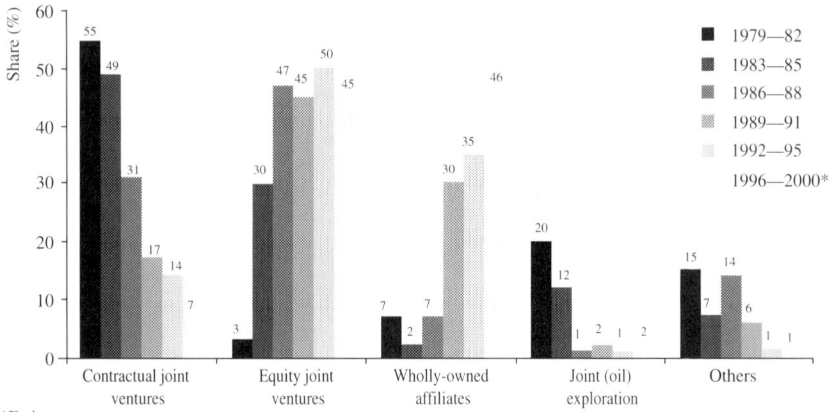

Source: MOFTEC, 1984–96.

Figure 5.7 Forms of inward FDI, China, 1979–2000

global TNCs with financial clout and international market access prefer this form. Those with very large investments have created holding companies to coordinate the activities of their numerous Chinese affiliates; these holding companies usually execute strategic business functions such as overall planning, executive recruitment, national advertising and legal affairs.[33]

5.3.4 China's outward investment position

China's outward FDI has developed very rapidly compared with other countries at a similar stage of development (Figure 5.8). It was the largest foreign investor among emerging economies, reporting an annual average of US$2.2 billion during 1994–97. By 1997, outward stock exceeded US$20 billion (Figure 5.9). China has thus reached Stage 3 of the IDP.[34] According to UNCTAD, over 900 Chinese TNCs had already established over 4600 foreign affiliates in 130 countries by 1994–95.[35] Chinese outward investment is concentrated in industrialized countries, especially those in the Asia–Pacific region: Canada (23 per cent); Australia (20 per cent); the United States (19 per cent);[36] Hong Kong (8 per cent) and Thailand (3 per cent).

The two main motives that incite Chinese companies to invest abroad are access and proximity to export markets (e.g. infrastructure FDI in North Africa and Southeast Asia) and a stable supply of natural resources (e.g. FDI in mineral extraction and aluminum smelting in Australia; timber in Canada). Investment in industrial production accounted for only 15–20 per cent of outward FDI in 1996, significantly less than in services (50 per cent) such as

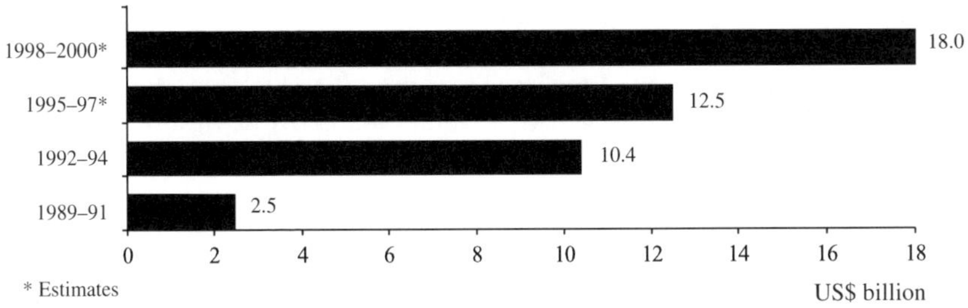

Source: UNCTAD, *World Investment Reports 1996, 1998.*

Figure 5.8 Cumulative outward FDI flows, China, 1989–2000

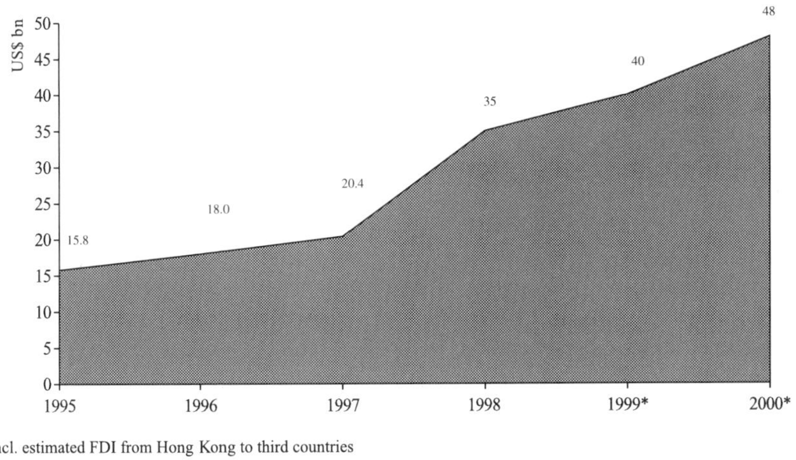

Source: UNCTAD, *World Investment Reports 1996, 1998.*

Figure 5.9 Outward FDI stock, China, 1995–2000

trading, ship repair, hotels and banking, or in raw materials extraction and processing (about 30 per cent).

In the 1980s outward investments were made almost exclusively by a small number of government-controlled organizations belonging to various ministries. State-owned organizations are still the most significant foreign investors, but starting from the mid-1990s private companies have started establishing foreign subsidiaries in western countries, Japan and Southeast Asia. Enterprise groups controlled by regional and city governments (e.g. Guangdong, Jiangsu, Shanghai) have also started making market-seeking and strategic investments abroad. Chinese operators engage in new business activities abroad to safeguard the survival or growth of their firms in the turbulent domestic market, and average Chinese FDI projects abroad are about half the size (US$1.2 million) of foreign investments in China (US$2.5 million). The most common forms of outward FDI are mergers and acquisitions (about 20 per cent), greenfield investments and joint ventures, depending on the expertise of the Chinese parent firm.

Growing foreign activities have led to the emergence of a professional managerial class with wide international experience and know-how, which is a major factor of international understanding and proves extremely useful for maintaining high inward investment levels.

5.4 Foreign investment legislation and incentives

Until the reform process was started in the early 1980s, China had no specific policy or laws on foreign investment and trade. The little foreign investment that entered the country was permitted only for very specific purposes: to acquire new technology, to ensure an adequate supply of capital and raw materials for domestic industries or to promote exports. Ever since, the country's FDI laws have been constantly refined and adjusted to the new global FDI context, which suddenly made the country's industries more competitive than other emerging countries of Asia (e.g. South Korea, ASEAN economies). The overall FDI regime was gradually liberalized and a legal and institutional framework created to facilitate and protect foreign investments. The new laws responded to complaints from western multinationals, which were not willing to accept arbitrary rules and procedures that hampered smooth business development.

FDI laws reflect the determination of national policy-makers to channel investment into selected sectors and regions. The three main laws on equity and contractual joint ventures, and wholly-owned subsidiaries stipulate that foreign investments are permitted on Chinese territory 'to expand international economic cooperation and technological exchange' (Article 1). All along, Chinese authorities have emphasized the aspect of transfer of technology and know-how to local operators. Foreign TNCs that fulfill this requirement can obtain licences rapidly. This approach is also reflected in the initial importance of contractual joint ventures for joint research and development.

China's FDI laws and policies are similar to those designed by other East Asian nations before it: Japan, South Korea, Singapore and Taiwan. These countries succeeded in systematically attracting international know-how, building competitive national industries and thus became serious competitors in most important consumer and capital goods industries. It is this determination to learn by acquiring foreign technology and directing FDI to those industries where the country has or wants to develop a particular strength that transformed China into a strong economy. These policies are supported by strong legislation. China has already managed to become the largest economic 'dragon' in Asia. This is the most important lesson to be drawn from China's FDI experience.

China's national FDI policy is expressed in a number of laws and texts that lay down the norms and application procedures for the various types of FDI (Box 5.2).

Box 5.2 Fundamental laws and texts governing FDI in China

- Law on equity joint ventures of 1 July 1979 (amended in 1990 and 1996).
- Law on wholly foreign-owned enterprises of 12 April 1986.
- Law on Chinese–foreign cooperative (contractual) joint ventures of 13 April 1988.
- Preliminary regulations for the establishment of the *China-Holding* of 4 April 1995.
- Catalogue guiding foreign investment in industries of China (1996, regular updates[37]).

5.4.1 Equity joint ventures

In most joint ventures, foreign equity ranges from 25 to 50 per cent. Generally, the western partner provides equipment, process know-how and funds, while the Chinese counterpart contributes the infrastructure (factory, offices, land), human resources and local contacts. Article 5 of the Law on Equity Joint Ventures (1979) states that 'technology and know-how contributed by the foreign party must be of advanced nature and suited to the needs of the country'. The local partner is expected to clarify legal issues with the respective government officials and local bodies. Foreign equity is protected by the Chinese State against nationalization or expropriation, which are only possible under special circumstances and upon provision of full compensation (Article 2, 1979 Law). This passage is similar to the corresponding provision in Russia's 1991 and 1999 FDI laws.[38]

Chinese authorities still pressure equity joint ventures to purchase raw and processed materials, energy and auxiliary equipment from domestic suppliers and to sell their output outside the territory of China (Article 9, 1979 Law). The export requirement was relaxed recently, especially in areas where domestic demand is not satisfied by local supplies (e.g. personal computers, telephone sets). Enforcement of the export clause improved export performance of domestic enterprises, which helped the State to accumulate record foreign reserves. (Russian legislation does not include such a clause.)

Foreign investors are entitled to remit their net profits abroad through special accounts opened with the Bank of China or, lately, other authorized banks (Article 10, 1979 Law). The 1979 Law also foresees conciliation or arbitration procedures in case the board of directors is unable to resolve disputes between the Chinese and foreign parties. Both partners can agree upon an arbitration institution in China or abroad when they apply for an authorization of the joint venture. Similar provisions apply to contractual joint ventures (1988 Law).

The Joint Venture Law was reviewed in 1990. The most important modification is the abolition of the contract duration applied to some joint ventures. It also allows foreign nationals to chair the board of directors of joint ventures. On 1 April 1996, several privileges for equity joint ventures (tax deductions and exemptions in case of reinvestments in China, as stipulated in Article 7, 1979 Law) were considerably curtailed for investments that were not considered essential for China's industrial and technological development. Priority is given to high-tech and certain services sectors (e.g. insurance, leasing) over consumer goods and labour-intensive industries.

5.4.2 Wholly-owned subsidiaries and holding companies

As FDI increases, the number of wholly foreign-owned ventures has risen in China. At the beginning of the reform process in the early 1980s, enterprises with 100 per cent foreign ownership were allowed only in the special economic zones. A Law promulgated in 1986 extended this form of operation to practically all parts of the country on condition that the venture uses advanced equipment and technology and is to a large extent export-oriented (Article 3, 1986 Law). Like joint ventures, wholly-owned subsidiaries enjoy special protection from nationalization or expropriation, but they must not harm the country's social and public interests (Articles 4 and 5, 1986 Law).

For large investments, a business licence is granted after systematic examination and approval by the Ministry of Foreign Trade and Economic Cooperation (MOFTEC), the supervisory authority (Articles 6–11, 20–23, 1986 Law).

As from 1 July 1996, the national currency is convertible on clearing accounts, according to the new foreign exchange regulations. This will allow wholly-owned subsidiaries (and joint ventures) to make necessary payments and to acquire foreign currency freely at local banks for trading operations, reimbursement of loans and profit repatriation.

Foreign operators now enjoy the same rights as Chinese companies, which were already permitted to acquire foreign currency from local banks in April 1994. The People's Bank of China has adequate foreign reserves to assure foreign investors that sufficient foreign currency is available to carry out the required capital transfer operations. Unlike the Russian rouble, however, the Chinese renmimbi is not yet freely convertible.

The 1995 Regulation on the establishment of China holding companies offers several advantages. Multinationals like Philips, Unilever and Siemens already operated through holding organizations, with the open consent of the Chinese authorities, even before the regulation was passed. Large TNCs are strong enough to finance their own lobbyists and to pressurize central and regional decision-makers. Based on the new rules, all foreign companies can establish holding operations for managing and administering equity participations and other forms of investments in the country. Three conditions must be met when establishing holding operations (Article 2, 1995 Holding Regulation):

- The company must be financially healthy, creditworthy, have a long presence in China, and possess combined foreign assets of at least US$400 million.
- It must have a domestic equity stake of over US$10 million.
- It must have received approval for at least three investment projects in China.

Alternatively, holding companies can be formed by TNCs that have conducted more than 10 investment projects in manufacturing or infrastructure in the country, representing a total paid-in capital of US$30 million. MOFTEC is the sole institution that can authorize the establishment of a Chinese holding. Upon approval, the foreign company must agree to an equity investment of US$30 million to be paid within two years in a freely convertible currency. Holding companies cannot be used as a tax shelter for reinvesting profits accumulated in local currency.

Nowadays, it is possible to admit a Chinese joint venture partner into the holding. The partner is also subject to the two-years rule, but is allowed to make the equity payment in local currency. The foreign parent company must act as a guarantor for the Chinese holding and should therefore have a strategic interest in its successful expansion in the country. The holding is authorized to provide support to attached Chinese affiliates in purchasing equipment, office space, supplies and raw materials. It can also assist in personnel recruitment, loan negotiations with banks and other financial institutions, borrowing, foreign exchange procurement and stock exchange operations.

The holding regime enables foreign TNCs to benefit from special tax exemption on dividend payments on behalf of their Chinese subsidiaries. In general, the corporate tax rate is 40 per cent. However, the Chinese holding regime excludes common tax advantages enjoyed by holding companies in Anglo-American countries and continental Europe (e.g. cutting profits by transfer pricing and by shifting gains and losses between various subcompanies). The advantages of this new legal form can only be gauged on an individual basis. The coming years will also show how far the holding regime will succeed in attracting additional FDI into China.

5.4.3 Industries to be promoted during 1996–2000

Following the examples of India and Mexico, China's State Planning Commission (SPC), the State Economic and Trade Commission, and MOFTEC drafted a catalogue of sectors where FDI will be favoured, permitted, limited or forbidden. The objective is to channel foreign investments into those sectors that are considered most important for China's economic development. The catalogue is expected to put an end to the so far anarchic situation of 'anything goes, if the investor has the right connections (*guanxi*)'.

The catalogue of industries, which has been published in Chinese and English, includes 17 main sectors with a description of subsectors to be developed through FDI.[39] The government intends to update it regularly and adapt it to new world scenarios in line with priority sectors to be promoted. Until 2000, FDI will be encouraged in agriculture, energy, environmental technology, essential raw materials, and infrastructure (roads, airports, telecommunications). High-tech sectors and new technology for product improvement, productivity enhancement and export development will also receive special attention. Such technologies concern last-generation computers, integrated digital telephone networks, recycling of raw materials, and pollution control techniques. About 170 branches are favoured, of which 24 are in machine building/mechanical engineering and 18 in electrical engineering and electronics.

FDI will be restricted in sectors having excess capacity and standard technologies. About 110 subsectors have been identified, including diesel motors, passenger and cargo ships, leaded batteries, simple equipment for polyester-filament production, container and lift production (subgroups of the sector machine building), and washing machines, refrigerators, radios and tape recorders, and radio and TV transmission systems (subgroups of the electrical/electronics sector). For 13 branches, including automobiles, colour TV sets, cameras, fax machines and copiers, special permission must be obtained from the respective ministries. FDI is not permitted if it adversely affects national security or the environment. Foreign investors are also not allowed into branches controlled by state monopolies, such as postal services, telecommunications, and air traffic control. Foreign companies will face no difficulties in sectors not explicitly mentioned in the catalogue.

5.4.4 Incentive mechanisms for foreign investors

A number of incentives are offered to attract FDI. These include tax breaks and exemptions, reduced tariffs for imports, easy entry and exit for expatriate employees, and relative autonomy in the management of local business operations. The incentive packages proposed to foreign investors are regularly adjusted by the central and regional authorities, according to the policy objectives stipulated in the current five-year plan. For example, special tax regimes and exemption from customs duties were granted to manufacturing units first in the special economic zones along the eastern coast and opposite Hong Kong and Macao, and later extended in the 1980s and early 1990s to new development areas in the Yangtse delta, Shandong province and Dalian (Liaoning province). Once the planned target is achieved, the incentive package is adjusted and new measures are announced.

Today, the incentives focus on interior regions, rather than the coastal areas and overcrowded city agglomerations, which had benefited from fiscal advantages and attracted the bulk of foreign capital during the early period of reforms. City authorities (Beijing and other large cities like Tianjin, Shanghai and Guangzhou) have established new development zones, high-tech parks and free trade areas to decongest urban areas, which also allows investors to be closer to their regional suppliers.[40] For example, investors in the Suzhou Industrial Park or Pudong Special Development Zone benefit from special facilities (warehouses, offices, housing for executives, schools); wide-ranging tax exemptions for a few years (especially corporate and property tax); free repatriation of profits; and duty-free imports of building materials, spare parts, company cars and office automation equipment.[41]

For investments below a certain level,[42] regional authorities are generally free to decide on the preferential treatment without seeking special permission from central bodies (MOFTEC). They can independently promote and develop local business with the help of FDI.

The overall aim is to attract a critical mass of FDI that will eventually allow the country to join the World Trade Organization and to adhere to the principles stipulated in its Charter, including the multilateral investment protection regime.[43]

5.5 Macroeconomic impact and industrial restructuring through FDI

The technology, innovation capabilities and skills brought by western TNCs have impacted significantly on China's economic performance (Figure 5.10). The positive results can be attributed to a combination of far-sighted policies not only for FDI, but also in different economic and financial spheres (strict monetary control, fiscal intervention, foreign trade

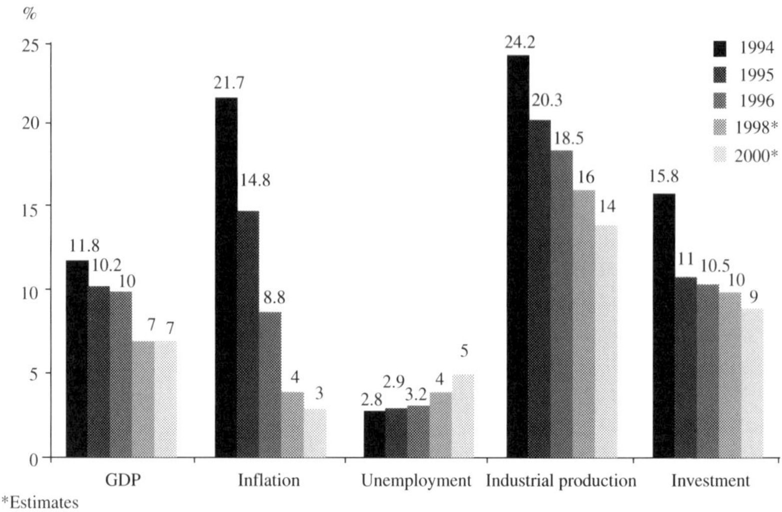

Source: State Statistical Bureau of the PRC; Austrian Trade Commission, *China Nachrichten*.

Figure 5.10 Main economic indicators, China, 1994–2000

promotion, industrial development measures and support to SMEs). Another factor is the willingness of leading TNCs to invest in the most populated country of the world.

Broadly speaking, technology and know-how imports through FDI have had four major consequences for the Chinese economy:

- They prompted the sectoral shift from agriculture[44] to industry and, increasingly, to financial and nonfinancial services.
- They transformed industry from being highly labour-intensive to knowledge- and capital-intensive.
- They led to GDP growth and raised living standards, exports, industrial output and employment.
- They generated tax revenue and foreign reserves.

Foreign companies have contributed to China's economic upswing by supplying a mutually-reinforcing package of capital, technology, organizational and managerial practices, and immediate access to new export markets. Investors who arrived in the 1980s and 1990s have produced a multiplier effect by increasing areas of interface between indigenous and foreign factors of production. The results are visible in all major cities of the country; construction and trade flourish, and business activity is slowly permeating to remote regions of the country.

FDI has played a catalytic role in the process of modernizing China's economy and raising the country's industrial competitiveness at a global level. Market opening and reforms have led to less dependence on foreign technologies. The market reforms have helped the country expand its export base and earn valuable foreign exchange, part of which is reinvested to upgrade priority sectors of the economy. Foreign investment is now systematically used by the Chinese government to undertake industrial restructuring across the country.

Robust economic growth, fuelled by the private sector, has shielded China from the impact of the Asian financial crisis. Even the devastating flood that rendered millions of people homeless during the summer of 1998 did not significantly affect the economy. Inflation stood at an all-time low in 1998 (4 per cent), and the benchmark one-year deposit rate, at 5.2 per cent, constitutes a further boost for domestic investment.

5.5.1 FDI-induced economic changes

Inward FDI has been instrumental in creating and strengthening a free market system based on competition, free price mechanisms and a more transparent legal system. China could thus improve its locational advantages through higher corporate competitiveness and a more diversified industrial base.

The country has emerged as one of the fastest-growing economies in the world, with above-average annual growth rates in the 1980s and 1990s. Although there were certain years of lower growth in the early 1990s as a consequence of the Tiananmen incident, the economic boom has never subsided (Figure 5.11). During 1990–96, the Chinese economy expanded at an average inflation-adjusted rate of about 9 per cent. In several instances, the growth rates forecast in the country's five-year plans were adjusted upwards.

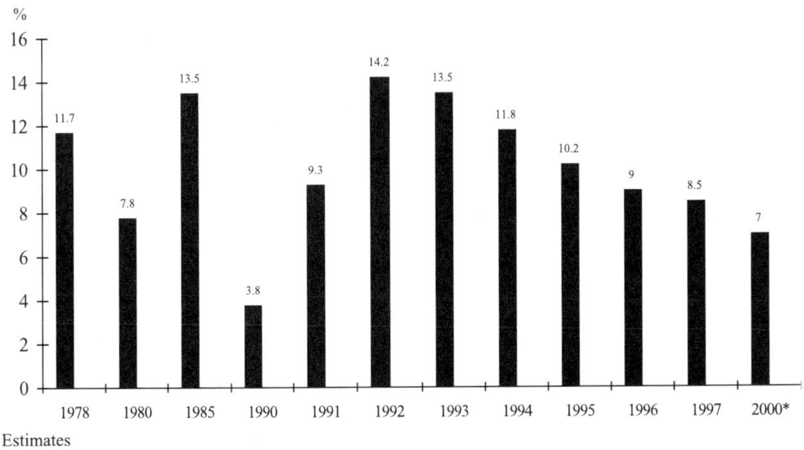

Sources: State Statistical Bureau of the PRC, 1998; *The Economist*, 1997–98.

Figure 5.11 GDP growth rates, China, 1978–2000

During 1992–93, a record growth rate of about 14 per cent compelled authorities to tighten credit by restricting the money supply and thus brake an overheated economy. Real growth for 1997 was around 9.5 per cent, when China's GDP reached a new record of RMB5800 billion (about US$630 billion). For 1998–99, China's State Statistical Bureau expects a real growth rate of 7–7.5 per cent. Barring a dramatic reversal, high economic growth is expected to continue well into the next decade.

The rise in absolute GDP has improved annual per capita income, which rose from US$70 to US$550 during 1980–97, placing the country well ahead of many other emerging economies, but still behind leading Latin American economies. Like other large emerging markets, China will continue to improve its position in the international ranking and become a major challenger to be reckoned with in the twenty-first century. Measured in purchasing power parties (PPP),[45] China's total GDP will rank third in the world by 2002, after the United States and Japan.

On the expenditure side, gross capital formation[46] accounted for about 40 per cent of GDP (RMB 2280 billion or US$285 billion) in 1996. Domestic investment was about five times the level of FDI, thus playing a much bigger role than in Russia and other LEMs. The fast development of domestic industry, construction and services would not have been possible without the inflow of large-scale foreign investment into key industries.

There is a correlation between the rise in FDI and investment activities of national operators, independently of their form of ownership. During 1995–96, two-digit growth rates were recorded for domestic investment activities undertaken by state enterprises (16.1 per cent), mixed enterprises (11.8 per cent) and private enterprises (small private companies: 20.8 per cent; large private companies: 35.3 per cent). Joint ventures run by the leading state enterprises in collaboration with strong foreign partners are the largest investors in the country.

Foreign investment inflows are changing the structure of the economy (Figure 5.12). Unlike in Russia, however, the change is gradual: the agricultural sector still represents about 20 per cent of GDP[47] (28 per cent in 1978). Altogether, FDI has contributed to a consolidation of industry, which accounts for about 52 per cent of GDP (9 percentage points more than in Russia). The services sector is low compared with industrialized countries (31.3 per cent of GDP, compared with 49 per cent in Russia), but progressive regional authorities (e.g. Shanghai, Nanjing, Guangzhou, Dalian) have increased investments in financial (banking and insurance) and nonfinancial services (retailing, transport, trading).

Increased foreign investment has also contributed to a significant rise in net household income over the past 10 years.[48] Average annual incomes in major industrial centres like Shenzhen, Beijing, Shanghai, Tianjin and Guangzhou rose to US$700–800 (compared with US$150–180 for farming

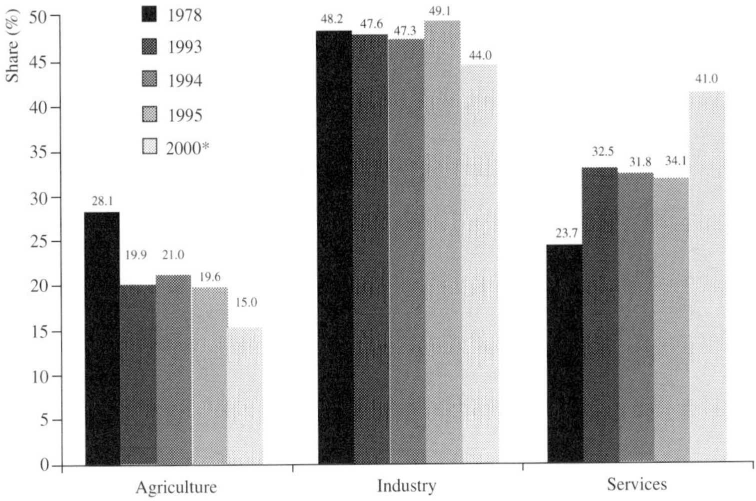

*Estimates

Sources: State Statistical Bureau of the PRC, *China Statistical Yearbook*, 1997, 1998.

Figure 5.12 Composition of GDP by economic sector, China, 1978–2000

communities in landlocked regions). Rapid growth and industrial expansion have also polarized incomes within Chinese society, where the gap is widening between haves and have-nots in the cities, and between urban and rural populations. Increasingly, rural people look for job opportunities in larger agglomerations, where labour supply already exceeds demand.[49] Income discrepancy is a growing concern for China's leaders, who are not only ideologically bound to equalize incomes but are increasingly concerned about the possibility of renewed social unrest. Faced with this situation, authorities attempt to channel FDI into smaller towns and rural areas so that new technologies and know-how will spread employment further inland.

Imports of necessary raw materials, energy products, and capital and consumer goods have stimulated foreign trade. During 1991–96, the trade volume grew at an annual average of 19.7 per cent compared with 10.6 per cent during 1986–90. In 1997, China's exports were US$183 billion (US$152 billion in 1996) while imports stood at US$142 billion (US$137 billion in 1996). If FDI rates grow as expected in the coming years, China's total foreign trade volume is likely to touch US$400 billion by 2001, making it one of the largest traders in the world, together with the leading industrialized nations. In 1997, foreign-funded enterprises accounted for 47 per cent of China's foreign trade (exports and imports).[50]

The remarkable increase in foreign reserves to a record volume of US$123 billion by the end of 1997 can also be largely attributed to FDI. It is also becoming an important tax generator for the central and regional governments, and its share in total tax revenue passed from 4 per cent in 1992 to 12 per cent by the end of 1997.[51]

5.5.2 Impact of FDI on domestic investment and private sector structures

Foreign capital is an important source of finance for medium- and long-term investments in China. While investment budgets allocated by the central government and regional authorities are gradually reduced, the share of FDI in equity capital of enterprises registered in China continues to rise. Direct capital contributions by foreign investors often allow domestic operators to overcome liquidity bottlenecks and to expand.

FDI is a catalyst for domestic investments, which also focus on large cities, the southern provinces and coastal areas,[52] all of which have experienced a consumption-led boom. Most domestic investment takes place in Guangdong (11.5 per cent), Jiangsu (9 per cent), Shanghai (7.3 per cent), Zhejiang (6.8 per cent) and Shandong (6.6 per cent), although interior provinces including those near the Russian border (e.g. Heilongjiang, Jilin) are also catching up.

The share of FDI in domestic investment rose from an insignificant 2 per cent in 1983 to 28 per cent in 1996 (Figure 5.13). The most notable jump in ratio occurred following the adoption of special investment measures during 1992–93. Before that, the Tiananmen square happenings had

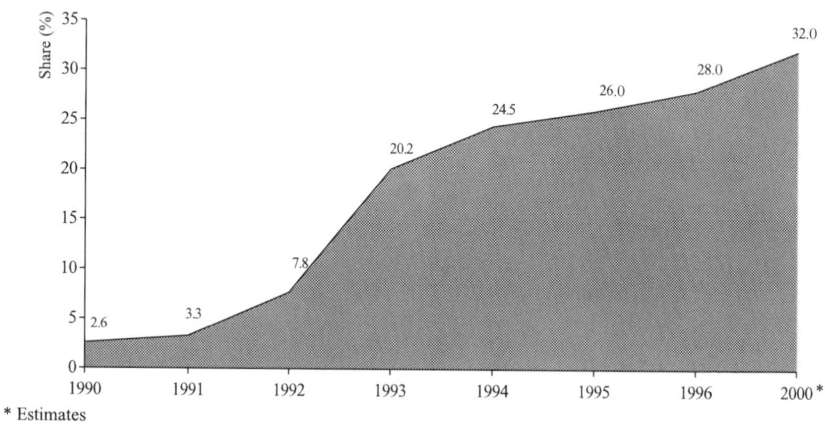

Source: UNCTAD, *World Investment Reports 1996, 1997.*

Figure 5.13 Share of FDI in total investment, China, 1990–2000

hindered foreign capital inflows. Altogether, gross fixed capital formation[53] represented around 40 per cent of GDP in 1996 (compared with 21 per cent in Russia[54]) and has become a major force behind China's economic and technological process, together with high consumer demand and rising exports.[55]

FDI has modified ownership patterns in industry (Figure 5.14), which now show a higher participation of the private sector. More than 60 per cent of industrial growth can be attributed to private companies in 1998 although they account for only 15 per cent of the enterprise population (5 per cent in 1990). Often, these companies are joint ventures with foreign equity or wholly-owned subsidiaries of TNCs. The state sector still accounts for more than half of domestic investment, but it generates only 34 per cent of industrial output (compared with 55 per cent in 1992). Private enterprises have become an important motor of economic and industrial development. Their share in domestic investment has increased at the expense of entirely state-owned or mixed enterprises. In 1996, it had already reached 32 per cent. In industrial output, private enterprises increased their share from practically nil in 1978 to over 30 per cent in 1997. The shares would be even higher, if they included the stake of private entrepreneurs in mixed enterprises. In 1995, private companies already employed 56 million people, 20 per cent more than in 1994.

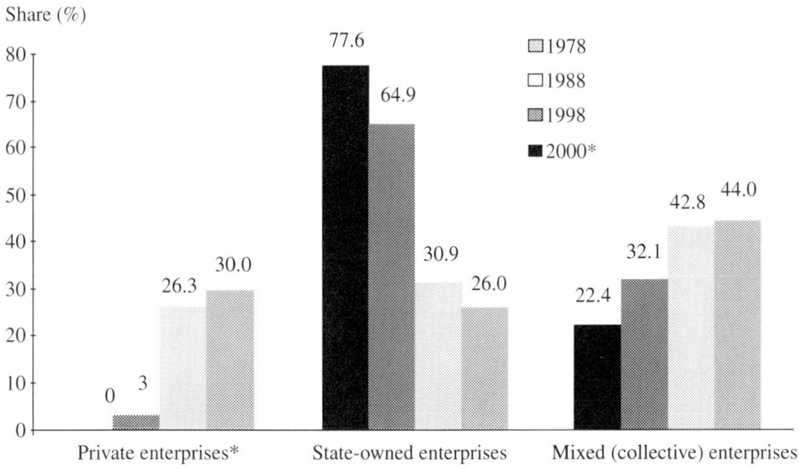

* Including foreign corporations

Source: *Zhongguo Tongji Zhaiyao*, 1996; Austrian Trade Commission, *China Aktuell*.

Figure 5.14 Industrial output by type of ownership, China, 1978–2000

Private equity is also represented in mixed enterprises, which accounted for a significantly higher share in industrial output (44 per cent in 1997) than entirely state-owned enterprises (26 per cent). Although FDI has led to visible reinforcement of private ownership, technological development of many important sectors is still hampered by inefficient state-owned enterprises (SOEs), which maintain a strong control over many basic industries (e.g. machine building, chemicals, automobiles, energy, and minerals and other raw materials). Accumulated debts and a precarious financial situation have turned SOEs into the Achilles heel of China's economy (Figure 5.15). In 1996, out of 102 000 SOEs half were making losses. The biggest losses are currently incurred by state companies in defence, nonferrous metals, coal and tobacco.[56]

The poor performance of SOEs is a major concern for the Chinese government as about 100 million workers are employed by them.[57] Most SOEs lack the funds to pay salaries on time or to buy the required raw materials and equipment. Antiquated production methods compel companies to produce low quality products, which do not find any sales outlets. Their main customers, other state-owned companies, pay extremely late (after up to 9 months) leading to a rise in triangular debts and high deficits in the state-owned banking sector, which strains the relationship between enterprises and the financial sector.

Personal connections between state enterprise directors and high-ranking government officials appear to still ensure the required flows of state subsidies in important industries. In 1996, subsidies allocated to state enter-

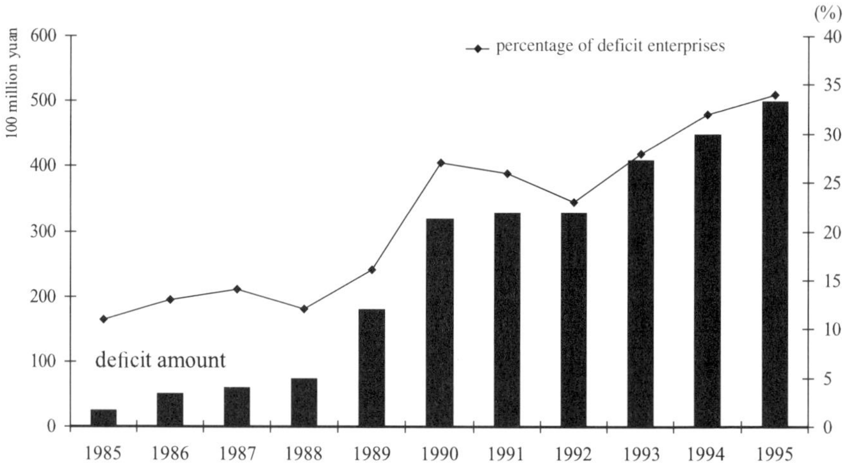

Source: State Statistical Bureau *China Statistics Yearbook*, 1996; Jetro, *China Newsletter*, vol. 4, 1997.

Figure 5.15 Performance of state-owned industrial enterprises, China, 1985–95

prises represented 80 per cent of China's budget deficit. But as the Chinese government is compelled to cut subsidies and direct assistance, the role of the state sector in the economy and share in total employment is bound to decline. Inspired by the success of inflation control measures in Europe and North America, Chinese leaders are determined to reduce the public deficit level[58] and to keep inflation under control. On a visit to Germany in October 1997, President Jiang Zemin declared that by 2000 China's budget deficit should not exceed the ceiling established by the EU Maastricht criteria (3 per cent of GDP). In the future, government subsidies will be limited to a small number of public players selected by the State Economic and Trade Commission. In June 1996, for example, about 300 state enterprises with good market prospects for their products were chosen as recipients of direct state assistance (e.g. Shanghai Petrochemical, Shanghai Tyre & Rubber, Guangzhou Shipyard, Luoyang Glass, Harbin Power, Tsingtao Brewery, Huaxin Cement).

Many SOEs are unable to adjust to the market, unlike the leading 'national champions'[59] or the dynamic foreign and smaller village and township enterprises (VTE). The Chinese government is therefore keen on identifying foreign joint venture partners for these SOEs. But the lack of interest on the part of TNCs in collaborating with large, unprofitable state conglomerates places the authorities in a dilemma: either to continue paying subsidies or to start a broad privatization campaign. Total privatization and restructuring of SOEs, however, will be a difficult task, because of the imponderables, especially the social consequences that such measures may involve. Although this issue must be addressed, so far no massive privatization programme has been launched as in Russia. Budgetary problems increasingly force authorities to close or restructure individual SOEs, but these companies often continue to depend on public assistance for survival even after restructuring. Moreover, ideological constraints rule out any radical change in policy. During the September 1997 Party Congress, Communist leaders spoke of the need for restructuring SOEs and allowing new forms of ownership, but instead of allowing the new owners the 'right to own', they granted them the 'right to use' for a period of 49 years.

As long as the ownership issue has not been truly resolved, SOEs will not become sufficiently attractive for the next wave of TNCs. Here lies Russia's chance to close the gap with China for FDI in the coming years, when the vast pool of medium-sized TNCs will look for opportunities in large emerging economies.

5.5.3 Impact of FDI on export performance and employment

A direct link can be established between China's improved export performance and FDI over the past 10 years (Figure 5.16). Japanese FDI in Southeast Asia brought similar results. Foreign affiliates helped significantly through

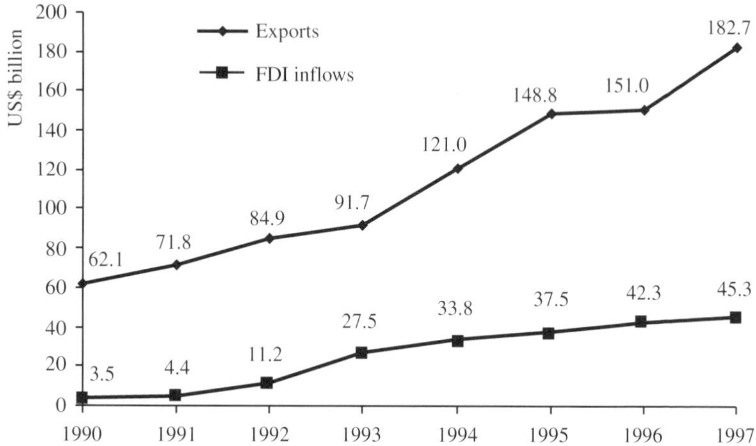

Source: State Statistical Office of the PRC, *A Statistical Survey of China*, 1998.

Figure 5.16 FDI inflows and exports, China, 1990–97

trade and investment in integrating China's production network into the 'flying geese' pattern of economic development across Asia.[60]

In 1996, exports by foreign affiliates (Figure 5.17) reached US$30 billion or almost one-third of China's total exports. Ten year earlier, their share in

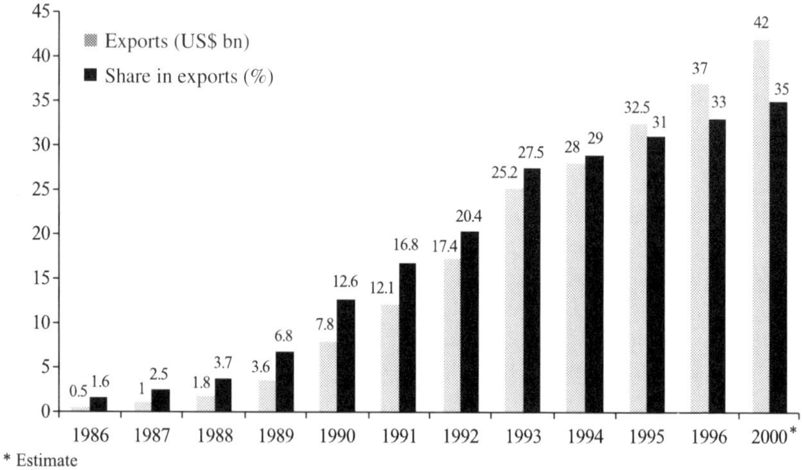

Source: MOFTEC, 1993–96.

Figure 5.17 Export performance of foreign affiliates, 1986–2000

total exports had only been 1.2 per cent in value terms. According to a recent study carried out by MOFTEC, foreign-funded firms export the bulk of their output:[61] for example, only 13 per cent of medicines produced in China are sold on the domestic market and 20 per cent of electronic goods, 32 per cent of detergents and 40 per cent of beverages.

Increased export activities have also led to more jobs in urban areas. The share of foreign affiliates and equity joint ventures in urban employment was about 5–6 per cent in 1996, about four times higher than in 1988. As a result, China's share in world exports trebled from just under 1 per cent in 1986 to 3.5 per cent in 1997, with average annual growth rates of 12–13 per cent. In absolute terms, foreign trade grew by 12 per cent in 1997 (19 per cent in 1996) to US$325 billion, making the country one of the world's most important trading nations in the world. Recently, export-oriented FDI also appears to have had a positive effect on the trade balance. During 1994–97, China expanded its surplus from US$5.3 billion to US$40.4 billion.[62] According to forecasts by the State Statistical Office of the PRC and China's Development Research Centre, exports will grow by 5–6 per cent annually during 1998–2000.[63]

The direct correlation between FDI inflows and foreign trade is also observed at regional level. Foreign trade activities are mostly concentrated in special economic zones and regions promoted by the government to receive FDI. Guangdong, where most of the country's FDI is concentrated, reports the highest foreign trade volume (37 per cent of the total), followed by Beijing (13 per cent) and Shanghai (9 per cent). FDI-induced exports are mainly directed towards developed economies bordering the Pacific Rim: Japan, the United States, Taiwan and South Korea. The United States has emerged as the leading export market, and it buys more products from China than it sells to China. The US market has become a major outlet not only for US-controlled ventures in China, but also for products manufactured in joint ventures with overseas Chinese, European, Japanese and South Korean participation.

The situation has reached a point where Chinese authorities are under pressure from the US Trade Department, which wants more balanced trade. In 1995, for the first time, the United States recorded a larger trade deficit with China than with Japan. Foreign trade was also expanded with South Korea (+45 per cent during 1994–95) and other ASEAN countries (+40 per cent), mainly following increased FDI from these countries. The largest market for Chinese products in the EU is Germany (3.8 per cent of Chinese exports and 6 per cent of imports), although it is not the leading European investor.[64]

In general, China's main trading partners are also major investors. Successful exporters to China have gradually become insiders and established local production facilities and joint venture operations. Investments undertaken by these TNCs have generally produced better results than FDI by complete newcomers.

Economic cooperation with Russia is based on different precepts. Although trade between the two countries rose significantly – by 9 per cent to US$7 billion during 1995–96, after a continuous fall since 1990 – it is not yet underpinned by reciprocal FDI. Today, Russia accounts for about 3 per cent of China's imports and 1 per cent of exports. Experts reckon that an increase in bilateral FDI would have a positive effect on trade, which could easily attain US$20 billion by 2003–05. Bilateral FDI is still comparatively low: in 1995, Russia invested US$22 million in China, while China invested US$40 million in Russia. Efforts to enhance FDI could be directed at those industries where each country imports from the other: power equipment, transport machinery, metals and chemicals for Russian FDI into China; food, consumer goods and light industrial and textile products for Chinese FDI into Russia. China's trade deficit with Russia was US$3.5 billion in 1995.

In spite of China's trade deficit with Russia, its exports structure appears to have higher potential. Contrary to the situation in Russia, there has been a continuous shift towards exports of finished products and components over the past five years, a result of systematic promotion by the Chinese of knowledge-intensive FDI. Finished products and medium- to high-tech components already represent 85 per cent of total Chinese exports, while raw materials, minerals and foodstuffs account for a negligible 15 per cent.

In recent years, China has become one of the world's largest producers of apparel, textiles, toys and other consumer goods. These industries are mainly located in the south and have been set up with capital contributed by overseas Chinese, western and Japanese entrepreneurs. Since the early 1990s, China has also set up factories for producing electrical devices, office equipment, telecommunications components, and a broad range of consumer electronics (alarm clocks, calculators, radios, tape recorders and TV sets). The quantum jump in exports of Chinese consumer goods and equipment would have been inconceivable in the early 1980s, when foreign investment was still low.

FDI in China has thus created efficient cross-border networks between suppliers and clients of capital, intermediate and consumer goods, stimulating overall trade and investment in the Asia–Pacific region. In a number of consumer goods segments, China has replaced Japan and South Korea as a 'magnet' pole of regional economic development. Russia could play a similar role as the future 'FDI locomotive' of eastern Europe, if targeted foreign technologies are acquired to create an efficient industry structure.

5.5.4 Industrial diversification at sectoral and regional level through FDI

China's main achievement in the past 10 years has been its structural shift away from heavy industry and mechanical engineering towards light industry segments producing all types of consumer goods and, increasingly, knowledge-intensive products. While heavy industries with significant capital requirements are still dominated by state-owned conglomerates struggling to maintain the same level of output and employment, private companies with both domestic and foreign equity participation have made significant inroads into the food processing and consumer goods sectors.

Healthy economic growth and domestic investment have favoured the development and modernization of China's consumer goods sector. The State Planning Commission (SPC) estimated overall growth of industrial output at 12–13 per cent for 1998 (14 per cent for 1997; 17 per cent for 1996), much of it generated by consumer goods (Figure 5.18). Private operators have been able to improve their market and financial position more successfully than larger, state-owned companies. China has succeeded in building a strong industrial base by directing domestic and foreign investment to strategically relevant sectors, including knowledge-intensive industries. Most product categories showed significant growth in industrial production from the early 1990s (Figure 5.19).

The government's attention will be directed at the following sectors in future years:[65]

- *Iron, steel and nonferrous metals*. China intends to reach full autonomy for basic steel products and to reduce its dependence on foreign technologies for specialty steels. Additional FDI is sought for expanding national aluminium production used for developing competitive aircraft, packaging and automotive components industries. Leading foreign investors for aluminium are TNCs from Canada, France, Israel and the United States.

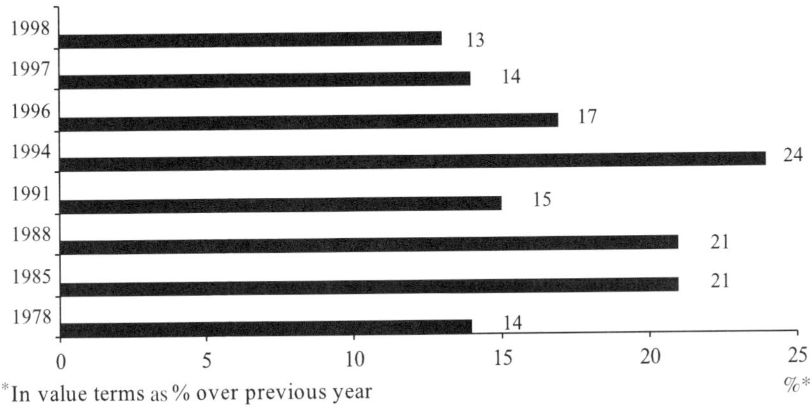

Source: State Statistical Bureau of the PRC, *A Statistical Survey of China*, 1998.

Figure 5.18 Growth of industrial production, China, 1978–98

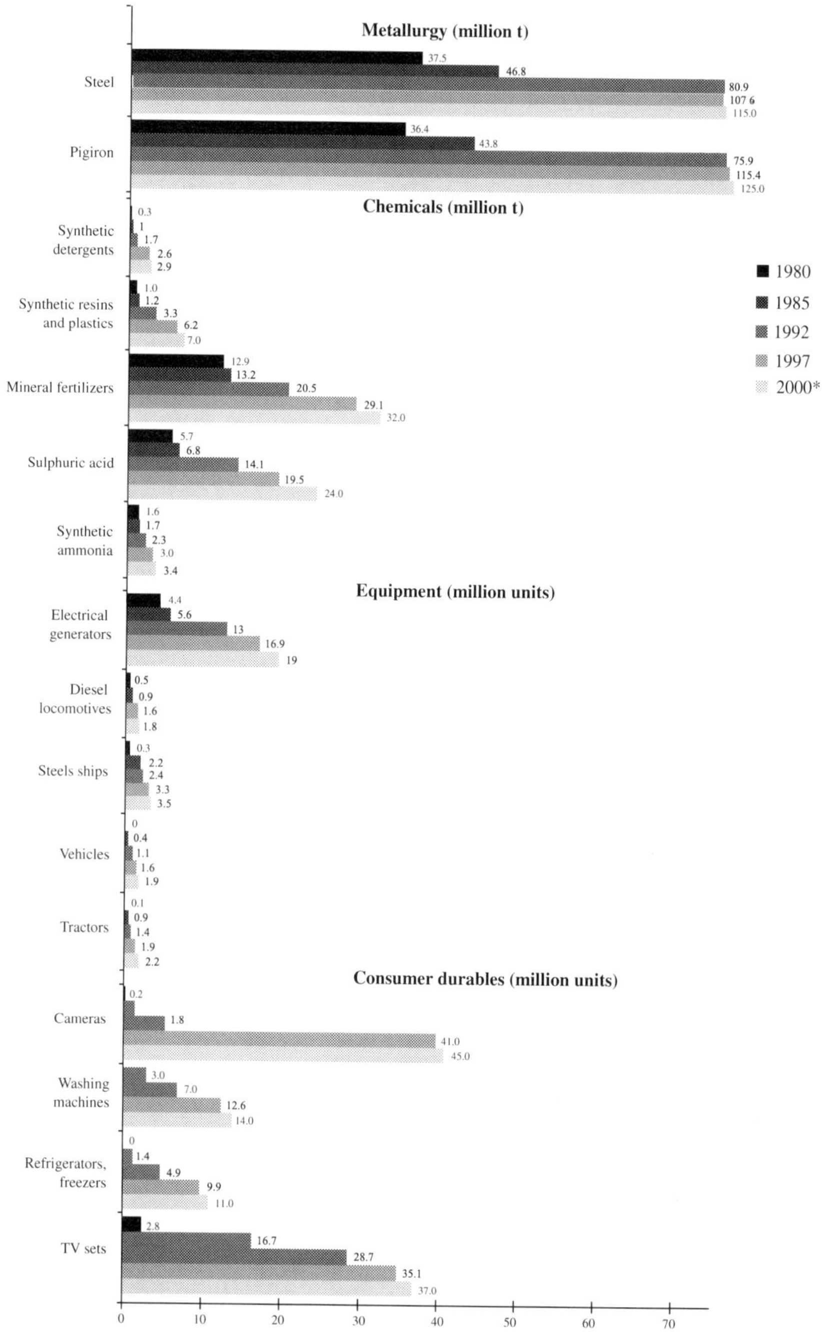

Source: State Statistical Bureau of the PRC, *A Statistical Survey of China*, 1998.

Figure 5.19 Changes in output of leading industries, China, 1980–2000

- *Machine tools*. The aim is to concentrate on applications for agriculture where there is still a frequent shortage of mechanical spare parts, hydraulic and pneumatic systems and ball bearings. Moreover, domestic manufacturing of packaging and food processing equipment is to be encouraged, as well as equipment for wood processing, gem cutting and pollution control. The equipment sector today accounts for more than 20 per cent of total exports (US$34 billion). In only one decade, China could move from almost total import dependence in machine tools to an almost balanced trade situation today. The Chinese government intends to raise the share of machine tools in total exports to about 25 per cent by 2000.
- *Automobiles*. About US$13 billion will be invested in 10 new plants with state-of-the-art equipment by 2000. These investments will be made by powerful joint ventures with substantial foreign equity and know-how in new processing technologies and management of such operations (Table 5.1). In the automobile sector, China competes with Brazil, India and Mexico. All these emerging countries seek to attract the most modern manufacturing technologies from western, Japanese and South Korean automobile multinationals. Most large manufacturers have already invested in China: Volkswagen (Shanghai), Audi (Changchun), Citroën (Wuhan), Peugeot (Guangzhou), Daihatsu (Tianjin), Chrysler (Beijing). In trucks, semitrailers and buses, China has attained a high degree of autonomy in only five years by using valuable know-how of global companies such as Daimler-Benz, Iveco and Volvo.

Table 5.1 FDI ventures in the automotive sector, China, 1996–98

TNCs	Equity (%)	Start of production (year)	Planned output (units)	Planned FDI (US$ mn)
Peugeot	32	1996	60 000	170
Ford	50	1996	125 000	800
General Motors	50	1996	25 000	100
Daewoo	51	1996	80 000	1 000
Mercedes Benz	51	1996	20 000	115
Honda	60	1997	30 000	260
Hyundai	100	1998	100 000	700

Source: *The Economist*, 2 March 1996.

- *Office equipment, computers and electronics*. In this sector, China's authorities are banking on US TNCs to continue setting up new production facilities that will reduce the country's high dependence on imports (over 50 per cent in 1996). Compaq and IBM are the leading foreign investors in the PC market, which reached a sales value of

US$1 billion in 1995/96 (world market: US$35–38 billion). By 2000, China's PC market could grow 8–10 times attracting more TNCs interested in gaining a share of this expanding market. In electronics, the aim of the authorities is to establish knowledge-intensive research and production facilities. In its ninth five-year plan (1996–2000), the Chinese government has foreseen a special fund of RMB1 billion (US$120 million) to finance R&D and production of high-tech components (e.g. wafers, processors, memory chips, networks).

- *Food and beverages*. As their purchasing power increases, Chinese consumers demand more sophisticated products. Examples of segments where western technology has become important are fruit juices, beer and diary products, especially ice cream and yoghurt which the young generation has started to relish. The Chinese authorities plan to approach medium-sized enterprises from Europe, but do not seem to have a well-conceived concept as yet.[66]
- *Chemicals and pharmaceuticals*. FDI in these sectors originates mainly from German, Swiss, US and UK companies. Since the inception of the open door policy, China's policy-makers have encouraged local production facilities for most healthcare products to reduce dependence on imports. This objective has been attained only partially, and China remains an important importer of high-tech chemicals and pharmaceuticals from western countries and Japan.
- *Petrochemicals, plastics and dyestuffs*. China is increasing its know-how base through FDI from Germany, Switzerland, Norway, the United States and Japan. France has also become an important investor following a major investment by Total, which built a US$800 million oil refinery on the outskirts of Dalian (Liaoning province).
- *Environmental control and energy saving*. Ever since these two areas have been declared a top priority in the current five-year plan, foreign technologies are systematically sought in the G7 countries.
- *Construction and building materials*. Foreign capital worth US$3 billion is expected to flow into this branch by 2000. Priority will be given to environment-friendly materials that also save energy. Currently, production is almost entirely absorbed by domestic demand, but the government plans to raise production levels so that by 2000 around 10 per cent of national output can be exported (as of 1996, exports already represent about 7 per cent of domestic output). Priority segments are specialty paints and glues, fibreglass, ceramics, insulation materials, double-layer and noise-resistant window frames, and sanitary fittings for bathrooms and kitchens. Many joint ventures were formed mainly with TNCs from Denmark, France, Germany, Italy and Japan. Certain special construction materials are still imported, mainly from Europe, Japan, the United States and South Korea, often via Hong Kong. The construction materials sector benefits considerably from the housing and real estate boom (shopping centres, department stores and office

buildings). The high demand for housing and offices that has been observed since 1995 is expected to persist into the next century. Today, the share of construction in the country's value-added is about 3.5 per cent (almost the same as in Russia, which is experiencing a similar construction boom). Lift and construction equipment manufacturers will also benefit substantially from these developments. The US TNC Caterpillar recently decided to build a new factory for dredges and excavators in Tianjin.

- *Services.* Not all services have been opened to FDI. The emphasis in future years will be placed on a number of financial (all types of insurance – health, life, nonlife), and nonfinancial services such as air transport, railways, telecommunications, retailing (medium-sized supermarket chains will be preferred to luxurious department stores and hypermarkets[67]) and tourism. Thousands of trading companies specialized in import–export operations for all important sectors of the economy sprang up soon after the reforms. Such companies no longer need licences to import goods and they can buy and sell products at prices determined by the market; most own warehouses. These new developments have enabled domestic and foreign suppliers to use sophisticated distribution networks. As in other fast-developing economies, trading companies thrive on the mutually beneficial effect of foreign trade operations and FDI.
- *Agroindustry.* A healthy agroindustry is of strategic importance, and at a high-level meeting in 1996 the Minister of Agriculture declared that FDI of US$7 billion was needed to modernize production plants and warehousing facilities in the agricultural sector. The government intends to substantially increase wheat and fertilizer production by 2000. According to recent information published by the Chinese Statistical Bureau, about 6000 agricultural enterprises received foreign equity during 1996; this is three times more than in 1994. A priority area for future FDI is agricultural machinery, particularly tractors and combines. Targeted investment is also expected to reduce income inequalities and growing polarization in agriculture. Independent, smallholdings already compete with large, heavily subsidized state organizations.[68]
- *Military-industrial complex.* As in Russia, former defence enterprises have become involved in the manufacture of civilian products requiring sophisticated know-how and technology. About half of China's motorcycles, 30 per cent of colour TVs, and 10 per cent of minivans are produced by converted military plants. The military sector is now able to produce 50 major categories of civilian products thus providing selective entry opportunities also for foreign TNCs.[69]

Most leading western, Japanese and South Korean TNCs have become insiders in China through FDI. Medium-sized TNCs are also looking at possibilities of participating in the expanding Chinese economy.

Chinese consumers, who were isolated from the rest of the world, can now purchase international brands in modern food and nonfood retail outlets across the country. They have a wide choice of goods ranging from beer, cosmetics, detergents and sportswear to cars, mobile phones, hardware and consumer electronics. Most of them are manufactured locally by joint ventures or wholly-owned subsidiaries of TNCs, unlike Russia where most are imported.

FDI has contributed to industrial diversification at the regional level,[70] and many coastal and interior provinces have developed competitive

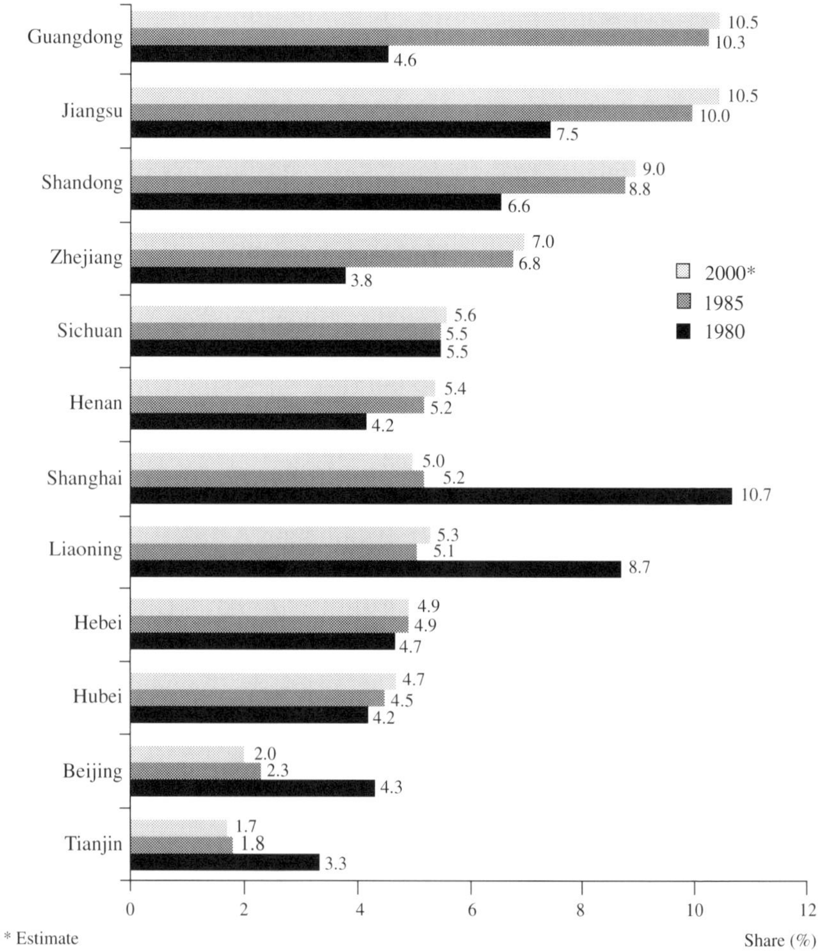

Source: State Statistical Bureau of the PRC, *A Statistical Survey of China*, 1998.

Figure 5.20 Economic weight of leading interior and coastal regions in industrial production, China, 1980, 1995, 2000

industries. Thus, the formerly isolated and neglected provinces of Anhui, Fujian and Guanxi each increased their share in national industrial production from around 1 per cent in 1980 to 3–4 per cent by 1997 (Figure 5.20). The three main cities of Beijing, Tianjin and Shanghai, however, have seen their importance diminish considerably since the country was opened to FDI (Beijing, from 4.5 per cent to 2 per cent; Tianjin, from 3.2 per cent to 1.7 per cent; Shanghai, from 11 per cent to 5 per cent). Decentralization has also occurred in services (e.g. finance, transport and distribution). The growing role of the regions is also reflected in the declining share of the large cities in national GDP (Figure 5.21). In 1997, only about 7 per cent of national income was generated by the three large metropolitan areas of Beijing, Shanghai and Tianjin (compared with a combined share of about 26 per cent in the late 1970s).[71]

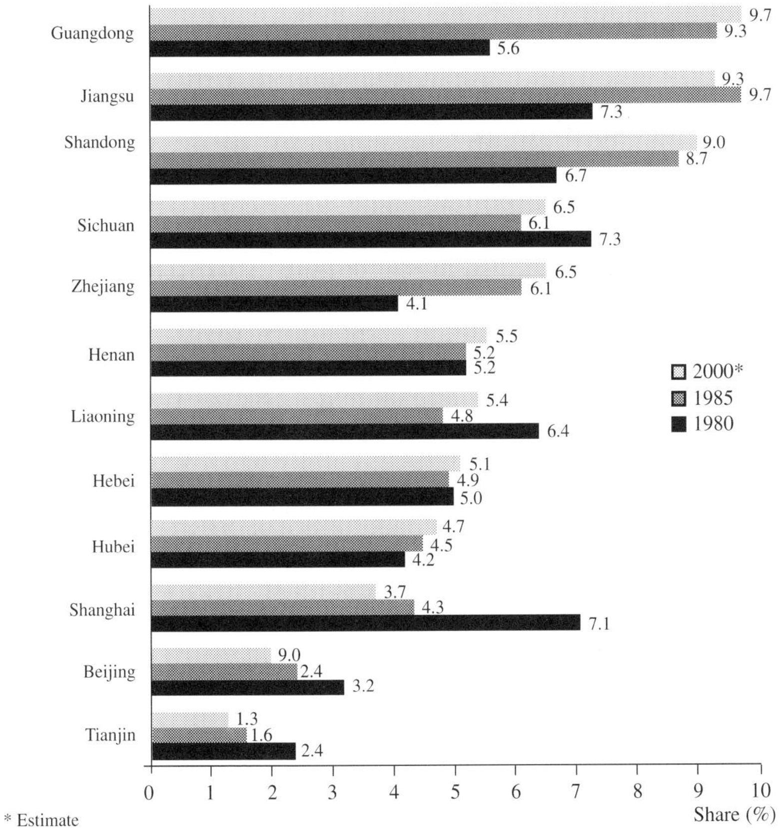

Source: State Statistical Bureau of the PRC, *A Statistical Survey of China*, 1998.

Figure 5.21 Economic weight of leading interior and coastal regions in GDP, China, 1980, 1995, 2000

China has so far been quite successful in diversifying FDI inflows on a sectoral and regional basis by delegating responsibilities to local bodies while maintaining firm central control over general policy issues which have wide-ranging macroeconomic impacts. China's overall FDI policy is coordinated by the Ministry of Foreign Trade and Economic Cooperation (MOFTEC) while regional governments (e.g. Guangdong, Shanghai, Tianjin) have increased their autonomy for carrying out their own promotion measures and offering adequate incentives.[72]

India provides a second case of regional and sectoral diversification through FDI, owing to the broad sectoral diversification of its economy in the first place, but also because its States (e.g. Maharashtra, Gujarat, Andhra Pradesh, Tamil Nadu, Karnataka) enjoy broad autonomy in FDI promotion and approval procedures.[73] Both China and India provide interesting examples of how FDI could help develop industries in the main regional markets of the Russian Federation and therefore warrant further analysis by Russia's FDI authorities.

Annex 5.1 Catalogue for the guidance of foreign investment industries, China, 1997–2002[74]

A: Encouraged foreign investment industries

I. Agriculture, forestry, animal husbandry, fishery and related industries
(e.g. Reclaiming and development of waste land; development of new, high-yielding varieties; reforestation; animal and fish production; safe agricultural chemicals including fertilizers; insecticides; storage and conservation technologies; agricultural machinery; water control and irrigation projects – the Chinese party will be the holding party or play a leading role).

II. Light industry
(e.g. Paper pulp, batteries, sewing machines, enzymes, freon substitutions).

III. Textile industry
(e.g. Synthetic fibres, special textiles, printing and dyeing).

IV. Communication and transportation, post and telecommunications services
(e.g. Locomotives and equipment for locomotives, equipment for highways, ports and city subways, construction and management of civil airports, digital telecommunication transmission equipment).

V. Coal industry

VI. Power industry
(e.g. Thermal, hydro, nuclear, alternative energy power stations).

VII. Ferrous metallurgical industry
(e.g. Processing and treatment of steel scrap, smelting of stainless steel, aluminium).

VIII. Nonferrous metal industry
(e.g. Silicone, tin alloys, nonferrous composite materials, copper, lead, aluminium mining).

IX. Petroleum, petrochemical and chemistry industries
(e.g. Ethylene, plastics and plastics alloys, synthetic rubber, fine chemicals for dyes, electronics, paper; oil and gas delivery pipes).

X. Mechanical industry
(e.g. Welding robots, insulation material, mining equipment, offset printing machines, turbine compressors, environment protection detecting equipment, hydraulic and pneumatic equipment, city sewage disposal equipment, precision bearings, key spare parts and components for cars, trucks, motorcycles, equipment for water quality detection and flood prevention).

XI. Electronic instruments
(e.g. Integrated circuits, sensors, computers and peripheral hardware, semiconductors, home electronics, CAD/CAM CAE equipment, satellite communication and traffic control equipment, optic fibres, ISDN telephone systems).

XII. Building materials equipment and other nonmetal mineral product industries
(e.g. Special glass, ceramics, new building materials, dry process cement, glass fibres, high-class refractory material used in furnaces for glass, glass fibre and ceramics production, machines for road planning, tunnelling and repair).

XIII. Medicine industry
(e.g. Chemical medicines under patent and administrative protection, analgesics, vitamins, cardio-vascular medicines, contraceptives, biotechnologies, diagnosis reagents for hepatitis and AIDS and radio immunity).

XIV. Medical equipment industry
(e.g. X-ray machines, electronic endoscopes, special tubes).

XV. Aerospace industry
(e.g. Civilian aircraft and components including engines, civilian satellites).

XVI. New industries
(e.g. Microelectronics, new materials, bioengineering, information and communication technologies, laser, ocean technology, seawater desalination, energy saving and antipollution technologies).

XVII. Service business
(e.g. Business and engineering consulting, services for enterprise incubation).

XVIII. Permitted projects, whose products are to be wholly exported

B: Restricted foreign investment industries

I. Light industry
(e.g. Washing machines, refrigerators, freezers, small compressors, table salts, nonalcoholic beverages, millet wines and famous spirits, tobacco processing, pig, cow and sheep hides).

II. Textile industry
(e.g. Viscose staple fibre, wool and cotton spinning, raw silk, fibre and polyester).

III. Petroleum, petrochemical industries
(e.g. Refineries with output capacity of less than 5 million t a year).

IV. Communication and transportation, post and telecommunications services
(e.g. Construction of main railway lines, transportation by water, air freight, general aviation – in all these cases, the Chinese party must take a leading role).

V. Power industry
(e.g. Conventional coal-fired power plants).

VI. Nonferrous metal industry
(e.g. Copper and aluminium alloys, mining and smelting of precious metals, mining of tin and rare-earth metals).

VII. Chemical industries
(e.g. Sensitive materials, sulphuric acid, synthetic fibre raw materials, radial tyres).

VIII. Mechanical industry
(e.g. Complete automobiles, car and motorcycle engines, air conditioners, fire power and hydroelectric equipment, duplicators and cameras).

IX. Electronic industry
(e.g. Colour TVs, video cameras, video recorders and magnetic heads, magnetic drums and movements of video recorders, analogue-type mobile communications systems, wireless beeper call and telephone, receiving equipment of satellite navigation and key parts – wholly foreign-owned enterprises are not allowed).

X. Building material equipment and other nonmetal product industries
(e.g. Exploration, mining and processing of diamond and other natural gems – wholly foreign-owned enterprises are not allowed).

XI. Medicine industry
(e.g. Traditional Chinese herb medicines, penicillin G, production of addiction narcotic and psychoactive drugs – the Chinese party will be the holding party or play a leading role. Vaccines against AIDS, type-C hepatitis – the Chinese party will be the holding party or play a leading role. Immunity vaccines included in the State's plan, production of Vitamin C and blood products).

XII. Medical apparatus and instruments industry
(e.g. Disposable injections, blood transfusion systems and bags, large medical treatment equipment such as CT, MRI and accelerators for medical use).

XIII. Shipping industry
(e.g. Repairing, design and manufacture of special ships; manufacture of diesel engines for ships – the Chinese party must play a leading role).

XIV. Domestic and foreign trade, tourism, real estate and service industry
(e.g. Domestic commerce, foreign trade, tourist agencies, cooperative schools, medical establishments, accounting, audit and legal services, luxury hotels).

XV. Finance
(e.g. Banks, trusts, leasing, insurance; wholesale and retail of gold, silver, gems and jewellery).

XVI. Miscellaneous
(e.g. Printing, publishing, testing and attestation of imported goods, video production and distribution).

C: Prohibited foreign investment industries

I. Agriculture, forestry, animal husbandry, fishery and related industries
(e.g. Wild animal and plant resources protected by the State, rare precious breeds, animal and plant natural reserves, processing of green and other special teas).

II. Light industry
(e.g. Ivory carving and tiger-bone processing, handmade carpets, lacquerware and enamel products, blue and white porcelain, Xuan paper, and ingot-shaped tablets of Chinese ink).

III. Power industry and urban public utility
(e.g. Construction and management of electricity networks, urban networks of water supply, water drainage, gas and thermal power).

IV. Exploration, processing of mining industry
(e.g. Smelting or processing of radioactive mineral products).

V. Petroleum industry, petrochemical industry and chemical industry
(e.g. Mining and processing of szaibelyite and celestine).

VI. Medicine industry
(e.g. Traditional Chinese medicines that have been listed, preparing techniques of traditional Chinese medicine in small pieces ready for decoction and products based on secret recipes).

VII. Transportation, and post and telecommunications service
(e.g. Post and telecommunications, air traffic control).

VIII. Trade and finance
(e.g. Commodity and financial futures, derivatives).

IX. Broadcasting and film industries
(e.g. Broadcasting and TV stations, launching and relay stations, film and video tape production and projection).

X. Journalism

XI. Manufacturing industry of weapons

XII. Miscellaneous
(e.g. Projects that endanger the safety and performance of military facilities; developing and processing of carcinogenic, teratogenic, and mutagenesis raw materials; race course, gambling, pornographic service).

XIII. Other industries prohibited by the State or by international treaties China has signed

Notes

1. China's economic policy is based on wide-ranging planning mechanisms to achieve set investor targets.
2. Lack of confidence is a major reason why most FDI still originates from overseas Chinese operators and large multinationals, but less from medium-sized TNCs.
3. Especially large TNCs.
4. Many interior regions remain undersupplied in technologies and know-how.
5. Chapter 5.4.
6. Chapters 3.3, 6 and 7.
7. Chapter 5.3.4.
8. Chapter 5.3.
9. Deng Xiaoping died at the age of 92 just before Hong Kong's integration into China in July 1997.
10. These joint ventures are based on simple agreements between the two parties without equity arrangements. See also Chapter 5.4.1.
11. Chapter 5.4.
12. J. H. Dunning, *Foreign Direct Investment and Governments. Catalysts for Economic Restructuring*, 1996.
13. Chapter 5.3, Figure 5.7.
14. Chapter 5.3.2.
15. The Chinese leadership places a special emphasis on social*ist* as compared to the social market economies in western Europe.
16. X. Zhang, *in* J. H. Dunning, *Foreign Direct Investment and Governments*, 1996, pp. 380–422.
17. UNCTAD, *World Investment Reports 1995, 1996, 1997.*
18. L. Brahm, *Red Capital. Hong Kong '97. China Money Takes Center Stage*, 1997, pp. 43–4.
19. *Ibid.*, pp. 59–66.
20. Powerful banks and insurance companies, such as the Bank of China, China Agriculture Bank, China Industry and Commerce Bank and The People's Insurance Company of China are excluded from the list.
21. As with Japan, trading houses played a fundamental role in China's economic development. Although this study focuses on industry, this aspect should not be overlooked by Russian policy-makers.
22. Altogether, there are about 700 listed companies in China (India: 5850; Brazil: 590; Mexico and Russia: both around 200). For China, see also *Asian Business*, 'The Thorn in China's Side', June 1998, pp. 34–35.
23. Chapter 5.5.2.
24. R. L. Nicholas, *China in the World Economy*, Institute for International Economics, 1994.
25. UNCTAD, *World Investment Report 1998*.
26. Together with Hong Kong, inward Chinese FDI stock today amounts to about US$250 billion. See Chapter 3.3.
27. Chapter 5.4.
28. However, lower than expected economic growth in 1999 combined with low average return on equity (3.1 per cent) of foreign-funded companies is likely to curtail FDI inflows by 10 to 15 per cent. *The Economist*, 'China's private surprise', 19 June 1999, pp. 89–90.

29. About 200 of the top 500 US TNCs have a stake in the Chinese economy. It is the objective of the government to attract the remaining 300 in the coming five years. See MOFTEC, *China Economic News*, no. 43, 10 November 1997.
30. MOFTEC, *China Economic News*, no. 43, 10 November 1997.
31. F. Zhaokui, 'Review of China's Foreign Capital Introduction', *China Newsletter*, no. 131, vol. 6, 1998.
32. Chapter 5.4.
33. Chapter 5.4.2.
34. Chapter 1.9.
35. UNCTAD, *World Investment Report 1995*, p. 56.
36. According to the US-based Association of Chinese Investors, about 400 Chinese TNCs have established branches in the United States. These companies currently hold more than US$60 million in US treasury bills. See MOFTEC, *China Economic News*, no. 43, 10 November 1997.
37. See Annex 5.1.
38. Chapter 9.4.2.
39. Annex 5.1.
40. Large municipalities focus FDI promotion for high-tech industries with a strong research component as well as modern financial services, retailing and hotel development.
41. T. Meng *et al, Business Opportunities in the Yangtse River Delta*, 1996, pp. 91–127.
42. Usually, US$30 million for larger cities, but this level is constantly being adjusted upwards as municipalities become more autonomous.
43. Chapter 2.4.
44. In the 1960s agriculture accounted for 35–40 per cent of GDP.
45. The PPP measure takes into account local price structures and allows more realistic inter-country comparisons.
46. Equivalent of domestic investment.
47. In Russia, the share of agriculture in GDP is 9 per cent.
48. Austrian Trade Commission, *China Nachrichten*, March 1996.
49. Unemployment is estimated at 6 million for the 10 largest cities of China.
50. MOFTEC, *China Economic News*, no. 43, 10 November 1997. See also Chapter 5.5.3.
51. MOFTEC, *ibid.*
52. Chapter 5.3.2.
53. Including both domestic and foreign investment.
54. OECD Economic Survey, *Russian Federation*, 1997, p. 245.
55. W. Lihong, *China Business Weekly*, 24–30 August 1997, no. 5269 p. 8.
56. BfaI, *Wirtschaftsdaten zur Jahresmitte* [Mid-term economic indicators], 1997.
57. In 1996, the active population totalled 730 million, of whom 360 million in agriculture, 200 million in industry and 170 million in trading and other services. Together with mixed enterprises where the State retains significant equity, SOEs account for about 70 per cent of the active population in industry or 150 million people.
58. The budget deficit was 8.2 per cent in 1996 compared with 13.1 per cent in 1992.
59. Chapter 5.2.3.
60. Chapter 1.6.
61. *China Business Weekly*, no. 5269, 24–30 August 1997.

62. In 1997, exports amounted to US$183 billion and imports to US$142 billion.
63. The recent financial crash in Southeast Asia, which constitutes a major market for Chinese goods, may call for slight adjustments of this forecast.
64. During 1990–97, the United Kingdom was the most important European investing nation.
65. Austrian Trade Commission, *China Nachrichten*, 1996, 1997.
66. Communicated by a MOFTEC source.
67. Two of the world's leading hypermarket operators, Wal-Mart (United States) and Carrefour (France), have intensified their presence in China despite a still unfavourable legislative environment. See also *Le Point*, 'La guerre Wal-Mart–Carrefour' [The war between Wal-Mart and Carrefour], 19–26 December 1998, p. 81.
68. Agricultural production is also an economic development priority in Russia. Considering current difficulties (e.g. transport and warehousing problems, obsolete machinery, lack of capital and training) following the disintegration of former *sovkhoz* and *kolkhoz*, the Chinese example may be worth monitoring. The role of FDI in farm modernization and restructuring, and small enterprise development at central and regional level should also be studied.
69. *China Daily*, 2 August 1997.
70. Chapter 5.3.2.
71. JETRO, *China Newsletter*, no. 132, 1998.
72. Small and medium-range investment projects up to US$30 million are decided directly by city councils or regional governments. Approval by the federal State Council is required when foreign investments exceed US$100 million. See also MOFTEC, *China Economic News*, no. 45, 24 November 1997.
73. Chapter 6.
74. Approved by the State Council on 29 December 1997 and promulgated by the State Planning Commission, the State Economic and Trade Commission and the Ministry of Foreign Trade and Economic Cooperation on 31 December 1997.

6
FDI Policies and Prospects in India

Map 6.1 India

6.1 Competitive advantages and lessons for Russia

6.1.1 India's future assets

In terms of population (981 million in 1999), India represents the second largest market in the world after China. Healthy growth and a steadily rising GDP (US$420 billion by 1999 and approximately 6 per cent annual growth during 1995–98) will eventually propel India into the top league of nations. If measured in purchasing power parities, India's national product already ranks fifth in the world, after the United States, Japan, Germany and China. Although per capita GDP is still lower than in China, personal disposable income has risen rapidly since 1991 and will double that of the 1990s over the coming decade. Consumption patterns of middle- and upper-class Indians are also shifting towards those of industrialized countries, particularly in urban areas where pre-1990s family values are giving way to individualism, self-expression and spontaneity (Table 6.1).[1]

Table 6.1 Number of people and households by income class, India, 1997

	Number of people	Number of households	Average annual income (US$)
The super rich	39 000	6 500	over 100 000
The sheer rich	144 000	24 000	50 000–100 000
The clearly rich	444 000	74 000	25 0 00–50 000
The near rich	1.55 million	250 000	10 000–25 000
The strivers	25 million	5 million	below 10 000
The climbers	45 million	8 million	
The aspirants	120 million	20 million	
The deprived	763 million	131 million	

Source: NCAER 1998.

India offers another important attraction – a significant share of the population is young (57 per cent are under 24 years), guaranteeing long-term business opportunities for foreign investors. Against the background of an ageing population in western economies and Japan, the large proportion of young people in emerging markets represents, for many companies, a tremendous potential not only for consumer products, but also for high-quality brands, high-tech goods (e.g. computers, telecommunications) and modern services (e.g. retailing, insurance, information and travel).

One of the country's main assets is its vast pool of highly qualified professionals,[2] and India's worldwide leadership in software engineering and information technologies among emerging countries can be largely attributed to their contribution. Most *Fortune 500*[3] software and electronics companies have established a base in the 'Silicon Valley' of Bangalore and, more recently, in Hyderabad.[4] Some, like AT&T, IBM, Intel, Microsoft and Motorola, have opened their own R&D facilities and training centres in the country. Worldwide booking services via satellite for a number of airlines such as Lufthansa and United Airlines are hosted in India.[5] The Indian government has understood the importance of attracting TNCs specializing in information and communication technologies and biotechnology, which will contribute to its objective of making India a world leader in these knowledge-based sectors.

During the past 50 years, India has further strengthened its higher education structure to meet its growing need for competent managerial, research and technical skills. The six Indian Institutes of Technology (IITs) and four Indian Institutes of Management (IIMs) have earned a worldwide reputation for excellence in their identified areas of specialization,[6] and their alumni are sought by TNCs in India and other countries. India's success in technical education already has a far reaching impact, and it demonstrates – as in Germany, Japan and South Korea – the importance of an intensive education policy as a strategic support for FDI.[7]

Underpinning these achievements are India's democratic tradition and entrepreneurial spirit. Private enterprises represent about 70 per cent of industry, and the country's 23 stock exchanges are evidence of the high degree of capitalization.[8] India's industrial houses have built vast empires over the decades and are now preparing to meet TNC competition in India and abroad. Among the well-known corporate groups are Tata, Ambani (Reliance), Bajaj, Birla, Goenka, Khaitan, Murugappa, Mittal, to name a few. Foreign investors find a diverse industrial structure, a mature entrepreneurial culture and a business milieu that needs no initiation. The private sector today covers all products and services required by the market from steel, cars and travel services to toothpaste; state-owned enterprises are concerned mainly with heavy industries, public services and infrastructure. Internally, the market was always open: before liberalization operators also competed for market share and consumers had a large choice of goods and services, even if competition was less fierce than when foreign TNCs made their entry in 1991.

As a corollary, India also has a vast private retail and wholesale network, and this represents both a support and a challenge to new entrants. Modern formats are emerging both in nonfood and food retailing, but the process is slow in inner city areas where space has become a problem. The supermarket concept has been successful mainly in southern (Bangalore, Chennai) and, to a certain extent, western (Gujarat) India, but it is spreading elsewhere as well. Distribution is a key factor of success and is often the main reason why TNCs seek a local joint venture partner.[9]

Private enterprise in manufacturing and retailing is perhaps India's main competitive advantage over other LEMs, which have yet to recover from sudden privatization (Russia) or are in the midst of state enterprise restructuring (China).

Further advantages for foreign investors are the widespread use of English as the working language and the country's geographic proximity to the markets of the Middle East, South Asia and Southeast Asia. Unlike China and Russia, which are still losing academics and specialists to foreign countries owing to a seemingly unstoppable brain drain, Indian émigrés are returning to the subcontinent, attracted by special incentives given to NRIs (non-resident Indians).[10] They also appreciate the government's efforts to reduce the country's two main weaknesses: inadequate infrastructure including telecommunications and a slow and unwieldy bureaucracy which, if improved, will accelerate growth considerably.

In addition to these factors, India has vast mineral and agricultural resources – the key inputs for its industries. It ranks first worldwide in tea and milk production; second for rice, wheat, groundnut and vegetables; and third for cotton, tobacco and fruit. This agricultural diversity makes it an attractive destination for FDI in food processing.

6.1.2 India's policy challenges and achievements

A major challenge before the Indian government is to sustain a minimum GDP growth rate of 5–6 per cent per annum, which will ensure a gradual improvement of general living standards and income levels. Economic growth must necessarily exceed the rate at which the population is increasing.[11] Economic policy aims to control fiscal deficit (currently at 5 per cent of GDP) and to push forward important reform projects (e.g. privatization of public sector units or state-owned corporations, development of infrastructure, streamlining of public services, review of obsolete laws including patent and labour laws, and land ownership limits or ceilings).

The Indian government introduced radical changes when it shifted to a more market-oriented economy in 1991. Stimulated by China's success,[12] the objective of the New Industrial Policy (NIP)[13] was to enhance the competitiveness of domestic industries through transfer of foreign technology and capital. The policy abolished the restrictive system of industrial licences except in 18 'sensitive' industries; these licences were earlier required for starting any business. The number of sectors reserved exclusively for the public sector was reduced from 17 to 6 during 1991–98,[14] and automatic approval was granted for foreign equity participation up to 51 per cent in 34 sectors that account for 50 per cent of the value-added in manufacturing. Since then, the equity limit has been raised and the number of sectors has been increased. Equity and debt markets were also opened to foreign investment institutions with certain controls and regulations.[15]

Economic liberalization in India was the outcome of international political and economic changes. Various external circumstances like the Gulf crisis and the collapse of the Soviet Union (one of India's main trading partners) provoked a balance of payments crisis. The World Bank and IMF intervened but imposed conditions that led the Indian government to liberalize the economy. As a signatory to the WTO agreement, India must remove quantitative restrictions and tariff barriers to imports. It is also committed to aligning its intellectual property laws to international regulations.

The NIP received a mixed reaction from the business community. While it welcomed the abolition of industrial licences, it was apprehensive about the opening of the Indian market to foreign TNCs. After decades of isolation during which they benefited from a protected market, Indian companies have to face competition from abroad. As in Russia, large groups exert pressure on the government to prevent hostile take-overs by foreign TNCs.[16] Consumers and industrial users have, however, benefited from a wider choice, innovative and new products, better quality and lower prices. The media also favours more open policies, although business practices of certain foreign corporations have been severely criticized.

Post-1991 budgets presented by successive governments (from different political parties – Congress, United Front, Bharatiya Janata Party) have sought to strike a balance between socioeconomic exigencies, pressure from local business lobbies to protect their markets ('level playing field' for both foreign and domestic enterprises), and external pressures to hasten economic reforms. Each budget and subsequent policy amendments have all aimed to further open the economy and facilitate FDI, particularly in sectors like infrastructure (energy, telecommunications, roads, railways, airports, ports), which have to be urgently upgraded to meet the growing needs of industry. All political parties unanimously recognize the need to pursue economic reforms and integration with global markets, although their proposed measures may differ. Proposals for improvement generally range from deregulation aimed at higher competition through FDI to selective protectionism in favour of Indian industry.

Since independence India has always pursued a well-defined strategy of industrialization. But only when the NIP was adopted in 1991, did the Indian government decide to achieve industrial aims through a more liberal policy based on a number of new measures: industry-specific foreign equity ceilings, export obligations and dividend balancing, an accelerated approval procedure, as well as special tax and other incentives for TNCs and export-oriented units (EOUs). Pillar or core industries are closely monitored against development targets established in five-year economic plans. Compared with China, India's approach is less interventionist and based mainly on indicative targets to be followed by industry and other economic operators.

The government constituted the Foreign Investment Promotion Board (FIPB) in 1991 to institutionalize FDI-related decisions within a central agency.[17] It serves as a single-window clearance agency for FDI proposals and is responsible for investment promotion. It has wide-ranging powers and has the flexibility to negotiate with foreign investors. As a recommendatory body, it advises government on FDI policies by identifying sectors where investment is needed in keeping with the five-year plan. That the FIPB was initially integrated in the Prime Minister's Office shows the importance given by the government to FDI. Today, its decisions on investment proposals are communicated through the Secretariat for Industrial Assistance (SIA) in the Ministry of Industry. The FIPB can also co-opt representatives from various ministries and government bodies because each proposal is vetted by the ministry corresponding to the specified activity. The success of the FIPB in gaining recognition within and outside India is proof of the relevance of a strong agency for channelling investments and technologies into targeted sectors.

The central bank, the Reserve Bank of India (RBI), was given the power to approve proposals for less than 74 per cent foreign equity.[18] Yet, although the scope of this mechanism has been widened, nearly 90 per cent of investment inflows have been channelled through the FIPB because foreign investors prefer a government authorization. Often, they opt for a direct clearance for 100 per cent equity although they may subsequently dilute their share. The Indian government attempts to orient FDI not only into projects that are considered beneficial to the Indian economy, but also to less-developed regions in an effort to distribute wealth evenly in the country. Decision-making at two levels – central and state governments – may have delayed certain projects, but on the whole it has been favourable to a more balanced economic development.

The government also launched the 100 per cent export-oriented units (EOUs) scheme for companies that export their entire production. These units are located mostly in export processing zones (EPZs) where production is organized on an internationally competitive basis with requisite infrastructure and duty-free imports. (There are six such zones: two in the west, one in the north, two in the south, and one in the east of the country.) Special incentives are offered such as exemption from customs duties on imported raw materials and components; no licence requirement for import of capital goods; exemption from central excise duty (tax on production) on products manufactured within the zone; complete tax holiday for a period of five years; exemption from tax on export earnings after the tax holiday; and simplification of procedures.

During 1991–97, several special EPZs and sector-oriented technology parks (e.g., electronics hardware, software technology, food processing) were created or expanded across the subcontinent (e.g. the cities of Bangalore, Chennai, Mumbai and New Delhi; the states of Andhra Pradesh, Gujarat, Karnataka and Kerala). Lately, Indian authorities have stepped up their public relations efforts overseas. Special budgets are allocated for trade and investment promotion officers, who are seconded to Indian embassies in the leading European and selected Pacific Rim countries including Australia, Japan and the United States. Information material on economic, sectoral and regional trends in the country and on

Doing Business with India is widely disseminated through the Indian embassies. Seminars and image-enhancement workshops are organized in the leading G7 countries in collaboration with local chambers of commerce and multilateral organizations like UNIDO. Chief Ministers of the different state governments, accompanied by high-level business delegations, periodically visit industrialized countries to promote their own state. The powerful Indian employers' association, the Confederation of Indian Industry (CII), has established representative offices in various countries to inform and advise potential foreign investors and also to assist CII's members in developing business outside India.

These efforts have already led to a better understanding and perception abroad of business prospects in India. Increased political dialogue and economic integration have also led to new trade and investment initiatives between India and a number of other emerging countries in Africa, Asia and Latin America. In Asia, Indian representatives are invited as dialogue partners to major summits and regional forums (e.g. ASEAN, APEC).

Although India opened its market only a decade ago, its performance is comparable to that of other countries during their first years of liberalization. Today, India fulfils all the conditions for becoming an attractive LEM for inward FDI. A closer look at India's new approach to FDI can yield valuable information to Russian policy-makers. Of particular relevance is the combining of instruments and incentives in a comprehensive policy package for reshaping priority branches of national industry and simultaneously activating the small business sector. Indian policy-makers systematically focus their efforts on approving investments that involve the transfer of useful technologies for the country's long-term socioeconomic development, particularly in rural areas.

Russian policy-makers should therefore study the functioning of India's FDI policy and its implications for other policy domains. They should also observe modifications and changes in the functioning of the FIPB in future years. Russia could adopt some of the winning features of India's approval system: a strong central institution, sector-oriented guidelines for foreign investors and a commitment to speedy delivery (the FIPB is committed to take binding decisions within six weeks of the application). Combined with appropriate promotional measures abroad, such a systemic approach could constitute a first basis for improving the FDI situation in Russia.

6.2 Foreign investment policy in preliberalization India

6.2.1 Prime Minister Nehru's socialist course and policy of self-reliance

After almost a century of colonial rule, India's first concern on gaining independence in 1947 was to safeguard its autonomy. For the economy, this concern translated as self-reliance and import substitution. The main idea was to seek a third way of economic development between the rigidly planned systems of the Soviet Union or China, and the 'free-for-all' capitalist system of the United States. The new economic systems being shaped in western Europe, especially in France, Germany and the United Kingdom, were considered better models for emulation.[19] Foreign policy was based on the principle of nonalignment,[20] which rejected association with either of the two blocs formed by the Soviet Union and the United States during the Cold War. This policy implied an independent path of socioeconomic development by nurturing competitive domestic industries with an initial focus on heavy industry (e.g. steel, metallurgy, chemicals, transport equipment).

Although India adopted a socialist system of economic planning, it did not compromise on its founding principles of democracy, political pluralism and rule of law. Civil liberties were respected and private entrepreneurship was encouraged. This distinguishes India most from many other emerging countries in Asia, which often preferred more authoritarian one-party rule, government intervention and nationalization of crucial means of production.

In keeping with the principle of self-reliance, the first five-year plan (1951–56) emphasized agriculture, irrigation, energy and transport to provide the necessary infrastructure for future expansion of industry. The second plan (1956–61) focused on heavy industries, including chemicals and defence. The industrial policy was amended to shift the primary responsibility of development to the public sector. Consumer industries were left to the private sector. India's development programme had attracted attention abroad and it received support from the Soviet Union, the United Kingdom and Germany for setting up three steel plants. At this time, several large European companies also established themselves in India. The companies of the first FDI wave included ABB, Bayer, Cadbury, Glaxo, Hoechst, Larsen & Toubro, Philips, Rhône-Poulenc, Siemens and Unilever, which are mostly perceived positively as 'Indian' companies even today.

Despite its nonaligned stance, India developed a privileged relationship with the Soviet Union, which was also India's main trading partner and supplier of defence technologies. Ideological differences did not affect relations between the two countries. Many joint projects in heavy engineering, science and defence were undertaken until the collapse of the Soviet Union.

In the 1960s and 1970s, the government gradually turned its attention to industrial sectors closer to consumption: light engineering, food, apparel, leather, sports goods, hardware and tools. Domestic production was encouraged and, even today, many Indian companies excel in these areas through well-established brands.[21] India's success in agro-industry and food production is most remarkable. Following two decades of poor harvests and food shortages due to poor monsoon rains and inefficient distribution, India finally managed to successfully implement its 'green revolution' by the late 1970s. Today, India is not only able to feed its people, but it has become a competitive exporter of agricultural commodities and food products and beverages to the Middle East, the neighbouring SAARC,[22] Southeast Asian and other countries. Besides agriculture and industry, important efforts were directed at education and research. Institutions providing general and technical education were upgraded, and significant public investments were channelled into research establishments.

In accordance with the principle of self-reliance, a complex licensing system was established in the 1960s which limited FDI to those industries that lacked the capacity to meet demand and targets set by the five-year plans. Indian authorities, however, remained suspicious of western multinationals and imposed wide ranging restrictions for many years. TNCs were expected to transfer know-how through licences or to accept a minority shareholding in operations controlled by Indian firms. Companies with foreign participation were supposed to be export-oriented, except those in high-tech industries or other priority sectors.

The Indian government steered industrial development by maintaining control over strategic sectors (infrastructure, heavy industries, defence), foreign trade and investment. However, internally, the economic system was largely based on free allocation of factors of production and open competition between economic agents. Foreign collaborations were not completely ignored as technology and investments were needed to accelerate development. The India Investment Centre (IIC) was set up as early as 1961, with offices in leading industrialized countries to foster inter-enterprise cooperation.[23] The Foreign Investment Board[24] was created within the government in 1968 to handle all cases involving FDI up to 40 per cent of equity.

6.2.2 The shift towards an open economy under Prime Minister Rajiv Gandhi

Throughout the 1960s and 1970s, nationalization of strategic sectors (banking, insurance, petroleum) and a strong emphasis on import substitution enabled Indian authorities to protect fledgling businesses and to develop a diversified industrial base. The complex licence system made it difficult for any foreign company to have its own manufacturing facilities in India. Large US multinationals like Coca-Cola and IBM had to withdraw in the late 1970s because of unfavourable framework conditions and the openly anti-FDI stance of then Prime Minister Indira Gandhi.

Import substitution – a policy that would be difficult to implement in this age of growing economic interchange and globalization – in those days enabled the building of strong indigenous industries. Leading Indian industrial houses (e.g. Bajaj, Birla, Goenka, Mittal, Reliance, Tata) have grown into 'national champions' with plants spread across the country and, increasingly, a presence in selected foreign markets.[25] Their brands enjoy an excellent reputation across India and among nonresident Indians (NRIs) abroad. These companies are family-owned and the fact that they decide on thousands of jobs has made them privileged advisors to the government.

But towards the mid-1980s the 'Indian model' had become inadequate and could not respond to the challenges of the international environment. Countermeasures were needed to stop the economic downturn and reduce the country's isolation. The first visible sign of change was the Maruti or people's car project proposed by Sanjay Gandhi. A foreign collaborator was sought for the project and an agreement was signed with Japanese car-maker Suzuki. Western TNCs again took an interest in Indian industry. Most foreign chemicals, drug and pharmaceuticals companies that had been exporting to India began to set up manufacturing subsidiaries on the subcontinent. The share of manufacturing in FDI stock jumped from 20 per cent just after independence to 68 per cent in 1974 and 85 per cent in 1990.[26] Food and beverages, vehicles (automobiles, trucks, scooters, motor-cycles), optical equipment, chemicals, pharmaceuticals and electrical goods industries were major FDI recipients during this period.

However, FDI for collaboration projects was still heavily regulated. Foreign parent companies had to first study a complex set of rules, which varied with the industry, for royalty payments, contract duration, or renewals of technology transfer agreements. Restrictions were applied to FDI proposals that were not accompanied by significant technology transfer and oriented towards nonpriority industries. Foreign TNCs and their Indian partners were also expected to work with Indian consultancy firms for setting up new plants or for carrying out collaborative technical projects. Through these early projects, Indian authorities acquired experience in adjusting FDI policies to the needs of Indian industry and in implementing them through a powerful institution advising the government on FDI.

When Rajiv Gandhi became prime minister in 1984, conditions for foreign investors were further relaxed, although the declared objective to preserve a high degree of self-reliance through protection of national industries still influenced policy measures. Globalization and trade liberalization could no longer be ignored and authorities became more receptive to new projects presented by TNCs as they were considered vital for long-term industrial modernization based on a combination of technology, management and global market access.

In 1988, a fast channel was set up for expediting clearance of FDI proposals from major investing countries: Germany, Japan, the United Kingdom and the United States. Towards the late 1980s, FDI reached levels that marked India's readiness to shift away from its earlier mixed economy towards a free market policy.

6.3 India's New Industrial Policy: economic reorientation through FDI

The collapse of the Soviet Union, India's major trading and defence partner, seriously dented India's foreign trade and foreign exchange reserves. Simultaneously, the Gulf conflict caused a balance of payments crisis as remittances from Indian workers in Kuwait and Saudi Arabia stopped. In mid-1991, foreign reserves sank to an all time low[27] and a drastic remedy was called for; 25 t of gold were moved to London to raise a loan. The government put a structural readjustment programme into action, which finally opened the economy through the New Industrial Policy (NIP).

Economic liberalization revealed new opportunities in India for foreign investors. US TNCs, with PepsiCo in the vanguard, were among the first to seize the opportunity. India's close relationship with the Soviet Union had been an obstacle for the United States, which had based its South Asia policy on amicable relations with Pakistan. The end of the East–West cold war allowed Indian policy-makers to extend their partnership to major economies in the East and West.

FDI enhancement represents an essential component in the government's multipronged approach to reorient and develop domestic industry, to liberalize foreign trade and capital markets, and to stimulate the economy by reducing state assets in a number of industries. The NIP also introduced broad tax reforms and removed foreign exchange controls. Although a protectionist mentality still persists,[28] economic reforms are unanimously considered an irreversible process by all major political factions.

In its 1997 budget, the United Front, a coalition of 14 parties that succeeded Congress, sought to ease the fiscal burden on companies in an attempt to stimulate growth. The BJP budget of 1998, despite certain nationalist overtones, sought to simplify procedures which it considers the main constraint to industrial growth. The government also plans to open the insurance and banking sectors to private players and foreign companies.[29] In industry, the focus will remain on high-tech and infrastructure-related sectors. Also in trading (including retailing), further liberalization is expected as India has agreed to remove restrictions on imports and reduce customs tariffs in compliance with WTO regulations.

One of the ways in which successive governments since 1991 have tried to open the market is by dereserving the small-scale sector. In India, several industries, mainly for consumer goods, are reserved exclusively for this sector. Foreign equity for such units cannot exceed 24 per cent and the investment limit is less than US$1 million. When an industry is 'dereserved', it is opened to large-scale, including foreign, investment as in any other sector – this is an indirect way for allowing FDI. Since 1991, several industries including branches of the food processing, textiles, leatherware and other consumer goods sectors have been dereserved. In general, the business community agrees that liberalization and the entry of TNCs have brought about many improvements (technological, managerial) and increased business opportunities. Many young Indian managers realize that alliances with western partners can be a winning strategy for staying competitive in the increasingly difficult world market. Even the main opponents to rapid economic reforms, the industrial families like Bajaj of the Bombay Club, are not averse to technical collaborations with foreign companies. The lowering of customs tariffs for raw materials, components, and equipment is also beneficial to them and other domestic companies.

The business community is represented through chambers of commerce, associations and federations. (Membership is not automatic as in many European countries.) The chambers and federations have been in existence since independence. The three main bodies, the Confederation of Indian Industry (CII), the All-India Association of Chambers of Commerce (ASSOCHAM) and the Federation of Indian Chambers of Commerce and Industry (FICCI), form a powerful lobby at government level. The CII has begun to actively promote inter-enterprise cooperation and technology transfer through FDI in its seminars, one-to-one business meetings between Indian and foreign companies, and its increasing trade fair and exhibition activities in India and abroad.

Through FDI, India also hopes to move entirely away from aid to trade. In view of the limited resources of the public sector and the need to develop infrastructure and strengthen India's industrial base, there is a growing realization that only large inflows of foreign capital will meet these needs as domestic savings and multilateral aid will not be adequate. Infrastructure modernization alone is estimated to require investments of US$200 billion until the year 2000. The Indian Government aims to attract US$10 billion in foreign investment each year starting from 1999–2000, so that economic growth can be sustained at the recent rate of 6–7 per cent, given that industrial output has been growing at a favourable 11–12 per cent. Current FDI levels are lower than the target, but the number of approvals has risen by over 20 per cent compared with previous years.[30] The government is also tapping another source by offering numerous incentives to nonresident Indians (NRIs) so that they are more motivated to invest in their country. NRI investments account for 30 per cent of total FDI[31] and they have grown significantly since 1991.

The current FDI policy reflects the recognition that inbound investment is a catalyst for know-how transfer, higher foreign currency reserves, and integration in the global economy. FDI approval procedures have been simplified to reduce the response time. Incentive packages are offered, particularly in priority areas. Through its FDI policy, the Indian government seeks to further develop those industries that are essential for the country's economic growth (priority industries) and that have significant export potential. It also aims to build lasting structures in 'framework' sectors: infrastructure (energy, roads, telecommunications, ports, airports), machinery and equipment for all sorts of applications, chemicals and pharmaceuticals. Incentives for these industries are more substantial than, for example, for consumer goods sectors. Indian authorities also promote industries that help strengthen backward linkages with the agribusiness and farm sector (e.g. food processing).

Information technology, knowledge-intensive and infrastructure-related projects are preferred by the government. TNCs operating in these areas are offered advantageous conditions including direct financial support. As a supplementary measure, capital markets are being liberalized and are now recognized as vehicles to attract and retain capital of NRIs and international investment houses.

The Indian government is aware that India will have to compete strongly with other emerging economies to tap the necessary capital and expertise for bringing its industry and infrastructure in line with requirements of a modern economy in the twenty-first century.

6.3.1 Key organizations and procedures for FDI approvals

Approvals for FDI can be obtained through two routes:

- automatic approval by the central bank, the Reserve Bank of India (RBI);
- approval on a case-to-case basis by the Foreign Investment Promotion Board (FIPB).

Automatic approval by the RBI

Depending on the sector, automatic approval is given for foreign equity limits up to 50 per cent, 51 per cent, 74 per cent or 100 per cent. Approvals are given by the RBI within 15 days starting from the day of application. Lists of industries for each equity limit are presented in Annexure III of the NIP document. When the new rule was introduced, 35 high-priority industries were selected for automatic approval up to 51 per cent. In January 1997, the Cabinet reacted positively to the proposal of the Ministry of Industry to add 13 industries for equity up to 51 per cent, three industries for equity up to 50 per cent, and nine industries for equity up to 74 per cent.[32]

TNCs that opt for a higher shareholding than the prescribed limits of 50 per cent, 51 per cent or 74 per cent, have to apply to the FIPB. Companies that have already been granted automatic approval and that subsequently wish to bring in additional capital for the approved activities also have to apply to the FIPB, which would recommend such cases for automatic approval. The expanded list of industries eligible for automatic approval covers a wide range of sectors including electricity generation, transmission, and distribution; mining services; storage and warehousing services; machinery and equipment; metallurgy; instrumentation; chemicals; hotels and tourism; agricultural production and food processing; textiles; renting and leasing; business services; health services; non-conventional energy; and transport. National associations estimate that altogether industries benefiting from automatic approval account for 45–50 per cent of manufacturing output in India. More industries are being added to the list each year.

Automatic approval is granted to foreign majority holdings (up to 51 per cent) in trading companies primarily engaged in export activities. In this way, the Indian government intends to ease access to international markets. Foreign investors keen on raising their equity from a minority holding to a 51 per cent participation in an Indian firm as part of an expansion programme can also benefit from automatic clearance if the transaction does not take place in one of the few reserved sectors. In case of licensing arrangements, royalty payments of up to 5 per cent (8 per cent for export-oriented units) are also cleared through the RBI.

Nonresident Indians enjoy special treatment and receive automatic approval for 100 per cent equity investments in all the high-priority industries listed in Annexure III. These benefits are also extended to overseas corporate bodies (OCBs) in which NRIs hold at least 60 per cent equity. Proposals concerning other industries have to be addressed to the FIPB. Through this measure the Indian authorities hope that at least part of Indian assets abroad worth several hundreds of billions of dollars are directed to the mother country. Such measures are envisaged also by other emerging countries, which had suffered from significant brain drain and capital exports in the past (e.g. Brazil, China, Mexico and Russia).

The RBI cannot grant automatic approval for any items or activities reserved for the small-scale sector or for those that require industrial licence. TNCs operating in these sectors have to apply to the FIPB.

Case-by-case approval by the FIPB

Approval from the FIPB is required for all proposals that are not eligible for automatic approval by the RBI. This implies all proposals for foreign equity exceeding the prescribed limits of 50 per cent, 51 per cent or 74 per cent depending on the industry, and those for industries not mentioned in the government's list as well as those that require an industrial licence. High-priority and nonlisted industries (e.g. specialty drugs, cellular mobile phones) require special permissions which are granted on a case by case basis, following formal application by the foreign investor.

Increasingly, TNCs tend to submit proposals for 100 per cent equity participation to obtain a 'once and for all' clearance, although they may start with a simple majority of 51 per cent and raise their stake whenever appropriate at a later stage. Applications are submitted to the Secretariat of Industrial Assistance (SIA), which serves as the secretariat for the FIPB. Special forms were designed to facilitate administrative processing, but individually prepared applications carrying all relevant details about the TNC and its intentions in India are also accepted. In keeping with its objective of expeditious clearance, the FIPB is committed to convey its decision within six weeks of the application to the Board. The Board consults the administrative ministry for the specified industry before taking a decision. There have been cases of disagreement between the two which have caused inordinate delays. Decisions are also sometimes delayed because certain policy changes have not been cleared. Some of the laws that have become obsolete due to rapid changes in the economic and business environment can be changed only through acts of parliament.

FDI approvals are generally difficult to obtain for consumer goods including food and beverages, which are already being produced in sufficient quantities in the country. In such cases the investment may be prohibited or tied to certain conditions. For example, dividend payments to foreign majority stakeholders or parent firms must be balanced by export earnings over a period of seven years. Furthermore, foreign TNCs are supposed to help market the output generated in India to third parties or within their own integrated network of subsidiaries abroad. Foreign equity must cover all foreign exchange requirements for imports of capital goods and equipment.

The central role of the FIPB in FDI approval and promotion

The FIPB is a regulatory body that functions as an independent public agency. It was specially created to consolidate, monitor and promote the inflow of FDI into India. Its main role is also to study whether the proposed investments are beneficial to the Indian economy, to facilitate realization of foreign investments in India and to undertake investment promotion activities.

To guarantee fast-track approvals and to present a serious partner for TNCs, the FIPB was originally (1991) placed under direct supervision of the Prime Minister's Office. It used to be headed by the Principal Secretary to the Prime Minister. The Finance Secretary (Ministry of Finance), the Commerce Secretary (Ministry of Commerce), and the Secretary of the Department of Industrial Policy and Promotion (Ministry of Industry) were also members of the Board. In 1996, the FIPB was moved out of the jurisdiction of the Prime Minister's Office to that of the Department of Industrial Policy and Promotion in the Ministry of Industry. The Board now has the following composition:

- Chairman: Industry Secretary (Secretary, Department of Industrial Policy and Promotion), Government of India;
- Finance Secretary, Government of India;
- Commerce Secretary, Government of India;
- Secretary (Economic Relations), Ministry of External Affairs, Government of India;
- Other secretaries to the Government of India and top officials of financial institutions, banks, and professional experts on industry and commerce can be co-opted as and when necessary.

The FIPB has retained its main powers, especially its role of interministerial coordination, which ensures that each proposal is vetted by the respective ministry. This system prevents any subsequent revision of a decision by a ministry. Proposals and applications are systematically vetted by senior officials from the corresponding ministry. An FDI project that is related to the food industry, for example, will involve the Ministry of Food Processing. The FDI-related experience of the FIPB staff and the possibility of consultation with officials from other ministries, government departments and, increasingly, regional authorities enable the FIPB to carry out technical, commercial and financial analyses of all types of proposals.

For high investments, this procedure involves the collection of all relevant data and information to prepare a comprehensive, customized incentives package (tax reductions, removal of import duties for equipment and other essential components required during the initial phases of the investment).

By providing the FIPB with the necessary flexibility and authority, the Indian government has introduced a liberal, transparent and effective procedure aimed at enhancing FDI in the coming years. The FIPB employs experienced professionals with broad experience who can conduct purposeful negotiations with representatives of foreign companies. The FIPB has privileged access to highly placed policy-makers and officials in the capital and the major regional (state) governments. Information gathering and contact establishment are thus facilitated for investments that are made in the states. Moreover, the Secretary of the Department of Industrial Policy and Promotion, who chairs the FIPB, oversees the industrial policy and promotion matters.

The FIPB is closely linked to a special Investment Promotion and Monitoring Cell, which was set up by the Ministry of Industry in 1992. The Cell functions under the overall responsibility of the Minister and attends to inquiries from entrepreneurs concerning licensing, tariffs and duties, corporate taxation and company law. Nodal officers have been designated in other ministries and state bodies (Ministries of Finance and of Commerce, Reserve Bank of India, Indian Investment Centre). This facilitation Cell organizes meetings with the officers concerned at the investor's request, in particular when the investment is expected to have significant macro-economic and employment impact. It also provides foreign companies and their Indian counterparts with information on infrastructure facilities and FDI incentives offered by the various state (regional) governments for setting up businesses. State authorities are connected through a computerized database and information network which is coordinated by the National Informatics Centre (NIC). Upon request, the Cell monitors the status of an application, the progress of implementation and the disbursement of public grants for various projects, which it can communicate to investors and state authorities at any time.

The FIPB also liases closely with the Cabinet Committee on Foreign Investment (CCFI) and the Foreign Investment Promotion Council (FIPC), which were constituted in 1997 as supporting institutions to raise inbound FDI to US$10 billion a year. Members of the FIPC include the Ministry of Industry and the chairmen of the three leading business associations ASSOCHAM, CII and FICCI; it systematically targets companies in source countries for sectors where FDI is required.

In spite of the FIPB's privileged access to other political and private bodies (Figure 6.1), FDI clearance is as far as possible kept free from lobby pressures or similar considerations. Guidelines were set in January 1997 to ensure objective evaluation of proposals, and evaluation is based on factual information (technical, socioeconomic and environmental assessment of the investment). The main criteria established in the guidelines are: sector priority, with emphasis on infrastructure; export potential; employment potential, particularly in rural areas; links or backward integration with agribusiness or agriculture; social relevance (hospitals, human resource development, life-saving drugs and equipment); and the transfer of technology or capital. As a rule, no proposal is rejected without giving foreign investors clear reasons, and possibilities of adapting the project in

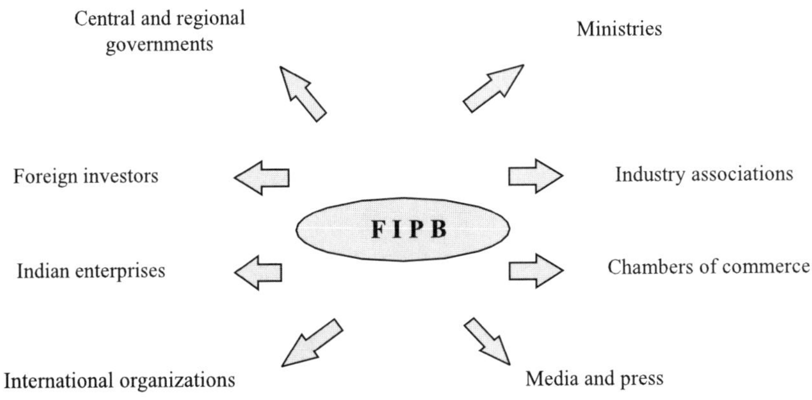

Figure 6.1 FIPB's privileged links, India

such a way that it is eventually approved are also indicated. This raises investor confidence and contributes to image enhancement in foreign countries.[33]

First actions consist in preparing sectoral profiles, on the basis of which selected foreign companies are to be approached on a branch or individual basis in the respective countries. Special site visits are also organized in India preceded by one-to-one dialogues with TNC board members to motivate them to invest in specific industries and regions. Upon request, the FIPB can recommend or mediate between the foreign investor and potential partner enterprises in India (Box 6.1).[34]

Box 6.1 Main responsibilities of the FIPB

- To ensure expeditious clearance of FDI proposals.
- To review periodically the implementation of proposals cleared by the Board.
- To review on a continuous basis the general and sectoral policy regimes relating to FDI, in consultation with administrative ministries and other concerned national and regional agencies, and develop a set of transparent guidelines.
- To undertake investment promotion activities including direct contacts with interested TNCs.
- To liase with related bodies, including those representing the Indian private sector (chambers of commerce, sectoral associations) and nongovernmental organizations.
- To identify sectors into which investments can be sought on the basis of national priorities and to keep in view specific world regions from which investment may be invited through special efforts.
- To undertake all relevant activities for promoting and facilitating FDI.
- To work closely with international organizations dealing with FDI issues.

By setting up the FIPB as an independent agency with broad political powers, the Indian government intends to expedite approval procedures and reduce bureaucratic delays.[35] The experience so far clearly shows the advantage of having a one-stop agency having the necessary regulatory powers, which liaises with different ministries. Its performance is increasingly measured on the basis of its ability to canvass foreign investors by generating and providing strategically relevant information about industrial and technological developments in India and technology sourcing potentials in overseas markets.

6.3.2 Prospects for FDI policy improvements until 2000

As in Russia, India's central government will, in the years to come, be confronted with three major challenges in its efforts to attract foreign companies to the country. First, it will need to make more effective use of the administrative apparatus so that bottlenecks are reduced, particularly those arising from conflict between the central and state governments. Its second task is to pursue the economic reforms introduced in 1991 and to underpin them with coherent, investor-friendly policies. Finally, infrastructure (e.g. energy, telecommunications, transport.) will need to be modernized and expanded.

International organizations and companies are pressing for total liberalization and opening of the Indian market. They advocate further improvements of the current FDI policy, which the Indian government has already begun to address, such as:[36]

- Enlarged scope for automatic approval for most industries and raising of the general foreign equity ceiling from 51 per cent to 74 per cent. There have already been many cases of foreign TNCs receiving permission for setting up wholly-owned subsidiaries or for raising their equity to 74 per cent, but such approvals do not yet apply across all major branches of industry.
- Increased policy transparency and stability by eliminating the sometimes discretionary case-by-case approach and by setting clear standard guidelines.
- Better interministerial and centre–state coordination to speed up approvals at all levels (FIPB and states).
- Delegation of more responsibilities to state authorities, which should be able to grant approvals in essential industries and up to predetermined capital ceilings.[37]
- Active FDI promotion and incentive mechanisms by means of attractive policy packages for strategic (roads, telecommunication, ports and energy) and ICT (software, computers, electronic components) sectors.
- Granting special loan facilities; public support for R&D and training; full or partial exemption of long-term capital gains tax, investment/reinvestment allowances, accelerated depreciation allowances, and longer tax holidays (up to 10 years for strategically relevant projects, e.g. infrastructure-related FDI).
- Faster project implementation by identifying and removing sources of delay; expanding and refining the single-window system and fast-track mechanism at FIPB level, including expediting communication with regional administrations.
- Acceleration of the removal of import restrictions in keeping with the WTO regulations and India's commitment to do so by 2000.

- Revising intellectual property laws to include product patents (at present India grants only process patents).

Some of these issues have been addressed by the government. In the 1998 budget, the government reiterated the high priority it accorded to the task of increasing private investment, including FDI, in industry. To this end, it would minimize bureaucratic and procedural hurdles in various ministries and state governments. The aim is to double FDI inflows during 2000–01.

The government decided to implement a monitoring system for every foreign investment proposal exceeding US$25 million. To assist foreign investors, an officer of the administrative ministry will be designated as monitoring officer to accelerate processing and implementation of the project, in conjunction with the central and state authorities. The officer will be responsible for obtaining the government's decision on the investment proposal within 90 days.

The government's earlier efforts to liberalize telecommunications have been acknowledged by the WTO. The 1998 budget, also proposed to open the insurance sector to competition from private Indian companies. This could be a back-door entry for foreign insurance companies, many of which have signed agreements with Indian partners. The Insurance Regulatory Authority will be converted into a statutory body, and the necessary legislation will be introduced by 2000. Subsequent statements announced that the government was also considering opening the agricultural and housing sectors to FDI.

As a signatory of the GATT agreement following the Uruguay Round, India is committed to amend its patent laws by 2005. Under the trade-related intellectual property rights (TRIPs) agreement signed by India in 1995, the government will have to allow product patents in all fields of technology, including pharmaceuticals and agriculture. By April 1999, it has to provide exclusive marketing rights (EMRs) for agrochemicals and pharmaceutical products, and a mailbox for receiving product patent applications in these two sectors. EMRs concern products for which patent applications are filed after the agreement came into force (January 1995). The patent holder can apply for EMR for five years even before the patent is granted in India. Mailbox provisions imply that India has to legislatively be in a position to accept product patent applications in the drugs, chemicals and agriculture sectors even if these are granted at a later date. These amendments are being examined by the various ministries to make the Indian Patents Act WTO-compatible.

Such legislation will allow India to benefit from new technology and protect its traditional knowledge (particularly its indigenous medical resources) and biodiversity from uncompensated commercial exploitation. Urgently needed legislation on plant and seed varieties, biodiversity and geographic appellations is also under study.

6.3.3 Investment incentives under the NIP

Examination of incentive schemes adopted in India at central and regional (state) levels to attract specific forms of FDI would provide Russian authorities with valuable information and ideas that could be modified and applied by certain regional bodies. Both central and state governments in India offer domestic and foreign investors a number of incentives with a view to stimulating industrial growth and exports. The focus is therefore on new industrial projects, infrastructure and IT projects and export-oriented units. These incentives are revised regularly to accommodate new industrial sectors that need to be promoted. Most incentives are fiscal in nature, mainly deduction of 30 per cent of group total income for 10 years for certain new industrial projects and five-year income tax holiday. State governments also supply power at concessional rates and offer capital subsidies, particularly if investors establish their units in specifically designed industrial and scientific parks (e.g. electronics industries in Bangalore, Mumbai).

The Ministry of Commerce set up seven export processing zones (EPZ), where export-oriented companies are given the requisite infrastructure and incentives, including duty-free imports, to support their activities. The development commissioner of each EPZ, who is responsible for management of the zone and development of exports from it, is also the licensing authority for the zone. The seven EPZs are located at:

- Kandla Free Trade Zone, Gujarat;
- Santacruz Electronics Export Processing Zone, Maharashtra;
- Falta Export Processing Zone, West Bengal;
- Madras Export Processing Zone, Tamil Nadu;
- Cochin Export Processing Zone, Kerala;
- NOIDA Export Processing Zone, Uttar Pradesh;
- Visakhapatnam Export Processing Zone, Andhra Pradesh.

FDI in 100 per cent export-oriented units (EOUs) benefits from even longer tax holidays (up to eight years). EOUs can be located within or outside EPZs, and approval for foreign investment in EOUs is automatic except in sectors that figure on the negative list of the government. The project should be 'technically superior' and 'required for the country's development'. In such cases, equipment that is delivered as part of the foreign TNC's equity contribution can be imported duty-free.

Approvals for EOUs are granted for a maximum period of 10 years, two years beyond the tax holiday period. EOUs can also use foreign exchange more freely. Other monetary and nonmonetary incentives given to ensure long-term competitiveness include:

- duty-free import of capital goods, raw materials, and components, without restrictions;

- permission to sell up to 25 per cent of the output in the domestic market;
- complete exemption from central and state taxes on production and sales;
- exemption from tax on export earnings after the period of tax holiday (eight years);
- freedom to borrow foreign currency loans at prime interest rates;
- decentralized single-window clearance of proposals by the administrative authorities of the respective EPZs;
- liberal loans and financing schemes by government-owned financial institutions;
- sales to other export units, which qualify for the purpose of meeting export obligations.

India has drawn level with other Asian countries, which offer similar attractive schemes (e.g. Malaysia, Singapore, Thailand). Before designing the package, an Indian expert team studied locational advantages of several countries in East and Southeast Asia, particularly the incentives offered to foreign TNCs involved in export-oriented activities.[38] The first results of the new EOU scheme, which was introduced in 1994–95, look promising, and many multinationals have already established production facilities in EPZs or have applied to do so in the near future. Areas of particular interest are gems and jewellery, pharmaceuticals, apparel and software.

In April 1995, the government decided to extend the five-year tax holidays to enterprises engaging in infrastructure projects (building and operating of highways, expressways, airports, mass rapid transport systems and bridges). For high-priority industrial projects, foreign investors can apply for a 30 per cent flat rate reduction of annual income for 10 years. Taxes are payable only after five years on the remaining 70 per cent of income generated in India.

Several state governments allow either total exemption from or deferral of sales tax. Depending on the state, foreign investors can receive substantial subsidies for capital investment, including the purchase of imported capital equipment. Often, it is also possible to deduct outlays for R&D expenditure from annual sales. The government of Gujarat, for example, reimburses up to 80 per cent of expenses for new equipment or R&D for two years from the start of an operation in predefined sectors (e.g. medical and orthopaedic equipment). Concessional tax rates are also accorded on dividends, royalties, technical services and interest on loans received by foreign companies in India through double taxation relief based on bilateral treaties with over 40 countries. Financial institutions are allowed to deduct up to 40 per cent of their taxable income derived from financing of such investments.

Attractive incentives schemes enable authorities to gradually orient FDI flows into strategically relevant sectors. Tax exemptions and the removal of foreign exchange restrictions for export-oriented firms and other important investors has stabilized the foreign exchange reserves situation. Many regional authorities offer incentives to attract investment into their territories (Table 6.2). Higher business activity through increased FDI translates as higher tax revenue, which may be reinvested in FDI projects with socio-economic impact.

6.4 FDI-related legislation and bilateral agreements

India does not have an FDI-specific law. National policy-makers are of the opinion that the general political climate and existing legal system are stable enough and therefore do not warrant specific FDI legislation (as in Russia). Foreign investors' rights and duties are enshrined in area-specific legislation (e.g. Foreign Exchange Regulation Act, Labour Act, Companies Act), but the FIPB has, however, laid down guidelines based on corresponding polices. All these documents are accessible to foreign investors. Besides, the Indian government plans to sign bilateral FDI agreements with over 50 countries during 1997–2000. The text of these agreements resembles those signed by Russia with its main trading partners over the past 5–6 years[39] and shows that investment protection and guarantees are given high priority by the Indian government. India signed its first bilateral agreement with the United Kingdom on 14 March 1994. Analogous agreements with France, Germany, Italy, Japan and the United States followed during 1994–95.

Bilateral agreements are meant to protect all kinds of assets, including intellectual property rights, goodwill, technical assistance and know-how. Special provisions oblige contracting parties to accord foreign TNCs the same treatment as domestic companies. The Indian government is expected to incorporate two fundamental principles of multilateral FDI in the bilateral agreements to be signed with other countries: the most favoured nation clause and the principle of national treatment.

As in Russia's bilateral agreements, nationalization or expropriation must be accompanied by prompt, adequate and effective compensation and prior review by a judicial or other important authority. Likewise, foreign capital invested in India, as well as profits and dividends earned, can be repatriated freely after payment of taxes. The Indian government also guarantees repatriation of foreign capital invested in India (including capital appreciation) in case of disinvestment, after payment of taxes. All foreign currency transactions related to repatriations, royalty payments and technical know-how fees have to be approved by the Reserve Bank of India. Dividends can be remitted abroad provided they are balanced by export earnings for a period of seven years from commencement of production. Beyond this period, balancing is not required.

Table 6.2 FDI incentives offered by India's southern states, 1996–97

State	Population (mn)	Capital	Technical parks (number)	Main incentives offered
Tamil Nadu	59	Chennai	5	• special grant up to INR10 million for mega projects • special grant for FDI in electronics industry • financial assistance for purchase of power generating sets • concessional power tariff
Karnataka	48	Bangalore	4	• single-window clearance facility • investment grant (15–25% of capital) • special assistance for installation of pollution control equipment • sales tax exemption for 3–5 years for selected zones (electronics cities of Mysore and Dharwar) and sectors (electronics, telecommunications, high-tech) • exemptions of import duty on raw materials used by 100% export units
Kerala	33	Trivandrum	2	• green channel scheme for expeditious clearance of projects • investment grant (15% of fixed capital) • cash incentives for setting up quality control laboratories • grant for installation of power generation sets • exemption/deferment of sales tax for 7 to 10 years • escort service for investments exceeding INR500 million (US$12 million)
Andhra Pradesh	75	Hyderabad	3	• investment grant (15–20% of capital) • sales tax deferment up to a period of 10 years

Source: T. T. Meng *et al.*, *Business Opportunities in India*, 1996, pp. 130–4.

Foreign companies can acquire or hold immovable property in India for carrying out their activities. India has thus a definite comparative advantage over China and Russia where foreign TNCs currently have only the right to use or lease land for a maximum period of 49 years.

India has fully subscribed to the World Bank's Multilateral Investment Guarantee Agency (MIGA) as of January 1994. As a consequence, all investments approved by the Indian government are additionally insured against the political risks of expropriation, nationalization, or war and civil disturbances. In its determination to enhance FDI flows, the Indian government will also introduce special trade policy initiatives (EXIM policy[40]), which are expected to have a direct impact on inbound FDI. They include the abolition of import licensing on all industrial inputs[41] and the reduction of import duties on these items (from a minimum of 0 per cent to a maximum of 65 per cent compared with 85 per cent before) and capital goods (down by 10 points to 25 per cent). Investors who participate in special export schemes can benefit from even lower rates. Items are also being phased out of the restricted import list in keeping with the commitment to the WTO.

Taxation of foreign investors has been adjusted to stimulate FDI inflows. Several legal acts were passed during 1996–97 including:

- simplification of tax administration;
- overall tax reductions and abolition of wealth tax on financial assets;
- tax deductions up to 65 per cent even for companies with headquarters outside of India;
- special rates for dividends, interest, royalty or technical fees received by foreign investors; these rates are lower than those applicable to domestic companies;
- complete tax exemption on profits derived from exports of goods;
- tax holiday for a period of 5 consecutive years in the case of 100 per cent export-oriented units and companies operating from export processing zones;
- reduction of multiple taxes between national and state levels.

Since 1 March 1993, foreign capital transactions and money transfers have been largely facilitated by the introduction of convertibility of the rupee for current account transfers, particularly for import–export operations and invisible transactions such as dividend payments, repatriation of proceeds, royalties, travel and other remittances (insurance payments, shipping, education). Foreign investors can also benefit from the liberalization of capital markets and the government's privatization programme. Full convertibility of the Indian rupee is also planned, but following the Southeast Asian crisis the government has decided to introduce this measure in phases.

Supportive legislation is foreseen in a number of other areas, the most important of which are:

- *Foreign exchange* regulations are being updated to adapt to the entry of foreign operators.
- The *labour* law will be streamlined for redeployment, retrenchment and retraining of labour, according to productivity levels and profit situation of the company.
- *The competition law* is laid out in the Monopolies and Restrictive Trade Practices Act, which will be reinforced to prohibit hostile take-overs, acquisitions and other actions aimed at suppressing competition and at creating powerful monopolistic or oligopolistic structures.
- The *intellectual property* laws are being reviewed to align them to WTO stipulations.
- India's *environmental law* now demands environmental impact assessment of projects to attract investments with low pollution levels (water treatment, disposal of effluents, etc.).

6.5 Foreign investment patterns in the 1990s: origin and destination

6.5.1 FDI approvals and inflows

In response to the liberal policy measures, FDI increased progressively in the post-reform period in terms of both approvals and actual inflows; according to UNCTAD, inflows amounted to about US$2 billion in 1995. Indian sources reported an inflow of US$3.5 billion for 1997 (end of year figure), bringing total inbound stock in India to approximately US$11–12 billion in 1998. This is a definite improvement compared with 1989–94 when annual inflows averaged only US$400 million. But per capital inward FDI is still low because of India's large population; during 1996–97 it was only US$3, which is eight times less than Russia. However, as the NIP slowly shows its effect and foreign companies turn into real investors, per capita FDI is expected to increase.

Indian authorities have only recently begun to provide detailed statistics on FDI inflows by sector and region. They also distinguish between FDI approvals (investments approved by the FIPB and the RBI) and actual inflows. Official statistics on foreign investment approvals and cash inflows suggest that there could be a gestation period of almost five years between initial approval and inflow of committed investments. The government had approved cumulative FDI proposals worth INR1588 billion (US$37 billion) during 1991–98,[42] but the cumulative actual inflows were only INR353 billion (US$8.2 billion) representing 22 per cent of the total value of approvals.

This discrepancy can be explained by the high concentration of FDI in large-scale infrastructure and turnkey projects with a long leadtime. There is also an administrative reason: any increase in equity by a foreign investor must be approved by the government. To avoid another approval procedure, applications to the FIPB usually state a maximum investment amount to cover future investments. The actual investment is therefore necessarily less than the stated amount. But difficulties during implementation such as procedural bottlenecks (particularly for infrastructure), land disputes, environmental clearance and labour issues also contribute to these delays. The authorities are therefore addressing these problems and are confident that procedural improvements will increase FDI substantially.

FDI approvals in 1998 stood at US$16 billion, almost one-third higher than the government's target of US$10 billion for actual inflows. All possible efforts will therefore be made in the coming years to raise the actual inflows/approvals ratio to 60–70 per cent. By 2002–03, actual inflows could already represent three-quarters of approvals. If the current momentum is maintained, inbound stocks could touch US$20 billion at the turn of the century. Authorities also believe that this increase in FDI will lead to higher exports (Figures 6.2 and 6.3).

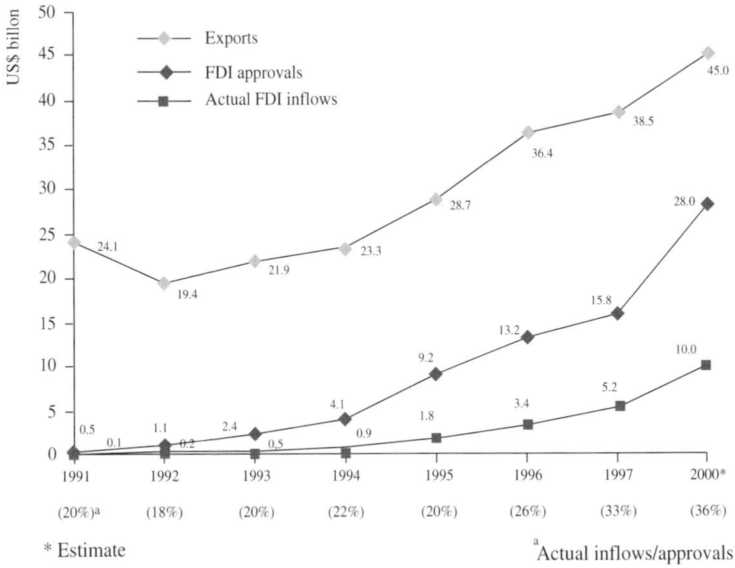

Source: *CII Newsletters; SIA Newsletters.*

Figure 6.2 FDI inflows, approvals and exports, India, 1991–2000

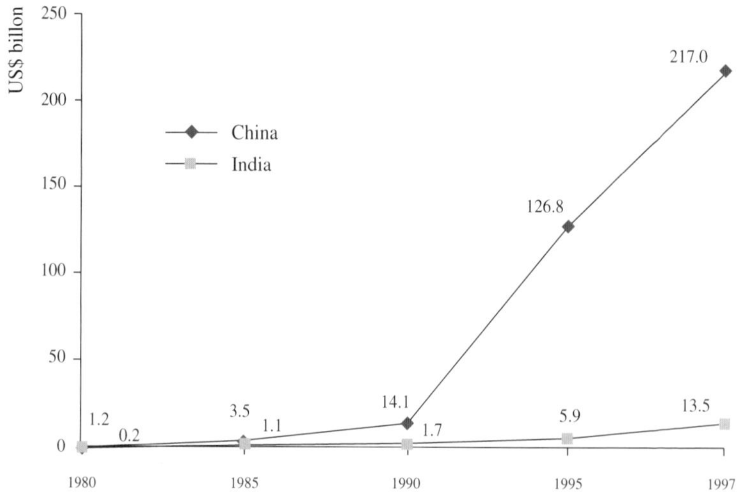

Source: Adapted from *SIA Newsletters*; UNCTAD, *World Investment Reports 1997, 1998*.

Figure 6.3 Inward FDI stock, China and India, 1980–97

6.5.2 Sectoral and regional distribution of FDI

The sectoral distribution of FDI approvals during 1991–96 (Figure 6.4) reveals a concentration on telecommunications (27 per cent) and fuels (20 per cent), followed by transport equipment and chemicals (each with a share of 7 per cent of all approvals). Consumer goods industries have a relatively minor share so far, primarily because of intense domestic competition and restrictions in these sectors. High inflows can be observed in infrastructure-related industries (energy, telecommunications, transport) and chemicals including pharmaceuticals. Other sectors with high FDI potential are tourism (hotels, catering), information technology, banking and nonfinancial services, whose average shares of total approved projects have been less than 3 per cent each so far.

US TNCs have so far made the biggest commitments, accounting for over one-quarter of total approvals (Figure 6.5). They have invested mainly in energy, telecommunications, services and software development. Similarly, UK TNCs – the second largest investors in India – are particularly active in energy and telecommunications, but also have major stakes in chemicals, like TNCs from Germany and Japan. Increasingly, companies from Australia, Malaysia, Singapore, South Korea and Thailand are entering the Indian market against the background of closer integration between India and the Asia–Pacific economies. Selected TNCs, irrespective of their country

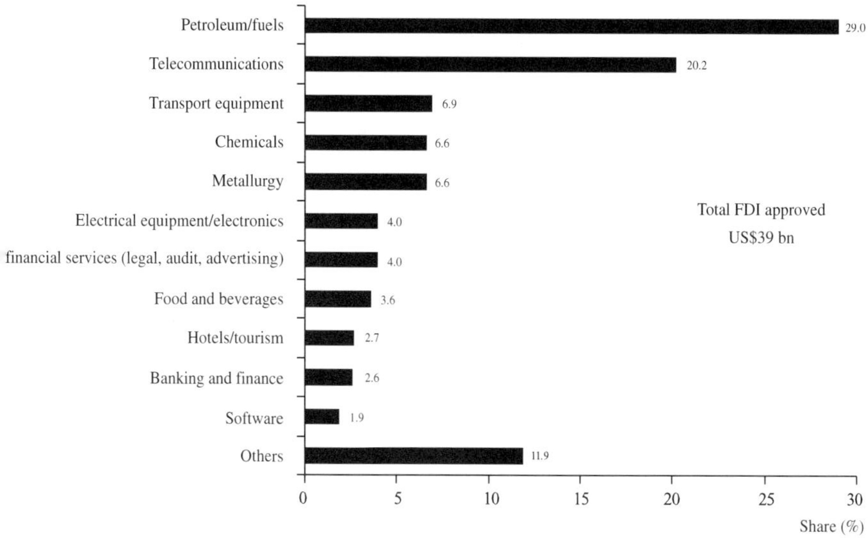

Source: *SIA Newsletters*.

Figure 6.4 Sectoral breakdown of FDI approvals, India, 1991–97

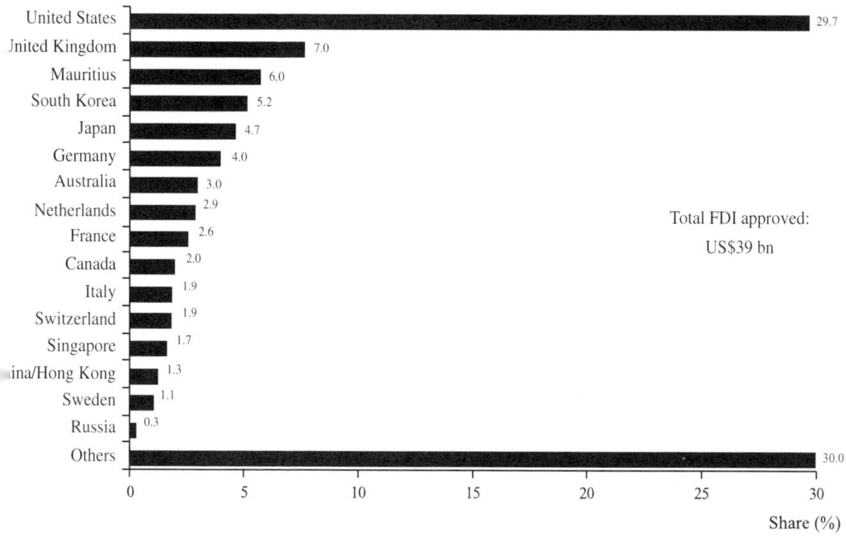

Source: *SIA Newsletters*.

Figure 6.5 FDI approvals by country of origin, India, 1991–97

of origin but often involving NRI equity, channel their investment through holdings located in Mauritius. They thus benefit from the agreement between India and Mauritius which reduces the tax burden on repatriated income.

A sectoral focus is observed in investments from different countries, often reflecting their global competitive advantages. FDI from Canada, Israel and Malaysia, for example, is almost exclusively in telecommunications. Italian TNCs have major stakes in leather, garments and engineering goods, while Japanese TNCs are involved in automobiles, motorcycles and consumer electronics. Germany and the United Kingdom control several chemical plants, US TNCs have particular interests in India's electronics and software industry.

Four states in India accounted for over half of the foreign investment approved between August 1991 and December 1996: New Delhi (24.5 per cent), Maharashtra with Mumbai (15.7 per cent), West Bengal with Calcutta (7 per cent), Tamil Nadu with Chennai (5.1 per cent). Thus, investors have shown a preference for major agglomerations with well-developed infrastructure and promising market prospects.

State government support, the level of urbanization, social infrastructure and economic prospects are major determinants for location of FDI projects. Therefore, politically stable and economically advanced states like Gujarat, Karnataka and Andhra Pradesh are expected to attract increased FDI volumes in coming years. Local governments in these states, which currently account for 2.5–4.5 per cent of total approvals each, offer many incentives and guarantee fast-track local approval and implementation mechanisms. Canvassing efforts are increasingly directed at nonresident Indians (NRIs), particularly in eastern and southern Africa, the Middle East, the United States, the United Kingdom and Southeast Asia.

6.5.3 India's outward FDI position

During the 1950s and 1960s, India's FDI position was typical of economies at Stage 1 of the IDP:[43] outbound investments were almost nonexistent and inbound FDI was low. The bulk of inward FDI stock was held by resource-seeking TNCs in petroleum, steel, minerals, agricultural products (jute, tea) and services (mainly trading and transport). Inbound FDI rose further during the 1970s, when resource-seeking FDI began to give way to cost-oriented FDI, which was mostly directed at export processing zones where foreign companies could benefit from India's low labour and energy costs. Since the late 1980s, there is a visible trend towards market-seeking inbound FDI as foreign companies intend to become insiders in India, one of the largest potential consumer markets of the world.

Outbound FDI remained negligible until the early 1980s when leading Indian enterprises began to establish sales subsidiaries overseas. With the help of foreign know-how and technologies acquired through inward FDI,

India could equip itself with the combination of OLI advantages it required for making the transition to Stage 2 of the IDP, which is characterized by rising outbound and inbound FDI.

Despite significant market expansion at home and the ensuing accumulation of financial reserves, Indian companies still struggle with cash shortfalls when it comes to conquering foreign markets. Unfavourable exchange rates and high prices, especially in the megacities of the developed world, generally reduce their chances of becoming significant outbound investors. But Indian companies are gradually emerging as important suppliers of industrial FDI to other emerging countries, including the transition economies of Central and Eastern Europe. By 1997, Indian outward FDI stock amounted to US$1.5 billion. Most investments went to developing and emerging economies in Africa and Southeast Asia. Recently, Middle East and CIS countries have become important target regions for Indian TNCs (Figure 6.6). FDI in Central and Eastern Europe focuses on leather and engineering industries, and trading subsidiaries. In industrialized countries, Indian FDI is mainly directed at North America (Canada, United States) and the European Union. These markets are of strategic importance, because they enable Indian TNCs to be close to technologically developed markets and potential clients (e.g. software development). Australia and Japan also attract increasing volumes of FDI flows from India.

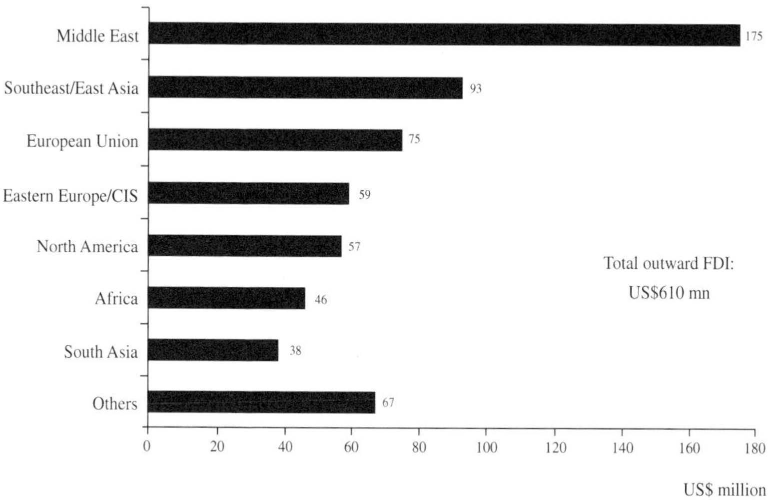

Source: Based on data from FIPB, *SIA Newsletter*.

Figure 6.6 Outward FDI by region, India, 1991–97

The bulk (80–90 per cent) of India's outward FDI is marked by self-generated competitive advantages in capital goods, turnkey plants and consultancy services including licensing and know-how transfer. The most prominent branches for outbound FDI are light engineering, textiles, chemicals, pharmaceuticals, leather products, and specific services (software development, trading). Competitive price–product–service combinations derived from managerial and technical expertise are decisive factors for establishing operations in foreign countries.

As part of the general economic opening and deregulation, the Indian government liberalized outward investment procedures on 17 August 1995. Indian TNCs can now buy equity in all types of foreign operations: joint ventures, majority–minority stakes and wholly-owned subsidiaries. By 1997, 400 approved wholly-owned subsidiaries of Indian TNCs had become operational in foreign countries, and Indian equity participation amounted to INR18.2 billion (US$423 million). Most subsidiaries are located in the United Kingdom, the United States, Singapore and Germany, and since 1992, a few dozen subsidiaries have been set up in Russia which is seen as an important market by Indian TNCs.

In recent years, the number of overseas Indo–foreign joint ventures has grown significantly. As early as 1974, an Inter-Ministerial Committee on Joint Ventures Abroad had been established within the Ministry of Commerce to approve proposals from Indian companies interested in opening subsidiaries abroad or cooperating with foreign counterparts. Although Indian ventures abroad increasingly receive official support as a means of promoting exports from India, cash and capital remittances to overseas ventures are still tightly checked and need to be justified because of foreign currency shortages in India.

By 1997, there were about 600 active joint ventures with Indian equity participation abroad (up from 214 in 1991), valued at INR20 billion (US$465 million). The main industries were: light engineering, chemicals and pharmaceuticals, food, iron and steel, rubber, commercial vehicles, glass, pulp and paper, and cement. In services, Indian TNCs invested mainly in hotels, restaurants, trading, consultancy and construction. Overseas joint ventures have been launched in the United Kingdom (46), Malaysia (42), the United States (38), the United Arab Emirates (36), Singapore (36), Sri Lanka (34) and Russia (28). Joint ventures with Russian counterparts are expected to increase as trade, which was interrupted following the collapse of the Soviet Union, resumes and Indian businesses expand their activities in the growing Russian market.

Indian joint ventures[44] in niche markets abroad, where larger TNCs have not shown any interest, enable medium-sized operations to share experience, expand capacity utilization and overcome domestic regulatory policies. They also help safeguard export markets and diversify business risks in the home market. Investments usually involve export of machinery and equipment, supply of technical know-how, export of goods and, more rarely, cash remittances.

6.5.4 Scope for Indo-Russian FDI

While foreign TNCs are increasingly penetrating the Indian market, Indian companies are expected to enhance their outbound investment operations in an effort to maintain or even expand strategic market positions. The excellent trade relations and business contacts established at the time of the former Soviet Union will form the foundation of future collaborations and business between India and Russia.

Indo-Russian trade turnover was at its highest level during 1989–91 when the two countries exchanged goods worth US$6–7 billion each year. The break-up of the Soviet Union led to sudden disruptions of deliveries from Russia while Indian companies continued to export food, textiles, apparel, pharmaceuticals and engineering goods. Bilateral trade reached around US$2 billion annually during 1995–97. In 1998 it was expected to reach US$2.7–3 billion, of which Indian exports to Russia were estimated to be 60 per cent.[45] Indian companies are particularly interested in increasing their market share in a number of sectors in Russia: food and beverages (processed fruit and vegetables, baby food, soybean products, rice, tea); textiles, readymade garments, footwear; household appliances; automotive components; iron and steel parts; shipbuilding; chemicals; pharmaceuticals; and paper and printing.

Leading Indian TNCs have established offices in Moscow as they perceive Russia as a major market for future business. It is interesting to note that numerous Indian organizations consider the Russian Ministry of Foreign Economic Relations the nodal agency for foreign investment although FDI policies in Russia are currently administered by the Ministry of Economy.[46] This may be an indicator that more efforts may be required on the Russian side to actively promote their country in major LEMs such as India where interest in investing in Russia is mounting.

The conversion of the military sector in Russia is expected to open new possibilities for collaborations and FDI in information and telecommunication technologies. India could gain from technology imports from Russia in iron and steel production, nuclear and thermal power stations, electricity generation, petrochemical products, polymers, heavy engineering goods, aviation and radar systems, infrastructure, water purification, heavy trucks and lorries, construction, fertilizers and agricultural equipment. India would be a particularly interesting partner for FDI in pharmaceuticals, electronics and a large number of consumer goods (textiles, apparel, footwear, and processed foods and beverages) which are commonly traded between the two countries.[47]

Collective initiatives on both sides are gaining ground to lobby for their members' interest. The Indian Business Association in Moscow already has more than 100 members and has strengthened its information, advisory and lobbying capabilities. The Indian Embassy has also set up a Business Development Cell to explore business opportunities and expedite projects.[48] The Russian authorities are now expected to follow suit so that trading and FDI opportunities in the growing Indian economy are not missed.

6.6 The macroeconomic impact of FDI and the role of 'national champions'

The Indian economy has undergone a phase of readjustment since the NIP was launched in 1991, but the positive effects of liberalization and deregulation started to appear in 1993–94. During the first two years of economic reforms economic activity slowed down owing to drastic cuts in state assistance (especially for agriculture and the public sector) and higher competition from foreign TNCs, but after 1993–94 the positive impact of liberalization and deregulation could be seen as GDP started to rise.

Industrial production and investment activity (both domestic and foreign) grew considerably after 1995 generating annual average growth rates of about 6–7 per cent compared with the extremely modest 'Hindu' rate of growth of 1–2 per cent during the 1980s (Figure 6.7). On the basis of present FDI policies and economic deregulation, analysts expect high growth to be maintained beyond 2000.[49] In 1996, industrial production rose by an unprecedented 12 per cent, almost 4 percentage points more than in 1995. Industrial production could stabilize at 7–8 per cent annually for the coming 5–7 years, especially if the government succeeds in improving infrastructure and in facilitating the creation of additional productive capacity through foreign investment.

Once markets were opened and monopolies abolished in several key industries (e.g. steel, automobiles), inflation was also brought under control, and in June 1999, India reported its lowest inflation rate (2.03 per cent) since two decades. During 1985–95 average annual inflation was 9.8 per cent. Higher revenue through portfolio and foreign direct investment helped reduce the budget deficit to 6 per cent of GDP (9 per cent in 1991). In 1997, more than 15 million jobs were created across the country in the industrial and agricultural sectors compared with 7 million in 1997.[50] Official unemployment remained at 7 per cent in 1997.

Economic liberalization and the removal of trade and FDI restrictions immediately impacted on the country's foreign trade, which grew by 30 per cent during 1995–97. Exports increased by 15 per cent to reach an all time high of US$33.1 billion in 1997, but growth rates were even higher for

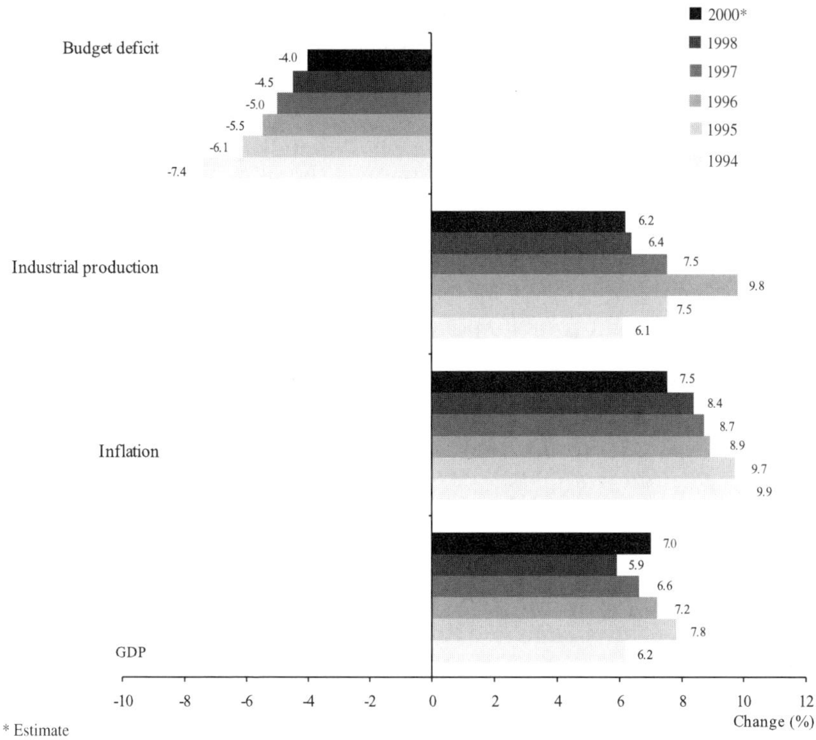

Source: IMF, BfAI, Deutsche Bank Research.

Figure 6.7 Main economic indicators, India, 1994–2000

imports, which rose by 47 per cent to US$38.6 billion. As the trade deficit widened to US$2.4 billion in 1995, US$4.6 billion in 1996 and then to US$5.5 billion in 1997 following trade and FDI liberalization, the government intensified efforts to increase exports and urge Indian industry to become more competitive abroad. Indian embassies abroad have been instructed to provide additional support to Indian companies trying to penetrate new foreign markets. The export volume in manufactured goods in 1997 was comparable to that of Russia[51] (estimate for 1997: US$24 billion), but it is significantly lower than China's (US$150 billion). The Reserve Bank of India's foreign exchange reserves swelled from US$1.5 billion in 1991 to over US$30 billion in 1998, mainly owing to increased exports and incoming FDI.

Major export markets for products from India are Europe, the United States, Japan and the Middle East. Owing to traditional ties with the former Soviet Union, India is also an important exporter to Russia, Kazakhstan, Uzbekistan and other CIS countries. Indian TNCs are increasingly targeting the nearby SAARC economies of Bangladesh, Pakistan and Sri Lanka, and negotiations are underway to reduce tariff barriers. Most important import items are oil, machinery and industrial equipment, chemicals and pharmaceuticals. Whereas finished products come mainly from OECD countries, the Middle Eastern economies are the main suppliers of crude oil and derivatives.

Owing to encouraging results in a number of crucial economic areas including the expanding services sector, protectionist forces in the government – although still vocal for political reasons – are losing ground.

Most Indian companies are now prepared to face foreign competition by designing new products, upgrading their manufacturing technologies, conquering new markets and entering into strategic alliances with foreign partners. Indian companies have been able to improve their position in the world market in a number of sectors, and some of India's leading companies (Figure 6.8) such as Tata, Birla, Ranbaxy and Larsen & Toubro have begun to invest abroad, including CIS countries.[52] The country has developed a strong base for services (software development), agricultural products (tea, coffee, wheat, food grain, fruit, vegetables), basic minerals, leather items, textiles, gems and jewellery, sports goods and light engineering goods, which are exported all over the world. Electronic components and customized computer software are produced according to specifications for US and Japanese TNCs, but also increasingly for domestic firms. India has developed a diversified domestic vehicle industry (automobiles, trucks, two- and three-wheelers). Major automobile companies (Daewoo, Fiat, Ford, General Motors, Honda, Hyundai, Mercedes Benz, Skoda, Suzuki, Toyota, Volvo) and their automotive components suppliers have already launched their models in India, some of them in collaboration with an Indian partner. The aim is to increase car exports to nearby regional markets by 20–30 per cent by 2000.

Over the past few years, Indian authorities have managed to considerably improve the investment climate in the country, but they need to open the economy further and drastically improve infrastructure to realize India's full potential as an FDI destination. They also need to pay more attention to the hidden champions (medium-sized TNCs). Compared with Russia, India already enjoys the confidence of a large number of executives from the world's top 500 TNCs (about 200 will have invested in India by 2002–03). They rely on India's democratic political system, rule of law, and a firm commitment to stability by the government. Indian authorities believe that these positive factors will eventually also incite technology-rich medium-sized TNCs to invest in India.

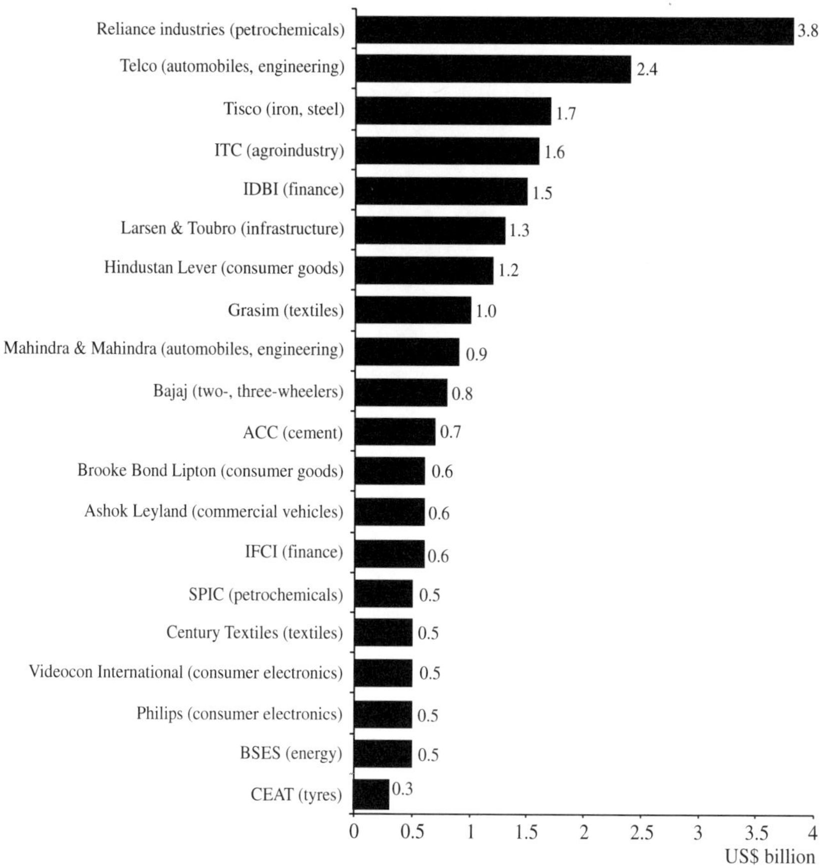

Source: 'The BT-500', *Business Today*, 7–21 September 1998.

Figure 6.8 Top 20 Indian companies by sales, 1997/98

Annex 6.1 List of industries and services open to FDI, India, 1997–98[53]

A: Automatic approval for foreign equity up to 50%

A–1 *Mining of iron ore*

A–2 *Mining of metal ores other than iron ore (excluding uranium group ores)*

Manganese ore.
Chromite.
Bauxite.
Copper ore.
Mining of lead and zinc ores.

A–3 *Mining of nonmetallic minerals*
Rock aggregates, sand and clays.
Construction minerals other than rock aggregates, sand and clays.
Fertilizer and chemical minerals.
Ceramic, refractory and glass minerals.
Salt mining and quarrying including crushing, screening and evaporating in pans.

B: Automatic approval for foreign equity up to 51%

Industries

B–1 *Agricultural production (certified high-yielding hybrid and synthetic seeds)*

B–2 *Plantation (certified high-yielding plantation developed through plant tissue culture)*

B–3 *Food products*
Preparation and preservation of meat.
Manufacture of dairy products (e.g. milk powder, ice-cream, condensed milk, baby milk foods, butter, cream, cheese, pasteurized milk in bottles/polythene packs).
Canning and preservation of fruits and vegetables (e.g. sun-drying, artificial dehydration of fruits and vegetables, fruit/vegetable juices, sauces, jams).
Processing, canning, and preserving of fish, crustacea and similar foods.
Grain milling (including flour).
Production of common salt.
Manufacture of cocoa products and sugar confectionery (including sweet-meats).
Manufacture of starch and its derivatives.

B–4 *Cotton textiles*

B–5 *Wool, silk and manmade fibre textiles*

B–7 *Paper, paper products, printing and publishing*

B–8 *Basic chemicals and chemical products (excluding petroleum, coal)*
Industrial organic and inorganic chemicals.
Fertilizers and pesticides.
Plastics in primary forms; manufacture of synthetic rubber.
Paints, varnishes, and related products; artists' colours and ink.
Drugs, medicines and allied products.
Manmade fibres.

B–9 *Rubber, plastic, petroleum and coal products*

B–10 *Nonmetallic mineral products*
Nonrefractory ceramic pipes, conduits, guttering and pipe fittings.
Nonrefractory flooring blocks, support or filler tiles and roofing tiles.
Glass and glass products.
Nonstructural ceramic ware (e.g. insulators and fittings for electric machines, appliances and equipment).
Cement, lime and plaster.

B–11 *Metal products*
Manufacture of fabricated metal products (e.g. railway and ship containers; gas cylinders; tanks, reservoirs and containers; reinforced safes, vaults, steel

trunks; sanitary and plumbing fixtures and fittings of metal; iron and steel pipes/tubes and fittings; welding electrodes).
Forging, pressing, stamping, and roll-forming of metal; powder metallurgy.

B–12 *Machinery and equipment other than transport equipment*
Agricultural machinery and equipment and parts thereof.
Machinery and equipment used by construction and mining industries.
Prime movers, boilers.
Industrial machinery for food (including bottling) and textile industries.
Refrigerators, air-conditioners and fire fighting equipment.
General purpose nonelectrical machinery/equipment.
Machine tools.
Office, computing and accounting machinery and parts.
Special purpose machinery including machines for sewing and knitting; weighing, washing and laundrying; filtering and purifying liquids and gases; distilling and rectifying plants.
Electrical industrial machinery including insulated wires and cables, accumulators, batteries, lamps, flash bulbs for photography, valves and tubes, radiographic X-ray apparatus and tubes.

B–13 *Transport equipment and parts*
Ships and boats.
Locomotives and parts.
Railway or tramway wagons and coaches, railways, tramways, etc.
Heavy motor vehicles.
Motor cars including jeeps and station wagons.
Motorcycles and scooters (including three-wheelers).

Services

B–14 *Restaurants and hotels*
B–15 *Land transport (support services)*
B–16 *Water transport (support services)*
B–18 *Renting and leasing*
B–19 *Business services*
Data processing, software development and computer consultancy services (including software supply).
Business and management consultancy activities (including market research services).
Technical testing and analysis services.
R&D services (excluding basic research and setting up of R&D/academic institutions that award degrees/diplomas/certificates).

B–20 *Health and medical services*

C: Automatic approval for foreign equity up to 74%

C–1 *Mining services*
Oil and gas field services, except exploration and production services.
Services incidental to mining including drilling, shafting, reclamation of mines, surveys/mapping; excluding services related to gold, silver, and precious/semiprecious stones.

C–2 *Basic metals and alloys industries*

Iron ore pellets, pig iron, sponge iron and steel in primary/semifinished/finished forms.

Semifinished iron and steel products in re-rolling, cold-rolling and wire drawing mills.

Ferro-alloys.

Copper manufacturing.

Brass manufacturing.

Aluminium manufacturing.

Zinc manufacturing.

Casting of metal.

Other nonferrous metal industries, excluding gold, silver and platinum.

C–3 *Other manufacturing industries*

Medical, surgical, scientific and measuring equipment except optical equipment (including orthopaedic appliances, laboratory and scientific instruments, thermometers, balancing machines, test benches).

Photographic, cinematographic and optical goods and equipment (excluding photo chemicals, sensitized paper and film).

Items based on solar energy like solar cells, cookers, air and water heating systems.

C–5 *Nonconventional energy generation and distribution*

C–6 *Construction and maintenance*

Roads, railbeds, bridges, tunnels, pipelines, ports, and harbours and runways.

Waterways and water reservoirs.

Hydroelectric projects.

Power plants.

Industrial plants.

C–7 *Land transport (excluding pipelines for petroleum products and natural gas)*

C–8 *Water transport (ocean and inland water transport)*

C–9 *Storage and warehousing services (especially for agricultural products with cold storage requirements)*

D: Automatic approval for foreign equity up to 100 per cent

D–1 *Electricity generation, transmission and distribution*

Generation and transmission of electric energy produced in hydroelectric power plants.

Generation and transmission of electric energy produced in coal or lignite-based thermal power plants.

Generation and transmission of electric energy produced in oil-based thermal power plants.

Generation and transmission of electric energy produced in gas-based thermal power plants.

Distribution of electric energy to households, industrial, commercial and other users.

Note: Foreign equity in projects under this category should not exceed Rs15 billion. Proposals involving generation, transmission and distribution of electric energy produced in atomic reactor power plants are not eligible for automatic approval.

Annex 6.2 List of industries reserved for the public sector, India, 1997–98

Arms, ammunition, defence aircraft and warships.
Atomic energy.
Coal and lignite.
Mineral oils.
Mining of iron ore, manganese ore, chrome ore, gypsum, sulphur, gold and diamonds.
Mining of copper, lead, zinc, tin, molybdenum and wolfram.
Minerals specified in the Schedule to the Atomic Energy Order, 1953.
Railway transport.

Notes

1. India's middle and upper class is estimated at 15–20% of the total population, i.e. 150–190 million people.
2. India has the second largest pool of skilled scientific, technical and managerial manpower in the world after the United States.
3. Leading US business journal which, every August, publishes annual rankings of the world's 500 largest corporations.
4. Capital of the state of Andhra Pradesh in central India.
5. Remote services including back-office facilities and knowledge centres are considered domains where India intends to attain international leadership. *The Economist*, 'Indian Business – Spice up your Services', 16 January 1999, p. 61.
6. IITs offer integrated courses for engineers in all specializations: chemistry, mechanical, automotive, electrical, electronics, nuclear, construction, plastics, food, etc.
7. Chapter 15.4.3.
8. India counts about 6000 listed companies – 10 times more than China and 30 times the number listed on Russian or Mexican stock exchanges.
9. In Russia, too, regional authorities are understanding the importance of developing an effective retail system to supplement industrial modernization.
10. Nonresident Indians live mainly in North America, United Kingdom, Southeast Asia and Australia.
11. Growing at an average annual rate of about 2–2.3 per cent, India's population is expected to exceed that of China by 2020–25.
12. Chapter 5.
13. Chapter 6.3.
14. In 1998, licensing was limited to six sectors: defence equipment, atomic energy, coal and lignite, mineral oil, minerals, railway transport.
15. Similar to other emerging markets, India has become an important destination for portfolio investments.
16. For a description of the position of India's leading business families concerning FDI see also G. Piramal, *Business Maharajas*, New Delhi, 1996.
17. Chapter 6.3.1.
18. *Ibid.*
19. At that time, India's elite had been largely educated in Europe, especially the United Kingdom. Both Mahatma Gandhi and Jawaharlal Nehru appreciated

the prevailing socioeconomic systems in Europe. Nehru was deeply influenced by the Fabian Society, like most Indian intellectuals of that time.

20. This movement found wide support in Indonesia, Egypt and Yugoslavia, which together with India spearheaded the formation of a grouping called the non-aligned countries. The first conference was held in Bandung, Indonesia, in 1957.
21. The strengths of Indian (and also Chinese) companies in consumer goods is a major distinction from the currently fairly precarious situation in Russia, which in these industries depends excessively on imports.
22. SAARC: South Asian Association of Regional Cooperation, expected to introduce a free-trade area between its members Bangladesh, India, Maldives, Nepal, Pakistan and Sri Lanka by 2001.
23. Today, the IIC constitutes a nodal agency for promoting investment by NRIs in India.
24. Predecessor of today's FIPB.
25. G. Piramal, *Business Maharajas*, 1996.
26. N. Kumar *in* J. H. Dunning, *Foreign Direct Investment and Governments*, 1996, p. 352.
27. In early 1991, foreign reserves fell to only a few million US dollars, just sufficient to pay for a few days of indispensable oil imports.
28. India's economic nationalism or *swadeshi* has been analyzed in major economic publications, often with special reference to FDI. It is now giving way to a certain pragmatism based on the priority of economic advancement. See *India Development Report*, Mumbai, pp. 129–42.
29. TNCs can hold up to 26 per cent in insurance companies, according to a recent statement.
30. Chapter 6.5.1.
31. Tata Service. *Statistical Outline of India*, 1997.
32. An updated list of industries is included in Annex 6.1. See also Nabhi, *Manual for Foreign Collaboration and Investment in India*, 1996, 1997, 1998.
33. Since the introduction of reforms and liberalization of FDI, India's economy has grown faster with the consequence that international credit agencies have upgraded its overall rating.
34. This function is limited to large-scale projects. Smaller projects are often handled by the different chambers, associations or business consultants.
35. On 27 July 1999, the Indian government set up the Foreign Investment Implementation Authority (FIIA) to act as a single point interface between foreign investors and various government agencies. It is an independent body that supports the FIPB.
36. All-India Association of Chambers of Commerce, workshop papers, International Conference on Prospects for FDI in India, 29–30 August 1996, New Delhi.
37. A recent example of efforts to decentralize FDI approvals is the power sector, where investments of up to INR15 billion (US$375 million) will be dealt with directly by state authorities, even if the foreign equity level is 100 per cent. See also S. Rangnekar, 'States Given More Latitude to Attract FDI in Core Sectors', *The Economic Times*, 7 May 1998.
38. Information sourced from officials responsible for FDI promotion. See also Nabhi, *Manual for Foreign Collaboration and Investment in India*, 1996, pp. 36–39.
39. Chapter 9.4.
40. Amendments to the export–import policy are usually announced each year before the national budget.

41. Including new and used capital goods, parts and machinery, but excluding certain consumer goods.
42. August 1991 to March 1998.
43. Chapter 1.9.
44. V. N. Gupta, 'Venturing Abroad', *Times of India*, 3 February 1996.
45. See also *The Economic Times*, 'Russian Maze', 17 May 1998; and *The Hindu*, 'Indo-Russia Buyer-Seller Meet in St. Petersburg', 31 March 1998. As a comparison, India's bilateral trade with China also rose to almost US$2 billion in 1997, with Indian exports accounting for US$900 million and imports from China standing at US$930 million.
46. This is still the case with many Indian executives, although the Ministry of Foreign Economic Relations has been abolished as part of public sector reshuffling in 1997. See Indo–CIS Trade Conference, background paper, 17–18 September 1996, New Delhi, p. 11.
47. These sectors were also defined as priority areas during the visit of Prime Minister Primakov to India in December 1998.
48. Today, about 85 per cent of Indian exports to Russia utilize the 'rupee trade route', which was established between the two countries to enable India to pay back the debt it had accumulated during Soviet times. A major challenge will consist in raising the 'free trade' share and in providing incentives for FDI to Russia.
49. Strategic planning by the Indian government has made the economy more resilient to external shocks like the Southeast Asian financial crisis of 1997–98. The US sanctions imposed after the nuclear tests in May 1998 had no significant impact on economic growth and FDI applications by foreign companies.
50. See recent study of the Confederation of Indian Industries (CII), New Delhi, 1998.
51. Out of Russia's total exports of US$86 billion in 1997, only about 30 per cent were manufactured goods, the rest being raw materials (fuels, minerals). The ratio for China was 85:15 in favour of manufactured goods. For India, the ratio is 75:25.
52. Birla invested in a rayon grade pulp plant in Russia as early as 1994.
53. This list is a condensed and simplified version of Annexure III of the NIP. The original list can be consulted on the Internet: <http://indmin.nic.in> On 11 February 2000, the Indian government decided to place all items and activities barring a few under the automatic approval route.

7
FDI Policies and Prospects in Mexico

Map 7.1 Mexico

7.1 Competitive advantages and lessons for Russia

Mexico, whose population will reach 100 million by the year 2000, is by far the most populated Spanish-speaking country in the world. In the Americas, it ranks third after the United States (270 million) and Brazil (160 million). Its total land area (almost 2 million sq. km) is the fourth largest after the United States, Brazil and Argentina. Mexico shares a common border of about 3100 km with the United States, its largest trading and investment partner, and its geographic proximity to the United States, the world's leading economy, is Mexico's most important location-specific asset for attracting inward FDI.

Since the formation of the North American Free Trade Association (NAFTA) in 1994, foreign investors can trade and establish operations freely within the economic grouping that also comprises Canada and the United States. TNCs from Europe, Asia and South America prefer Mexico as a regional manufacturing platform for exports to Canada and the United States, just as they select Ireland and the United Kingdom for continental Europe, or Hong Kong for China. However, geographic closeness to the US market and NAFTA membership are not the only assets of this LEM, Mexico offers

- a highly educated population, especially in the larger cities[1] (Mexico, Monterrey, Guadalajara, Leon, Puebla), but also in areas bordering the United States (Tijuana, Mexicali, Ciudad Juarez, Nuevo Laredo);
- an extremely young workforce – in 1997, 40 per cent of the total population or about 35 million people were under 18 years of age (similar to other LEMs except Russia, where the percentage is only 22 per cent);
- an abundance of natural resources, especially energy (oil and gas), minerals, a wide variety of food crops (tropical fruit, vegetables) and fish;
- an increasingly diversified industrial sector owing to the successful *maquiladora* industrial development programme;[2]
- excellent trade and economic relations with Latin America, the Pacific Rim and EU countries.[3]

The creation of NAFTA with Mexico's participation has benefited the domestic economy,[4] as it brought fiscal stability, economic growth, a stable currency and industrial and technological diversification. Ever since, politicians have become active promoters of free trade and liberal investment regimes across even wider regional groupings.[5] Mexico, which is considered progressive by regional standards, now serves as a model for other Latin American economies (Colombia, Peru, Venezuela) as they move towards more liberal FDI regimes and greater integration in the world economy.

The Mexican economy has come a long way from the severe recessions of the early 1980s, which did not reassure foreign investors. Chronic capital shortages because of high debts and restrictive macropolicies had lowered the country's credit ratings and financial possibilities. But globalization and greater economic integration with the rest of the world compelled the Mexican leadership to introduce wide-ranging policies to liberalize and deregulate the economy and improve domestic investment conditions. Mexican industry – similar to that of Russia today – was not knowledge-intensive and exports comprised mainly raw materials and low value-added products such as agricultural produce, textiles, mechanical parts and steel rods, which were often repacked and processed across the border in the United States.

The Mexican government started by opening basic infrastructure facilities (roads, ports and telecommunications) to foreign investors in the early 1990s. Deregulation and strong economic performance were prerequisites for admission to the OECD and WTO in 1995. Since Mexico joined the OECD club of advanced economies, its economic performance[6] has come under regular scrutiny by the organization. In return, Mexico benefits from special assistance and advisory mechanisms to enable member countries coordinate their economic policies to maintain high growth, cut inflation, stimulate world trade and reduce unemployment. Mexico is the only large emerging economy that has joined the OECD so far.[7] Together with Brazil, it has become the most popular destination economy for FDI in Latin America.

Attracted by a domestic market that expands at an average rate of 6–7 per cent annually, most of the world's top 200 companies have set up manufacturing or sales subsidiaries in Mexico. The Mexican authorities maintain close contact with these companies, mainly through the network of embassies and consulates in other OECD countries. The Mexican government is also interested in attracting medium-sized TNCs.

For Russian FDI authorities, Mexico represents an interesting case for two main reasons. First, it demonstrates the positive impact of belonging to a wider regional grouping that includes powerful members like Canada and the United States, where many of the world's top TNCs are headquartered.[8] Regional integration through NAFTA opened access to international capital markets and public finance, which supported the economy even during the 1994 crisis. Mexico's recovery that year was much faster than in the 1980s[9] or compared with other less-integrated – and therefore more vulnerable – South American economies. Russia would also benefit from closer cooperation with the geographically close CIS (Ukraine, Kazakhstan) and Central European countries, and EU member states. Secondly, the Mexican example also shows how closely economic revival is linked to a consistent policy of FDI liberalization at home and the systematic promotion of location-specific advantages abroad. Continuous publicity by the Mexican

FDI authorities has paid off as investors from all important Triad regions (EU, Asia, North and South America) have established their manufacturing platforms and regional headquarters in Mexico.

Following the last 1994 crisis, which was partly provoked and then intensified by capital withdrawals by institutional investors (similar to Russia's August 1998 crash), the Mexican government is expected to place even more emphasis on FDI (as opposed to portfolio investment), which makes economic recovery much more sustainable. US, European and Asian manufacturing operations in Mexico in fact helped the country to overcome the crisis by maintaining high production and export levels. The *maquiladora* scheme[10] comprises attractive incentives to foreign companies investing in specially designed industrial zones. Mexico thus became a preferred location for consumer and capital goods industries, which raised domestic employment significantly and brought stability against fluctuations on the capital markets.

To consolidate its position, Mexico will need to focus on high value-added manufacturing rather than raw materials processing, which still represents about 40 per cent of state revenue.[11] The 1997 fall of international oil prices had serious consequences for Mexico's balance of payments, although oil now represents only around 10 per cent of the country's exports (compared with 25 per cent in the mid-1980s). The Mexican government is keen on further reducing its dependence on the US market and identifying alternative trading partners. In 1997, almost 80 per cent of the country's exports went to United States, which also accounts for 60–64 per cent of inward FDI stock.[12]

7.2 Inward FDI policy and structural reforms

Mexico's post independence period[13] was marked by *laissez-faire* capitalism that allowed foreign operators to hold significant stakes in the national economy including important companies. In the early 1920s, this situation was exploited by US and European corporations determined to secure their supplies of oil, strategic minerals and essential agricultural resources. Resentment against foreign influence in the national economy rose and in 1938 President Cardenas resorted to the nationalization of oil refineries. For many years, the Mexican authorities tried to shield their economy from foreign influence, and when the Partido Revolucionario Institucional (PRI) consolidated its power in the 1960s, capital inflows were still subjected to strict controls with the objective of protecting Mexican enterprises and property.

The government continued to adopt restrictive policies throughout the 1970s and 1980s, when only a limited number of sectors were opened to foreign investors so that domestic companies could consolidate market shares at home. The objective was to raise self-reliance and thus reduce expensive imports. By checking FDI inflows, national politicians intended to stop the sell-out of key industries to large TNCs, which benefited from a favourable exchange rate and mostly pursued short-term objectives of profit maximization to the detriment of long-term socioeconomic development. Against the background of worldwide trade liberalization and global competition, the self-reliance strategy had to be partially abandoned in the mid-1980s. In a highly protected environment, domestic enterprises could not match international competitiveness and technological progress of their foreign counterparts. Mexico's over dependence on imports of knowledge-intensive products and components[14] and persisting economic recession eventually forced the Mexican government to adopt policies that facilitated restructuring of enterprises, privatization, fiscal reorientation and FDI liberalization.

But FDI was not completely liberalized as political groups connected with the national union movement pressed hard for legislation that restricted foreign investment to only specific industries. At the same time, a new export-oriented, outward-looking business class favoured radical socioeconomic transformation. The government embarked on a policy of greater international integration of the Mexican economy which eventually raised economic growth and standards of living. Although the upward cycle was temporarily interrupted by the peso crisis of 1994–5, this policy visibly modernized manufacturing, banking, retailing and transport.

As with India, the change in policy was made inevitable by the serious financial problems of the public sector and ensuing pressure by leading industrialized countries and international organizations. The United States was the strongest advocate of economic liberalization and deregulation in Mexico because many US companies, especially from California, New Mexico and Texas, had built up vital interests in the Mexican economy.

Structural adjustment was pursued rigorously through a consistent privatization programme covering the entire economy during 1994–98. Direct and portfolio foreign investment brought in significant amounts of capital, which redressed the balance of payments. The first wave of privatizations, approved under the administration of President Carlos Salinas in 1988, spurred the private sector and reoriented business activities towards services and higher value-added technologies. Corporate and state resources were allocated more effectively, private entrepreneurship received an impetus, and export performance improved. By mid-1996, more than 1200 state-owned enterprises had been privatized, generating a total revenue of US$25 billion for the government. Recently, strategic sectors on which the state still maintained control – such as railways, ports, roads, and airports – were also privatized. The government encourages entrepreneurship through tax advantages, more flexible labour laws, and the possibility for foreign companies to own real estate. In addition, it has established training and applied science institutions of higher learning to raise education standards that meet the needs of a modern economy.

Privatization has been extended to practically all important sectors: hotels, airlines, most banks, the state telephone company (Telmex), mining (Minera Cananea), paper mills, TV channels (TV Azteca), sugar mills, seafood distribution, fishing companies, automobile assembly and steel companies. The current programme includes sectors that were highly protected in the past: ports, petrochemicals, highways, airports and railways. About 120 enterprises are still state-owned, half of which will probably be passed on to private owners by 2000–03. Privatization opens new business prospects for foreign investors who can thus gain access to sectors formerly limited exclusively to the Mexican state and nationals.

The strategy of the government of President Zedillo – as during President Salinas' term – consists in attracting FDI in manufacturing which, unlike simple portfolio investment,[15] will upgrade and restructure key industries and raise employment levels. To attract foreign manufacturers, more economic sectors were opened to FDI (100 per cent ownership in banking), and location-specific assets were systematically developed through special incentive mechanisms (tax breaks and holidays, financial support for staff training, advisory services). Economic reorientation is closely linked to the country's northward integration with the United States and Canada through NAFTA. It allows Mexican companies access to the world's largest consumer market and the latest manufacturing technologies. Other emerging economies of Latin America such as Argentina, Brazil and Chile have to rely more on themselves and on regional alliances with neighbouring countries (MERCOSUR) to maintain the high-growth momentum.

A special government agency, the Secretaria de Comercio y Fomento Industrial (SECOFI), was entrusted the task of promoting industrial development, coordinating the country's FDI policy and approving large-scale foreign investment projects. Located in the capital, it is presided over by the Minister of Industry and Trade, who is also a permanent cabinet member. SECOFI is assisted by the specially created Mexican Investment Board (MIB), a nonprofit organization jointly sponsored by the government (Ministry of Trade and Industrial Development, Ministry of Foreign Affairs), the business community and major banks. MIB guides and informs foreign investors about sales prospects, legal changes and local finance (website <www.mib.org.mx>).

7.3 Foreign investment legislation

7.3.1 The 1973 and 1993 FDI laws

In 1973, the Mexican parliament passed the Law to Promote Mexican Investment and Regulate Foreign Investment. This rather restrictive law reflected the intention of the authorities to strictly control all foreign investment activities in Mexico. During the 1970s, direct investment by foreign operators remained tightly regulated, monitored, and almost entirely restricted to minority participation in a few economic sectors. A change in approach to FDI during the first half of the 1980s translated into a more liberal interpretation of the 1973 Law. In 1989, a special regulation permitted, for the first time, foreign equity participation of 49 per cent and above, without prior authorization. It was applied immediately to 73 per cent of industries and services.[16] Automatic approval was granted for foreign investment up to US$100 million.

Completely overhauled legislation which totally liberalized FDI was eventually passed in December 1993 by the Mexican parliament, as the country prepared itself to ratify the NAFTA treaty. The 1993 Foreign Investment Law (FIL) reflects a three-pronged strategy:

- to clear key economic sectors for majority participation by foreign corporations;
- to simplify the screening process;
- to streamline the activities of various government departments responsible for promoting FDI.

The Foreign Investment Commission (FIC) was specially created and made the sole and exclusive authority to implement and enforce the new law. Whereas the main tenet of the previous (1973) law was controlled expansion of multinationals so that only requisite technology could be transferred to Mexican industry, the 1993 law aims to upgrade all pillar industries through FDI. Officers in Mexican embassies and consulates were specially trained for promoting FDI; they also directly approach medium-sized companies from leading industrialized countries, which have been recognized as major targets in the coming years. Since the new law came into force, several hundred large and medium-sized TNCs from Canada, the United States and Europe have invested in the Mexican economy.

The 1993 law nullifies all previous provisions that restricted foreign participation to predetermined economic activities; foreign companies are now allowed to control up to 100 per cent equity in Mexican enterprises. The repealed 1973 law had limited FDI to 49 per cent participation, unless expressly authorized under special provisions, whereas, under the new law, only in certain strategic sectors is foreign participation forbidden or restricted to minority holdings.[17] Following the outflow of capital during the 1994 financial crisis, the government was compelled to allow greater foreign participation, even in sectors that were earlier totally protected: railways, ports, airports, telecommunications and most financial services. Nevertheless, the FIC has to issue a special permission in case of acquisition of majority stakes in 'economically indispensable' Mexican companies. FIL authorizes foreign companies to own real estate for nonresidential purposes (as in Russia today, only long-term leases were permitted earlier). NAFTA and non-NAFTA companies are subject to the same stipulations, with a few exceptions specified in Articles 5–7 of the 1993 law.

7.3.2 Supplementary legislation

Mexico's government has launched a process of economic modernization by adopting unprecedented actions to reduce government intervention in the economy and to open it to international competition. Being an OECD member, Mexico had to adapt its entire legislation to western standards. The country's legal framework today consists of a series of interdependent mechanisms which mostly offer foreign operators national treatment and the security needed to plan and undertake long-term FDI projects. The most important areas, which have been regulated in a fairly transparent manner, are:

- ***Tax legislation***: The Income Tax Law specifies tax rates for private and corporate operators, including foreign investors. Other taxes affecting FDI are the value-added tax and business asset tax. Mexico has also signed double-taxation treaties with almost all OECD countries. The country's tax treaty with the United States, which came into effect with the start of NAFTA, reduced withholding taxes on interest, royalties and capital gains as an additional incentive for encouraging foreign direct and portfolio investment.
- ***Labour regulations***: The Federal Labour Law dates from 1970. It governs all aspects of employer–employee relations, including collective bargaining, the right to strike, minimum wage rates, working hours, compensation and occupational health and safety. The law establishes employee rights which sometimes even go beyond the guarantees provided by other OECD countries. Provisions that may deter foreign investors and may be amended in the coming years concern mandatory profit-sharing for employees, limited number of justifiable causes for layoffs and high severance and seniority pay in cases of redundancy.
- ***Liberal exchange control regime***: Convertibility restrictions have been abolished since November 1991. Similar to China and India, foreign currency may be purchased from authorized banks and exchange houses at quoted rates and upon availability of such foreign currency. Although there is no exchange control, bank accounts may not be denominated in foreign currency, except in few cases for individuals and *maquiladora* operations in border areas with the United States. No limitations are imposed on capital remittances when operations are wound down or dissolved in case of repatriations following disinvestment by foreign entities.
- ***Competition law***: The Competition Law effective as of 1993 aims to regulate trusts and to check unfair trade practices. It is meant to promote fair and open competition in the country. Thus, price-fixing agreements among oligopolistic competitors and suppliers (vertical agreements) are tightly controlled. The law also imposes limitations on mergers and

acquisitions deals when these result in market domination and distortions. Large-scale FDI projects involving possible acquisitions of leading national players have come under close scrutiny by the Mexican authorities.

- ***Industrial property***: The Industrial Property Law, which was amended on 2 August 1994, protects all forms of intellectual property: patents, utility models, industrial designs and secrets, trade marks and brands, and copyright (including software).
- ***Environmental regulation***: Mexico enacted the Environmental Law in 1988 with the purpose of checking water, soil and air pollution, determining the parameters to preserve nature and wildlife, promoting rational use of natural resources, and securing the health of the population. Foreign companies planning to build manufacturing plants have to comply with increasingly strict regulations.

7.4 Foreign investment patterns in the 1990s: origin and destination

7.4.1 FDI inflows and stock

The opening of the Mexican economy to foreign capital led to a noticeable rise in FDI inflows starting from the early 1990s (Figure 7.1). Average inflows during 1991–97 were US$6.5 billion, whereas in the 1980s average annual inflows amounted to only about US$2 billion, the level reached by

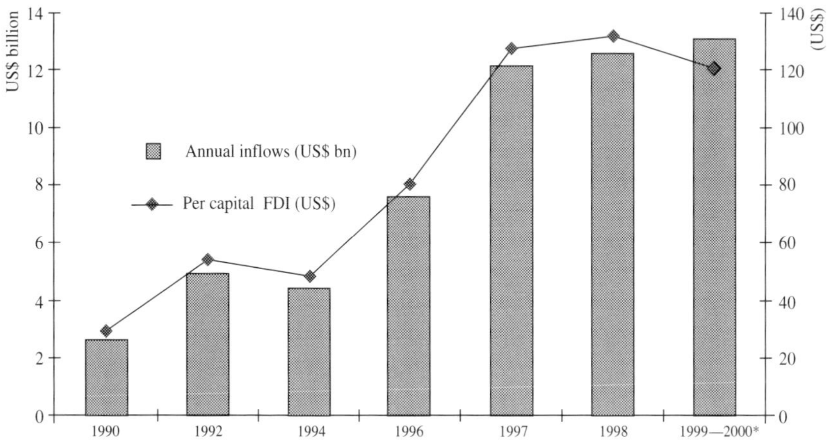

*Estimates

Sources: SECOFI; UNCTAD, *World Investment Reports 1996, 1997, 1998.*

Figure 7.1 Annual and per capita FDI, Mexico, 1990–2000

Russia today. The drop in the value of the Mexican currency coupled with the government's extension of the *maquiladora* programme increased inward investment further during 1995–97. In 1997, inflows touched a new record of US$12 billion and are expected to rise to US$13–14 billion annually during 1999–2002. In 1997, annual per capita inflows reached US$125 – three to four times higher than in Russia.

Current FDI inflows account for about 5–6 per cent of GDP and 17–20 per cent of domestic investment. The Mexican government aims to maintain annual inflows of US$12–14 billion, which seems an achievable target given the country's economic potential and geostrategic location as a manufacturing hub for the North and Latin American markets.

By 2000, Mexico's overall FDI stock is expected to exceed US$100 billion or 60–65 per cent of Canada's level (Figure 7.2). Per capita FDI stock will amount to US$1050 in 1998 (US$915 in 1997), the highest among LEMs but still lower than that of the other two NAFTA members (about three times lower than the United States and five times lower than Canada). In 1997, Mexico's accumulated FDI stock already represented one-quarter of the country's GDP – the highest share among Latin American countries.

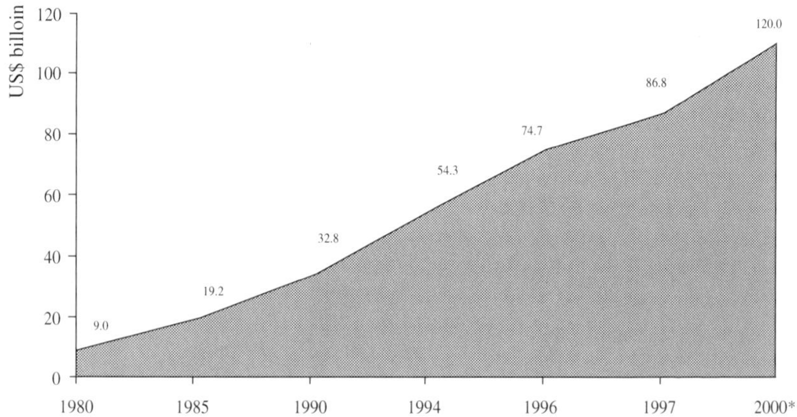

*Estimate

Sources: SECOFI; UNCTAD, *World Investment Reports 1996, 1997, 1998, 1999.*

Figure 7.2 Inward FDI stock, Mexico, 1980–2000

The largest source country for FDI (Figure 7.3) so far has been the United States (59 per cent of stocks), followed by the United Kingdom (8 per cent), Japan (5 per cent) and Germany (4 per cent). By promoting their country in Europe and Asia, Mexican authorities managed to reduce overdependence on US TNCs during 1985–95 (from 65 per cent to 55 per cent of inward FDI stock). However, since the NAFTA treaty was ratified by the Mexican parlia-

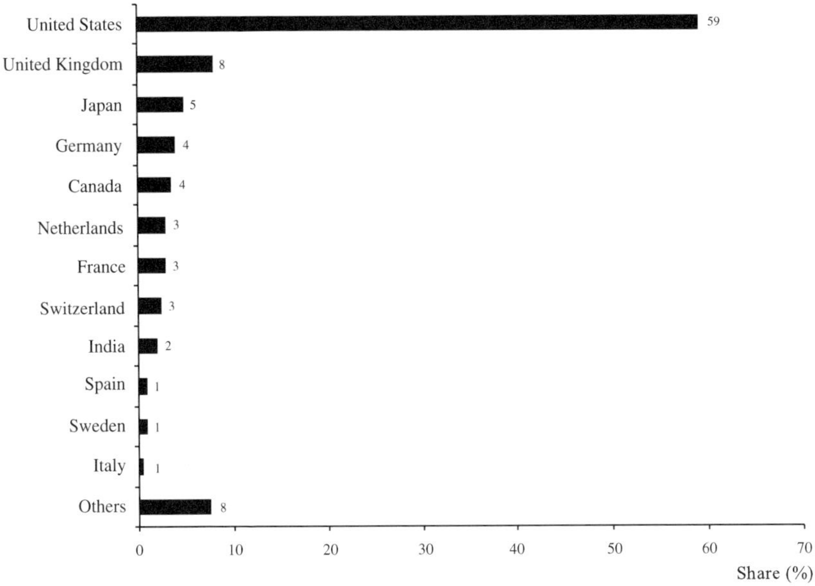

Sources: INEGI, 1998; Banco de Mexico, 1998.

Figure 7.3 Inward FDI by country of origin, Mexico, 1990–97

ment, FDI from the United States has grown steadily leading to a record level of accumulated stock by US operators who by 1998 again held a share of about 65 per cent of total FDI. Japanese FDI also grew considerably following the creation of NAFTA, from only US$61 million in 1983 to about US$2 billion in 1997.[18] Germany's investment that year stood at the same level.

South Korean TNCs had started to invest massively in manufacturing plants for consumer electronics, office automation equipment, automotive components, textiles and consumer goods (white goods, toys), but some of these investments have ground to a halt following the 1998 financial crisis in South Korea.

Japanese FDI projects have also been cut down following economic recession in Asia, but, altogether, traditionally cautious Japanese TNCs regard Mexico as a more stable country than Russia and as an important manufacturing platform for sales to the large US market.[19] Among Asian TNCs, only South Korean companies seem to view Mexico and Russia as two equally important LEMs for the coming decades.[20]

7.4.2 Sectoral and regional distribution of FDI

Foreign investment in Mexico followed the typical pattern of an emerging economy. While the 1940s and 1950s saw the entry of TNCs seeking access to strategic raw materials and natural resources, the 1960s and 1970s were marked by a rise in investments in labour-intensive industries. Mexico thus strengthened its role as an export platform to the United States. Today, the two initial types of investment (raw materials and labour-oriented) have been replaced mostly by market- and strategic asset-seeking FDI accompanied by portfolio operations.

Industry accounts for the bulk of FDI inflows into Mexico: about 70 per cent, compared with 28 per cent for services. Although the tertiary sector (finance, transport, trading, tourism) has grown in importance in the domestic economy, manufacturing ventures predominate. The share of industry has been stable during the 1990s. Inbound FDI is concentrated in a few pillar industries: automobiles (18 per cent); food, beverages and tobacco (16 per cent); chemicals (14 per cent); electricity industry and electronics (6 per cent); metallurgy (5 per cent); oil derivatives, mechanical engineering, paper and printing technologies (4 per cent each) (Figure 7.4). In these industries, FDI has definitely contributed to a number of improvements through skill and capital transfers, technology infusion and increased competition. Many competitive Mexican companies (e.g. Cemex, construction; Gruma, food; Grupo Televisa, media) have emerged, which in turn are studying investment opportunities abroad. In the services sector, the bulk of FDI has so far been

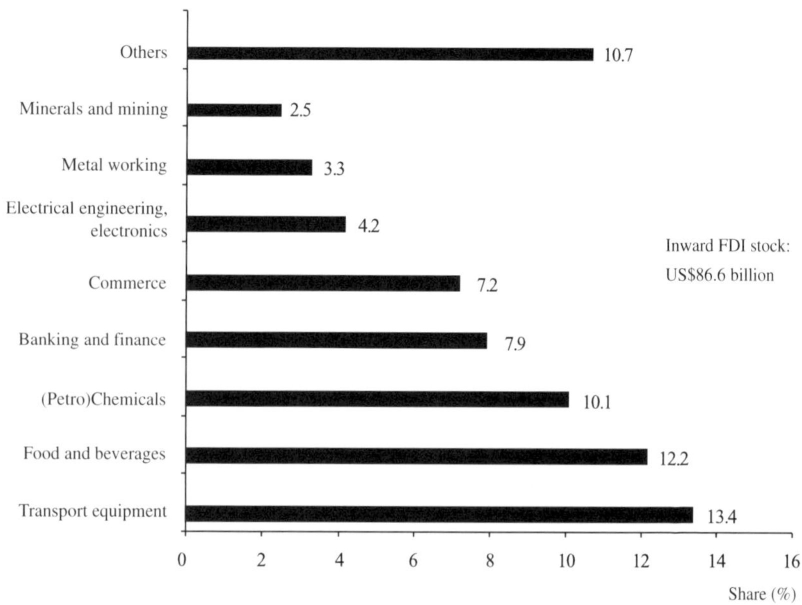

Source: OECD, *International Direct Investment Statistics Yearbook 1997*; SECOFI.

Figure 7.4 Sectoral distribution of FDI, Mexico, 1997

in banking, insurance, and business services (10 per cent); retailing and wholesale trade (7 per cent); and telecommunications (4 per cent).

Although FDI in manufacturing industries is growing,[21] the share of services in total FDI has also risen each year since the early 1990s. Today services account for about 40 per cent of inward FDI stock against 55 per cent for industry (in 1985, only 16 per cent of the stock was in services). It is expected that by 2003–04, services may draw even with industry as services sectors are liberalized. Banks and hotel operators have particular interest in the growing Mexican market.

For many years, FDI has followed a certain regional pattern with above-average concentration in the capital Mexico City and other leading cities such as Guadalajara (Jalisco), Monterrey (Nuevo Leon), and the border cities of Ciudad Juarex and Tijuana. The economically motivated uprising in the southern province of Chiapas demonstrated the importance of balanced regional development for political stability and investment generation. Ever since, the Mexican government has decided to provide additional incentives for FDI projects in more remote regions of the interior.

7.4.3 Mexico's outward investment position

Until the early 1950s, Mexico's location-specific advantages were insufficient to attract significant FDI, with the exception of investments in mining, oil extraction and agriculture. Some domestic companies had begun to export mostly low value-added consumer goods, textiles and processed food to the United States, but they had yet to gain the necessary financial strength to upgrade their technology, or even consider setting up production facilities abroad. Until the mid-1980s, Mexico's economy was considered to still be at Stage 1 of the investment development path,[22] which is characterized by low inbound investment and almost nonexistent outbound FDI. Since the early 1990s, the country has gradually moved to stage 2 of the IDP (rising inbound and negligible outbound FDI).

Following the systematic modernization of mechanical, chemical and textile industries and the development of advanced information technologies, leading Mexican operators are gradually emerging as foreign investors in markets such the United States, Canada, Latin America and western Europe (especially Spain). Large Mexican TNCs[23] have started buying stakes in foreign companies in an effort to undertake market-seeking and strategic investments. Since 1988, mergers and acquisitions originating from Mexican operators (including foreign-equity enterprises) have more than trebled, from US$800 million to US$3 billion.[24] Large Mexican banks have followed their clients abroad and contribute to further expansion of outward FDI.

Outward Mexican FDI is mainly concentrated in certain production and service sectors such as cement, glass, automotive components and agribusiness.[25] In terms of outward stock (US$3.3 billion in 1997), Mexico trails a number of other Latin American countries, including Brazil (US$8.7 billion), Chile (US$5.8 billion) and Venezuela (US$3.4 billion) (Figure 7.5).

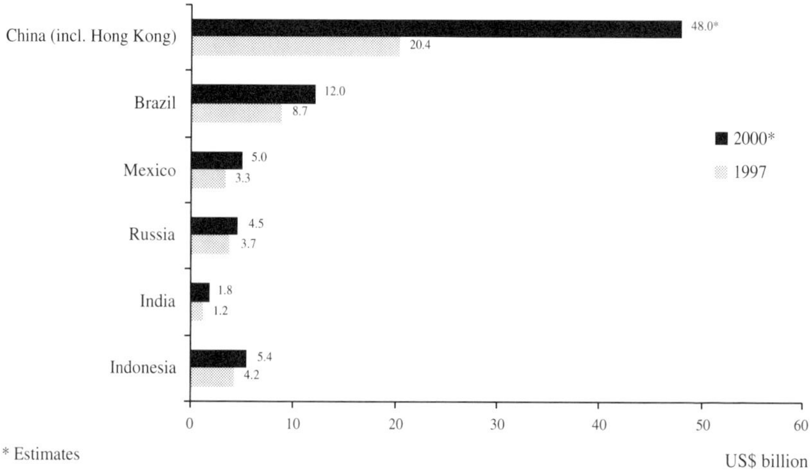

Source: UNCTAD, *World Investment Reports 1996, 1997*; SECOFI.

Figure 7.5 Outward FDI stock, Mexico and other LEMs, 1997, 2000

The formation of NAFTA has stimulated outward expansion. But, altogether, inflows still outpace outflows, which indicates that the country has not yet reached stage 3 of the IDP. Most outward investors are long established market leaders. Otherwise, Mexican companies in general do not yet appear to be strong enough to invest abroad and thus compensate at least partially for the investments made by foreign operators in the domestic market. In fact, the gap between inward and outward FDI is expected to widen as Mexico's high economic growth in the coming years will attract even more foreign operators. Moreover, the country has still to recover completely from the 1994 financial crisis, which made domestic companies financially vulnerable and the country highly dependent on FDI for modernizing its industries. The country's net outward investment (NOI) position is therefore expected to remain negative for at least 10–15 years.

7.4.4 The NAFTA factor

The NAFTA founders had the following major objectives in mind:

- to eliminate trade barriers between member countries;
- to foster conditions required for achieving fair competition;
- to increase opportunities for foreign investment;

- to guarantee adequate protection of intellectual property rights;
- to establish effective arbitration procedures for the resolution of legal cases;
- to reinforce trilateral cooperation between the United States, Canada and Mexico;
- to promote regional and multilateral exchange of know-how on the basis of inter-enterprise cooperation and cultural programmes; and
- to contribute to a better protection of the environment.

The grouping today offers a US$7 trillion consumer market of around 400 million people making it even more important than the EU in terms of total population and combined purchasing power. It has intensified inter-government cooperation and further economic integration and coordination. NAFTA has also favoured foreign trade and trilateral FDI between Canada, Mexico and the United States. Foreign companies located in Mexico can now trade and do business more effectively than before. This is one of the main marketing argument of Mexico's FDI authorities in their efforts to promote their country's locational advantages and to canvass foreign investors.

The NAFTA Treaty specifically stipulates, in Articles 1102 and 1103, the three principles encouraged by the WTO: nondiscrimination, most favoured nation and national treatment. These obligations apply to all activities related to the 'establishment, acquisition, expansion, management, conduct, operation, and sale or other disposition of investment'. In addition to these general provisions, certain commonly encountered forms of discrimination, such as requirements that a minimum level of equity be held by local nationals or that certain senior management positions be reserved to local nationals, have been abolished. Currency convertibility at market rates is also guaranteed. NAFTA prohibits expropriation, except for public purposes on a nondiscriminating basis and in accordance with due process of law and with compensation paid without delay at a pre-expropriation fair market value with applicable interest (Articles 1109 and 1110).[26] Besides offering ample protection mechanisms for foreign investors, NAFTA provides for cascading tariff reductions,[27] facilitation of immigration and work permit procedures of NAFTA citizens, special allowances for government procurement contracts and for special labour and environmental protection agreements.

The effects of NAFTA on the Mexican economy were studied in econometric models developed by Mexican and US economists in the early 1990s. Depending on the underlying assumptions, the NAFTA effect on GDP ranges from 0.5 per cent (constant return hypothesis) to over 8 per cent (growing return hypothesis coupled with free movement of capital). The trade and economic gains of NAFTA have so far exceeded all expectations. If the temporary 1994 crash is excluded, GDP rose by an average of 6 per cent during 1991–97, which almost corresponds to the constant or gradual return forecasts.[28]

The positive experience of NAFTA encouraged Mexican policy-makers to intensify trading links with the main Central and South American economies, with whom free trade agreements exist (Colombia, Venezuela, Brazil, Argentina, Chile). A proposal has also been mooted to start formal negotiations towards uniting all major groupings (NAFTA, MERCOSUR, Andes Pact, Central American Common Market) into a Free Trade Area of the Americas.

Whereas the Mexican government and the Clinton administration seek to expand NAFTA to the south, there is strong congressional opposition to US involvement in a larger agreement. Following Mexico's last financial crisis, which led to large-scale bail-out operations through international – especially US – banking institutions, a mega grouping raises the spectre of increased money transfers from the United States to the poorer southern countries. But intense competition from European and Asian TNCs for a share in Latin American markets may spur the US Congress to grant the 'fast track' authority[29] for further economic integration with leading South American countries (first Chile, then Brazil, Argentina and Venezuela). With or without NAFTA, the trend towards global trade and FDI liberalization appears to be unstoppable in the Americas, where a homogeneous free-trade and investment area is in the making from Alaska to Terra del Fuego.[30]

Ever since NAFTA was formed, FDI inflows from Australia, New Zealand and Asian countries have increased. Many Asian TNCs from South Korea, Japan, Taiwan, China and ASEAN opted for Mexico as their main manufacturing platform in the Americas. Mexico signed a free-trade agreement with the EU in 1999. Increasingly, FDI has become a significant issue in bilateral and multilateral conventions. This would certainly raise investors' awareness of Mexico's juridical accountability, political stability,[31] liberal FDI policy and economic growth 'just across the US border'.

Future efforts at regional integration will not be limited to the American and European continents. Asian nations are also moving forward in this respect[32] and it is in Russia's interest to pursue integrative efforts with its CIS and European neighbours. This includes an early ratification of the CIS convention on the protection of foreign investors' rights by the different CIS parliaments (*Gosdumas*) during the course of 1999.[33]

7.5 Macroeconomic impact and industrial restructuring through FDI

7.5.1 FDI-induced economic changes

NAFTA, privatization and economic deregulation have brought a continuous flow of foreign investment from third countries. Mexico's overall economic performance has, as a result, improved strongly since the early 1990s. All key indicators show significant improvements especially during 1996–98: GDP, gross capital formation (domestic investment), consumption, foreign trade and employment (Figure 7.6). GDP fell, however, following the 1994 peso crisis (–6 per cent in 1995), when increased government and corporate debt, compounded by political instability in the Chiapas province in southern Mexico, incited financial speculators to disinvest massively from the country's securities markets. The rapid recovery of the economy in about 15 months (mid-1996) indicates the resilience of the Mexican economy.

In 1998, Mexico's GDP is expected to exceed US$350 billion, propelling the country to rank 5 among LEMs (rank 2 in per capita terms after Brazil). Real GDP now looks set to grow by at least 4–5 per cent annually until 2000 and beyond, placing the country among the fastest growing Latin American economies. During 1990–97, per capita GDP rose by over 40 per cent, from US$2490 to almost US$3500.[34]

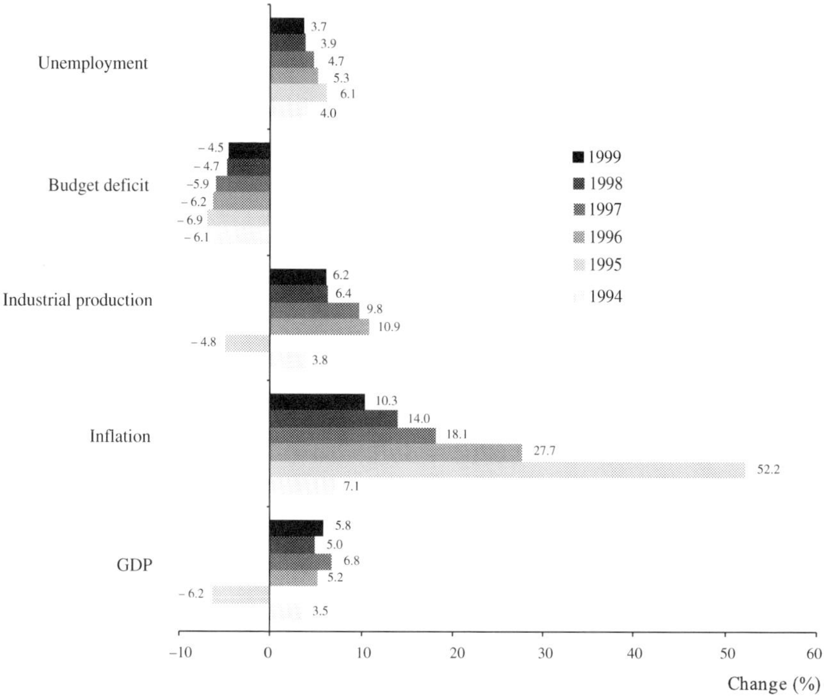

Sources: INEGI, OECD, BfAI, Statistisches Bundesamt, *The Economist*.

Figure 7.6 Main economic indicators, Mexico, 1994–99

Budgetary discipline stabilized the economy starting from early 1996, when the consolidated state budget showed a relatively low deficit of about 2 per cent (Russia, 4 per cent). The budget could have been almost balanced had the government not faced a drop in taxes and duties to the order of –21 per cent during 1994/95 (–34 per cent for import duties, –24 per cent for income tax). State debt was curtailed to 20 per cent of GDP, compared with 68 per cent in 1988. Short-term interest for monthly treasury bonds dropped from 47 per cent in 1995 to 26 per cent in 1996, owing to a cautious monetary policy and budgetary restraints. Low interest rates have benefited both domestic and foreign investment.

The inflation rate (30 per cent in 1996; 25 per cent in 1997), which rose to 52 per cent during the crisis in 1994/95, came down to 16 per cent in 1998. Although this is higher than the government's target of 10–14 per cent, the remarkable drop in the inflation rate is still a positive sign of successful policy implementation.

By mid-1997, the country's foreign reserves amounted to US$22 billion, against a remaining external debt of US$90 billion (US$130 billion in 1996).[35] The IMF provides support through a special loan facility of US$15 billion. During the peso crisis, state authorities estimated that about US$14 billion (mainly private funds) fled the country as capital exports, adding to the estimated US$30–40 billion already accumulated in foreign bank accounts by Mexican nationals (especially in the United States). Although Mexico has managed to attract inward FDI worth US$7–8 billion per annum since 1996, these transfers could hardly compensate the losses caused by capital flight. The government's main concern, therefore, is to maintain high international confidence in the country's economic and political stability.

Unemployment is a relatively new phenomenon. It stands at about 6 per cent of the country's workforce, double that before the 1994–95 crisis. There are signs that industrial restructuring and consequent automation of manufacturing processes will lead to higher unemployment in the coming year if the workforce is not retrained for other skills.

7.5.2 Impact on national export performance

Until 1982, Mexico was a protected and inward looking economy. Earlier, 78 per cent of exports were derived from only one product, oil, whereas today manufactured goods represent 82 per cent of all export sales. Industrial diversification through FDI has improved enterprise competitiveness. As a result of massive capital and technology inflows, exports recorded exponential growth.[36] Since 1990, each additional dollar of FDI has been accompanied by several dollars of exports (Figure 7.7), which has been an important factor for overcoming the 1994 crisis. Although export performance is often attributed to other factors (e.g. privatizations, tax reductions), FDI has unquestionably contributed to industrial diversification, which has improved trade performance.

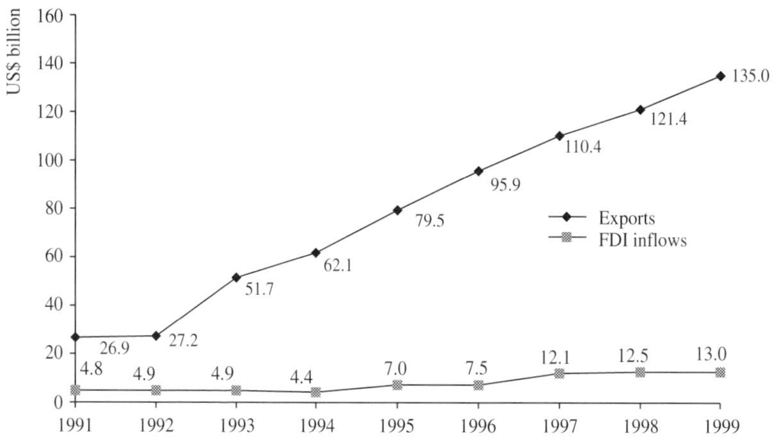

Sources: SECOFI; UNCTAD, *World Investment Report 1998*.

Figure 7.7 FDI inflows and exports, Mexico, 1990–99

Exports rose by over 23 per cent during 1995–97 to reach a record volume of US$110 billion (US$121.4 billion in 1998). Mexico's trade volume is now almost double that of Brazil and four times that of Argentina. Export activities by foreign investment enterprises have made Mexico the world's tenth largest exporting nation accounting for 40 per cent of Latin American shipments overseas. Exports are forecast to rise to US$135 billion in 1999. For the first time in many years, Mexico's trade balance turned positive again in 1995 and 1996, closing with a surplus of US$7.1 billion and US$2.5 billion, respectively. The rapid growth in exports is a significant achievement considering that the trade deficit was US$18.5 billion in 1994.

But Mexico's current foreign trade position also hides structural weaknesses. Trade is almost entirely focused on the US market, which accounted for about 84 per cent of exports and 76 per cent of imports in 1997 (Figure 7.8). Since Mexico joined NAFTA, foreign trade with its northern neighbours Canada and the United States has increased. The United States will continue to rank the highest as Mexico's trading partner; meanwhile Japan (5 per cent of imports) and Germany (4 per cent of imports) are gradually increasing their share. The largest importers (United States, Japan and Germany) are also the biggest investors. On the export side, Canada has replaced Japan as the second most important client market. Third comes Spain, the former colonial power.

Diversification of FDI to the *maquiladora* industries[37] has upgraded exports from labour-intensive products (textiles, apparel, footwear) to more finished and high value-added goods (automotive components, elec-

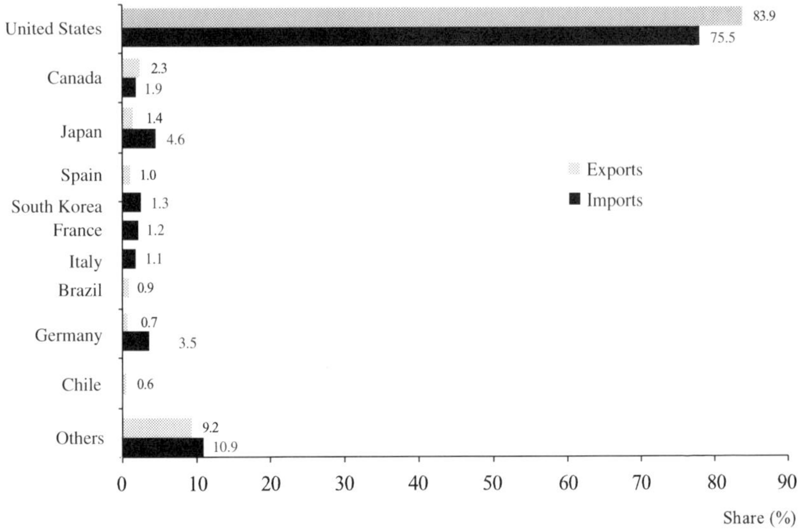

Source: INEGI, 1998.

Figure 7.8 Mexico's major trading partners, 1997

tronics, chemicals). Today, energy-related products represent only about 12 per cent and agricultural produce about 4 per cent of exports, compared with almost 50 per cent (combined total for both categories) of the total volume in the early 1970s. This is a clear sign of the improved international competitiveness of Mexico's industrial enterprises. Non-oil exports have continued to rise by 20 per cent annually since 1995. They comprise a significant share of intermediary products such as textiles, leather and metallic parts mostly destined for further processing in the United States and EU countries. Altogether, however, the share of high value-added goods (passenger buses, freight trucks, automotive components and electrical equipment) has increased since the 1980s. The value of consumer goods exports rose to almost US$7 billion in 1997; they now include household appliances, toys and sports goods.

Despite visible improvement in exports, the Mexican economy is still dependent on imports of essential transport equipment (11 per cent of imports), machine tools and other capital goods (15 per cent), consumer electronics (19 per cent), and chemicals and plastics (15 per cent). FDI is increasingly directed to non-*maquiladora* industries, whose exports rose by 22 per cent in 1997. In 1995, non-*maquiladora* exports for the first time exceeded *maquiladora* exports, and in 1996 the gap widened to over US$6 billion (US$43.4 billion for non-*maquiladoras*, against US$36.9 billion for *maquiladoras*).

Foreign firms account for a disproportionate share of Mexico's foreign trade. Since the early 1990s, their share of exports stands almost unchanged at 55–60 per cent. The automotive industry still accounts for the largest share of total exports by foreign firms (about 50 per cent), followed by electrical and electronic devices (14 per cent), basic chemicals (10 per cent), nonferrous metals (4 per cent) and pharmaceuticals (3 per cent).[38]

7.5.3 Industrial restructuring through FDI

The Mexican economy has undergone visible changes since the inflow of FDI, which has oriented it towards value-added industries and services. Raw materials (especially crude oil) and agroindustries no longer dominate the economy as in the early 1980s. Nevertheless, Mexico still remains an important producer of crude oil – 5 per cent of world output – and ranks fifth after Saudi Arabia (13 per cent of world output), the United States (11.5 per cent), Russia (10.5 per cent) and Iran (5.5 per cent).[39]

The share of agriculture in GDP has dropped below 7 per cent (similar to Russia).[40] The share of industry in GDP – 29 per cent, including mining and construction – is about 14 percentage points lower than in Russia, but it is an important sector (Figure 7.9) in Mexico as it generates employment and attracts considerable foreign investment. Altogether, Mexico's services sector has the largest share in GDP among LEMs and it is expected that FDI in services, especially from the other two NAFTA members, the United States and Canada, will in future years increase further providing additional stimulus to the economy.

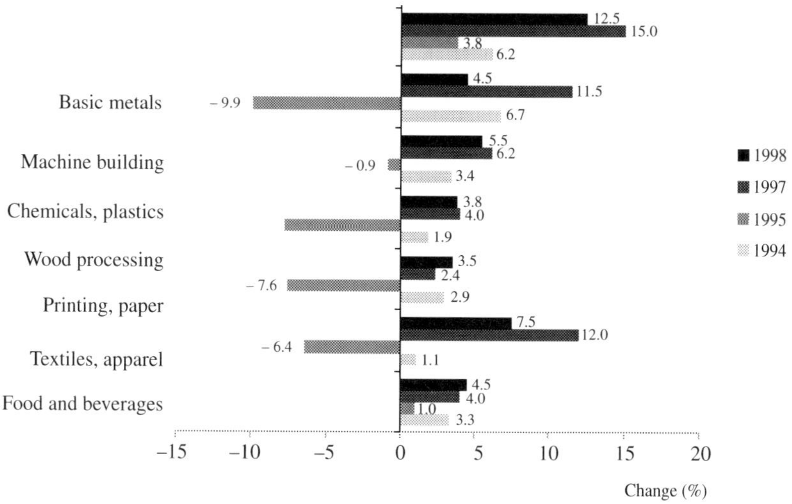

Source: BfAI, Banco de Mexico.

Figure 7.9 Industrial production, Mexico, 1994–98

Mexico's services sector – 67 per cent of GDP – is about 12 percentage points higher than in Russia, where services have also grown in importance following the disintegration of state structures and central planning. Market services, including financial services such as banking and insurance, are developing rapidly. Tourism, transport, trading and catering have become significant employers and income generators. As in other LEMs, nonmarket or public services have also remained very important in Mexico.

The Mexican government's strategy is to rely on FDI inflows to diversify the country's industrial tissue and to improve its export position. During 1998–2000 it plans to attract US$10 billion worth of FDI by offering new location-specific advantages, most probably by opening up new sectors for FDI (e.g. 100 per cent ownership in banking and insurance) and further privatization (e.g. transport infrastructure and satellite communications). TNCs have contributed more to economic restructuring and industrial competitiveness in Mexico than in India or Russia, where FDI commitments in industry are comparatively low. TNCs are key catalysts of structural change in Mexico. They also lead in exports to the United States, largely through intra-company transactions. The government actively promotes technological collaboration between Mexican and foreign companies with the aim of accelerating industrial diversification and modernization.

Foreign companies have so far been attracted by developments in five major industries that, after a significant contraction during 1995–96, have started recovering since 1997:[41]

- iron and steel: +14.9 per cent
- textiles: +9.6 per cent
- metal working: +8.5 per cent
- food and beverages: +3.6 per cent
- plastics and chemicals: +2.9 per cent

Most other industries reported stagnating or even receding output for 1997. With losses of 8 per cent, paper and wood transformation was the worst hit sector. Other sectors where the recovery has so far been difficult were machinery, and 'parts and appliances for the IT sector'. High-tech sectors are still underdeveloped in Mexico, although the government strives to attract foreign expertise in knowledge-intensive, high-growth industries like computers and peripherals, and telecommunications equipment. Within services there is an emphasis on banking, insurance, leasing and real estate.

Certain industries have seen the emergence of fairly large corporate players (Figure 7.10). Sales of the leading Mexican companies range between US$0.8 billion and US$3.4 billion (except Petroleos Mexicanos, US$14.4 billion). They increasingly export and invest in non-NAFTA economies. Some of them may also one day become potential candidates for investments in Russia. The Mexican authorities constantly study and

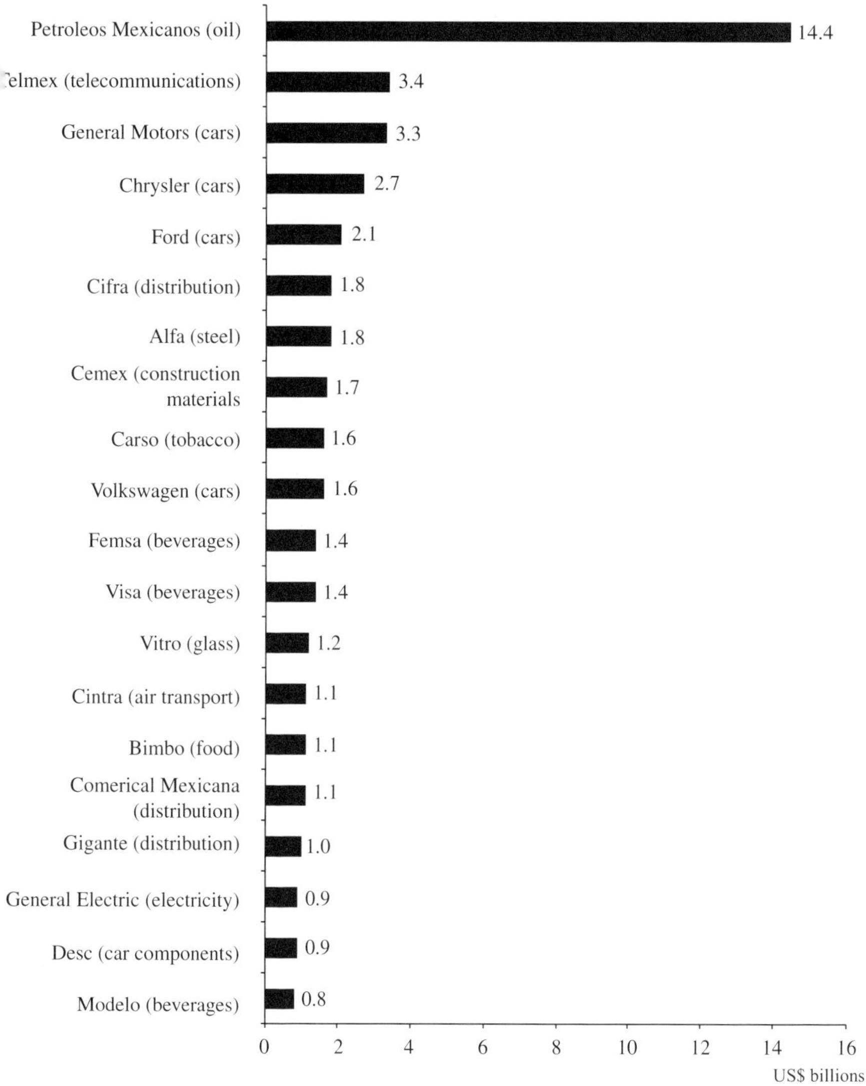

Sources: *Handelsblatt*, 17 September 1998; *Fortune 500*, 3 August 1998.

Figure 7.10 Top 20 Mexican companies by sales, 1997/98

observe developments in other countries. The ultimate aim is to reduce dependence on external know-how. In software development and computer engineering, for example, they look at reasons for success in India. South Korea and Taiwan provide examples for developing electronics and computer-controlled equipment industries. To develop its aeronautics industry, Mexico looks towards Brazil's and Russia's efforts in aerospace and helicopter construction.

7.5.4 The *maquiladora* concept and industrial modernization

Maquiladoras are a special feature of the Mexican economy. Basically, they are industrial enterprises dedicated to the assembly or transformation of foreign inputs (components, semimanufactures) temporarily imported free of customs duties and reexported after assembly or processing.[42] The *Maquiladora* Decree established four categories of authorized free imports:

- *Category 1*: Raw materials, containers, packing material, labels and brochures required to complement production.
- *Category 2*: Tools, equipment and accessories for industrial production and security; products necessary for hygiene and sanitation, pollution control; work manuals, industrial drawings; telecommunication devices and computers.
- *Category 3*: Machinery, apparatus, instruments and spare parts for the production process; laboratory and testing equipment and information products required for quality control; personnel training; and operations management.
- *Category 4*: Trailer bodies and containers.

Most of these imports may remain in the country for up to one year (category 1) or as long as the authorized *maquiladora* programme is still in effect (categories 2 and 3). Consistent with the NAFTA treaty, the *Maquiladora* Decree was amended in 1994 to authorize *maquiladoras* to sell a specified percentage of their output in the domestic market. *Maquiladoras* are given the possibility of becoming truly independent manufacturing establishments as long as their management raises autonomy levels and the unit manufactures competitive products for an entirely new customer base. Today, more than half the *maquiladora* production is already sold domestically, with a tendency for further growth in the years to come. By 2001, the Mexican government plans to remove all restrictions on *maquiladora* sales to the domestic market. On the other hand, *maquiladoras* will lose the benefit of exemption from customs duties and tax.[43] In keeping with the latest regulations from the Ministry of Commerce, *maquiladoras* must report domestic sales on a bimonthly basis, and sales in Mexico are subject to the general import duty on foreign parts and components originally imported duty free. All *maquiladoras* must pay a corporate tax on their profits. In practice, most *maquiladoras* report minimum profits, but, recently, special tax legislation was enacted to regulate transfer pricing between affiliates. At the same time, wide-ranging incentives have been maintained to divert US investments to the Mexican side of the border. Some of these investments would otherwise most probably go to California and Texas. *Maquiladoras* are no longer established solely for their labour cost advantages as in the 1970s and 1980s, when investments focused on the apparel, textiles and metal parts processing industries. They have turned into capital-intensive and higher-skill industries that have to maintain the global competitiveness requirements of investing TNCs. In the 1980s, *maquiladoras* were established mostly in the following sectors: electronic and electrical goods (43 per cent of total production), automotive components and transport equipment (30 per cent), textiles and apparel (6 per cent), wooden and metal furniture (5 per cent).[44]

About half of today's *maquiladoras* are US owned, 30–35 per cent are controlled by Mexican owners, and the rest mainly by Japanese, German and other European investors. The number of US- and Canadian-controlled *maquiladoras* has risen since the signing of the NAFTA treaty.[45] About 80 per cent (95 per cent in the 1980s) of these companies are located in areas close to the US border (especially in the regions of Baja California, Sonora, Chihuahua, Coahuila, Nuevo Leon and Tamaulipas), thus allowing US-based TNCs to take advantage of the production-sharing provisions of the Harmonized Tariff Schedule of the United States. Such companies can also benefit from reduced tariffs for specified imported goods that are assembled outside the United States using US components. *Maquiladoras* have become an important link in the global production network of leading North American operators.

Even during the peso crisis, when overall industrial production declined by almost 7 per cent, the *maquiladora* sector continued to grow in number (8.6 per cent p.a.) and employment (9.8 per cent p.a.). Today, *maquiladoras* are Mexico's second most significant foreign currency earner. The government needs, however, to be alert to prevent social degradation of workers, poor living conditions, and ecological problems. The average daily pay in a *maquiladora* plant amounts to just under US$5. In 1997, there were over 3800 *maquiladora* plants operating in Mexico and providing jobs to nearly 1 million employees[46] (Figure 7.11). Fifteen years earlier, there were only 600 *maquiladora* firms, employing just over 150 000 people. Today, *maquiladoras* produce goods whose value-added is worth over Mex$280 billion (US$35 billion). That puts them second only to oil in the Mexican economy. By 2005, the authorities expect the number to reach 5000, and employment to total over 1.5 million people; their share in GDP is also expected to rise from the current 6 per cent to 9–10 per cent, and in domestic manufacturing from 25 per cent to 33 per cent.

Among the early arrivals in Mexico were US automotive component manufacturers seeking cheap labour opportunities to assemble seat covers, dash boards and fuel systems. They were followed by American car assembly plants (General Motors, Ford, Chrysler) and investors from Japan and other Asian countries. The area around Tijuana, in the Mexican state of

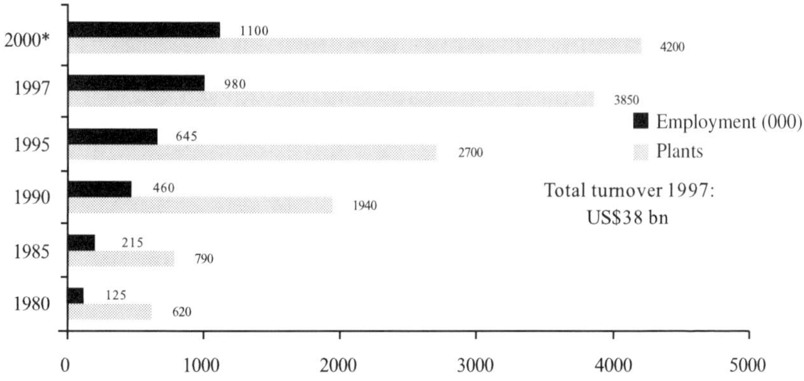

* Estimates

Sources: Banco de Mexico, INEGI.

Figure 7.11 Development of *maquiladora* industries, Mexico, 1980–2000

Baja California, is home to the largest and most technically advanced *maquiladoras*. There, about 1000 firms employ over 200 000 workers in a region directly connected by road and rail with California, the largest and richest US state. The most important products in Baja California are still automotive components and consumer electronics, particularly television sets, of which some 15 million are exported every year, mostly across the border to the United States.

The Korean company Samsung has been operating in the area since 1988; it makes cameras and TV monitors in a vast US$2 billion plant. Hyundai has a large factory that manufactures transport containers and truck trailers. Japan is represented by consumer electronics firms Sony, Hitachi, Matsushita and Sanyo. In early 1997, Sanyo North America moved its headquarters from New York to the outskirts of San Diego from where it can manage its Mexican *maquiladora* operations more easily.

The *maquiladora* scheme will soon need to be updated. It was put in place in the early 1970s when FDI into emerging economies was driven by cost rather than market or strategic concerns. Foreign investments provided TNCs with a manufacturing platform in a low labour cost country where environmental issues were not a priority. The trade unions resent foreign control and deem that the technology and know-how transfers in the *maquiladoras* are inadequate to raise the welfare of workers. Growing labour unrest has become an issue that Mexican authorities increasingly need to address. Another criticism of the scheme is that it has not created competitive medium-sized companies, nor widened the range of their activities. Instead, most companies continue working as subcontractors to larger foreign TNCs. Smaller Mexican industrial outfits face financial problems and depend on their foreign clients or co-owners for investments in human and technical resources to maintain their competitive position. Some of the companies have also applied for public assistance or capital increase by foreign – mainly US – investors.

Being run as subsidiaries from abroad, it is also difficult for *maquiladoras* to attract portfolio capital, which is increasingly diverted to sectors undergoing privatization (e.g. telecommunications, chemicals, petroleum, railways). The *maquiladora* concept, therefore, needs to be embedded in an overall strategy that aims at developing a strong industrial base which includes medium-sized enterprises.

The government has understood the importance of attracting SMEs from investing countries as counterparts for same-sized domestic companies. Such companies are offered many incentives as part of Mexico's SME support programme. Mexican investment promotion bureaus abroad are now canvassing medium-sized companies in the main source countries.[47] These SMEs prefer to invest exclusively in cooperation with their larger client firms, with whom they have long-term delivery contracts. Larger stand-alone investments by medium-sized foreign players are still infrequent owing to several risk factors: difficulty in understanding legislative changes, fear of being left alone, strict labour regulations, language and cultural barriers.

The existence of a direct border with the United States, its rich northern neighbour, makes Mexico a special case. The *maquiladora* concept is not entirely suited to Russia. As a traditionally industrialized country in the northern part of Eurasia, Russia could hardly benefit from a scheme based on the provision of labour-intensive goods to another developed economy, which could act as a 'locomotive'. It must immediately aim at developing pillar industries independently of whether they are labour- (textiles, chemicals) or technology- (electronics, machinery, aerospace) intensive.

Although *maquiladoras* have helped to raise general activity and employment levels in Mexico, the scheme is biased towards border regions and neglects interior territories where skilled labour would also be available. Despite this drawback, a detailed analysis of the key factors of success of the leading *maquiladora* companies (Mexican or foreign majority ownership) would yield interesting lessons for Russian authorities. Some of these companies have grown tremendously over the past 5–6 years because of efficient managerial skills, modern production technologies, aggressive marketing techniques, and quick incorporation into the global production and distribution network of parent or client TNCs. It would also be interesting to analyze further the context in which *maquiladoras* operate (industrial parks, cooperation with regional authorities).

The incentives and promotion mechanisms adopted by Mexican FDI authorities to induce leading TNCs to invest in the *maquiladora* programme should also be studied. By applying some of the progressive techniques adopted by the Mexican authorities, Russia could exploit its major asset, namely its geopolitical location at the very centre of the Eurasian continent, for acquiring FDI from many diverse economies.

Annex 7.1 Restricted sectors, Mexico, 1997–98

A: Activities reserved for the State (strategic sectors)

- Production and refining of oil and basic petrochemicals.
- Electricity distribution and sale.
- Nuclear power generation and production of radioactive materials.
- Telecommunications via satellite.
- Postal, telegraph and radiotelegraph services.
- Bill issuance and coin minting.
- Control, supervision and surveillance of ports, airports and heliports.

B: Activities reserved for Mexican (national) investors

- Domestic land transportation of passengers, tourists and cargo (excluding special delivery and express services).
- Retail distribution of petroleum and liquid gas.
- Radio broadcasting and television services (except cable TV, where foreign participation is allowed up to 49 per cent).
- Credit unions and development banks.
- International land transportation of passengers, tourists and cargo between points on Mexican territory (as from 18 December 1995, foreign equity up to 49 per cent in the capital stock of Mexican companies; as from 1 January 2001, foreign equity up to 51 per cent; as from 1 January 2004, foreign equity up to 100 per cent).

C: Activities subject to limited equity participation

- 10 per cent in cooperative production companies.
- 25 per cent in domestic and specialized air transportation and shuttle services.
- 49 per cent in the following activities:
  (1) holding companies of financial groups, commercial banks, brokerage houses and stock specialists; manufacture and commercialization of explosives and firearms,
  (2) printing and publication of newspapers,
  (3) cable TV and basic telephone services,

(4) videotext and package changeover services,
(5) fishing in freshwater, along the coast and in the exclusive economic zones, except aquaculture,
(6) port administration,
(7) supply of fuel and lubricants for ships, aircraft and railway equipment,
(8) manufacture and assembly of automotive components (as from 1 January 1999, FDI up to 100 per cent).

- Majority participation upon prior approval:
  (1) port services,
  (2) naval companies engaged in high-seas traffic,
  (3) administration of air terminals,
  (4) private education services,
  (5) legal services,
  (6) credit information companies,
  (7) institutions for categorization of securities,
  (8) insurance agencies,
  (9) cellular telephone services,
  (10) oil and gas well drilling,
  (11) construction and civil engineering projects.

Notes

1. Educated people continue to move from larger cities to the US–Mexican border towns to seize interesting job opportunities offered for managers, engineers and computer experts by TNCs operating *maquiladora* plants.
2. Chapter 7.5.4
3. A free-trade agreement between the EU and Mexico was signed in 1999.
4. Chapter 7.5.
5. Moves towards other groupings can be explained by the political aim to reduce dependence on the dominating US economy. See Chapters 7.4.1 and 7.5.2.
6. Chapter 7.5.
7. Russia has also applied for membership but was still considered a 'distant' candidate during a visit of the OECD Secretary-General in early October 1997; *The Moscow Times*, 9 October 1997.
8. FDI from the US west coast (Washington state and California) could, for example, be similarly intensified to develop raw materials resources (oil, wood, fishing) in Siberia and improve living conditions across the region.
9. It took the country almost seven years to recover from the 1982–83 crisis.
10. Chapter 7.5.4.
11. In this respect, Mexico is in a similar position to Russia; 'Poslednaya fyesta Zediyo' [The last party of President Zedillo], *Expert*, vol. 24, 29 June 1998, pp. 18–20.
12. Out of total exports of US$110.4 billion in 1997, goods worth US$86 billion were shipped to the United States.
13. Mexico gained its independence from Spain as early as 1821, but it remained the playing ball of colonial powers until 1967 when Austria and France were compelled to leave. Long civil wars and political instability plagued the first independent governments of the country until 1940.
14. Similar to Russia's situation today.

15. The 1995 financial crisis was triggered by overspeculation. Ever since, the government has focused even more on attracting capital in combination with know-how and technologies by way of FDI.
16. D. Colombo, *El Nafta – En el Marco del Desafio Americano al Mercado Unico* [NAFTA – against the background of the American challenge towards a single market], 1995, p. 140.
17. See list of sectors in Annex 7.1.
18. OECD, *International Direct Investment Statistics Yearbook*, 1997; Mexican Statistical Office (INEGI), SECOFI, 1996–98.
19. Chapter 13.4.2.
20. Companies like Samsung and Daewoo study FDI manufacturing projects in both Russia and Mexico, whereas Japanese companies focus on China, Mexico and Brazil.
21. Chapter 7.5.4.
22. Chapter 1.9.
23. Chapter 4, Annex 4.2.
24. See UNCTAD, *World Investment Report 1997*, M&A statistics.
25. OECD, *Regional Development and Structural Policy in Mexico*, 1997.
26. B. Kryzdal *et al.*, *Mexico – Business Opportunities and Legal Framework*, 1995, pp. 20–21.
27. Fifty per cent of tariffs on all US and Canadian exports to Mexico were abolished on 1 January 1994, the day NAFTA entered into force. By January 1999, this will be raised to 65 per cent of tariffs on all US and Canadian goods entering the country, and by January 2009 all tariffs on NAFTA imports will be removed.
28. D. Colombo, *El Nafta – En el Marco del Desafio Americano al Mercado Unico*, [NAFTA – against the background of the American challenge towards a single market], 1995, pp. 145–8.
29. This coincides with the Mexican government's position. See also *The Cargill Bulletin*, 'NAFTA – The Mexico Factor', April 1997.
30. BfAI, Mexico, *Wirtschaftstrends zur Jahresmitte*, 1997, p. 9.
31. Stability was dented in 1997 because of two main events: uprising in the southern Chiapas region and dwindling majority of the ruling Partido Revolucionario Institucional (PRI) in parliament.
32. Chapter 2.3.
33. Chapter 17.2.8
34. INEGI.
35. The highest foreign debt level in South America after Brazil (US$120 billion in 1997, similar to Russia). *The Economist* indicators, 1997–98.
36. CEPII report, *Compétitivité des Nations* [Competitiveness of nations], 1998, pp. 28–31.
37. Chapter 7.5.4.
38. Direccion General de Inversion Extranjera (General Directorate of Foreign Investment, SECOFI).
39. Tata Services, A *Statistical Outline of India*, International comparisons, 1998, p. 244.
40. For sector shares in GDP, refer to Chapter 8.3.1, Figure 8.3.
41. INEGI, Banco de Mexico. See also J. Dunning, *Foreign Direct Investment and Governments*, 1996, pp. 256–70.
42. B. Kryzdal *et al.*, *Mexico – Business Opportunities and Legal Framework*, 1995.
43. 'Mexikos Einbindung in die NAFTA' [Mexico's integration into NAFTA], *Handelsblatt*, 8 April 1998.

44. D. Colombo, *El Nafta – En el Marco del Desafio Americano al Mercado Unico* [NAFTA – against the background of the American challenge towards the single market], 1995.
45. J.H. Dunning, *Foreign Direct Investment and Governments*, 1996.
46. *The Economist*, 'Manufacturing Survey. The Tijuana Triangle', 20 June 1998, pp. 15–16.
47. Communication from a source with the Mexican FDI authorities in Bonn, Germany (November 1997).

Part IV

Russia's Key Industries and FDI Achievements in the 1990s

Map 8.1 Russia

8
Russia's Economic and Industrial Performance during Transition

Introduction

Breaking away from communism, Russia has opted for a new economic system based on private enterprise, entrepreneurship and free trade. After decades of isolation, ideological barriers have been removed so that the country now has a unique opportunity to raise living standards and to improve employment conditions by linking up domestic industrial capacity to developments in international markets.

While the establishment of a free trade regime and full rouble convertibility has started a practically irreversible process of integration of Russia's economy with world markets, it also means total exposure of Russian enterprises to foreign competition. So far, it has been extremely difficult for national enterprises to adjust to the new economic environment. Handicapped by outdated technologies, lack of capital, and slow development of management practices and competitive products, most factories in Russia run below capacity and often struggle for survival in the new economic environment.[1] Meanwhile, numerous foreign companies have made inroads into the Russian market, mostly through exports and local sales operations.

As a result of the rouble devaluation following the August 1998 crisis, imports have dropped sharply, giving national manufacturers in many industries a real chance to conquer market share.[2] To strengthen this process, inter-enterprise cooperation – drawing on historical and cultural ties with Europe[3] – should be sought more systematically to develop a number of industries whose performance has been far from satisfactory since market reforms were introduced in 1991: aerospace, automobiles and trucks; construction and agricultural machinery; timber, paper processing and furniture manufacturing; mechanical and electrical engineering; computer hardware and software; chemicals and pharmaceuticals; food and beverages; and consumer goods.

Overall FDI in local manufacturing remains low[4] because of the generally negative perception of the investment climate in Russia, which foreign companies do not consider conducive to heavy financial commitments. Russia still suffers from negative publicity in the international media, although this is not always justified[5] and hardly reflects future business prospects in the country. In most industries, there is a sharp contrast between the manufacturing possibilities and know-know Russia can offer and actual FDI inflows. Factual information is not widely disseminated among foreign companies, who often lack the necessary advisory channels for effective implementation of their investment in Russia.[6]

Given its many assets, Russia has a realistic chance of attracting substantially more FDI beyond the year 2000 to revive its industrial sector, but market forces alone will not be sufficient to bring about the desired reshaping and upgrading of the industrial sector. Without state support measures and indicative guidance during the entire transition period, available resources will not be automatically put to effective use. Enterprises will not be able to take advantage of the potential offered by the new global environment and will eventually disappear as they are caught in a vicious circle of low funding for indispensable investments and declining demand for their products and services.[7] Such a situation will hinder the country's industrial and technological advancement and endanger its status as an industrial nation. The government's major challenge will consist in designing a far-sighted strategy to raise the competitiveness of Russian enterprises at home and abroad.[8] To succeed, the government must take into account foreign investors' needs and expectations[9] and match them with the country's overall goals and industrial potential at national, regional, sectoral and enterprise level. In the medium term, there is no alternative to seeking western expertise, technologies and funding for systematic upgrading of specific industries in which Russia wishes to excel in the twenty-first century.

For the government, additional FDI has two immediate advantages. Increased inflow of private capital would allow it to drastically cut subsidies for larger companies and simultaneously entire industries could be reengineered with the help of western know-how. This would raise the market value of many companies, open new opportunities for local managers and improve prospects for further privatizations, reengineering of enterprises and sectors, and development of export potential for finished products. A successful FDI policy presupposes continuous assessment and monitoring of Russia's economic and industrial achievements at regional, sectoral and enterprise levels.[10] FDI targets[11] will need to be linked to the development of major economic and industrial indicators so that the regulatory framework[12] can be adjusted to help raise performance levels through sector-oriented capital and FDI infusions. Concrete proposals and incentive packages can then be formulated and made accessible to innovative enterprises – preferably technology leaders – in the major FDI source countries.[13]

8.1 Socioeconomic transformation since independence

8.1.1 Impact of economic reforms and structural adjustments

Dramatic structural changes have occurred in the Russian economy as a result of the disappearance of central planning, which was biased in favour of heavy industry and defence-related sectors over consumer goods and services as well as oligopolistic structures over small and medium-sized companies. Structural change was accelerated by the government's determined pursuit of market-oriented reforms based on free trade, rapid price deregulation and demonopolization of state-run enterprises. The ongoing reform process is far from completed, but measures implemented so far have already resulted in a wide-ranging reorganization of Russia's industrial capacity. However, rising imports and a decline in industrial competitiveness have sharply depressed industrial output and led to the closure or restructuring of inefficient enterprises.

High taxes, price hikes and low average returns from industrial plants have driven Russia's new entrepreneurs towards commerce and finance, where money can be earned faster and earnings concealed more easily than in industry. Investments in industry are more capital intensive, very costly due to high interest rates[14] and less rewarding than financial transactions. Potential foreign investors have been wary of investing in manufacturing operations owing to contradictory legislation and inadequate information on possible sites and partner organizations in the main regional markets. Bureaucratic barriers and legal inconsistencies represent another important obstacle for industrial start-ups or plant expansion projects, which require long-term planning and legal certainty to be carried out effectively.

The widespread preference of Russian and foreign entrepreneurs for short-term gains rather than investment in industry, where pay-back periods are longer, is not conducive to the country's long-term economic development. Besides, full rouble convertibility has encouraged flight of large amounts of capital. In 1999, foreign exchange held by Russians in banks abroad reached an alarming level of US$130–140 billion. Economic reforms have so far had mixed results (Figure 8.1), but after four difficult years of transition first signs of recovery were observed in 1995. The IMF, the World Bank and the OECD interpreted these results as a rather positive outcome of macroeconomic stabilization measures taken by the Russian government.[15] For the first time since 1991, important economic indicators such as GDP, industrial production and investment were moving upwards again after a sharp fall during 1991–94. In 1995, GDP fell by only 4 per cent compared with 13 per cent in 1994 and 9 per cent in 1993. Before the financial crisis of mid-August 1998,[16] GDP growth was forecast to attain 2–3 per cent by 1999–2000. Successful implementation of a cautious monetary policy, in conjunction with the IMF, substantially reduced monthly inflation levels to 2–5 per cent after July 1995, compared with 15–20 per cent throughout 1994.

Industrial output contracted by 3 per cent and 4 per cent in 1995 and 1996, respectively, compared with 23 per cent in 1994, the worst year for Russian industry since the beginning of the transition process in 1991. For the first time in seven years, industrial production was expected to stabilize and even rise again during 1997–99,[17] but recovery is still restricted to heavy industries: energy, ferrous and nonferrous metallurgy, and petrochemicals.[18]

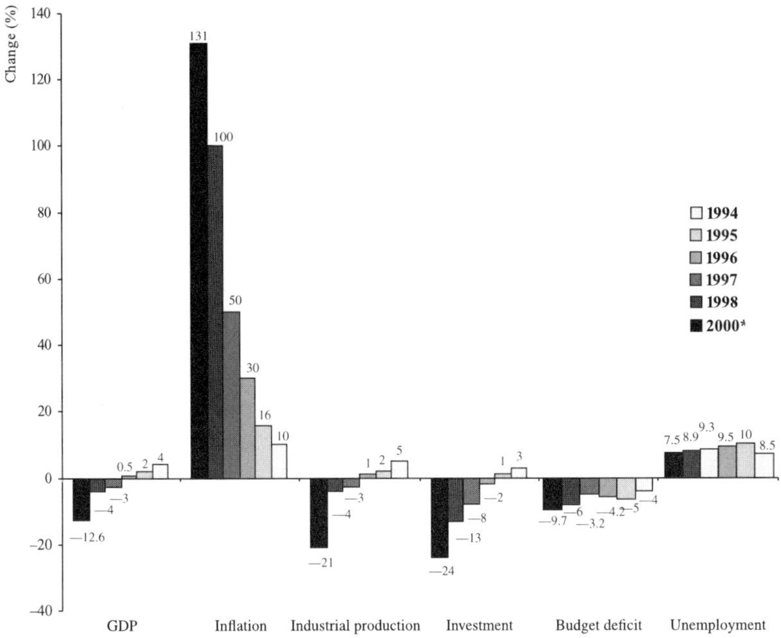

* Forecast before the August 1998 crisis.

Sources: Goskomtat, OECD, IMF, BfAI, Deutsche Bank Research.

Figure 8.1 Main economic indicators, Russia, 1994–2000

Investment levels remain the critical factor among the indicators used by international organizations to measure Russia's economic performance. The pace of decline in domestic investment has been checked, but it is still high compared with other indicators: –7 per cent in 1998 (as a direct result of the crisis), –2 per cent in 1997, –8 per cent in 1996, –13 per cent in 1995; –24 per cent in 1994; –12 per cent in 1993; –40 per cent in 1992. Although capital outlays have picked up again in housing and construction, investment in the industrial sector continues to fall in absolute and relative terms. In 1997, industry represented less than one-third of capital investments in Russia, compared with over 40 per cent in 1992. Domestic investment, despite government support (faster depreciation, tax advantages), is insufficient to ensure the reengineering of existing factories and production processes, and to maintain a stable level of employment in industry. Higher financial and technological participation of foreign enterprises could check attempts by the management of large national enterprises to form lobbies for more subsidies and higher tariffs on imported products.

Export earnings[19] enabled the central bank to accumulate foreign exchange reserves of about US$24 billion in 1997[20] allowing the government to reduce its budget deficit and to orient available resources towards high-growth industries. During 1994–96, Russia's budget deficit was reduced from 10.2 per cent to 3.2 per cent of GDP (4.2 per cent in 1997). The aim is to maintain low deficit levels, through drastic cuts in expenditure and higher tax revenue generation. During 1998–99, financial constraints will compel the government to drastically reduce expenditure for industrial development, energy, construction and agriculture. Foreign investment in these areas would be crucial to their performance.

As in many western economies, unemployment has become a serious problem in Russia; during 1995–96, plummeting sales and output in Russian industry pushed it to record levels. In early 1997, the records showed 8.9 million registered unemployed, corresponding to almost 14 per cent of the economically active population (8.9 per cent before the 1998 crisis). But these official figures mask the fact that many people are compelled to work in the informal economy as unemployment benefits are practically nonexistent. 'Undeclared' employment mainly in the services sector enables people to have a remunerated activity, which can be higher paid than official jobs in the state sector or in industry. But increases in knowledge-intensive jobs are not likely without focused industrial restructuring and higher FDI inflows. Although foreign investment is still relatively low, it already serves as a catalyst for creating jobs in main and ancillary industries.

Positive results in the economic arena presuppose a focused approach at government level that will trigger off a sustainable industrial upswing and ensure full utilization of available industrial capacity. A well-balanced FDI policy should serve as a support instrument to other adjustment policies envisaged until 2005.[21] Efforts aimed at enhancing FDI should be linked with industrial and R&D policies aimed at improving domestic investment levels in the industrial sector.

8.1.2 Foreign trade performance

In only a few years, the Russian government succeeded in fully integrating the country's economy with world markets by liberalizing foreign trade. Like China, Russia applied to join the Geneva-based World Trade Organization, a move that confirms the country's commitment to free trade and investment liberalization. From a situation of totally controlled trade and high self-sufficiency during the Soviet era, Russia has in a few years become the second most integrated LEM after China, with 1.6 per cent of world exports and 1.2 per cent of world imports in 1997[22] (Figure 8.2). Exports alone account for about 20 per cent of GDP against only 5–6 per cent during the Soviet era.

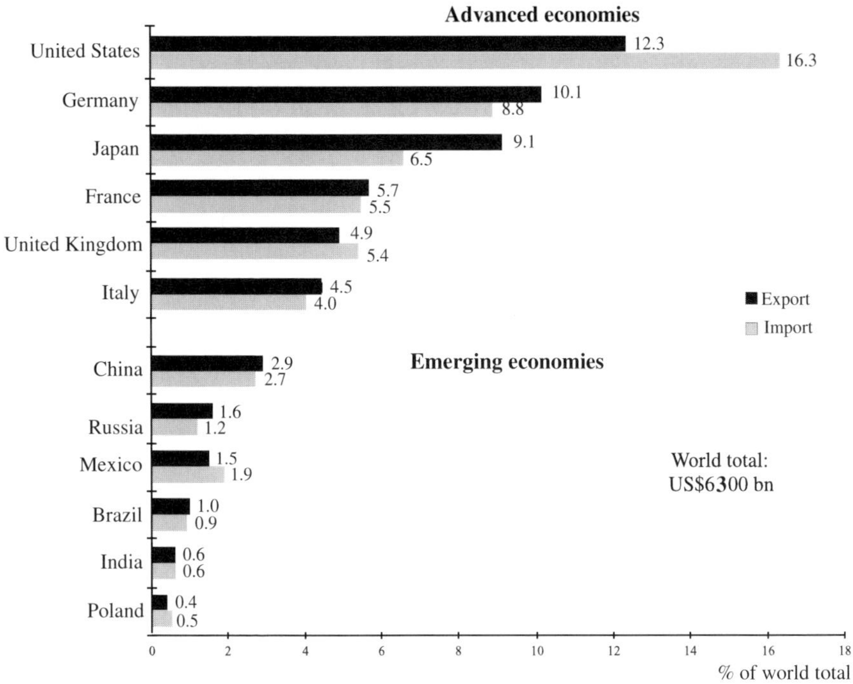

Sources: United Nations, OECD.

Figure 8.2 Foreign trade with major world economies, 1997

Unlike other LEMs, Russia's trade balance has been positive each year since 1991, and its trade surplus rose to a record level of US$20 billion during 1995–96. It contracted to under US$15 billion annually during 1997–98.[23] On the export side, Russia succeeded in expanding its position as a major supplier of raw materials to the EU, CIS and selected Asian economies. However, exports comprised mainly fuels (natural gas, oil), minerals, metal products and precious stones, which are exposed to significant price fluctuations on the world market. Together with wood, pulp and paper products, these categories represented about three-quarters of Russia's exports during 1997–98 (Table 8.1). Finished products, food and equipment do not yet meet international quality standards; they are mainly exported to other CIS countries.

For finished goods, imports outweigh exports, indicating a low level of competitiveness in value-added branches of the economy. Whereas raw materials supplies abroad have reached record levels, finished goods exports are still very low, creating a situation of overdependence on value-added imports from Europe, Asia and North America. During 1994–95, imports increased by almost 21 per cent; they included mostly consumer durables,

Table 8.1 Foreign trade, Russia, 1994–98

a. Trade balance (US$ billion), 1994–98

	1994	1995	1996	1997	1998
• *Total trade turnover* (exports+imports)	118.1	142.0	157.4	162.0	133.4
Export	67.5	81.1	88.6	88.4	73.9
Import	50.6	60.9	68.8	73.6	59.5
• *Trade surplus* (exports–imports)	16.9	20.2	19.8	14.8	14.4

b. Composition of Russia's exports and imports (1997–98)

	Exports (%)		Imports (%)	
	1997	1998	1997	1998
Fuels and minerals	47.8	42.7	5.8	5.7
Metal products, precious stones	24.0	27.5	7.1	7.2
Chemicals	8.3	8.4	14.4	15.3
Wood, pulp and paper	4.7	5.5	3.9	4.2
Food and agricultural products	2.8	3.1	25.1	24.5
Machinery and equipment	10.3	10.9	35.3	35.7
Textiles and footwear	1.1	1.1	4.5	3.9
Other	1.0	1.0	3.9	3.5
Total	100	100	100	100

Source: Goskomstat.

food items, chemicals, pharmaceuticals and machine tools. In 1996 and 1997, imports stalled owing to higher duties introduced for a number of product categories by the Russian authorities. They picked up again during the first half of 1998 (+3 per cent). Following the summer 1998 crisis, imports were severely curtailed and domestic producers began to introduce new technologies and take away market share from foreign suppliers, especially in the food and beverages sectors.[24]

Although Russia is expected to record a positive trade balance again in 1999, it is questionable whether in the long term imports with high value-added and know-how can be financed through raw materials exports. National resources are not unlimited and the only viable strategy for the medium term is to instead channel these resources into the country's own industries. The Russian government increasingly resorts to levying higher import duties on finished goods so that investors are incited to produce in the country. But these rather short-term measures will not have the same sustainable impact as a systematic upgrading of Russian industry through FDI. Moreover, if Russia intends to join the WTO free-trade mechanism, it will gradually need to abandon this policy.

In the coming years, analysts expect a significant reduction of the surplus and a deterioration of Russia's terms of trade.[25] A major challenge, therefore, will consist in rectifying structural deficiencies of the trade

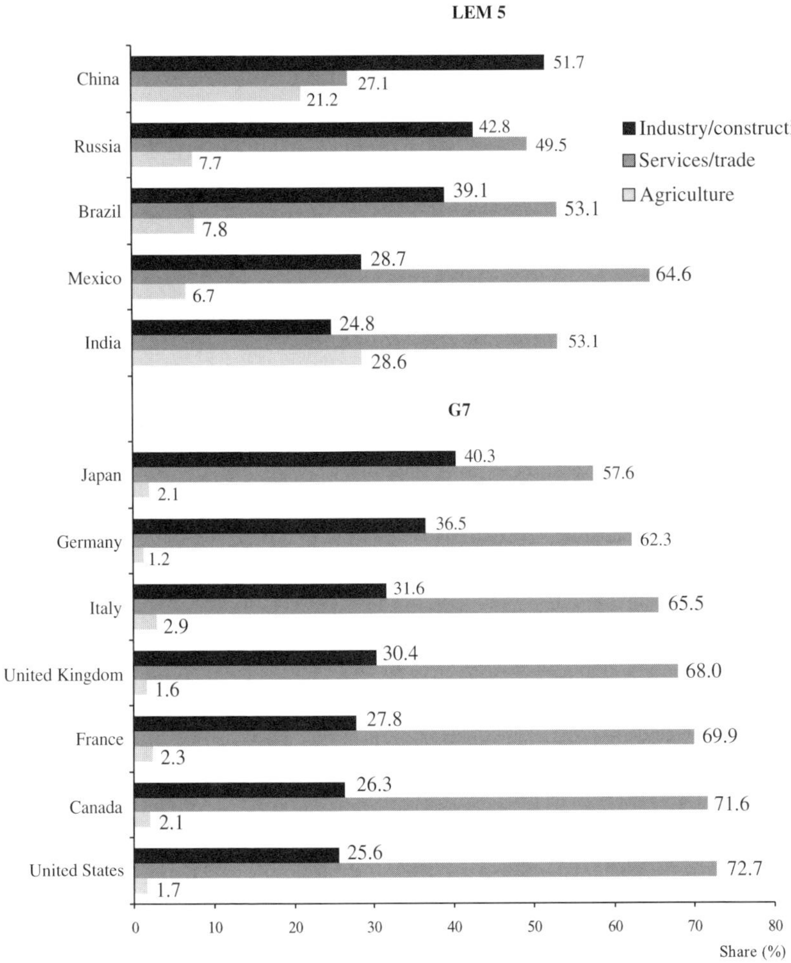

Sources: Goskomstat, *United Nations Statistical Yearbook*, 1997.

Figure 8.3 Importance of industry in the GDP of leading economies, 1996

balance, which being almost entirely based on raw material exports and finished goods imports could endanger the country's long-term position in international trade. FDI becomes crucial in this context, not only for increasing domestic production, but also for raising overall export levels and reorientating them towards more value-added and knowledge-intensive products.

8.2 Russia's industrial potential: highlights and prospects

8.2.1 Economic significance of Russian industry during transition

As in most other industrialized economies, Russia's manufacturing sector lost its position as the main employment and wealth generator to services (Figure 8.3). Employment patterns have followed general trends in production and developments linked to company closures in the various regions of the Russian Federation. The level of employment in Russian industry dropped from 23 million in the late 1980s to just above 14 million by 1998, (Figure 8.4). Industry thus represents 22 per cent of total employment; 9 points less than in 1990. These figures should be interpreted with caution as another 5–10 per cent of the people employed in industry are expected to lose their jobs by 2000–02, if domestic and foreign investment levels do not rise significantly.

Many companies are kept afloat through state subsidies, and 'hidden' unemployment in Russian industry may translate into real figures after 1998–99. National unemployment statistics are based on registrations with public unemployment offices instead of household surveys,[26] which probably show a more accurate picture of employment in Russia. The downward trend in industrial employment is an indicator of ongoing rationalization and cost-cutting efforts; it also reflects the breaking up of large companies into smaller units, which is usually accompanied by lay-offs due to closure of nonproductive departments. The trend also

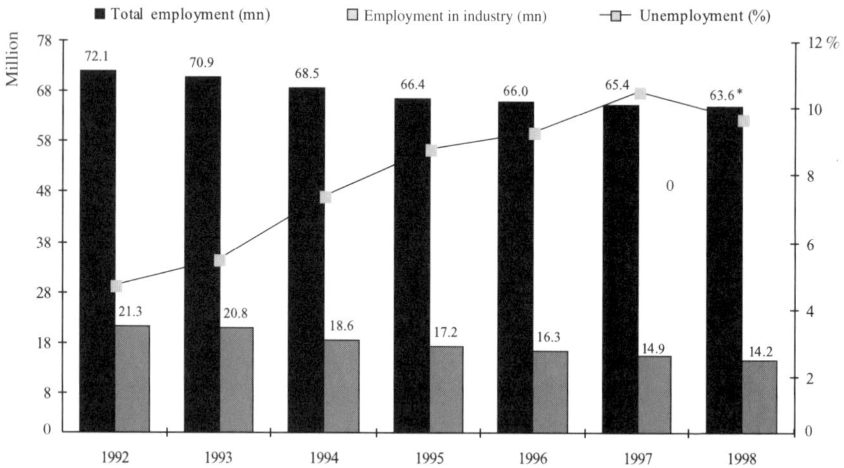

* Estimate

Sources: Goskomstat, *Russia in Figures*, 1997, 1998, 1999.

Figure 8.4 Employment trends in Russian industry, 1992–98

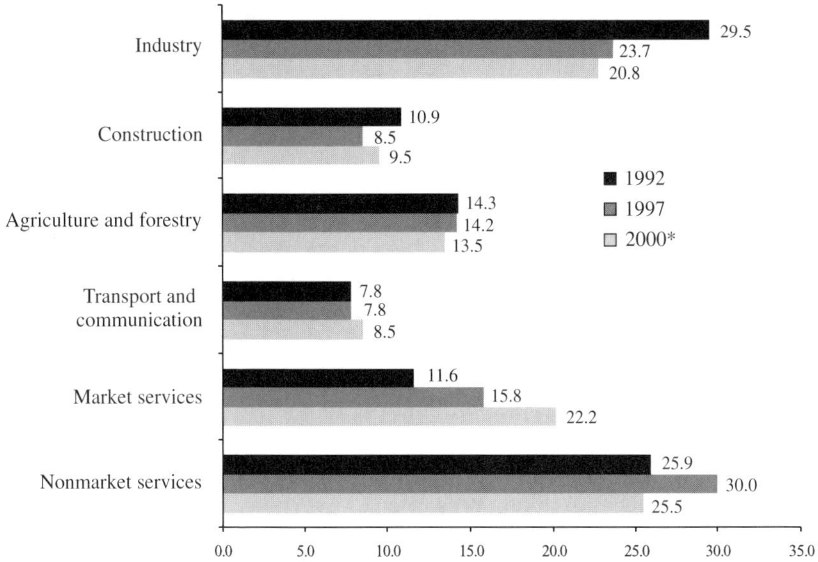

* Estimates

Sources: Goskomstat, *Russia in Figures*, 1997, 1998, 1999.

Figure 8.5 Employment by main economic sector, Russia, 1992–2000

reflects the first effects of the new bankruptcy legislation, which allows companies in default to file for closure.

The shift towards commercial and financial services (import/export, hotels and catering, retailing banking and advertising) will continue to erode the share in employment and GDP of the manufacturing sector (Figure 8.5). Within the industrial sector, the focus on energy and raw materials production for the world market has sidelined high-tech and knowledge-intensive industries (e.g. aeronautics, space technologies, nuclear power industry), which are exposed to increased competition from abroad and to brain drain. Also, most segments of the consumer goods and food sectors have yet to recover from decades of socialistic neglect, which hindered the development of a technology base.

On the other hand, Russia has a long industrial tradition and can offer domestic and foreign investors significant manufacturing capabilities in a number of branches.[27] The development potential is evidenced by the successful conversion of several military plants – often with western assistance – to units producing much needed consumer durables (e.g. computers, refrigerators, TV sets, washing machines). Certain domestic industries possess managerial competence and highly-qualified staff, but lack modern equipment, reliable techniques and venture capital. They could be rapidly reengineered with western capital, expertise and high-quality second-hand equipment. Despite the growing role of services, industry could regain its position as an important generator of income and wealth in Russia well into the twenty-first century. In 1996, the industrial sector, including energy and construction, accounted for almost 43 per cent of GDP, almost 8 percentage points less than in 1989. Current levels are similar to those in China and Brazil and the most industrially advanced countries (e.g. Germany, Italy, Japan). In the remaining G7 economies, services already account for around 70 per cent of GDP. Compared with LEMs, advanced economies are characterized by a highly productive agricultural sector, employing only 2–3 per cent of the workforce.

The increasing share of services is a natural outcome of the information age and the integration of Russia's economy with world markets. Nevertheless, Russia's future economic competitiveness will also be measured against its capacity to generate sufficient revenue from exports of machine tools, consumer goods and high-tech products. Despite present difficulties, Russia has the most developed industrial sector in the CIS. Almost the entire CIS output of passenger cars, trucks, metal-cutting equipment, chemicals, paper, fabrics, footwear and TV sets originates in Russia.

8.2.2 Industrial production and capacity levels

Russia's industries are facing the challenge of adjusting to the new market realities of a free and globalized economy, a revival for these industries is hardly thinkable without government intervention.[28] Policies should focus on the existing industrial base and harness its potential. The situation is particularly dramatic in the agroindustrial complex, which is a major link in the national food chain.[29]

As a consequence of economic transition, practically all 'pillar' industries in Russia suffer from considerable losses in output and employment. During 1992–93, production levels remained quite stable only in a few sectors such as automobiles and electrical appliances. Starting from 1994, however, output started plummeting in practically all sectors, with further falls recorded well into 1997 (Figure 8.6). The decline in industrial growth was arrested briefly in 1995, when output fell by only 5 per cent, compared with 23 per cent in 1993. The government's stabilization policies are showing some effect, and a turnaround is within reach. But it will take several years before industrial production will attain the late 1980s level. Food and light industries were the worst hit as they could not match international quality standards. They directly felt the shift of consumer demand towards foreign products of reliable and higher quality. During 1990–97, output fell most dramatically for finished goods: textiles and clothing (to about one-fifth of the 1990 level); meat and dairy products; pulp, paper, and wood processing; and machine building (to about 40 per cent of the 1990 level). Further upstream, losses were less

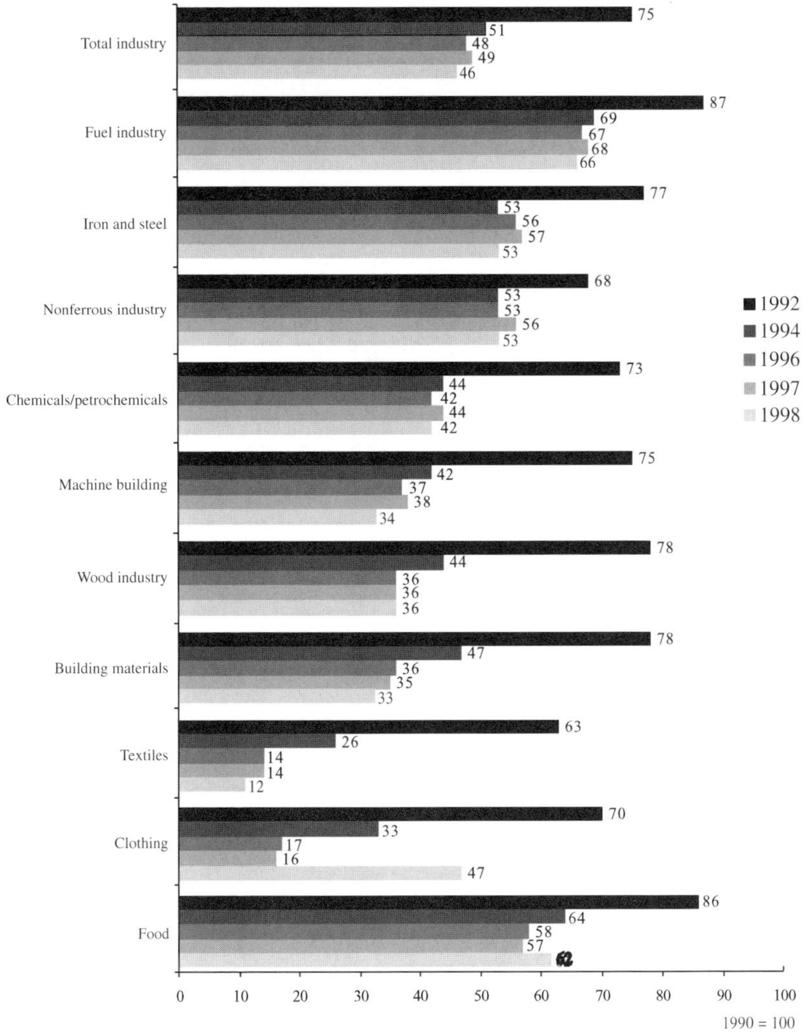

Source: Goskomstat, *Russia in Figures*, 1999

Figure 8.6 Index of industrial production, Russia, 1992–98

pronounced for intermediate goods: building materials, chemicals and petrochemicals, iron and steel. Raw materials was the only sector where production levels could be maintained because of favourable demand conditions in export markets (mainly from the EU and other CIS countries). During 1998–99, the situation improved slightly in sectors such as food, beverages and household goods because of lower imports

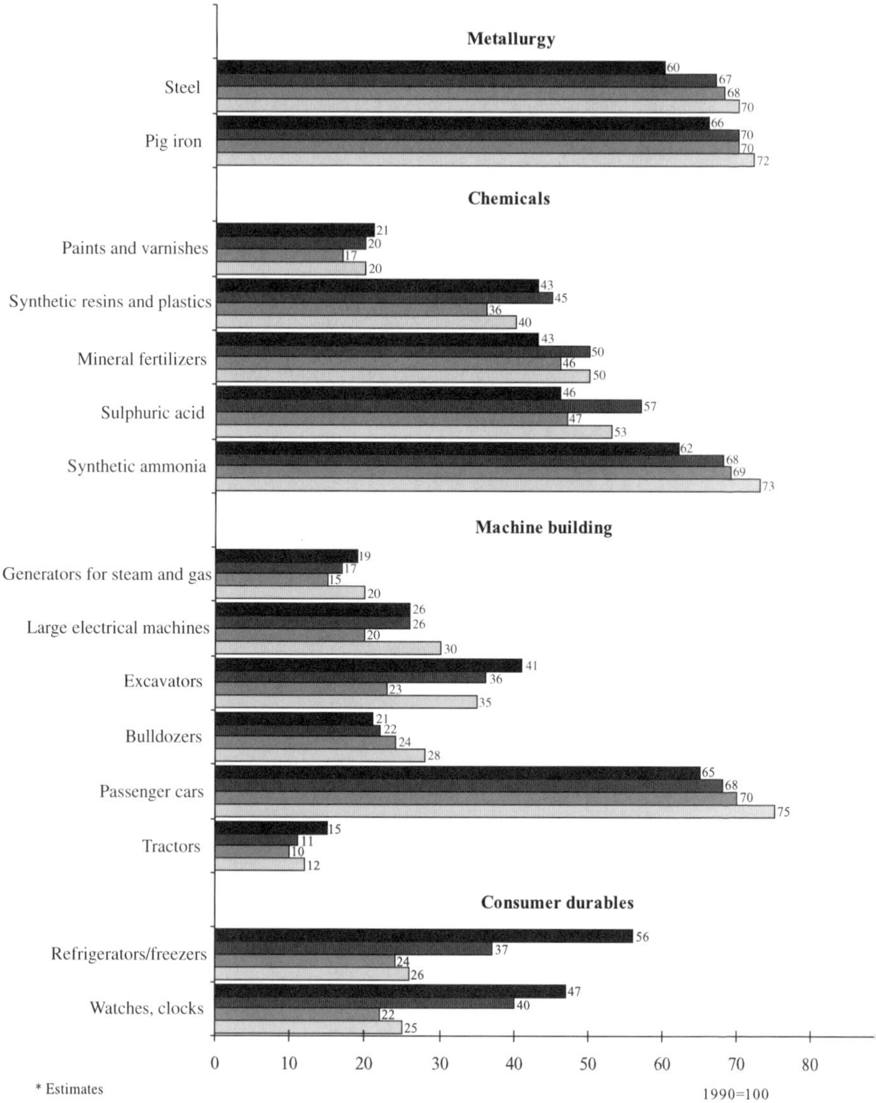

Sources: Goskomstat, *Russia in Figures*, 1998.

Figure 8.7 Capacity utilization in leading industries, Russia, 1994–2000

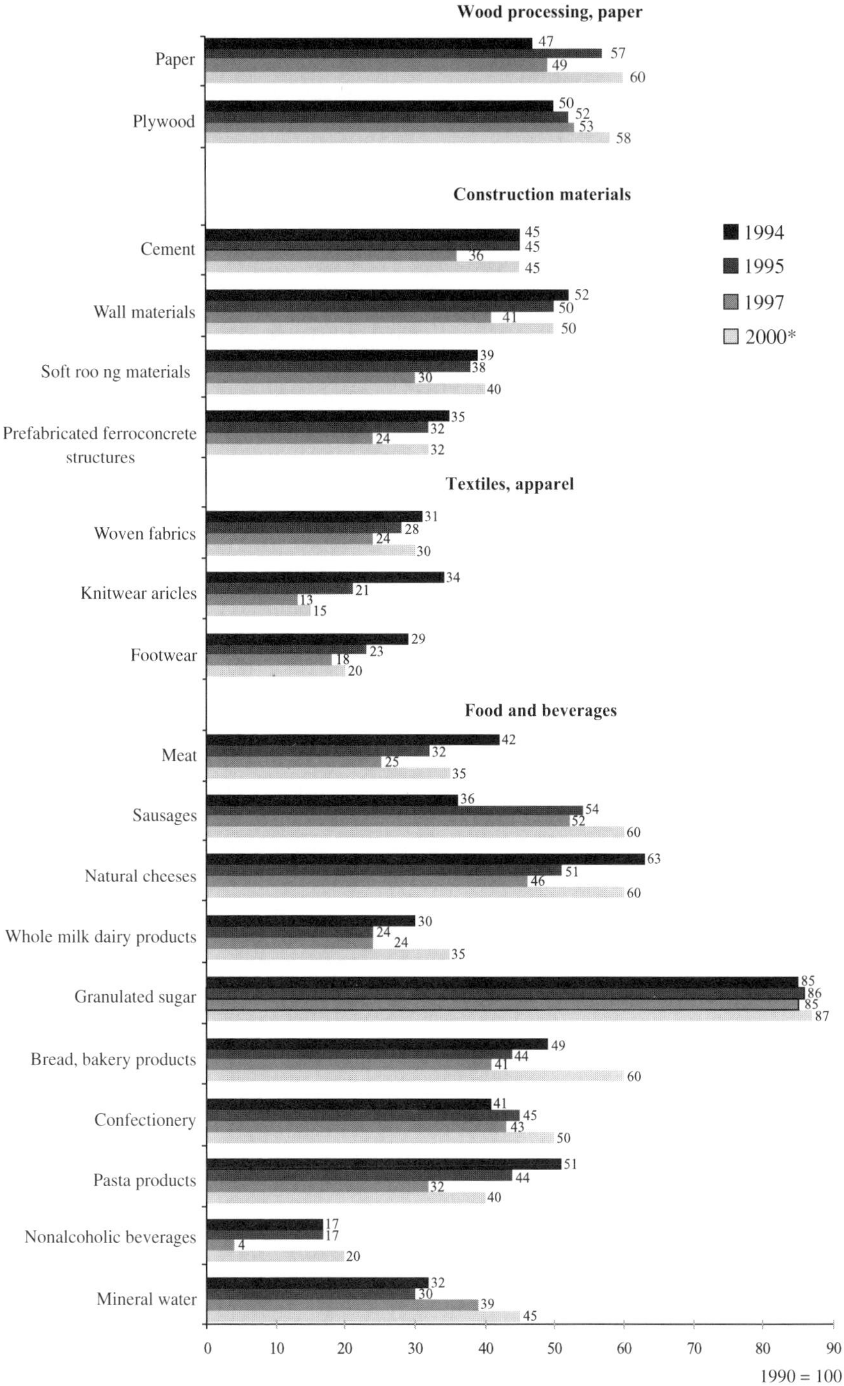

Figure 8.7 (*continued*)

following the devaluation of the rouble. But these improvements will only be temporary, if no appropriate political measures are taken to stabilize Russia's real economy.

Owing to increased competition from imports and the slow replacement of depreciated equipment, overall capacity utilization has dropped to extremely low levels in most industries as companies have not been able to generate sufficient revenue for building up capital (Figure 8.7). In 1996, capacity utilization rates picked up again in upstream metallurgy, engineering and chemical industries. Conversely, capacity utilization dropped below 50 per cent in most segments of the building materials branch (cement, pipes, soft roofings, porous fillings, panels, steel structures for construction). Consumer goods industries were worst hit; utilization rates dropped to just 20–35 per cent for segments like knitwear, hosiery, footwear, and meat and dairy products.

Conversion of high-tech companies belonging to the military–industrial complex may offer an excellent solution for reviving the capital goods and certain durable consumer goods sectors. More than 2 million jobs were lost and production decreased by two-thirds during 1990–97 following structural adjustment. Losses were particularly severe in electronics (–85 per cent), ammunition (–80 per cent), and aircraft and tank technologies (–75 per cent). The average capacity utilization rate in the defence sector is just 15–20 per cent. The government's conversion programme has so far had some impact; a few defence plants have been successfully restructured and now produce vacuum cleaners, refrigerators, kitchen utensils and home appliances. These plants do not produce strategically important goods any more; they have been privatized and become joint-stock companies.

Experts in Russia agree that the speed and success of conversion could be enhanced considerably through increasing collaboration with foreign TNCs. There are over 1000 large enterprises in the military–industrial complex, which employ about 600 000 highly qualified scientists and engineers. A number of sectors could therefore be systematically converted for civilian use: electronics, computers, telecommunications, light trucks, ships, helicopters and aircraft. Military conversion has become necessary with the change in the economic system, the opening of markets, the steady rise of domestic consumption and the overall reduction in defence spending.

The consumer goods sector holds a high priority for Russia's policy-makers, the aim being to reduce the country's dependence on imports. Plants also need to be reengineered in crucial intermediate industries such as chemicals and machine building. Several sector associations which often still operate under the old 'committee' structures have elaborated investment proposals, giving a detailed profile of leading enterprises. But these efforts would need to be embedded in a comprehensive policy package including an 'access strategy' to reach suitable partner firms in the major

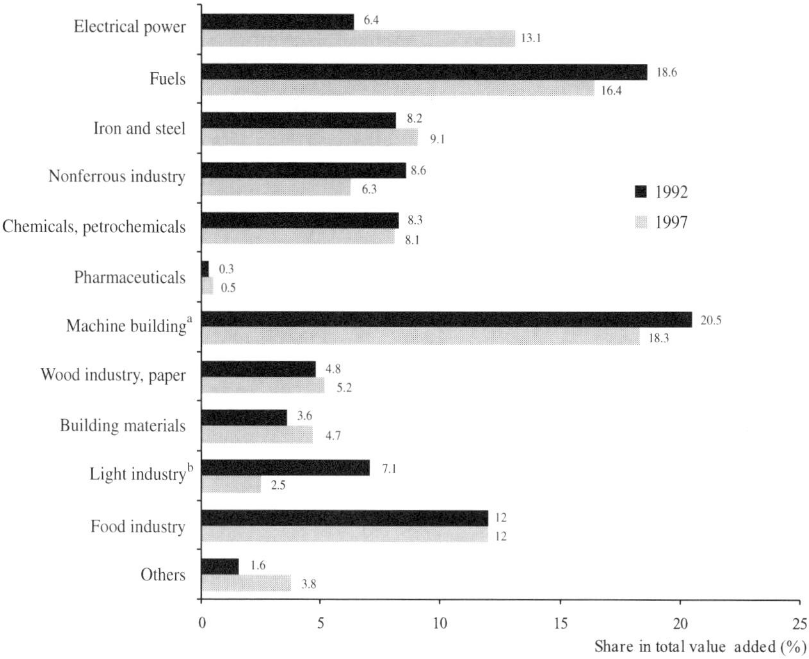

[a] including consumer electronics, transport equipment
[b] including textiles, knitwear, footwear

Source: Goskomstat, *Statistical Yearbooks*, 1996, 1997.

Figure 8.8 Russia's leading industries, 1992–97

markets. Proactive measures for attracting foreign investment should be undertaken in cooperation with FDI promotion offices in selected source countries.

8.2.3 Russia's key industries

Recent trends in the main industrial sectors[30] (Figure 8.8) are described in the following subsections. They have been analyzed to highlight restructuring and growth prospects for foreign investors. Together with services, these industries should be included in any master plan designed to attract higher volumes of FDI into Russia.[31] In most branches, although consumption is rising, local production is declining because of lack of capital investment and know-how. These constraints should be seen as opportunities for foreign investors seeking new markets, who would benefit from the lower cost of labour, energy and raw materials in Russia, and also have direct access to a large market. Several foreign companies have already recognized this potential and set up operations in Russia. If FDI and

Table 8.2 Output of selected chemicals, Russia, 1992–98

Industry	Output (000 tonnes)							
	1992	1993	1994	1995	1996	1997	1998	Trend 2000
Mineral fertilizers	12 300	9 900	8 300	9 600	9 100	9 500	9 300	↑
Chemical fibres and yarn	474	349	198	216	135	128	130	→
Synthetic resins and plastics	2 544	2 246	1 669	1 804	1 411	1 563	1 591	↑
Synthetic detergents	532	441	344	334	313	310	252	↑
Toilet soap	114	82	56	61	65	70	68	↑
Caustic soda	1 836	1 423	1 137	1 156	871	946	830	→
Synthetic rubber	1 610	1 102	632	837	796	704	621	↑
Tyres for vehicles[a]	42	36	20	19	21	25	24	↑

[a]In million units, including tyres for motor vehicles, agricultural machines, motor cycles and scooters.
Source: Goskomstat.

domestic investment pick up as expected, most key industries could regain their 1989 production levels by 2000–05.

Chemical and petrochemical industry

Russia's chemical sector comprises about 800 large enterprises operating in five main areas: bulk chemicals, specialty chemicals, petrochemicals, agricultural chemicals and biochemicals. Chemical companies have always played a key role in the country's economy owing to their links with upstream (energy, machine building) and downstream (consumer goods, agroindustry, automobiles and transport) industries. The sector is strongly represented in the Central, North-Western, Ural and West Siberia economic areas.[32]

Unlike other industrial sectors, chemicals have shown a visible recovery during 1995 (Table 8.2), with an overall growth rate of almost 11 per cent in that year. Production of synthetic rubber rose by 33 per cent, polyethylene by 36 per cent, and mineral fertilizers by 16 per cent. During 1996–97, similar trends were observed. Exports were the main motor for this good performance. In 1995, for example, exports of synthetic rubber rose by 125 per cent and those of polyethylene by 150 per cent. With an annual export volume of US$4.5 billion during 1996–97, chemicals were the third most important export item after oil and gas. Main customers are located in western European countries, China and the United States. The Russian chemicals industry has a reputation for high quality and reliable delivery, and has excellent know-how for producing mineral fertilizers, ammoniac, synthetic fibres, synthetic rubber and organic products. In 1997, certain branches of the chemical industry (e.g. chemical fibres, synthetic detergents, synthetic rubber) experienced a decline in output, which could only partly be compensated by higher prices. The 1998 crisis led to further decline in most of these and other branches.

The committee for the chemical and petrochemical industry, Roskomchimnefteprom, defines and implements policies for the industry. Measures aim at streamlining about 120 plants and building new capacity for the production of essential chemical products which have to be imported now (e.g. paints, coatings, environment-friendly chemicals, specialty chemicals, special detergents). The Committee plans to significantly expand current fertilizer production by 2000. Its programme includes the implementation of 50 investment projects in 24 selected agroindustrial enterprises and the setting of stringent conditions for participating companies regarding pay-off period, environmental impact and social sustainability. The programme will be launched in the four most industrialized regions (Central, Volga, Ural, West Siberia), and later extended to other geographic areas. A special fund of US$50 million has been earmarked for the purchase of foreign equipment. The Committee also aims to attract FDI worth US$3 billion over the next five years for modernizing and developing the sector. It is an ambitious target given that FDI levels in the chemical sector totalled only US$82 million in 1997 (US$165 million in 1996). The Committee will use a special 'pull' strategy to canvass companies in foreign countries, and plans to organize special workshop cycles and presentations of candidate firms to achieve its objective. A national FDI masterplan should in fact utilize the valuable know-how and policy experience acquired by sectoral committees, associations with foreign operators and specialized research and education institutes.

Table 8.3 Output of machine tools and mechanical equipment, Russia, 1992–96

	Output (000 units)					
Industries	1992	1993	1994	1995	1996	Trend
Metal-cutting lathes	53.4	41.9	20.1	17.6	11.4	→
of which, numerically-controlled	5.0	1.4	0.5	0.3	0.2	→
Milling machines	50.0	22.5	11.8	11.6	9.8	→
Forging and pressing machines	21.0	5.8	2.3	1.9	1.7	→
CNC machines	14.9	1.2	0.4	0.3	0.2	→
of which, machining centres	2.0	0.3	0.1	0.07	0.02	→
Wood processing machines	18.7	11.4	5.9	6.5	5.4	→
Spinning machines	1.1	0.5	0.2	0.1	0.05	→
Weaving looms	11.9	5.4	1.3	1.9	2.1	→

Source: Glawstankoprom, Goskomstat.

Machine building industry

Producers of machines and equipment have been among the worst hit by recession (Table 8.3). In 1994, production in this branch dropped by 43 per cent, which was 22 percentage points lower than in the industrial sector as a whole. In 1995, output levels fell again by 7 per cent and a real recovery is not yet noticeable. The only exceptions are heavy-duty machines and special equipment for the oil and gas sector. Elsewhere, the situation is quite critical considering that equipment sales were an important source of revenue during the Soviet era, when machines were exported to COMECON countries, the Middle East, Asia[33] and Africa. In the late 1980s, Russian equipment manufacturers used to export about 20 per cent of their production, against hardly 5 per cent today. Exports were practically halved during 1992–94. In 1995, exports rose again by 10 per cent to reach a value of approximately US$1 billion. Today's main export markets for Russian equipment are the other CIS countries, Central European economies and China. Altogether, Russia's world market position in machine tools has declined since 1990.

Essential machine tools are imported mainly from Germany, Italy and the United States, but the import volume (US$35–50 million) has dropped to only 2 per cent of what it was at the time of the Soviet Union (US$2 billion). Formerly, purchases were centrally coordinated by the state-owned import organization Stankoimport, but during 1992–96, the buying structure in Russia changed completely. Earlier, the main equipment users were large conglomerates, whereas today they are medium-sized plants which need special machinery that is produced only in small quantities by Russian factories. The economic upturn since 1995 has already impacted the equipment manufacturing branch as the demand for numerically-controlled machining centres and modern precision machines is almost 20 times higher than domestic production. The 1998 crisis led to further reduction in purchasing power, obliging authorities to move away from import dependence towards modernization of the domestic machine tool industry.

In 1996, out of the 3 million units of equipment in the industrial sector, at last two-thirds were obsolete or in poor condition. Financial problems make it difficult for users in the automobile, textile, electrical, aeronautics and shipbuilding sectors to import the much needed equipment. About 30 joint ventures have been signed of which only three started producing by early 1997. The main asset of the equipment industry is the well-developed iron and steel industry in Russia.

There is a great need for food processing and packaging equipment. The country's food industry is developing fast (especially meat processing, bakery products and beverages) and already represents the third largest FDI recipient sector after petrochemicals and the energy and fuel complex. Modern equipment is needed so that local companies can compete with high-quality imports, particularly for processed foods, beverages, confectionery, dairy products and baby foods. For 1997, the market volume for food processing and packaging equipment is estimated at almost US$900 million, of which 60 per cent will need to be imported.[34]

Transport equipment and the automobile industry

There is a pent-up demand for passenger cars and all types of commercial vehicles in Russia. In Soviet times, cars were a luxury item that only few privileged people could afford; state organizations or enterprises received a certain quota of duty cars, light vans and transport trucks. The private sector was then too underdeveloped to represent a significant market, but the situation has changed since the Russian economy was liberalized and former monopolies privatized into smaller units. Today, an increasing number of organizations are directly passing orders to acquire entire fleets of vehicles, and an all-Russia network of private dealerships offers a vast range of domestic and foreign brands. Driven by higher purchasing power, user preference is shifting towards high-quality foreign brands: cars from Germany and Sweden; trucks from France, Germany and Sweden; buses from Germany, Sweden and Turkey.

In 1997, car production picked up by 13 per cent from 1996 to almost 1 million units (compared with an increase of 4 per cent from 1995 to 1996) and thus exceeded the 1992 and 1993 levels (Table 8.4). In 1998, production contracted by 15 per cent because of the financial crisis. Foreign brands, which are of superior quality, are seriously indenting the market

Table 8.4 Output of transport equipment, Russia, 1992–98

	Output (000 units)							
Industries	1992	1993	1994	1995	1996	1997	1998	Trend 2000
Trucks	583	467	183	142	134	146	142	↑
Trolleybuses (units)	1685	1695	714	340	127	116	123	→
Passenger cars	963	956	798	835	868	985	836	↑
Motor cycles and scooters	604	526	199	71	39	54	24	→
Bicycles	2402	1812	869	563	348	424	361	→
Railway wagons (freight)	17	12	8	7	7	5	4	→
Tractors	137	89	29	21	14	13	10	→
Combines								
grain harvesters	42.2	33	12.1	6.3	2.5	2.3	1.0	→
potato harvesters	3.2	0.6	0.1	–	–	–	–	→
fodder harvesters	8.5	2.5	1.4	0.4	0.5	0.3	0.2	→
Excavators	15.4	12.6	6.5	5.2	3.5	4.5	3.2	→
Bulldozers	12.2	6.5	2.2	2.4	2.7	2.5	1.6	→

Source: Goskomstat.

share of domestic manufacturers. Russian car makers are therefore overhauling their production plants in an effort to bring out new models, if possible in collaboration with foreign partners. In 1997, almost half a million cars were imported into Russia, equivalent to almost 60 per cent of domestic output in terms of units sold, but the value of imports already exceeds that of national production. World market leaders such as Daewoo, Fiat, Mercedes, General Motors and Skoda[35] are considering opening production facilities in Russia during 1998–2000.[36]

Output of trucks and buses dropped significantly during 1992–96, and there is a visible deficit of buses for city transport. During 1996–97, 11 000 buses had to be imported into Russia, mainly from western Europe, Hungary[37] and Turkey. Manufacturers of agricultural and construction vehicles also reported substantial losses; output of tractors and combines fell appreciably during 1992–98, and in 1998 only 1000 grain harvesters were produced compared with 42 200 in 1992. Cooperation was therefore reactivated with manufacturers in other CIS countries, especially Belarus and Ukraine. Russian authorities are also approaching western companies, some of which (e.g. John Deere) have already invested in the country. In 1998, the number of bulldozers dropped to 13 per cent of the 1992 level and that of excavators to 20 per cent.

Electrical and electronics industry

Since Russia opened its market for electrical and electronic goods, domestic manufacturers have suffered severe losses. Foreign generators, car batteries

Table 8.5 Output of selected electrical goods industries, Russia, 1992–98

	Output (000 units)							
Industries	1992	1993	1994	1995	1996	1997	1998	Trend 2000
Radio receivers	4015	2806	1087	988	477	342	225	→
TV sets	3672	3987	2240	1005	313	329	324	→
Tape recorders	2775	2215	731	348	102	39	10	→
Video recorders	445	269	85	23	7	0.01	5.4	→
Cameras	1607	852	442	296	217	143	60	→
Watches and clocks (mn units)	58	60	26	18	8	5	4	→
Refrigerators	3184	3481	2662	1789	1064	1186	1043	→
Washing machines	4289	3901	2122	1294	762	801	852	↑
Vacuum cleaners	4319	3657	1533	1001	691	610	445	→
Electric irons	7718	7647	2736	1954	1256	953	697	→
Sewing machines	1624	1420	411	98	43	12	8	→
Batteries (mn units)	267	191	101	50	25	14	4.5	↑

Source: Goskomstat.

and small motors used for household appliances have increasingly replaced domestic products, which are too expensive and mostly of inferior quality. Domestic output of batteries dropped almost 60 times, from 267 million units in 1992 to 4.5 million in 1998. Transformers are the only market in the electrical branch where domestic products hold a market share of 40–50 per cent. Further downstream, foreign brands have gained total control of the market for audio and video equipment, and partial control of white goods (refrigerators, washing machines, electric irons, sewing machines, vacuum cleaners).

Up to 1993, domestic production rose only for TV sets and refrigerators owing to lower prices of local brands. Output of washing machines, vacuum cleaners, irons and sewing machines decreased slightly in 1993 and then fell steeply during 1994–98 (Table 8.5). Domestic demand has now almost entirely shifted towards imported brands. In 1996, for example, the country imported 3.1 million TV sets worth US$575 million, ten times the level of domestic output. Production of TV sets dropped by more than half during 1994–95 and again by two-thirds during 1996–98. In 1998, only 324 000 TV sets were manufactured in Russia, compared with almost 4 million in 1993. A slight recovery was recorded during 1997/98. Domestic producers of refrigerators, washing machines and vacuum cleaners reported a less significant fall in output, but they are also struggling with outdated technologies. In the long run, imports can be reduced only if foreign manufacturers (mainly from Europe, Japan and South Korea) contribute to the renewal of the manufacturing base for consumer durables in the country.

Certain domestic manufacturers have, however, managed to retain their market. Producers of specialized quartzes, optical equipment and electronic components (e.g. Angstrem, Mikron, Ekran) are running at full capacity;[38] they export up to 50 per cent of their production and generate sufficient revenue to invest in R&D. The expanding telecommunication market holds good prospects for optical fibre cables, switches, digital systems, telephone sets and cellular phones. FDI in the telecommunications sector rose from US$200 million in 1993 to US$600 million in 1997, and indication of this sector's potential is that so far no western cooperation partners who invested in it have withdrawn their commitment.

The situation is quite different for computers and related software. Computer components, hardware and peripherals (printers, disk drives, scanners, faxes, copiers) are imported mainly from Asia, and increasingly western Europe and the United States (for the more expensive brands). However, equipment assembled and produced in Russia is gaining market share and reached 66 per cent of domestic sales in 1997. Leading Russian manufacturers like R&K, R Style and Wiener PC have managed to build a certain brand equity and report good sales.[39]

Table 8.6 Output of selected textile and light industries, Russia, 1992–98

	Output (million)							
Industries	1992	1993	1994	1995	1996	1997	1998	Trend 2000
Fabrics, all types (m^2)	5090	3739	2197	1774	1431	1577	1395	↑
cotton	3292	2327	1529	1240	1023	1202	1088	→
wool	276	206	91	72	50	47	40	→
flax and jute	415	316	162	133	116	107	68	→
silk	731	596	246	198	139	134	111	→
Knitwear (units)	456	340	190	108	61	53	43	→
Footwear (pairs)	220	146	77	52	37	32	24	→
Sports shoes (pairs)	9.7	5.4	3.4	2.3	1.8	1.7	1.5	→
Carpets (m^2)	34	35	21	13	10	9	8	→
Jackets (units)	28.4	20.4	10.7	7.3	5.3	4.9	5.4	→
Suits (units)	13.3	11.5	6.6	5.4	5.7	5.3	6.0	↑
Dresses (units)	57.1	30.8	22.5	10.7	8.6	5.8	4.9	→
Trousers (units)	30.1	20.9	12.9	7.9	5.5	5.6	5.1	→
Skirts (units)	10.6	5.9	2.4	1.6	1.5	1.3	1.2	→
Coats (units)	17.2	13.4	5.1	3.1	2.1	2.3	2.5	→

Source: Goskomstat.

Textile and apparel industry

The textiles branch used to be one of the most profitable industries in Russia before the economic changes in 1991, and textile groups were important employers and taxpayers. The picture is quite different today. Since the early 1990s, the entire sector suffered from a sharp decline in output that exceeded the average recorded in the industrial sector as a whole. Textiles and apparel plants are located mainly in the regions of Ivanovo,[40] Tver, Vladimir, Moscow and St Petersburg. They have the highest production capacity in the country, but are lying practically idle today. During 1992–96, production dropped for all types of fabrics: silk (–81 per cent), wool (–82 per cent), woven flax and jute (–73 per cent) and cotton (–69 per cent). In 1997, the cotton sector showed the first signs of recovery; the remaining textile sectors recorded less pronounced declines (Table 8.6). In 1998, the situation worsened again owing to the negative effects of rouble devaluation.

The recession and high imports partly explain the losses in production. Other factors are shortage of cotton and other raw materials from Uzbekistan and other Central Asian states, and rising energy costs. Earlier, cotton was sourced from Uzbekistan at 30 per cent below world prices. Today, all the Central Asian republics demand payment in foreign currency, and Uzbekistan has started exporting to all major world markets and reduced supply to Russia. Moreover, obsolete textile machinery cannot be replaced owing to lack of funds; about one-fifth of the existing equipment has been in operation for more than 20 years. Technology imported from former Czechoslovakia and East Germany is still used in a majority of textile mills. Increasingly, machines are imported from Germany, Italy and Taiwan.

In the apparel sector, production of jackets, dresses, trousers and skirts has decreased sharply. Only production of coats, suits and jackets picked up slightly during 1997–98. Production of children's suits and overcoats practically stopped. Currently, Russia produces only about 0.02 coats and less than 0.1 trousers per inhabitant, the lowest level in 60 years. Output of footwear and sports shoes was 7–9 times lower in 1998 than in 1992.

The opening of the Russian economy to foreign competition has not been favourable to apparel manufacturers; Russian consumers prefer western products for their better quality and design. Most imports come from low-cost countries like China, Turkey and South Korea, while upmarket clothes are increasingly imported from western Europe and the United States. Today, domestic production accounts for only 13–15 per cent of national demand (40–45 per cent in 1989), although the Russian market for garments (trousers, jeans, jackets, suits, shirts, coats, skirts, dresses and hosiery) is expected to grow by 15–20 per cent annually until 2005.

Collaboration with foreign suppliers would revitalize Russia's textile and apparel industry, but potential investors are wary of political instability in the major producing regions, the overall legal context and the state of certain mills. Most Russian privatized enterprises (more than 90 per cent of the total) have to take up bank loans or go public (those with better performance levels) to raise capital. Well-conceived promotion and information campaigns in foreign markets (e.g. France, Germany, Italy, Spain, the United Kingdom and the United States) would help establish confidence for more FDI in this strategically important industry.[41]

Building materials industry

Russian building materials companies are slowly reengineering their production units as they adapt to the shift away from uniform high-rise buildings to small, compact housing units. The main constraint of the building materials factories (about 400 at the end of 1998) has been lack of capital for acquiring equipment and technology from western firms. In recent years, many small firms have been created, some as spin-offs of larger enterprises. These companies do not represent a large share of the Russian building materials market, but they are flexible, have a distribution network and could be potential partners for foreign TNCs. The sector specializes in standard materials such as cement, prefabricated ferro-concrete and steel structures, slates and standard bricks (Table 8.7). High-quality materials (insulation, environment-friendly roofings, special bricks, linoleum, soft

Table 8.7 Prospects for selected building materials, Russia, 1992–2000

	Output (million)			
Industries	1992	1995	1997	2000*
Cement (tonnes)	62	37	27	45
Prefabricated ferro-concrete structures (m^3)	59	28	16	35
Bricks (bn units)	22	14	10	25
Window panes (m^2)	118	66	70	90
Heat insulation materials (m^3)	35	7	9	15
Asbestos-cement sheets (units)	4517	1666	1263	1450
Linoleum (m^3)	93	57	46	65
Ceramic floor tiles (m^2)	7.6	6.4	5.3	4.7
Ceramic wall tiles (m^2)	30.7	20.7	17.5	15.9

*Estimates
Sources: *Finansowyie iswestia*; Goskomstat.

roofing and combination materials, high-tech materials such as paints, special glues and coatings, etc.) would logically be a potential area for foreign collaboration.

The demand for modern building materials, including paints, anti-corrosion varnishes and coatings, is rising not only in the large agglomerations of Moscow and St Petersburg, but also in all other large cities (Russia has 13 cities with a population exceeding 1 million inhabitants). The need for traditional materials such as asbestos-cement sheets is expected to decrease considerably in the coming 2–3 years. Modern building techniques are also spreading into the regions. The building materials sector is closely connected with ancillary industries supplying doors, window frames, sanitary and other items (e.g. fittings, bathroom and kitchen equipment, paints and coatings). Although detailed statistics on all these segments are not readily available, their growth potential can be said to be comparable to that in the building materials segment, at about 10–15 per cent annually until 2000, now that the industry is on the upswing after the decline in 1991–95.

There is a visible boom in the construction sector across the country. In 1997, newly built areas totalled 34 million sq m, and the share of housing built by individual households on their own account rose from 12 per cent in 1992 to almost 30 per cent in 1997.[42] Russia is rapidly becoming a major market for all sorts of construction projects: office and commercial buildings, hotels, luxury villas, middle-class housing complexes, country homes and renovation of old buildings. The interest in new building projects is rising proportionately with income and purchasing power of the population. Several TNCs (e.g. Lafarge, Heidelberger Zement, Dyckerhoff, Atlanta Cement) have begun to enter into strategic alliances with

Russian partners, and investments have already taken place in cement, prefabricated concrete, linoleum, coatings and resins.

Food and beverages industry

Russia's food industry, like the consumer durables sector, was not allowed to develop by the centrally planned system; competition and demand for foods and beverages were strictly controlled. Today, the situation has changed and Russian consumers can choose from a vast range of food

Table 8.8 Output of selected food and beverage industries, Russia, 1992–98

	Output (000 tonne)							
Industry	1992	1993	1994	1995	1996	1977	1998	Trend 2000
Foods								
Meat	4 784	4 041	3 282	2 416	1 937	1 464	1 307	↑
Sausages	1 547	1 493	1 545	1 293	1 296	1 139	992	↑
Dairy products	9 800	8 400	7 200	5 600	5 300	5 200	5 300	↑
Cheeses[a]	299	313	285	218	193	165	178	↑
Animal butter	762	732	488	421	323	277	271	↑
Margarine	560	438	278	198	200	222	237	↑
Fish[b]	3 300	2 800	2 400	2 400	2 400	2 700	2 500	↑
Bread and bakery products	16 800	15 000	12 400	11 200	9 900	8 900	8 200	↑
Flour	20 400	18 200	16 000	14 000	11 800	10 900	11 200	↑
Pasta products	1 102	836	680	603	444	455	546	↑
Confectionery	1 829	1 746	1 530	1 372	1 262	1 347	1 310	↑
Salt (extraction)	3 600	2 200	2 200	3 100	2 100	2 100	2 200	↑
Sugar								
granulated	3 923	3 918	2 736	3 155	3 294	3 765	4 726	↑
refined	747	443	214	126	127	112	98	↑
Canned products (mn cans)	5 353	4 517	2 817	2 428	2 158	2 162	2 142	↑
Jams	213	173	60	34	30	28	40	↑
Beverages								
Natural juices (mn dl)[c]	718	447	242	211	220	265	315	↑
Mineral water (mn dl)	21.6	15.4	20	27.6	30.3	37.7	47.0	↑
Wine (mn dl)	39.8	24.9	21.1	15.2	11.3	11.9	12.5	↑
Sparkling wine	7.6	8.6	8.5	8.2	9.2	9.7	9.2	→
Brandies and spirits (000 dl)	31 821	1 652	1 766	887	1 156	922	1 100	↑
Beer (mn dl)	279	247	218	213	208	261	324	↑

[a]Fat content exceeding 20% of dry matter.
[b]Canned fish included.
[c]dl: decalitre (10 l)

Source: Goskomstat.

items. Most foods and beverages are, however, imported to the detriment of local production. Food imports are highest for dairy products, prepared and frozen foods, juices, bakery products, confectionery and baby food, and they affect local production of basic products like meat, sausages and bread. Meat and dairy production practically halved during 1992–97 (Table 8.8). A large number of food plants had to close down, or were restructured and downsized to remain competitive. The beverages sector (mineral water, juices, alcoholic drinks) is the only industry where Russian companies have succeeded in regaining important market shares after heavy losses during 1992–95.

The food sector being of strategic importance, urgent reforms are needed to rectify this situation. The sharp devaluation of the rouble during the second half of 1998 increased the demand for locally produced food items and beverages. The Russian food manufacturer Wimm-Bill-Dann conquered a market share of almost 35 per cent for fruit juices and 15 per cent for milk products in Greater Moscow during 1998–99. Manufacturers now have a real chance to expand their market share, but they will need to modernize equipment and expand capacity.

Russian consumers have maintained a strong preference for domestically produced beverages and food, especially meat and dairy products but also jams and confectionery. There is therefore a good opportunity for western TNCs to cooperate closely with well-established Russian or CIS manufacturers. By 2000–01, FDI is expected to rise to over US$1 billion in the local production of cheese, bakery products, yoghurts, chocolates and other confectionery, and a large number of alcoholic and nonalcoholic drinks. Collaboration between local plants and foreign investors could maintain an adequate level of production in Russia, generate employment and support domestic growth through more competitive prices.

8.3 Russia's regions: industrial concentration and employment

A policy that aims to improve Russia's industrial competitiveness must take into account regional patterns and the sectoral potential of the country's leading economic areas. An exhaustive overview of the industrial potential in all the regions is difficult because of the country's size. Besides, information is scarce although central and regional authorities have recently started producing industry-specific company information to encourage exports, to attract more TNCs, and to enable those operating through representative offices to identify business opportunities in major regional markets outside Greater Moscow.

In the 1920s, long before its formal political independence, Russia was already subdivided into regional entities. The aim was to improve planning and to ensure economic and industrial development at regional level.

Today, the Russian Federation is formed by 89 'federation subjects' including 21 republics with a very high degree of political autonomy. Since the adoption of a new constitution in 1993 and the subsequent law on compulsory election of local leaders by the end of 1996, the balance of power has shifted towards regional authorities. Compared with earlier times when regional governors were mere appointees reporting directly to the Kremlin, they are now answerable mainly to their electorate.

The central government increasingly negotiates economic development and tax issues with regional power brokers represented in the Federation Council, the upper house of parliament where all the regions are represented. Most regional leaders claim quasi-sovereign powers similar to those enjoyed by autonomous republics, and private diplomacy efforts of some local leaders have already led to the setting up of their own overseas offices (e.g. office of the Yaroslavl region in Germany) and the signing of bilateral trade and investment agreements. Russia's central government will need to cooperate closely with regional authorities so that the country's industry as a whole will eventually benefit from higher inflows of 'selected' FDI.

Industrial development in the regions is determined mainly by available natural and human resources, and the economic policy direction followed by local governments. Since reforms were introduced, certain regions such as the Nizhny Novgorod *oblast* and Tatarstan and Bashkortostan republics focus on making their industries competitive for international markets.

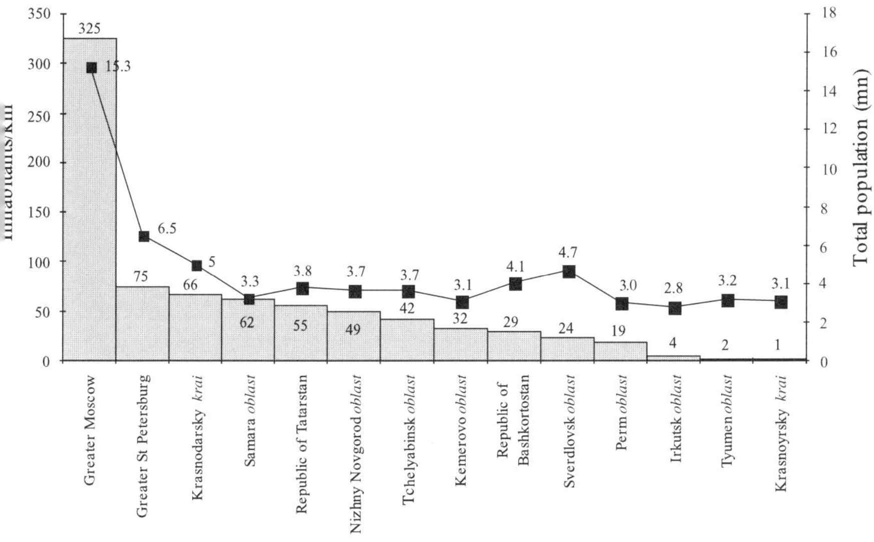

Source: Goskomstat, *Regioni Rossyi*, 1997, 1998.

Figure 8.9 Most populated regions, Russia, 1997

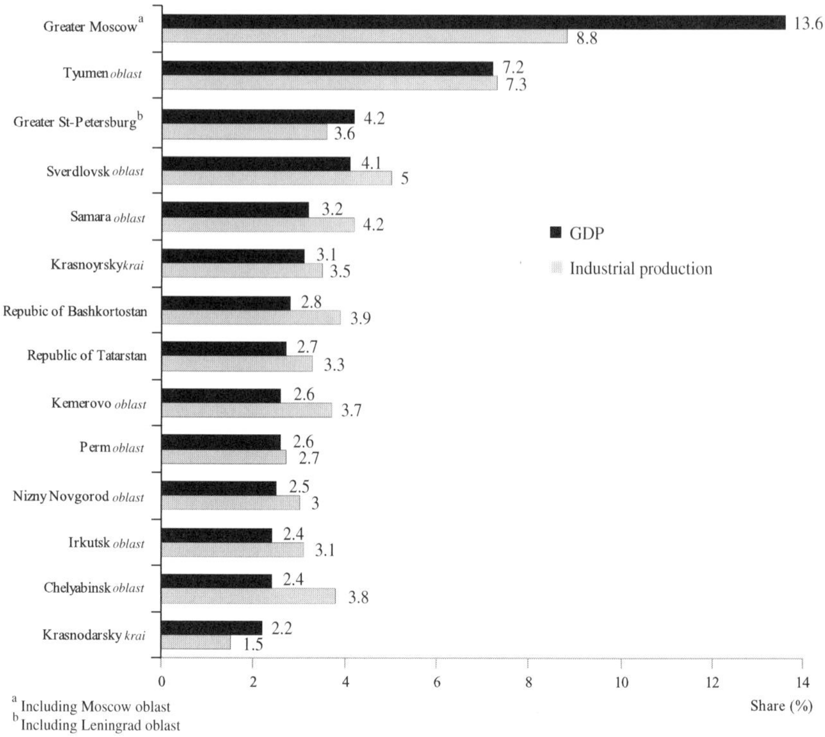

Source: Goskomstat, *Regioni Rossyi*, 1998.

Figure 8.10 Main industrial regions, Russia, 1997

Others like the Ulyanovsk *oblast* or Buratya republic opted for gradual industrial transformation and privatization. People with higher purchasing power tend to live in the more populated regions of European Russia (Figure 8.9), which constitute the main industrial centres for most of Russia's finished goods and components industries. Almost 80 per cent of Russia's population – about 120 million people – lives in the European part of the country. In terms of GDP (Figure 8.10), Greater Moscow (city and *oblast*) ranks first (14 per cent), followed by Tyumen *oblast* (7 per cent), Greater St Petersburg (4 per cent), Greater Sverdlovsk (4 per cent), Samara (3 per cent) and Krasnoyarsk (3 per cent). These city agglomerations account for the highest concentration of population.

Russia's regions are grouped into 11 'greater economic areas' with their specific industrial patterns.[43] During 1990–93, these economic areas formed political associations aimed at socioeconomic cooperation, foreign trade and FDI enhancement, and agricultural, industrial, energy and infrastructure development.[44] As a rule, regions close to the large markets of

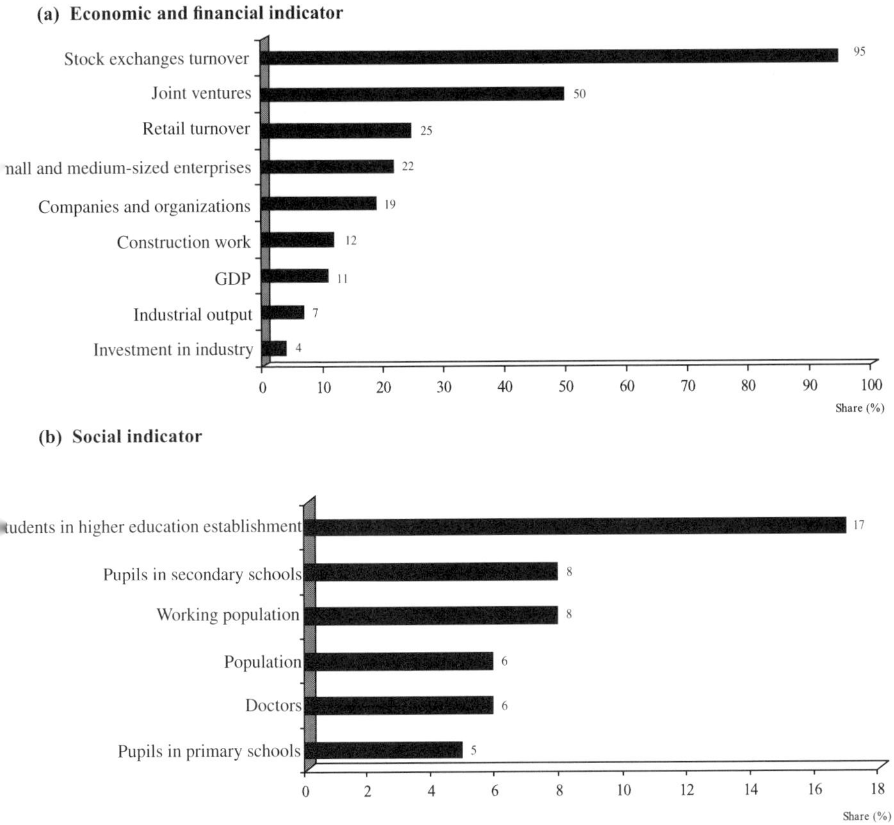

Sources: Mosvneshinform, *Business in Moscow Today*, 1997; Goskomstat, *Regioni Rossyi*, 1997.

Figure 8.11 Moscow's role in the Russian economy, 1997

Greater Moscow and St Petersburg have more diversified industrial sectors than the more isolated regions east of the Urals. Most capital equipment and chemical plants are located in the Central, North-Western, Greater Volga and Ural economic areas. Together with the Volgo-Viatsky, Central Black Earth, and North Caucasus economic areas, they are the country's main providers of food products, consumer durables, textiles and apparel, cars and trucks, and electrical appliances. They also attract most foreign investments.[45] Regions located east of the Urals (Siberia, Far East) are rich in natural resources; they supply oil, gas, minerals, and fishery products to the rest of the country and for export.

In the European part of the country, there is a fairly balanced distribution of major industries with many regions offering interesting prospects for investment and enterprise development. Although the capital Moscow has emerged as a major trading (25 per cent of retail sales in 1997) and financial centre (95 per cent of stock exchange turnover), its overall share in industrial production never exceeded 7 per cent (Figure 8.11).

The key industries in the major economic areas are (industry shares in regional output in brackets):[46]

- *Central Economic Area*, with Moscow as the industrial centre: machine tools and metal working (25 per cent); food (16 per cent); building materials, chemicals, light industry and consumer goods (each 7 per cent). The Tula *oblast* is the most prominent with its relatively high share of the chemical branch (24 per cent) in industrial production. In Moscow, the share of machinery is 30 per cent, that of chemicals 11 per cent.
- *Northwestern Economic Area*, with St Petersburg as the industrial centre: machine tools and metal working (26 per cent); food (19 per cent); wood processing and paper (9 per cent). The Leningrad and Novgorod *oblasts* are major centres for timber processing and paper production (11 per cent and 12 per cent of industrial output, respectively), together with Karelia republic and Archangelsk *oblast*, which both belong to the Northern Economic Area. In St Petersburg, machine building (35 per cent) and food processing prevail (25 per cent).
- *Northern Economic Area*: mainly wood processing and paper industries (over 50 per cent of industrial production) in the Karelia republic and Archangelsk *oblast*).
- *Urals Economic Area*: iron and steel (22 per cent); machine tools and mechanical engineering (16 per cent); gas, coal and other fuels (14 per cent). In this economic area, the fuel industry represents 31–33 per cent of industrial output in the Republic of Bashkortostan and the Orenburg *oblast*. Perm *oblast* and the Bashkortostan republic are characterized by a relatively high share of chemical production (20–22 per cent).
- *Povolsky Economic Area* hosts several industrial centres for aerospace and automotive engineering (Samara), petrochemicals (Kazan) and agricultural machinery (Volgograd).
- *Volgo–Vyatsky Economic Area*, with the industrial centre Nizhny Novogorod: machine building, especially automotive industry (41 per cent).
- *North Caucasian Economic Area:* strong focus on food (up to 44 per cent).
- *West and East Siberia* and the *Far East* are known mainly for their gold and diamonds reserves (especially Yakutia and Magadan), and petroleum and gas extraction industries (Tomsk, Omsk). Mechanical engineering, light industry and food processing are weakly developed.

The region with the highest number of industrial employees and workers is the Central Economic Area (4.2 million), followed by the Urals (3 million) and the Povolsky (2.3 million) Economic Areas. These economic regions are known for their high concentration of industrial enterprises in a number of territories and *oblasts* such as Greater Moscow (44 per cent of industrial employment of the Central region), Bashkortostan, Samara, Saratov, Sverdlovsk, Tatarstan, Tschelyabinsk and Volgograd. Industrial employment is very low in East Siberia and Russia's Far East. These two regions combine only 10 per cent of total employment of the Russian Federation. The share of blue-collar workers has remained stable over the years, at 80–83 per cent of total industrial employment. This is higher than the shares of most industrialized countries (60–65 per cent), where the proportion of white-collar workers has been rising with the introduction of new production technologies since the late 1970s.

8.4 Structural changes at enterprise level

The reciprocal impact of structural changes in Russian industry and enterprise transformation following demonopolization and privatization has accelerated change. New types of legal forms appeared for the first time in 70 years, in particular limited liability and joint stock companies. During 1991–98, the enterprise population in industry (Figure 8.12)[47] increased several times as a result of the breaking up of highly-diversified state conglomerates and new start-ups. Monopolies are now limited to only a

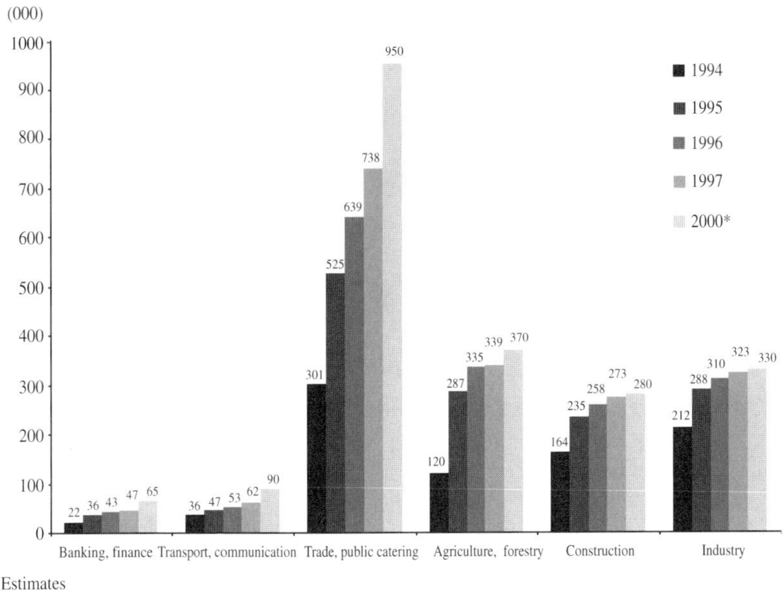

Source: Goskomstat, *Statistical Yearbooks*, 1997–98.

Figure 8.12 Number of enterprises by main economic branches, Russia, 1994–2000

few upstream industries, such as coal mining, machine building and chemicals, where a few large companies still concentrate a large portion of output. Large companies represent less than 1 per cent of output and employment in light engineering and food processing industries. The choice of potential Russian partners has therefore increased considerably for foreign investors.

Most manufacturing companies are not in a position to generate sufficient revenue for new product development and market expansion. Traditional commercial and technological ties with suppliers and customers in Central Europe and the former Soviet republics were severed following political changes, although inter-republic ties between enterprises are being slowly reestablished. But business relations within the CIS are hampered by lack of finance and credit facilities and are mostly based on advance payments in hard currency (usually US dollars). Cuts in defence expenditure in 1992 affected not only the military–industrial complex, but also important ancillary industries and suppliers in the energy, machine building, chemicals and other branches. Corporate expansion has become extremely difficult for most enterprises for lack of sufficient liquidity and cash flow. Moreover, qualified managerial and technical staff are moving to new assignments in foreign joint ventures, banks and service firms.

Today only very few Russian companies, mostly belonging to the petroleum, natural gas and aerospace sectors, can meet international quality standards for exports and earn sufficient foreign currency for business expansion. Nonetheless, as in services (e.g. banks, insurance companies, trading houses), a growing number of manufacturing companies are run by dynamic managers familiar with modern management techniques, strategic planning, information and communication technologies, and financial management. Some of them use market intelligence on their export markets and approach partners to evaluate export/import, technology transfer and joint venture opportunities. On the whole, there is a growing interest among Russian entrepreneurs to identify suitable foreign partners to jointly invest in new equipment and competitive products for the world market.

In most consumer goods, food and services segments, a number of western and Asian TNCs have conquered large market shares. Leading international players already enjoy a comfortable lead in technology, information and marketing know-how over domestic enterprises. These companies invested in existing factories, created joint ventures or built their own plants, despite negative media coverage of Russia, which still deters medium-sized investors.

But the Russian government needs to offer a better information system and intelligence infrastructure,[48] and financial support to medium-sized enterprises interested in developing their business with foreign partners. The more precise and up-to-date the information at enterprise level, the higher will be the chances of attracting FDI. Foreign TNCs could be approached more systematically if detailed information on the enterprise potential in the country is accessible to potential investors, both at sectoral and regional levels. Detailed company profiles including information on the history, management, product range, markets and financial situation of companies would be very useful. The analysis at enterprise level should be fine-tuned in cooperation with regional administrations. More targeted assistance should also be sought from international donors at bilateral (FDI-exporting nations and their main regional authorities, federations of industries) and multilateral (international organizations, development banks) levels.

8.4.1 Privatization and ownership patterns

State ownership in Russian industry has declined since the reform process was started in 1991, and in no other country has the privatization of assets matched the size and scope of the Russian exercise. The Russian government's far-reaching privatization programme has transformed ownership patterns and increased the number of companies. A large number of public enterprises have been converted into joint stock companies and new businesses have been established. Although the tertiary sector benefited most from these developments, the share of private companies in the industrial sector also increased from 15 per cent in 1990 to 72 per cent in 1996. This rate is higher than in many industrialized countries where state companies still play an important role (e.g. France, Japan, Spain).

Entirely private companies in Russia are usually much smaller than mixed or state enterprises. In 1996, the share of private enterprises in total

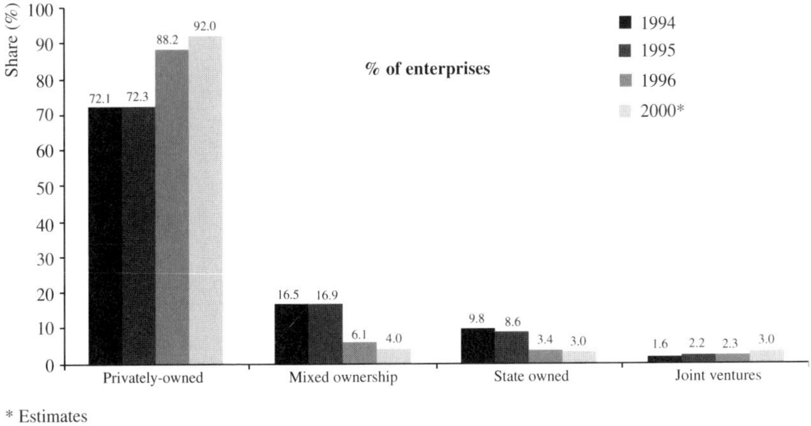

Figure 8.13 Russian industry by type of ownership, 1994–2000

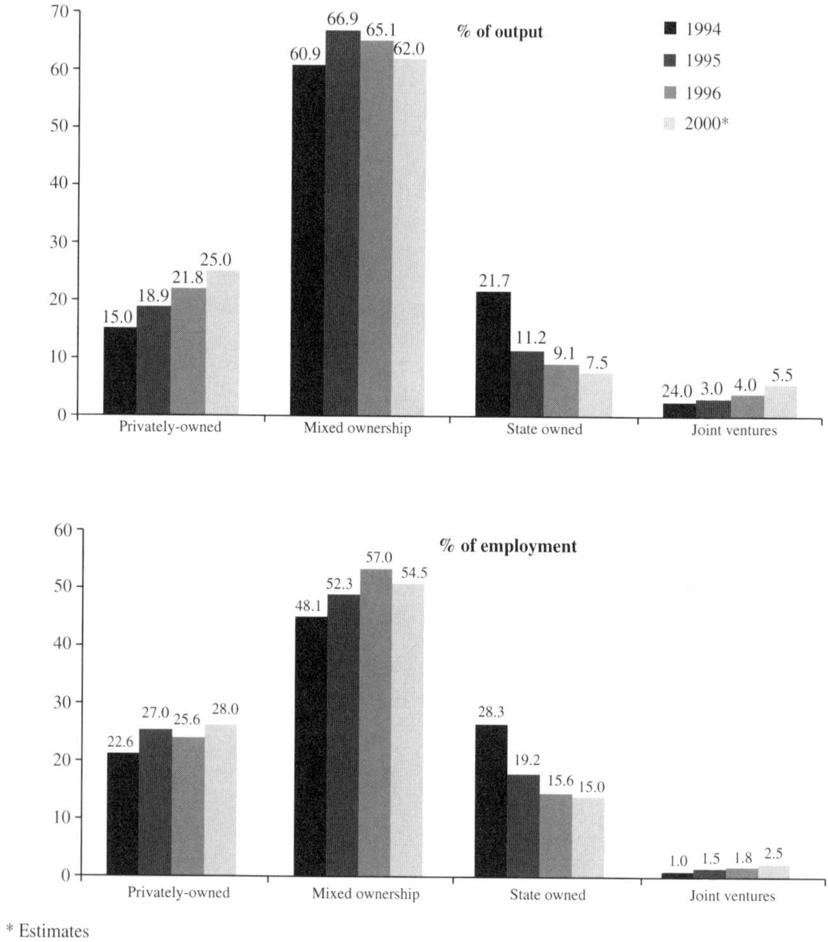

Source: Goskomstat, *Statistical Yearbook*, 1997; *Russia in Figures*, 1997.

Figure 8.13 (*continued*)

industrial output and employment was already 22 per cent (19 per cent in 1995, 15 per cent in 1994) and 26 per cent (27 per cent in 1995, 23 per cent in 1994), respectively (Figure 8.13). Their share in output is expected to rise as industrial transformation and foreign participation continue. In 1996, joint ventures with foreign partners represented only 2 per cent of Russia's industrial enterprise population, 4 per cent of industrial output and 2 per cent of industrial employment.

The initial enthusiasm about privatization has subsided and, in critical sectors, the State still holds on to its stake. In 1996, only 670 industrial establishments were privatized, down from almost 12 000 in the peak year of 1993 (5230 in 1994, 1465 in 1995).[49] Several lobby groups campaign for less privatization by referring to the negative effects of the hasty sale of state property. Sectors with the highest state participation[50] are energy, metallurgy, coal mining and telecommunications. Companies owned by the federal state, regional authorities and municipalities in these sectors continue to be subsidized, and the original plans to privatize them have been postponed. Private companies are strongest in light industries, food and beverages, and wood processing, pulp and paper.

Although companies with foreign participation are growing in number, their weight in Russian industry is still minimal. The preferred sectors are wood-processing – mainly due to investments from Scandinavian countries – and light industry, particularly consumer goods and processed foods and beverages. The number of industrial joint ventures in the Russian Federation rose from 1200 in 1991 (as of 1 January) to almost 4000 in 1997, of which one-third were from non-CIS countries.[51]

Unlike in advanced economies, the share of SMEs in industrial production and employment is still negligible.[52] SMEs have become indispensable players in the light and food industries, where their share was around 75 per cent of total output and employment. Very large companies control all branches of heavy industry and raw materials extraction: ferrous and nonferrous metallurgy, chemicals, machinery and metal working.

Altogether, corporate restructuring, privatization and the sale of state assets has advanced faster in Russia than in Brazil or China, where authorities are still reluctant to privatize important state conglomerates. In many cases, transformation has been mainly juridical and often without due attention to productivity and industrial competitiveness. On the whole, however, privatization has spawned a large number of players in many branches of industry, and there are good prospects for attracting foreign capital and raising domestic investment levels.

8.4.2 The geographic spread of enterprises

Almost 85 per cent of the enterprises are located in the European part of the Russian Federation. Greater Moscow (city and *oblast*), the country's main industrial centre accounting for about 14 per cent of Russian GDP,[53] has a wide diversity of enterprises belonging to various industrial branches. Over one-fifth of all Russian enterprises and two-thirds of all companies in the Central Economic Area are concentrated there. The City of Moscow has seen the most dramatic rise in the number of industrial companies. In only four years (1992–96), the number rose more than 16 times to almost 17 000 units.

Similarly, by 1996 Moscow *oblast* recorded about 6500 units, compared with 5300 in 1995. By 1997, the number of industrial enterprises in Greater Moscow reached about 25 000 and was still rising slowly.

The main reasons for these developments has been the breaking-up of state conglomerates following a wave of privatizations. New companies have been spun off mainly as joint-stock companies in a number of sectors, especially food processing, chemicals and plastics processing, and mechanical and electrical engineering. The increase in the number of companies is due less to entirely new creations as in the services sector.

Many privatizations were also conducted in St Petersburg, where the number of industrial enterprises increased from 542 in 1991 to over 6000 in 1996. In 1998, the number rose to over 7000. As in Moscow, the pace of privatization has slowed down somewhat starting from 1995, mainly owing to apprehensions caused by the steady rise in popularity of the Communist party which strongly objects to the restructuring of large corporations and the ensuing job losses. While privatization of small enterprises, especially in the services and light industries, is practically complete, that of the state-owned mammoths is slow and has even suffered a setback.

The process of creation of enterprises is slower in the eastern part of the country. In several republics and territories from the East Siberia and Far East economic areas, privatization was not a high priority as the regional authorities were more concerned about preserving minimum levels of employment in existing companies. Moreover, as the companies belong mainly to the raw materials extraction and energy sectors, local policy-makers and industrialists are more reticent about privatization and restructuring than their counterparts in the European part of the Russian Federation and West Siberia (e.g. Novosibirsk, Omsk). New company formations in upstream sectors are more complicated than, for example, in consumer goods. Nonetheless, technology needs to be upgraded even in the upstream sectors, and local authorities in the eastern regions are also campaigning actively to attract foreign investors.

Hardly any new industrial companies were created in the remote East Siberia and Far East economic areas. In regions close to the Chinese border (e.g. Chita, Buryata, Irkutsk and Amur), growth averaged only 5–10 per cent annually during 1992–97. Increased trade with Japan and China has, however, led to the establishment of new production units on the Russian side. In the coming years, higher investment flows are expected between China and Russia. A case in point is the Primorsk *oblast* (capital: Vladivostok), where the number of companies more than doubled during 1993–97 after privatization of the fish processing and other food-related industries. The port of Vladivostok has also recorded an increase in the number of joint ventures between Chinese, Japanese, South Korean and US TNCs and Russian operators.

Notes

1. Chapter 8.2
2. See also 'Nastoyashiye Russkoye Varenye' [Real Russian-made jam], *Itogi*, 10 November 1998, pp. 54–6.
3. Chapter 9.1
4. Chapter 9.3
5. Recently, positive signals have also been given by Russian courts, which have passed judgements in favour of western companies (e.g. Microsoft) in copyright cases and against their Russian joint venture partners.
6. Chapters 16.3, 16.4 and 16.5.
7. Capacity levels in most industries have dropped to precariously low levels endangering the survival of many key enterprises in the regions. See also Chapter 8.2.2.
8. See strategic concept suggested in Part V.
9. P. Fischer, *Enterprise Survey Evaluation and Conclusions for the Strategic Orientations and Launch of an International Consultancy Agency*, internal report, MESI, Moscow, July 1996.
10. Chapters 8.1 to 8.4. The economic and industrial overview proposed here is certainly not exhaustive and should therefore be refined, especially at sector and enterprise levels, during policy implementation.
11. Chapter 14.
12. Chapter 9.4.
13. Chapters 13 and 16.
14. 150–200 per cent during 1995 and 1996. The situation started improving in 1997, when annual interest on loans dropped to 30 per cent in certain banks.
15. OECD, *Russian Investment Guide*, 1996, p. 40.
16. The growth forecast was revised downward, to –5 per cent as a direct consequence of the financial crisis.
17. This forecast had to be revised following the 1998 financial crisis.
18. Chapter 8.2.3.
19. Chapter 8.1.2.
20. By the end of 1998, foreign reserves fell to only US$12 billion as a consequence of the financial crash.
21. Part VI.
22. Russia's share of world imports fell to about 0.8 per cent in 1998 following a fourfold rouble devaluation.
23. Paradoxically, Russia's foreign currency reserves no longer grow despite a comfortable trade surplus. Apparently, Russia's official imports are highly underestimated as about one-quarter of shipments are not declared. M. Sarafanov, Mogila Ispravit [Hopeless situation], *Expert,* 5 July 1999, p. 16.
24. In 1998, Russia's foreign trade volume fell by 17 per cent, but the country still reported a comfortable trade balance of US$13 billion (exports: US$73 billion; imports: US$60 billion), which should help ease debt servicing while launching a long-term industrial development policy.
25. First signs of deterioration became visible in early 1998, when world oil prices dropped to unprecedented low levels reducing Russia's import revenue by almost 30 per cent. Oil prices are volatile even if they rose again in 1999.
26. Based on the methodology developed by the International Labour Office (ILO).

27. Chapter 8.2.3.
28. Part VI.
29. Russia'a dependence on imported food items is one of the major problems the government will be confronted with in the coming years.
30. Raw materials industries will not be covered owing to their fairly high level of development. For industrial competitiveness and development potential in Russia, refer to Chapter 12.
31. Part V.
32. For industrial structures in the key economic areas; see section 8.3.
33. Especially China, India, Laos and Vietnam.
34. US Department of Commerce, 1997.
35. Belongs to the German Volkswagen group.
36. Because of the financial crisis, most of these projects have been postponed by two years at least.
37. The Hungarian flagship company Ikarus received capital infusion from Russian financial–industrial groups (FIGs).
38. Information collected before August 1998.
39. 'Telenet', special report in *Kapital*, October 1997, p. 8.
40. In the former Soviet Union, every fourth metre of cloth was produced in this region.
41. Chapters 16.3 and 16.4.
42. Goskomstat, *Russia in Figures*, 1997, 1998.
43. Goskomstat, *Regioni Rossyi* [Russia's regions], 1997, 1998. See also Chapter 12.4 of this publication.
44. T. G. Morozova *et al.*, *Regionalnaya ekonomika* [Regional economy], 1995.
45. Chapter 9.3.
46. Goskomstat, *Regioni Rossyi* [Russia's regions], 1997, Vol. 2, pp. 190–5.
47. The enterprise population also increased dramatically in other economic sectors, especially agriculture, construction and distributive trades.
48. Chapter 16.3.
49. Goskomstat, *Russia in Figures*, 1997, p. 388.
50. Including mixed enterprises with state participation.
51. The total number (all economic sectors included) of joint ventures and foreign companies rose from around 2500 in 1992 to over 16 000 in 1996; Goskomstat, *Russia in Figures*, 1997, p. 372.
52. The Russian threshold to distinguish between small and large companies in industry is 200 employees, which is significantly higher than in other industrialized countries, where the ceiling is set at 20–25 employees.
53. See Figure 8.10.

9
Salient Features of FDI in Russia

9.1 Milestones of FDI into Russia

The foundation of Russia's industry was laid by Peter the Great, who invited western partners to transfer the required technology for setting up the first manufacturing units in Petersburg, Novgorod and Yaroslavl. The Romanov tsars who succeeded him continued these efforts, convinced that cultural, financial and know-how exchange with the other European nations could only benefit Russia. During 1895–1914, inflows of foreign capital into Russia were as high as 55–60 per cent of domestic investment,[1] whereas today FDI equals only 1–2 per cent of domestic investment.[2] The main investing nations were Germany (28 per cent of FDI in 1913), France (19 per cent), the United Kingdom (17 per cent) and Belgium (11 per cent) (Figure 9.1). In those days companies from western Europe predominated;

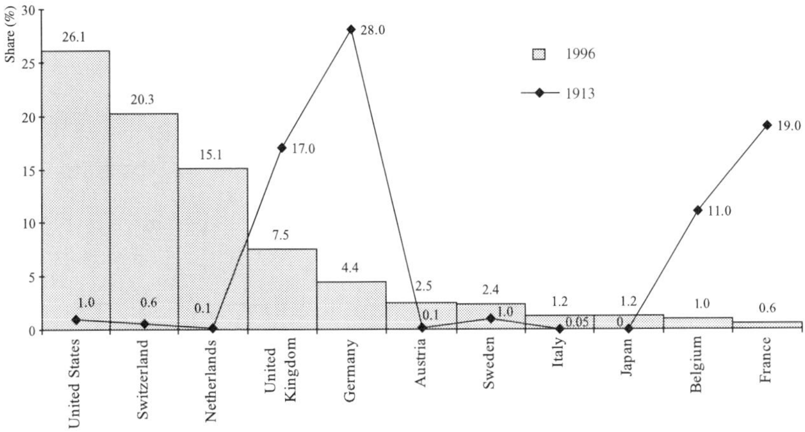

Source: Boguslavski, 1999; Goskomstat.

Figure 9.1 Share of FDI by main investing country, Russia, 1913, 1996

for the United States, Russia was too far away as a destination country (1 per cent of FDI).

Russia depended on foreign technology for manufacturing skills in all sectors. Western European companies assisted in extending the Trans-Siberian railway line into the Far East regions and in the establishment of large metallurgical, petrochemical and power plants. The production of Russian passenger and military ships and the development of diesel motors for domestically produced trucks and cars also date back to the pre-First World War era, when Russian companies cooperated closely with their western partners. Unlike today, Russia was a net importer of raw materials and exported value-added products. Foreign capital was invested not only in industry, but also in trading, banking and transport. At the beginning of the twentieth century, although no special legislation protected these foreign investments, the favourable business climate was sufficient incentive for the European companies to develop their activities in Russia. Special laws for banking, trading and stock exchange adequately protected foreign ownership and guaranteed repatriation of profits.

The situation changed abruptly after the Communists took over. The new Soviet government under Lenin initially favoured FDI as it was considered important for industrial modernization, and special concessions were granted for raw materials extraction, especially in the oil sector. In 1922, special committees were established to monitor concessions (under the Gosplan) and joint venture operations (under the Council for Labour and Defence Issues). But this partial open-door policy was totally abandoned towards the late 1920s, no new concessions were granted after 1928 and many large TNCs lost their assets between the 1920s and 1940s.

Under the succeeding governments of Stalin and Chrouchtschov, FDI dropped to an extremely low level until the mid-1980s. The Communist regime aimed at economic self-sufficiency, with emphasis on the development of heavy industry and military-related technologies, upstream industries such as machine building and chemicals were promoted by the central planning authorities. But the absence of competition isolated Russian industry and slowed its development compared with the industrialized countries of Europe and Asia. The production of consumer goods was neglected altogether (it still remains an Achilles heel of post-communist Russia).

Under Party Secretary-General Gorbachev, the economic situation deteriorated considerably, especially in agroindustry but also in most light and heavy industries. On 19 August 1986, the Council of Ministers passed a special law on joint ventures so that more foreign know-how could be transferred to the country, especially for developing a stronger manufacturing base for consumer goods.[3] Foreign companies were allowed to control 49 per cent equity in joint ventures, and later this ceiling was lifted through a special regulation passed by the Council of Ministers on 2 December 1988, when foreign operators were allowed to increase their stake up to 100 per cent subject to negotiations between the partners. Another law passed on 6 March 1990 guaranteed profit repatriation, land ownership and compensation rights (in case of forced expropriations).

For the first time, special economic zones were established for foreign companies, which were offered special fiscal, financial and import duty advantages. Subsequent laws further improved the rights, guarantees and protection mechanisms for those companies. The new laws entitled TNCs to full ownership of operations, portfolio investments, long-term land use, and freedom to reinvest profits; henceforth, they enjoyed the same rights as domestic investors. The Soviet leadership had started to see FDI as an essential catalyst for economic renovation, and although this process was briefly stopped in 1991 it resumed shortly after Russia entered a new era of economic development under a market economy.

9.2 The domestic investment situation and capital requirements

At the time of the Soviet Union, all important investment decisions were taken by the State. Central planning authorities allocated financial resources for plant expansion or modernization to industrial enterprises on the basis of agreed production targets. Most such enterprises were large and responsible for a very diversified product range; those belonging to strategic sectors that employed a large number of workers were given special privileges. Targets were defined exclusively in terms of output; quality considerations were secondary, and interaction with foreign partners was almost nonexistent. Glasnost and perestroika brought back the first private investors in the late 1980s, but until 1989 private capital still amounted to no more than 10–15 per cent of total investment.

The reforms of 1991–92 reduced the role of the federal and regional authorities in resource allocation (Figure 9.2). In 1996 only 20 per cent of capital investments were funded from the state budget[4] compared with 37 per cent in 1990. Company profits, depreciation allocations, and portfolio investments became the main source of investments. There is a tendency for operators to take the lead from state-owned entities in many industries except for large infrastructure and construction projects, which as in other countries remain under the control of the public sector. Bank loans are still underutilized as a source of finance as interest rates for short- and long-term loans are too high. Most companies prefer to rely on their own resources to pay for modernization of equipment and plant expansion. Against the background of reduced state subsidies, they increasingly look for partnerships with foreign companies, which are considered an important source of finance for investment projects in industry.

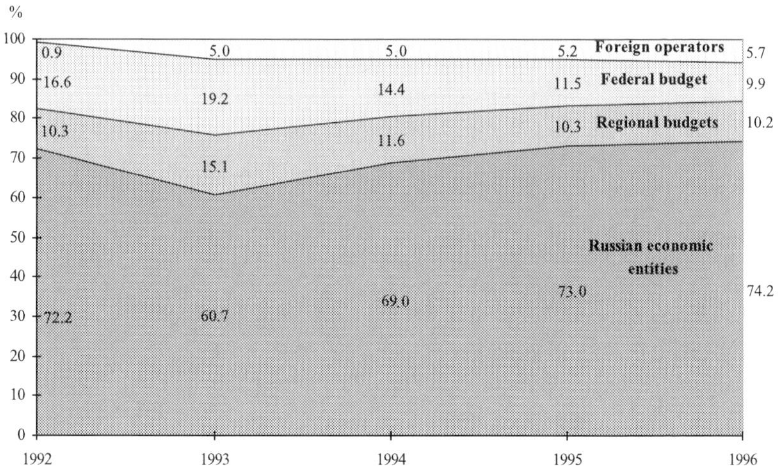

Source: Goskomstat, *Russia in Figures*, 1997.

Figure 9.2 Capital investments by source of financing, Russia, 1992–96

In 1997, gross fixed capital formation declined to only 20 per cent of GDP – 11 percentage points less than before the reform process started (Figure 9.3). Industry accounted for only 36 per cent of capital formation – 5 percentage points less than in 1992 (Figure 9.4). Although a slight recovery was noticeable in industry in 1997, services advanced to become the most important investor in Russia. Transport companies, for example, increased their share from 8 to 15 per cent during 1992–97, and similar trends were reported for retailers, wholesalers and financial institutions. Housing construction[5] is also increasingly dominated by the private sector. Another big loser from economic transition is agriculture, which saw its share in overall investment dwindle from almost 11 per cent in 1992 to

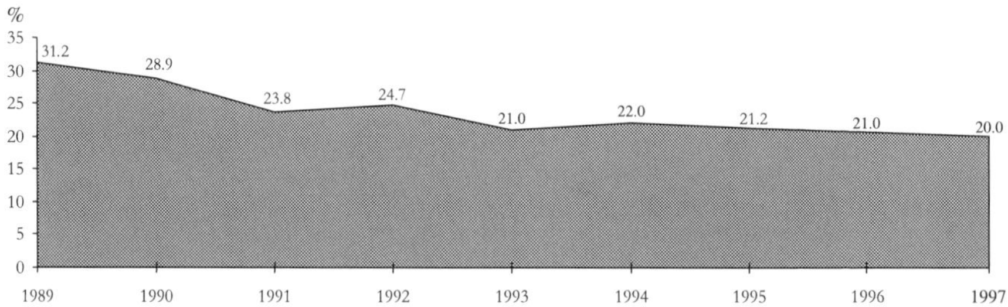

Source: Goskomstat; OECD, *Economic Survey – Russia.*

Figure 9.3 Gross capital formation/GDP, Russia, 1989–97

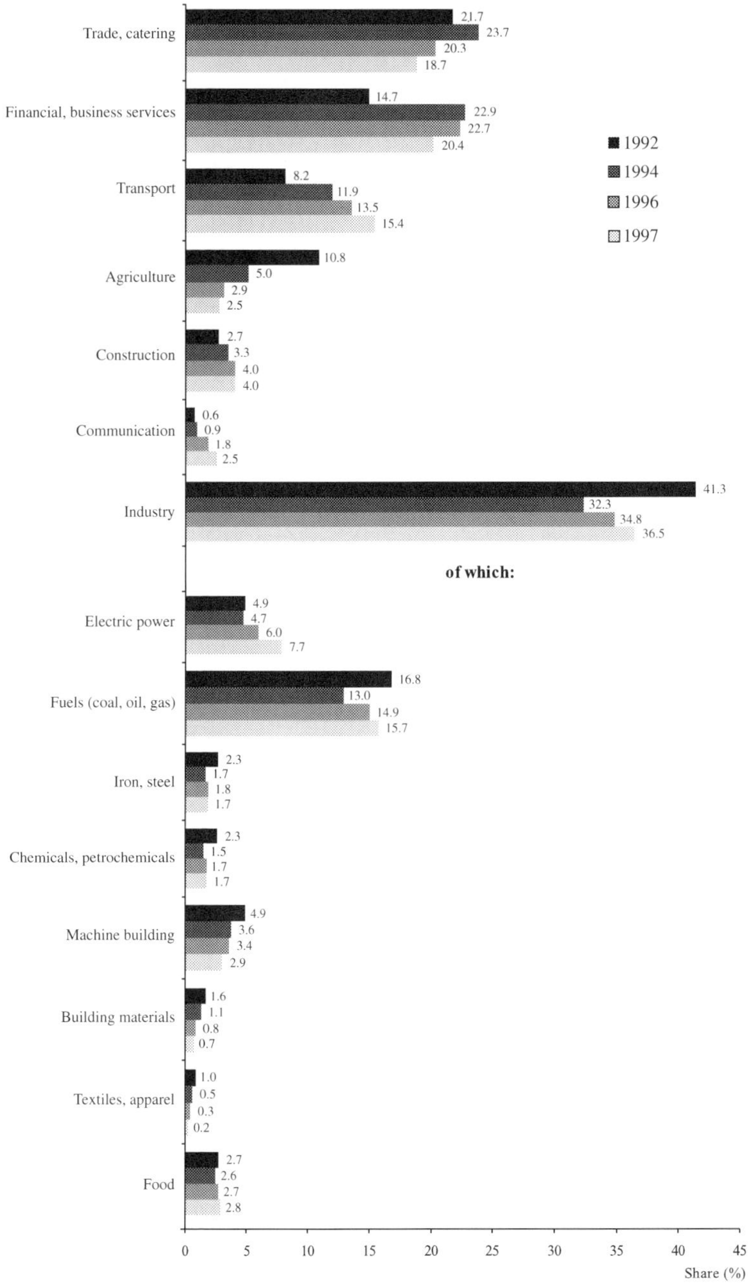

Source: Goskomstat, *Russia in Figures*, 1998.

Figure 9.4 Breakdown of capital investments by economic sector, Russia, 1992–97

2.5 per cent in 1997. The task before the government in the years to come will be to reestablish a certain balance by providing guidance and support to the industrial and agricultural sectors. For example, modernization and development of the food industry in Russia has a high priority, and its future will depend on the existence of an efficient rural base.[6]

Resources allocated to investment are based on the financial performance of companies. By the beginning of 1997, already about 50 per cent of private companies (43 per cent for industrial companies)[7] in Russia reported losses, compared with 14 per cent in 1993. In a number of industries, loss-makers already represent over half of the existing companies: forest products/paper (63 per cent), nonferrous metals (61 per cent), coal (60 per cent), transport (58 per cent) and textiles/apparel (56 per cent).[8] Loss-making triggers off a vicious circle of tax defaults, bankruptcies and staff layoffs. As bank loans have become inaccessible to most operators, the only recourse for these companies is to seek state assistance, but the government has curtailed subsidies for plant expansion, training and R&D in an effort to reduce the public deficit.

The federal budget, which was approved on 26 March 1998, allocated insignificant funding for crucial industries:[9]

- aerospace (Rb1636 million or US$104 million),
- electrical engineering/electronics (Rb1246 million or US$40.3 million),
- shipbuilding (Rb1154 million or US$25.2 million),
- telecommunications (Rb1113 million or US$18.5 million),
- metallurgy (Rb123 million or US$3.8 million),
- biotechnologies (Rb15.9 million or US$970 000),
- machine building (Rb14.7 million or US$780 000).

Only strategic industries (military, infrastructure, agriculture and mining) receive some assistance. At the same time, revenue through corporate taxes cannot be accrued if companies cannot redress their finances. The situation was aggravated by the financial crisis that shook Russia starting from August 1998.

Rigid rules of international organizations will not break the vicious circle. For example, the IMF – the largest international donor – makes disbursement of bridging loans[10] dependent on higher state revenue generation, which is only possible through a combination of a more efficient tax collection system and drastic curbs in spending, including that for indispensable social services such as education, health and culture. The growing pressure for budgetary stabilization is one of the reasons for budget cuts and tax increases by the Russian government. Both Russian and foreign companies are adversely affected by these measures, which lack a long-term strategy to systematically rebuild Russia's industrial sector.

Funds provided by the IMF or other international aid programmes are immediately used to fill financial gaps in the administrative–political sphere (e.g. payment of salaries in the public sector and financing of the government apparatus) and rarely reach social organizations (e.g. schools, hospitals) and the privatized industrial sector. Exceptions are special financial envelopes made available through the bilateral Transform (Germany) and Know-how (United Kingdom) funds, and venture capital funds (including minority participations) offered by the London-based EBRD. But these funds can hardly cover the financial needs of Russian industry. Moreover, public funding requires expensive administrative structures, which absorb a significant share of the aid programme. Russian companies can rarely meet their need for new technology and know-how from such programmes. The most important catalyst for sustainable industrial development in Russia during transition is through FDI and foreign collaboration.

Russia's annual capital needs until 2005–10 amount to about US$100–150 billion or 15–20 per cent of GDP.[11] But even this estimate is low considering the enormous task of expanding domestic infrastructure and reengineering Russia's industry, handicapped by 70 years of planned economy.[12] Up to US$25–30 billion is needed only for conversion of defence-related enterprises.[13] In 1997, Russian companies managed to generate Rb1300 trillion (or US$55 billion). Following continuous decline, the state budget (federal and regional) only managed to generate about Rb175 trillion (about US$14 billion),[14] which is far from what would be needed to rebuild national industry, agriculture and infrastructure.

Disbursements of international aid amounted to just US$6–7 billion during 1995–96 and even these are expected to be cut drastically in the years to come owing to budgetary constraints in the donor economies. A more promising route can be opened by enhancing FDI inflows, which now stand at only US$2–2.5 billion a year.[15] This source of finance and technology is the most effective as investments are made directly where they are needed; the Russian authorities should recognize its significance and step up their efforts to attract more investors from abroad.

9.3 Foreign investment patterns and trends: origin and destination

9.3.1 FDI flows and stock

According to UNCTAD, FDI inflows averaged about US$2 billion during 1992–97 which represented 0.9–1.0 per cent of gross capital formation (GCF). Foreign portfolio investments in Russia were more than four times higher than FDI during this period. Although the Russian statistical services

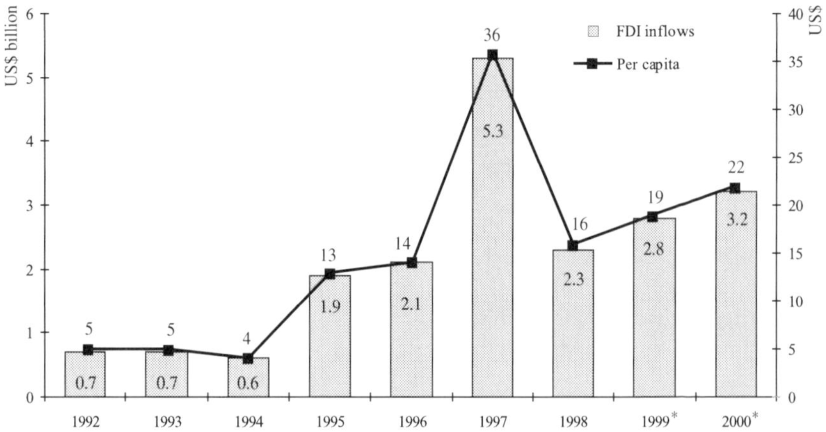

* Estimates

Sources: UNCTAD; Goskomstat.

Figure 9.5 FDI inflows, Russia, 1992–2000

(Goskomstat) reported a higher share in GCF (i.e. 2.5–3 per cent),[16] the ratio is still well below the average in other large economies. Considering the country's potential, 6–8 per cent of GCF[17] is a realistic target for capital and technology inflows. For 1997, Goskomstat reported record inflows of US$5.3 billion, but in 1998 inflows dropped again to US$3.4 billion.[18] FDI inflows are expected to stay below the US$3 billion mark during 1999–2000, if no determined countermeasures[19] are taken (Figure 9.5). Higher FDI inflows would have a beneficial effect on other types of investment including portfolio operations, which dropped to an all-time low of US$91 million in 1998.

Although FDI represents a significant source of additional finance, particularly for emerging and transition economies, in Russia it has so far not had the desired macroeconomic impact. Only one-third of annual inflows[20] benefited the industrial sector during 1996–98. By comparison, more than half of the FDI flowing into China (US$45 billion in 1997) and India (US$2.5–3 billion) were directed at the industrial and infrastructure sectors.[21] As FDI inflows are measured in foreign currency (compared with roubles for domestic investment), more substantial transfers by western standards could have a significant impact on Russia's economy. In 1997, accumulated FDI stock amounted to only US$11.5 billion compared with US$217 billion for China, US$126 billion for Brazil and US$87 billion for Mexico.[22]

Russian FDI originates mainly in western European countries and the United States. In 1997, US TNCs were by far the largest foreign

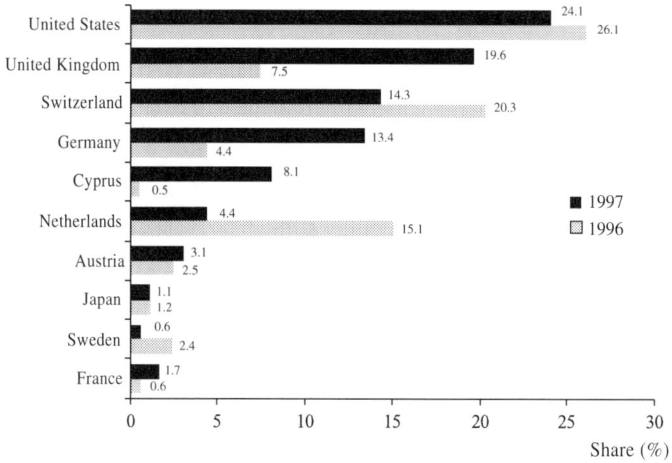

Source: Goskomstat.

Figure 9.6 Major foreign investors, Russia, 1996–97

investors with over 24 per cent of inbound FDI (Figure 9.6). Investment from the United Kingdom was 20 per cent. Next came Swiss (14 per cent) and German (13 per cent) investors.[23] The prominent ranking of Switzerland suggests – as with Cyprus (8 per cent) – that part of FDI represents repatriation of Russian capital that had left the country earlier.[24] In spite of increased interest on the part of Japanese and South Korean firms, their share in total investment remains quite modest. Japanese TNCs, for example, accounted for only 1 per cent of total investment during 1996–97. Combined investment from other CIS countries represented less than 1 per cent. In 1997 Ukraine, with total investment of about US$24 million, was the largest investor among CIS countries, followed by Belarus (US$17.5 million) and Kazakhstan (US$14 million).[25]

Foreign investors from the OECD countries have become even more cautious after the 1998 financial crisis. With the exception of US and Dutch operators, who invested a total of US$1.2 billion and US$610 million, respectively, FDI from other countries was restricted: Germany (US$330 million), United Kingdom (US$205 million), Finland (US$140 million), Sweden (US$70 million) and France (US$15 million).[26]

The number of joint ventures with foreign partners and foreign wholly-owned subsidiaries increased from 2533 in 1992 to 16 079 in 1996. In 1997, there were only 14 700 foreign investment companies[27] following several withdrawals and dissolutions, especially in trading and transport services (Figure 9.7). Most joint ventures were established with companies

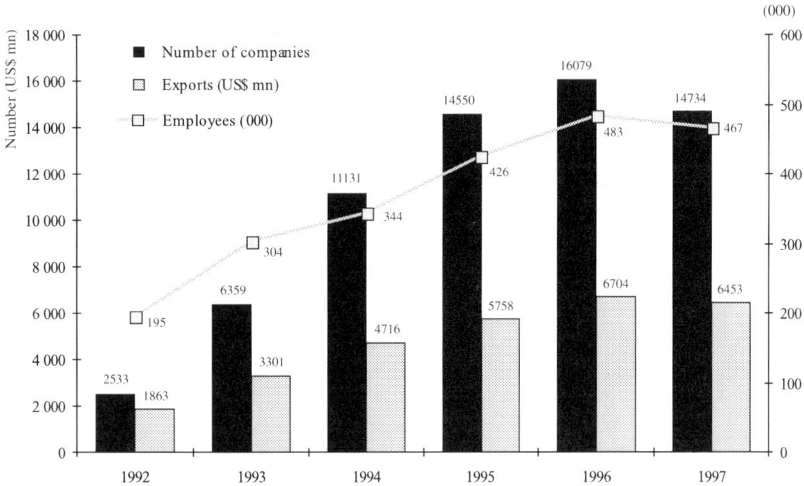

Source: Goskomstat, *Russia in Figures*, 1997, 1998.

Figure 9.7 Joint ventures and wholly-owned subsidiaries, Russia, 1992–97

in the United States (19 per cent), Germany (13 per cent), China (9 per cent) and the United Kingdom (8 per cent). The combined share of these four countries in the total authorized capital of joint ventures amounted to about 40 per cent. Companies from Austria, Finland, Italy and Poland also formed strategic alliances with Russian partners. Country-wise distribution for wholly-owned subsidiaries is similar; US companies lead, followed by enterprises from China, the United Kingdom and Germany.

Joint ventures remain the most important form of FDI in terms of employment (about 470 000 employees by end 1997) and exports (about US$6.5 billion). They are the preferred mode of entry of medium-sized players, who represent a significant potential that should be canvassed by the Russian FDI authorities.[28]

9.3.2 Regional and sectoral distribution of FDI

In 1997, the bulk of inbound investment was still directed at financial services and trading activities (together about 65 per cent or almost US$8 billion). Measured in US dollars, FDI in industry is extremely low compared with other LEMs. Leading FDI recipient industries were fuels (US$1.7 billion), food (US$704 million), machine building (US$274 million) and wood processing (US$202 million) (Figure 9.8). In future, more FDI should be directed into agroindustry, chemicals and plastics, consumer goods and high-tech industries. Domestic skills and resources in these sectors need to be developed to reduce the current dependence on imports, which could wipe out local industry if they continue unchecked.

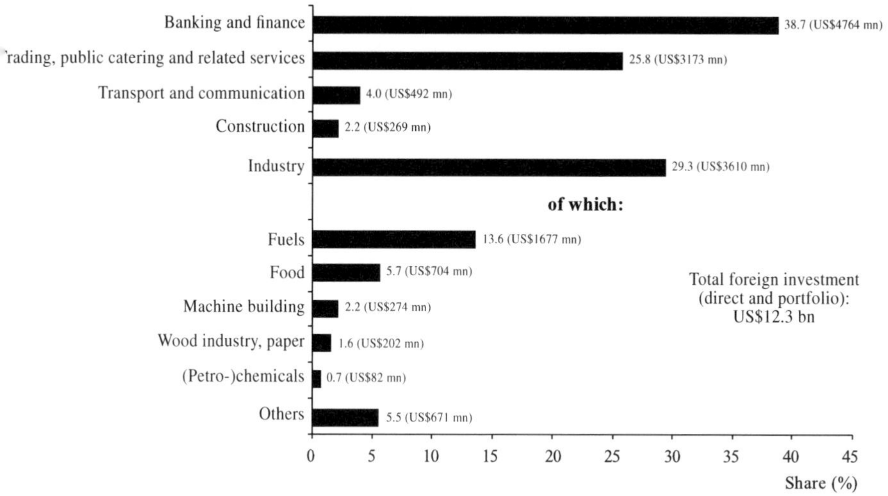

Source: Goskomstat, *Russia in Figures, Statistical Yearbook*, 1998.

Figure 9.8 Sectoral distribution of FDI, Russia, 1997

Almost 60 per cent of inbound FDI is concentrated in the Central region, where Greater Moscow (city and *oblast*) acts as a magnet (Figure 9.9). Moscow continues to attract the bulk of foreign investment, because of its diversified industrial structure and continuous promotional efforts by the city administration.[29] Greater St Petersburg (city and Leningrad *oblast*) also accounts for a significant share of FDI inflows. Likewise, the republic of Tatarstan (capital: Kazan) and the *oblasts* of Tyumen, Samara and Nizhny Novgorod are becoming preferred destinations for many western firms.

Many regions still suffer from the earlier dependence on heavy industry. They will need to define priority industries to be developed through FDI. As the domestic consumer market grows, FDI must be promoted into regional markets to reduce dependence on external supplies. A more balanced distribution of FDI will need to include the Volga and West Siberia economic areas (about 18 per cent of inbound FDI), which include very diverse industries that need to be urgently modernized.

Since 1995, US, South Korean and even Japanese companies have shown increased interest in Vladivostok and Sachalin (Far East). Other high potential regions are Chabarovsk, Krasnodarsky *krai*, Perm and Saratov in the European part of the country.[30] Regional authorities have begun to canvass foreign investors through special promotion offices in major source countries. In Germany, for example, a number of representations were established during 1995–96 by the regions of Altai and Tjumen, the city of Kaliningrad, Novosibirsk *oblast*, and the republics of Chakassia and Tuva. But a lot remains to be done to coordinate policy efforts and increase inflows to promising industrial sectors.[31]

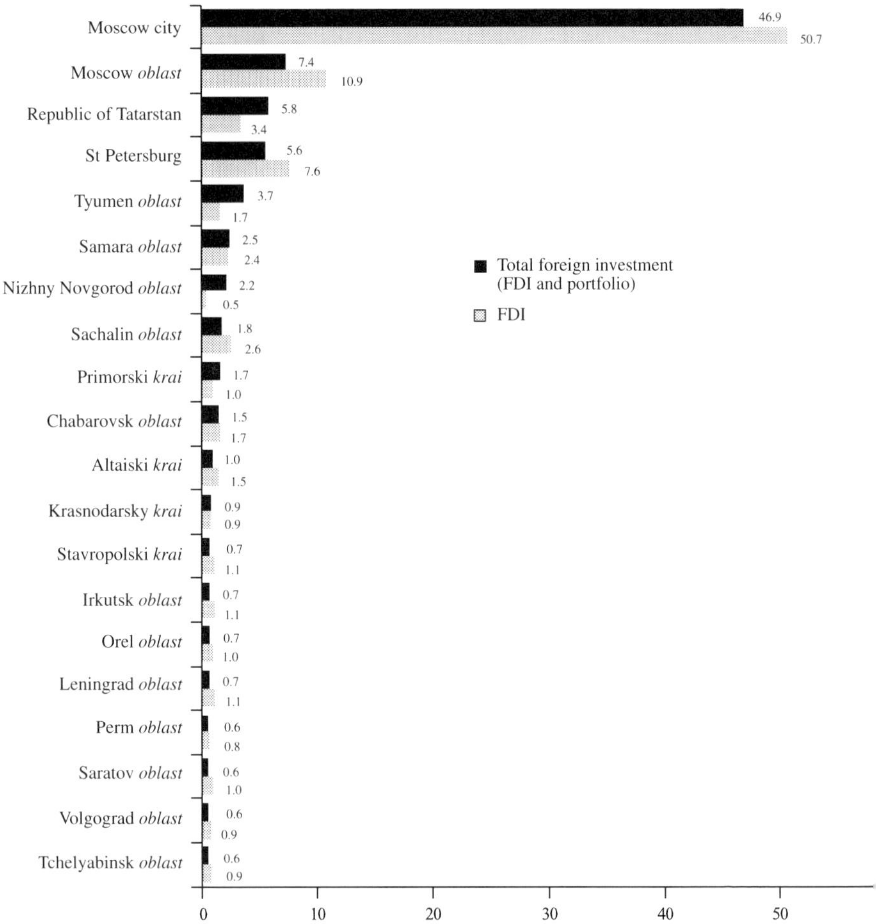

Source: Goskomstat, *Regioni Rossyi*, 1997, 1998.

Figure 9.9 FDI by main economic region, Russia, 1997

9.4 Legislation related to foreign investment

9.4.1 General legal situation

In industrialized countries, economic and political stability obviates the need for specific legislation to protect foreign capital and investment. Solid legal foundations in these countries guarantee nondiscrimination against foreign companies for establishment (e.g. registration procedures, guaranteed property rights), profit generation (e.g. homogeneous and predictable tax laws, depreciation allowances, and nondiscriminatory incentives) and litigation (e.g. transparent labour laws, possibilities of arbitration, clear antimonopoly regulations). However, framework conditions are less stable in transition and emerging economies. Most of these countries, therefore, had to adopt special legislation for protecting and regulating foreign investment. Comprehensive legislation has been instrumental in ensuring regular FDI inflows. Policies were designed to orient foreign investments into specific industrial sectors that need to be developed. Examples of successful policy implementation on the basis of clear legislation can be found in ASEAN countries, China and India. Leading Latin American countries (e.g. Argentina, Brazil, Chile, Mexico) have also adopted FDI laws to attract more foreign capital and technologies.

Russia is going in a similar direction with its specific FDI laws that are supplemented by a series of regulations in other policy areas. FDI-related laws and policies must reinforce one another and together contribute to an increase in FDI inflows into the country. Foreign investors should also be able to contact a 'one-stop' agency, which is in a position to inform about FDI-related regulations and provide assistance in project implementation.[32] This approach is useful for raising confidence levels and clarifying Russia's FDI priorities.

Already before the break-up of the Soviet Union, most policy areas were covered by specific legislation. These laws were subsequently fine-tuned by modifying certain acts to create a more investor-friendly environment and to promote private entrepreneurship. A series of updates and new laws concerning FDI are under preparation for submission to the Duma during 1999 (e.g. a new tax code, land code, FDI protection rights and a special fund for small business development). These laws will clarify issues still unclear to foreign investors already operating or planning to set up manufacturing activities in Russia. These issues refer to property rights, dispute settlement and protection mechanisms, and law enforcement in regional markets outside Greater Moscow and St Petersburg.

Through improved legal mechanisms,[33] Russian authorities also hope to channel back funds held by Russian citizens and organizations in banks outside the country. If repatriated even partially, these funds (about US$120–140 billion in 1999) could contribute significantly to rebuilding Russia's manufacturing base.[34] Since 1990, the Russian authorities have enacted a number of laws to facilitate foreign investment. All essential laws have come into force, with sufficient protection and legal remedy possibilities for foreign operators. The most fundamental legal source is the new Russian Constitution, which was adopted by national referendum on 12 December 1993. The Constitution protects private property (Article 35), and enshrines the right of all individuals to engage in entrepreneurial and other economic activities (Article 34); foreigners are basically accorded the same rights as Russian citizens (Article 62). Another important legal source is the new Civil Code, which was adopted by the State Duma on the basis of the German codex on 21 December 1994. The Code determines the legal status of individuals and legal entities, establishes the legal basis for the right to property, and provides general norms for contractual and other civil obligations. The Civil Code is based on five fundamental principles: equality of all participants regulated by civil law, inviolability of private property, freedom of contract, free exercise of civil rights, and judicial protection of civil rights. The second part of the Civil Code that came into effect on 1 March 1996 covers various forms of obligations: purchase and sale, rent, leasing, borrowing and lending, payments, insurance, agency commission and public tender.

However, linguistic barriers, a lack of reliable information, and the fact that FDI is governed by an array of rules and provisions that overlap and leave room for divergent interpretation make the current legal situation appear intransparent and confusing to most foreign investors. Moreover, as legislation is passed both by national and regional authorities, the regulatory kaleidoscope becomes even more confusing. Investors also complain about not receiving timely information on legal changes concerning their rights and responsibilities.[35] Russian embassies and trade missions are not trained to treat requests from potential investors in a satisfactory way. There are very few FDI specialists who provide complete information on Russia's investment potential and laws. Rigorous training and organizational efforts are required so that all representations of the Russian Federation abroad understand the impact of FDI and feel more responsible about canvassing and informing foreign TNCs.

9.4.2 FDI-specific legislation

Since the introduction of a market economy, Russian legislators have passed a number of laws and regulations to improve the foreign investment climate in the country. Those relevant for foreign companies are:

- Law on Property in the Russian Federation of 24 December 1990 (Property Law).
- Law on Companies and Enterprise Activity of 25 December 1990 (Enterprise Law): it regulates types of admitted legal forms of companies operating in Russia.
- Regulation on Public Limited Companies of 25 December 1990.
- Law on Privatization of Public and Communal Enterprises in the Russian Federation of 4 July 1991 (Privatization Law): it defines objectives of the privatization programme and conditions for participation in public tenders.
- Law on Foreign Investment in the Russian Federation (FIL) of 4 July 1991, which was supplemented by the 1999 FIL.
- Law on Investment Activities in the Russian Federation of 25 February 1999.
- Law on Foreign Investment of the Russian Federation of 9 July 1999.

The Foreign Investment Law (FIL) of 1991 was the first *lex specialis* for all business activities conducted by foreign enterprises in Russia. Until the new FIL came into effect in July 1999, this law represented the most important legal act governing FDI in Russia. For the first time, FDI had become the subject of a separate law that grants broad freedom to foreign investors in the country. FIL distinguishes four types of foreign investors (Article 1):

- legal entities founded according to provisions in their countries of origin;
- foreign citizens, provided that they are registered and entitled to carry out a business activity in their country of origin;
- foreign governments; and
- international organizations.

Foreign investors are so far not allowed to own land directly; their property is limited to material assets (e.g. equipment) and intellectual property (Article 2). But foreign companies are now free to participate in joint ventures, to establish fully-owned (100 per cent) subsidiaries, and to acquire (totally or partially) existing enterprises, including their assets and intellectual property rights (Article 3).

All foreign investors, irrespective of their origin, have the same rights to invest and to determine the amount, direction and form of their investments (Article 5). No prior government approval (licensing) is required except in the following cases:

- large enterprises with substantial foreign participation;
- investments in banking and insurance;
- large-scale construction and infrastructure projects (after preliminary evaluation by specially appointed experts);
- expansion investments or new plants in environmentally risky sectors such as chemicals and paper processing (monitored by environmental and health authorities);
- exploitation of natural resources (subject to special conditions and rules, in particular production sharing or concessionary arrangements with Russian partners and subject to a special law enacted on 21 February 1992).

FDI is not permitted in the following areas: production of weapons and drugs, pharmaceuticals, liquors, tobacco, precious metals and stones (Presidential Decree No. 179 of 22 February 1992). The government is currently preparing a draft law aimed at specifying those sectors where automatic approval can be obtained, and those where FDI is limited or entirely forbidden. It was supposed to be submitted to the Duma in the course of 1997–98, but it has been contested by representatives of leading TNCs and the liberal forces in the country.

Foreign investors have a number of options for the legal form of their venture in Russia (FIL, Article 12; Enterprise Law, Article 9). As in most other countries, they can choose between partnership (owners are fully liable) and limited-liability companies. Generally, foreign investors prefer to operate through joint stock companies, of which three types can be distinguished: open (OAO) and closed (ZAO) public limited companies, and private limited companies (OOO). Closed public limited companies are a typically Russian form of operation; third parties can acquire shares of such companies only upon approval of the majority of a restricted circle of shareholders. The minimum capital requirement for public limited companies was raised by Presidential Decree No. 1482 of 8 July 1994 to an amount equivalent to thousand times the minimum monthly wage.[36]

FIL contains special guarantees for foreign investors against nationalization.[37] Requisition and confiscation by the State have to be justified by socioeconomic constraints. In such cases, the law protects foreign investors from arbitrary discrimination and entitles them to adequate and rapid compensation in the currency initially used for the investment or in any currency acceptable to the foreign investor (Article 7). FIL explicitly reiterates the principles of 'national treatment' and 'nondiscrimination', in line with multilateral commitments made at the OECD and WTO. Foreign investors thus enjoy the same rights as national enterprises across the entire federal territory (Article 6). These principles are also explicitly mentioned in the Presidential Decree on Perfection of Work concerning Foreign Investment (No. 1466 of 27 September 1993). Activities of foreign investors on the territory of the Russian Federation can be restricted only by federal legislation and presidential decrees, which can invalidate provisions and rules issued by regional (local) governments.[38] The Presidential Decree, which aims at raising confidence levels among foreign investors, recommends nondiscriminatory treatment of foreign investors in the privatization process. It calls upon the Russian executive powers to develop new proposals concerning special taxation and preferential treatment of FDI in the form of draft legislation to be submitted to the lower chamber of the Parliament (State Duma). Following the example of countries like India and Mexico, the Decree also recommends the adoption of a priority list of industries and a negative list of prohibited sectors or activities for FDI. The Decree also proposes a reorganization of government bodies and institutions responsible for attracting, protecting and regulating FDI and for vetting proposals. So far, only certain provisions of the Decree have been translated into appropriate normative acts and measures at national and regional levels. There would, for example, be sufficient legislative room for reinforcing the status of the present FDI agency and give it the necessary authority and powers to enhance FDI into the country.[39]

The uncertain economic situation at federal and regional levels makes it difficult for the regional governments to respect entirely and unconditionally the guidelines set by the Decree. The 'grandfather's clause' of the Decree, which stipulates a freeze of investment conditions and regulations for a period of three years to increase predictability, is particularly difficult to implement. Financial constraints can prompt sudden changes in originally agreed stipulations and hinder public authorities from making the necessary concessions. The overall situation is, however, improving as regional bodies recognize the importance of inbound FDI for local employment and generation of export earnings.

Further improvements are expected from the new Law on Foreign Investment signed by the President of the Russian Federation on 9 July 1999. The Law enjoins the Russian government to elaborate and implement a federal FDI policy. In cooperation with the regional authorities,[40] the government will also propose new FDI-related legislation and establish updated lists of priority projects for the sectors and regions to be developed (Article 23). The new Law stipulates a series of additional guarantees for foreign investors: national treatment, legal protection, compensation in case of nationalization and expropriation and overall stability for investment projects for a period of up to 7 years. The problem of land acquisition by foreign investors, a major factor hindering FDI inflows, is not addressed by the new legislation. Today, Russian legislation covers all the focal areas of particular interest to foreign investors:

- taxation
- labour
- acquisition and lease of property
- customs tariffs and foreign trade[41]
- copyright issues and patents
- foreign exchange and securities markets
- antimonopoly requirements
- enterprise privatization
- dispute settlement mechanisms.

9.4.3 Tax legislation

Foreign investors in Russia are confronted with a complex taxation system which has been frequently modified since 1991. All Russian companies, including those with foreign equity are subject to the same tax laws (FIL, Article 28). Tax Law No. 2118–1, passed on 27 December 1991, distinguishes three levels of taxes: federal, regional and local. Typical federal taxes are corporate tax, income tax on physical person, value-added tax, tax on foreign exchange operations and securities transactions, and special taxes for the use of natural resources, as well as excise and customs duties.

As in other countries, certain taxes are payable directly to federal authorities, others are partly payable to local bodies (e.g. corporate and income tax). Regional authorities levy special taxes: for example, on the property of a company, timber exploitation and water use. Local authorities collect land taxes, levies on company registrations and trading rights and taxes on the property of physical persons.

The Presidential Decree of 22 December 1993 (No. 2270) regulates tax distribution between the centre and the regions. Regional authorities are free to set the level of profit (corporate) tax within a maximum limit of 22 per cent (but 30 per cent for banks and insurance companies) and that of property and assets tax up to 2 per cent. Foreign companies from countries having double taxation treaties with Russia usually apply for tax exemption in Russia.

All foreign entities with a permanent representation or establishment in Russia (e.g. wholly-owned subsidiary, majority joint venture) are liable to pay corporate or profit taxes, which are calculated from profits earned by the Russian operation. Russian companies, on the other hand, are taxed on their worldwide income. The corporate tax rate varies according to the location of the enterprise. The maximum rate is 35 per cent of profits from sale of goods and services, including net income from nontrading activities such as leasing and capital gains. Corporate tax consists of a federal (13 per cent) and a regional component (maximum 22 per cent in the City of Moscow). Taxable profits can be reduced through a variety of deductions. For example, interest paid on bank loans used for the purchase of current assets is tax deductible, but not loans for fixed assets and equipment.[42] Foreign companies that do not operate through a permanent representation pay lower taxes: 20 per cent on income from sales, 15 per cent on dividends and interest, and 6 per cent on income from freight (usually for transport agents).

Two specific tax incentives are offered to foreign investors:[43]

- Tax holidays of 2 years for investments exceeding US$10 million and minimum foreign equity of 30 per cent; in years 3 and 4 these companies have to pay a corporate tax of 25–50 per cent of the generally applied tax rate;
- During 5 years, foreign SME investors are guaranteed preferential corporate tax treatment similar to that applied to domestic enterprises.

Exceptional tax breaks may also be granted for some time to companies engaged in certain sectors such as medical equipment, pharmaceuticals and food industries. Besides the central government, regional authorities have started introducing their own tax incentives to attract foreign investors. A recent Presidential Decree of February 1998 determines special tax privileges for foreign investors in the Russian automotive sector.[44]

Value-added tax currently stands at 20 per cent for all goods and services, except for children's goods (10 per cent) and food products, which are not subject to VAT. Foreign investments are also subject to property or assets tax, which is levied on the annual balance sheet value of fixed and current assets less receivables and cash holdings. The tax is set by regional governments (e.g. 1.5 per cent for Moscow) and has to be paid on a quarterly basis.

Compared with other economies, Russia still has too many taxes, which are often collected at short intervals (e.g. every quarter or even two months for VAT). Besides, authorities – both federal and regional – tend to modify the rules according to the budget situation. So far, all attempts to streamline tax laws and types of taxes have failed. The success of a targeted FDI policy will largely depend on the speed at which the current taxation system can be simplified[45] and brought in line with international practices. The new Tax Code of 31 July 1998 (first part[46]) defines the overall functioning of the tax collection system in Russia and the different types of taxes at federal and regonal levels. Future tax laws are expected to improve transparency and predictability for foreign and Russian operators.

9.4.4 Labour and land legislation

The 1991 Foreign Investment Law stipulates that foreign enterprises and Russian enterprises with foreign participation must comply with minimum standards set by Russian labour laws. The prevailing laws apply to all Russian employees but not to foreign staff members, who must, however, obtain a working permit from the federal immigration authorities. Labour relations are regulated by the following acts:

- Russian Labour Code of 9 December 1971 (modified by the Law of 22 December 1992);
- Law on Employment of the Population (1990);
- Law on Trade Unions (1990);
- Legislation on Minimum Wages (revised periodically to compensate for inflation);
- Law on the Resolution of Labour Disputes (1991);
- Law on State Pensions of 1990 (amended by Presidential Decree of 24 December 1994);
- Law on Medical Insurance of 1992 (amended by Presidential Decree of 24 December 1993);
- Regulation on Social Insurance (26 October 1993);
- Law on Unemployment Insurance (1992).

At the time of the Soviet Union, foreign companies were compelled to use the services of intermediary trading organizations. Today, accredited representative offices, joint ventures and wholly-owned subsidiaries can directly employ Russian citizens with whom they sign contracts stipulating tasks, salary, working hours (no more than 40 hours per week), probation (usually 3 months), paid leave (20 days, nonconvertible into cash) and dispute resolution. The Russian Labour Code always take precedence over employment contracts in case of disputes. For example, overtime cannot exceed a total of 120 hours a year no matter what is agreed between the employer and employee.

In contrast with common practice in most industrialized countries, Russian law allows its citizens to undertake supplementary jobs in addition to their full time employment. This stipulation in the Code can only be modified if economic prosperity raises wages to international standards. Most foreign employers are advised to protect themselves from abuses by including special provisions in employment contracts, which specify that employees should devote full attention to the employer during working hours and that any other activities during this time would be considered a violation of the contract. The Labour Code formally prohibits employers to make unilateral changes or to force the employee to perform tasks not mentioned in the contract. Employment duties set out in contracts should be reasonably broad and comprehensive. In case of sick leave, the employee is asked to submit a medical certificate, but foreign companies usually include stricter notification in their employment contracts.

Employers must transfer directly to the local tax inspectorate the income withheld from an employee's salary for tax payment. They must also contribute to social insurance, health insurance and pension schemes, which are calculated as a percentage of the employee's total remuneration (overall contribution of 39 per cent in 1995). In addition to the state health insurance, employees can subscribe to private health insurance schemes. The employer can finance such schemes as part of a perks package.

Foreign companies that plan greenfield investments or direct acquisition of Russian enterprises (majority or minority stake) need to be assured that their right to own property (land, plant and other immovables) is respected. The 1991 FDI Law grants foreign investors the right to own a variety of assets such as companies, parts of companies, buildings and securities. They have the right to use land, but cannot own it. However, a special draft law on land ownership rights (Land Code) has been submitted to the Russian Parliament for deliberation. The recent historic auction of private land in the Saratov region is expected to break an important deadlock on private ownership of farmland. Other regions such as neighbouring Samara and Tatarstan are now also moving in that direction.[47] These reformist regions are expected to become very attractive for foreign companies in the years to come. Land use rights vary with the regions. The Moscow government, for example, grants leases of up to 49 years through a tender system. There are also short-term leases of five years. A recent presidential decree enables owners of privatized immovable property in the

Moscow region to acquire an automatic 49-year lease for the land upon which such immovable property is located.

Although the Russian Constitution of 1993 legalized private ownership of land and the Civil Code of 1994 extended this right to sell and purchase land to companies, the Land Code is needed because general statements have so far had little impact on foreign investors as they have hardly committed funds at regional and local levels.

9.4.5 Foreign trade and customs regulations

Russia's foreign trade regime has swung radically from extreme restrictions during the time of the Soviet Union to almost complete liberalization today. Imports were freed of administrative controls and the system of export quotas and licences abolished. Licences are required, however, for exports and imports of strategically important or environmentally damaging goods: nuclear and chemical materials and technologies, industrial waste, military technology and weapons of all sorts, and medicines. Because of international obligations, export quotas and licences are also required for textiles, unprocessed aluminium, silicon carbide and ammonium nitrate. These quotas have become the most delicate topic of discussion between Russian and EU negotiators. Decrees on procedures are issued by the State Customs Committee.[48] Importers must submit various documents (cargo declaration, licence, safety certificate and proof of payment) to clear the goods.

Both foreign and domestic goods must comply with the safety requirements set by the State Committee of Standardization, Metrology and Certification. Russia's national certification system is based on international ISO 9000 standards. The Law on Protection of Consumer Rights requires safety guarantees for a number of products: toys, children's apparel, food, chemicals for domestic use, perfumes and cosmetics, consumer electronics, electrical measuring instruments, pesticides, mineral fertilizers, petroleum products, transportation vehicles, hunting and sporting weapons, and furniture. Most of these products also need to be certified that they meet sanitary and phytosanitary standards before they can be released in the market. Imported goods must also fulfill these conditions.

As a rule, FDI increases as import restrictions are removed. Since the early 1990s, tariffs have been reduced to harmonize them with those in industrialized countries. Average import duties now range between 5 and 30 per cent. Some basic products such as cocoa, tobacco, pharmaceuticals, sugar can be imported duty-free while the export of strategic raw materials (e.g. cereals, wood, nonferrous metals, ships, arms and ammunition) is tightly controlled.

FIL offers a number of concessions to foreign investors. Fully-owned subsidiaries, for example, do not need to pay customs duties on imports destined as equity for a new venture in Russia (Article 24). Joint ventures with a minimum foreign equity also enjoy special privileges (Article 25); they can export products and import inputs according to their needs and without a special licence. Joint ventures registered before 1 January 1992, continue to enjoy duty-free import of gas, oil and products that they process in Russia. Equity-related imports – e.g. machinery, semimanufactured goods, as a contribution of these joint ventures to the authorized capital – are exempt from import duties and taxation.

However, protectionist tendencies still remain. Certain communist-led regional governments have joined forces with large local enterprises to demand protection, especially in the automotive, chemical and food industries, thus exerting pressure on the central government for higher duties and stricter certification for foreign companies. But, on the whole, Russia seems to be on the path to full trade liberalization. However, as it prepares to joint the WTO, which promotes free trade and worldwide FDI protection, Russia will need to further liberalize its foreign trade regime.

Notes

1. M. M. Boguslavski, *Inostrannyie investitsii* [Foreign investment], 1996, pp. 1–12.
2. Total capital forming investment as opposed to gross capital formation, which does not include repairs and investment in nonmaterial and circulating assets. See Goskomstat, *Russia in Figures*, 1997, p. 229; *Russian Statistical Yearbook*, 1997, p. 405.
3. See also Chapter 9.4.
4. Federal budget plus budgets of federation subjects (regions) and local authorities.
5. Housing and construction activities accounted for Rb1225.8 trillion or US$41 billion in 1996 – about 60 per cent of gross capital formation.
6. According to official statistics, not even US$2 million were invested in agriculture by foreign companies in 1996. See Goskomstat, *Statistical Yearbook*, 1997, p. 415.
7. Goskomstat, *Statistical Yearbook*, p. 530.
8. OECD, *Economic Survey: Russian Federation*, 1997, Paris, pp. 113–23.
9. BfAI, 'Rußland, fast durchwegs Kürzungen bei staatlichen Investitionen' [Russia, cuts almost everywhere in public-sector investment], *Info Osteuropa*, November 1998, pp. 8–9.
10. These loans are known as systemic transformation facility or STF.
11. In 1996, GDP was US$625 billion in PPP or US$440 billion in nominal value.
12. Annual transfers to former East Germany, whose population is less than 10 per cent that of Russia, have averaged DM120–150 billion or US$70–90 billion per year since unification in 1990.
13. OECD, *Economic Survey: Russian Federation*, 1997.
14. Goskomstat, *Russian Statistical Yearbook*, 1997, pp. 406–9.
15. Chapter 9.3.1.
16. Goskomstat, *Russian Statistical Yearbooks*, 1997, 1998, 1999.
17. Chapter 14.

18. According to UNCTAD, FDI inflows were even higher – US$6.2 billion. Considering the critical state of Russian industry, both figures (Goskomstat and UNCTAD) could be overestimated as only about two-thirds of approved FDI is actually received (the ratio may be much lower in 1998 owing to the negative impact of the financial crisis). To avoid misunderstandings and to measure real flows, Russia should consider publishing precise figures for investment approvals and actual FDI, as is done in China and India. Current statistics do not clearly distinguish between FDI, portfolio and other types of investments, in particular trade credits and credits from foreign governments guaranteed by the Government of the Russian Federation. The inclusion of trade credits, which represent up to 70 per cent of the 'foreign investment' total, is particularly confusing as these amounts are not real capital inflows into Russia's economy.
19. The legal basis for government intervention is provided by the new Law on Foreign Investment of 9 July 1999 (Articles 23 and 24). See Chapter 9.4.2.
20. Including portfolio investments.
21. Chapters 5 and 6.
22. Chapter 3.3.2.
23. These shares have remained quite stable over the years, which suggests similar country contributions to Russia's accumulated FDI stock.
24. OECD, *Economic Survey: Russian Federation*, 1997, pp. 69–70.
25. Goskomstat, *Russia in Figures*, 1997, p. 252.
26. Goskomstat, *Socio-economic Situation in Russia,* January 1999.
27. Of which about 7800 in trading, 3000 in industry and 1100 in construction.
28. Chapters 4.2 and 14.5.
29. In 1998, the Moscow City government launched the Moscow International Business Association (MIBA) to attract foreign investors who are also invited to join the association as members. The association mainly undertakes lobbying assignments at the level of the Moscow City authorities. See *Moskauer Deutsche Zeitung*, 'Gemeinsam gegen die Krise' [United against the crisis], February 1999.
30. For industrial structures in Russia's regions, refer to Chapter 8.4.
31. Chapter 17.
32. Chapter 17.
33. Chapter 15.2.
34. In 1947, the Italian government introduced a general amnesty on funds repatriated by overseas Italians, if they were used for the realization of FDI projects including the purchase of equipment. This measure contributed significantly to the economic miracle of postwar Italy.
35. Chapter 17.1.
36. This provision is also covered in the special Regulation on Public Limited Companies.
37. The fundamental guarantees and protection mechanisms have been included in the CIS Convention on the Protection of Foreign Investors' Rights, which has been approved by a number of CIS Parliaments. The text of the Convention has so far not been officially translated into English (as of March 1999).
38. Autonomous regional authorities like Tatarstan have their own FDI-specific legislation, which is fundamentally similar to the federal FIL.
39. Chapter 17.
40. Some regions such as the Novgord, Samara and Moscow *oblasts* have already adopted more specific FDI legislation to promote selected industries and areas of economic development through fiscal and other incentives.

41. According to diplomatic sources in Moscow, laws and regulations related to Russia's Customs Authority and duty collection mechanisms need to be overhauled to allow free trade and investment. Another area of concern to foreign enterprises is arbitrary certification. These two issues were the main points of discussion during the official visit of the Italian Prime Minister Massimo d'Alema to Moscow on 8–10 February 1999.
42. This rule will need to be relaxed if enterprises are to be stimulated to engage in long-term manufacturing activities for which they need to acquire fixed assets and equipment.
43. Presidential Decree of 23 May 1994, No. 1004.
44. The need for single decrees with a sector focus (to determine incentives and protect investors' rights in key industries such as oil and automobiles) is the result of lack of coherent planning in the framework of an overall FDI policy and legislation scheme.
45. At the time of finalizing this chapter (September 1999), the Russian government was starting a process of tax simplification and reduction to relaunch business activity following the 1998 crisis.
46. The second part of the Tax Code is scheduled to be approved by the two legislative Houses (Duma, Federation Council) during 1999.
47. 'Yeltsin Vows to Fight for Private Land', *Moscow Times*, 7 March 1998, pp. 1–2.
48. For recent changes in the export–import regime, refer to 'Izmeneniya v Mekhanizme Gosregulirovaniya Vneshnetorgovoi Deyatelnosti' [Changes in the mechanism of government regulations concerning foreign trade activities], *Expert*, 8 March 1999, pp. 68– 69.

Part V

Towards a Long-term FDI Strategy for Russia

10
Strategic State Guidance for FDI

10.1 Russia's difficult road to becoming a modern industrial nation

An advanced economy is characterized by rising productivity at home and relocation of specific production processes to countries with better factor conditions through FDI and global sourcing. Burdened by the total collapse of domestic production and the replacement of domestic products by imports, the Russian economy is still very far from this stage.

Compared with industrialized countries, which record a fairly balanced FDI situation after decades of intensive trade leading to high economic integration, Russia has apparently not progressed beyond the initial stages of the investment development path.[1] Overall inward FDI has remained negligible and most incoming projects have only targeted raw materials or low value-added industries.[2] Finished and high value-added products are mostly imported. Financial and managerial weaknesses prevent Russian enterprises from acquiring domestic market share, let alone acquiring stakes in foreign companies. Outward FDI flows, which would be an additional sign of economic progress, are lower than at the time of the Soviet Union.

Russia's overdependence on imports of essential finished products strains the country's balance of payments. More favourable conditions for TNCs would attract knowledge-intensive industries so that Russia could move beyond the purely factor-driven stage of economic development – focus on raw materials sectors and labour-intensive industries – typical of a developing rather than an advanced economy (Figure 10.1). To catch up with China, India, Mexico and other competing emerging economies,[3] Russia should proceed to the subsequent investment- and innovation-driven stages by better use of its scientific base and raw material resources.

With each passing year since the reform process started, Russia has experienced a deterioration of its economy (capital stock, plants and

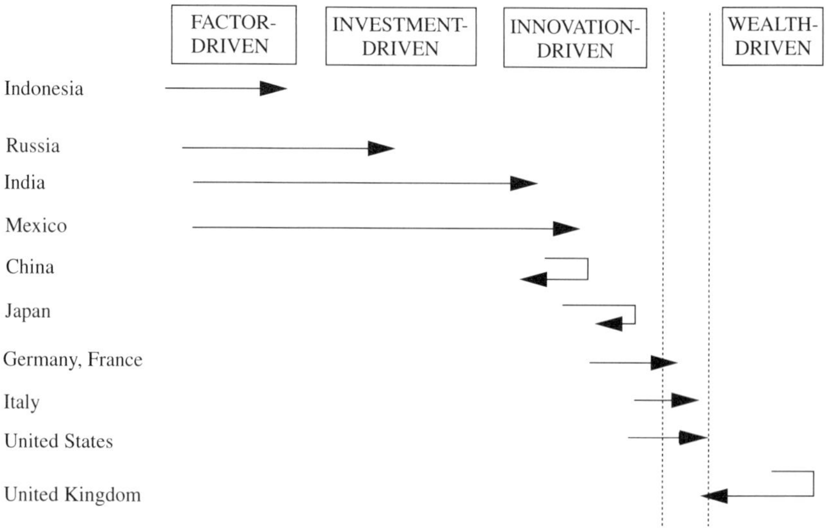

Source: Adapted from M. Porter, *Competitiveness of nations*, 1990.

Figure 10.1 National competitiveness in the late 1990s

equipment, technology). In many respects, the country has thus fallen two stages behind the industrialized economies of Europe, North America and Asia who are approaching or have already advanced to the wealth-driven stage of economic development, which is marked by a high degree of competition, consumer satisfaction through a wide variety of domestically produced and imported goods and overall socioeconomic and legal stability.

Being a country with abundant raw materials reserves, Russia faces a true 'oil or industry' dilemma. This was also the situation in the Netherlands in the early 1970s,[4] when the discovery of large gas sites gradually moved employment away from industry towards less value-added activities. As the market was not able to strike a balance, the Dutch government was compelled to intervene with targeted industrial policies. Eventually, industrial 'desertification' was averted and today the Netherlands' high-tech and services sectors have placed it among the most developed and diversified economies in the world. Russia finds itself at similar crossroads, but it must overcome excessive dependence on raw materials exports to rebuild the economy.[5] Growth based exclusively on the development of the primary sector is not sustainable.

In the consumer goods and capital equipment industries, a vicious circle of factory closures, dismissals, falling purchasing power levels and low demand has formed in the leading economic areas outside Greater Moscow and St Petersburg. Attempts by the authorities to protect local industries through higher import duties and nontariff barriers have failed. Excessive trade regulation is not a strategy for industrial upgrading and diversification. A better long-term option is to design a strategic industrial policy and to systematically target foreign technologies, capital and know-how.

Russia needs massive funds for industrial restructuring and modernization, rebuilding and expansion of its infrastructure, conversion of its defence sector, and rectifying the severe environmental problems left by communism. It must invest in the engines of growth and stability: the agroindustrial complex; machinery; chemicals; electronics; road, rail, air and sea transport; telecommunications; energy conservation; medical equipment and many others. Substantial investments are also required to modernize indispensable social services such as hospitals and educational establishments, warehousing capacities to optimize trading (retail and wholesale structures) and transport, as well as the hotel sector to develop tourism.[6] At present, Russia is not investing anywhere near the level necessary for maintaining an acceptable economic momentum. Since the collapse of the Soviet Union, gross capital formation has dropped to unprecedented low levels.[7]

The Russian government has the possibility of raising its bargaining power by creating a favourable environment for foreign investors, irrespective of their size. Once investor interest in Russia increases, the government will be encouraged to shift its focus from large foreign corporations (in most cases, FDI originates from the world's top 100 companies) to medium-sized operators and eventually to the domestic economy, thus orienting all enterprises towards specific long-term development objectives.

One of the greatest challenges before Russia's policy-makers in the coming decades will be to transform its industry into a modern, operational structure. The central concern will be the capacity of the country's key companies to reach high levels of productivity and international competitiveness. The success of technological and managerial transformation at enterprise level will ultimately translate into the emergence of a strong middle class, signifying that a majority of Russians enjoy improved living standards, economic prosperity and durable social stability.

10.2 Urgency for an FDI strategy

The continuing decline in Russia's industry calls for a far-sighted strategy supported by the government to attract the manufacturing technology, managerial know-how and financial resources it needs from abroad. Such a strategy should be based on a clear vision and concept. It implies:

- accurate and continued monitoring of major competitor LEMs (Chapter 11), FDI sourcing possibilities in G5 and other advanced economies (Chapter 13) and the country's industrial potential (Chapter 12);
- setting of targets for essential industries and technologies (Chapter 14);
- designing effective policy instruments to prospect and absorb the desired type of investment (Chapter 16); and
- policy implementation and monitoring through a coordinating agency (Chapter 17).

Russia cannot afford to lose any time. Its main competitors – Brazil, China, India, Indonesia and Mexico – are progressing rapidly in formulating more favourable FDI policies. Over the past five years, these large emerging markets (LEMs) have succeeded in increasing investment inflows significantly through a combination of FDI-specific legislation and integrated policy instruments.[8] Former socialist countries of Eastern Europe, particularly the Czech Republic, Hungary, Poland and Ukraine have also intensified efforts to create specific FDI-friendly laws and policies. Governments in Asia, Latin America and Eastern Europe have decided not to leave the vital issue of foreign investment to chance and turned into active promoters of their markets in the international arena. Even industrialized countries, which are the larger recipients of FDI, continue to improve investment conditions. Formerly indifferent countries (e.g. Germany) have eased investment approval procedures and try to optimize framework conditions for foreign companies[9] in an effort to accelerate industrial growth and employment. The visible success of liberal economies (e.g. Ireland, United Kingdom, United States) has also prompted generally protectionist countries like France and Japan to turn to foreign investors as new employment and tax revenue generators.

While a few countries already have a consistent and dedicated FDI strategy,[10] most governments have begun to approach inward FDI in a much more systematic way than in the 1980s. In progressive economies, the task of formulating and implementing FDI strategies is increasingly entrusted to independent investment development or promotion agencies.[11] These agencies are usually organized like semipublic institutions and are run by professionals with close links to the private sector. Abroad, they operate through their own promotion offices (in major source markets) and by seconding FDI experts to the home country's embassies in other important markets.

In spite of intense competition worldwide, Russia is in a good position to approach leading TNCs and has an edge over its competitor LEMs if it optimizes its advantages. Russia offers:

- a large pool of highly trained specialists and an excellent educational system,
- an abundance of raw materials,
- better physical infrastructure,
- a large consumer population that is rapidly catching up with those in industrialized countries,
- cultural affinity with other European and North American countries,
- geographic proximity to both European and Asian investors, and
- a base for expanding operations into the new CIS markets.

To turn these assets into a timely advantage, the Russian authorities need to formulate a viable FDI strategy and implement it rapidly so that the country's industrial decline and brain drain[12] can be arrested, jobs preserved and tax revenue generated. A strategic focus will help increase the level of productive rather than speculative investment. Manufacturing in the country will replace trading, finance and import–export activities so that Russia can reposition itself as a major industrial power. Moreover, the introduction of better and cleaner technologies would limit environmental hazards in Russia.

The country's framework conditions, especially instability caused by frequently changing and burdensome taxes and customs regulations, need to be considerably improved. Transparent policies and clear laws on labour, foreign trade, property and environment, and the enactment of an equitable and stimulating taxation system will help foreign investors 'feel more at home' in Russia.[13]

FDI enhancement and promotion measures demonstrating the government's firm intention to improve the situation through a clear strategy would raise international confidence levels considerably. Such a strategy will involve speedy implementation of transparent instruments.[14] Data collection mechanisms also need to be improved as potential investors need a prior evaluation of the economic performance of key national players and their manufacturing capabilities. Central and regional authorities should work together so that efforts are coordinated and not needlessly duplicated.

The need for political guidance for industrial development through FDI will decline with Russia's economic advancement. But such support measures will remain crucial[15] throughout the transition period, at least until 2010–15. Russia's current difficulties can be compared to those already faced by other industrialized countries. Japan, for example, was obliged to take far-reaching steps to raise industrial competitiveness during economic reconstruction in the 1960s and 1970s. To ensure the transfer of know-how, the Japanese favoured joint ventures rather than fully-owned subsidiaries through special legal acts and incentive mechanisms (e.g. tax breaks). The policy of selective technology absorption was abandoned only in the 1980s, when Japanese companies had become world leaders in a number of advanced industries. In postwar Germany, Italy and South Korea, strategic state guidance was also instrumental in accelerating industrial restructuring and modernization.

10.3 Political implications of an FDI strategy

A strategic FDI policy for Russia must receive the necessary administrative support and intellectual input from the highest policy- and law-making institutions: the legislature (State Duma and Federation Council), the President's and Prime Minister's Offices, the main ministries (economy, finance, industry, agriculture, trade, labour, education, science, foreign relations), and the judiciary system. An integrated approach involving all major political forces will help optimize synergies and avoid unnecessary delays, misunderstandings and overlapping of authority. The notion that FDI can contribute to industrial upgrading if properly channelled should permeate leading ministries, which will have to give all their support to make it succeed.

Not all leading political forces of the country are fully aware of this urgency. The idea of strategic state guidance still encounters opposition from liberal politicians striving for a market economy with minimal state interference because they seek to remove all vestiges of the earlier rigid and centralized command system. At the other end of the spectrum, some communist and extreme-right politicians combat the increased influence of foreign capital, often without distinguishing between speculative and indispensable productive investments in Russia's industrial sector and geographic regions. While certain members of the State Duma regard FDI enhancement measures as an important complement for improving the general state of the Russian economy, ideological prejudice sometimes supplants systematic and profound diagnosis of possible benefits of FDI. The lengthy debates conducted in the Duma during March 1997 on the extension of the 'grandfather's clause'[16] to provide foreign investors with a five-year guarantee of legal and policy stability demonstrate how difficult it still is to rally opposing political views around a consistent nationwide approach to FDI.

Russia will have come to terms with this policy dilemma arising from the sudden economic and political change to a free market system. The top leadership will eventually need to develop a clearer understanding of the internationally proven advantages of a correct mix of foreign and domestic investment. In the interest of economic advancement, policy-makers across party lines will have to work closely for a common cause – to raise the country's industrial competitiveness through enhanced FDI. Consensus at the highest political level is a common denominator in all countries that have been most successful at industrial modernization based on innovative and well-conceived incentives for foreign investors. The success of a national FDI strategy will depend on the implementation of a series of instruments and general international confidence in Russia's long-term stability.

Industrialized countries have adopted judicial norms (e.g. land issues, property rights and employment) and reliable legislation related to foreign trade, banking, labour and taxation. Ensuring a healthy investment climate for national and foreign companies alike, these countries enjoy a reputation of being reliable destination economies. Similarly, Russia will need to strive for conducive framework conditions by adjusting and improving current policies. Information, communication and promotion efforts must be intensified and widened to reach a much larger international audience.[17] Public relations and lobbying campaigns should be conducted systematically in major FDI-exporting countries (western Europe, United States and selected Asian economies) with the aim of presenting Russia as a promising location for future FDI. The high cost of such activities warrants attentive planning by the top echelons of Russia's political establishment.[18]

To function effectively, FDI specialists should be able to operate autonomously, without interference from other government departments. They should report directly to the highest political level in the country (President, Prime Minister, Cabinet of Ministers). It may therefore be worthwhile to look at options to create – as practiced by other successful recipient governments – a truly independent authority (agency or even ministry) responsible for systematically enhancing FDI into Russia. Foreign investors gain confidence when they deal with a neutral body not hindered by conflicting ministerial interest but truly concerned with the level, type, and focus of FDI. At the same time, the agency would maintain close ties with all relevant ministries, thus ensuring the required information flow for a smooth implementation of a focused FDI policy.

The timing is favourable for a government-backed FDI programme. Russia's overall macroeconomic situation shows signs of improvement and there is a growing recognition of the urgent need to promote industrial development. Besides, the world's top TNCs and a sizeable population of larger medium-sized TNCs based in OECD countries are preparing to position themselves in the larger emerging economies, including Russia, in anticipation of increased global competition in the coming decade.

10.4 Strategic orientations for FDI policy-making

There is hardly a term that is employed more frequently – and even abusively – in modern business and policy-making jargon than 'strategy'. Originally derived from the Greek[19] to describe military talent and the faculty to steer an army through obstacles towards victory over the enemy, the concept of strategy was adopted by business scholars who extended it to the general management of organizations. Basic concepts of strategic management can be usefully applied to FDI as it is a domain to be developed through close interaction between public authorities and the private sector.

In this case, strategic thinking implies clarity concerning the overall direction of the country in terms of industrial development and FDI. A strategic FDI policy is characterized by:

- clear and achievable targets,
- tangible results,
- an acceptable timeframe, and
- phased action plans.

The attribute 'strategic' implies that the highest political level is involved in the planning, implementation and supervision of FDI concepts. Applied to FDI, strategic planning aims at:

- recognizing and exploiting global FDI opportunities,
- minimizing the danger of losing essential manufacturing projects to competing economies,
- extending strengths and assets of Russian industry, and
- systematically removing weaknesses within 'pillar' industries, which will determine Russia's economic progress and the country's future role as an industrial power.

In strategic planning, key factors of success are identified and optimized on a continuous basis. In the case of inbound foreign investment, these success factors mainly include domestic assets and locational advantages:[20]

- quality of political and economic leadership at central and regional levels;
- growth potential of leading industrial sectors;
- national research facilities;
- availability of skilled labour and raw materials;
- favourable business conditions beyond the year 2000.

Success factors are constantly threatened by an evolving international environment, especially changing demand (e.g. global competition for FDI among recipient countries) and supply (e.g. increasing bargaining power of large and certain medium-sized global players) patterns. Global competition compels every nation to design effective policy packages so that success factors are maintained and, preferably, extended, while weaknesses are minimized. The government needs to recognize threats so that opportunities offered by a dynamic world environment can be fully exploited (Figure 10.2).

The outlined strategy will need to be fine-tuned during implementation as more detailed subsector data become available through regional authorities and the statistical services.[21] Finally, appropriate policy instruments

Strengths	Weaknesses
• Human resources and education • Raw materials base • Democratic political system • Strong industrial base • Scientific leadership	• Managerial deficiencies when dealing with foreign countries • Neglect of important industries during communist regime • Environmental problems • Lack of quality orientation in manufacturing and low competitiveness of domestic enterprises
Opportunities • Worldwide economic integration • Saturation and intense competition in western markets • Shift from foreign trade to FDI in the twenty-first century • Interest of TNCs in Russia's immense natural resources	**Threats** • Failure of reform process • Further fall in industrial output • Political destabilization • Competition from other LEMs • Bargaining power of foreign TNCs • Internal resistance to change

Figure 10.2 SWOT analysis for Russia

will be recommended that could enable the Russian authorities to attain established targets by 2005 through long-term action plans.[22]

10.4.1 Overall strategic approach to FDI enhancement

In the 1980s, most LEM governments saw FDI as a necessary evil. In many industrialized countries (e.g. France, Italy, Japan, Spain), leading foreign investors were considered more as unwelcome competitors to domestic producers than as potential providers of jobs and new technologies. The mostly interventionist industrial policies translated into a defensive reaction to FDI as they aimed at protecting job-intensive industries even if they had become uncompetitive in world markets: coal, steel, metallurgy, shipbuilding and automobiles.[23]

Since the beginning of the 1990s, state intervention in the economy has been reduced and, as a result, more investor-friendly and proactive strategies for developing FDI have been adopted. Many governments still pursue a merely across-the-board (horizontal) rather than a sector-oriented FDI strategy. Foreign companies are offered favourable investment conditions including generalized incentives, no matter which industry they belong to or try to develop in the host country. Russia has the opportunity to demarcate itself and take the lead very early by developing a two-pronged concept optimizing both the horizontal and sectoral aspects. In addition, being a large country, Russia will also need to include a regional component.

To have a long-term impact on industrial development, Russia's FDI policy will need to be truly offensive and aim at industrial (sectoral) and socioeconomic (horizontal) improvement (Table 10.1). It should:

- be proactive and dynamic;
- aim at achieving tangible improvements at sectoral and macroeconomic levels;
- yield a series of effective instruments to revamp selected industries in Russia's main economic areas;
- comprise a package of transparent and consistent incentives which will need to be adapted and even upgraded according to the economic significance of the investment.[24]

A strategic FDI policy can be formulated within the framework of related policies, such as industrial (e.g. India) or R&D (e.g. certain federal states in the United States) policy, or developed separately as an independent policy. For an emerging and transition economy the size of Russia, an independent FDI policy would be the most effective way of dealing with specific investor needs and requirements.

The existence of a specific FDI policy will also facilitate the measurement of results against defined targets and selected instruments. It is easier to adjust an independent policy to changing global conditions. A separately formulated FDI policy does not mean, however, that it will function in a

Table 10.1 Generic[25] strategy options for FDI enhancement

	Offensive, proactive strategy Adopted by a majority of progressive governments in the 1990s, most promising for Russia	**Defensive, reactive strategy** Most common in the 1980s among industrialized and emerging economies
Sectoral	Targeted support of specific growth industries with global impact, through a combined industrial and FDI policy: electronics, avionics, satellite-based communications, specialty chemicals, new materials, automotive sector	Support and protection of critical sectors by yielding to pressure from lobbies (e.g. steel, automobiles, shipbuilding, food, textiles, military–industrial complex), restrictive FDI policy
Horizontal	Comprehensive system of policy measures, legislation and incentives to enhance FDI in lead sectors with high impact on the rest of the economy	General protectionism: high customs duties and FDI restrictions for a majority of sectors; selective relaxation of barriers under international pressure

vacuum without interlinks with other policy areas, especially industrial, foreign trade, labour, fiscal, monetary, social, education and environmental policies. In fact, a separate FDI policy could act as a spearhead for other policy areas, as it fosters technology exchange, capital transfers and inter-enterprise cooperation, which form the basis of a healthy economy.

The ultimate aim will be to construct a transparent window to the outside world for Russia's industry through an independent strategic concept for inward FDI. The proposed measures provide a general framework containing fundamental guidelines, which Russian authorities could integrate into their annual programmes for economic development through investment generation and industrial modernization.[26]

10.4.2 Strategic planning for FDI policy-making

Consistent planning of measures and budgeting of required financial, human and technical resources are crucial for FDI enhancement. Plans result from determined efforts aiming at continued monitoring of FDI developments outside Russia and studying developments in Russian industry. The best plans will, however, have no effect if they are not translated into immediate action and if the envisaged operations are not carried out within a tight timeframe (e.g. giving a specialized agency the necessary political support to function autonomously, hiring professionals for canvassing among leading TNCs in selected countries, carrying out promotional campaigns and establishing the required contacts with leading international media, etc.)

Designing a viable FDI concept involves a step-by-step approach (Figure 10.3). Once the strategic orientation of the FDI policy has been decided, both the external environment and domestic factors need to be evaluated carefully (intelligence phase). The information indicates realistic targets to be achieved through an attractive policy package. The policy algorithm is improved as the national FDI enhancement programme advances, demanding continuous upgrading of the information infrastructure and adaptation mechanisms.

All efforts should be aimed at a systematic upgrading of Russia's industrial portfolio through higher involvement of progressive TNCs with a long-term interest in the Russian market. Confidence among foreign investors will increase as existing policies are fine-tuned in the light of more accurate intelligence.

The study of the external environment and industrial potential (intelligence phase) is a prerequisite for the subsequent stages of the planning process. Accurate and timely information on global FDI opportunities (potential source countries, technologies and companies) and competition from other economies, and developments in major industries in Russia will facilitate the targeting of efforts and serve to define the required policy instruments.

Step 1 FDI strategy orientation

- Design of an appropriate overall FDI strategy: defensive, offensive, sectoral, horizontal, combined
- Establishment of a long-term FDI policy direction to be supported by all major political and industrial forces in Russia, at central and regional levels

↓

Step 2 FDI intelligence

- Study and monitoring of external environment: economic, industrial and technological trends in advanced economies, global FDI developments and flows, business policies and investment motivations of leading TNCs (multinationals, hidden champions)
- Analysis of competitive environment: FDI policies, legislation and promotion mechanisms adopted by major competitor countries, industrial progress through FDI in major competitor economies
- Assessment of internal environment ('domestic factor'): national resources and industrial assets and capabilities compared with competing economies (benchmarking)

↓

Step 3 FDI target setting

- Formulation of realistic, achievable FDI targets (overall annual inflows, per capita inflows, relation between FDI/GDP and FDI/domestic investment)
- Selection of domestic 'pillar' industries to be upgraded through FDI
- Targeting of strategic technologies and innovative TNCs in FDI-exporting countries
- Ensuring compatibility with national goals

↓

Step 4 FDI policy implementation

- Evaluation of strategic options for industrial upgrading: focused budgetary resource allocation, industrial specialization vs diversification, cluster building, corporate restructuring, cost-cutting, disinvestment vs expansion through FDI
- Optimization of FDI framework conditions: fiscal and monetary policies, legal framework, foreign trade and employment regulations
- Devising attractive incentive mechanisms
- Establishment of special zones for industrial development
- Information, promotion, and image building campaigns
- Designing of high-level advisory services for corporate executives
- Financial engineering in cooperation with national banking institutions

↓

Step 5 FDI coordination and control

- Establishment of an independent FDI agency
- Planning and allocation of the necessary resources for FDI enhancement
- Monitoring and evaluation of performance
- Cooperation at national and international levels to strengthen Russia's FDI position
- Organization and management of strategic change

Figure 10.3 Five-step process for strategic FDI enhancement

10.4.3 Strategic intelligence for industrial upgrading

Russia's authorities have to attract more FDI in a context of intense competition from other countries. To capture a greater share of FDI for Russia's industry, they need to formulate policies and strategies based on up-to-date and reliable information and strategic business intelligence.

Russia's capacity to attract and absorb the required foreign technologies will therefore depend on its leadership's understanding and mastering of the four major forces governing international competition for FDI (Figure 10.4):

- Market forces, industrial structures and economic prospects in advanced countries (Russia's FDI target markets).
- Behaviour and motivations of leading TNCs (Russia's FDI clients).
- Bargaining power and strategies of other FDI recipients, especially LEMs (Russia's FDI competitors).
- Development of domestic industries (Russia's industry portfolio).

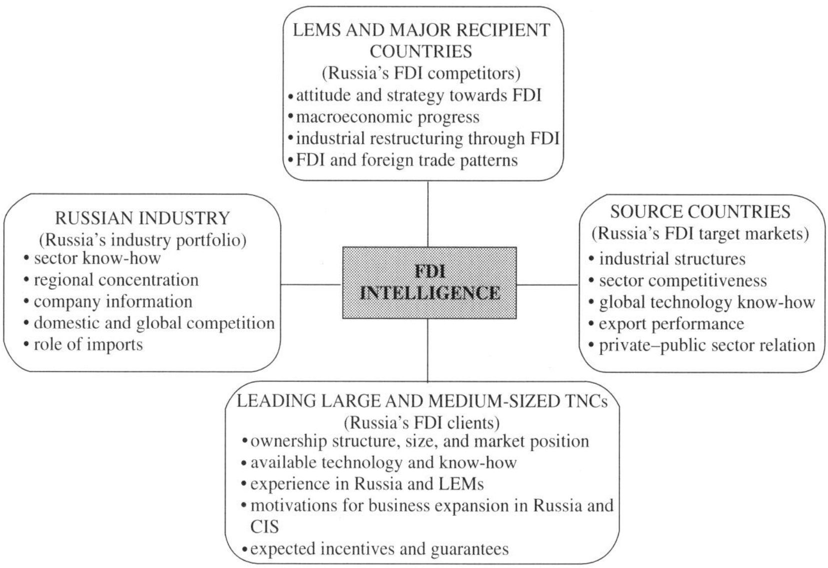

Figure 10.4 Focal areas of FDI intelligence

Russia must develop the ability to evaluate and anticipate these forces through consistent information and intelligence efforts. Each of the four forces represents a focal area of intelligence that should be covered by the FDI agency in a separate functional area (information and intelligence service).[27]

Information and intelligence are indispensable for:

- identifying industrial sectors where FDI would have a beneficial impact on the local economy;
- locating the appropriate investors who match these requirements;
- supplying information for benchmarking[28] Russia's FDI performance with that of other countries;
- formulating FDI policies and adjusting the strategic orientation rapidly to new developments in Russia and the world;
- preparing 'marketing' and promotion campaigns.

In the following chapters, current FDI inflows into Russia and its future expansion potential will be assessed with respect to other LEMs so that achievable targets can be set concerning prospective FDI-exporting countries as well as industrial sectors and regions to be promoted in Russia. Specific assets of Russia's manufacturing capability will be highlighted on the basis of previously researched sector information.[29]

Notes

1. Chapter 1.9.
2. Chapter 9.3.
3. Chapter 11.
4. The economic problems Dutch policy-makers were confronted with at that time are referred to as 'Dutch disease'. See also T. Barker and V. Brailovski, *Oil or Industry? Energy, Industrialization and Economic Policy in Canada, Mexico, the Netherlands, Norway, and the United Kingdom*, 1981.
5. The only other LEMs currently facing similar problems of raw materials dependence are Indonesia and Nigeria.
6. Although this study focuses on the importance of FDI for industrial restructuring, essential services and the primary sectors of the economy (agriculture, forestry) can also be positively affected.
7. Chapter 9.2.
8. Chapters 3.3, 5, 6 and 7.
9. Germany's broad tax reform project, which was put forward by the leading coalition government in late 1997 but has so far failed to win the support of the opposition, was initially conceived to stimulate domestic investment and attract foreign investors after inward FDI had reached an all time low of US1.5 billion in 1996.
10. Examples are Ireland, Malaysia and Singapore.
11. See efforts undertaken by selected LEM governments highlighted in Part III.
12. Every year, Russia loses thousands of scientists and engineers to North America, western Europe, and Australia.
13. Chapter 15.
14. Chapter 16.
15. About the need for policy guidance in industry, see also 'Kagda rynku nada pamogat' [When it is indispensable to support the market], *Expert*, 6 October 1997, pp. 12–15; A. Martynov, 'Aktivisatsyia investizionnoi politiki' [Activization of investment policy], *Ekonomist*, no. 9, 1997.

16. Chapter 9.4.
17. Chapters 16.3. and 16.4.
18. Chapter 17.
19. Strategos (Greek) = army commander.
20. See also 'eclectic paradigm theory', Chapter 1.8.
21. The largest international information groups (Dun & Bradstreet, Reuters, Financial Times and others) are also actively involved in developing the local information environment. Data-collection mechanisms and the general status of the Russian information market are therefore expected to improve further in the coming years.
22. Part VI.
23. In 1999, French and Italian authorities still impose quotas to protect national car manufacturers (Peugeot, Renault, Citroën, Fiat) from Japanese and South Korean competition.
24. Chapter 16.1.
25. The overall strategic direction is called 'generic' in current business management theory.
26. The Ministry of the Economy formulated a medium-term development plan for 1997–2000, which has been only partially implemented so far.
27. Chapter 17.1.3.
28. Benchmarking is a relatively new term in business science describing all efforts aimed at comparing an organization's performance with that of its major competitors.
29. Chapter 8.2.3.

11
Russia and its Competitor LEMs

As an emerging market, Russia faces direct competition from a number of neighbouring countries that offer higher levels of economic and political stability (transition economies of Central and Eastern Europe) or from those representing an equally significant market potential (other LEMs). This chapter will compare FDI patterns in Russia and major LEM competitor economies.[1]

11.1 Global importance and FDI position of LEMs

LEMs have significant populations with rising purchasing power, skilled labour and abundant raw material and agricultural resources. Growing at much faster rates than the leading OECD markets, these countries offer sustainable expansion prospects for large and medium-sized TNCs, which are increasingly compelled to globalize their operations owing to the shrinking of their home markets. Compared with smaller emerging and transition countries with limited market potential and natural resources (e.g. Hungary, Poland, Malaysia), LEMs are in a position to attract all types of FDI, including market-seeking, raw materials-seeking, export-oriented and strategic investments meant to 'contain' competition even before the market potential can be fully realized.[2]

Poland was included in this comparative analysis despite its smaller population size and market potential than LEMs. In Eastern Europe, Poland (population: 40 million) represents the third most populated country after Russia (148 million) and Ukraine (50 million); it continues to attract FDI following the introduction of investor-friendly policies in 1993. Other emerging economies such as Argentina, Chile, Malaysia, Thailand and Turkey also receive a growing portion of FDI, but their success in economic transformation through FDI cannot match that of Poland. It benefited significantly from western European and US investments in anticipation of the country's integration into the EU.[3]

By 2000, the six LEMs, which today already make up about half[4] of the world's population, will account for a combined GDP exceeding that of the United States and Japan.[5] Measured in purchasing power parities, the GDPs of China and India already exceed that of either the United Kingdom, France or Italy (Figures 11.1 and 11.2). Brazil (US$850 billion) and

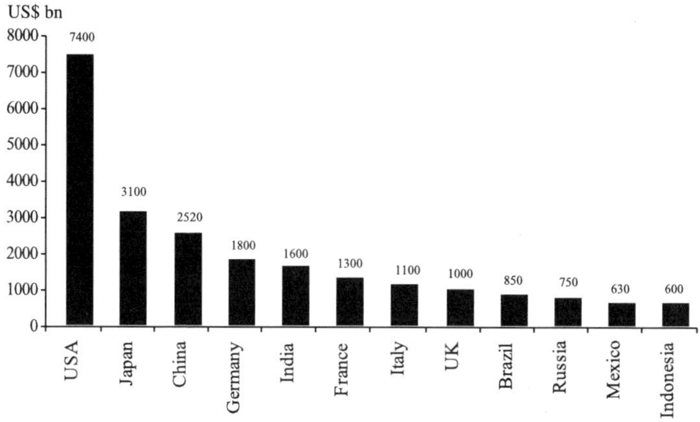

Sources: Adapted from United Nations; *The Economist.*

Figure 11.1 GDP in purchasing power parities, leading world economies, 1997

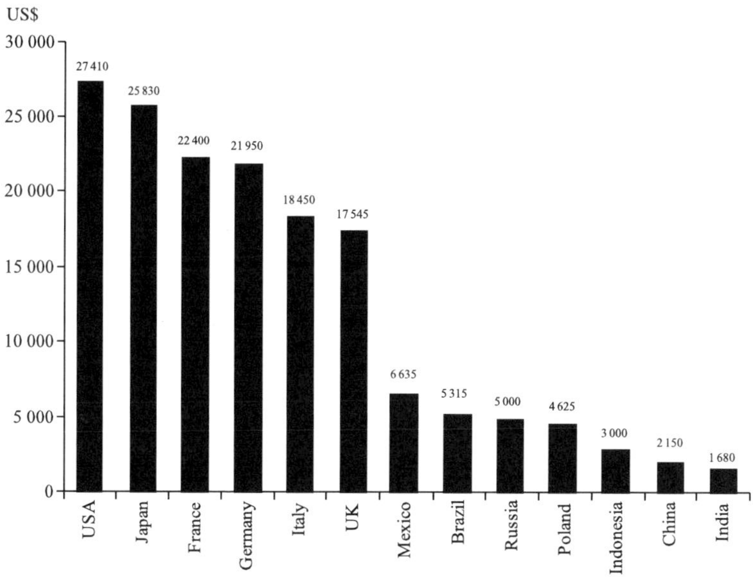

Source: Adapted from United Nations, *The Economist.*

Figure 11.2 Per capita GDP in purchasing power parities, leading world economies, 1997

Indonesia (US$600 billion) have a higher GDP than either Spain or South Korea. Today, all LEMs (excluding Poland) already figure among the 10 leading economies in the world.[6] LEMs have also strengthened their position in international trade. By 1998, the combined share of the six LEMs and Poland in world exports will exceed 11 per cent; twice as high as in the mid-1980s. LEMs already account for a higher combined export volume than any advanced economy, except the United States with whom they are expected to draw even.[7]

Benchmarking Russia[8] with other LEMs (Table11.1) is useful for defining objectives for inward FDI over the next few years.[9] Various FDI-related indicators can be studied for this purpose:

- overall FDI inflows and stocks;
- share of FDI in overall investment;
- inflows by major FDI-exporting countries;
- inflows by major industries;
- inflows by type of enterprise and form of investment;
- import flows by main product categories and countries of origin as first 'signal' of potential FDI.

Table 11.1 Economic performance of the world's largest emerging economies, 1997

Country	Population (mn)	GDP index[a]	Economic growth[b]	Industrial production index[a]	Industrial production growth[b]	Exports (US$ bn)	Foreign reserves (US$ bn)
Brazil	160	119	6	115	7	52	62
China	1250	182	7	185	7.5	160	112
India	950	121	4	134	4.5	35	25
Indonesia	190	131	2	119	1.5	50	21
Mexico	100	111	5	107	5	95	23
Poland	40	132	6	131	5.5	26	15
Russia	150	59	1	53	1	92	18

[a] 1990 = 100
[b] % change 1998/1997

Source: Adapted from United Nations, national statistical offices, *The Economist*.

A glance at Russia's position in comparison with competitor LEMs will enable Russian authorities to define possible objectives for inward FDI during 2000–05. Each year, achieved results can then be compared with fixed objectives. Dynamic realities in the global FDI arena will demand close monitoring and fast adjustment mechanisms.

China is by far the largest FDI recipient among LEMs.[10] Inflows have risen considerably since the early 1990s enabling the country to accumulate stocks worth almost US$220 billion, which is higher than the combined stock of

Brazil and Mexico the second and third LEM recipients. Over the late 1990s, other LEM governments have intensified their efforts to boost inflows into selected industries and regions. Brazil, India, Indonesia and Mexico have all liberalized their policies and now allow foreign investors to acquire majority stakes in a number of sectors that were formerly closed to them: automobiles, computers, telecommunications, energy, metallurgy, food processing and consumer goods. Russia's stock in 1997[11] was US$11.5 billion. If the present trend continues, inflows into Russia are expected to be at the most 5 per cent of China's, which will not be sufficient to modernize domestic industries. Much smaller economies of Eastern Europe (Czech Republic, Hungary, Poland) have been more successful, mainly owing to investor confidence and the strict stability orientations of their national governments.

Owing to its large population and development potential, Russia could easily attract as much FDI annually as Mexico and easily exceed the per capita levels of Indonesia or China. Most LEM governments have defined ambitious targets for future FDI (Table 11.2). Political farsightedness will be required to prevent useful technology being diverted away from Russia to competitor LEMs in the coming years.

Table 11.2 FDI inflows and stock in large emerging economies, 1995–2000

Country	FDI inflows (US$ bn)				FDI stock 1997	Per capita inward FDI 1996–1997*
	1995	1996	1997	2000 (T)	(US$ bn)	(US$)
Brazil	4.9	9.5	16.3	18–20	126.3	80
China	37.5	42.3	45.3	50–55	217.3	37
India	1.8	2.6	3.3	8–10	11.2	3
Indonesia	4.5	8.0	5.4	7–9	62.1	34
Mexico	7.0	7.5	12.1	12–15	86.8	103
Poland	2.5	5.2	5.0	6.5–10	16.5	127
Russia	2.0	2.1	5.3	5–7[a]	11.5	25
LEMs	**60.2**	**67.7**	**92.7**	**106.5–126.0**	**531.7**	–
World share (%)	**19.1**	**19.4**	**23.1**	**24–25**	**15.4**	–

*Annual averages; T denotes annual targets set by national governments; [a] a focused FDI strategy could raise this level to US$9–10 billion.

The FDI/domestic investment ratio measures the speed of industrial modernization through FDI, the dependence of national industries on imported technology and their role in the international division of labour. FDI represents only about 0.9 per cent of total gross capital formation (domestic investment) in Russia, four times less than in India and five to seven times less than in Brazil and Indonesia. Considering that this share is based on low gross capital formation levels expressed in Russian roubles, there is sufficient potential for expanding the ratio to 7–9 per cent by 2005.[12] This level could ensure the inflow of technologies needed for Russia's industrial transformation. China, Mexico and Poland where the reform process started relatively early, report ratios of well over 15 per cent. In China, foreign affiliates have become important players in the national economy; their contribution was equivalent to 26 per cent of domestic investment in 1996–97, three times higher than 10 years before.

Besides the FDI/domestic investment ratio, other indicators (some are shown in Figure 11.3 for the major LEMs) that should be monitored closely with respect to competitor economies are:

- the share of inward FDI in GDP;
- the share of inward FDI in imports;
- FDI inflows compared with outflows;
- inward FDI stock compared with outward stock;
- the share of foreign affiliates in employment and exports;
- the tax contribution of TNCs as a share of total tax revenue; and
- the average value of FDI projects (in US$ million).

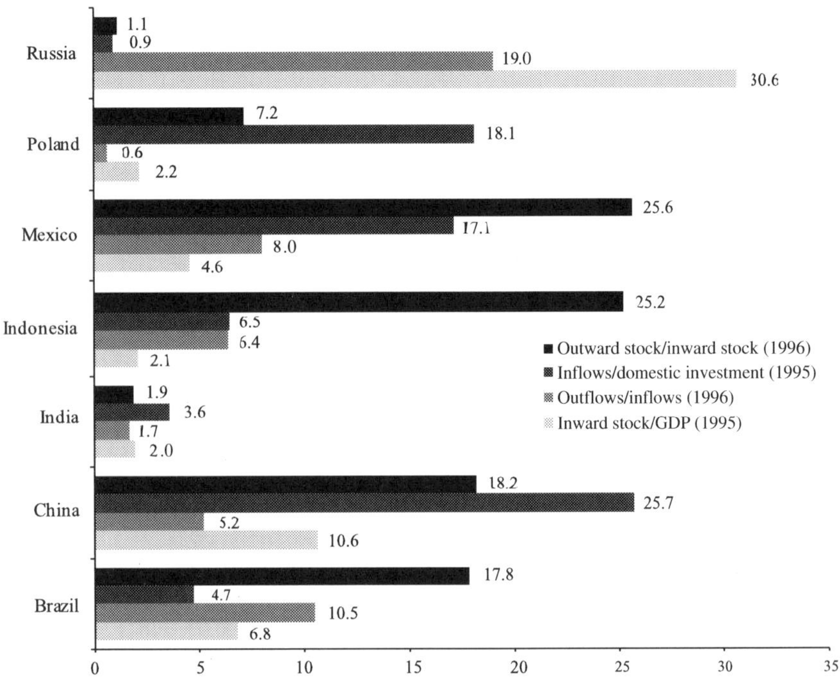

Source: Based on UNCTAD, Goskomstat (for Russia).

Figure 11.3 Main FDI ratios, LEMs, 1996 and 1997

FDI authorities in other LEM governments (e.g. China, India) have also started using a series of indicators to monitor developments in FDI. The indicators are benchmarked against a desirable value to indicate the importance attached to the transfer of skills and technologies from abroad over a long period of time. High initial ratios decrease over time as dependence on foreign know-how reduces. Effective absorption of FDI that is oriented towards the development of specific industries and regions is therefore significant.

11.2 FDI sourcing patterns of LEMs

In an era of rapid communication and travel, geographic distance has become only one among many criteria for investing abroad. Nowadays, a location is evaluated by a set of criteria including legal stability, high economic growth coupled with rising purchasing power, and political readiness to offer special incentives for high-volume FDI. In most LEM countries, FDI authorities have understood this and increasingly try to attract foreign companies not only from nearby Triad economies, but also from more distant regions (Table 11.3). Brazilian and Mexican FDI promoters, for example, are canvassing in Europe, Japan and South Korea now that most important North American (US and Canadian) TNCs have already invested in the two countries.

Table 11.3 Trends in FDI to LEMs from major Triad markets

	United States, Canada (Triad 1)		EU countries (Triad 2)		Japan, South Korea (Triad 3)		Other emerging countries (incl. LEMs)	
	Importance	Trend	Importance	Trend	Importance	Trend	Importance	Trend
Brazil	++	↑	++	↑	+	↑	+	↑
China	+++	→	+++	→	+++	↑	+	↑
India	+++	↑	+++	↑	+++	→	+	→
Indonesia	+	→	+	↑	++	→	++	↑
Mexico	+++	→	++	↑	++	→	+	↑
Poland	+++	→	+++	→	+	↑	+	↑
Russia	+++	→	+++	↑	+	↑	+	↑

+++ very significant; ++ significant; + moderate; → no development; ↑ upward trend

A major sales argument is the large domestic market and the possibility of accessing markets across the regional groupings such as NAFTA (case of Mexico), MERCOSUR (case of Brazil) and ASEAN (case of Indonesia). India is fostering integration within the SAARC, a regional grouping that also comprises Bangladesh, the Maldives, Nepal, Pakistan and Sri Lanka, which will eventually offer a consumer market of approximately 1.5 billion people to foreign investors. China is so far the only LEM that does not belong to a larger grouping.[13] In the coming decades, there will be a growing tendency for LEMs to create regional subclusters within their sphere of influence. As core economies, these countries would then offer investment platforms for exports into neighbouring markets thus contributing to regional economic development.

To compete with other LEMs, Russia will need to promote its own regional integration project within the CIS. Once the existing free-trade area with selected countries (e.g. Belarus, Kazakhstan, Kirgystan) evolves into a wider customs – perhaps monetary – union, foreign companies could radiate from a manufacturing site in Russia and sell to an enlarged CIS market of almost 300 million consumers.[14] Given its unique geographic spread across the Eurasian continent, Russia is in an ideal position to canvass potential investors from all Triad countries and the emerging economies in Asia (South Korea, China, India) and Central Europe (e.g. Poland). Some of these companies already have sales offices in Russia to support their trading activities. They will soon be interested in setting up local manufacturing or assembly facilities to reduce transport costs and avoid customs duties.

Sectors that could be of interest to China and India include engineering, textiles, apparel, consumer goods, and construction and engineering projects related to tourism (e.g. hotels, resorts). Russian authorities have a wide range of options to increase inward FDI; they therefore need to concentrate resources on priority market–sector combinations.[15] The EU being the nearest FDI source should be a priority region for attracting FDI. Paradoxically, although Russia is the closest LEM for western European companies, it receives less FDI than China, India or Mexico (Figure 11.4). The same is true for FDI from the United States and Japan (the most important source countries), which could be increased significantly.[16] Russian emigrants in the United States and other countries could also be investors, just as the overseas Chinese, nonresident Indians and Mexicans residing in California and Texas who return home as significant investors. Here, too, Russia trails far behind other LEMs.

11.3 FDI priorities by main industries

LEMs cannot afford to neglect essential industries in their industrial development policies. All LEM governments strive for national competitiveness in strategic sectors with a high knowledge component: chemicals, machine tools, electronics, automobiles, aerospace, pharmaceuticals, building materials, environmental technologies and others. Subsequently, efforts will also be directed at possible synergies between key industries and important service sectors such as finance, retailing and tourism (Table 11.4).

China and India have successfully built strong indigenous industries by minimizing dependency levels in lead sectors such as food and beverages, chemicals, pharmaceuticals, machine tools, electronics and transport

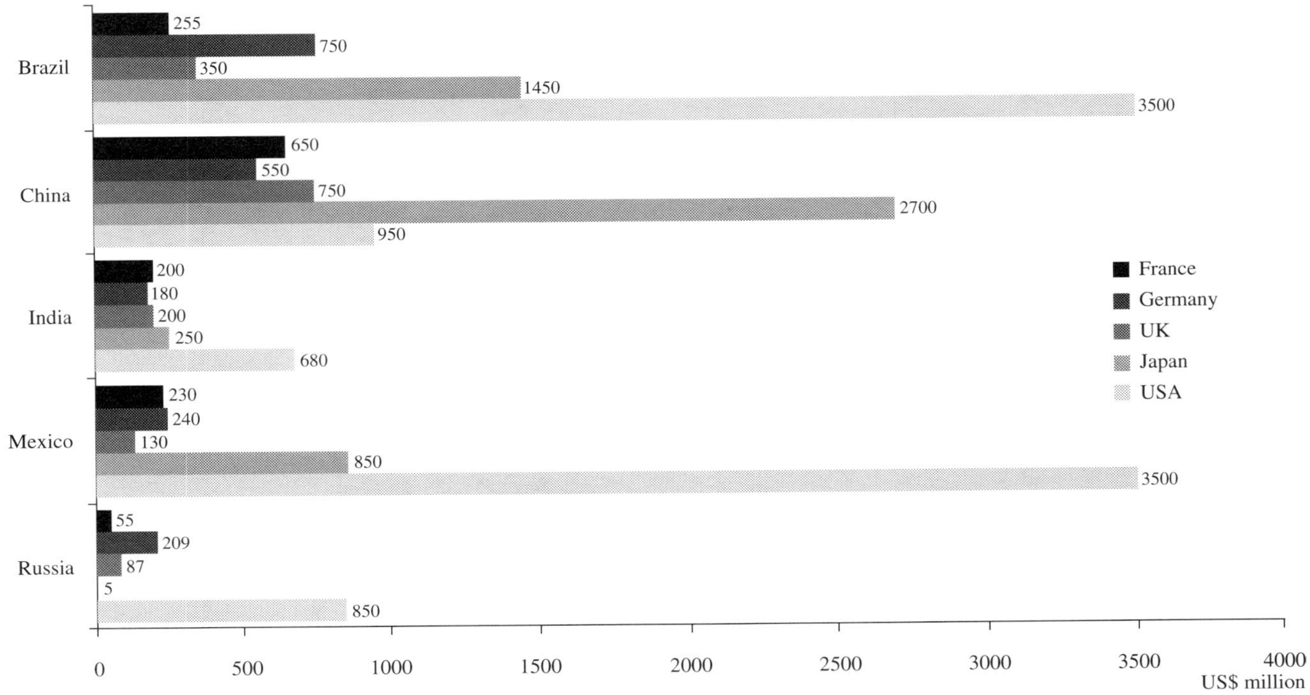

Source: Based on data from OECD, UNCTAD, Goskomstat (Russia), Banco de Mexico, MOFTEC (China).

Figure 11.4 FDI flows to LEMs from G5 countries, 1996

Table 11.4 FDI policy priorities by main industrial sectors, LEMs

Sectors	Brazil	China	India	Indonesia	Mexico	Poland	Russia
Primary sectors							
Energy	+	+	+++	+	+	+	+
Iron and steel	+	+	+	++	+	+	+
Mining and strategic raw materials	+	+	+	++	++	+	+
Construction materials	++	+++	++	++	++	++	+++
Secondary sectors							
Food, beverages	++	+	+++	+	+	++	+++
Textiles	+	+	+	+	+	+	+++
Light consumer goods	++	+	+	++	+	++	+++
Bulk and specialty chemicals	+++	+++	+++	++	++	++	++
Pharmaceuticals	+++	+++	+++	++	+++	+++	+++
Automobiles	+++	+++	+++	+++	++	+++	+++
Electrical engineering	+	+	++	++	+	+	+
Machine building	++	+++	+++	++	+	++	+++
High-tech industries	++	+++	+++	+	++	++	+++
Environmental technologies	++	+++	+++	+	++	++	+++
Tertiary sectors							
Retailing	+	+	+	+	++	++	++
Tourism	++	++	++	++	++	+	++
Banking and finance	++	+	+	+	++	+	+

+, ++ and +++ denote the importance attached to FDI for industrial and economic development.

equipment. Both countries achieved industrial diversification through a combined FDI-cum-industrial policy aimed at upgrading of specific national industries through a 'cluster' approach.[17] Competitive advantage was systematically strengthened by stressing essential factors of success: upgrading of management skills and education levels in the national educational establishments, providing practical on-the-job training in enterprises, maintaining R&D capabilities and a proactive government policy. Similarly, Brazil, Indonesia, Mexico and Poland have succeeded in diversifying their industrial base by enhancing FDI inflows considerably since the early 1990s.

Russia should continue to develop competitive advantages in those industries where it holds leadership: aerospace, electronics, chemicals, optics, vehicles and engineering industries. Output levels in these lead sectors have dropped dramatically because of lack of investment in modern and innovative technology. Compared with other LEMs, Russia's FDI is still concentrated in a few raw materials and service-intensive areas. Oil, gas, retailing, wholesaling and banking represent about 45 per cent of current FDI into Russia.[18]

Usually LEM governments attempt to build competitive advantage in sectors suffering from factory closures because of high import penetration. China, for example, successfully built a solid tissue of light and consumer goods industries such as textiles, toys, sports goods and household appliances. These sectors, which were developed during the first wave of FDI in the 1980s, still contribute significantly to national wealth, especially in landlocked areas receiving special priority as new investment locations. Today, the Chinese government focuses on automobiles and light machinery, as well as a number of high-tech segments (electronics, telecommunications equipment, personal computers, composite materials, specialty chemicals), for which it tries to promote the country as a regional manufacturing platform.

China has been very successful in attracting the most diversified range of industrial FDI among LEMs. In several value-added industries that were highly dependent on imports, China has succeeded in taking away export market shares from industrialized countries. The country has become a major regional supplier of telephone sets, computer components (microchips, semiconductors), machinery (textile, packaging, and metal processing), consumer electronics and certain types of pharmaceuticals.

India is moving in a similar direction and its aim is to catch up with other LEMs, especially China which is considered its biggest competitor. India's large consumer base has made it a promising location for FDI in automotive, machinery, chemicals and selected high-tech industries.[19] Simultaneously, the Indian government encourages FDI in infrastructure-related sectors (energy, transport, telecommunications), information technology, optics and pharmaceuticals. India's chances for attracting more FDI in these sectors look promising owing to the large pool of highly educated engineers and strong indigenous producers who represent potential partners for investing TNCs. The trend towards more diversified FDI is accelerated by the global convergence of consumer behaviour in many sectors and the increasing demand for high-quality international brands.

Mexico has focused on light vehicles, consumer goods, chemicals and pharmaceuticals, initially in the framework of its *maquiladora*[20] programme, but now increasingly through 'stand-alone' FDI across the whole country. As in India, export requirements have been relaxed and foreign investors are allowed to compete openly with domestic manufacturers. For many European and Asian TNCs, Mexico's *maquiladora* plants along the US–Mexican border represent significant export platforms for entering the North American markets for a number of light industries (e.g. toys, apparel, textiles, footwear, automotive and electronic parts).

Conversely, market-seeking TNCs have until now selected Brazil and Indonesia mainly for developing strong domestic businesses. They increasingly look at these two LEMs as potential bases for exports to neighbouring countries and connected regional markets (MERCOSUR, ASEAN). Already, cars, and electronic and chemical products produced in Brazil are sold to

Argentina and Chile; cosmetics and sports goods manufactured in Indonesia are exported to Malaysia, Philippines and Singapore. In all these cases, the existence of surrounding markets belonging to the same economic grouping attracts investments for a wide range of industries. Governments in the 'core' LEMs can thus pursue a strategic policy of industrial diversification.

Industrial diversification was also the creed of the Polish government when it decided to open the national economy to FDI. In only five to six years, Poland reduced its dependence on imported products with medium technology content (building materials, processed food, nonalcoholic drinks, office supplies, furniture, packaging materials and basic pharmaceuticals). These products are now manufactured in the country and account for a considerable share of domestic employment. Poland has already become an important export platform to Belarus, the Czech Republic, Hungary, Russia and Slovakia.

11.4 FDI trends by type of investor

LEMs, including Russia, have so far not been able to provide a consistently stable environment for foreign investors. Economic difficulties, political instability, language barriers and cultural particularities make these emerging countries difficult to penetrate for foreign companies. The degree of penetration of large and medium-sized TNCs has a direct impact on industrial and economic development; it reflects the country's position on the IDP.[21] Only large multinational operators have the necessary financial resources, staying power, high-level contacts and access to strategic information to be able to invest in emerging economies during the initial stages of economic transition and international integration (Russia's situation today).

Medium-sized TNCs can rarely afford to invest on their own at this stage, without having the assurance of a sufficiently wide client base.[22] Geographic distance and political imponderables are more important criteria for these firms than for their larger counterparts. Medium-sized companies pursue a more cautious and gradual strategy of market penetration than large TNCs. They gain experience as exporters before opening representative offices or sales subsidiaries. They establish their own production units only when they have built a large market in which their imports are no longer price competitive.

In spite of difficulties, medium-sized TNCs are making inroads into LEMs, starting with China, which is most advanced on the IDP.[23] Large TNCs from Europe, Japan and the United States, which had invested in the 1980s, now expect total quality management (TQM) from their international suppliers, including product reliability, timely deliveries and after-sales service. Their vendors need a local presence to guarantee these requirements. Smaller capital goods and components companies are therefore compelled to follow their (usually much larger) customers abroad and to invest in their own production facilities. This is especially true for mature[24] industries where critical order volumes have been reached: cars, chemicals, computers and certain food and nonfood industries (e.g. cleaning products, housewares). In China, the 'follow the leader' strategy has become a precondition for medium-sized operators to stay in business and even to maintain privileged relations with their large multinational customers worldwide.

All LEMs will increasingly benefit from a natural shift of industries away from high-cost[25] countries towards low-cost and high-growth transition economies. 'Second wave' LEMs such as India and Indonesia still face difficulties in attracting medium-sized TNCs from Europe or the United States, mainly because of insufficient market penetration by larger western players. Like China, Indonesia has become a preferred destination of smaller companies from Hong Kong, Taiwan and Singapore. These companies, which are owned mostly by overseas Chinese families, find familiar cultural ground for cooperating with local partners. A similar situation can be observed in Brazil and Mexico, where a western European diaspora attracts FDI from medium-sized businesses from the EU.

Besides geographic proximity, cultural affinities are a major factor enabling Mexico (NAFTA) and Poland (EU) to attract numerous medium-sized foreign investors from adjacent regions.[26]

Within the medium-sized camp, TNC behaviour can differ considerably depending on the sector of activity: component suppliers, food or consumer goods manufacturers, engineering and high-tech goods providers. While the first category has begun to internationalize business through FDI, the food, consumer and high-tech goods TNCs prefer market penetration through exports for a long time before deciding to invest in distant markets. FDI decisions depend on global export volume, OEM[27] supplier agreements, and, most important, the relationship with local and foreign distributors.[28] A host government's decision to raise import taxes or introduce quotas can also prompt companies to enter into manufacturing ventures in important markets.

Similar trends can be observed in Russia today. Following a wave of investment from large TNCs, medium-sized food and consumer goods companies from Europe and North America are beginning to look at opportunities to cooperate with local producers. They also hope to be able to sell to CIS markets from a manufacturing platform in Russia. In this context, Russian authorities will need to understand FDI motivations depending on size of operator and sector of activity so that proper incentive schemes can be designed. Economies with a high proportion of SMEs such as Germany and Italy will deserve special attention. Cultural and geographic affinities make Russia a predestined market for medium-sized operators from Central[29] and western Europe. Economic relations will eventually improve between Russia and Japan, which like Canada, the

United States and China is developing an interest in exploiting resources in Russia's Far East. An effective FDI strategy for Russia will have to take into account the needs of leading TNCs in the major Triad economies.

The world's top 200 companies control major business stakes in practically all LEMs, if not in manufacturing then through assembly operations, sales or representative offices (Table 11.5). A local presence also enables them to directly develop customer relations and to inform headquarters about developments and unexplored sales potentials in the country. These companies will need to be approached one by one by the Russian FDI authorities.[30] It is difficult to accurately categorize large and medium-sized TNCs as definitions of size vary according to the country. Over the long run, Russian authorities will need to establish their own criteria of classification for a systematic approach to TNC canvassing.[31]

Table 11.5 TNC strategies in LEMs by size category

	Large TNCs	Medium-sized TNCs	Small TNCs
Brazil	P, SO	SO, X	RO, X
China	P, SO	P, SO	X
India	P, SO	P, SO	X
Indonesia	P, SO	*Asian TNCs*: P, SO, X *EU, US TNCs*: SO, RO, X	*Asian TNCs*: SO, X *EU TNCs*: X
Mexico	P, SO	*US TNCs*: P, SO, X *EU, Asian TNCs*: SO, X	*US TNCs*: P, SO, X *EU, Asian TNCs*: X
Poland	P, SO	*EU TNCs*: P, SO, X *US, Asian TNCs*: SO, X	*EU TNCs*: RO, X *US, Asian TNCs*: X
Russia	P, SO	*EU TNCs*: SO, X *US, Asian TNCs*: SO, X	*EU TNCs*: X *US, Asian TNCs*: X

Notes:
Large TNCs: turnover above US$10 billion.
Medium-sized TNCs: turnover of US$500 million–10 billion.
Smaller TNCs: turnover below US$500 million.
Stages of market penetration: P (production), SO (sales office), RO (representative office), X (export).

Russia, although a latecomer on the global FDI scene, has been able to narrow the gap significantly with competing FDI-recipient countries. Most of the world's leading multinationals have opened offices in Moscow, St Petersburg and other large cities such as Samara, Kazan, Yekaterinburg, Ufa and Novosibirsk. From these offices, specialists observe economic and political developments to inform top management at headquarters about the strategy to be followed for future FDI in distribution and manufacturing.

Russian authorities will need to enhance information supply so that sales and FDI-related activities of TNC subsidiaries are encouraged and extended. Regular contacts with the heads of subsidiaries of important TNCs in Moscow must be maintained to help convince top decision-makers at headquarters about business prospects in Russia. Even these actions should be embedded in an overall strategic plan to enhance FDI to Russia.

11.5 FDI trends by form of investment

In terms of forms of investment, practically all LEMs except Russia – which joined the international economic community only at the beginning of the 1990s – initially tried to upgrade their industries by imposing an import substitution model, which restricted FDI significantly.[32] Foreign companies were allowed to invest on condition that they cooperated closely with local manufacturers so that transfer of know-how was ensured. In most cases prevailing regulations stipulated that local partners should have majority stakes in manufacturing joint ventures. This approach enabled China and India to build up strong local industries through targeted foreign collaboration.[33]

But growing competition among FDI-recipient economies tilted bargaining power in favour of large TNCs, which now increasingly consider wholly-owned subsidiaries as the only acceptable mode of entry (Table 11.6). For greater efficiency, companies prefer to internalize their technology and to themselves determine the degree of market penetration and expansion in the country.[34] The preference for wholly-owned subsidiaries is the result of many

Table 11.6 Preferences of market entry modes by type of TNC, LEMs

	Joint venture		Majority participation, acquisition		Greenfield, 'stand alone' investment	
Indonesia	LSO	MSO	LSO	MSO	LSO	MSO
Brazil	–	+	+	++	++	–
China	+	++	–	++	++	–
India	+	+	–	++	+	–
Indonesia	+	+	–	+	+	–
Mexico	–	+	+	++	++	+
Poland	–	++	+	++	++	+
Russia	+	++	+	–	++	+

LSO: Large-scale operators; MSO: medium-sized operators.
++ strong tendency; + emergence of trend; – low preference.

negative experiences with local partners. By 2000, experts reckon that wholly-owned subsidiaries will represent half of all foreign investments in China, whereas equity joint ventures will become less common.[35] Confronted with declining FDI and the need for foreign capital and technology, public authorities are compelled to accept these conditions. China was the first to promulgate a law on wholly-owned subsidiaries (1986), but many companies have not yet made use of it.

During the 1980s, joint ventures were seen as the only possible route for market entry into countries like China, India and Indonesia. In several industries, wholly-owned subsidiaries were not allowed. Foreign investors found that local firms familiar with market conditions and contacts were useful for steering the venture through the administrative and legal formalities. Today, a growing number of TNCs find that they lost valuable time and market opportunities because of differences in business practices, philosophy and goals with their local partners. In countries like China or Indonesia, larger state-owned companies were frequently selected as privileged partners. Because of negative cash flow, these companies often pursue short-term (quick profits) rather than long-term aims (building market share). Foreign companies in Brazil and India face similar situations with local partners. Large TNCs with significant market shares and financial clout have therefore started increasing their stakes in local joint venture operations and, if possible, buying out their partners.[36] Greenfield investments are becoming more common, although they are more complicated in China than in India[37] or Mexico.[38] In China, foreign cooperation partners are being accused of introducing their own trademarks at the expense of established local brands.[39]

Russia is the latest LEM to arrive on the world FDI scene. Its bargaining possibilities for imposing a certain mode of entry on foreign companies are therefore reduced to a minimum. In industries where Russia lacks modern technologies, but still possesses a clear competitive advantage (e.g. avionics, automobiles, chemicals, food processing, new materials), joint ventures could be signed with local manufacturers. This way, know-how and technology could be transferred more effectively. At the same time it will be extremely difficult, against the backdrop of worldwide liberalization, to impose the legal form of joint venture, as China did in the 1980s. The only viable strategy would therefore be to provide TNCs with supportive mechanisms (including information and incentives) for certain types of investment; the ultimate decisions about the type of investment will however lie with the foreign investor in most cases.

Joint ventures could be imposed in strategic sectors (e.g. oil, gas, aerospace) where only a limited number of world players exist and where Russia will need to keep control over its technology and raw materials base. In most other sectors (e.g. light and consumer goods industries, mechanical engineering, chemicals), TNCs would opt for a joint venture out of technical rather than strategic considerations. In some cases joint ventures may not always be the ideal form for business development. When existing plants and machinery cannot be refurbished, stand-alone solutions may be more appropriate. The Russian market will, however, remain difficult for 'go-alone' strategies, irrespective of the sector and size of the TNC.[40] Only the commitment of local management (e.g. in form of a minority equity) could help the venture succeed over the long run. It will be the task of Russian FDI authorities to keep track of all successful ventures and promote them in Russia and abroad as models to attract new projects.

The mode of entry largely depends on the size and motivations of the TNC. Raw material-seeking investors (generally multinational companies) prefer concessionary arrangements during the contractual period. If the principal reason is low labour costs (efficiency-seeking FDI), companies are as a rule more easily prepared to buy majority stakes in existing operations to ensure supply flow. Otherwise, larger market-seeking TNCs invest in greenfield investments with greater determination than medium-sized operators, which would prefer to export to Russia for a long time before undertaking any manufacturing FDI. With growing competition, however, many medium-sized companies will be confronted with a steady deterioration of sales margins. Starting from 1999–2000, hundreds of smaller TNCs are expected to start looking at possible manufacturing partners in Russia; they will represent an enormous potential for restructuring Russia's industrial sector within 5–7 years.

11.6 The competitive scenario and opportunities for higher FDI into Russia

Limited to large corporations up to the late 1980s, FDI is now also adopted as a strategic option by even medium-sized and small TNCs. With worldwide liberalization and the opening of formerly closed markets, FDI flows are expected to grow considerably in the coming 7–10 years. Experts forecast global FDI flows to exceed US$1000 billion per annum (US$425 billion in 1997) by 2005–07. Russia will miss an excellent opportunity to upgrade its industries if it does not position itself well to take advantage of these growing investment flows. These opportunities stem from a favourable convergence of external factors.[41]

- efforts by TNCs worldwide to internationalize their manufacturing capabilities and to expand their business by seeking lower-cost production facilities and proximity to local markets and raw materials sources;
- intense competition and economic recession in major industrialized countries obliging even medium-sized operators to seek new distribution and manufacturing outlets in emerging markets, including Russia;

- first signs of crisis for the average SME in a number of key industries in western Europe, which could become privileged suppliers of technologies and know-how to Russia owing to cultural affinities, geographic proximity and technological synergies;
- difficulties experienced by other LEMs, which lack sufficient energy resources and the geographic advantage;[42]
- the spread of new information and communication technologies facilitating canvassing and promotion.

In the present global setting, opportunities for multiplying FDI into Russia outweigh threats from major competitor economies. Of the emerging countries studied, Poland represents a rival in the medium term, as it continues to be an attractive destination for manufacturing FDI from western European, North American and, increasingly, Asian companies (especially from South Korea and Japan). Poland has become a base for medium-sized German TNCs keen on expanding their production and trading facilities eastwards.

Internationally outright acquisitions have become the preferred mode of entry for the larger foreign groups. In Russia, however, it is difficult to identify operational plants, and foreign investors often have to resort to more costly stand-alone options. Medium-sized companies belonging to the 'new FDI wave' may also consider building new plants further East (Belarus, Russia and Ukraine) as the Russian authorities have raised import duties and nontariff barriers (norms and standards), and Central European markets are becoming easily accessible for exports from nearby manufacturing locations in Austria and Germany. Besides, a growing number of companies expect Central European countries (e.g. Hungary, Czech Republic, Poland) to become full EU members, offering the possibility of duty-free trade.

Russia can become an interesting destination for EU companies, particularly for heavy and light engineering goods and perishables. The size of the market and the fear of protectionist measures is an important motive for becoming an insider. Foreign TNCs that produce in Poland, Hungary and the Czech Republic and trade with Russia are all potential investors for Russia.[43]

In the long run, China is considered a more serious challenger even if it cannot represent a viable option for every foreign manufacturer. For western Europeans, China is still a distant market, geographically and culturally, demanding substantial financial resources, personal commitment and patience.[44] Medium-sized TNCs are particularly concerned about their business prospects in China. Compared with larger TNCs, they depend more on partnerships with local companies, which are not always easy to handle, besides they are already highly competitive in a number of sectors.[45]

Leading multinationals will, however, seek a strong presence on the Chinese market out of geostrategic reasons. China already attracts significant investment from nearby Japan, South Korea and Southeast Asian

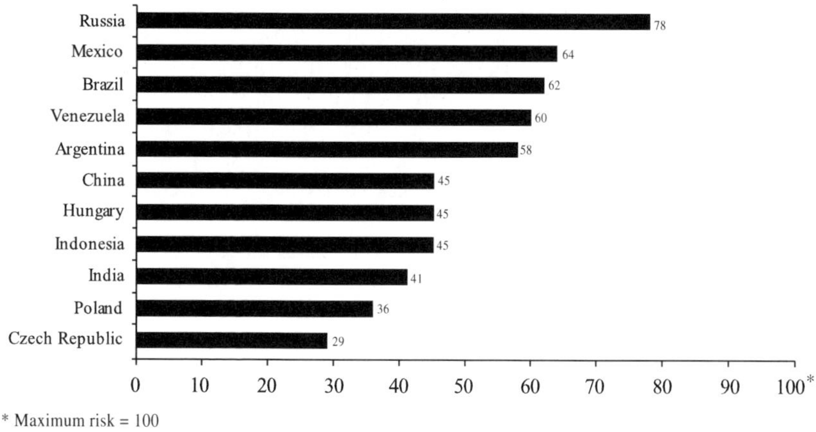

Source: EIU, Country risk service, 1998.

Figure 11.5 Country risk ratings of emerging markets, 1998

countries. As of now, most US and Asian TNCs sill consider China a less risky market than Russia (Figure 11.5). Although China represents a serious competitor, its improving economic relations with Russia will open possibilities of developing FDI between the two countries.[46]

India is the other Asian alternative to China for foreign investors. However, many European and US companies consider it a difficult market owing to geographic distance, high diversity and social organization. Following the government's liberalization measures, many TNCs have established businesses and production sites in the country. However, the slow pace of reforms and changes in government tend to hinder new investors. Certain large TNCs (e.g. Siemens, Mercedes Benz) use India as a base for triangular business with Russia[47] and other CIS economies, especially Kazakhstan, Turkmenistan and Uzbekistan. India's trade links with former USSR countries date back to the socialist era, mainly for construction, hotel management, light and heavy engineering, chemicals and military equipment.

In 1993, Indian and Russian authorities agreed to establish a special clearing facility to enable India to repay debts with the former USSR through exports labeled in rupees. Indo–Russian FDI is expected to develop as trade between the two counties increases (e.g. pharmaceuticals and services FDI into Russia, steel and infrastructure FDI into India). By cooperating closely with Indian authorities, synergies could be found for mutual FDI enhancement. The Indian mentality – probably because of the shared Indo–European past – is closer than that of East or Southeast Asian countries. India is both a competitor and a partner for Russia.

Mexico mainly competes for FDI from the United States, US companies prefer Mexico to Russia as an FDI destination because geographic proximity allows them to better monitor and control their investments. Japanese and South Korean TNCs have also become very active in Mexico where they have invested in a large number of plants. Both China and Mexico benefit from the unresolved border dispute over the Kurile islands in the Pacific Ocean, which prevents Russia from becoming a truly alternative destination.

EU companies invest in Mexico for reexports to the US, Canadian and South American markets, and to a certain extent the domestic market. EU companies generally report positively about their investments in Mexico, especially since it joined NAFTA but also because of the country's efforts to establish a free-trade zone with other important Central and South American markets. Russia will be able to compete better against the Mexico option if it can offer foreign investors an enlarged CIS market of 300 million consumers. The establishment of a real free-trade area or even a single market based on free movement of people, goods, services and capital would enable investors to sell to an equally large market[48] as NAFTA from a single production site in Russia.

Due to geographic distance and quite different locational advantages based on distinct climatic conditions and raw materials, Brazil and Indonesia cannot be considered as direct competitors of Russia. Larger investments in either country will therefore hardly replace investments in Russia. Besides, the economies of Brazil and Indonesia are strongly raw materials-based, without the scientific and research capabilities that Russia offers in addition. Moreover, both countries have experienced several economic and financial crashes demonstrating the risk of being overdependent on raw materials, without having a strong manufacturing and technological base. The US$23 billion rescue package for Indonesia – the second largest international fund at that time – following a stock exchange crash in October 1997, will make the country even more dependent on international donors.[49] The international bail-out package accorded to Brazil following the latest financial crash of January 1999 is even higher (US$41.5 billion) raising the country's external debt to a record level of US$280 billion. Brazil's financial difficulties are compounded by a trade deficit of US$33 billion (1997).[50] Like Russia and other LEMs, the two countries have significantly large consumer markets. Their governments' efforts to develop finished goods and capital-intensive industries like aerospace, automobile, information technology and electronics have already attracted increasing volumes of FDI.

The world's leading multinationals will sooner or later need a solid presence with manufacturing capabilities in all major LEMs. Depending on the type of investment (market-seeking, resource-seeking, strategic), FDI will take the form of majority participation, joint ventures or greenfield factories.

In spite of growing competition, Russia stands a good chance of attracting significant technologies and know-how through FDI, but it must move rapidly to reform FDI mechanisms. Valuable investments may otherwise be lost during these crucial years when TNCs are taking decisions on foreign investments. Opportunities lost to competing economies will impact negatively on Russia's economic stability during its critical transition phase.

Russia must take its main challengers seriously. Practically all LEM governments strive to attract FDI from all important source regions. Knowing that most companies can commit human and financial resources to only one country at a time,[51] governments strive to improve their 'pitch' with customized incentive packages. In addition, Russia can build a highly competitive position by also upgrading its human resources.

Notes

1. For information on other recipient countries, see Chapter 3.2.
2. For types of FDI, see Appendix: Definitions and Explanatory Notes.
3. See Chapter 3.3.3.
4. The combined population of the six LEMs is almost 3 billion.
5. If current growth rates persist, the combined GDP of the six LEMs will attain the level of US$8500–9000 billion at the turn of the century.
6. On the basis of GDP measured in PPP.
7. By 1998–99, the combined global export share of the six LEMs will roughly correspond to that of the United States (around 11 per cent).
8. See also Parts III and IV.
9. Chapter 14.
10. Chapter 5.
11. Chapters 3.4 and 9.3.
12. Chapter 14.2.
13. However, it is a member of the Asia-Pacific Economic Council (APEC), a loose grouping uniting practically all the countries bordering the Pacific.
14. Chapter 2.3.
15. Chapters 12.3 and 13.2.
16. Chapter 13.4.
17. Chapter 12.3.
18. Chapter 9.3.2.
19. India is the leading LEM for software development.
20. *Maquiladora* industries were originally set up in border regions with the United States to offer foreign investors special tax allowances and other incentives. See also Chapter 7.5.4.
21. Chapter 1.9.
22. Including vendor agreements with large TNCs, who are already their clients in home markets.
23. China can be considered to have attained phase 3 of the IDP, which is characterized by high inward FDI in a number of sectors coupled with still small but growing volumes of capital exports.
24. In terms of FDI.
25. In terms of labour, taxes and raw materials.

26. For cultural implications of FDI, refer to Chapter 15.4.
27. OEM (original equipment manufacturers) designates a business relationship whereby a smaller supplier company sells components or semifinished products for further processing or assembling by larger organizations (e.g. tier one automotive component manufacturers, computer component manufacturers).
28. Hence, the importance to develop a modern retail and wholesale (including warehousing) infrastructure for parallel FDI enhancement in consumer goods.
29. Czech, Hungarian and Polish companies have already started investing in Russia.
30. See also Chapter 14.5.
31. In Table 11.5, a turnover criterion was applied (large TNCs starting from US$10 billion). As the analysis is refined, a combined set of criteria similar to the one used by UNCTAD to calculate the transnationality index may be more accurate (e.g. turnover, employees, exports). Additionally, technology-related indicators (e.g. R&D outlays) could be defined to channel the transfer of indispensable know-how. See also Chapter 4.1.
32. Chapter 2.1.
33. Japan and South Korea successfully pursued a similar strategy in the 1950s and 1960s.
34. See internalization strategy, Chapter 1.5.
35. 'Multinational Companies in China: Winners and Losers', *The Economist Intelligence Unit*, 1997. See also Chapter 5.
36. As in the case of most automobile joint ventures in India, but also in consumer goods among medium-sized players.
37. Joint ventures have become easier since the New Industrial Policy was adopted in 1991. See Chapter 6.
38. Several *maquiladora* operations are based on joint ventures with local enterprises. See Chapter 7.
39. JETRO, *Newsletter* no. 132, 1998.
40. Go-alone strategies involve mainly the building of own plants with employed management.
41. Part II.
42. Owing to its geographic spread, Russia could benefit from FDI from all Triad markets: Japan, western Europe and the United States.
43. Hence, the importance of monitoring the product composition of foreign trade between these countries and Russia.
44. Asian companies, on the contrary, feel a closer cultural affinity to China.
45. 'Chinese Companies. Silicon Valley, PRC', *The Economist,* 27 June 1998.
46. Chapter 5.5.3.
47. Chapter 6.5.4.
48. Provided purchasing power will constantly increase in CIS countries.
49. 'Indonesian Economy Gets US$23 Billion Rescue Package', *The Moscow Times,* 3 November 1997.
50. *Frankfurter Allgemeine Zeitung,* 'Die Krise in Brasilien – Das Vertrauen internationaler Anleger ist erschüttert' [The Brasilian crisis – the confidence of international investors is shattered], 19 January 1999, p. 10.
51. This is also true for the world's leading multinationals, which increasingly focus on one or a maximum of two countries when they undertake major manufacturing investments overseas.

12
The Competitiveness of Russian Industry at the Threshold of the Twenty-first Century

This chapter attempts to provide conceptual guidelines for studying and monitoring sector developments in Russia. The conceptual framework is based on statistical indicators and trend analyses of the main industries described earlier;[1] it will need to be expanded and constantly updated to take into account the dynamic changes in Russia's industrial sector.

The intention is by no means to provide a regulatory framework for upgrading specific industries through FDI, but rather to design a strategic concept which will accompany and shape in a positive way the industrial selection process imposed by a market economy.

12.1 Strengths and weaknesses of Russian industry

Since 1991 Russia has made significant strides towards a market-friendly economic system. The most visible achievements so far have been:

- an extensive and committed privatization programme leading to a greater role of entrepreneurship and free enterprise;
- a substantial reduction of inflation;
- a concerted effort to maintain a stable rouble exchange rate vis-à-vis the US dollar and D-mark even after the crisis;[2]
- a comfortable and even expanding trade surplus;
- closer economic integration with world markets.

In spite of these achievements, Russia's industrial sector remains in a critical state. The sudden introduction of a new market system based on competition and innovation has disrupted a number of industries, production in most key industries has dropped to about half the 1989 level when market reforms were introduced.[3] At the same time, a number of new players have given the sector fresh impetus and shown the potential to attract more FDI.

Besides large raw materials and energy conglomerates (e.g. Lukoil, Gasprom, Norilsk), an increasing number of domestic enterprises has begun to develop new products, to invest in modern equipment and process technologies and to 'go public' for additional capital.[4] Some of these enterprises are dynamic spin-offs of former state enterprises following privatization.[5] So far, most of today's success stories are based on close cooperation between domestic banks and enterprises,[6] Russian and foreign enterprises, or wholly-owned foreign operations and their Russian management. Future success will definitely involve international cooperation that aims to raise the overall competitiveness of domestic industries.

The dynamic changes occurring in the industrial sector demand constant monitoring of developments: a prerequisite for the formulation of any FDI strategy. A database must be established at a specialized FDI agency to update policy-makers and foreign investors on key industrial indicators. It will also monitor, for example, how major players in the military–industrial complex are gradually switching to the production of consumer and engineering goods. The strong focus on national defence and heavy industry during Soviet times has left a valuable heritage of technical skills, production capacities and advanced R&D facilities in a number of sectors.[7] Other industries could be systematically modernized in clusters around this nucleus:[8] capital goods, transport equipment, chemicals, heavy and light engineering goods, consumer electronics and durables. Such projects are already under way with financial and technical backing from foreign companies.

Industrial and FDI strategies can also be derived from a continuous study of the export and import situation by major product categories. A close look at Russia's trade balance should supplement the study of the situation in domestic industry. It will show, for example, the degree of import penetration and, set against capacity utilization in the main industries, provide an important indicator for what could be done to upgrade finished goods industries. Partnerships with foreign companies should, for example, be envisaged in sectors where the gap between imports and domestic production has to be narrowed and where capacity levels are insufficient to maintain acceptable employment levels. It will be important to study the industrial production gap for all major product categories (Figure 12.1).

As no country operates in a vacuum, Russia's policy-making efforts to establish competitive industries and enhance industrial performance will be measured against those achieved by major competitor economies. Compared with industrialized countries and other LEMs, Russia's industrial sector is still in an unfavourable situation marked by chronic shortages of capital for new investments and by inadequate salaries and wages.[9] While FDI policies are being implemented, the competitiveness of major industries should be

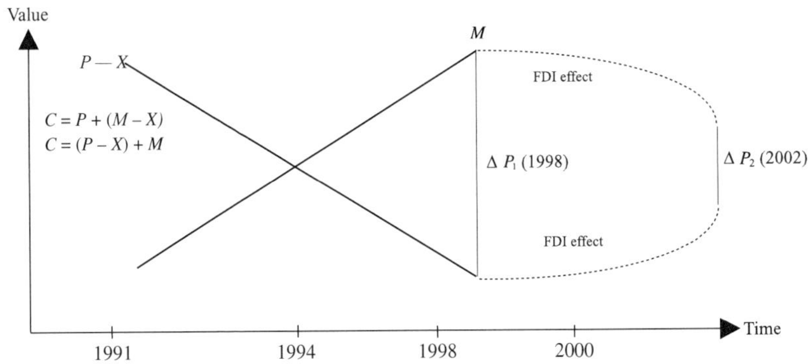

C: Consumption; *P*: Production; *M*: Import; *X*: Export; Δ*P*: Production gap.

Figure 12.1 Industrial production gap, Russia, 1991–2000

compared with others in Russia and with the same sectors in other LEM competitor economies (Box 12.1). An attempt to compare the competitiveness of Russian industry as a whole with that of other major LEMs is made in Table 12.1.

Box 12.1 Key industrial indicators to be monitored for an FDI strategy

- Industry-wise privatization (applications and realizations).
- Ownership patterns by industry.
- Number of enterprises by key industry.
- Size classes by turnover and number of employees for main industries.
- Concentration rates in the major industrial sectors.
- Indices of industrial production.
- Changes in sales and order volumes by industry.
- Capacity utilization by industry.
- Investment activity: total figures by sector and type of investment (R&D, equipment, buildings and other assets).
- Role of foreign investors in asset creation and sales performance.
- Import/domestic production ratio for all essential industries (at NACE group and class levels[10]).

Undercapitalization represents one of the greatest weaknesses of Russian factories, as a result of which they cannot fund R&D, product improvement and diversification projects. Other obstacles to modernization are related to

Table 12.1 Competitiveness of Russian industry compared with China and India

Criteria	Rating				
	5	4	3	2	1
A: Management skills					
Leadership experience, motivation and dynamism of top management			I C R		
Marketing and demand-oriented selling by operational management		I		C R	
Information about and experience in foreign markets		I	C	R	
Intercultural skills to develop cooperation with foreign partners		I	CR		
B: Labour force					
Educated and skilled labour force		I C R			
Availability of young trainees		I C		R	
Training and HRD		I	C	R	
C: Technology and equipment					
Modern machinery			I C	R	
Domestic availability of modern process technologies			I C	R	
Cost-efficient use of equipment			I C	R	
D: Capital					
Capital for regular investment in renewal of equipment			I C		R
Development of new products through adequate R&D budgets			I C		R
Adequate pay and incentives for staff			I	C	R
E: Raw material supplies					
Availability of inputs for production	R		C	I	
Easy access to raw materials through modern infrastructure		R	C	I	
F: Political support					
Assistance of central government		C	I	R	
Support from regional authorities		C	IR		
G: Supplier–client relationship					
Existence of financially strong buyers		I	C	R	
Existence of technically advanced suppliers		I	C	R	

1 = lowest score; 5 = highest score. R: Russia; C: China; I: India.

management skills (e.g. languages, understanding of foreign cultures) and lack of sufficient support by local and national political leaders. On the other hand, foreign investors have the resources to employ the qualified local management required for a successful venture.[11]

Current weaknesses are related to general economic and social conditions, but these can be alleviated by improving overall framework conditions.[12] Regional authorities play a decisive role and must be involved in all efforts to improve the factors of success of key industries at local level. Only then can competitiveness be raised through FDI to consolidate Russia's position in the global marketplace.

12.2 Industry portfolio analysis

Targeted resource allocation will reduce weaknesses and build strengths of Russia's major industries. For this, their attractiveness (measured in terms of future market and employment potential) and competitive position (measured in terms of market share relative to imports[13]) need to be analyzed and monitored carefully. The industry portfolio analysis proposed here has been designed for this specific purpose.

Industrial sectors are prioritized according to their contribution to the national economy (in terms of value-added and employment) and their share in world supply (in terms of global market share). The idea is to direct FDI towards important industries that show promising demand prospects, but which record a low market share because of high import penetration. Although many industries will need to be developed in parallel, budget limitations will impose a certain differentiation right from the beginning of the FDI strategy formulation process. Prioritization will therefore ensure systematic development. Priorities need to be set first at industry level, then, as implementation of the FDI policy progresses, at subsectoral (group) and segment (class) levels. A preliminary selection of key industries and their subsectors is provided as an example (Table 12.2).

A two-dimensional portfolio analysis will highlight the competitiveness and need for FDI input for each industry. In a second step, the concept can be extended to subsectors, which can also be positioned on a specially designed matrix. Similar to the portfolio practice in corporate management,[14] the *x*-axis will describe the relative competitiveness of an industry, which can be influenced by authorities while the *y*-axis will show the influence of market developments on the industry. An industry's location on the matrix shows its strengths and weaknesses in relation to other industries, and is a first indicator of the type of government action required in terms of FDI policy.

For each key industry, separate portfolios will assemble the most important subsectors (groups) that need prior attention. The food products portfolio, for example, will highlight the importance of the dairy, bakery,

Table 12.2 Examples of activity classification within manufacturing[15]

Key industry	Priority scale	Subsector (group)	Segment (class)
Food and beverages	A+++	Dairy products, meat products, bread and bakery products, confectionery, frozen foods, baby foods, delicatessen, spices, canned food, juices, soft drinks, etc.	E.g. dairy products: condensed milk, sweet condensed milk, hard cheese, soft cheese, yoghurt, desserts.
Nonfood consumer goods (light industries)	A++	Textiles, knitwear, apparel, personal care products, household care products, housewares, sports goods, office supplies, tools, etc.	E.g. apparel: children's, men's and women's wear; sportswear; outerwear, etc.
Construction materials	A++	Basic materials (cement), nonbasic materials (e.g. coatings).	E.g. materials: varnishes, paints, anticorrosion coatings.
Interior fittings	A++	Fittings, frames, windows, doors, furniture, locks.	E.g. furniture: for offices, kitchens, living rooms, bathrooms, chairs, tables, etc.
Chemicals	A++	Bulk chemicals, plastics processing, synthetic rubber, fertilizers, adhesives, new materials.	E.g. plastics: PVC, polypropylene, compounds.
Pharmaceuticals, medical supplies	A++	Drugs (including biotechnology-based), disposables.	E.g. drugs: antidepressants, analgesics, antiinflammatory, pressure reducing.
Wood and paper	A++	Pulp, paper, cardboard, wood products, stationery.	E.g. wood products: panels, boards, doors, window frames, floorings, matches, cases, etc.

continued ...

Table 12.2 (*continued*)

Key industry	Priority scale	Subsector (group)	Segment (class)
Transport	A+	Automobiles, trucks, buses, ships, motorcycles, bicycles, etc.	E.g. automobiles, mechanical and electronic boats, aircraft, components, window screens, transmissions, seals and rubber products, tyres.
Electronic and electric goods	A++	Consumer electronics, lighting, batteries, transformers, generators, switchgear, medical and scientific equipment.	E.g. medical and scientific equipment: laboratory equipment, diagnostic equipment, surgical aids, etc.
Information and communication technology	A++	Computer hardware, telephone and facsimile instruments, cables, smart cards, telecommunication equipment.	E.g. computers: semiconductors, wafers, chips, diskettes, computer drives, printer devices, monitors.
Environment technologies	A++	Water treatment, waste disposal, air purification, recycling.	E.g. waste disposal: incineration plants, filter systems, exhaust devices, collection equipment.
Capital goods	A++	Equipment for food processing, plastics processing, textiles, car assembly, hydraulic equipment, conveyor belts, etc.	E.g. food processing equipment: machines for meat processing, dairy products sterilization machinery, bottling and packaging equipment lines.

meat, baby food and frozen foods industries which suffer from exceptionally high import penetration.[16] To provide a valuable decision-making tool for FDI policy-makers, the portfolios should subsequently be established at subsector (group) level. These portfolios will show the competitiveness of the leading segments in a given subsector. A dairy foods portfolio will, for example, highlight the position of spread cheese, hard cheese, yogurt and condensed milk produced in the country. The portfolio method will enable policy-makers to visualize the position of essential industries and their subsectors, and thus recognize the urgency for action. Through regular monitoring and portfolio updates, the effect of FDI on developments in key industries such as foods and beverages, construction materials, chemicals, pharmaceuticals, automobiles can be evaluated.

To illustrate the methodology, selected pillar industries are positioned on a specially designed matrix (Figure 12.2). The economic importance of key industrial sectors[17] needs to be weighted on the basis of four criteria:

- their share in total industrial value-added,
- their share in industrial employment,
- their domestic market share (import dependence and FDI attractiveness), and
- their growth potential in Russia and at a global level (through exports and outward FDI).

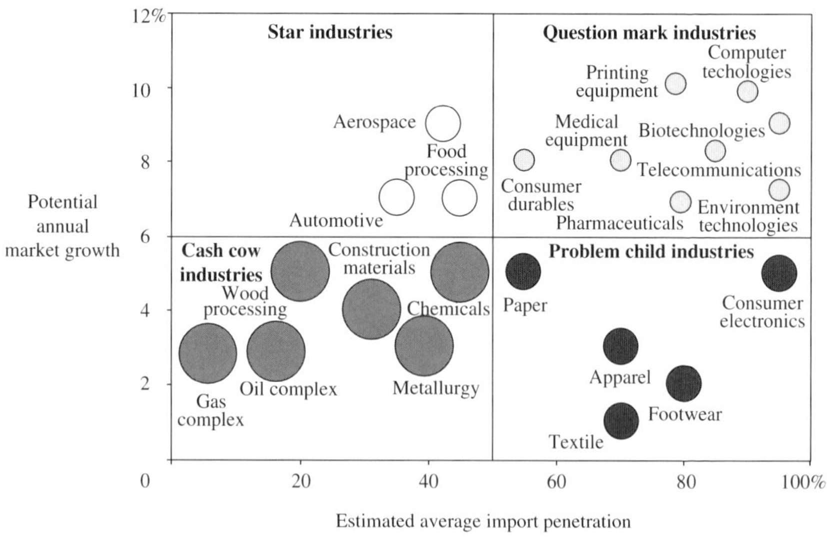

Figure 12.2 Russia's industry portfolio, 2000–05

Selected industries are represented by circles and positioned in one of the quadrants of the market growth/relative market share (in relation to imports) matrix. The importance of each industry is reflected by the size of the circle. The position of each industry in the matrix is based on estimates of future growth and import penetration.[18]

Industry portfolios can assist Russia's FDI specialists in evaluating industrial developments, deriving strategies and allocating resources for implementing policies. The exercise will require fine-tuning at subsectoral level as the FDI enhancement process continues, and priorities will be re-adjusted well into the first decade of the twenty-first century (Figure 12.3).

To gain time and increase economic impact, FDI instruments should initially be directed at 'star' and 'question mark' industries, which could

Long–term attractiveness / Relative competitive advantage	High	Medium to low
High	**Star industries** Promising industries in terms of growth and profits; they therefore warrant high FDI focus to upgrade domestic manufacturing capabilities *Examples*: Automotive industry, aerospace, processed food *FDI strategy*: To achieve LEM leadership, to adopt a focused FDI approach for all relevant industries, to allocate resources	**Question mark industries** Industries facing competition from other LEMs and advanced economies; they require high investments to become competitive and therefore involve certain risks. FDI is important if they can be developed into stars, otherwise it should be combined with a targeted import strategy to cover domestic needs. Efforts should focus on selected potential star sectors to raise impact; risks should be evaluated carefully *Examples*: All consumer goods, light industries, microelectronics, medical devices, environment technologies pharmaceuticals *FDI strategy*: To reduce import dependence; to adopt a targeted FDI approach for selected sectors
Low to medium	**Cash cow industries** Industries that have reached a high degree of maturity, but generate significant resources for economic development and domestic investment (mainly through exports) *Examples*: All raw materials industries including petroleum, natural gas and derivatives (bulk chemicals and plastics), metals and minerals *FDI strategy*: To modernize profitable sectors to achieve highest possible cash flow over the longest possible period. Sufficient cash generation does not warrant FDI in these industries and downstream sectors	**Problem child industries** Industries with low comparative advantage on a global scale; they represent mature businesses that need to be subsidized to generate profits *Examples*: Textiles, apparel, footwear, consumer electronics, paper *FDI strategy*: To divest and reduce subsidies; to allow market forces to 'cleanse' portfolios; to adopt a targeted FDI approach for selected sectors

Figure 12.3 Attractiveness and competitive advantage, selected Russian industries

generate high earnings and employment through FDI. 'Cash cow' sectors such as natural gas, fuel and their derivatives are also important revenue generators, but they are fairly self-sufficient and less dependent on FDI. However, an industry that is in the 'cash cow' quadrant may still need FDI for its upstream or downstream branches, which may represent 'star' or 'question mark' industries within the subsector portfolio (e.g. plastics processing within the petrochemicals sector). Industry portfolios should therefore be produced for the lowest possible sectoral level and look at entire clusters of industries.

Advanced economies are characterized by mixed industry portfolios implying that a number of lead sectors are located in the upper-left part of the matrix (star sectors). Long-term competitiveness of these countries is determined by market leadership in established industries that enable the economy to generate the cash flow (through domestic sales and exports) required for investments in new technology areas in the 'embryonic phase'.[19] To compete with these economies, Russia's industrial development must follow the path from 'question marks' to 'star' and 'cash cow' sectors. About 70–80 per cent of all existing factories will need to belong to such sectors leaving a maximum of 30 per cent for the 'problem child' industries. FDI can initially be a strong motor of innovation and introduction of new technologies so that 'problem children' are gradually converted into 'stars' and 'cash cows'. Integrating the life-cycle of each essential industry extends the portfolio analysis (Figure 12.4). The life-cycle approach is useful for classifying industries according to their stage of maturity and competitive position at three levels: domestic market, LEM or – more difficult to achieve – global level. Industries can thus be grouped according to five stages of development: introduction, growth, maturity, saturation and decline.

Applied to key industries, the method shows that Russia is far from balanced in its industrial development. It includes practically no important sectors with global or LEM leadership at the initial phases of a life-cycle (introduction or growth). Most operational industries are domestically oriented and located between maturity and decline (C, D, E and F sectors in Figure 12.4). This situation is rather precarious and endangers Russia's future role as an equal negotiator among industrialized countries.

Several useful strategy elements can be deduced for Russian industry from a life-cycle scheme highlighting the country's competitive position relative to other world regions:[20]

- **A** industries such as defence-oriented avionics, shipbuilding and telecommunication are absolute star sectors. They enjoy a relatively high market share and low import penetration. Russia disposes of a strong scientific base and holds a strong competitive position in these sectors, even at a global level. The knowledge and skills accumulated in these industries form a solid base for systematic development of new products and related technologies especially for civilian purposes (e.g. electronics, satellite-

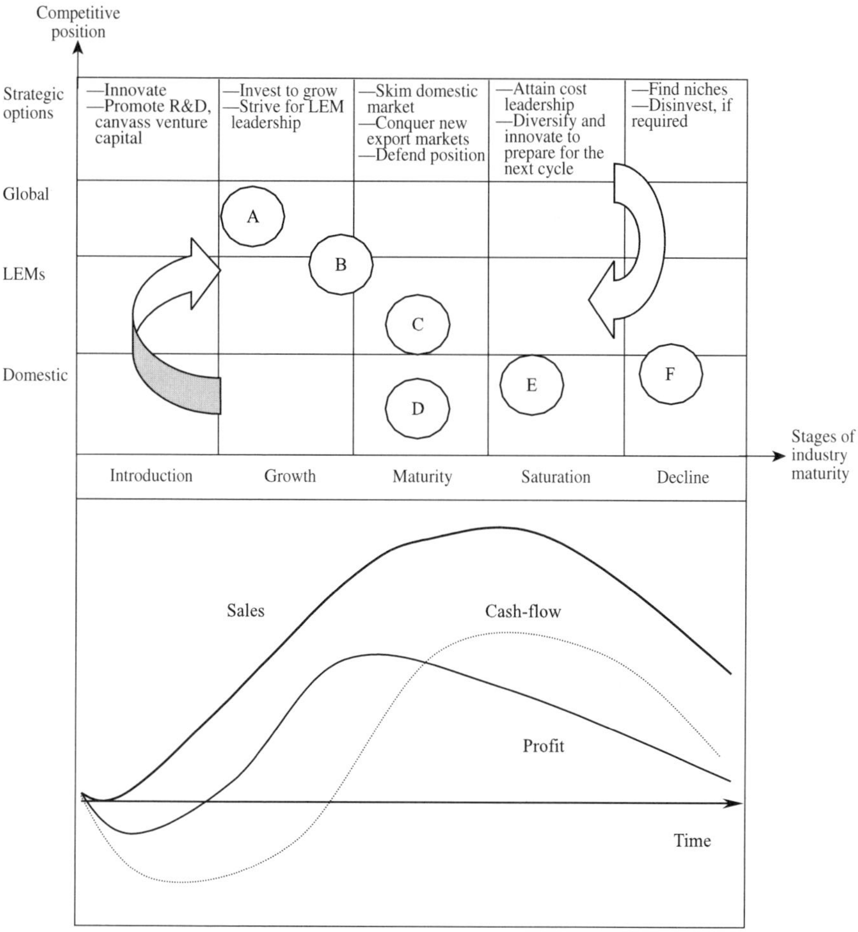

Figure 12.4 Russia's industry life-cycle

based and earth-to-earth telecommunication) and for maintaining high national competitiveness. Star sectors and related industries in their introduction and growth stages should therefore be given top priority for resource allocation to enhance FDI. Western technologies with or without TNC partners would contribute to the modernization of these industries. This becomes a prerequisite against the background of rising international competition even from LEMs (e.g. China's efforts to extend its own space programme, Brazil for short-haul aircraft).

- **B** industries (e.g. oil and gas, petrochemicals) have a relatively large share of the domestic market and high export potential due to a relatively strong competitive position. They are well-positioned on the life-cycle matrix, but focused investments are needed to modernize the sector and maintain a high degree of international competitiveness. They need support for infrastructure development (e.g. international gas pipelines). Although these industries are not top priority for FDI resource allocation, they warrant special attention for the development of downstream activities (e.g. specialty chemicals, plastics).

- **C** industries (e.g. ferrous and nonferrous minerals, new materials-based alloys) are already good foreign exchange generators. FDI enhancement measures will need to be designed for modernizing equipment (e.g. conveyor and transport systems, extraction technologies). **B** and **C** industries are extremely vulnerable as they depend on the availability of natural resources.
- **D** industries such as automobiles, trucks, buses, railway technologies and selected chemicals have reached their maturity stage, but need to be reactivated through 'attached' technologies that improve the final product. National demand is fairly high, but other LEMs (e.g. China for automobiles and shipbuilding, India and Mexico for light and heavy vehicles, India and Indonesia for motorcycles) also master the required technologies and dispose of fairly transparent market information owing to mostly oligopolist industry structures at global level.[21] In these sectors, imports into Russia have risen dramatically since 1991, making it difficult for Russian companies to expand their domestic and global market share. A targeted FDI strategy would raise international competitiveness as new products using modern manufacturing techniques can be introduced (e.g. electric cars for city traffic, minivans, all-purpose jeeps).
- **E** industries include domestically produced machine tools, selected food products, pharmaceuticals and most consumer durables (refrigerators, TVs, videorecorders); they have a very small domestic market share and suffer from a weak competitive position. Subsidies may not be the appropriate answer, whereas FDI incentive mechanisms would attract the required investments to stretch the maturity phase of these industries (e.g. modern packaging technologies for foods and beverages) and to establish modern plants in Russia.
- **F** industries (e.g. textiles, apparel, footwear and toys) have entered the phase of decline. International competition is intense, especially from products manufactured in other LEMs like China and India, but also in other low labour-cost markets in ASEAN (particularly since the devaluation of the Southeast Asian currencies following the crisis), Turkey and Middle East economies. State subsidies and efforts to enhance FDI could help reactivate certain subsectors within selected industries (e.g. hosiery, sports shoes). In the medium and long term, however, part of the workforce will need to be redeployed to other more promising industries.

Strategic options – resource allocations, disinvestment, diversification, cost cutting and 'skimming' – for industrial upgrading can be deduced directly from the four quadrants of the industry portfolio and life-cycle curve. On the whole, Russia should aim at a balanced mix between traditional and high-tech sectors. The importance of traditional, labour-intensive industries such as apparel, sports goods, household appliances, glassware and ceramics should not be underestimated considering that labour costs are still much lower in Russia than in western economies. With upgraded technology, these industries could even compete with low-cost products from economically less-advanced countries.

FDI should be channelled into high potential sectors, where Russian enterprises possess the preconditions required for global comparative advantage, but cannot exploit available resources effectively to generate value-added products demanded by the domestic and international markets. Initially, the focus should be placed on pillar industries that can create cascade effects on the rest of the economy. Many of these crucial industries had either been neglected in the past or have lost their technological and market edge in the process of economic transformation. They include sectors such as innovative chemicals and pharmaceuticals, new materials, industrial and transport equipment, telecommunications, shipbuilding, food processing and construction equipment and materials. High-tech sectors to be developed relate to environment, information and health-related technologies.[22]

For an accurate analysis and strategy formulation, the Russian statistical office, Goskomstat, as well as the customs authority and sectoral associations will need to provide policy-makers regularly with comprehensive industrial and foreign trade statistics at subsectoral (e.g. dairy), branch (e.g. yoghurt) and regional levels.

12.3 Clustering of interdependent industries

In advanced economies, interdependent upstream and downstream industries constitute fairly homogeneous clusters where enterprises work together to optimize different production stages in vertical value chains: raw materials and component suppliers, end-product manufacturers, dealer and service networks. Within clusters, strong enterprises may seek to increase efficiency levels through vertical integration strategies by acquiring majority stakes. Vertical macrosector links also exist between industry, agriculture and services, which are mutually supportive in a smoothly functioning economy. Cluster analysis introduces a vertical approach to industrial monitoring and supplements the results of portfolio analysis, which determines the competitiveness and FDI requirements of industries belonging to the same or related sectors of activity (horizontal approach).

Cluster analysis suggests that individual industries should not be viewed as separate entities for strategic FDI enhancement, but should be developed systematically by exploring synergies between vertically interrelated sectors. A large and diversified country like Russia can, for example, more easily attain a competitive position in the automotive sector if it manages to upgrade the main upstream sectors supplying high-performance steel, mechanical and composite parts, engines, gear boxes, pistons, spark plugs, tyres, rubber seals and electrical components. Modern forms of distribution and car dealership will automatically emerge to satisfy higher demand levels. The development of the core industry can thus have a cascade effect on upstream and downstream industries or services belonging to the cluster.

A country cannot be competitive in all spheres of activity at the same time. In all advanced economies, international competitiveness originally developed around specific clusters. Sweden's competitiveness in pulp and paper, for example, extends to timber-handling and paper processing equipment, conveyor systems and certain downstream wood-based industries (e.g. matches), while Denmark developed specific industrial technologies for the agribusiness and food industries (Table 12.3). Similarly, German carmakers and capital goods industries benefit from the existence of highly competitive components suppliers. In Italy, special clusters have formed in industrial districts specialized in metal working–cutlery, fashion–design, leather–shoes or wood processing–furniture value chains.[23]

Clustering can be observed in all economies. Larger nations normally have a larger number of key industries than smaller countries. However, economic success is not always a function of quantity, but of cluster quality, which can be determined and shaped by appropriate investment policies by the government, preferably at the beginning of a sustainable process of economic growth. Successful smaller economies such as Sweden, the Netherlands or Canada prove how essential it is for a government to nurture knowledge-intensive clusters with a strong international position such as transport equipment, machinery, advanced information technologies, biotechnologies and value-added services.

Leading OECD economies furnish innumerable examples that highlight the sociopolitical and economic importance of cluster building. Once key industrial clusters started forming in economies like Germany (chemicals, mechanical engineering, automotive) and France (food processing, cosmetics) in the 1950s and 1960s, entire groups of industries became mutually supporting within the cluster to create a multiplier effect in terms of employment and technology transfer across the economy. US know-how in consumer durables and nondurables contributed to US leadership in agricultural processes, packaging and mechanization (upstream sectors) as well

Table 12.3 Industrial clusters in selected advanced economies

Country	Key industries	Upstream (input) sectors	Downstream (output) sectors
Denmark	Food processing (dairy, meat, beer)	Yeast, enzymes, refrigeration equipment	Modern distribution systems
	Biotechnology, pharmachemical complex	Chemical components, medical equipment, instrumentation	Pharmaceuticals, vitamins
	Furniture	Wood processing	Designer furniture, chairs, cupboards
Sweden	Pulp and paper	Wood processing equipment, pulp-making and paper-drying machinery, sulphur boilers, chemicals used in pulp making	Office supplies, specialty paper
	Metallurgy	Mining equipment	Metal working
Italy	Fashion	Textiles, yarn, dyes	Designer clothes
	Food processing	Agricultural produce, food packaging machinery	Baby food
	Furnishings, furniture	Wood processing	Office and kitchen furniture
Germany	Transport equipment	Metal working, steel, automotive components, tyres, metal-steel alloys	Cars, buses, locomotives and railway cars, ships
	Chemicals	Chemical polymers	Bulk and specialty molecules, for agriculture, healthcare, new materials
	Printing	Pulp and paper industry, printing machines	Advertising
	Electrical equipment	Electrical components	Consumer electronics, electrical appliances
USA	Information technology	Semiconductors, complex logic chips	Computer hardware, telecommunications equipment
Japan	Consumer electronics	Memory chips, integrated circuits, semiconductors	Notebook computers, facsimile machines, television sets, calculators, audio-video equipment
	Transport equipment	Electrical, electronic, and mechanical components	Sports cars and limousines, minivans, motor cycles

as advertising and financial engineering (downstream sectors). Japanese strength in consumer electronics led to the successful development of memory chips and integrated circuits, whereas US firms are global leaders in complex logic chips used in computers, telecommunications equipment and defence electronics.[24]

Experience shows that any highly competitive pillar industry helps to create strong supplier and client industries in a mutually reinforcing process. Small and medium-sized enterprises form satellites around larger groups and supply their global markets. Diversification efforts of key players can also lead to the establishment of new industries that use technology and know-how transferred from the parent company. But the new trend, even for larger companies worldwide, is to focus on core competences and farm out production of intermediary products or essential services. This is why cluster building is recognized as having a significant impact on small business development. The strong international position of a world-class buyer industry at home not only benefits suppliers domestically, but also motivates them to move to other markets where the buyer has operations. German and Japanese automotive components suppliers, for example, have followed national carmakers by setting up factories in emerging and advanced markets and have thus been able to maintain their world leadership position.

The success of clusters often depends on the organization and interrelation of firms belonging to the cluster. In Japan and South Korea, for example, large groups (*keiretsu*) have shareholding links with important supplier and client firms, as well as banks and trading companies. Companies within the cluster thus represent guaranteed markets for each other enabling them to optimize the value chain, to exchange information, and finally to become world leaders in their line of business. Long-term stability is achieved through vertical trade associations, which encompass groups of related sectors and their supplier industries, but also through coordinating efforts by government ministries (e.g. MITI in Japan). In Italy, Germany and Switzerland, many companies are linked together by family or quasi-family ties facilitating continuous interchange and product improvements. Geographic proximity can also help foster informal ties. Overseas Chinese firms operate in a similar way for spreading their business networks across Asia–Pacific Rim countries including the United States, Canada and selected Latin American countries.

As the competitiveness of an advanced nation is linked to strong intersectoral links, Russia must also strive to systematically develop integrated clusters around key industries. Clusters should also include services (modern distribution and banking systems) as they bring products and technologies closer to the end-users. Food and consumer goods manufacturers depend on supermarkets, hypermarkets and megastores for sales outlets. In advanced economies, the entire value chain functions at high-quality level: raw materials processing, production of strategic components (semimanufactures) and specialized machines; manufacturing of end products; modern distribution systems supplying end-users and consumers. Economic efficiency requires that essential upstream industries are located within acceptable geographic distance from core industries for just-in-time deliveries.[25]

In Russia, over 70 years of planned economy have disrupted the practice of efficient clustering, which was more common at the beginning of this century when the country was in the midst of the industrial revolution. Smaller clusters had formed under communism around monopoly suppliers, but on the whole industrial diversity was hampered by 'monoculture' practices. The introduction of free markets in the early 1990s has led to cross-shareholdings and the emergence of strong financial–industrial groups (FIGs), without, however, contributing substantially to diversified industrial structures. A few clusters around key industries such as the chemical, oil and gas, automotive, metallurgy, machine building and shipbuilding industries have begun to function, but critical equipment, parts and components still have to be purchased through foreign suppliers. The country's leading chemical and mechanical engineering plants, for example, were established close to important users, mainly in the Central and Urals economic areas. Conversely, wood cutting and processing (pulp and paper production) was concentrated in the Northwestern, North and Far East economic areas.[26] But these structures are very fragile and can hardly be compared to real clusters consisting of a dynamic network of many highly competitive supplier and client companies.

It will take Russia many more years to create internationally competitive client and supplier industries in key areas like electronics, telecommunications, automobiles and chemicals. It is a real challenge as the earlier economic system was based on only output targets that did not take quality requirements into account and on state control of means of production, which led to the formation of industrial oligopolies. But the process of establishing dynamic industrial clusters could be accelerated through targeted domestic and foreign investment. Russia's favourable raw materials supply base would enable it to ensure bottom-up integration in a number of crucial areas such as machinery, chemicals, transport equipment, and paper and printing.

When grouping or clustering industries, all vertical (supplier, buyer) and horizontal (common customers, technology and distribution channels) links must be taken into consideration including those with foreign countries. In the first phase, know-how and technologies needed for the different manufacturing stages will need to be acquired from other advanced economies depending on their traditional global strengths built over the years. Gradually, competitive supplier industries should be developed in Russia around pillar sectors (e.g. agroindustrial complex, automotive sector, shipbuilding, heavy-duty machinery for mining and raw material extraction) or cross-cutting activities (e.g. health, home, communication, leisure, education). If the issue is addressed early enough, Russia could gradually rebuild the main industrial clusters by 2015–20.

Clusters can be formed systematically in regions where there is already a high geographic concentration of interdependent industries (e.g. machinery and equipment in Moscow and St Petersburg; automotive sector around Togliatti; chemicals in Moscow *oblast*, Nizhny Novgorod and Tula). Additional capital and technology for such clusters can be acquired through FDI. One option could consist in declaring major economic regions, cities or agglomerations special development zones, where foreign investors can benefit from special incentives if they contribute to developing specific industrial clusters. Competition between local and foreign companies will stimulate ideas, skills, diversification and R&D development. Strong industrial clusters developed against the background of global competition can become significant vehicles for overcoming information deficit and management shortcomings marked by an inward focus, inflexibility and lack of innovation.

When building clusters, authorities and businessmen need to take into consideration a series of sociocultural elements that determine goal congruence and compatibility among cluster members (Table 12.4). State and local governments can guide these elements and thus play a prominent role in developing competitive industries.[27] Falling communication and transportation costs and the lowering of barriers to trade and international

Table 12.4 Factors contributing to industrial cluster building

Factor	Situation
Family or quasi-family ties	+
Personal relationships developed at school, military service	0
Common ownership within an industrial or financial group	–
Cross-shareholdings and interlocking management	–
Community ties due to geographic proximity*	–
Trade associations encompassing clusters	–
Ties through the scientific community and professional associations**	+
Common values such as belief in continuity and long-term relationships	0
Strong national identity	+

Situation in Russia: strong +, medium 0, weak –
* either traditionally or through the establishment of technology parks or industrial zones.
** e.g. chambers of commerce in Germany.

competition make efforts to systematically build locational and competitive advantages through industrial clusters even more indispensable. These advantages are increasingly determined by differential knowledge, skills and rates of innovation, well-trained specialists and organizational routines.[28] Capacity building should be undertaken at regional and even local levels. It is at *oblast* level that Russian firms must be systematically encouraged to cooperate within clusters and thus generate true competitive advantages to penetrate international markets.

Russia has a real chance to build competitive clusters with the help of FDI. International changes in competitive patterns are raising factor costs in key sectors of the leading economies, where opportunities in more productive activities can lead to the disappearance of entire clusters (e.g. consumer electronics in Austria and Germany). Inter-country competition makes industries where technology is the least sophisticated or products are the least differentiated gradually lose their competitive advantage in certain economies. Activities in the value chain that are least productive are then relocated to countries with lower factor costs (e.g. production of sports shoes in China, leather goods in India or textiles in Brazil). With rising industry maturity, national firms are compelled to relocate standard technologies abroad and to innovate and upgrade their production processes to stay competitive at home.

All key industries, however, need to generate the ability to create knowledge and adopt advanced technologies. Even in traditional or seemingly simple technologies, 'mature' businesses can be converted into growth areas as the Japanese (e.g. development from walkman to walk-CD) or Italian (e.g. leather shoes, apparel) TNCs have demonstrated repeatedly. The same is true with sectors close to raw materials extraction. They can be upgraded by adding value in terms of know-how, technologies and skills. Authorities in some of the oil producing regions of the Russian Federation have already understood this; they have been diversifying downstream towards industrial exploitation of natural resources. The semi-autonomous republic of Tatarstan, for example, is building a modern oil processing plant which will produce 1.2 million t of diesel and 670 000 t of high-quality gasoline for cars, 315 000 t of special kerosene for aircraft and a series of other value-added items including specialty motor oils.[29]

Competitive advantage emerges from pressure, challenge and adversity.[30] As international competition intensifies, Russian enterprises should form the required clusters in close collaboration with selected foreign partners and on the basis of selected imported technologies. More efficient clusters in Russia will enable domestic enterprises to link up to globally integrated value chains.[31] Targeted FDI could act as a valuable vehicle for faster cluster building in Russia. The national FDI policy must therefore be conceived in close cooperation with regional authorities who should be involved from the start in analyzing existing capacities in terms of factories and projects to be developed jointly.

12.4 The regional dimension of Russia's industry

Any FDI strategy would be incomplete without taking into account the regional dimension of existing and potential industrial patterns and the general economic factor conditions and assets in the regional markets.[32] In a large country like Russia, industrial patterns can differ significantly from one region to another. Natural resources including climatic and soil conditions determine factor availability and are reflected in historical and current industrial priorities of regional administrations.[33]

Investing in manufacturing operations in a regionally diverse economy such as Russia requires careful location analysis and a long-term strategy for any foreign company. It needs careful consideration of not only the current situation (economic, social, regulatory) but also the future potential (new regional markets). Should the plant be located near Moscow because of the large sales potential and existing trading and client relations? Or would it be more convenient to choose other sites at an acceptable distance from the main Greater Moscow market, but close to the raw material base and possibly other important agglomerations which will develop in future years?[34] Is the manufacturing project meant exclusively for sales in Russia or also as an export platform to neighbouring CIS economies? What possibilities exist to obtain energy and water, to recruit and support qualified management and staff, and would there be any important research facilities in the environs?

As payback periods can be rather long for manufacturing projects, the future sales potential must be assessed carefully and all possible risk factors taken into account.[35] Corporate executives normally undertake a detailed and comprehensive analysis of the external and internal environment of the investment project. In complex markets like Russia, a project team of various experts would need to study the feasibility of the FDI project in two or three alternative locations, by evaluating each on the basis of prevailing market and factor conditions as well as incentives offered by regional authorities.

The most important factor conditions to be assessed in the regional markets are:

- water supply and discharge (chemical, textile and paper plants);
- energy availability (steel and aluminium plants, paper mills);
- raw materials supply base (machinery and equipment, chemicals, forest products, food processing);
- logistics, transport and communications (wood processing, furniture, heavy engineering, all high-tech sectors);

- qualified workers and engineers, information, labor relations and laws (all sectors, especially knowledge-intensive and high-tech industries);
- distribution systems, proximity to markets (perishable items, fast-moving consumer goods).

When formulating a national strategy, statistical data should be supplemented with qualitative information (based on interviews) on industrial assets and deficiencies in the greater economic areas (GEAs).[36] A regionally focused study on industrial strengths and weaknesses serves as a useful supplement to a national portfolio and cluster analysis. As industrial modernization and diversification progresses, the study should be refined and extended to describe the situation more precisely at subregional (*oblast, rayon*) level.

Regional and local authorities can contribute to the establishment of portfolios for industrial subsectors (groups) and segments (classes) at subregional level as specific sectors may be located and expanded in some regions but not in others. For example, the Central or Ural GEAs are home to clusters of downstream and upstream industries (e.g. automobiles, chemicals) covering the complete value chain between suppliers and clients. In such cases, the weak links should be identified and then systematically strengthened through FDI. The regional approach is particularly useful for attracting foreign companies into the European part of the Russian Federation, which accounts for about 80 per cent of the country's population (117 million, out of a total population of 148 million) and industrial potential. To canvass potential investors, especially from nearby western and Central Europe, concrete information should be disseminated and advice provided on sector structures, enterprises, possible partnerships and other strategic options (e.g. new plants) in the different *oblast* markets.[37]

To channel FDI to the eastern part of the country (West and East Siberian GEA, Far Eastern GEA), its abundant natural resources should be highlighted to foreign investors from Asia, Europe and North America. In this way, mining and raw materials extraction and processing industries could be upgraded in these regions, which could become important suppliers of essential inputs to key industrial users within and outside Russia. Increased FDI will raise raw material demand within Russia; at present, most raw materials are exported because of low output of other domestic industries.

To illustrate this approach, a preliminary overview has been prepared of industrial strengths and weaknesses and possible measures for improvement at GEA level (Table 12.5). This exercise constitutes only the first step in a long-term process of analysis, monitoring and cooperation at regional level,[38] but could serve as a model for more detailed regional portfolios at *oblast* level.

Table 12.5 Industrial strengths and weaknesses of Russia's greater economic areas[39]

Greater economic areas (GEA)	Major agglomerations (mn inhabitants)	Main industries	Assets	Drawbacks	Policy aims through increased FDI
Northern GEA Area: 1466 000 km² Population: 6 mn	Archangelsk (1.7) Vologda (1.4) Murmansk (1.2)	Metallurgy, forestry products, wood processing, furniture, fisheries, chemicals	• Abundant natural resources • Clean environment • Proximity to developed Scandinavian markets	• Lack of human resources • Poor physical and technological infrastructure	• Management training • Infrastructure development • Industrial zone development
Northwestern GEA Area: 197 000 km² Population: 8 mn	St Petersburg (6.0) Pskov (1.0)	Forestry products including paper, printing; iron and steel, aluminium; ship building, farm machinery, capital goods; fertilizers and bulk chemicals; pharmaceuticals; consumer goods, light industries, food processing	• Highly qualified human resources • Leadership in paper industry (50% of national newsprint production) • Abundant raw materials (gas, oil, iron ore, minerals) and electric energy • Crossroads between Scandinavia and Russia • Access to sea ports and river system • St Petersburg as industrial, commercial and research centre	• Lack of technicians and engineers • Unequal distribution of population • Pollution and environmental problems	• Industrial conversion • Management training • Improvement of social services (hospitals, schools) • Environmental protection
Central GEA Area: 483 000 km² Population: 30 mn	Moscow (9.2) Tver (1.7) Yaroslavl (1.6) Ryasan (1.4) Smolensk (1.3)	Very diversified industrial base, leading region in aircraft, car and truck manufacturing; chemicals; food processing	• Presence of practically all essential industries and services • Major scientific and research base • Long industrial tradition • Qualified technical staff • Modern infrastructure • Central geographic location in European Russia • Moscow as administrative, political, financial and services capital	• Poor in natural resources and energy • Landlocked region without proper access to sea ports	• Reorganization of industrial sector • Enterprise conversion in the military–industrial complex • Strengthening of research base • Development of know-how intensive sectors (information and biotechnologies)

Table 12.5 (*continued*)

Greater economic areas (GEA)	Major agglomerations (mn inhabitants)	Main industries	Assets	Drawbacks	Policy aims through increased FDI
Volgo-Viatsky GEA Area: 265 000 km^2 Population: 9 mn	Nizhny Novgorod (3.9) Kirov (1.8)	Machinery, transport and construction equipment; electrical devices and instruments; petrochemicals, rubber, tyres, fertilizers; wood processing, paper; building materials; food processing	• Large raw materials base for construction • Educated workforce and broad engineering base	• Limited water resources • Soil erosion owing to intensive agriculture • Environmental pollution	• Human resources development • Development of high-tech industries
Central Black Earth GEA Area: 168 000 km^2 Population: 8 mn	Voronezh (2.5) Belgorod (1.5) Kursk (1.4) Tambov (1.3)	Food processing, agricultural equipment; petrochemicals, synthetic fibres and rubber, resins, tyres, detergents; cement; textiles and apparel	• Fertile soils • Mineral resources • Qualified manpower especially for food processing • Favourable geographic location for access to the major consumer markets (Greater Moscow, Rostov, Volgograd, Samara)	• Critical demographic situation (aging population, migration to Moscow and St Petersburg) • Energy deficit	• Human resources development • Improvement of research facilities • Canvassing of sophisticated food processing industries • Industrial zone development

continued...

Table 12.5 (continued)

Greater economic areas (GEA)	Major agglomerations (mn inhabitants)	Main industries	Assets	Drawbacks	Policy aims through increased FDI
Povolsky GEA Area: 537 000 km^2 Population: 17 mn	Kazan (3.9) Samara (3.5) Saratov (2.9) Volgograd (2.7) Penza (1.6) Ulyanowsk (1.5)	Food processing; petrochemicals, fertilizers, plastics; automobiles and trucks; light and heavy industry, agricultural machinery; building materials	• Qualified human resources • Network of research institutions • Proximity to the Urals GEA for raw materials and energy • Fertile soils • Access to the Caspian and Black seas via the Volga river and a network of canals and waterways	• Dependence on energy and raw materials from other regions (especially coal, chemicals, minerals)	• Development of chemical and high-tech industries • Improvement of the agroindustrial sector • Upgrading of research facilities
North Caucasus GEA Area: 355 000 km^2 Population: 18 mn	Krasnodar (5.0) Rostov (4.5) Stavropol (2.6)	Livestock production, food processing; agricultural machinery; metallurgy; chemicals	• Abundant energy (coal, oil, gas) • Natural resources • Diversified agroindustry • Access to Mediterranean sea through Black sea • High tourism potential	• Proximity to regions with ethnic tensions • Soil erosion • Water shortages • River and sea pollution • Low degree of industrial diversification	• Human resources development • Improvement of research facilities • Canvassing of sophisticated food processing industries • Industrial zone development
Urals GEA Area: 824 000 km^2 Population: 21 mn	Sverdlovsk (4.8) Yekaterinburg (3.7) Ufa (2.5) Perm (3.1) Orenburg (2.3)	Metallurgy; capital equipment (particularly for chemical industry), automotive components, construction equipment	• Second most important industrial region after Central GEA • Diversified industry • Abundant raw materials (iron ore, wood) • Abundant energy resources (coal, gas, oil) • Qualified labour force	• Gradual raw materials depletion • Industrial deterioration • Poor transport infrastructure	• Improvement of warehousing and transport • Canvassing of environmentally-clean industries

Table 12.5 (*continued*)

Greater economic areas (GEA)	Major agglomerations (mn inhabitants)	Main industries	Assets	Drawbacks	Policy aims through increased FDI
West-Siberian GEA Area: 2 427 000 km^2 Population: 15 mn	Novosibirsk (2.5) Omsk (2.2) Tomsk (1.2)	Industries and technologies for oil and gas extraction, metallurgy, wood processing, machinery, agroindustry	• Vast reserves of oil and gas (largest export base from Russia) • Abundance of iron ore and other minerals and metals • Water resources • Wood resources (12% of Russia's forests)	• Low population density (6.2 inhabitants/km^2) • Shortage of scientists and engineers compared with the economic potential • Very low FDI inflows • Severe soil pollution environmental problems	• Human resources development • Improvement of infrastructure (roads, rail links, airports)
East Siberian GEA Area: 4 123 000 km^2 Population: 9 mn	Krasnoyarsk (2.5) Irkutsk (2.4)	Coal and mineral mining; aluminium; electrical engineering; wood processing, paper; machinery; chemicals (caustic soda, synthetic fibres and rubber, resins, tyres, fertilizers, plastics, paints), cement, glass and other building materials; agroindustry (canned products, flour, bakery products)	• Abundant hydroenergy resources for electricity generation • Abundance of coal • Metal resources (cobalt, nickel, tin)	• Nationality factor: people of diverse ethnic origin living under extreme climatic and difficult social conditions • Low overall density of population (2.2 people/km^2) • Shortage of scientists and engineers compared with economic potential • Very low FDI inflows • Soil pollution and environmental problems	• Human resources development • Improvement of infrastructure (roads, rail links, airports) • Modernization of extraction industries

Table 12.5 (*continued*)

Greater economic areas (GEA)	Major agglomerations (mn inhabitants)	Main industries	Assets	Drawbacks	Policy aims through increased FDI
Far Eastern GEA Area: 6 216 000 km^2 Population: 8 mn	Vladivostok (2.0) Khabarovsk (1.7)	Mineral resources, diamonds; wood processing, paper; shipbuilding; furs, fisheries (largest in Russia); steel, capital equipment; meat processing	• Gateway to Asia and North America • Abundance in fish and marine resources • Vast mineral reserves (diamonds, gold, precious metals) • Energy reserves (coal, oil and gas) • Forestry resources	• Extremely harsh climatic conditions • Very small population for exploiting natural potential • Environmental problems	• Human resources development • Improvement of infrastructure (roads, rail links, airports) • Development of food processing industries

Notes

1. Chapter 8.3.
2. After 3 years of stability, the rouble started losing ground *vis-à-vis* major world currencies as a result of the August 1998 financial crisis.
3. For the situation of major branches of Russian industry, see Chapter 8.2.
4. A few hundred companies are already listed on the Moscow or St Petersburg stock exchange. Enterprises like Lukoil and Gasprom finance a large part of their operations by issuing securities, which are also traded on the world's leading stock exchanges.
5. E.g. Uralmash in Yekaterinburg, which has a 60–65 per cent share of the Russian market for metallurgical and drilling equipment and quarry excavators (*The Economist*, 14 May 1997).
6. Financial–industrial groups (FIGs).
7. Russia disposes of specialized research institutes with world class scientists and experts in practically all important sectors. These are currently undersupplied with public funding and orders from the private sector.
8. Chapter 12.3.
9. The situation is most dramatic in the agroindustrial complex, where many factories run at 25 per cent capacity and have resorted to barter trade and other activities not related to their core competence. For example, a dairy or cheese plant may also sell mineral water, beer, vodka or offer mechanical repair services for farming equipment. See also Chapter 8.3.
10. For industry classification according to NACE Rev. 1, see Appendix: Definitions and Explanatory Notes, 4.3.
11. Examples of successful ventures in Russia are Coca-Cola, PepsiCo, Mars, Nestlé, Procter & Gamble, Unilever.
12. Chapter 15.
13. At a later stage, the competitive position can be calculated on a global scale, particularly for those industries that have attained a strong international position (e.g. aerospace, satellite communication and high-tech sectors emerging from the military–industrial complex).
14. See Ph. Kotler, *Marketing Management*, 1994, pp. 70–6.
15. In Russia, statistical services plan to replace the existing activity classification (see Appendix: Definitions and Explanatory Notes, 4.1) with the European NACE Rev. 1.
16. A slight recovery is noticeable in some of these industries as imports became more expensive following the devaluation of the rouble.
17. A similar approach could be used for upgrading essential services sectors such as banking, insurance, transport, tourism and retailing.
18. As industries develop through increased FDI, this analysis can be extended to include, in the x-axis, global market shares or comparative market shares with other LEMs (instead of market share relative to imports).
19. For further details concerning the life-cycle theory applied to business, see also Ph. Kotler, *Marketing Management,* 1994, p. 70–82.
20. The scheme can be used also to compare Russia with individual countries or any other world regions (e.g. EU, Visegrad countries of Central Europe). It can be also be extended to subsectors, if these form homogeneous groups that can be compared internationally (this will increasingly be the case as statistical definitions and collection methodologies are harmonized).

21. Only a few global players operate in these industries. They are therefore approached directly by FDI authorities in other LEMs to expand their manufacturing facilities and thus contribute to local employment.
22. Both for medical and pharmaceutical purposes.
23. See also Chapter 16.2.2.
24. See M. Porter, *The Competitive Advantage of Nations*, 1994.
25. Hence the importance of establishing special development zones in regions with sophisticated supplier–client networks (clusters). This practice is observed in China and other LEMs. See also Chapter 16.2.
26. Chapter 12.4.
27. See Chapter 15.4
28. M. Porter, *The Competitive Advantage of Nations*, 1990.
29. See 'Regions of the Russian Federation', special report, *Expert*, no. 38, 6 October 1997, p. 9.
30. M. Porter, *Competitive Advantage of Nations*, London, 1990, p. 174.
31. Each year, more companies are using the global information and communication infrastructure offered by the Internet to optimize cross-border contacts with buyers and sellers (e-commerce). See *The Economist*, 'The Net Imperative', 26 June 1999.
32. The regional dimension applies to all LEMs and is one of the most crucial factors in national policy-making.
33. Some regional leaders already make determined efforts to support large enterprises inherited from the Soviet system and to develop new, knowledge-intensive industries. In the republic of Tatarstan, the leadership strives not only to sustain industrial heavyweights such as the truck manufacturer KAMAZ, but also to look for opportunities to develop new industries (e.g. value-added products derived from the republic's large oil industry).
34. A cheese factory could, for example, be located in the Voronezh *oblast*, which is a traditional milk processing and cheese producing region; it is ecologically clean and close to the raw materials base (livestock, milk).
35. Unlike solely financial investments, speculation is more difficult in manufacturing, which requires long-term planning and careful preliminary analysis.
36. Statistics alone are not a sufficient source of information as they are produced with a certain time lag and are therefore not always adequate for decision-making for foreign investors, especially during a transition period marked by incredibly fast and dynamic economic changes.
37. Chapters 16.3 and 16.5.
38. Owing to the vastness of Russia's territory, it would be a daunting task to present a comprehensive overview of the regional development potential for each subregional (e.g. *oblast*) level in the framework of this study.
39. Summarized from several official publications and V. A. Gorbanyov, *Ekonomitscheskaya y Sozialnaya Geografiya Rossiyi y stran SNG* [Economic and social geography of Russia and CIS countries], 1996.

13
FDI Sourcing Potential in the World's Leading Economies

13.1 Focus on G7 economies

To rebuild its industries, Russia will have to increase foreign investments from the current level and it will need to source FDI from the EU, North America and the leading Asian economies.[1] A good understanding of the industry structure in these countries will enable it to identify suitable companies and to approach them systematically. Together with continuous benchmarking with the major competitor LEM economies[2] and monitoring of Russia's own industrial assets,[3] the observation of macroeconomic and industrial developments in the world's most advanced nations is essential for formulating and implementing an effective FDI strategy. Gradually, the overall technology sourcing potential will thus become more transparent enabling Russia's FDI authorities to attract appropriate players.

The leading OECD countries – G5, G7[4] and the rest – constitute the centrepiece of Russia's foreign and international economic policy. In 1995, Russia was officially invited to participate in the G7 summits of heads of state and government. At these summits, global economic and financial issues are discussed so that adequate steps can be taken for macroeconomic stabilization. These meetings are now referred to as G7 + 1 or G8 summits in recognition of Russia's participation.

Today, the Russian government coordinates policy areas concerning trade, finance, environment, defence and internal security (combat of international terrorism and drug traffic) with its G7 partners. The governments of France, Germany, Japan, the United Kingdom and the United States also provide technical assistance to Russia's fledgling market economy. They also decide on multilateral finance and debt rescheduling for Russia at international organizations such as the IMF, World Bank, WTO and OECD.[5]

Triangular summits between the heads of state and government of Russia, France and Germany started officially in 1996. Efforts at policy coordination and mutual confidence building are expected to positively influence relations of other EU countries with Russia. A political framework has thus been created for Russian authorities to tap the industrial and technological potential available in the larger EU economies (France, Germany, Italy, Spain and the United Kingdom) and the smaller ones (Austria, Belgium, Denmark, Finland, the Netherlands and Sweden). Switzerland is not part of the EU, but is closely linked to it; it has some of the most powerful TNCs.

Russia's geographic, cultural and historical links with Europe offer a favourable background for further developing trade and investment relations. EU members of the OECD account for over 50 per cent of Russia's foreign trade volume,[6] and often serve as a trading and investment bridge between North America and Eastern Europe.[7] Closer interenterprise cooperation between Europe and Russia could become a major factor for promoting European integration and the formation of a new European identity, and contribute towards a situation of well-balanced international relations on the Eurasian continent. Bilateral meetings with selected advanced countries can also be excellent fora for attracting more FDI. Important trade and investment agreements are usually signed during such gatherings; they mostly concern the large TNCs, which are well connected with the upper political echelons in their countries.[8] Large-scale, politically motivated projects are door openers for other FDI projects by smaller players.

To garner a larger share of the global FDI market, Russian FDI specialists must in fact start approaching medium-sized technology leaders who will generate the desired multiplier effect for building clusters in Russia's regions. The thousands of medium-sized players in the OECD countries represent an enormous FDI potential. What makes these companies particularly interesting is their inherent preference for joint ventures and other forms of interenterprise alliances with local counterparts, unlike the larger TNCs, which prefer greenfield investments with reduced involvement of local know-how. More accurate information will therefore need to be collected on the market standing, technological capabilities and financial strength of leading medium-sized players.

This chapter presents an overview of industrial structures and their specificity in the seven largest and most populated OECD economies: France, Germany, Italy, Japan, Spain, the United Kingdom and the United States.[9] For each country, a list of top companies will be given. As true multinationals these companies have important subsidiaries in other OECD countries. Given the vast scope of sectors and companies in the G7 countries, the leading medium-sized operators could not be researched in-depth.[10] Industrial patterns are described as closely as possible so that Russian FDI specialists can approach market leaders at a later stage.

Before presenting key indicators of industrial realities in the world's largest economies, a search methodology was elaborated that could later be extended to identify companies in the smaller OECD and other economies. An effective FDI information system allowing continuous updates and quick access to reliable company data will constitute an indispensable instrument of Russia's FDI policy.[11] LEMs like China, India and Mexico are both competitors and sources of FDI.[12] Their large-scale TNCs are already active or could be interested in investing in Russia once the country demonstrates that it is a stable investment destination; it will be important to gradually set up a monitoring system for these countries as well.[13]

13.2 Developing a sector–country methodology

Matching an appropriate country to a sector can lead to:

- the formulation of sector-specific FDI projects with the world's key players,
- a concentration of resources, and
- a better overall impact of FDI policy measures.

An FDI enhancement programme is most successful in countries where companies have sound strategic reasons to invest in Russia.[14] It is the task of FDI specialists based abroad to supply the necessary background information about key players in their region so that communication campaigns (promotion, information workshops and advisory missions) can be planned to obtain the highest possible cost–benefit impact.[15] Such information can be reliably obtained from a range of sources in the target country:[16] business databases, corporate brochures, media, political and semiofficial bodies (e.g. ministries, chambers of commerce, trade associations, training establishments). Information must be collected systematically at each level: country, industry, company, opinion leaders (Table 13.1). Desk research should be supplemented by interviews and discussions with industry specialists.

Information and communication efforts should also be driven by the sectoral priorities set by the Russian authorities. If, for example, new technologies and expertise are to be attracted for modernizing the national pharmaceuticals industry, the leading targets should be top players in the G5 economies, plus Switzerland and Belgium. Information from Russian missions in other countries (Canada, Finland, the Netherlands, Sweden and Switzerland) would also reveal world leaders in those countries. An understanding of the pharmaceutical sector in each target country (structure, concentration rates, market volumes and shares, growth trends) will

Table 13.1 Cascading approach to assess the technology potential in advanced economies

Level	Parameters to be monitored	Main information sources
Country	• Economic growth • Industrial production index • Foreign trade • Outward FDI performance • Competitive advantage of major industries	• National statistics offices • International organizations • Economic press
Industry	• Structure and trends • Employment • Turnover of sector • Share in total value-added • Number of players, concentration levels • Degree of internationalization of sector	• National statistics offices • Trade associations • Chambers of commerce • Specialized press
TNCs	• Legal form • Governance, ownership structures • Products, technologies, image • Intellectual property (patents) • Number of employees • Sales turnover • International activities (exports/turnover, licensing arrangements)	• Annual reports (large TNCs) • Other company information • Special information providers • Company directories
Opinion leaders	• Trends and development of economy and sectors • Influence on corporate decisions	• Publicity materials • Announcements • Seminars

provide FDI specialists with essential facts needed to present and negotiate investment projects for Russia.

The country–sector focus serves more as a guidance for identifying potential investors, it is not a rigid rule. The authorities should be open to project proposals from nontargeted countries (e.g. China, India, South Korea, Turkey) if the opportunity arises and they offer attractive terms. In highly concentrated industries such as chemicals and transport equipment the search will need to focus on the world's top players instead of limiting the analysis to certain countries. Although Russia is large enough to accommodate several players in the same sector, the investment capacity of the target companies should also be considered. They may not all be prepared to invest, perhaps because of FDI commitments in other countries, other projects like an acquisition, or a lack of strategic interest in Russia, lack of human and financial resources in the case of medium-sized companies or an imminent takeover of the company. The list of target companies should therefore be as exhaustive as possible to cover such contingencies.

As the 'playing field' is immense in terms of regions, sectors and technologies, budgetary and time constraints have to be taken into account, especially in OECD countries. In these countries, many sectors such as food processing, furniture, office supplies or paper production are dominated by medium-sized players who adopt a cautious and conservative approach. Most often these companies prefer to export than to invest in emerging markets. Irrespective of the industry that is targeted, Russian authorities should pursue a multicountry approach. Such an approach reduces dependence on a single country and generates healthy competition among potential investors from different countries, which will give the federal and regional FDI authorities high bargaining power.

The sector–country approach can be represented as a matrix, where the sectors form the *x*-axis and countries the *y*-axis. First, target G7 or OECD countries are selected according to major sectors; then each important industry is subdivided into major subsectors (see example for the food sector in Figure 13.1). Finally, all top players are identified and listed for each subsector. As the search is refined and extended, more subsectors and companies are added. This method helps FDI specialists rapidly visualize the options for various sectors and target the top players. They can then set realistic objectives (number of companies to be contacted, FDI projects to be canvassed per quarter) and measure the results achieved. It is the priority sector for Russia that should determine the target countries and companies, and not vice versa.

Top players are prioritized according to their sector ranking and technology potential. Market leaders should be targeted first as they generally demonstrate a higher readiness to invest in a difficult market like Russia than smaller players, who prefer to operate in more familiar environments. The country– sector searches should not concentrate on only large TNCs, but also include leading medium-sized companies.[17] Such systematic searches will help the Russian authorities better understand the sectoral structure and identify top players in each of the target markets. These top players will need to be contacted individually, irrespective of their size.

For each important FDI source market, the larger groups are listed in the respective country chapter.[18] These companies attain annual sales volumes of several billion US dollars and represent large suppliers of capital, technologies and know-how at a global level. Russia's FDI authorities need to monitor the strategic intentions and financial performance (e.g. sales, earnings before tax, cash flow, export share, investment levels, labour productivity, main financial ratios) of these enterprises and propose

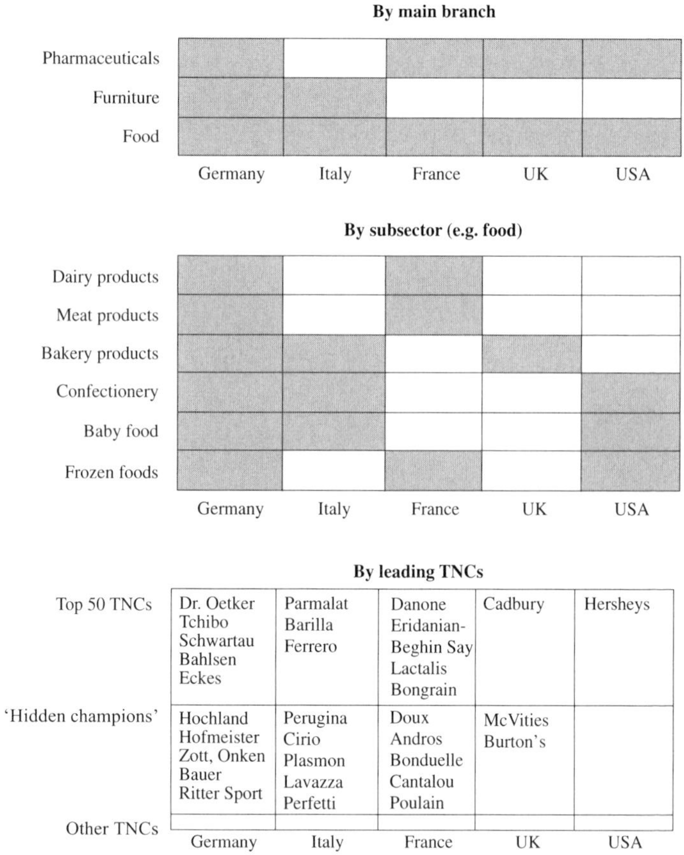

Figure 13.1 Sector–country matrix

attractive investment projects in Russia's regions. Only a small percentage of the accumulated earnings of a few selected large-scale and medium-sized players in the G7 and other OECD countries would be sufficient to trigger off a process of sustainable industrial modernization across Russia.

13.3 Monitoring economic performance of leading industrialized countries

The FDI authorities will find it difficult to identify appropriate potential investors without a proper system for monitoring macroeconomic and industry trends in the target countries. Such a system will help define the role that each country could play in restructuring Russia's industry. It should monitor important indicators such as:

- overall economic growth;
- the share of major industries in value-added and employment;
- the industrial production index of major branches;
- the performance and background information of market leaders by industrial sector – legal form, ownership, employment, turnover, export volume, etc.[19]
- export performance and trade balance by product category and by trade partner (including Russia);
- FDI outflows and balance (outflows minus inflows) by major industry; and
- FDI trends for Russia.

GDP growth rates average 1–3 per cent in most industrialized countries – much lower than in emerging markets, but their base is much higher. Ireland, the United Kingdom and the United States are, however, expected to grow faster by a few percentage points during 1998–2002.[20] Low growth in the other countries can be attributed to:

- stagnant, sometimes receding, consumer demand, mainly because of rising unemployment and high taxes, which reduce overall purchasing power;
- saturated markets marked by intense domestic and international competition;
- costly social security systems to finance an ageing population, usually at the expense of corporate players (high taxes, low incentives).

Despite and sometimes because of this difficult context, large and medium-sized companies look for new markets with greater expansion potential, such as Russia.

The annual production index is an indicator of domestic demand and export potential of leading industries. A declining index is a sign of market stagnation at home and increased competition in world markets. Governments of industrialized countries strive to reduce the impact of a slowdown on employment and corporate tax revenues. Although industrial growth has slowed down and the overall share of industry in GDP has fallen in most industrialized economies, the leading manufacturing industries have remained important employers and tax payers. Most service sectors depend on their performance. Governments are therefore interested in supporting international expansion of companies through trade and FDI, and Russia's FDI authorities should capitalize on this situation.

The competitiveness of a country's industries is reflected in the trade balance.[21] A high correlation is generally observed between a country's export performance and its companies' foreign investment capacity. Usually, industries with high export shares are a significant source of technology and industrial know-how. It is often in these sectors that important potential investors can be identified. Companies having a strong overall export sales ratio may look for greater market penetration in growing markets like Russia. Hence, the importance of closely monitoring foreign trade and FDI.

The main indicators for the top priority countries (Table 13.2) should be regularly updated and supplemented by other information related to industrial competitiveness; data collection should subsequently be extended to smaller OECD economies and major LEMs.

13.4 Industrial competitiveness of major Triad economies

Initially, FDI enhancement efforts should focus on the large Triad countries:

- the EU's big five – France, Italy, Germany, Spain and the United Kingdom;
- Japan;
- the United States.

These economies lead in terms of GDP, industrial potential, exports and annual FDI outflows. Over 80 per cent of the world's top 500 TNCs are headquartered in these countries (Figure 13.2).

The search strategy for each country should take into consideration industry strengths, institutional structures, business habits and cultures. In

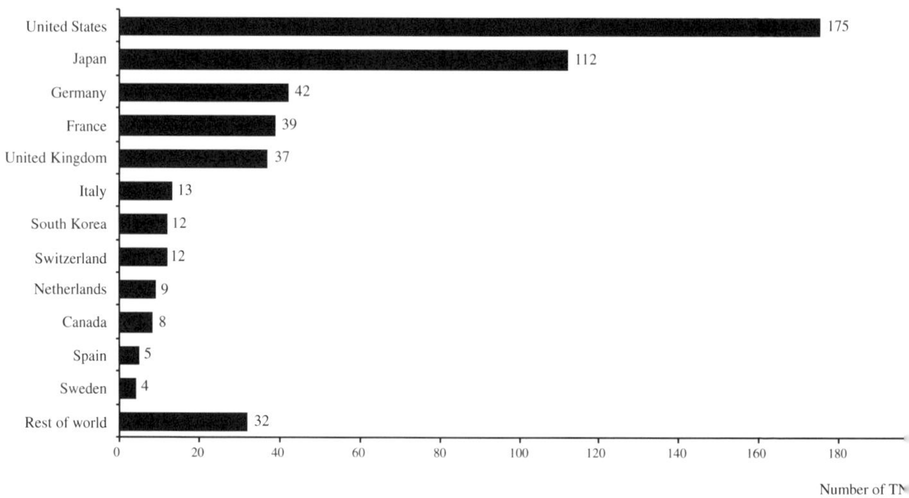

Source: *Fortune 500*, 3 August 1998.

Figure 13.2 Country representation in the top 500 TNC league, 1997

Table 13.2 Economic performance of leading OECD economies, 1998–2000

Country	GDP 1998 (US$ bn)	Per capita GDP 1998 (US$)	Annual economic growth 1999–2000* (% change)	Industrial production 1999–2000* (% change)	Exports 1998 (US$ bn)	FDI outflows 1997 (US$ bn)	Population (mn)
United States	8230	30 481	3.5–4.0	2.5–3.5	683	132.8	270
Japan	3784	31 533	1.0–1.5	0.5–1.0	457	24.1	125
Germany	2136	26 050	2.0–2.5	1.0–1.5	570	86.6	82
France	1424	24 550	1.5–2.5	1.0–1.5	369	40.6	58
United Kingdom	1357	23 807	2.5–3.5	2.0–2.5	341	114.2	57
Italy	1172	20 561	1.5–2.0	1.5–2.0	322	12.1	57
Canada	581.7	20 775	2.5–3.5	2.5–3.5	225	26.6	28
Spain	553.0	13 488	2.0–3.0	1.5–2.5	148	18.4	41
Netherlands	377.5	23 593	2.5–3.5	2.0–2.5	213	38.3	16
South Korea	297.9[a]	4 885	1.0–2.0	1.0–1.5	157	4.8	61
Switzerland	264.6	42 000	1.5–2.0	1.5–2.0	106	17.4	6
Belgium	250.5	24 300	1.5–2.0	1.5–2.0	184	23.1	10
Sweden	226.9	28 750	2.0–2.5	2.0–2.5	101	22.5	8
Austria	212.3	28 428	1.5–2.5	1.5–2.0	93	3.0	7

Sources: OECD, *Main Economic Indicators*, 1999; National statistical offices; *The Economist*; UNCTAD, *World Investment Report 1999*.

[a] Before the effect of the financial crisis, national GDP stood at US$484.6 (1996) and US$442.5 (1997).

* Estimates

most industrialized countries the economy is dominated by a few industries which also have high shares in GDP[22] (Table 13.3):

- United States: information and communication technologies, aerospace, pharmaceuticals, chemicals, food and beverages, raw materials-related sectors (mineral and oil extraction, wood and paper, etc.).
- Japan: consumer electronics, automobiles, machinery, electrical goods.
- Germany: machine tools, automobiles, electrical engineering, chemicals, plastics, food and beverages.
- France: cosmetics and personal care, food and beverages, railway technologies, telecommunication.
- Italy: apparel, furniture, machinery, metal products, chemicals, plastics, household appliances, food and beverages.
- United Kingdom: food and beverages, petroleum products, metal products.
- Spain: food and beverages, automotive components, metal products, selected bulk chemicals.

Table 13.3 Sector–country competitiveness matrix, leading OECD economies

Industry	USA	Japan	Germany	France	Italy	UK	Spain
Food, beverages	+++	+	+++	+++	+++	++	+
Textiles	+	+	++	+	+++	+	++
Apparel	+	+	++	++	+++	+	++
Footwear, leather articles	–	–	++	+	+++	+	+++
Wood processing	+++	+	++	+	++	–	–
Paper products	+++	+	++	++	++	+	+
Coke and petroleum products	+++	+	+	++	++	++	–
Chemicals	++	+	+++	+	++	+	–
Rubber, plastics	++	++	+++	+	++	+	+
Glass, ceramics	++	++	++	++	+	+	+
Metal products	++	++	+++	+	++	+	+
Machinery	+	++	+++	+	++	+	–
Office automation, computing	+++	+++	++	+	–	+	–
Consumer electronics, communication	+++	+++	++	+	–	+	–
Medical and precision instruments	++	++	+++	+	+	+	–
Motor vehicles and parts	++	+++	+++	++	++	+	+
Other transport equipment	++	+	+	+	+	+	–

High competitiveness +++; medium competitiveness ++; low competitiveness +; very low technology sourcing potential –

Among OECD countries, Germany and Italy represent particularly interesting, but extremely difficult, targets as they host a large population of medium-sized companies spread over the entire territory. These medium-sized players account for a large share of industrial production. But they are not always easy to identify and canvassing them involves significant travel and promotional budgets.[23]

Each leading source economy will be reviewed in the following chapters, mainly the key industries and companies that have a high level of international competitiveness which makes them potential long-term investors for Russia.[24] Although industrial structures in the smaller OECD countries and the LEMs China and India are not reviewed in detail, the technology and investment potential of these economies should not be undervalued. Depending on the technology to be attracted, these countries could in fact offer interesting alternatives to the large OECD countries (e.g. mining technologies from Australia; food processing, leather goods, textiles and engineering products from India; electronics, apparel, toys, sports goods from China). They should be at least lightly monitored to prevent missing a substantial investment opportunity when it arises in these countries. Once the information system for priority countries is in place, the model could be used to study other countries of potential interest.

13.4.1 United States

The United States is the largest economy in the world, whose GDP will exceed US$8000 billion by 1999. Economic and trade relations between Russia and the United States have improved steadily since a democratic and free market system was instituted in Russia after the break-up of the Soviet Union. The US Chamber of Commerce in Moscow plays an active role in promoting bilateral trade and technology contacts. It offers US companies advice, training, finance and lobbying support for their business with Russia. The Chamber fosters long-lasting alliances between medium-sized US and Russian companies in manufacturing.[25] Special export and investment promotion programmes are also organized by the US authorities to support medium-sized companies in overseas markets.

The United States has built substantial know-how in many high-tech industries: information and communication technologies, chemicals and bioengineering; aviation, aerospace, and satellite technologies; and raw materials processing. Russian aircraft producers already cooperate with US airframe, avionics and engine manufacturers. These alliances are bolstered by the US government's intention to grant airworthiness certification to new civilian airplanes manufactured in Russia, which are proposed for the growing Asia–Pacific markets.[26] Its size, resources and overall industrial strength make the United States a global technology provider for various types of consumer, capital and high-tech goods as well as services. US TNCs control many subsidiaries in western Europe, which are responsible for planning, implementing and supervising FDI decisions in Eastern Europe including Russia and the CIS. US firms remain the largest investors in Russia and accounted for about one-quarter of inward FDI during 1991–97.

US companies have reached a high degree of international competitiveness in a number of important industries:

- aerospace
- energy-related technologies
- agricultural machinery
- automobiles and automotive components
- specialty chemicals
- pharmaceuticals and biotechnologies
- healthcare equipment
- sports goods and leisurewear
- durable and fast-moving consumer goods
- information technologies for offices and homes (hardware and software)
- telecommunications equipment
- new materials based on ceramics, plastics and fibreglass
- food processing
- financial and nonfinancial services
- hotels and fast-food services

Under consistent attack by Japanese and European rivals, the United States is losing its position as the world's main technology provider in a number of important industries. German and Swiss TNCs are superior, for example, in chemicals, new materials, specialized machine tools, electrical equipment, and DIY goods and tools, whereas Italy has distanced the United States and other countries for footwear and apparel, home furnishings and design-oriented industries. France dominates the cosmetics market and is strong in foods. Japan offers a greater variety of consumer electronics.[27] In chemicals, synthetic rubber, plastics, paper processing and printing, US technologies are challenged by Germany, Sweden and Finland.

In 1997, about 20 per cent of the world's top 100 TNCs were of US origin (Figure 13.3). Market leaders are listed on the stock exchanges (NYSE, NAFTAC) and information is easily available. Although the stereotype of US industry is the large American corporation, there are more than 22 million small and medium-sized businesses which employ well over half the workforce and generate more than half the country's GDP.[28] Many of these companies are in service sectors[29] and oriented towards the domestic market, but an increasing number also supply US multinationals or sell directly to other countries. They could serve as sources of technology for Russia in areas such as automotive components and special instrumentation for the chemical and petrochemical sectors. Industries with a large number of

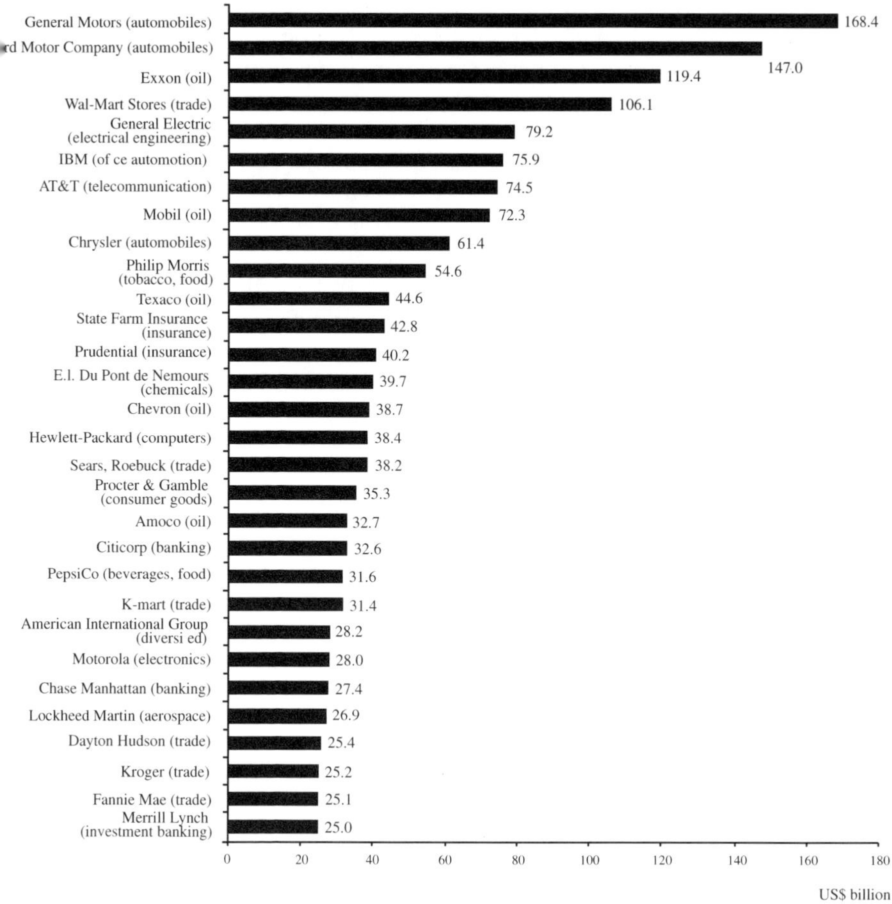

Source: *Fortune 500* Index; *Handelsblatt*, 'USA – Warmer Gewinnregen für die Top 100' [USA – good profits for the top 100], 2 March 1998.

Figure 13.3 Top 30 US TNCs by sales, 1997

medium-sized establishments include (Figure 13.4): metal products (47 800), food and beverages (27 200), plastic products (20 200), and radio, TV and communication equipment (18 600).

Three factors will favour FDI from the United States in the coming years:

- the inherent dynamism and eagerness of US corporate executives and businessmen to discover new markets;
- the capability of US multinationals to offer state-of-the-art technologies;

- the existence of powerful bilateral institutions such as the US Chamber of Commerce and the Commission of Economic and Technological Cooperation,[30] which have become important catalysts for cross-border trade and FDI. During the visit of former Prime Minister Tschernomyrdin to the United States in March 1998, numerous agreements were signed for space and satellite technology, and healthcare. The positive results achieved so far through these agreements may incite other US companies to build plants in Russia.

The United States has stepped up its efforts to integrate Central and South American countries into a continental trade area of the Americas by 2005. Despite the reluctance of the US Congress to accept the fast track approval mechanism, the emergence of this trade region is inevitable as the country prepares to face competition from the EU and its single currency.[32] The United States is also an active promoter of economic integration with Asian Pacific Rim countries. Most US outward FDI

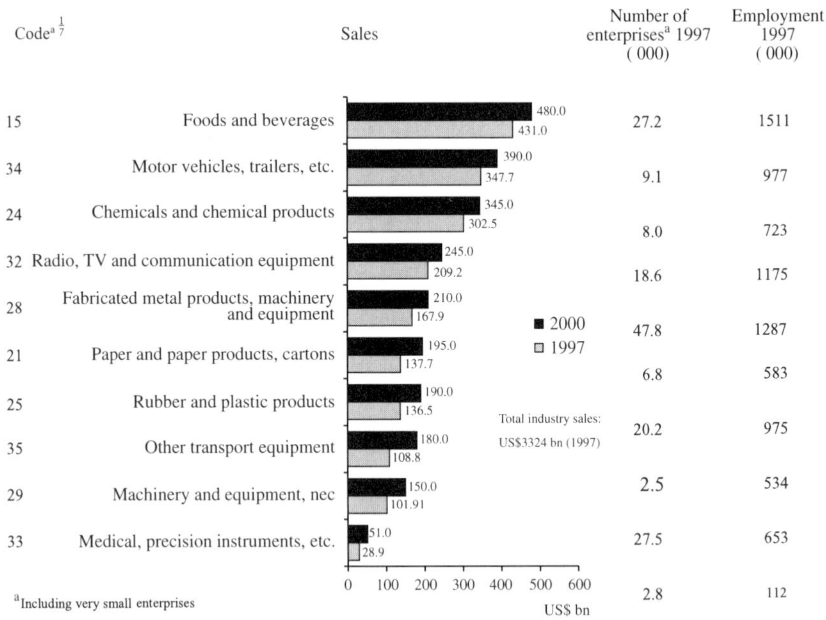

Source: adapted from OECD, *Industrial Structure Statistics*, 1997, 1998.

Figure 13.4 Industrial competitiveness, United States, 1997, 2000

to emerging economies is concentrated in Asia and Latin America (Figure 13.5). Hungary was the largest recipient among Eastern European transition economies in 1996. Russia's inward FDI stock from the United States reached almost US$1 billion by 1996, which was the highest among OECD countries but still 14–23 times less than US investments in Brazil, China and Mexico.

Considering the global orientations of US TNCs, FDI promotional efforts should be intensified for expanding factories and plants that have been set up and for attracting new investors. Prospective US investors can be identified by studying past and present FDI outflows and export structures. US industries with a high share in FDI outflows at the global level should be analyzed further and matched with industrial requirements in Russia's main regional markets.

13.4.2 Japan

It took Japan only three decades to rebuild its shattered economy after the Second World War and emerge as the second most important industrial power, with a GDP expected to exceed US$4000 billion in 1998. The country's remarkable transition in the 1970s from a factor-driven to an innovation-driven economy has given its companies a competitive technology and price edge.[33] Today, Japan is the leading global supplier of electronic components, electrical devices, consumer electronics, cars and motorcycles. Japanese industry has also achieved a high level of industrial competitiveness in medical instruments, machinery and food ingredients. It is the second largest investor in the Asia–Pacific region; it has remained highly competitive despite a domestic slowdown and the Southeast Asian crisis of late 1997.

The Japanese economy is dominated by *zaibatsus* or large integrated companies (Figure 13.6) which usually group several industrial and services enterprises (including banks, insurance companies and trading houses). The SME sector (about 60 per cent of total) comprises mostly domestic players, who are not international investors. Some SMEs, which are exclusive suppliers to large groups, may follow their clients, particularly to Triad markets in Asia, Europe and North America. Japan's relations with Russia are still strained because of the territorial dispute over the Kuril Islands, to the north of Japan's Hokkaido island in the Pacific ocean. Japan pledges to increase trade and FDI once the islands, which it says were annexed by the former Soviet Union under Stalin in August 1945, are returned. Recently, the two governments have shown a certain readiness to base their relationship less on territorial disputes and more on mutual economic gain. Russia still needs to improve its legal and physical infrastructure to reassure Japanese companies that their investments will be safeguarded.[34]

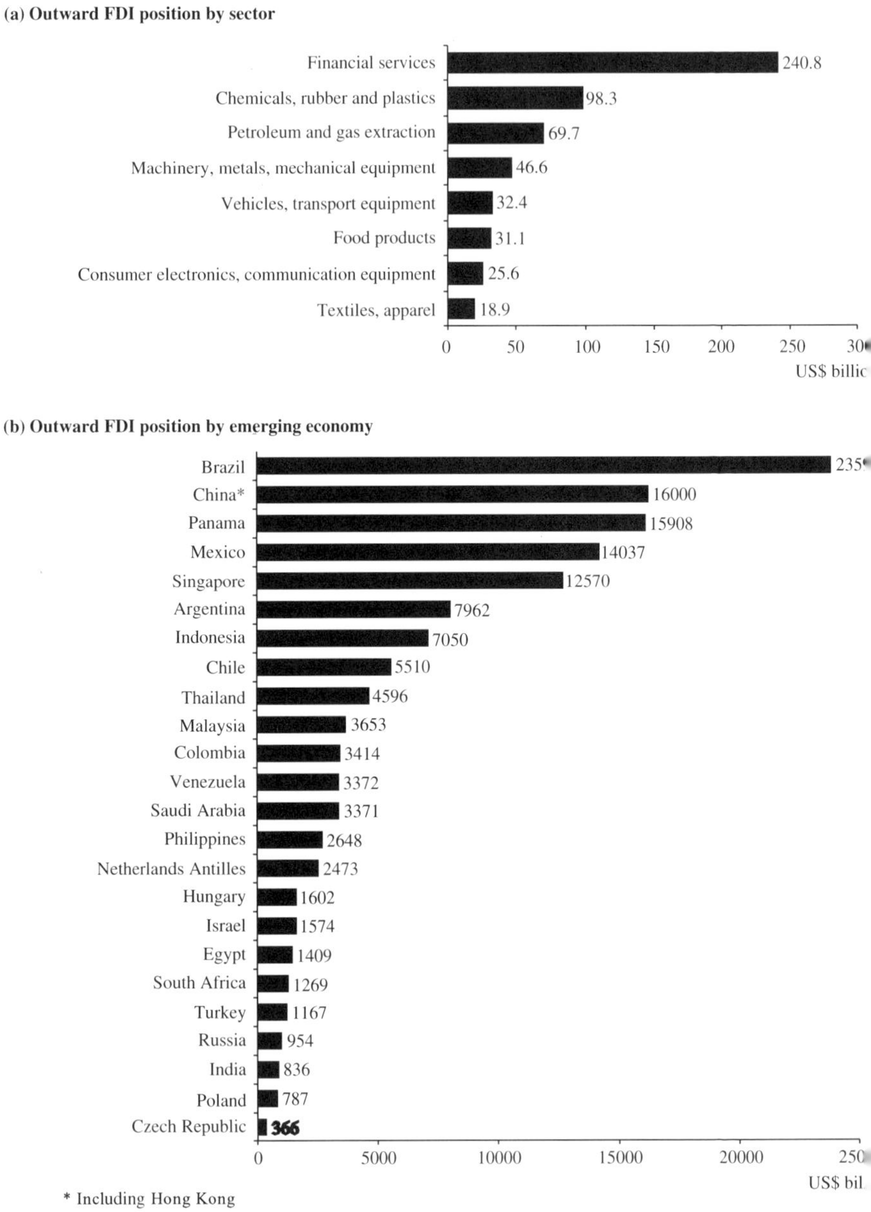

Source: Adapted from OECD, *FDI Statistics Yearbook*, 1997.

Figure 13.5 FDI performance by sector and region, United States, 1996

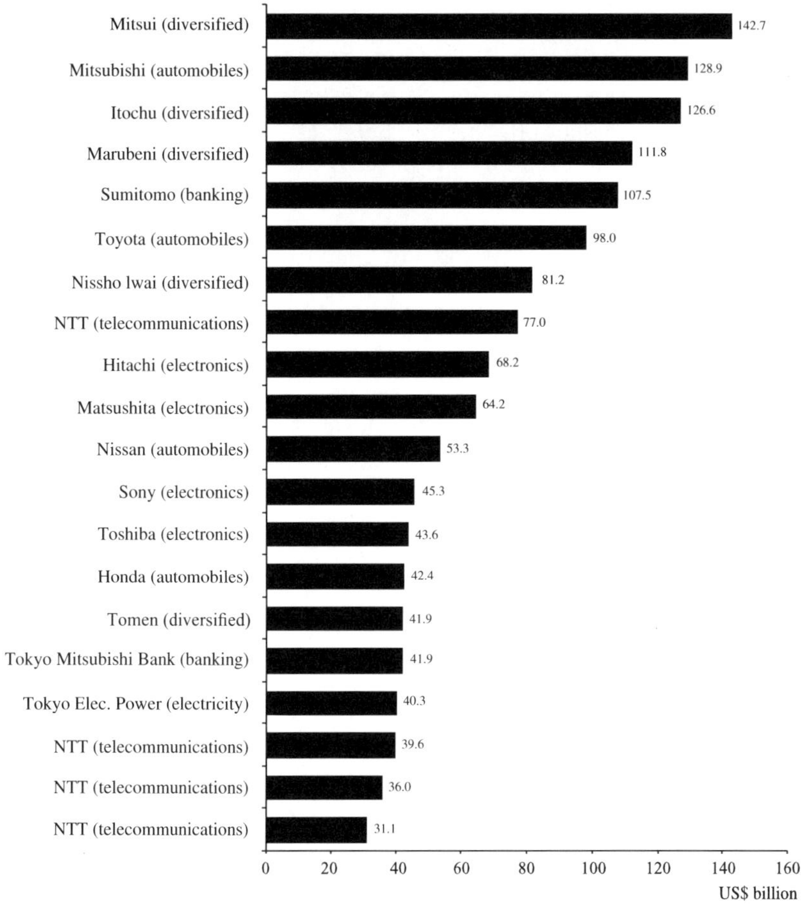

Source: Tokyo Kenzai Inc., *Japanese Corporate Groups,* 1997; *Fortune 500,* August 1998.

Figure 13.6 Top 20 Japanese TNCs by sales, 1997

Bilateral negotiations have begun on a number of multibillion dollar oil and gas exploration, and pipeline projects. While Japan depends on external supply to meet its energy requirements, it has developed modern technology for exploration, exploitation and transport. There are innumerable possibilities for joint projects between Japan and Russia, including tapping and transporting of gas from the Irkutsk fields in Siberia to the markets of China and South Korea, drilling for gas and oil off the island of Sakhalin, mining and petroleum refining projects in Siberia, and the joint exploitation of wind and solar energy on the disputed Kuril Islands.[35] These projects could be catalysts for developing closer ties among northeast Asian countries in the coming decades. With Japan's financial and technical assistance, eastern Siberia could be developed into an energy and raw materials base for northern China, the two Koreas, Japan and certain Southeast Asian economies. A Russian–Japanese consortium, under the aegis of the Russian Ministry of Energy Technology and the Japanese MITI, is supposed to bring together dozens of companies and banks of the two countries for exploration and exploitation of Siberian gas, oil and minerals.

Apart from FDI in energy and raw materials in the eastern regions, Japanese companies could bring in technology and know-how in a number of downstream industries in the European part of the Russian Federation, including:

- specialty steels and metals, new materials;
- consumer electronics, watches and optical devices;
- vehicles including cars, jeeps, vans and motorcycles;
- computer components and peripherals;
- telecommunications technology;
- healthcare equipment;
- instruments for laboratories.

These industries account for the highest output and number of employees in Japan, and comprise thousands of establishments (Figure 13.7), ranging from small firms catering to the domestic market to large multinationals operating at a global level. Attention should be focused on sectoral leaders who are most likely to be interested in expanding their operations to new large-scale markets such as Russia and the surrounding CIS countries.

The structure of Japanese industry is unique: it is polarized between global players and midget companies that sell exclusively to nearby markets or are integrated into larger systems as component suppliers to the big TNCs. Large independent medium-sized players with sufficient financial clout to venture alone in foreign markets are rare. Identification of large TNCs is therefore simplified, and the information can be obtained from industry associations and the powerful employers' federation *Keidanren*, which represents Japan's top 200 TNCs abroad.

Following two years of recession, the Japanese government now feels obliged to cut corporate taxes and carry out broad structural reforms (direct funding of infrastructure and R&D programmes, development of high-tech industries, deregulation of state oligopolies, reduction of ministries and administrative staff). This will raise the competitiveness of its industries.

Japan's tax system, which dates back to the late 1960s, constrains profit generation and effective allocation of resources by domestic companies.[36] This has led to falling FDI outflows, which were halved from over US$40 billion in the early 1990s to just about US$20 billion by 1997.[37] Following

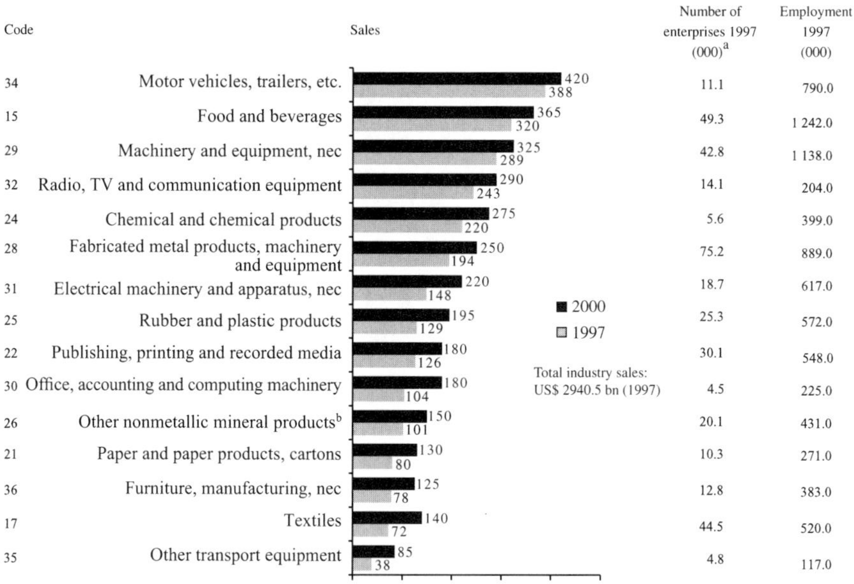

[a] Including very small enterprises
[b] Mainly glass and ceramics

Source: Adapted from OECD, *Industrial Structure Statistics*, 1997, 1998.

Figure 13.7 Industrial competitiveness, Japan, 1997, 2000

these structural and fiscal reforms, Japanese FDI into Russia should gain pace provided an acceptable solution is found to the Kuril Islands issue and political stability increases in Russia.

Japanese TNCs are extremely cautious investors; they adopt a 'wait and watch' attitude until all relevant economic and political indicators point upwards. Political stability is considered a high priority for FDI. Japanese TNCs are interconnected and rely on the green light from the top political circles and superior bodies (Ministries of Foreign Affairs and of the Economy, MITI, industry associations, large banks). Once a destination country meets with general approval, large waves of Japanese FDI can be expected.

Total Japanese FDI in Russia in 1996–97 was extremely low (about US$400 million) compared with its high technology and investment potential (Figure 13.8). In 1997, Japan was the world's third largest investor (in terms of accumulated stock) after the United States and the United Kingdom,[38] but following years of diminishing outflows during 1994–97, Japan is being challenged by Germany, whose medium-sized TNCs are pressing abroad as investors. In Russia, Japanese investors even trail behind South Korea, although on a worldwide basis South Korean FDI represents only 14 per cent of Japan's outflows and about 4 per cent of

(a) Outward FDI position by sector

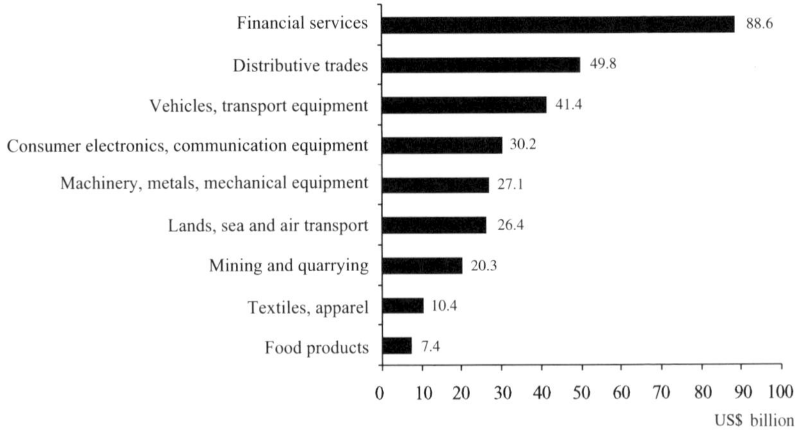

(b) Outward FDI position by emerging economy

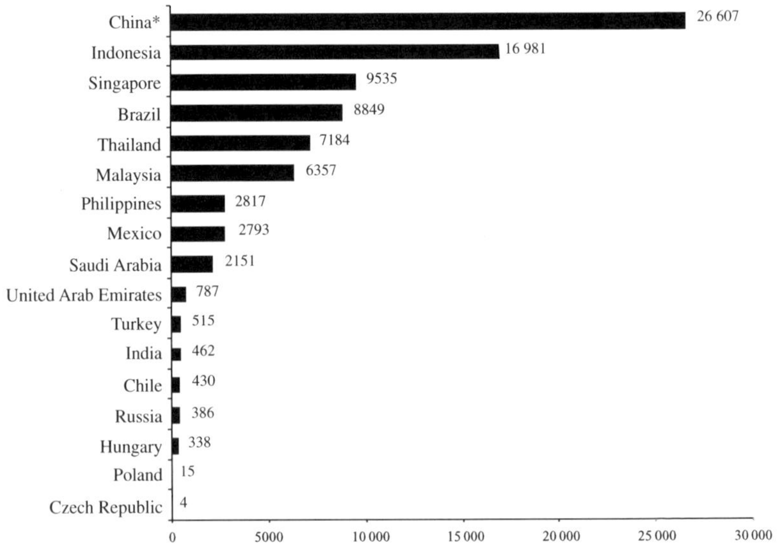

* Including Hong Kong

Source: Adapted from OECD, *FDI Statistics Yearbook*, 1997.

Figure 13.8 FDI performance by sector and region, Japan, 1996

outward stock. Japanese investment has so far been directed mainly to the emerging markets of Asia, especially China and the ASEAN economies, but increasingly also to Latin America. Japanese FDI stock in Brazil is 20 times and in Mexico 9 times higher than in Russia.

13.4.3 The EU's big five: Germany, France, Italy, United Kingdom, Spain

Together, the 15 EU member states today account for over one-third of the world's industrial production and employment. EU industry is highly diversified and has a large population of medium-sized players in both small and large member states. Therefore, Russian FDI authorities will find a vast potential of new technologies for almost every industry. The EU's common currency project is expected to stimulate industrial competitiveness and also motivate companies to invest in Eastern European economies (Figure 13.9).

But the atomized industry structure and diversity of languages and mentalities can complicate search and canvassing efforts. There are about 16 million industrial and services enterprises in the EU, over three-quarters of which are located in the five big member states (Germany, France, Italy,

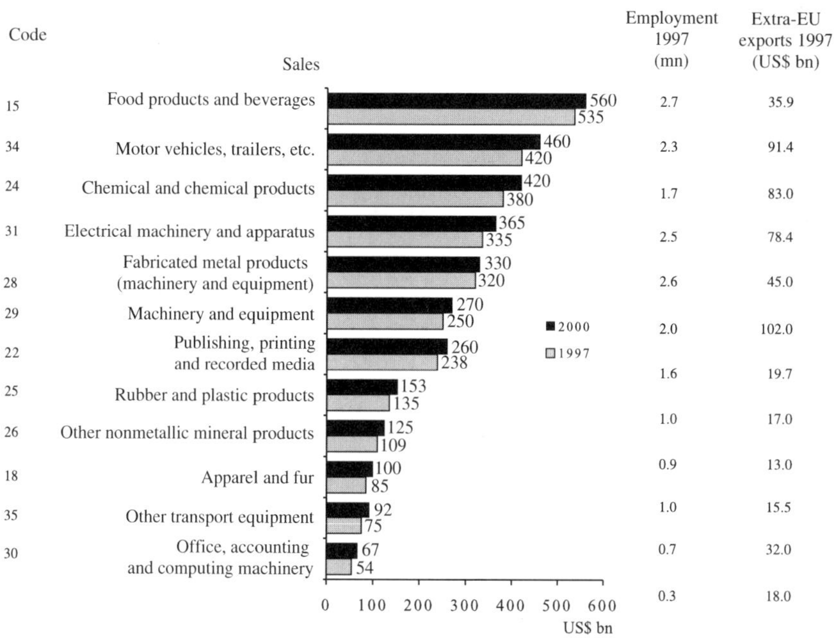

Source: Based on European Commission, *EU Industrial Outlook*, 1996, 1997, 1998

Figure 13.9 Industrial competitiveness, leading EU economies, 1997, 2000

the United Kingdom and Spain) and account for about 80 per cent of employment and turnover.[39] Manufacturing enterprises (5.6 million) represent about 35 per cent of the total enterprise population in the EU.

The objective is to find medium-sized industrial companies that are sufficiently large and financially strong to pursue a long-term strategy in Russia.[40] Together with the very large TNCs, this target group represents at the most 1 per cent of the total enterprise population, but almost half of total industrial turnover in the EU. Most of the financially strong TNCs are headquartered in the larger EU countries, but many important players are also located in the smaller member states (the Netherlands, Belgium, Sweden, Finland and Denmark). The difficulty lies in distinguishing between potential medium-sized investors and very small players, which account for the bulk of EU enterprises, cater to the domestic or EU markets and are unlikely to be interested in investing in large emerging markets like Russia.[41]

Germany constitutes the most populated and strongest EU economy. It leads in many industries in terms of market volume, available technologies and number of suitable TNCs. The other large EU countries France, Italy, the United Kingdom and Spain also offer a number of companies in innovative industries, which should be approached. A brief overview is given of general industrial structures and sector competitiveness levels in the five major EU member states: Germany, France, Italy, the United Kingdom and Spain.

Germany

Germany is the economic powerhouse of the EU and the third largest economy in the world after the United States and Japan; its GDP in 1999 is expected to exceed €2000 billion. Since re-unification in 1990, Germany has transformed itself into a political interface between Eastern and western Europe. Within the EU, Germany follows a philosophy of Europe-wide stability, which inspired the common currency project.[42] Because of geographic and historical reasons, it is in Germany's interest to see Russia's economy prosper and its industry develop quickly.

An entrepreneurial tradition and strong engineering capacity have seen Germany's industry through the two crippling world wars. Political determination, a well-organized administration and open dialogue with the unions enabled the country's industry to regain its strength within two decades. Today, German industry is one of the most diversified, innovative and competitive in the world (Figure 13.10). It is composed of large groups (Figure 13.11) and thousands of small and medium-sized companies (*Mittelstand*) which together represent an invaluable source of technology and know-how that could contribute to the modernization of Russian industry. Latest figures estimate the number of medium-sized manufacturing companies at just under 90 000 (over 90 per cent of

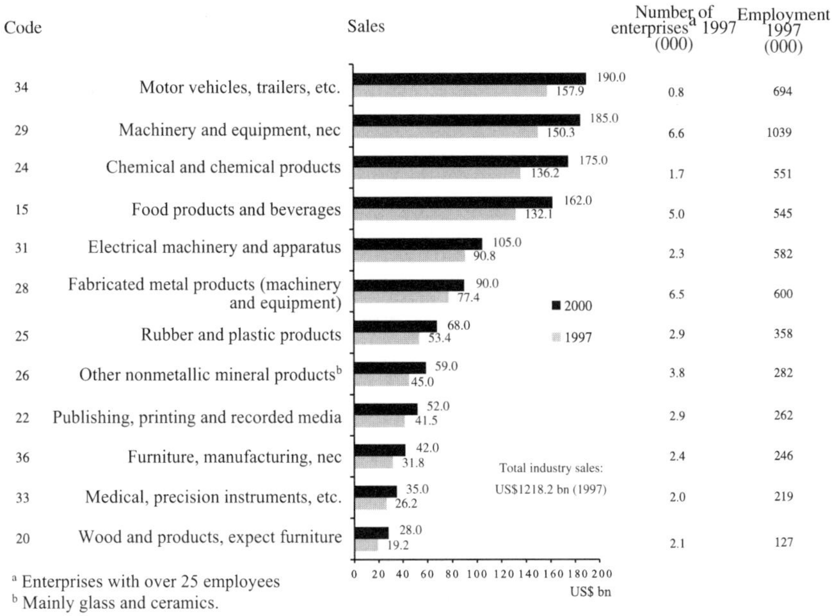

Source: Adapted from OECD, *Industrial Structure Statistics*, 1997, 1998.

Figure 13.10 Industrial competitiveness, Germany, 1997

all industrial enterprises). In 1997, they accounted for 42 per cent of the total industrial workforce (2.7 million out of 6.5 million) and 36 per cent of total turnover generated by industry (DM712 billion out of DM1.9 trillion).[43]

The term *Mittelstand* includes a variety of companies of different sizes. The qualitative attribute (companies still run by owner families and not belonging to public limited companies with listed shares) generally supersedes the quantitative attribute in terms of number of employees or turnover. Owner-managed or owner-controlled companies can have a workforce of up to several thousand employees. Such 'hidden champions'[44] often develop better technologies in their specific fields of business than diversified multinational corporations. Russian FDI authorities should also focus on appropriate medium-sized players for investments in Russia. The time to approach the German *Mittelstand* is favourable. Following more than three decades of uninterrupted growth and prosperity, their entrepreneurial and innovation capacity is checked by an increasingly unaffordable social security system, high corporate taxes and labour costs (the highest worldwide), and inflexible labour market regulations.

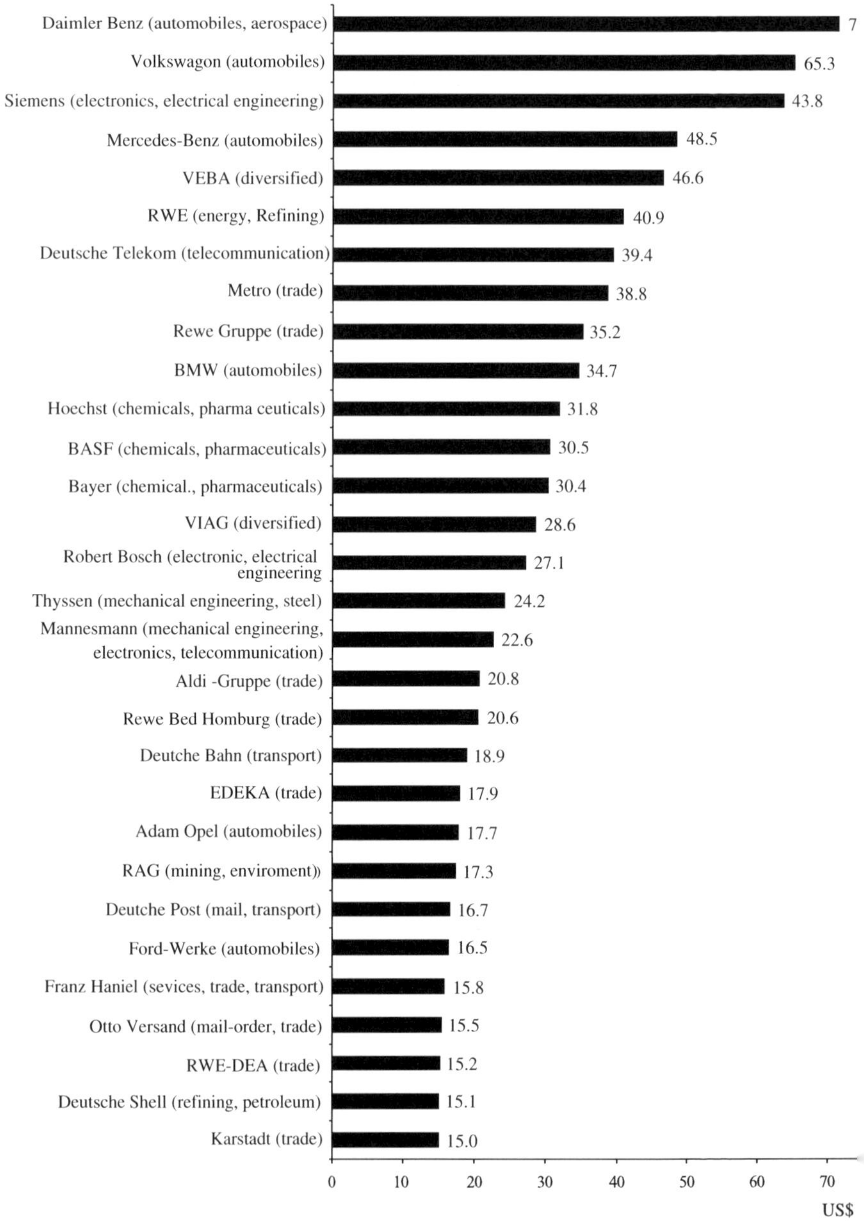

Sources: Schmacke, *Die Grossen 500 auf einen Blick* [The big 500 at a glance], 1997, 1998; *Fortune 500*, August 1998.

Figure 13.11 Top 30 German TNCs by sales, 1997

These constraints are compounded by fierce competition, a saturated market, risk of hostile takeovers, a sluggish economy (GDP growth 1.5–2 per cent in 1999) and problems of succession. In 1998, over 30 000 enterprises were closed down (9 per cent more than during 1996–97) in Germany.[45] German industry will be compelled to increase its investments abroad in the coming years. Geographic proximity and old historical ties make Russia a privileged partner. But company owners and managers still need to be convinced that business prospects in Russia are better than in other LEMs such as Brazil, China, India and Mexico. They also watch the course of economic reforms and the restructuring of Russia's banking sector following the 1998 financial crisis.

German family-owned companies are traditionally extremely cautious and prefer exports to investment projects which have a high risk component. (This attitude has had disastrous consequences for a number of companies, which had to either close down or were bought out by foreign competitors, mainly from the United States, Japan, France, Sweden, the Netherlands and Italy.)

Germany's companies are not only diversified, but also decentralized, with the respective *Länder* governments playing an important role in R&D support, and advisory and financial services for overseas market expansion. Companies are spread across the entire territory. Unlike certain countries where industries are concentrated in the north, Germany's high-tech belt is located in the south, mainly in Bayern and Baden-Württemberg. Any promotion effort directed at German industrial groups should take into consideration the strong ties between industry and local chambers of commerce and political authorities.

Compared with Central European countries, German FDI stock in Russia is still negligible (Figure 13.12). The Czech Republic, Hungary and Poland have so far attracted 3–6 times more foreign investors from Germany compared with Russia.

France

The French economy is characterized by a strong public sector which still controls many strategic, high-tech and heavy industries, and part of the banking and insurance network. Large-scale industrial development is often promoted through state investments and state-funded R&D. Over the past 15 years, successive governments have intermittently promoted or slowed down the process of privatization. Socialist governments are particularly concerned about layoffs following the transfer of companies to private owners, because of already high unemployment levels. Fiscal discipline imposed by the EU monetary union and competition are expected to bring about a change.

While large and mostly state-owned enterprises control many important sectors, the role of medium-sized players should not be underestimated

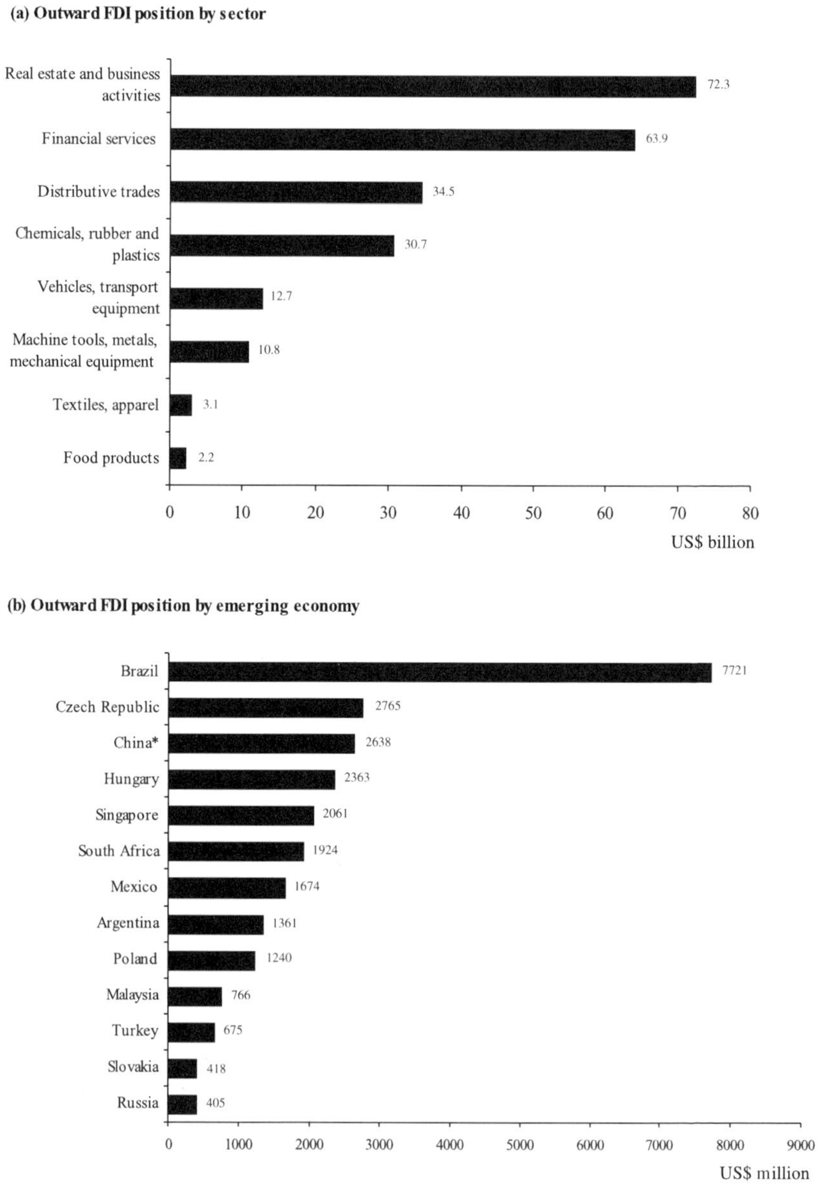

* Including Hong Kong

Source: Adapted from OECD, *FDI Statistics Yearbook*, 1997.

Figure 13.12 FDI performance by sector and region, Germany, 1996

(Figure 13.13). Corporate restructuring, divestments and privatization have energized this segment of French industry over the past 15 years. Unlike the large companies, which have their headquarters in and around Paris, medium-sized enterprises are scattered across the country. As in other EU countries, these companies are mostly family-owned private companies; some of them have become European and even world leaders in their industries and would include investors and technology suppliers for Russia.

French companies are innovative and open to new ideas, particularly if they enhance productivity. French TNCs have also increased their stakes in foreign companies over the past two decades and emerged as the world's fifth largest investors. In 1996, French outward FDI stock already exceeded US$200 billion. French companies are among the world leaders in the following sectors (Figure 13.14):

- telecommunications and electricity;
- railways;
- aerospace;
- water management;
- construction and construction materials;
- food and beverages;
- personal care and cosmetics;
- household equipment;
- automobiles;
- automotive components including electronic devices;
- tyres;
- glass technology;
- banking, finance and insurance;
- tourism;
- retail services.

Owing to widespread state ownership and government intervention in a number of important sectors, negotiations for cooperation or strategic alliances will often have to be conducted at a high political level. They can be initiated during visits of politicians, who are usually accompanied by business delegations. Political lobbying is common practice for large-scale and strategic projects in important markets such as Russia.

The deep interest of the French in Russian culture and history is an advantage. Such 'soft' factors need to be understood and promoted together with the 'hard' realities of Russian industry as they could make projects far more interesting to potential industrial partners from France.

The emerging economies of Latin America and Asia have so far benefited the most from French foreign investments (Figure 13.15). The main destinations have been Brazil (just under US$4 billion by 1996), Argentina (US$1.4 billion), Singapore and China (both around US$1.2 billion).

Source: *L'Expansion,* 'Les 1200 premiers groupes industriels et entreprises de services et leurs filiales' [The top 1200 industrial and services enterprises and their subsidiaries], 1998.

Figure 13.13 Top 30 French TNCs by turnover, 1997

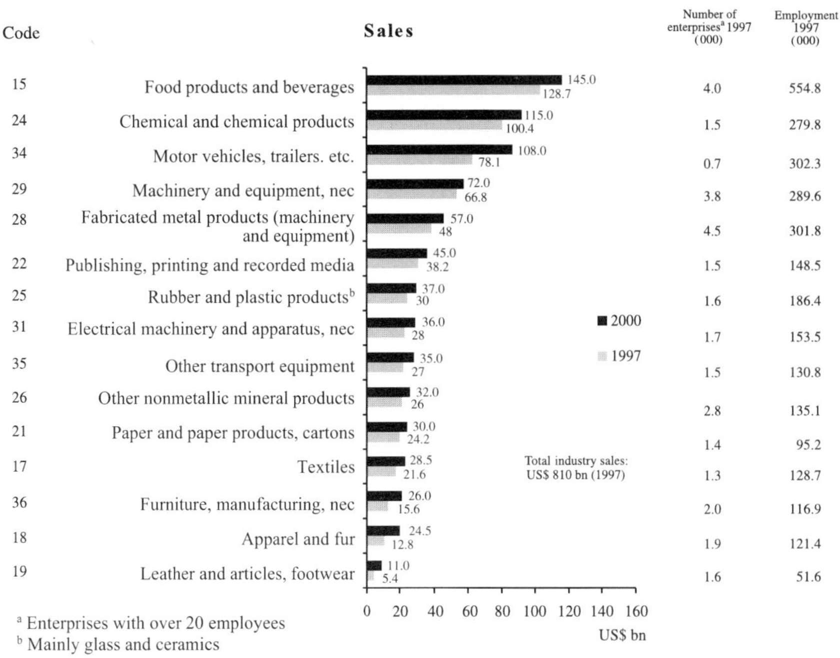

Source: Adapted from OECD, *Industrial Structure Statistics*, 1997, 1998.

Figure 13.14 Industrial competitiveness, France, 1997

Selected North African and Middle East countries (e.g. Morocco, Turkey, Lebanon) are also frequent destinations because of former colonial ties. Altogether, France's outward investment position is rather weak in Central and Eastern Europe. By 1996, only US$90 million had flowed to Russia. The French authorities are studying possibilities of assisting industry in its efforts to strengthen its position in Eastern Europe.

Italy

Italy's integration into the EU (1957) and its government's determination to end a policy of lira devaluation, which prevailed in the 1960s, prompted Italian firms to upgrade product and process technology. Since then the country's comparative advantage has shifted from low labour costs to innovation. Italian industry has shown a remarkable ability in developing new products and in introducing state-of-the-art manufacturing technologies in small and medium-sized companies, which – as in Germany – dominate the national economy. The concomitant rise in purchasing power and quality consciousness among consumers have supported the growth of these enterprises.

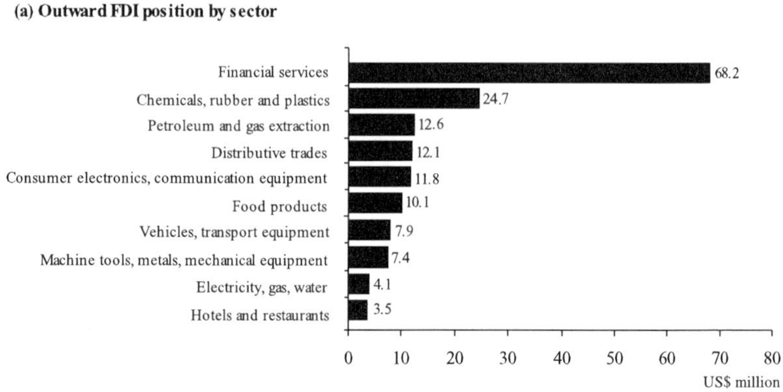

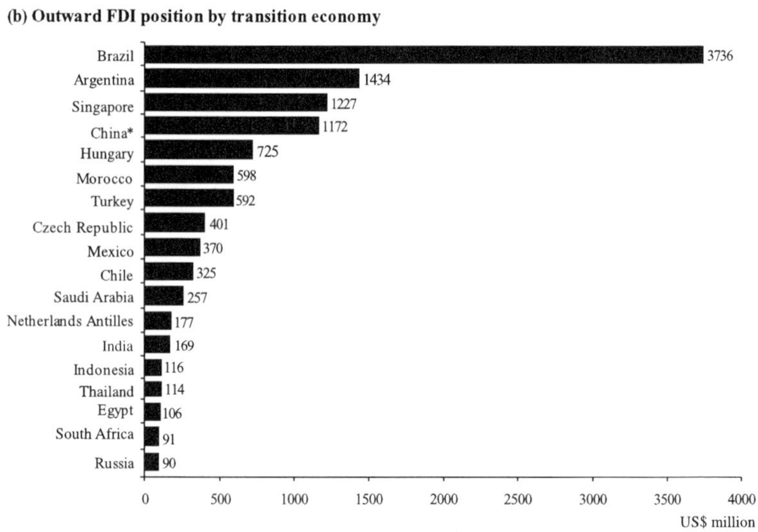

* Including Hong Kong

Source: Adapted from OECD, *FDI Statistics Yearbook*, 1997.

Figure 13.15 FDI performance by sector and region, France, 1996

Highly competitive clusters of world-class supplier industries gradually emerged around key industrial sectors, especially in the northern provinces of Lombardy, Piemont, Veneto, Emilia Romagna and Trentino. The natural entrepreneurial spirit and talent for design have made the Italians leaders in design-based industries in addition to others (Figure 13.16):

- textiles and apparel
- leather goods and footwear
- household goods, white goods
- furniture
- sanitary equipment, heating systems
- machine tools for all types of applications, particularly textile, plastics, and food processing industries
- automobiles, buses
- scooters, bicycles
- ceramics, plastics, new materials
- food
- cosmetics

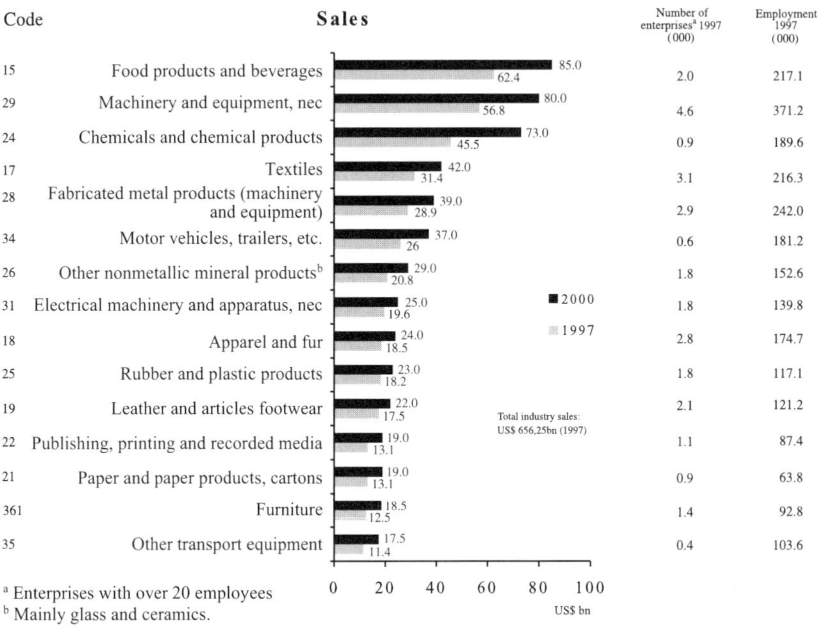

[a] Enterprises with over 20 employees
[b] Mainly glass and ceramics.

Source: Adapted from OECD, *Industrial Structure Statistics*, 1997, 1998.

Figure 13.16 Industrial competitiveness, Italy, 1997

- toys
- pharmaceuticals

Many of Italy's thousands of family-owned medium-sized companies have gained a worldwide reputation for their products and brands. There are not many large global players, but these companies along with their subsidiaries account for a substantial share of total turnover in Italian industry (24 per cent in 1997), but their share in employment is minimal (7 per cent in 1997). Companies like Eni (oil), Fiat (automobiles), Telecom Italia (telecommunications) and Montedison (pharmaceuticals) now rank among the global top 100 (Figure 13.17).

Research on Italian companies should first distinguish between purely Italian groups and companies controlled by foreign shareholders. In the past five years, many well-known Italian brands have been acquired by foreign companies. For example, the brands Buitoni (sauces for pasta), Motta (ice cream) and Perugina (confectionery) were bought over by the Swiss food group Nestlé, Galbani (cheese) by the French group Danone, and Zanussi (white goods) by the Swedish competitor Electrolux. German, French and US groups have also become important investors in Italian industry, mainly through mergers and acquisitions. A recent example is Mannesmann from Germany, which acquired a large stake in the Italian telecom equipment business from Olivetti. Foreign influence is particularly pronounced in the Italian food industry, where already one-third of Italy's top 25 companies are foreign-owned or controlled by foreign capital.[46]

In cases of foreign ownership, the management structure should indicate whether the Italian company still has the power to decide on FDI or if all international business development decisions are taken elsewhere.

Italian companies are generally smaller than their US, German or French competitors, but they are more flexible with quick decision-making. They are usually more open to joint ventures and strategic alliances rather than cost-intensive greenfield investments. Italy has become the world's fifth largest exporter, but in terms of outward investment the companies are more reserved. Only larger groups are gradually drawing even with their competitors from other leading OECD economies (Figure 13.18).

Italy still has the lowest outward FDI/GDP among G7 countries, but selected companies have progressed considerably as insiders in large emerging economies including Russia. Many large projects have been initiated or are at the planning phase with firms like Fiat (car production in Niznhy Novgorod), Breda-Finmeccanica (urban transport services in St Petersburg and northwestern towns), Eni (natural gas), Merloni (production of white goods in Moscow *oblast*), Parmalat (dairy products manufacturing in Nizhny Novgorod), Tecnimont (polypropylene unit in Ufa), Fata (agroindustry project in Karelia), Ferrero (packaging unit in Nizhny Novgorod) or Telecom-Stet (telecommunications).[47] But, altogether, Russia still plays a minor role

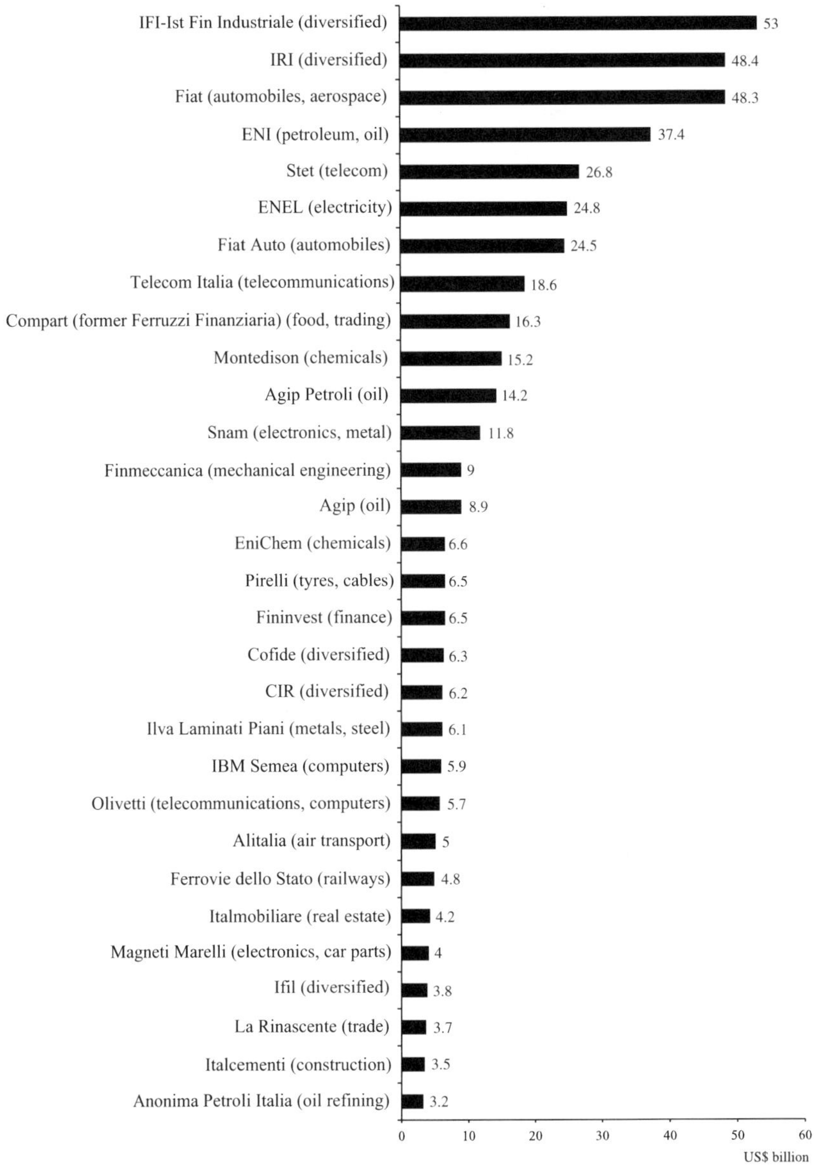

Source: *Mediobanca*, 'Il Mondo Economico. I primi 309 gruppi industriali e societari' [The first 309 industrial groupings], 1997.

Figure 13.17 Top 30 Italian TNCs by sales, 1997

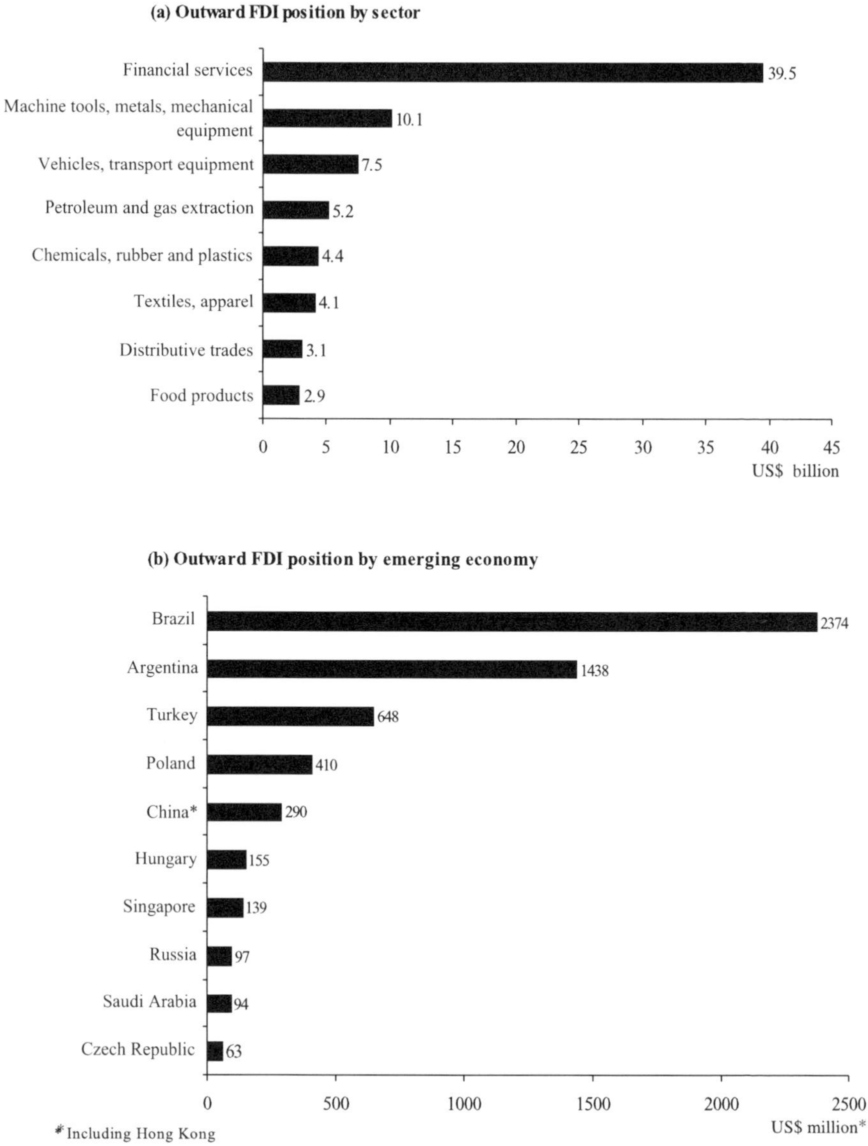

Source: Adapted from OECD, *FDI Statistics Yearbook*, 1997.

Figure 13.18 FDI performance by sector and region, Italy, 1996

for Italian companies, which have so far preferred to invest in Brazil (US$2.4 billion by 1996), Argentina (US$1.4 billion), Turkey (US$650 million) and Poland (US$410 million).

United Kingdom

It was in Great Britain that the industrial revolution began with the invention of the steam engine. It was the basic element for the development of railways, shipbuilding, and steel and textile mills. The country maintained its position as the world's leading industrial power until the First World War. After the Second World War and the loss of its colonies, especially on the Indian subcontinent and in Africa, Great Britain was overtaken by other industrialized countries. Today, many manufacturing industries have practically disappeared or are under foreign control (e.g. automotive sector).

Although investment and employment levels declined drastically in industry, successive UK governments relied on market forces and decided not to intervene and check the downward production cycle. Weaknesses in pillar sectors (infrastructure, consumer durables, construction) quickly spread to other industries, creating a downward spiral of low innovation, unemployment and a gradual shift away from manufacturing towards services. The situation was aggravated by aggressive trade union movements in the 1970s and 1980s. The government of Prime Minister Thatcher curtailed the power of the unions and further deregulated the economy. The country was thus set once again on a high-growth course, but with a clear focus on services and selected high-tech industries (pharmaceuticals, telecommunications).

In 1999, the United Kingdom has become one of the fastest growing EU economies. While certain industries such as machinery, motorcycles and automobiles were abandoned altogether, others were reengineered and a large number of service sectors reinforced (e.g. insurance, banking, air transport, express services, shipping, etc.). Many modern industries were created or kept afloat with the help of investments by European (Germany, France and the Netherlands), North American (Canada and the United States) and Asian (Japan and South Korea) TNCs, which were offered significant fiscal incentives and subsidies by local authorities and the central government (Figure 13.19). Among the most competitive UK industries (Figure 13.20) are the following:

- chemicals and petrochemicals,
- pharmaceuticals,
- food and beverages,
- chemicals,
- houseware and household appliances,
- components for computer and telecommunication hardware, and
- services (investment banking, insurance, advertising, consulting).

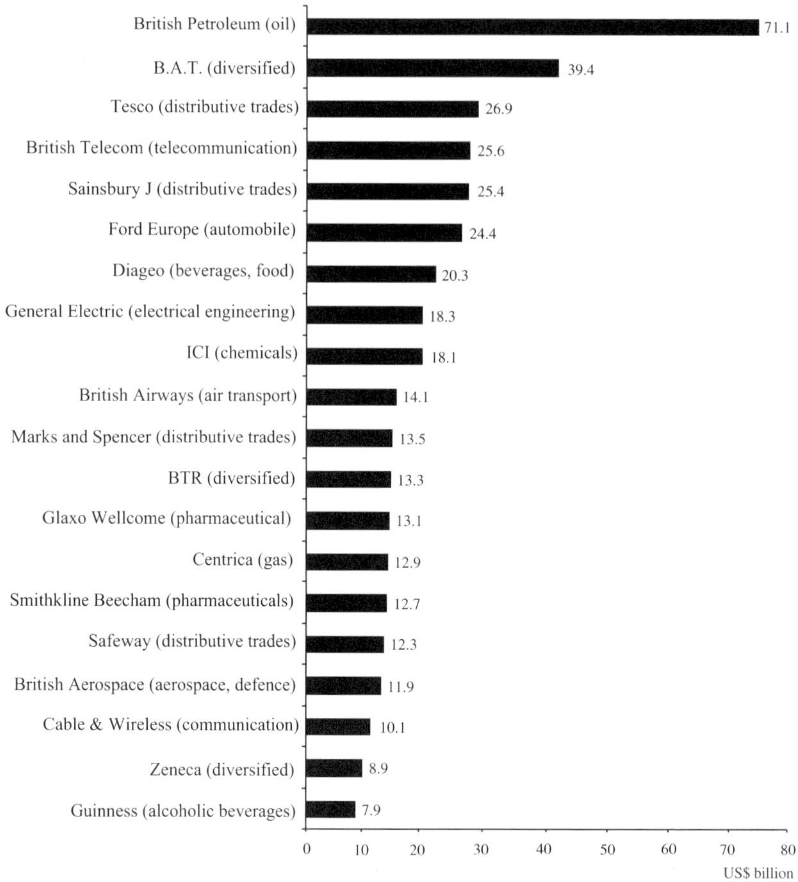

Sources: *Financial Times*, FT 500, 22 January 1998; *Handelsblatt*, 'Die 100 größten Unternehmen Europas' [The 100 largest European companies], 9 June 1998.

Figure 13.19 Top 20 UK TNCs by sales, 1997

UK industry has always maintained stronger trade and investment links with English-speaking countries, particularly the United States, Canada and Australia. But it constantly seeks new markets and could also be interested in Russia, which still ranks low among FDI destinations from emerging markets (Figure 13.21) compared with other destinations (e.g. Singapore, China, South Africa, Brazil, Malaysia).

Spain

Spain is the fifth largest economy in the EU. Also a Mediterranean country, it competes with Italy in a number of industries, particularly food and

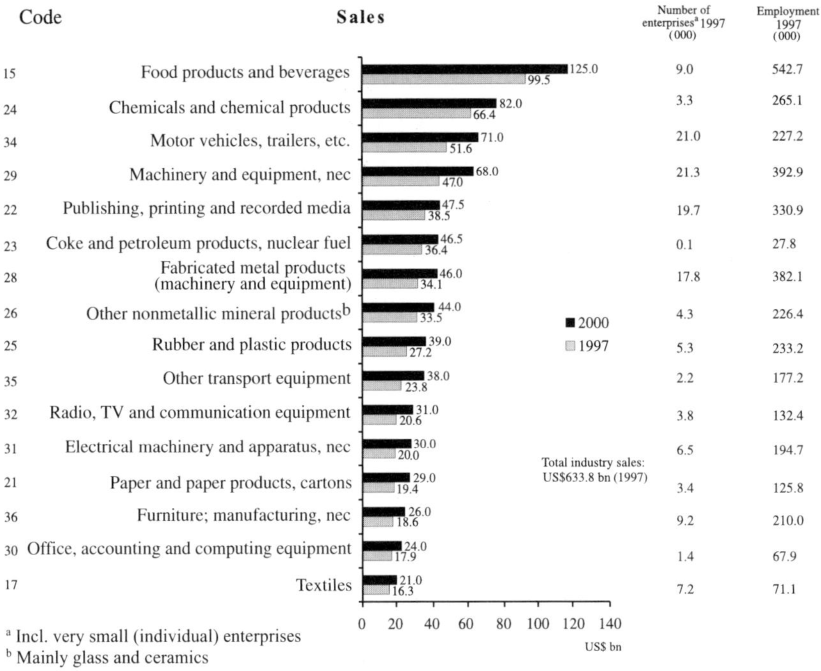

Source: Adapted from OECD, *Industrial Structure Statistics*, 1997, 1998.

Figure 13.20 Industrial competitiveness, United Kingdom, 1997

fashion (shoes, apparel, leather goods, jewellery). Spain still has a comparative advantage in labour costs. Owing to increased inward FDI over the past few years the country has also become an important producer of automobiles (Seat), automotive components and engineering goods (Figures 13.22 and 13.23). Spain also exports significant quantities of beverages (wines, juices) and fresh and frozen foods to northern and Eastern Europe and other parts of the world. Recently, Russia has also become an important destination for fresh and processed foods from Spain.

Spain's main destination countries for exports and outward FDI are other EU member states, the United States and the larger Latin American economies (Argentina, Brazil, Mexico, Peru and Chile) (Figure 13.24). In Latin America, it has become an important investor in the services sector: finance (insurance, banks), transport, tourism, telecommunications.[48] Apart from food processing and metal working, there are few investments in the manufacturing sector in foreign countries. Spanish authorities therefore try to provide financial and other incentives for Spanish TNCs to expand their presence through more exports and FDI.

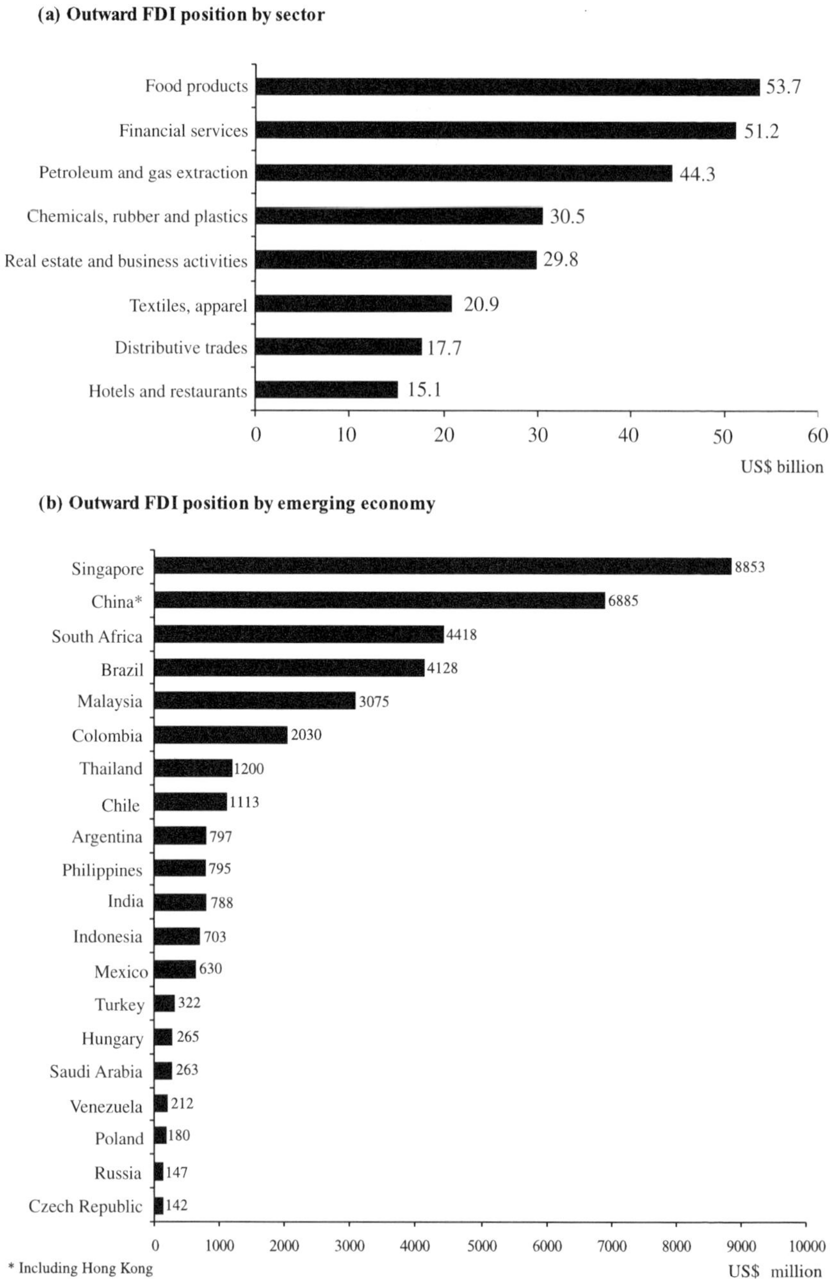

Source: Adapted from OECD, *FDI Statistics Yearbook*, 1997.

Figure 13.21 FDI performance by sector and region, United Kingdom, 1996

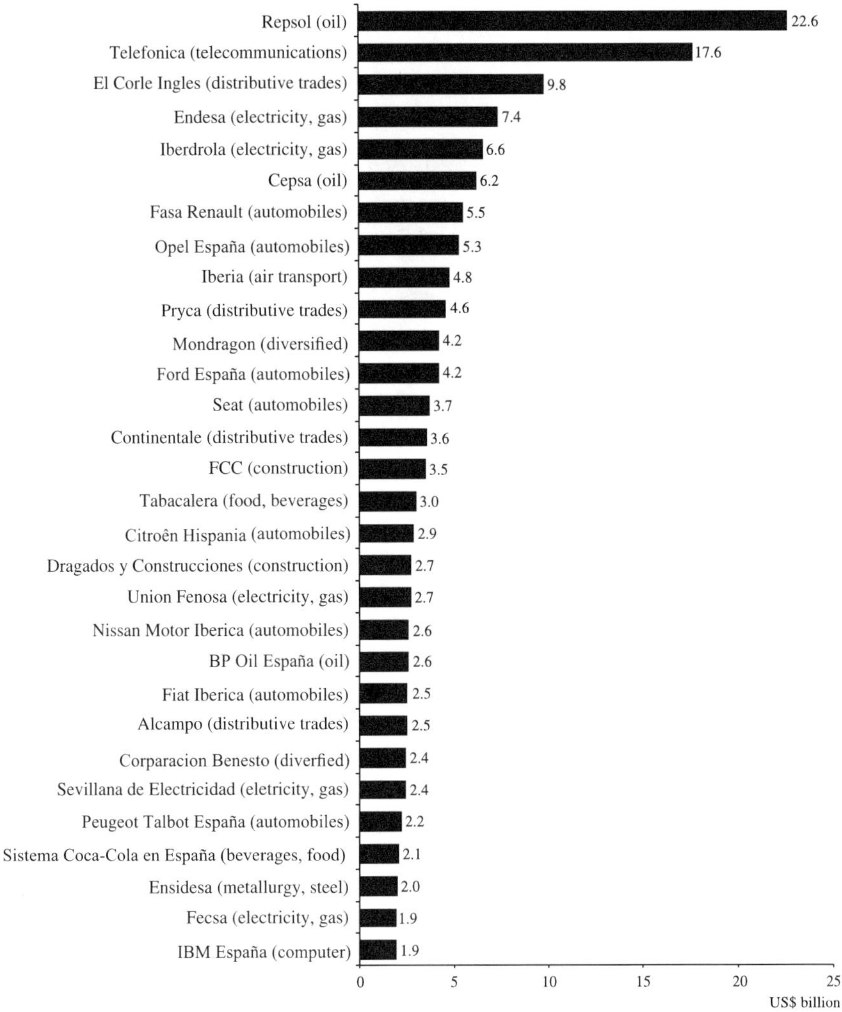

Source: *El Mundo economico*, 1997.

Figure 13.22 Top 30 Spanish TNCs by sales, 1997

Culturally and historically, Russia is not as closely linked to Spain as the Spanish-speaking Latin American countries, some of which are former colonies. However, the Spanish national press has repeatedly pointed out the need to diversify the country portfolio both for exports and outward FDI. Spain's overdependence on the EU and Latin American markets is considered a weakness that has to be rectified by moving to new markets.

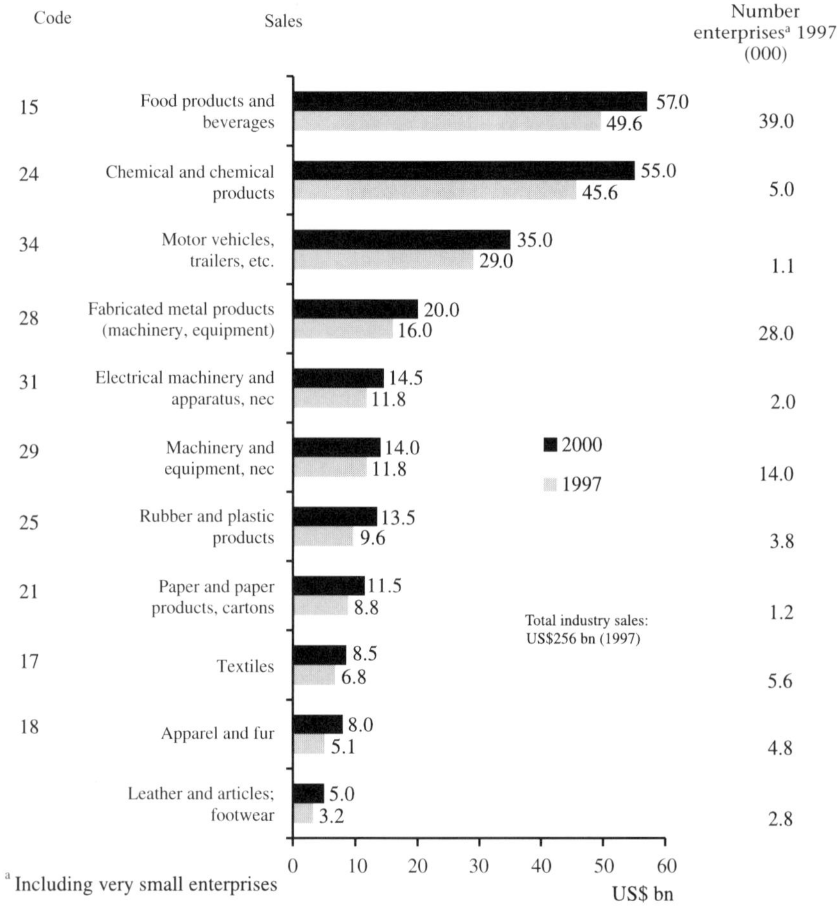

Source: Adapted from OECD, *Industrial Structure Statistics*, 1997, 1998.

Figure 13.23 Industrial competitiveness, Spain, 1997

Russia and other Eastern European economies, together with China and India, are considered promising alternative markets to Brazil and Mexico where Spanish firms are already quite strongly represented. Spain's leading 50 or so corporations account for 80–90 per cent of the country's exports and outgoing FDI. During 1990–96, only about US$30 million were invested in Eastern European countries by Spanish TNCs.[49] This level of penetration is very low compared with the country's importance in Europe and the industrial potential of the recipient countries.

As in Italy, several Spanish companies have been acquired by foreign TNCs. The ownership structure of Spanish companies should be studied to identify the real decision-making divisions even if they have been transferred to offices outside Spain.[50]

(a) Outward FDI position by sector:

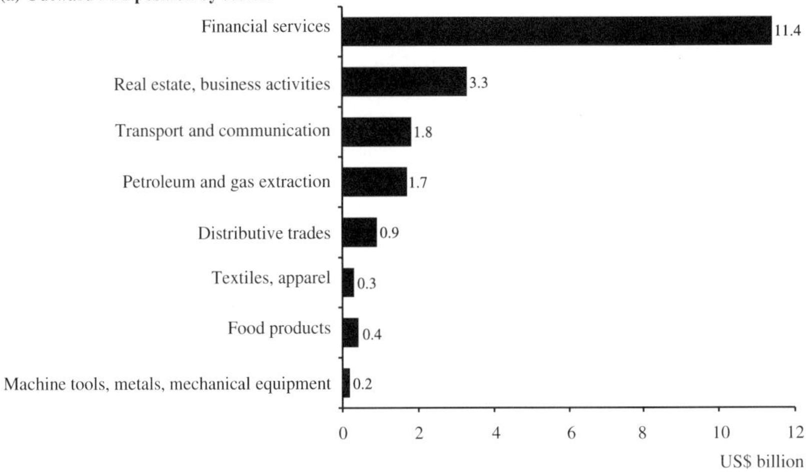

(b) Outward FDI position by emerging economy:

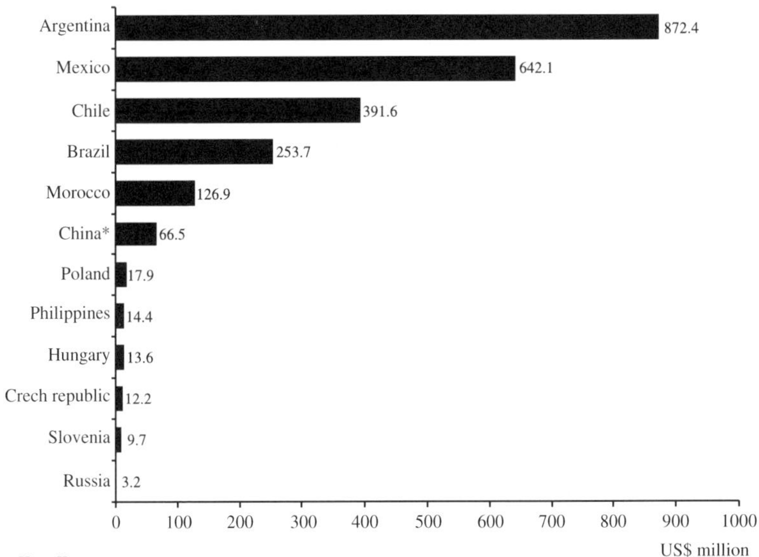

* Including Hong Kong

Source: Adapted from OECD, *FDI Statistics Yearbook*, 1997.

Figure 13.24 FDI performance by sector and region, Spain, 1996

13.4.4 The smaller OECD economies

Other important source countries for FDI into Russia are Austria, Denmark, Finland, the Netherlands, Sweden and Switzerland in Europe, and Canada in North America. Many well-known large and medium-sized TNCs are located in these countries and belong to a variety of sectors (Figure 13.25):

- telecommunications (Nokia from Finland, Ericsson from Sweden);
- automobiles (Volvo and Saab from Sweden);
- trucks and motorcycles (Steyr from Austria);

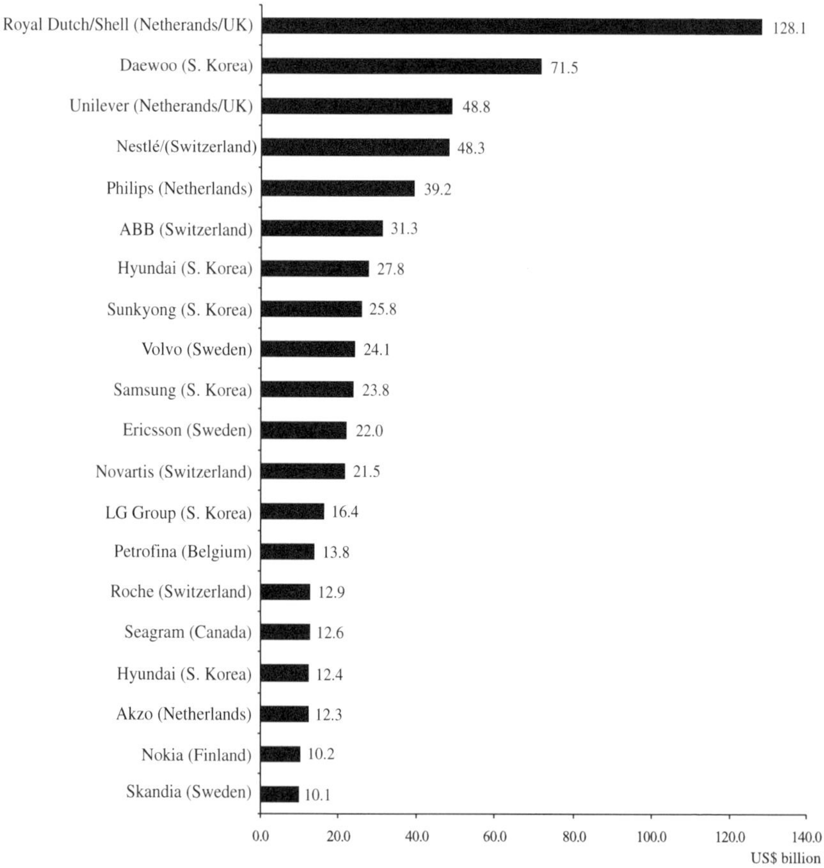

Source: *Fortune 500*, 3 August 1998.

Figure 13.25 Top industrial TNCs from smaller OECD countries by sales, 1997

- mechanical engineering (Voest from Austria, several machine tool companies from Switzerland);
- chemicals, pharmaceuticals (Novartis from Switzerland);
- fast-moving consumer goods (Unilever from the Netherlands/United Kingdom);
- food (Nestlé from Switzerland);
- beverages (Heineken from the Netherlands);
- toys (Lego from Denmark);
- beverages and alcoholic drinks (Seagram from Canada).

All these countries have relatively small domestic markets and their industries need to find outlets abroad. Most of the smaller OECD countries record much higher ratios of outward FDI/GDP than the larger countries (e.g. Netherlands and Switzerland: 6 per cent compared with under 2 per cent for France, Germany and the United States).[51]

The most populated of the smaller EU countries, the Netherlands, has many TNCs that could be canvassed for raising FDI to Russia. Some of the global players such as Philips (electronics, medical instruments), Akzo (pharmaceuticals, paints, chemicals) and the Anglo-Dutch TNCs, Unilever (fast-moving consumer goods, foods) and Shell (oil), have already made several investments in Russia, and are consolidating their operations or preparing for further expansion into regional markets. Many US, Japanese and South Korean TNCs have their European headquarters in the Netherlands[52] where important FDI decisions are taken for Central and Eastern Europe. The Dutch government is actively sponsoring FDI-related projects in Russia and other CIS countries.[53]

Swedish industry is clustered around a few large companies. R&D investment is high so that companies can innovate and raise productivity levels to compensate for high labour costs. But the domestic market of 9 million people is too small and Swedish companies have to look for opportunities in overseas markets where they offer vanguard technologies to foreign buyers. The multinationals have built global networks of sales and manufacturing subsidiaries. Throughout the 1980s, the Swedish economy suffered from over-regulation, high taxes and wages, and an overvalued national currency. Since the government began to reduce its role in industry and banking, Swedish firms have regained their competitiveness and have become global leaders in a number of technical sectors:

- telecommunications equipment, especially mobile telephony;
- aerospace;
- automobiles, trucks and buses;
- shipbuilding;
- household appliances;
- knock-down furniture and floor coverings;

- pharmaceuticals;
- high-tech chemicals; and
- wood processing and paper.

Switzerland is another important target for sourcing FDI. The country is mainly known as the world's leading financial centre, but this should not mask the fact that Swiss industry has developed advanced products, equipment and technologies over the past four decades. As in Belgium, the Netherlands and Sweden, the domestic market is small and companies have to seek foreign markets. Swiss products enjoy a high reputation in the following areas:

- watches and jewellery;
- specialized machine tools for cutting, drilling, metal shaping and all sorts of downstream applications such as textiles, packaging and electronics;
- pharmaceuticals and specialty chemicals;
- food processing;
- environmental control equipment;
- medical equipment; and
- insurance.

For the past three years, Switzerland has occupied a top position among foreign investors in Russia. Although part of these flows are most probably related to Russian capital returning home for more productive investments, the competitiveness of Swiss companies should not be underestimated. During 1991–97, Switzerland was one of the world's largest exporters of capital. On a per capita basis, about US$1440 were transferred abroad, which is 3–4 times higher than the larger EU countries, and 7 times higher than the United States and Japan.[54]

In Europe, Austria plays an important role as a natural interface between East and West. Historically, Austrian trading and barter companies were special mediators for western enterprises trying to expand their business east of the 'Iron Curtain'. The opening of borders benefited Austrian TNCs, who were quick at seizing new opportunities offered by privatizations and a general increase of demand for consumer goods and equipment. Hungary and the Czech Republic are the most popular destination countries. Larger companies such as Voest Alpine (steel, mechanical engineering), Maculan (construction), Weinberger and Heraklith (building materials) would have good chances to expand their sales and investments in Russia. In the past few years, many Austrian companies were acquired by foreign groups, mostly from Germany and the United States.

On the North American continent, Canada could also become a major investor in Russia with whom it shares many similarities. Canada is a northern hemisphere country, disposes of a huge landmass (second largest in the world in terms of territory) and has a large resource base like Russia. Its raw materials processing industries (wood processing, metal and raw materials extraction and processing equipment, chemicals) could supply technology and know-how relevant to Russia's needs. Many Canadian TNCs invest abroad indirectly under piggy-back schemes as suppliers of components or semimanufacturers to US multinationals (automobile or computer sectors). But Canada's own TNCs are in a position to take their own investment decisions and are committed to strengthen their position in the world's large emerging markets.

Finally, in Asia, South Korea could be another interesting target. Large TNCs like Samsung, Hyundai, Lucky Goldstar (LG) and Daewoo have remained foreign investors in spite of the crisis that hit the economy at the end of 1997. South Korea offers interesting technologies in automobiles, shipbuilding, electronics, metal working (iron and steel) and machine building.

Notes

1. Chapter 3.2.
2. Chapter 11.
3. Chapters 8.3 and 12.
4. G5: France, Germany, Japan, United Kingdom, United States; G7: G5 plus Canada and Italy.
5. Developing countries (e.g. Cuba, India, Vietnam, Laos) owe Russia an estimated US$100 billion. This outstanding debt was a major reason for Russia's admission to the G7.
6. Boris Rodyonov, 'Schto sulit racschirenyie Evrosoyuza na Vostok' [Eastward expansion of the European Union], *Modus vivendi*, 1(2), 1998.
7. An increasing number of US and Canadian TNCs use their western European headquarters for expanding their business eastward to Russia and the CIS.
8. A trade and investment agreement was signed between Russia and Italy on 10 February 1998 during President Yeltsin's visit to Rome. Since the financial crash, international policy-makers have turned their attention to general issues (e.g. debt repayment, customs, certification) instead of paving the way for FDI-oriented projects to save Russia's economy.
9. Chapter 13.4.3.
10. All EU countries together host tens of thousands of SMEs, which could be approached systematically by the Russian authorities.
11. Chapter 16.3.
12. Currently, Russia is in a weaker position in terms of inward FDI. In 1996, companies from the G5 countries invested much more in the other important LEMs: China, India, Brazil, Mexico. Increasingly, other emerging economies are signing bilateral investment agreements with Russia. A recent example is Argentina; see 'Argentina signs agreement with Russia', *Expert*, no. 24, 29 July 1998, p. 5.
13. For current economic performance and key players in LEMs, refer to Chapters 5–7 and 10.3.

14. AG. Wint, 'Public Marketing of Foreign Investment: Successful International Offices Stand Alone', *International Journal of Public Sector Management*, 5(5), pp. 36–37.
15. For FDI policies, refer to Part VI.
16. Mostly, publications are available only in the local languages; Russian FDI authorities will require the assistance of competent advisors 'to read between the lines' of certain studies and analyses.
17. Chapter 14.5.
18. Chapter 13.4.
19. For large players, such information can be obtained through annual reports. As most medium-sized companies are closely held private companies, this information is not often made public by the company, but could be obtained from secondary sources.
20. These three countries have more flexible economic policies, especially lower taxes and incentives for developing entrepreneurial activity.
21. Once a certain export volume is reached, a company must become an insider to remain competitive. FDI becomes the only viable means for a company to secure a market in the long term.
22. For details see Chapter 14.
23. Chapter 16.4.
24. For current FDI performance of leading industrialized countries, see Chapter 3.2.
25. *American Chamber News*, no. 3, September–October 1997, Moscow.
26. *Moscow Times*, 24 March 1998.
27. See Chapter 14.
28. *American Chamber News*, no. 3, September–October 1997, Moscow.
29. Services already account for over 70 per cent of US GDP.
30. The Commission was established in 1993 and is known by the name of Gore–Tschernomyrdin Commission (after the US Vice President and former Russian Prime Minister).
31. In this and the following chapters, the UN activity classification (ISIC Rev. 3) was used to allow comparisons between the United States, Japan and EU countries (where the standard is the EU NACE Rev. 1 classification). See Appendix: Definitions and Explanatory Notes.
32. The decision to accelerate integration was taken at the Summit of the Heads of State of the Americas that took place in Santiago de Chile during 17–19 April 1998.
33. M. Porter, *The Competitive Advantage of Nations*, 1990, p. 685.
34. *The Economist*, 'A Warm Russo–Japanese Bath', 1 November 1997, p. 28.
35. P. Lardner, 'Japan Warms to Russia', *The Moscow Times*, 15 September 1997, p. 6.
36. *The Economist*, 'Tax Reform Runs Late', 8 November 1997, p. 87.
37. Chapter 3.2.
38. Chapter 3.2.2.
39. Eurostat, *Les enterprises en Europe* [Enterprises in Europe], 1996.
40. Chapter 14.5.
41. The selection criterion for larger medium-sized players in industry should be the number of employees (preferably over 250 employees for industrial enterprises). See also European Commission, *Panorama of EU Industry*, 1996, p. 187.
42. Following the summit of EU heads of state and government on 2 May 1998 in Brussels, the common currency, the euro, was officially introduced for banking transactions starting from 1 January 1999.

43. *Handelsblatt*, 'BDI: Insbesondere der Mittelstand leidet unter dem Bonner Reformstau' [Medium-sized German firms suffer from stalling reforms], 13 November 1997, p. 8.
44. H. Simon, *Hidden Champions, Lessons from the World's Best Unknown Companies*, 1996. See also Chapter 4.2.
45. In 1997, the total debt of these companies amounted to DM27.5 billion. In 1998, a slight recovery was reported for the western *Länder*. See also *Handelsblatt*, 'Mittelstand-Konjunktur in West und Ost gespalten' [Mittelstand is divided between West and East], 15 April 1998.
46. Istituto Guglielmo Tagliacarne, 'Le piccole e medie imprese dell'industria alimentare italiana – caratteristiche strutturali e strategie competitive' [Small and medium-sized Italian food companies – structural characteristics and competitive strategies], 1997, p. 87.
47. Fiat's investment plan, which was postponed because of financial difficulties of the potential Russian partner following the August 1998 crisis, would have represented the largest FDI operation by an Italian firm (US$850 million), followed by Merloni (US$100 million) and Parmalat (US$12 million), according to a source at the Milan Chamber of Commerce, Moscow branch, in November 1998. See also *Yustizinform*, 'Diritto ed Economia in Russia e nella CIS', [Law and economics in Russia and the CIS], nos 1–2, 1998, pp. 5–7.
48. Important Spanish TNCs in Latin America are: Telefonica (telecommunications), Ficosa (automotive components), Banco Santander (banking), Mapfre (insurance) and Repsol (oil refining, filling stations).
49. J. Duran, *Multinacionales espanolas, algunos casos relevantes* [Spain's multinationals, selected case studies], 1996, p. 36.
50. Of the 100 leading exporting companies about half are subsidiaries of foreign multinationals. Approximately the same ratio applies to outgoing FDI. See J. Duran *Multinacionales espanolas, algunos casos relevantes* [Spain's multinationals, selected case studies], 1996.
51. OECD; *The Economist*, 'Foreign Direct Investment', 18 July 1998, p. 107.
52. After the United Kingdom, the Netherlands is the most important location for overseas TNCs, practically on par with Belgium (in terms of number of established companies).
53. 'Niderlandi' [The Netherlands], *Delovyie Lyudi*, special report, September 1997.
54. Société de Banque Suisse, *Le Mois* 1(2), 1998, p. 18.

14
Strategic Target Setting for Russian FDI during 2000–05

14.1 Compatibility with national goals

To be successful, an FDI strategy must be based on realistic objectives concerning annual inflows, targeted TNCs and sectors to be developed in Russia's key economic areas. Foreign investment operations must also be in line with Russia's overall socioeconomic goals and global aspirations. FDI targets should therefore be embedded in the national goals that determine the country's long-term orientation and ambitions. Compatibility between FDI targets and national goals will prevent discord between planned FDI actions and other important policy areas. In turn, clear FDI targets will allow policy-makers to adjust other policies, which would otherwise hinder FDI enhancement.

Target setting, a precondition for designing appropriate FDI instruments,[1] cannot be an entirely objective exercise. It is mostly related to the intentions and ambitions of decision-makers at the highest political level. Nevertheless, targets must be realistic and based on accurate analysis of the international environment (global FDI trends, competitor countries, TNC motivations) and Russia's potential to develop certain competitive advantages on the basis of key factors of success (industrial and locational strengths, including R&D capabilities and special labour skills). To set them, policy-makers need to answer the questions:

- What is needed?
- Where are we headed to?
- How do we attain the targets, through which policy instruments?
- Which institutional set-up is required to adjust targets and implement actions?

The FDI targets proposed here are meant to provide overall guidelines for Russian policy-makers. These targets are based on realistic assumptions about the possibilities offered within specific sectors of Russian industry (Box 14.1). They take into account the current FDI situation and its prospects worldwide,

Box 14.1 National goals for the Russian Federation

A: All-encompassing goals

- To ensure a long-lasting place for Russia in the ongoing process of international economic integration ('Russia must go global as a country').
- To promote close political cooperation with the United States, EU member states and all other leading nations.
- To accelerate economic integration within the CIS.
- To work towards the resolution of international conflicts.
- To promote Russia's membership in all important international organizations and fora.

B: Functional policy goals

Economic goals

- To rebuild technological competitiveness of Russian enterprises.
- To improve Russia's terms of trade by gradually shifting towards manufacturing and export of value-added goods.
- To stabilize and maintain the value of the Russian rouble.
- To pursue industrial restructuring and to carry on with privatization.
- To develop high-tech sectors and to become a world leader in knowledge-intensive industries of the twenty-first century.
- To continue with the conversion of the military–industrial complex.
- To upgrade efficiency and productivity through increased FDI.

Social and cultural goals

- To strengthen social cohesion by alleviating tensions, eliminating conflicts and ensuring internal security.
- To develop a social conscience and a sense of justice.
- To preserve national heritage in religion and the arts.

Military and security goals

- To safeguard the country's borders and territorial integrity.
- To develop good partnership with NATO.
- To pursue military cooperation with CIS and other neighbours.
- To promote the principles of nuclear nonproliferation.
- To revamp nuclear power plants and to dispose of nuclear waste.
- To maintain good-neighbourly relations with Asian, European and North American nations.

Environmental goals

- To protect Russia's environment and wildlife.
- To raise living standards through sustainable economic development on the basis of environment-friendly standards and technologies.
- To sanitize infested and environmentally hazardous regions (e.g. Baikal, Tyumen).

including sourcing options in the world's leading economies[2] and investment motivations of the world's leading TNCs.

14.2 Overall targets for FDI enhancement

During 1996–97, FDI inflows into Russia amounted to US$7.4 billion, corresponding to a per capita level of only US$25. Most international FDI specialists consider this volume far too low to upgrade industrial competitiveness. Annual FDI inflows could be raised to US$6–8 billion starting from 2000–02, and even up to US$10 billion after 2003.[3] The aim should be to reach an average annual per capita level of US$60–70 (Table 14.1).

Table 14.1 Targets for inward FDI to Russia, 2000–05

FDI indicators, ratios	Actual FDI	Expected FDI	Annual targets	
	1996–97*	1998–99	2000–02	2003–05
Annual FDI inflows (US$ bn)	3.7	4–6	6–8	8–10
Per capita FDI inflows (US$)	25.0	27–40	40–54	54–67
Accumulated inward FDI stock (US$ bn)	11.5	16–20	35–45	50–70
FDI/domestic investment ratio (%)	0.9	3–5	5–7	7–9
Inward FDI stock/GDP ratio (%)	1.1	2–3	3–6	6–9

*Annual average

This is a realistic target considering current global FDI trends, the country's large consumer market of 150 million and another 140 million in the adjacent Russian-speaking CIS economies and Russia's geographic proximity to the EU and the fast-developing economies of Central Europe (some of which will become EU members by 2002–03). Thousands of large and medium-sized enterprises from the EU face saturated markets at home in a context of intense competition. To avoid collapse or hostile takeovers, they will be compelled, sooner or later, to invest in the large emerging economies. Russia could attract a total of several billion dollars from its European neighbours.[4]

China and India do not enjoy the same locational advantages as Russia. Although China is close to technology-rich Japan, South Korea and Taiwan, it is (this also applies to India) geographically very distant from Europe, which represents the largest economic region in the world with a combined GDP of US$8500 billion (western and Central Europe). Russia should also try to attract more FDI from North American (Canada, United States), and developed and fast-growing Asian economies (China, India, Japan). These countries could contribute at least US$3–4 billion each year to industrial modernization in Russia.

If properly channelled, FDI from Europe, North America and Asia could bring about a second industrial revolution in Russia, similar to those in Germany, Japan or South Korea after the Second World War.[5] This presupposes that Russia gradually builds an FDI stock of about US$50–70 billion by 2008–10, which should be a feasible target considering the needs and absorption capacity of Russia's industry.

14.3 Sectoral priorities for FDI in Russia's main economic regions

Relaunching a large and diversified economy like Russia's cannot be done without setting regional and sectoral priorities. This ensures that investment efforts generate the highest yields through a cascade effect across the economy. The aim will be to encourage FDI in pillar industries so that clusters can be formed and sectors strengthened upstream (agriculture, raw materials processing) and downstream (e.g. market and nonmarket services).[6] Industrial sectors to be upgraded through FDI should be selected on the basis of a detailed portfolio and cluster analysis as described earlier,[7] and the analysis will need to take into account the government's pluriannual plans to raise domestic investment levels.[8] Basic sectors such as steel, cement, paper, machinery, chemicals, transport equipment and infrastructure will serve as a launching pad for the rest of industry and should receive capital and know-how through FDI to supplement inadequate state assistance and domestic private sector investment.

The recommended classifications for target-setting are the international standard industrial classification (ISIC)[9] or the derived European activity classification NACE Rev. 1.[10] Both classifications still differ from Russia's current industrial classification, but are expected to become the common standard of the Russian statistical services starting from 2000. The idea is to target key industries that would have a significant multiplier impact in an economically advanced country. Obviously, these priorities will need to be aligned with Russia's overall objectives of industrial development. Following further analysis of the target economies,[11] FDI authorities will thus have to define concrete targets for FDI by industry. The intention here is to develop a consistent methodology for setting targets based on priorities. Targets must be established and revised regularly on the basis of accurate information on the potential to attract global FDI.[12]

Regional priorities based on industrial requirements in the leading republics, territories and *oblasts* should be set to achieve balanced development throughout the Russian Federation. Regions with high development potential could act as motors for less centrally located areas. In other LEMs, a spillover effect from major regions to other parts of the country can also be observed:

- The growing importance of China's and India's inner regions, which are now considered possible investment destinations by foreign TNCs.[13]
- Mexico City still accounts for about 40 per cent of Mexico's GDP and FDI, although border regions close to the United States are becoming more important since the 1990s, owing to the *maquiladora* concept of turnkey plants.[14]
- The state of Sao Paulo, which accounts for 35 per cent of Brazil's GDP, has so far attracted over 60 per cent of inward FDI but its share is gradually falling to the benefit of other inner and coastal regions (e.g. Santa Caterina, Mato Grosso do Sul, Anapolis, Bahia, Maranhao).

In Russia, Greater Moscow currently receives about half of Russia's inward FDI, but an increasing number of foreign ventures are selecting other regions (e.g. St Petersburg, Nizhni Novgorod, Samara, Yekaterinburg, Kazan, Novosibirsk). Altogether, FDI seems to be more evenly distributed in China and India, where several economic centres have emerged (Shanghai, Kanton, Tianjin, Beijing for China; Mumbai, New Delhi, Bangalore, Hyderabad, Chennai, Calcutta, Pune for India).

The priority scale (Table 14.2) was derived from the significance of these industries for developing Russia's economy, but also their importance in major competitor markets, especially China, India and Mexico. The industries should be targeted for productive FDI rather than exports to meet growing domestic consumption. Thus, telecommunications equipment is given a B priority for manufacturing in Russia, although its use and application should be encouraged across Russia as a major pillar sector for infrastructure and communications. Initially, Russia will depend on high-tech imports, but it should slowly try and develop its own advanced sectors, especially those that have a large domestic market (e.g. telephone sets, office equipment, computers, software). As Russia's industrial tissue develops over the next 5–10 years, sectors classified as B will move on to category A.

Leading LEMs followed a similar path which was based on long-term target setting for key industries. It took China, for example, 10–12 years of industrial development before it could advance from light industries to more sophisticated value-added items including automobiles, aircraft, machine tools and telecommunications.

Mexico also developed its light industries to increase exports to advanced markets, thus helping the government earn the necessary foreign exchange for embarking on industrial diversification and development towards knowledge-intensive sectors. India chose a slightly different direction; it originally focused FDI more on its heavy industries (engineering goods, chemicals) and, with the introduction of the New Industrial Policy, increasingly diversified towards consumer goods and software development, in which it has now become a world leader.

Russia could skip the labour-intensive light industry phase as it has abundant raw materials and highly educated and skilled human resources.

Table 14.2 Priority industries to be targeted, Russia, 2000–05

Target sectors	2000–02		2003–05	
	P	T	P	T
Oil and gas	AA		AA	
Ferrous and nonferrous metallurgy	AA		AA	
Food and beverages	AA		AA	
Wood-based products: sheets, plywood, boards, carpentry, joinery	A		A	
Paper and related products, including publishing and printing	AA		AA	
Construction materials, including paints, glues and dyes	AA		A	
Basic chemicals, rubber and plastics	AA		A	
Pharmaceuticals	AA		A	
Furniture for homes and offices, sanitary systems	A		A	
Aircraft and aerospace technology	A		A	
Apparel, textiles, footwear and leather goods	A		B	
New materials of glass, ceramics and fibres	B		A	
Machine tools and equipment for various applications (e.g. agriculture, textiles, mining, construction), pumps, compressors, CNC machines	B		A	
Transport equipment: automobiles, trailers, buses, ships, locomotives, aircraft and spacecraft	B		A	
Office equipment, computers, and telecommunications equipment	B		B	
Equipment for waste disposal and water purification	B		B	
Domestic appliances	B		B	
Sports goods, musical instruments, toys, jewelry	C		B	

P: Priority industries to be upgraded through FDI (priorities: AA, A, B, C).
T: Targeted FDI in US$ million, to be determined by Russia's FDI authorities before each planning session.

It could directly move on to upgrading of traditional industries while simultaneously developing high value-added sectors. This will enable it to catch up with other LEMs[15] and regain its competitiveness *vis-à-vis* the leading industrialized countries. For practical reasons, policy-makers should concentrate first on sectors with a high FDI and revenue potential such as oil and gas, nonferrous minerals and metallurgy. Being a country rich in raw materials, Russia could thus attract sufficient financial resources to systematically develop manufacturing sectors and thus gradually diversify towards technologies for finished and high-tech product categories. A series of legislative proposals concerning the development of the raw materials sector through FDI have recently been put before the two Houses of Parliament (Duma, Federation Council). According to the Oil Consultation Forum, a think-tank and advisory committee based in Moscow, FDI volumes in this area could attain US$64 billion during 1998–2008, and US$200 billion during the next 50 years.[16] The funds raised through FDI could then be used to develop oil fields[17] and possibly other downstream manufacturing industries (e.g. plastics, paints, varnishes and glues).

14.4 Targeting FDI exporting countries

FDI source countries should be selected after comparing information on sectoral competitiveness, technology level, export performance and outward FDI.[18] G5 economies offer the best prospects as well as some other smaller highly-developed OECD countries (e.g. Austria, the Netherlands, Sweden, Switzerland). These countries, which together form the Triad regions, account for the largest trade and FDI volume at global level; they are characterized by relative economic stability and sophisticated technologies, and their companies need to expand abroad through FDI. They are therefore categorized as priority A countries (Table 14.3).

Table 14.3 Target countries for increasing inward FDI, 2000–05

Priorities	Target countries	Annual FDI target*
Priority AA countries (always important)	EU top five (France, Germany, Italy, United Kingdom, Spain); United States; Japan	US$5–6 billion
Priority A countries (short-term concern, 2000–02)	Smaller EU countries (Austria, Belgium, Finland, Netherlands, Sweden, Norway); other OECD countries (Switzerland, Canada)	US$2–3 billion
Priority B countries (medium-term concern, 2002–04)	Australia, China, India, Poland, Hungary	US$500–900 million
Priority C countries (long-term concern, after 2004)	Mexico, Brazil, Romania, Indonesia, South Korea, Taiwan, Malaysia, Singapore	US$300–500 million

* Targeted FDI in US$, to be determined by the Russian FDI authorities before each planning session. In this table, realistic targets are suggested for the period 2000–05.

The two main competitor LEMs, China and India, were categorized as priority B, as they are advancing rapidly. India has long-standing trade links and good political relations with Russia. Talks are under way to dollarize its debt and this should facilitate investments in and from Russia. In the longer term, other relatively successful economies in the Triad or its peripheral regions (the emerging economics of Central Europe, South America and Southeast Asia) could also be targeted.

Priority AA countries are those where FDI promotion and public relations should be undertaken immediately. These countries rank highest as investors and exporters, and almost all the global *Fortune* 500[19] companies are headquartered here. Even the medium-sized technology leaders from these countries, the 'hidden champions', have started investing outside their home markets. An information and monitoring system should be set up so that FDI specialists can effectively and rapidly reach target TNCs through promotion and communication campaigns.

Setting country priorities does not mean that projects from nonpriority countries should be disregarded. Smaller budgets may be made available, for example for selected information materials and conferences but costly campaigns and direct company visits should focus on the main markets. Targeting will enable funds to be channelled effectively according to national priorities. Work on priority B and C countries should begin gradually and only after a positive track record has been established in priority AA and A economies.

14.5 Targeting FDI players: top 200 and hidden champions

The most important step in target setting is the identification of the most suitable TNCs that will fill the technology and know-how gaps in specified sectors of Russian industry. Companies can be contacted directly (large TNCs) and indirectly (through industry associations for medium-sized players) in the major source countries.

The process can be divided into several steps:

Step 1 All large-scale TNCs in the targeted countries are listed independently of the sector;[20] they require separate target setting and canvassing efforts (e.g. direct visits and presentations).

Step 2 The leading medium-sized players are identified, preferably by key industries. They will form the second wave of investors after 2003–05.

Step 3 All important companies must be screened on the basis of the relevance of their technologies to Russia's needs.

Step 4 The companies should be contacted and sensitized about the business potential in Russia. An action is only successful if a targeted player embarks on the first phase of an FDI project in Russia.

Monitoring and canvassing are continuing efforts as new investors can emerge owing to changing situations in Russia and these countries.

The targeted 'large medium-sized' TNCs will preferably have the following profile:

- more than 500 employees;
- a turnover exceeding US$200 million;
- a global presence through own sales and production subsidiaries;
- portfolio of well-known brands;
- a solid reputation in the global market as providers of state-of-the-art technologies.

Preliminary corporate targets have been identified on the basis of sectoral structures and company size (large vs medium-sized TNCs). Although the targets presented here refer to companies in the top priority (AA) countries, the list should gradually be expanded to A and B countries as FDI specialists gain information on sector–country combinations in the major FDI source economies[21] (Table 14.4).

The diversity and large population of medium-sized TNCs make it more difficult to differentiate and target potential investors. Research and reconnaissance missions, and close cooperation with local experts are indispensable for shortlisting medium-sized players. Russia's FDI authority will be able to refine its targets and adopt a suitable incentives policy by monitoring changes in the corporate sector. It should therefore establish a modern information system supported by accessible databanks and company databases (including contact persons and main financial and nonfinancial indicators).[22] Timing and speed will be vital as technologies worldwide are limited and corporate decision-makers are already preparing to establish manufacturing facilities in the growing emerging markets. Once a TNC has set up a manufacturing unit in a specific market, it is tied to that market for a long time and that particular type of investment is definitively lost to a competing host economy. Approaching profitable market leaders in the main FDI source economies would give the Russian FDI authorities a head start over competing government agencies from other countries.

Table 14.4 Target industries and companies in priority AA countries, 2000–05

Target country	Industry	Type of TNCs	Main targets* (players)
United States	Chemicals	Large TNCs: Top 10	
	Automobiles	Large TNCs: Top 5	
	Food processing	Large TNCs: Top 20	
	Electronics, computers	Large TNCs: Top 10	
	Wood processing, paper	Large TNCs: Top 10	
Germany	Electrical goods	Large TNCs: Top 10 Medium-sized TNCs	
	Automobiles	Large TNCs: Top 5	
	Automotive components	Medium-sized TNCs	
	Food processing	Medium-sized TNCs	
	Construction materials	Large TNCs: Top 5 Medium-sized TNCs	
	Office supplies	Top-15 medium-sized players	
	Printing technologies	Top-5 medium-sized players	
Japan	Electronics	Large TNCs: Top 10 Medium-sized TNCs	
	Automobiles	Large TNCs: Top 5	
	Automotive components	Medium-sized TNCs	
	Chemicals, cosmetics	Large TNCs: Top 5 Medium-sized TNCs	
France	Automobiles	Large TNCs: Top 5	
	Automotive components	Medium-sized TNCs	
	Food processing	Medium-sized TNCs	
Italy	Chemicals	Large TNCs: Top 5 Medium-sized TNCs	
	Food processing	Medium-sized TNCs	

* Targeted FDI in US$, to be determined by Russia's FDI authorities before each planning session.

Notes

1. Chapter 16.
2. Chapter 13.
3. Chapter 11.1.
4. The basis for these efforts could be provided by the special partnership and cooperation agreement signed in 1995 between Russia and the EU, which ultimately aims at removing trade restrictions between the two regions.
5. For global FDI data see Chapter 3.
6. Although not studied specifically in this report, increased FDI in services is equally important. It will automatically benefit from industrial revival in Russia.
7. Chapter 12.3.
8. Chapter 9.2.
9. OECD, *Industrial Structure Statistics*, 1997, pp. 340–2.
10. Eurostat, *Statistical Classification of Economic Activity of the European Community, NACE Rev. 1*, Statistical Document 2E, 1996. See also Appendix: Definitions and Explanatory Notes.

11. Chapters 13 and 14.4.
12. Chapter 3.2.
13. Until the late 1980s, FDI was mainly directed at larger cities (e.g. Beijing, Shanghai, Guangzhou in China; Mumbai, Bangalore and New Delhi in India) or coastal areas (e.g. China's special economic zones; ports in Gujarat and Tamil Nadu in India). See Chapters 5.5.4 and 6.5.2.
14. Chapter 7.5.4.
15. Brazil and Indonesia, although much further away geographically than China or India, will increasingly compete in the world market with some of Russia's major industries, especially minerals and metals, but also aircraft, helicopters and pharmaceuticals.
16. V. Visloguzov, 'Para delitsya' [It is time to share], *Itogi*, 27 October 1998, pp. 50–3.
17. According to Duma experts, oil output could contract from 300 million t to 200 million t if FDI is not mobilized rapidly.
18. Chapter 13.4.
19. *Fortune* is a monthly US business magazine, which publishes enterprise rankings on an annual basis.
20. Chapter 13.4.
21. Chapter 13.2.
22. Chapter 16.3.

Part VI

Policy Instruments for Enhancing FDI during 2000–05

Introduction

The strategy concept for enhancing FDI inflows is developed on the basis of global FDI data and specific targets: FDI flows expected, main FDI ratios, type of foreign companies to be canvassed, national industries to be upgraded, and regions to be promoted.[1] The success of the strategy will depend on the definition of effective instruments and implementation of appropriate actions. The commitment of political leaders to industrial revival will influence regional, national and international decision-makers positively and create the expected impact. The vision of modernizing Russian industry must then be translated into realistic FDI policy formulation and implementation.

During 1995–96, Russian authorities formulated a national programme to raise overall investment levels with a view to promoting specific industries and regions in future years. The need to raise foreign investment levels was addressed for the first time, but a drastic fall in private sector profits eroded state revenue, forcing the government to make radical fiscal adjustments. Most of the measures proposed in the programme had to be postponed.

In 1997, the Ministry of the Economy launched a new development plan to be implemented by 2000. Compared with the 1995 programme, which also included the creation of a coordinating unit under the Ministry of the Economy and legislation to stimulate domestic and foreign investment, the new programme strengthened the role of the government in mobilizing and allocating resources. A central element of the programme was the launch of an extra-budgetary development fund to be financed partly through borrowings from the World Bank and the European Bank of Reconstruction and Development (EBRD). According to the target, state guarantees and loans for productive investment should have been increased to Rb50–60 trillion (US$8–10 billion, at 1997 prices) annually.

The assumption underlying the plan is that FDI will increase from US$6 billion to US$10 billion during 1997–2000, which already appears to be a very ambitious target (FDI has stagnated at US$2–3 billion since 1996). Moreover, no clear strategy was put into place to systematically approach leading large and medium-sized TNCs. Only 10 per cent of state investment finance for industry was allocated because of state budget constraints and financial difficulties of enterprises, which could not honour their coinvestment commitments.[2] Share prices fell to unprecedentedly low levels (by more than 10 per cent[3]) in early 1998, forcing the central bank to tighten the money supply, thus pushing up interest rates. The stock exchange crash, which followed in August–September 1998, aggravated the situation even further. For the government, the high cost of refinancing and strict IMF provisions left little room for implementing the plan. Besides, volatility of international oil prices (Russia's main source of foreign currency income) makes long-term planning difficult.

According to experts,[4] the plan laid out by the Ministry is too ambitious in relation to available resources. Neither does it distinguish between internally generated investment and FDI for industrial restructuring. The formulation and implementation of a separate FDI policy that fosters international cooperation and exchange of know-how among enterprises would ultimately improve the financial situation of economic operators in Russia so that they can contribute more effectively to a government plan for technological and social development. General framework conditions should be improved before concrete FDI policy instruments[5] can be implemented. The most important task will be to define the optimum combination of macro and FDI-related measures for achieving the desired results, with a minimum of resources and within set deadlines. The time factor is important in policy formulation and implementation.

Policy efforts for FDI should be directed to seven main areas:

- improving general framework conditions: law, taxation, public administration and macroeconomic indicators;
- offering incentives packages for important projects;
- assigning special zones for economic and technological development;
- carrying out proactive training, information, promotion and image-building campaigns in Russia and abroad;
- building an FDI advisory network;
- providing financial engineering for important industrial projects;
- establishing an internationally recognized FDI agency.

The measures described in the following chapters aim to raise issues and offer guidelines rather than strict policy mechanisms. A government programme to intensify investment must strike a careful balance of cultural, political, social and economic choices. Budgetary constraints and trade-offs with other vital socioeconomic issues (e.g. indexation of pensions, unemployment benefits, upgrading of the healthcare system, environmental protection) should be taken into account.

Notes

1. Chapter 14.
2. Urinson, 'Perspektivy investitionnoi aktivnosti' [Prospects of investment activity], *Ekonomist*, no. 2, 1997, pp. 3–9; OECD, *Economic Survey. Russian Federation*, 1997, pp. 128–9.

3. D. Polikarpov, 'Stock Market Crash Viewed as Long-term Crisis', *Moscow Times*, 30 January 1998, pp. 1–2.
4. Discussions at the CIS Inter-State Committee for the Economic Union (MEK), Moscow, during 1997–8.
5. Chapter 16.

15
Framework Conditions for Foreign Investors

Like other leading transition economies, Russia has adopted a series of instruments to improve the overall investment climate, but many investors are concerned about the grey areas which discourage decision-makers from planning and executing FDI projects. These areas are:

- political instabilities,
- malfunctioning of the judiciary,
- poor economic and infrastructure conditions,
- high energy costs,[1]
- imponderabilities with taxation,[2] and
- the still unresolved land ownership issue.[3]

In their efforts to facilitate matters for foreign companies, successive governments have formulated a series of draft laws which have been submitted for approval to the State Duma.

The future success of Russia's FDI policy will be determined by progress made in the country's macro-systems (Figure 15.1). These systems need to be improved through appropriate measures.

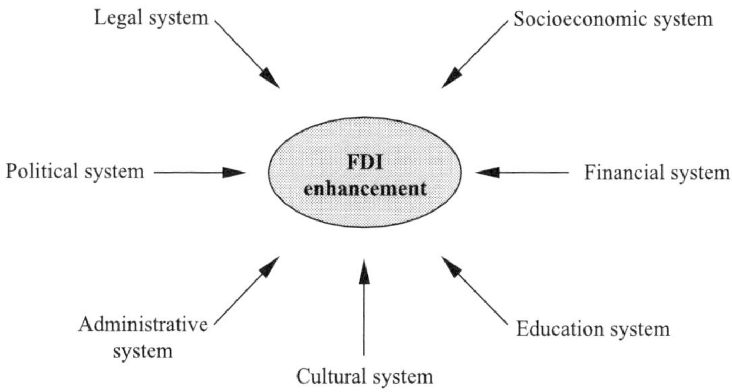

Figure 15.1 Macrosystems to be optimized for FDI enhancement

Table 15.1 Comparative analysis of macrosystems, LEMs, late 1990s

	Rating[a] (C I R)					Rating[a] (B M R)				
	5	4	3	2	1	5	4	3	2	1
Legal system										
Democratic constitutional framework: rule of law and democratic pluralism		I	R	C			M	R B		
Transparency of legal procedure		I	C	R				M B	R	
Credibility of courts		I	C	R			M	B	R	
Independence of judiciary		I	R	C				M B R		
Existence of unambiguous FDI laws		I	C	R				M B	R	
Legal protection mechanisms for foreign investors (expropriation guarantees, profit and capital repatriation, dispute settlement, etc.)		I	C	R			M	B	R	
Consumer, patent and trademark protection laws		I	C	R			M	B	R	
Equitable antitrust and competition law		I	R	C				B M R		
Political system										
Stable political leadership		C I	R				M	B	R	
Overall political stability		C I	R				M	B	R	
Low potential for civil disturbance		C	I	R			M	B	R	
Provisions for public safety and protection of corporate interest			C I	R			M	B	R	
Pluralism of political parties and leading interest groups		I R			C		R	M B		
Accord between regions and central government		C	I R					B M R		
Restrained union activity		R		C I			R	B	M	
Fair elections		R I			C		R	B M		
Good standing at international organizations		C	I	R			M	B	R	
Stable external relations with neighbouring countries			C I R				M B	R		
Political risk rating			C I R				M	B	R	
Administrative system										
Government efforts to reduce bureaucracy			C I	R			M B		R	
Transparent FDI screening and approval procedures			C I		R			M B		R
Integrity of public sector officials			C	I R				M B	R	
Effectiveness and motivation of national administration			C	I R			M B	R		
Economic system										
GDP annual growth exceeding 5%	C	I		R		M	B		R	
Low inflation (preferably below growth rate)		R	C I				B M R			
Stable national currency		C I	R					B M R		
Low tariffs and quotas on imports and exports			C	I R				M	B R	
Low unemployment level (maximum 8% of workforce)			I	C R					B M R	
Flexible employment rules including simplified procedure for work permits for expatriates			R	I C				B M R		
Good transport and communication infrastructure		R	C	I			R	M	B	
Adequate energy supply		R	C	I			R	M	B	
Existence of small and medium-sized businesses		I R	C				R	M B		

continued...

Table 15.1 (*continued*)

	Rating[a] (C I R)					Rating[a] (B M R)				
	5	4	3	2	1	5	4	3	2	1
Financial system										
Stable monetary and fiscal policies		C	R	I				MB	R	
Operational regional banking network		I	R	C					BMR	
Simplified foreign exchange transactions		R	C	I			MR	B		
Truly operational stock market across the country		I	C	R				MB	R	
Availability of local finance (leasing, venture capital)			I	C	R				MBR	
Education system										
Abundance of educated and skilled manpower	I	C	R					R	MB	
Innovative and decentralized education system enabling permament skill development		R	CI				R	MB		
Corporate and public sector investment in R&D and innovation			C	I	R				MBR	
Cultural system										
Readiness of local management to cooperate with foreign partners		I	R	C				BMR		
Openness to new tasks and technologies		I	R	C				BMR		
Intercultural and multilingual skills of managers		I	CR					BMR		
Proclivity of employees towards increased international integration		IR		C			RM	B		

C: China, I: India, R: Russia
B: Brazil, M: Mexico, R: Russia
[a] Scale: 5, highest; 1, lowest.

Starting from the early 1990s, practically all leading LEM governments have introduced new macro policies in an effort to make general framework conditions more conducive to foreign investors. They are in line with basic policy recommendations recently made by the World Bank following a survey of 3600 entrepreneurs in 69 countries. The Bank has established a list of basic government tasks for attracting FDI:

- building a solid legal foundation,
- maintaining macroeconomic stability,
- investing in basic social services and infrastructure,
- protecting the socially weak and the environment.[4]

The performance of competitor LEMs and their impact can offer useful lessons for Russian policy-makers. The following checklist could be used for coordinating and monitoring those areas where Russia scores low compared with other LEMs (Table 15.1). The assessment is based on survey results and discussions with European entrepreneurs.[5] The preliminary analysis shows that Russia is competitive in a number of areas. Concerted awareness and marketing campaigns that highlight success stories and planned measures would help Russia improve its image.

15.1 Determining the extent of macro guidance

While other LEMs such as China and India have adopted strict macro control mechanisms to guide the structural reform process of their economies, Russia relied almost entirely on the capability of markets to determine the allocation of its national resources. Partly influenced by foreign advisors from bilateral or its multilateral technical assistance programmes, partly because of its determination to abolish the command economy, the new Russian leadership embarked on a large-scale programme of enterprise privatization, price liberalization and economic deregulation during 1992–94. Although this 'shock therapy'[6] accelerated the introduction of a free market system, it could not prevent industrial and social decline.

Taking the US economic system as a model, the Russian State abruptly withdrew from most industries, assuming that private operators would adjust better to the new market economy. The government retained control of large state-owned and strategically important enterprises. All others had to face increased competition from within and outside the country. Despite privatization, the government's greatest challenge has remained: winding down the huge and unprofitable state-owned conglomerates for which markets no longer exist.[7]

Against the background of contracting national output and declining standard of living, the Russian government is now compelled to pursue a more moderate course of economic transformation based on targeted intervention to ensure the revitalization of critical areas of the economy. Internal political lobbying has risen in favour of higher government guidance and control, especially in industry, capital investment, foreign trade and high-tech projects. The new course is a response to economic problems and factory closures in the regions; it reflects the government's willingness to create jobs in industry and reduce overdependence on imported consumer goods.

This tendency now goes across party lines, and its proponents include most leading reformers who have transformed themselves into *gosudarstvenniki* (supporters of a strong State).[8] As President Yeltsin stated, 'for the transition to durable economic growth, economic freedom alone is not enough. What is needed is a new economic order',[9] signalling a shift from pure market mechanisms to a greater role of the State in the economy, but ruling out a return to Soviet-style planning.

The debate no longer centres on a radical choice between the two extremes of free markets and central planning; the issue in the coming years will be to determine an appropriate middle path, a Russian-style market economy. This would include a strong social component and the implementation of coherent industrial policies to enhance transfers of capital, technology and know-how through FDI. FDI can shape industrial development in Russia. It should be a strategic policy area where indicative government intervention enables foreign operators to establish mutually beneficial partnerships with local companies.

The implementation of a federal FDI policy implies close coordination of the policies of important ministries particularly in those areas that could negatively affect incoming investments (Box 15.1). Countries like China have understood

> the necessity of establishing macro-management bodies at central government level to coordinate economic policies and specific administrative functions of multiple commissions and ministries, each with their own power base and concerns over political territory, not to mention the various personalities who would definitely involve themselves in local and regional conflicts which arise when supplies must cross provincial boundaries.[10]

By contrast, Russia did not opt for such bodies as China's State Economy and Trade Commission or Japan's powerful Ministry of Industry and Trade (MITI).

Box 15.1 Major issues to be addressed by macro guidance

1. Overall macroeconomic instabilities.
2. Declining domestic and foreign investment.
3. Unbalanced industrial structure: disproportionately high ratio of heavy and military industry compared with light and high-tech sectors.
4. Declining competitiveness of agriculture.
5. Mounting interenterprise (triangular) debt leading to scarcity of funds and supply problems across the country.
6. Financial difficulties of large state-owned enterprises.
7. Long process of economic unification within the CIS.
8. Deterioration of the national scientific and research base and drastic reduction in both state-funded and private sector R&D budgets.
9. Economic potential disabled by insufficient macroeconomic planning and control.
10. Deteriorating social conditions and political instability due to divergent views held by the numerous parties.

Source: L. Nankuan, 'Ten Big Obstacles Preventing Economic Progress in Russia', *in Yearbook of the World Chinese Enterpreneurs* (in Chinese), 1996.

Russia could become an alternative FDI destination if it succeeds in projecting an image of overall socioeconomic stability and political credibility. Stability to foreign investors is associated with a government that shapes but does not interfere directly in the economic process.[11]

15.2 Promoting a transparent legal framework

Stable laws, reliable legal procedures and an independent judiciary are prerequisites for an evolving democracy. The weight of FDI-specific legislation and institutional enforcement are important indicators of a government's commitment to attract foreign investors, especially in a transition economy.[12] The scope of normative acts related to FDI reflects the current balance of power in legislative assemblies, but also the role of the executive and the importance it attaches to creating investor-friendly framework conditions.[13]

Russia's 1999 Foreign Investment Law provides ample protection and guarantees for foreign investors. Apart from property rights, which for foreigners are limited to the right to use (foreign investors cannot directly buy, own or resell immovable property within the Russian Federation), the sensitive areas related to FDI (protection from expropriation, freedom to repatriate profits and even capital in case of disinvestment) have been addressed by the authorities. To raise confidence levels, an ombudsman needs to be appointed to mediate and hear cases involving foreign investors. Foreign corporations should be kept informed about the favourable changes in the legal framework, particularly the new protection mechanisms. The relevant laws should be accurately translated and publicized through Russia's foreign missions. A consistent information, marketing and promotion effort would help foreign opinion leaders and corporate executives to understand the functioning of the Russian judiciary. These campaigns should highlight the increasing legal accountability of Russian partners and therefore constitute a major argument in favour of FDI.[14]

Russia should opt for a prescriptive rather than a proscriptive legal regime. Proscriptive regimes prohibit all activities that are not specifically permitted. Important LEMs like Brazil, India, Indonesia and Mexico have all abandoned such regimes which were based on the heavy use of licensing, high tariffs and complex nontariff barriers that overamplified the government's supervisory role and deterred foreign companies from making investment commitments. Liberal or prescriptive regimes, on the other hand, adopt the principle of 'everything is allowed except when it is specifically forbidden'. Such a regime is usually accompanied by attractive incentives and FDI-inducing policy mechanisms. In their current debate over the legislative enactment of a detailed catalogue of forbidden and permitted industries, Russian policy-makers will need to bear in mind that transparent and fair FDI legislation will be more conducive to the development of indigenous industrial capabilities than restrictive measures. In the future, Russian courts will have to apply internationally accepted principles, which are mostly enshrined in the new legislation:

- national treatment;
- protection of property and adequate compensation in case of expropriation;
- free transfer of profits;
- possibility of disinvestment;
- right to use land and other immovables;
- fair competition policy and antitrust regulations;
- effective consumer protection mechanisms;
- environment protection.

Land ownership remains a contentious issue for foreign investors in Russia. President Yeltsin is committed to removing this last vestige of communism and openly favours legalizing the private sale, purchase and rent of land. The President of the Federation Council, Yegor Stroyev, officially declared his support, thus taking a different stand than the majority of the Duma members who fear that fertile land areas could be taken by speculators.[15] Russian policy-makers will need to address this pressing issue. The current limitations on private land ownership are considered a major stumbling block not only for additional FDI, but also for the urgently needed reform of the strategically important agroindustrial sector.

15.3 Improving sociopolitical and macroeconomic framework conditions

Parallel to transparent legislation, foreign investors request a stable political and administrative system: low rotation in political leadership; reduction of tensions between the ruling party and opposition, and central and regional authorities; integrity, motivation and high competence of government officials; public safety provisions and protection of foreign interests; peaceful conflict resolution between employers and unions; transparent FDI screening and approval procedures; and so on.

On the economic front, a predictable environment is reflected by a set of key variables: sustainable growth; low inflation; rising purchase power; secure employment conditions; stable exchange rate of the rouble; and good infrastructure for transport, energy and telecommunications. Progress made towards gradual improvement of the general socioeconomic climate will contribute considerably to higher confidence levels within the international business community. Macroeconomic stability hinges on the availability of financial resources and solid banking structures. Foreign suppliers of indispensable equipment such as digital printing, plastics processing and other high-tech machinery to the Russian Federation will be able to extend their business into major economic regions if special installments or leasing contracts can be negotiated with potential buyers and their banks. Although substantial progress has been made in improving the financial and banking sector, more needs to be done so that foreign companies gradually turn to opening sales subsidiaries with technical after-sales facilities, which would accelerate technology and know-how transfer to Russian enterprises and increase FDI.

Multinational companies examine economic and political framework conditions closely before responding to tax incentives or other financial inducements offered by host governments. FDI enhancement policies should therefore be seen in a broader context of general socioeconomic progress based on coordinated measures in areas affecting foreign investors: taxation, labour, privatization, research, and overall macroeconomic and monetary adjustment. Business expansion into a market like Russia is interesting only if the sales or production facility fits into the investor's global production, sales, and technology networks. All stability and accountability criteria need to be met so that such a network can function effectively.

FDI policies cannot be seen separately from other major economic and industrial policy issues. There is undoubtedly a need to integrate investment, technology and trade policies with fiscal[16] and monetary policies as they have a reciprocal effect. Comprehensive and coordinated policies can restrain the volatility of FDI and allow it to develop to an advanced stage. Consistent macroeconomic stability and microeconomic competitiveness are both needed to maintain high levels of foreign investment.

15.4 Developing a national vision through intercultural understanding

Cultural attitudes and beliefs influence a people's way of life and thinking, its relation to time, change, authority, family, decision-making, risk and nature. Culture also shapes its general approach to more tangible socioeconomic realities: industrial organization, social cohesion and general policy-making. A society's value system determines its attitude towards innovation and entrepreneurship, and as such it is considered a determining factor for a country's global economic position and technological advancement.[17]

The formulation of Russia's economic advancement strategies and policy instruments is embedded in a typically Russian sociocultural context. In a democracy, this is partly reflected in the expectations of the electorate. The new global situation holds both opportunities and constraints for Russia's long-term development, but at the same time a high degree of intercultural awareness, openness and empathy is expected from decision-makers in government and industry when dealing with foreign partners from other sociocultural contexts. An FDI strategy that is insensitive or runs counter to cultural patterns at home and abroad is therefore bound to fail.

15.4.1 Attempting to categorize culture

Cultures in the contemporary world can be seen as combinations or variations of two types: individualism, and communitarianism or collectivism.[18] Individualism suggests an atomistic structure of society, emphasizing individual initiative, decision-making and achievement. Communitarianism, by contrast, takes a more organic view, stressing the value of belonging to groups and organizations that make decisions and protect people in exchange for their loyalty.[19] The fast economic development of the East Asian countries, for example, was driven by strong group orientation and interorganizational cooperation, emphasizing indicative state planning and strategic guidance. By contrast, Anglo-Saxon cultures favour *laissez-faire* policies characterized by the least possible State interference. Such economies are not guided by active industrial policies, and national governments mainly intervene when strategically important sectors are in danger of falling behind international competition.[20] The social market economy practiced in most countries of continental Europe lies between *laissez-faire* and strategic State macro planning of the Asian type.

Since the debate between communism and capitalism is over, international scholars speak of different versions of capitalism, specifically the individualistic variants of capitalism and the communitarian forms of capitalism.[21] This view, which, for example, classifies the German and East Asian economic models under the same category of communitarian capitalism,[22] may lead to a certain oversimplification of facts. Cultural attitudes and their impact on overall socioeconomic behaviour and performance are extremely complex and so diverse that countries cannot be grouped under two broad categories, but rather under more specific subcategories.

Numerous variations and combinations are possible, as reflected by the divergent foreign, industrial, fiscal and monetary policy approaches of France and Germany.[23] In another example, entirely different enterprise ownership patterns and political governance models have resulted in different industrial and FDI policy choices by India and China.[24] Communitarian value systems, typical of Asian societies, can vary significantly depending on whether they are conditioned by underlying Muslim (Pakistan, Indonesia), Hindu (India), Buddhist and Shinto (Japan, Southeast Asia) or Confucian (China, Taiwan) religious practices and beliefs. Similarly, the individualistic value system of the Scandinavian, Anglo-Saxon, Germanic and Latin countries has led to distinct economic models and industrial performance.

World cultures can be categorized by broad world regions (Figure 15.2)[25] although even this classification does not explain the differences in economic policy approaches of neighbouring countries such as Thailand and Malaysia[26] or South Korea and Japan, which have built their own type of capitalism during the twentieth century. Sociocultural subtleties should be

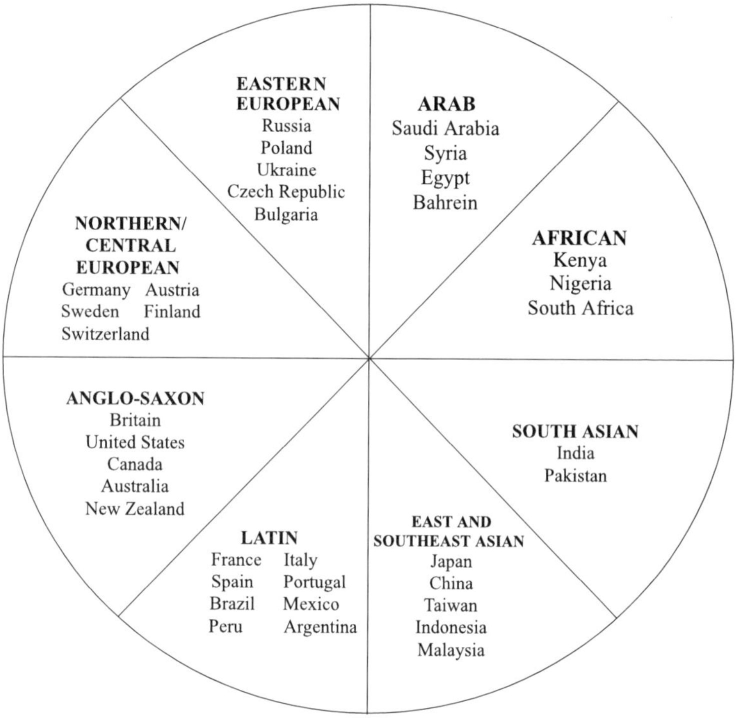

Figure 15.2 Categories of cultures by world regions

taken into account by Russian policy-makers when designing effective country-specific intelligence, promotion and canvassing instruments.[27]

15.4.2 Culture and economic growth

Opinions differ on the reasons and the extent to which certain cultural values encourage, or hamper, economic growth and development. Leading economists and business strategists increasingly question the influence of culture on a country's economic upswing.[28] Is the rise of the miracle economies in East and Southeast Asia, for example, attributable to inherent Confucian culture or rather to a series of historical coincidences and the pressure of foreign competition?[29] Opponents of the 'culture theory' point out how the very Confucianism that was blamed for holding back East Asia during the industrial revolution is now claimed to be the motor behind the economic miracles of the region; it is possibly held responsible today for excessive financial speculation and the currency crisis.[30]

Again, culture seems to have been the driving force behind the spectacular advance of the West since the 19th century. Max Weber[31] stressed the importance of the Protestant work ethic for economic progress. It focused on hard work, frugality and honesty, and was combined with demands for more liberal political rights. The combination brought success to largely Protestant northern Europe and North America which soon assumed world leadership.

But Catholic Italy and Spain became the fastest growing economies in Europe in the second half of the twentieth century. The dramatic rise of Latin America and many Asian economics in the past two decades in spite of traditional cultural and social values provides sufficient arguments that culture probably is a decisive factor, but it must be reinforced by favourable global economic and technological conditions.

No country enjoys the benefits of an eternal status quo. Western and northern Europe, for example, which had enjoyed decades of growth after the Second World War now face a socioeconomic crisis, rising unemployment and falling industrial competitiveness. Expensive social systems and a lack of political vision seem to be the cause rather than unfavourable culture-related conditions. Governments are called to rethink their policies and to question elements of their existing value system which have been outstripped by global developments. Socioeconomic systems periodically change, compelling the leadership to give a new focus to social values, including private initiative and entrepreneurship. These changes have to be based on the country's vision of its role in the world community.

Over the centuries, Russia has developed its own rules of social cohesion. Slavophiles still remark that 'Russia does not belong to any of the great families of mankind, neither to the East nor to the West'. This feeling of uniqueness, which is common to many nations, is reflected in the recently passed religion bill that attempts to protect Orthodox concepts and beliefs from other, mostly imported, religious and philosophical currents.[32] Some go as far as to say that Russia's 'collectivist-communist soul' represents a handicap for private enterprise and a free market economy,[33] although the rise of entrepreneurship in larger cities like Moscow and St Petersburg provide sufficient evidence for dismissing such generalizations.

Although each national culture is unique, communication is creating a global village leading to a certain convergence of views and attitudes, especially in business management and consumer behaviour.[34] However, mentality-related factors can be decisive in the success or failure of foreign investment projects where intercultural management issues become significant. They should therefore not to be overlooked while implementing a strategic FDI policy.

15.4.3 Intercultural management and adaptability to global changes

New challenges and situations make cultures dynamic. Exposed to global influences, cultural values are pressured to change, reorganize and adjust.[35] In a fast changing global environment, a country's leadership must forge a new national vision based on attainable goals for its citizens.[36]

Following the break-up of the Soviet empire, Russia is also in search of a new national identity, a *nationalnaya ideya*.[37] A viable vision for the twenty-first century will see further integration of the Russian people in the world economy. Targets for guiding domestic enterprises towards higher levels of competitiveness and technological progress would make this vision more realistic. If Russia succeeds, it could become a fast-growing economy. Culture is reflected in the education system. Strong intercultural understanding needs to be fostered right from school; this requires an education policy with a strong focus on foreign languages and teaching of other civilizations and cultures.

Russian managers will need to be prepared and trained for future collaborations with foreign partners. Training programmes on the 'soft factors' of cross-border management are now common in western Europe; they include special management and language courses for all staff levels (managers, technicians, support staff). Such courses should be included in university programmes.

The government has begun efforts to sensitize managers and students to international business. Under a new presidential scheme, for example, selected young Russians are sent abroad for top management training in the G7 countries.[38] For the five-year programme, travel costs are met by the Russian government, while host countries and enterprises cover training expenses. Unfortunately, the project was discontinued because of the financial crisis. The EU finances training of young Russian managers who are sent for practical training to European companies.[39]

Notes

1. Currently, oligopolist utility companies or *energos* provide industry with electricity and other energy (gas, oil) at much higher rates to compensate low household rates. A dispute between the federal and regional authorities has broken out over energy costs for industrial companies, which are major contributors to tax revenue and employment. See also *Moscow Times*, 'Regions Raise Storm over Electricity Costs', 1 November 1997.
2. Despite the new tax code which came into effect in April 1998, foreign investors still have to struggle with innumerable tax regulations and forms, which may differ from one region to another.
3. Chapter 9.4.4.
4. World Bank, *World Development Report 1997; The Economist*, 'The World Bank Says that Successful Economies need Effective Administration', 28 June 1997, pp. 93–5.
5. See also P. Fischer, *Enterprise Survey Evaluation and Conclusions for the Strategic Orientations and Launch of an International Consultancy Agency*, internal report, MESI, July 1996.
6. As opposed to the 'gradualist' approach of Hungary. See also Ph. Kotler *et al*, *The Marketing of Nations*, 1997, pp. 37–9.
7. G. W. Lapidus, *The New Russia. Troubled Transformation*, 1995; D. Yergin and Th. Gustafson, *Russia 2010*, 1995.

8. R. MacFarquhar, 'The Necessity of State Control', *The Moscow Tribune*, 27 September 1997, p. 8.
9. *The Moscow Tribune*, 'Hand of the State', editorial note, 27 September 1997, p. 8.
10. L. J. Brahm, *China as No. 1*, 1986, p. 82.
11. See examples of Germany and Japan in V. Golubovitch, *Ekonomicheskaya istoriya zarubezhnykh stran* [Economic history of foreign countries], 1998.
12. Chapter 9.4.
13. Presidential decrees were issued for important decisions on FDI (see Chapter 9.4).
14. Concrete case studies already exist of foreign companies that have won in legal proceedings against their Russian partners including regional entities (e.g. German cement manufacturer Knauf, see *Handelsblatt*, 'Grossinvestition in Russland gefaehrdet' [Large investments in Russia at risk], 19 October 1998).
15. *Moscow Times*, 24 September 1997, p. 5.
16. For details concerning the government's effort to improve the tax system, refer to Chapter 9.4 and A. Chmelev, 'A Balance Sheet on Russian Taxes', *American Chamber of Commerce Yearbook*, 1996–97, pp. 44–6.
17. R. Franke *et al*, 'Cultural Roots of Economic Performance: A Research Note', *Strategic Management Journal*, no. 12, 1991, pp. 165–73.
18. D. Hickson and D. Pugh, *Management Worldwide. The Impact of Social Culture on Organizations around the Globe*, 1995, p. 25.
19. G. Lodge *et al*, *Ideology and National Competitiveness: An Analysis of Nine Countries*, 1987, pp. 9–10.
20. As an example, the US government started intervening in the semiconductor market in the late 1980s, when Japanese companies were threatening the supremacy of the United States. As a result of this, many US companies (e.g. Intel, Motorola) joined forces under the aegis of the US authorities who also provided special R&D budgets and other financial assistance.
21. L. Thurow, 'Who Owns the 21st Century', *Sloan Management Review*, Spring 1992, p. 6.
22. Ph. Kotler, *The Marketing of Nations*, 1997, p. 113.
23. While France defends a rather interventionist doctrine in industry and the economy as a whole, German politicians are convinced that the State should limit its role to providing stable framework conditions. See also the article by W. Proissl, 'Die blockierte Gesellschaft' [The blocked society], *Die Zeit*, 19 September 1997, p. 41.
24. Chapters 5 and 6. See also D. Lal, 'India and China: Contrasts in Economic Liberalization', in *India in the World Economy*, 1999, pp. 71–99.
25. D. Hickson and D. Pugh, *Management Worldwide. The Impact of Societal Culture on Organizations around the Globe*, 1995.
26. Similar to banks in Arab countries, some of the state banks in Malaysia do not provide loans against interest (the Koran forbids this) but rather on the basis of share participation in a venture.
27. Chapters 10.4.3 and 16.4.
28. Davos symposium papers, 1997.
29. Confucianism had a political tradition of unquestioning loyalty to authority which hindered deep questioning and new institutions needed to break out of the feudal mould.
30. The stock exchange and currency crash that occurred in Japan (1996), South Korea (1997) and Southeast Asia (1997) was a direct result of an overheated economy which led to overspeculation.

31. German sociologist and political economist, 1864–1920.
32. The bill, which limits activities of most religious groups on Russian soil, was passed by the Duma, approved by the Federation Council and signed into law by President Yeltsin in September 1997. The new legislation stipulates that churches wanting to operate on Russian territory must prove their existence in Russia for 15 years, otherwise they are banned from founding schools, preaching in hospitals or prisons, printing or publishing religious literature or having their own media. See also *The Moscow Tribune*, 'Yeltsin Blesses Revised Religion Bill', 27 September 1997, p. 2.
33. *The Economist* 'Russian Exceptionalism', 15 June 1996, pp. 19–21; also see S. Filatov and L. Vorontsova, *Remaking Russia: In Search of a National Identity*, 1997.
34. For more details concerning the 'convergence thesis' as opposed to the 'culture-specific thesis', see also D. Hickson and D. Pugh, *Management Worldwide – The Impact of Societal Culture on Organizations Around the Globe*, 1995, pp. 277–9.
35. M. Porter, *The Competitiveness of Nations*, 1990.
36. N. Dhokalia, 'The Marketing of Development: An Exploration of Strategic Forms of Development', in *Marketing and Development: Toward Broader Dimensions*, 1988, pp. 63–78.
37. *Moscow Times*, 'Yeltsin Wants a New Idea for Russia', 3 August 1997; *Süddeutsche Zeitung*, 'Eine Idee für Rußland bringt 3000 Mark' [An idea for Russia earns 3000 marks], 3 August 1997.
38. *Moscow Tribune*, '"Russia's Finest" Sent Abroad', 6 February 1998, p. 1.
39. TACIS Productivity Initiative (PIP) and Work Attachment Program (WAP).

16
FDI-related Policy Instruments

Favourable legal, macroeconomic and political framework conditions alone cannot directly influence FDI inflows; they must be supplemented (Figure 16.1) by:

- special incentives for FDI in designated industries and regions;
- creation of special development zones to promote particular regions or technologies;
- establishment of an investor information system;
- promotion and image-building campaigns;
- advisory services intended for the management of leading large (the world's top 500) and medium-sized TNCs (hidden champions);
- financial engineering; and,
- creation of an FDI agency, which serves the regions.[1]

These FDI measures should be planned at federal level in consultation with regional authorities.

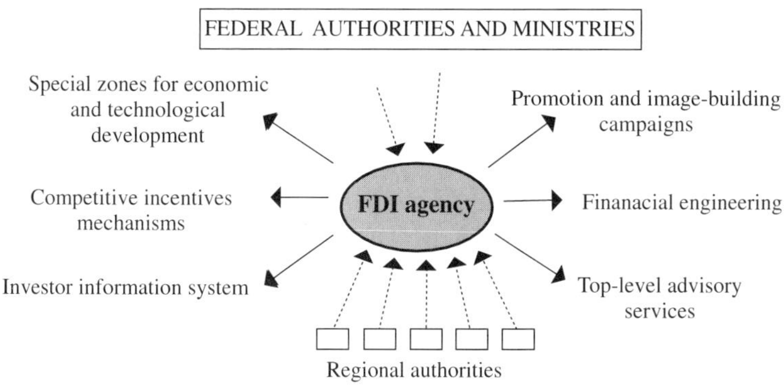

Figure 16.1 FDI-related instruments

16.1 Designing incentive mechanisms

Attractive incentives add to the advantages of overall sociopolitical stability and long-term sales prospects offered by an economy. The incentives package should be transparent and compatible with expectations of investors, and it should also compete with schemes offered by competitor economies. Incentives can become an important factor in favour of Russia once corporate expert teams have shortlisted it as a possible investment site. An attractive incentives package also facilitates the task of FDI promotion specialists responsible for international image-enhancement campaigns. On the other hand, too many incentives can have counter-productive effects. As countries bid for FDI, they tend to give away many concessions (financial incentives, long tax holidays, etc.). Such measures, taken on political rather than economic grounds, strain government budgets. While the exigency of acquiring technology and capital for rapidly building a comparative advantage may justify such measures, they should be counterbalanced by antimonopoly and takeover laws to prevent the rise of oligopolies and consequent market distortions.

Incentives should be an essential but not the only component of an FDI policy. The incentive schemes need to be adjusted according to the strengths and FDI requirements of key industries and regions.

16.1.1 Types of incentives

Incentives serve to win over foreign investors who are assessing the advantages of various destinations. Designed to attract and retain FDI, incentives consist of specific measures aimed at either increasing the rate of return of a particular FDI project or to reduce its costs or risks. The scope and type of incentives generally reflect the objectives and financial possibilities of host governments. The most important types are fiscal incentives and direct financial contributions (Box 16.1).

A growing number of transition economies propose specific incentives geared to priority industries and regions. Often, special qualifying conditions or restrictions such as export, employment, and training requirements are attached to these incentives granted to TNCs. These restrictions can deter foreign investors in spite of sometimes generous overall incentives. Restrictions are generally introduced after an industry has been successfully established and domestic companies become competitive.

China and India, for example, offer generous tax holidays for joint ventures and wholly-owned subsidiaries in high-tech industries with high export, employment, technology and local sourcing content. However, sectors having well-established local industries (most consumer goods, food and light engineering sectors) do not benefit from such incentives as the authorities want to keep a level playing field for both domestic and foreign players (Table 16.1).

Box 16.1 Types of FDI incentives

- **Fiscal incentives.** Measures aimed at reducing the general tax burden and payback period of the investment (e.g. tax holidays, tax breaks in the form of reduced corporate or value-added tax, abolition of certain taxes such as property and commercial tax).
- **Financial incentives.** Direct payments and contributions by national, regional or local administrations of the host or home[2] country to attract important projects or to direct investment flows; partial reimbursement of investment in land, buildings and equipment (in France); offsetting R&D expenditure against profits made in the same year (in Ireland).
- **Nonfinancial incentives:** Measures meant to improve technical and operational conditions for foreign companies, for example:
  - Public funding for infrastructure facilities such as special access roads, railway tracks or port facilities; improvement of the telephone, water supply and drainage systems, energy supply; etc. (in China, India, the United States).
  - Funding of special training programmes for the local workforce (in the United Kingdom).
  - Possibility for foreign companies to participate in open tenders on equal terms as domestic enterprises (in Brazil, Indonesia).
  - Investor tours and study visits paid by the host country (in France).
  - Speedy approval mechanisms: fast-track approval through single-window clearance within a one-stop agency (in India, Mexico, Poland).

Faced with increased competition and trade liberalization requirements by international bodies, LEMs are not as rigorous about export performance as before. Like other performance requirements, such conditions are proscriptive. Experience shows that better results are obtained by inducing investors to bring technology and know-how that will produce internationally competitive products, which could then be profitably exported.

16.1.2 International incentives practice

Both emerging and industrialized economies compete to offer incentives that will move investment decisions in their favour; the most common practice is to offer fiscal incentives in the form of tax exemption or alleviation. Direct financial assistance is also given for important investment projects that promote regional development and new technologies. Budgetary constraints may compel governments to focus more on large ventures rather than medium-sized TNCs.

Table 16.1 Conditions for FDI in mature industries, LEMs

Type	Conditions	Trend
Financial conditions	Mandated minimum exports	↗
	Foreign exchange control	→
	Capital repatriation restrictions	↘
	Profit repatriation restrictions	↘
	Dividend balancing against exports	↗
	Compulsory foreign financing	↗
Employment and supply conditions	Minimum employment levels	↗
	Restricted appointments of foreign managers to board	↗
	Compulsory staff training	↗
	Restrictions on work permits for foreign personnel	→
	Limits to foreign supplies (local content rule)	↗
	Mandatory minimum local R&D	↗
Ownership conditions	Equity ownership limitations	↗
	Restricted diversification/expansion	↗
	Limited protection of intellectual property rights	→
	Prohibition for foreigners to own land/ business premises	↘

Trend: upward ↗, stable →, downward ↘

Significant financial incentives can be offered only by countries with a strong revenue base. Ireland, the United Kingdom and several US state governments managed to attract leading blue-chip TNCs by offering low-interest grants, partial reimbursements of expenses for land and buildings, and financing of infrastructure (access roads and railway, power and water systems, etc.). In most cases, FDI had significant impact on local employment and regional development (BMW plant in South Carolina, Mercedes Benz plant in Alabama, the Siemens R&D facility for telecommunications in the United Kingdom, Seiko in France[3]). Similarly, Ireland managed to overcome its economic recession of the early 1980s by proposing fiscal concessions to leading US, Japanese, and European companies in information and communication technologies.

To save costs, authorities increasingly prefer to offer nonfinancial incentives (e.g. open tenders, access to government orders) and special loan facilities for certain types of investments. California, for example, provides pollution control and public infrastructure financing, small-business loan guarantees, low-interest environmental loans, direct loans for hazardous waste reduction, and recycling loans.[4] Many LEM governments also combine nonfinancial and direct incentives by adjusting certain schemes according to capital needs and overall national objectives (Table 16.2).

Incentive schemes and priorities in the six competitor LEMs have remained stable since their reform processes were launched in the early 1990s. In addition, regional authorities may offer their own incentives. In

Table 16.2 FDI incentives offered by LEMs

FDI incentive	Brazil	China	India	Indonesia	Mexico	Russia
Low corporate tax	+	0	0	+	+	++
Tax holidays	+	+	+	+	+	0
Accelerated depreciation	+	+	0	+	+	0
(Re)investment allowance	0	0	+	0	+	0
Reduced social security contributions	+	0	0	0	+	0
Lower value-added tax	+	0	0	0	+	+
Exemption from import duties for essential inputs	+	+	+	+	++	+

++ very important, + important, 0 indifferent.

India, for example, certain states such as Andhra Pradesh and Gujarat can extend tax holidays and the duration during which machinery can be imported duty-free.

Among the CIS countries, Belarus, Kazakhstan, Ukraine and Uzbekistan have turned investor friendly to divert FDI that would otherwise be destined for Russia. Uzbekistan and Ukraine intend to build an automotive industry, and Ukraine passed a special Law on the Stimulation of Automobile Production in 1996. For a period of 10 years, TNCs investing at least US$150 million in the industry are to be granted substantial tax concessions and other incentives. Daewoo from South Korea intends to pay in the required minimum sum as charter capital, and until 2003 the company wants to invest an additional US$1.3 billion to expand its capacity to 255 000 cars. Half the output will be exported, mainly to Russia.[5] The 1996 Law has already aroused the interest of other global car makers as FDI will be exempt from value-added tax, and import duties and customs tariffs on equipment and parts used in production.[6] Foreign companies will also be given breaks for corporate and property taxes.

In a recent agreement between China and Kazakhstan to develop three oil fields in northwestern Kazakhstan (investment: US$9.5 billion), the Kazakh government allocated land for the pipelines and guaranteed safety.[7] Fiscal concessions were also made to the Chinese side. Kazakhstan pursues an ambitious plan to become the world's sixth largest oil producer by 2010, and it has already attracted several billions of US dollars in investments.

Regional and local authorities show considerable imagination in designing incentives. French local authorities, for example, sell or rent land and buildings on generous terms or partially reimburse the cost of a new building, warehouse or other immovables. In case of important industrial projects, the Délégation à l'Aménagement du Territoire et à l'Action Régionale (DATAR) subsidizes up to 25 per cent of investments in land, buildings and equipment acquired during the first three years of an operation. Criteria for eligibility are the location (generally, backward regions are promoted), the number of jobs created (minimum of 20 in the first three years), and the financial capacity of the investor (turnover of at least FF300 million, investment of more than FF20 million during three years).[8] The French government also finances investor tours; representatives of large TNCs are invited for a fact-finding mission, which includes a three-day holiday and a meeting with the Minister of Commerce.[9] Belgium and the Netherlands also organize similar programmes for important foreign investors, who receive ministerial backing for their projects.

Usually, an integrated package of incentives is more effective than independent, disjointed measures. The Irish authorities managed to attract US$5 billion of FDI during 1994–96[10] by offering an incentives package to foreign companies engaged in manufacturing (Box 16.2). Similarly, Poland offers a variety of fiscal and nonfiscal incentives.[11] These include tax benefits up to 100 per cent of capital provided that the foreign investors' capital contribution exceeds €2 million (already calculated in euro in preparation of their integration into the EU). Further tax breaks are given to businesses that import technology, but export a minimum of 20 per cent of their goods and services, especially if they are located in designated development zones. Exemptions from corporate income tax (currently 40 per cent, 5 percentage points higher than in Russia) can last up to three years after start-up and are linked to a number of clearly set criteria.

16.1.3 Which incentives strategy for Russia?

Certain guidelines can be drawn from the experience of other countries for developing a Russia-specific incentives package:

- corporate preferential tax not above 35 per cent;

Box 16.2 Ireland's FDI incentives package, 1997

- Corporate tax reduced by up to 10 per cent for up to 5 years in target industries.
- Technology acquisition funds of up to 50 per cent, subject to a maximum of IR£250 000, for any one project.
- R&D funding up to 50 per cent of the total amount but subject to a maximum of IR£250 000, for any one project.
- Rent subsidies of up to 45 per cent (up to 60 per cent in designated areas).[12]
- Grants for fixed assets (up to 45 per cent; 60 per cent in designated areas), employment (full cost of a negotiable number of workers for a determined duration), management training (for a determined duration) and project feasibility studies (up to a maximum of IR£15 000 per project).

- tax holidays for an initial period of two years, after which rates are scaled up each year until full domestic treatment is applied after a period of five years;
- accelerated depreciation of assets according to internationally recognized accounting standards;
- a special customs regime for imports of machinery or spare parts;
- assistance from regional authorities for selecting the most appropriate investment site and availing the best possible facilities (e.g. access to main road, electricity supply, water supply and drainage);
- special treatment for FDI in designated areas;
- a one-stop agency to accelerate approvals, particularly for investments with socioeconomic impact and exceeding a certain value (US$30 million in China, for example).

Larger TNCs expect privileged treatment before committing large investments for modernizing existing plants or establishing new production facilities in Russia. Not all will agree to reinvest generated earnings in the country. Most of them expect to be able to remit profits to their home countries without restrictions, or to repatriate funds in case they decide to wind down their operations.[13] Accelerated depreciation schemes and special allowances for reinvestment represent additional fiscal incentives.

Current programmes in Russia are too general and not industry-specific. Under pressure from international donors, the government is compelled to raise domestic tax levels instead of using its resources for giving tax breaks for productive FDI. Conversely, regional authorities tend to make excessive concessions including long tax holidays and the right of duty-free imports over longer periods. Often these schemes, which aim to maintain industrial output and employment levels, have to be repealed when local enterprises complain about unfair competition. The damage can be significant for all parties involved: the foreign investor, the workforce and regional authorities.

Incentive proposals must be transparent and understandable to newcomers; they should not be modified too frequently without justification.[14] Clarity will be improved by streamlining incentives and by defining high-priority industries targeted for modernization. Incentives should be based on objective priorities – real advantages for the Russian economy, the respective industry and overall regional development – and not on the size of the investor. Large TNCs with greater bargaining power should not be favoured automatically over small investors.

TNCs expect incentives to be transparent, nondiscretionary and stable over time. Too many restrictions, case-by-case approvals, exceptional incentives for certain investors and lengthy delays in investment approvals may divert potential FDI to other emerging markets.

Decisions on the types of FDI incentives should be taken after careful deliberations with executing authorities at federal, regional and local levels because measures such as lower tax rates, duty-free imports, and special depreciation allowances may involve long-term gains, but also short-term losses. The impact of each incentive needs to be studied, and the measures should be planned and coordinated carefully so that negative effects are minimized and costs for local communities kept below their long-term benefits. Competition between regions, if not controlled, leads to excessive and uneconomical concessions. Similar tax and other incentives should be offered when regional administrations have identical sector development priorities. The Federation Council could serve as a forum where regional authorities can align their programmes to adopt measures that meet national objectives. Special incentives packages could thus be designed for remote or backward regions and the respective promotional bodies actively encouraged to participate in the national effort of coordinated FDI promotion.

Industries that already attract investments because of their high potential do not need further incentives. In the military–industrial complex or in the oil processing sector, for example, numerous foreign corporations are keen on acquiring controlling stakes of profitable local companies even without incentives. Industry-specific inducements to FDI should be accompanied by performance requirements. For example, incentives could be made conditional on the export of a certain proportion of output, transfer of state-of-the-art technology or training programmes for local employees and managers. Export criteria could be introduced to prevent companies exclusively interested in capitalizing on the domestic market, which would not improve Russia's balance of payments. In India, for example, foreign investors are expected to state their commitments to socioeconomic development when they apply for government approvals.

A dual regime of incentives could be adopted: a general regime with few limitations but no special incentives, and a special regime for companies investing in priority areas. Investors benefitting from the special regime would be given more generous incentives, but they need to be selected according to rigorous criteria. Foreign companies that bring other investors could also be rewarded depending on the importance of the mediated investment.[15]

Duty exemptions should be extended to imports of machinery and equipment that are not available in Russia. Equipment imports should be exempt from duty for both foreign and domestic investors to the extent that these are not available locally and can be offset against exports. The duty structure for raw materials and semi-manufactures should be rationalized to avoid anachronistic situations; for example, import duties on linoleum floorings are lower than on the PVC raw material, which hinders development of potentially competitive local industries.

The incentives package should be reviewed and evaluated periodically. The financial and human cost of each incentive (input) should be regularly compared with the results obtained (output).

Once the incentives are defined, they should be presented clearly through appropriate promotional materials, seminars and similar investor awareness actions. Broad categories of incentives could be highlighted in a specific FDI master plan or agenda,[16] administrative capacities also need to be sufficiently upgraded to implement and monitor incentive schemes effectively.

16.2 Assigning special zones for economic and technological development

16.2.1 Trends in international zone development and the role of regional authorities

Many industrialized and emerging countries have created special development zones (SDZs) for foreign investors. These areas offer excellent technical and industrial infrastructure to expand business: a skilled workforce, easy access to airports and motorways, banking and financial institutions, easy permit and approval procedures, a business-friendly atmosphere and privileged treatment in the form of incentives. In the 1980s, when zone development schemes were launched in emerging economies, foreign investors could qualify only if they established an export-oriented venture. Today, most host countries allow TNCs to select their own type of operation including production and services for the domestic market or purely strategic investments. The underlying idea is to transform these 'islands of development' into technological hubs with spillover effects into the surrounding regions.

The level of involvement of central and regional authorities in the establishment of such zones varies with the devolution of power to the regions. In China, every development park needs prior approval from the central government, whereas more federally structured states (e.g. India) design their own schemes, sometimes in collaboration with private (including foreign) developers. In Brazil, Indonesia and Mexico there is also a tendency to decentralize the decision-making process, but to retain the promotion function for the central government which can make use of its international network of embassies and trade commissions.

Central authorities can assist in obtaining financial and technical assistance for bilaterally funded ventures, such as China's Dalian Development Zone established in collaboration with Japan, or its Suzhou Science Park partly funded by Singapore. Bilateral technology parks between emerging and industrialized countries are an interesting option for LEMs, especially if the foreign partner has many suitable large-scale and medium-sized investors. The Ukrainian government, for example, signed a collaboration agreement with the German authorities to set up three technology development zones in Kiev, Kharkov and Zaporozhye.[17] The aim is to encourage partnerships between German manufacturers and dynamic local enterprises for jointly developing new products and technologies.[18]

In a large economy like Russia coordination at federal level would prevent unnecessary duplication and competition between regions. However, the federal park development concept should consider the requirements of the different regions.

Industrialized countries are increasingly decentralizing initiatives for zone development. The State of California, for example, has undertaken an innovative Enterprise Zone Program to foster partnerships between the state, local governments and foreign investors (Box 16.3). Thirty-six areas have been designated through special incentives, which are not available to investors outside the zones.

Box 16.3 California's Enterprise Zone Program, 1997

- Tax credits for sales tax on the first US$20 million of purchased machinery.
- Hiring credits for wages paid to qualified staff during 5 years.
- 15-year carryover of up to 100 per cent of net operating losses.
- Deduction of interests for loans from corporate tax.
- Reduced costs for land and buildings.
- Exemption from fees for construction.
- Expeditious approval of plans and issuing of permits by authorities.
- Assistance in personnel recruitment.
- Attractive financing facilities and low-interest revolving loans through the local banks.

16.2.2 From export processing zones to high-tech parks with sector focus

Export processing zones were popular in the 1980s among cash-poor countries with abundant cheap labour, their purpose being to accumulate foreign exchange reserves by inducing foreign investors to export their entire output to overseas markets. Export development zones are giving way to other schemes now that more governments are shifting away from low-tech, labour-intensive industries to know-how and technology-intensive industries in a more competitive global context (Table 16.3).

Emerging countries realize that science and high-tech parks, which focus on R&D, the supplier–buyer relationship and local skill development, can contribute more to their objective of establishing value-added and less-polluting industries. Such high-tech parks were started in the industrialized countries and are mostly located near larger agglomerations as they require research facilities, educational institutions and skilled manpower. The best-known park is Silicon Valley near Los Angeles, California, which acquired international fame in the 1980s when high-tech multinationals such as

Table 16.3 Zone development strategies, emerging markets, 1980s and 1990s

Raw materials-oriented FDI	Export- or labour-oriented FDI	Market-oriented FDI	Strategic FDI
Concessionary areas	Export processing zones, free trade areas	Centres of excellence, sector-specific high-tech parks	Diversified parks with high R&D component
1980s, large countries	1980s, 1990s for smaller countries	1990s, all countries	1990s, large countries

Microsoft, Compaq, Intel and Motorola opened their research centres there. Since then, other parks have been opened in many other countries, including the Patras and Thessaloniki parks in Greece, the Nagoya and Osaka high-tech parks in Japan, France's numerous *technopoles*, and the Technologie parks of Bavaria in Germany.

As the number of science parks increases, they tend to specialize in specific industries or technologies. In France, for example, health and telecommunications research is concentrated in Sophia-Antipolis on the outskirts of Nice, whereas computer-aided manufacturing techniques are developed in Angers (Figure 16.2). Agroindustry parks are located near agriculture universities and research centres in Montpellier, Clermont Ferrand and Reims. *Technopoles* have contributed to the creation of new enterprises and overall regional development. In Brest over 40 new companies were founded during 1991–97, creating more than 1000 jobs. Sophia-Antipolis, one of the oldest science parks in Europe, has attracted some thousand enterprises from all over the world, providing work for more than 20 000 people in the park itself and the nearby city of Nice.

The concept of the science park has also been adapted by Germany and Italy. Several such parks are located in Germany's southern high-tech belt near the regional capitals of Munich and Stuttgart. In northern Italy, various city municipalities (Bergamo, Brescia, Como, Florence, Prato, Modena) have implemented or are studying proposals for similar concepts. The Italian 'industrial district' scheme is more oriented towards innovation and cluster building (e.g. leather–shoes, textiles–apparel, wood processing–furniture, metal processing–household products) among national SMEs and promoting 'Made in Italy' abroad rather than attracting FDI.[20]

Sectoral specialization implies the existence of a domestic client base, a good network of supplier firms and the availability of infrastructure, including research facilities. The positive effect of sector-specific parks on technological development, advanced education and tax generation incites a growing number of regions and cities to do the same.

In Germany, the municipality of Hamm, a medium-sized town located between the Ruhr and Westfalia, set up an *Öko-Zentrum* for innovative

Map 16.2 France's *technopoles*[19]

enterprises in the field of environment technologies.[21] The aim is to cooperate with leading European companies and to form a network with similar parks in other countries. Leading emerging economies are also following this example, mainly to develop new industries through FDI. China and India count as leaders among LEMs in park development.

After successfully developing special economic zones (SEZ) designed to attract general FDI with a strong export focus around Hong Kong, Macao and in accessible areas along the southeastern coast, the Chinese authorities are now moving towards more industry-specific high-tech parks around major cities providing the necessary facilities and human skills (Beijing, Shanghai, Guangzhou, Dalian, Tianjin). The Dalian High-Tech Industrial Park[22] is broader in scope than most high-tech parks; it nevertheless focuses on knowledge-intensive and high value-added industries with a strong R&D component (e.g. electronics, machine tools, new materials, speciality chemicals). The Dalian Park groups 11 institutions of higher learning, 40 independent research organizations, 51 research centres of various kinds, 20 large and medium-sized industrial enterprises and over 600 innovative high-tech enterprises.[23] The Suzhou High-Tech park was built along similar lines.[24]

For its high-tech parks, China collaborates with other countries from which it can source technologies, know-how, management skills and capital. The Dalian Industrial Park, about 27 km from the centre of the northeastern city of Dalian (Liaoning province), was developed through a Sino–Japanese agreement. The Japanese government cofinanced major infrastructure projects including a container port, and a modern exhibition and conference hall. The Suzhou industrial park, about 200 km southwest of the city of Shanghai, was established in 1995 in collaboration with the government of Singapore. A similar scheme is being developed, in collaboration with Germany, in Tianjin, China's third largest city. The Chinese authorities now plan to use the know-how acquired through these collaborations for developing similar high-tech parks in the interior of the country.

In India, the software development park outside Bangalore focuses on software and hardware development (chips, switching systems, components for satellite technologies, digital medical equipment, etc.) in keeping with the global trend towards ISDN and multimedia. Companies are free to develop their products and services, which are exported or sold to the domestic market.

16.2.3 Towards integrated concepts of regional development

Authorities of countries with high FDI inflows are moving towards comprehensive regional development concepts based on sector specific parks. Technology park planners must ensure that wealth generated in the zones gradually spreads to the surrounding areas and then to the rest of the country. Without this diffusion, the high concentration of capital and know-how in special zones would entail the risk of creating islands of wealth, and their proximity to much poorer regions could lead to social unrest.

The original aim of establishing special zones exclusively for generating foreign exchange reserves or to protect local industry (initial efforts in China and India) must therefore be replaced by a broader aim of regional development. Parks can thus become centres of excellence and the motors of economic integration of surrounding regions.

The 50 sq km Dalian Economic and Technological Development Zone (DETDZ)[25] offers an interesting example of the ripple effect of an SDZ and how it merges with SDZs from other regional capitals.

Foreign investors in Dalian cooperate closely with suppliers and users in the cities of Shenyang, Tianjin and Beijing. They can acquire land, standard plant buildings and offices at rates far below city-centre levels, as well as high-standard housing (apartments and villas). There are also warehousing, shipping and business centres. The Dalian municipality built an expressway to the airport and established a special tourism and recreation park on the outskirts of Dalian. Providing these facilities in an emerging economy like China required a substantial planning effort by the local authorities, but it has paid off. By the end of 1997, the DETDZ attracted over a thousand foreign investors with total contracted FDI of US$4 billion (equivalent to the total for Russia during 1991–96). The main investors are Japanese, South Korean and US companies. Negotiations are under way with potential investors from France and Germany as a result of successful FDI promotion missions by the top officials of the zone and the active involvement of the city's mayor. The zone is becoming a major hub for supplying to northern China and other parts of East Asia (Japan, South Korea, eastern Russia).

16.2.4 Which special zone strategy for Russia?

The creation of SDZs can be useful for large and diversified economies with considerable disparities, which are compelled to strike a more equitable balance between the various regional markets. For Russia, SDZs can also represent an effective instrument of socioeconomic development in the regions, if the government succeeds in attracting competitive TNCs with high scientific and export potential. To increase SDZ awareness among foreign investors, the strategy and promotional activities need to be coordinated between the central FDI authority and regional administrations. This is especially crucial as large numbers of SDZs are created throughout the world and competition for capital and technology transfers from FDI-exporting countries increases.[26]

During 1990–97, several economic zones were established in Russia with a focus on free-trade and processing for exports, but their legal base is not clear to most foreign investors. Most of these zones apparently do not function at all.[27] No government department is able to confirm exactly which zones are operational, which facilities are available and what are the general conditions for potential foreign investors. A Federal Law on Free Economic Zones would help unify the legal status and treatment of these special areas. So far, each development zone is based on a separate legislative act, either in the form of a federal law, presidential decree, or even legislation dating back to the Soviet era. Russia's most important SDZs are located in coastal areas with port facilities and close to export markets. Among the 24 existing SDZs, four in the European part and two in the Far East are worth mentioning:

- St Petersburg SDZ, one of the largest SDZs in the world, has attracted a number of high-tech companies from northern Europe and the United States.[28]
- Vyborg SDZ, which was set up in collaboration with the Finnish authorities near the Russian–Finnish border, represents the first high-tech park established on Russian soil.

- The free port area of Yantar in Kaliningrad focuses on FDI from the EU (especially Germany).
- The high-tech park Zelenograd on the outskirts of Moscow is meant to attract advanced technologies from all over the world.
- Nakhodka SDZ and Sakhalin SDZ, both in the Far East close to the potential high-tech suppliers Japan and South Korea and the growing market of China; these two zones have already attracted investments from South Korean, Canadian and US TNCs interested in developing business at this increasingly important hub in northeastern Asia.
- Magadan SDZ in the Far East for the development of precious metals and other valuable raw materials.

The free zone of Sheremetyevo north of Moscow also has good prospects for development as it lies outside the domestic tariff area and offers TNCs fast access to the international airport.

In spite of initial government efforts to promote SDZs on Russia's territory, the concept has so far not generated the desired results. A number of factors complicate implementation:

- The difficult socioeconomic situation in the regions.
- The geographic and cultural distance of certain SDZs from potential investors.
- A lack of socioeconomic and technological infrastructure and other framework conditions.
- A lack of integrated strategy and coordination between the regions and centre.
- Insufficient promotion in foreign countries to attract the required technologies.
- Absence of cooperation with authorities from industrialized countries to promote the concept.

Being a country with long scientific and research traditions, high technology-oriented park schemes could be a particularly interesting option for industrial modernization in Russia. It may be useful to cooperate with selected industrialized countries. Bilateral park schemes could be developed in cooperation with the authorities from Finland, France, Germany, Italy, the Netherlands, the United Kingdom, the United States, Japan, China and India. Relative newcomers such as Spain and Portugal have also accumulated useful know-how for joint projects.

Most countries have followed their own paths of development and may contribute differently to zone creation and upgrading in Russia's regions. France and the United States, for example, have acquired expertise in service parks grouping high-tech firms with a need for common research, consulting and other support facilities. The German concept is typically more industry-oriented including component suppliers and large-scale warehousing facilities. Russia's regions may require different concepts depending on their industrial structures and need to create clusters. Most of them will have to opt directly for the fourth and fifth generation concepts without passing through the earlier stages of the 1970s and 1980s (Box 16.4).

Box 16.4 Phases of park development

- *First generation parks* (early 1970s): industrial parks with enormous warehousing facilities (80–85 per cent of the area) and access for large trailers, usually characterized by a high level of noise and pollution.
- *Second generation parks* (end 1970s): separation of offices from warehouses; larger parking areas.
- *Third generation parks* (early 1980s): arrival of more service companies to support the industrial side of the park; offices became more modern and attracted a large number of white collar workers.
- *Fourth generation parks* (mid–late 1980s): focus on light and clean industries as well as services with modern office areas and smaller warehousing facilities; this way, parks started competing directly with office areas in city centres.
- *Fifth generation parks* (1990s): modern park schemes supplying all the necessary facilities for locals and expatriates: restaurants, hotels, schools, fitness centres and cultural services: they are designed to attract leading players.

Instead of authorizing scattered SDZs across the Russian territory, poles of excellence should be developed at accessible distances from major agglomerations. Initially, these schemes could be sited around cities with over 1 million inhabitants.[29] Major cities offer forward and backward linkages with local supplier–client firms,[30] R&D centres, educational establishments and leisure facilities. After successful pilot projects in the larger regional capitals, the concept could be extended to smaller cities.

16.3 Establishing an investor information system

16.3.1 Information needs of foreign investors

Investors need to be informed in detail about long-term business prospects, prevailing legislation and possibilities of cooperating with Russian partners in the respective industries and regions. Dissemination of qualitative and quantitative information is therefore essential for any FDI promotion and image-enhancement strategy. An effective investor information system (IIS) should be set up so that relevant data can be made available to interested companies and opinion leaders through modern electronic data transfer technologies, including Internet.

The importance of information and data collection for an investment decision cannot be overstated. Most foreign companies today are uninformed about even basic facts on the economy, industry and legal developments in Russia and other CIS countries. Such information would significantly change their perception of Russia, particularly since sensational news reports often given an incorrect description of realities and can deter investment. Foreign businessmen are mainly interested in domestic and international competition, prospects in major client markets, distribution channels, the status of technological development and legal issues. In short, they should be given the entire spectrum of data and contacts that will enable them to evaluate the business environment and possibilities of industrial cooperation before formulating their entry or expansion strategy. They need to assess to what extent the political, macroeconomic and legal environment ensures the required stability, and how many administrative hurdles need to be overcome before obtaining final approval for the envisaged investment.

Foreign investors need to know how FDI is developing in their industry and related sectors. Such information allows them to schedule their entry at the opportune time to secure their market share before the arrival of competitors, which would raise the cost of entry. Such information should also be disseminated among opinion leaders, representatives of technical assistance bodies and other FDI catalysts. The information should, however be consistent; at present there are significant differences between FDI and industry-related data published by Russian (Goskomstat, Central Bank) and international (OECD, UNIDO, UNCTAD, EBRD, World Bank) organizations. Official statistics published by the statistical office Goskomstat and the Customs Authority can be used for a preliminary assessment of the market. These organizations and certain ministries with statistical capacity (e.g. Ministry of Science and Technology) have adopted international definitions and standards to facilitate comparison of data. In a dynamic environment, statistics age fast and authorities have to make special efforts to provide up-to-date and reliable figures. Statistics should, however, be accompanied by qualitative information including analyses of economic conditions, changes and developments, production, consumption, employment and key players in a particular industry. The information should also cover promising areas of investment (regions, sectors, companies, projects) and be disseminated through Internet.

Usually, potential investors start the familiarization process by contacting the Russian trade commission of diplomatic missions in their home countries. Foreign missions should therefore be regularly supplied with consistent figures and FDI-specific information materials (e.g. brochures describing regional economic and industrial assets, tax advantages, incentives offered in specific development zones, demand and supply conditions in major regions) by the concerned official bodies. Russian diplomatic staff should be trained to increase their insight into foreign investors' information needs.

16.3.2 Experience of other countries

Most countries disseminate information and promotional material. The Indian government, for example, issues a set of publications giving a detailed overview of FDI regulations, fast-track approval mechanisms, incentives and sectoral potential available to foreign companies in India. All reports are available in English from the Indian embassies, consulates and bilateral chambers of commerce. As India is anglophone, preparing material in good English is not so difficult. Attention has also been paid to presentation (design and printing) so that it is acceptable to foreign investors for whom presentation is as important as content. This attention to details shows a country's commitment to its FDI programme.

Ireland's Investment Development Agency (IDA) brings out three types of promotional publications, which are updated every two years:

- A general brochure describing Ireland's assets and advantages as an investment location: its investor-friendly administration and laws; labour costs and tax savings; highly-educated human resources; state-of-the-art information and telecommunications technologies; a modern banking system; and a promising and enabling business climate.
- Sector-specific brochures, including experiences of selected foreign investors, and information on major industries such as electronics, software, healthcare, teleservice and call centres, and financial services.
- Guideline reports covering facts on FDI: taxation and financial incentives including grants; direct financial contributions of national and regional bodies; corporate taxation; employers' social security contributions; banking and finance; and the legal environment.

Many regional bodies in industrialized countries disseminate information through their country's diplomatic missions, especially when they do not have their own representative office in the host country. Only in a few cases have stand-alone offices been opened by regional authorities. The US State of California, for example, introduces itself to the international business community through a variety of brochures specifying the economic potential and state incentives such as tax reductions, financial assistance (e.g. for employee training) and low-interest loans. It is disseminated through a number of California Investment Promotion offices abroad (e.g. Belgium for Europe, Japan for Asia). On the other hand, leading French regions (e.g. Alsace, Rhône-Alpes, Auvergne) and some of the larger cities (e.g. Paris, Nantes, Bordeaux) provide French embassies and trade commissions abroad with their latest brochures specifying incentives for foreign investors and contact addresses.

Russia needs to highlight its locational advantages through similar introductory information and promotion materials. Information gathering, production and dissemination all need to be coordinated with the regional authorities in charge of FDI promotion and expansion. Optimizing the regional data supply will represent a major factor of success of the country's information programme.

Most regional administrations of the Russian Federation also disseminate brochures about the history, challenges and industrial potential of their regions.[31] But their brochures are mostly available on-site, less so in Moscow and hardly outside Russia. Moreover, they are available only in Russian. Information on the locational assets and incentives offered by the leading regions should be disseminated more intensively through Russia's consular network, and particular attention should be drawn to key industries and enterprises in agglomerations with over 0.5 million inhabitants. For lack of strong coordination by a national agency, some of Russia's regional authorities have begun to cooperate directly with selected industrialized countries.[32] This type of cooperation may involve some exchange of publications and information, but its coverage is limited. The establishment of a reliable information system is essential for coordinating actions between the central government and regional bodies.[33] FDI specialists in Russia need to be informed by the relevant ministries, sector associations, statistical services and media.

16.3.3 Publications and other information products

A number of general and specialized publications should be produced under the responsibility of the federal FDI agency. A publication programme must be conceived that takes into consideration the specific needs of the foreign investor community, and should include:

- general publications (e.g. on the Russian economy);
- sectoral reports on different industries;
- reports on regions;
- information on potential investment projects;[34] and
- promotional materials[35] (including information on approval mechanisms, incentives and legal conditions).

Selected general publications can also be sourced from private publishers or other organizations (ministries, universities). Publications that require in-depth research and analysis could be prepared in collaboration with the regions, state bodies and statistical services (Table 16.4). All important publications should be produced in English; other foreign language versions (e.g. French, German, Japanese, Spanish) can follow at a later stage. Important documents (e.g. laws, approval procedures, incentive schemes,

Table 16.4 Proposed publications programme, 2000–05

Publication	Format	Frequency	Contents	User groups	Dissemination channel	Co-publishers
A: General economy series						
Socioeconomic trends in Russia[a]	A 5 50–60 pages Text and data	1 year	General socioeconomic overview: macroeconomic trends, changes in major economic and monetary variables, demographics, standard of living, employment, foreign trade, regional developments	Potential investors, opinion leaders, international organizations, university professors and students	Diplomatic missions, bookshops, international trade fairs, industry associations and chambers of commerce	FDI agency, universities, Goskomstat, private publishers
Pocket statistical yearbook[b]	A5 80–90 pages Only data	1 year	Main statistical indicators of economic and social trends	Potential investors, opinion leaders, international organizations	Diplomatic missions, bookshops, airports and flights, international trade fairs, industry associations and chambers of commerce	FDI agency, Goskomstat
B: Regional and sectoral series						
Russia's regional markets	A4 120–130 pages Text and data	1 year	Socioeconomic developments in major regional markets	Potential investors, international organizations	Diplomatic missions, bookshops, industry associations	FDI agency, universities, regional authorities, chambers of commerce
Russia's major industry and services markets[c]	A4 130–140 pages Text and data	1 year	Brief economic overview; general trends in industry (output, employment, ownership); profiles of leading industries	Potential investors	Diplomatic missions, bookshops, industry associations and chambers of commerce	FDI agency, regional authorities, universities, private publishers

continued …

Table 16.4 (*continued*)

Publication	Format	Frequency	Contents	User groups	Dissemination channel	Co-publishers
C: Business series						
Russia's top 300 companies	A4 120–120 pages Short texts and data	1 year	Brief company profiles and financial data of key players by sector and region	Potential investors, international consultants	Diplomatic missions, bookshops, industry associations and chambers of commerce	FDI agency, regional authorities, universities, private publishers
Privatization in Russia	A4 50–60 pages	1 year	Economic effects of privatization on different sectors, performance of enterprises, scope for M&A and FDI	Potential investors, international consultants	Diplomatic missions, bookshops, industry associations and chambers of commerce	FDI agency, universities, private publishers
Small and medium-sized enterprises (SMEs) in Russia	A4 50–60 pages mainly text	1 year	SME developments, privatization, breakup by sector and region, SME and FDI	Potential investors, international consultants	Diplomatic missions, bookshops, industry associations and chambers of commerce	FDI agency, universities, private publishers
D: FDI in Russia series						
Priority investment projects	A4 100–200 pages Text and data	1 year	Details of main investment projects in the regions (3–5 per participating region)	Potential investors, political leaders	Direct presentation	Regional authorities
FDI in Russia	A4 50–60 pages Text and data	1 year	FDI trends and forecasts, inbound and outbound FDI, origin and destination, sectors, regions, FDI by type, FDI legislation and approval mechanisms, administrative structure, FDI incentives, recommendations for TNCs	Potential investors, international consultants	Diplomatic missions, bookshops, industry associations and chambers of commerce	FDI agency, universities

continued …

Table 16.4 (*continued*)

Publication	Format	Frequency	Contents	User groups	Dissemination channel	Co-publishers
FDI case studies	A4 80–90 pages mainly text	1 year	Concise overview of most successful foreign investors and their Russian partners; reasons for success, management, marketing, export activity, technology transfer, human resources management	Potential investors, international consultants	Diplomatic missions, bookshops, industry associations and chamber of commerce	FDI agency, universities, private publishers
E: General publications						
Russia's main political bodies and organizations	A4 50–60 pages mainly text	1 year	Addresses and brief profiles of main political and semiofficial institutions, including industry associations	Potential investors, international consultants	Diplomatic missions, bookshops, industry associations and chambers of commerce	FDI agency, national administration, private information and research agencies, government information service
Promotional folders[d] on Russia and major regions	A4 20–25 pages mainly text folders with leaflets		Major industries, greater economic areas, legislation and incentives for foreign investors	Potential investors, international consultants	Diplomatic missions, industry associations and chambers of commerce	FDI agency

[a]Example: *Tableaux de l'économie française,* French statistical office, INSEE, annual publication.
[b]Example: Statistical pocket booklets issued by several national statistical authorities.
[c]Example: *EU Industrial Outlook*, European Commission, annual publication.
[d]Example: *Doing Business with India*.

special sector analyses) intended specifically for an important FDI source country should be published preferably in its language.

CD-ROMs and diskettes can sometimes be a more cost-effective support for certain types of information (essential data on the Russian economy, legislation for foreign investors). For example, the Indian Ministry of External Affairs produces a diskette *Doing Business in India*, which is distributed through the country's foreign missions.[36] The information products could use the large variety of supports now available for storing and disseminating business intelligence:

- brochures;
- reports, statistical booklets, sector overviews, economic studies;
- databases on diskettes and CD-ROMs;
- websites with feedback forms; and
- e-mail.

The human and financial resources required to produce and disseminate high-quality information materials should not be underestimated. The FDI agency will need to work with or employ professional writers, editors, translators and designers. All possible channels should be used to achieve wide international dissemination: Russia's embassy and consular network, international organizations, chambers of commerce, bookshops, fairs and direct mailing to leading enterprises. Relevant FDI publications should also be advertised on relevant websites. Attractive public awareness booklets on Russia could also be distributed on flights to and from Russia and at major domestic airports.

The FDI agency must have a website[37] as Internet is fast becoming a primary source of information that cannot be ignored. Potential investors are bound to check this source first as it is easily accessible and gives instant information. The site should be interactive, regularly updated and should publicize other documents that give more detailed information. This multimedia support offers abundant possibilities for presenting information in the most user-friendly way (text, image, animation, sound).

Setting up an investor information system calls for inputs from specialists with an international and private-sector background, and experience in marketing, public relations and strategic planning. The system should be linked to the federal FDI agency.

16.4 Planning proactive promotion and confidence-building campaigns[38]

16.4.1 International practice

Authorities in the major recipient countries used to react to FDI proposals instead of proactively searching potential investors from major FDI-exporting countries and promoting their location-specific advantages.

Often, they do not have a clear strategy for identifying suitable investors and for approaching them directly or through opinion leaders.

In most cases, promotion efforts are not convincing and costly actions are frequently abandoned halfway because they have not been thought through and unplanned budgets make further implementation difficult (Figure 16.2). General seminars and conferences are conducted, outdated and unclear brochures disseminated and ineffective advertisements placed in expensive western newspapers and business magazines. Buyer–seller meetings,[39] a recent phenomenon, are not having the expected effect, mostly because they focus on companies that are too small or belong to industries with limited potential in the destination country.

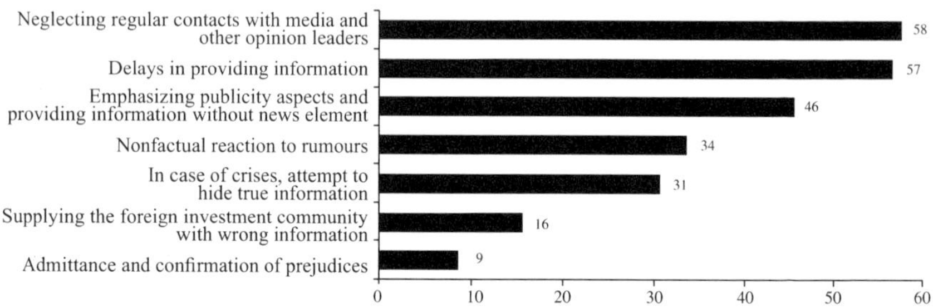

Source: K. S Pauli, *Leitfaden für die Pressearbeit* [Guidelines for press relations], 1993.

Figure 16.2 Most common mistakes in public communication

Promotions in high-cost countries can strain the limited budgets of FDI agencies from emerging economies. Canvassing TNCs requires local presence, attractive promotion material and proper media planning to gain publicity, all of which are high-cost factors.[40] A more focused approach and stricter cost control have enabled a few progressive countries to carry out successful campaigns. Ireland, Malaysia, Singapore and Taiwan are small countries but they continue to report record inflows in spite of their rather limited overseas offices and staff. In contrast, many large countries (including Russia) disposing of a much wider network of foreign missions are less successful despite their costly infrastructure.

Inspired by the success of its smaller competitors, the Indian government has special investment promotion officers in its embassies in the major Triad markets. They are in charge of information dissemination, and press and public relations. Mexico is also using its foreign missions to channel its promotions in North America and western Europe, where Mexican FDI experts directly interact with companies. Their well-designed brochures contain useful economic and legal information, and FDI successes are publicized through news releases. The impact of such efforts is seen in the country's FDI performance since 1996. Mexico's experience now serves as an example to the Brazilian authorities.

China is an exception in this regard because it was the pioneer LEM and it required less effort. Moreover, as a substantial part of FDI came from overseas Chinese, it did not have to deploy the same efforts as the new LEMs like Russia, who have to face stiff competition and economic slowdown in important source countries. China today hosts most of the world's top 200 companies, without having undertaken the type of government efforts that would be required if it were a newcomer today. The main concern of China's authorities now is to ensure steady FDI inflows from the second wave of foreign investors – the medium-sized TNCs. China will have to step up its promotional efforts in the coming years as competition increases from other LEMs.

Generally, countries like India and Russia that were isolated from the world because of their import substitution policies need to strive harder to make their target audience change its perception (and prejudices). They can draw lessons from Southeast Asian countries, which were also historically isolated. They also need to reduce the gap with industrialized countries, which remain the most successful recipients of FDI.

Aggressive governments also link up FDI measures with other policy areas such as culture, history and tourism for improving the country's overall image.[41]

16.4.2 Communication strategy for Russia

Communication and public relations activities must be geared to general image enhancement and confidence building at home and abroad. The idea is to generate higher FDI by acting at three levels:[42]

- Image-building efforts: regular public relations and public awareness campaigns including communication to the media and participation in important international exhibitions and trade fairs; use of a striking visual identity by the FDI agency to build 'brand equity' through high-quality services and investor orientation.
- Investment generating efforts: presentations at headquarters of multinationals and at trade associations (useful to approach medium-sized TNCs).
- Investment facilitation efforts: quick response services from federal and regional authorities regarding queries from investors.

The major objectives of a communication strategy in relation to FDI for Russia are:

- To create a favourable image of Russia as an investment destination;
- To change the longstanding perception of Russia as a socialist, investor-unfriendly economy;

- To inform the international public and media about the transition to a market economy that rewards investment.

It is an accepted fact that a country's image influences international trade and investment. It is no coincidence that the EU countries and the United States, which rank highest among FDI recipients, also enjoy reputations of economic stability and prosperity. Companies feel reassured that their investments would be safe in these low-risk countries. A good image can see a country through a crisis. Japan currently faces a serious economic slowdown. During 1997–98 Japan faced negative publicity, but its image as a major industrial power still holds. Even countries with a favourable image need to maintain it through continuing communication efforts.

The task before the emerging economies is different: they have to change stereotyped perceptions of their past performance and create a new modern image of themselves. So far, only a few emerging countries in Asia (Malaysia, Singapore, Taiwan), Eastern Europe (Czech Republic, Hungary, Poland, Slovenia) and Latin America (Chile) have succeeded in attaining a stability rating as average industrialized countries. While even international risk ratings published by private banks and research bodies are not completely objective and are partly influenced by image-conditioned factors, these countries have succeeded in publicizing their achievements and also have their own 'brands' – Southeast Asian Tigers and Dragons.

On the other hand, India, which has made good progress in liberalizing its economy, is still burdened by the image of a 'Hindu rate of growth'. During his visit to India in 1998, French President Chirac regretted that the 'image deficit' has hampered growth of trade and investment between the two countries. India often loses out on FDI because of its poor image, and to overcome this the government has created an India Brand Equity Fund to intensify its communication efforts.

History, culture and the prevailing economic situation all combine to fashion a country's image. Russia's history and culture (literature, art, music) are known and appreciated the world over, and its scientific achievements, despite the socialist regime, have been acknowledged. Since the fall of communism its negative image of the Evil Empire that repressed liberty has been cleared, but the achievements of the transition economy have not yet convinced the international community. Although a few open-minded investors from the United States, and western and Central European countries have begun to discover the 'thrill of doing business in a dynamic and promising environment like Russia', the social, industrial and political disruption and the growing threat of crime have tarnished the country's image.

Russian authorities should also draw on experiences of large companies who engage in image upgrading and repositioning, brand management and corporate communication to support their marketing strategy (Box 16.5).

Systematic image building involves continuous communication to a broad spectrum of target groups within and outside Russia. A variety of instruments

Box 16.5 Process of building an effective communication programme[43]

Step 1 *Problem analysis*: The problem that has prompted this exercise is that Russia's image has to be overhauled as the country positions itself as a favourable investment destination following the introduction of a democratic system.

Step 2 *Situation analysis*: This step focuses on three aspects:

- Regular image audits will reveal what the target groups think of Russia, its perceived strengths and weaknesses. Several audit techniques have been developed by advertising and PR agencies.
- Information on target markets and TNCs can be obtained through the investor information system and supplemented by regular interviews of key players.
- The competition analysis will focus on all other large emerging markets, which are also FDI destinations.

Step 3 *Gap analysis*: The divergence between the actual and desired images will highlight the issues that need to be addressed for repositioning Russia.

Step 4 *Translation into communicative profiling*: The research findings and strategic positioning need to be transformed into communication products. The central values are defined at an abstract level so that they can be easily translated into messages for the different target groups and areas of communication (PR, advertising, etc.). This ensures consistency in the messages and long-term planning of actions.

Step 5 *Implementation*: The overall budget for communication has to be established at the outset to avoid overambitious programmes that cannot be sustained (this would have a negative effect). The message content is defined and the appropriate media are chosen. Actions are scheduled and resources allocated according to priorities. The process should be iterative and not static.

Step 6 *Evaluation*: Evaluation is necessary to control the effectiveness of the planned actions in achieving the desired results. Midcourse corrections can then be carried out if necessary.

are available depending on the significance of the target group (Figure 16.3). Special attention should be paid to crisis management communication. Russian authorities have the option of subcontracting some of these activities out to advertising and public relations agencies that specialize in image building for governments and public organizations.

Budgetary constraints will demand a focused approach with respect to specific countries, sectors and companies. Initially, promotion and public relations actions should preferably be focused on the G7 economies and then extended to other potential source countries. A proposed programme for possible PR measures to be conducted during 2000–05 is presented in Table 16.5. The total budget will depend on the number of countries targeted and the choice of professional organizations.

Regular enterprise and media surveys (see example of California) are useful for assessing Russia's evolving image abroad and capturing early warning signals (Box 16.6). FDI authorities in countries like Ireland use similar mechanisms that are considered a barometer for monitoring the impact of promotional and image-enhancement measures.

16.5 Providing top-level advisory services

Foreign investors need strategic guidance for taking decisions on their market entry or expansion. Large TNCs have the resources to assign managers specifically for a new market and to monitor the target markets closely from headquarters. They often work with international and local consultants. Medium-sized TNCs do not have the financial and human resources for such monitoring and advisory services. But the number of investors among them is set to increase. A dedicated FDI agency could assist them through the different steps of the investment process. It could also help those engaged in purely export activities to take the decision to invest if the business potential warrants it. Such decisions are weighty for a medium-sized company and without advisory support it may prefer to pursue its export strategy even if a change would be more beneficial. Large companies could also improve their market position by receiving strategic information and advice on time. They often lack insider knowledge about local partners, manufacturing sites and legal changes, especially in the regions.

Both project advice and coaching are indispensable for the implementation of investment decisions. FDI-oriented strategic advice should be customized to meet a company's needs and to focus on the long term. Accurate assessment of market potential, scenario planning[44] and business intelligence are required by foreign investors, irrespective of their size and degree of market penetration.

The federal FDI agency should set up a coordinated external advisory network that caters to the needs of potential investors as it does not have

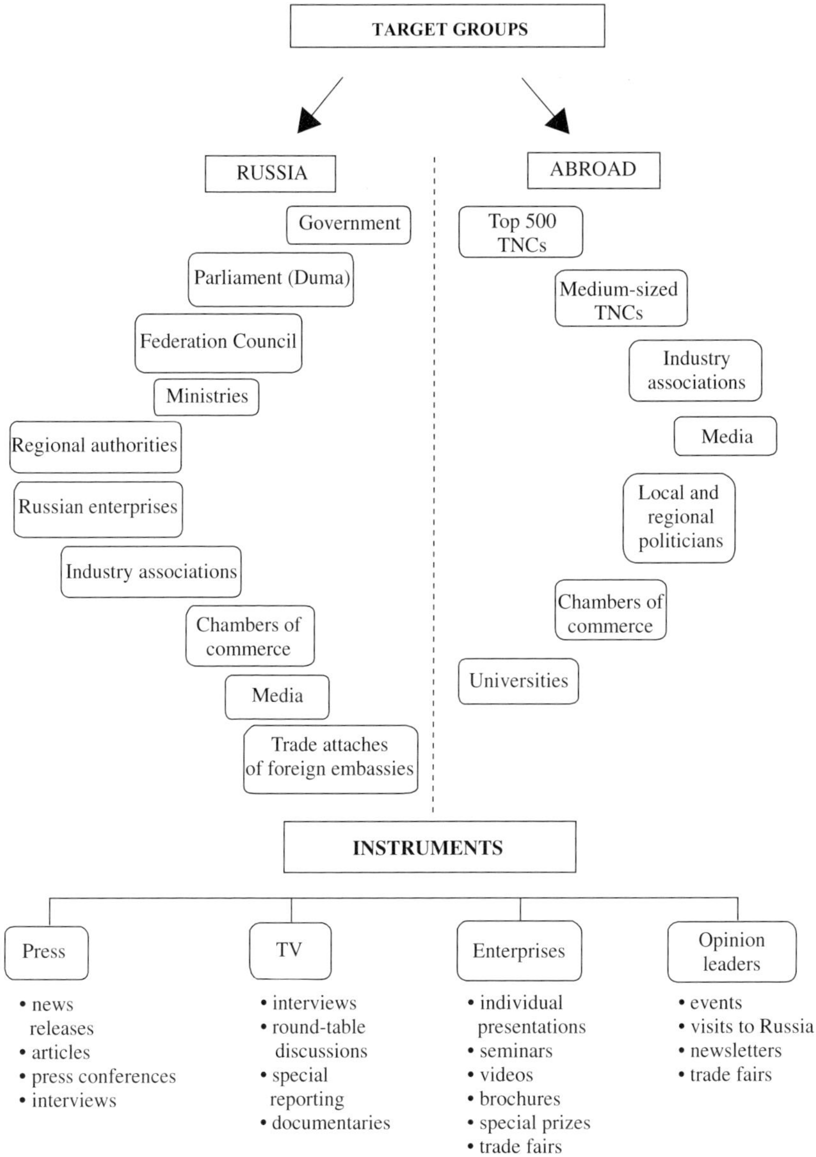

Figure 16.3 FDI communication components

Table 16.5 Proposed programme for public relations, 2000–01

Activity	Frequency	Objectives	Target groups	Examples
A: Investment-generating activities (mainly at enterprise level)				
Top-level investment missions and visits with sector-specific presentations	Minimum of 10 company visits per quarter in each target country	To establish and cultivate contacts with corporate executives, opinion leaders, industry associations, chambers of commerce, banks and the press.	Large TNCs and 'hidden champions' medium-sized TNCs	For large TNCs: FDI authorities of Ireland, Malaysia and Singapore For medium-sized TNCs: no established strategy so far by any FDI promotion authority
Russian FDI information seminars	1 seminar every six months in the G5 countries	To inform potential investors about general economic and political outlook, legal framework, case studies, corporate strategies, intercultural management aspects	Potential investors, opinion leaders, international consultants, university professors, media	Management Circle, Frost & Sullivan, but at a lower participation fee (private companies charge up to US$3000 per event lasting 1–2 days)
Participation in selected trade fairs	2–3 fair participations per year in G7 countries and LEMs	To create exposure and broad understanding of Russia's industrial and technological potential	Potential investors, opinion leaders, international consultants	Confederation of Indian Industry (CII)
Website	Regular updates	To provide general information on the state of Russia's economy and industry To propose investment projects from the regions	Potential investors, international consultants, opinion leaders, general public	<www.idaireland.com > website of the Irish Development Agency

continued ...

Table 16.5 (*continued*)

Activity	Frequency	Objectives	Target groups	Examples
B: Image building and support activities (press and public relations via media)				
Image brochures[a]	Regular updates (in cooperation with the regions) 10 image brochures of greater economic areas (GEAs)	To inform foreign publics and investors of the regional potential Brochures need to highlight economic prospects for industrial and services TNCs, but also educational (universities, research centres) and cultural facilities (cuisine and museums), fairs and exhibitions, infrastructure (airports, road network), etc.	Potential investors, international consultants, opinion leaders, general public	Image brochures of the Indian Ministry of External Affairs or Thai Investment Promotion Board
Media campaigns and advertising in general media and specialized press	Regular exposure	Special relation with western press (e.g. *The Economist*, *Expansion*, *Wirtschaftswoche*, *Il Sole 24 Ore*, etc.)	Potential investors, public and semi-public bodies, general public Target countries: G7, other OECD, LEMs	Bavarian Ministry of Economic Affairs, Transport, and Technology; Taiwan Industrial Development and Investment Centre of the Ministry of Economic Affairs

continued …

Table 16.5 (*continued*)

Activity	Frequency	Objectives	Target groups	Examples
Press releases, FDI newsletters	Regular press releases Bimonthly newsletter	To provide information on big FDI projects, news and views, policies of local authorities, seminars, advertisements	Potential investors, international consultants, media	Polish Investment Agency in Poland, Indian Embassy quarterly newsletter *Patrika*, monthly *Business Ireland* of the Irish Development Agency, *CEBANOR* of the Normandy Economic Development Agency in France, monthly *Hong Kong Trade* by Hong Kong Trade Development Council, etc.
Special articles and documentaries on industrial, technological and economic developments in international newspapers	1–2 articles and documentaries per year in each target country (G5)	Special reports should cover Russia's overall socioeconomic developments and prospects for foreign companies in the regional markets as well as case studies	Potential investors, opinion leaders, international consultants, general public	Dailies: *Wallstreet Journal* (USA), *Handelsblatt* (D), *Financial Times* (UK), *Les Echos* (F), *Il Sole 24 ore* (I) Weeklies: *The Economist* (UK), *Wirtschaftswoche* (D), *Express* (F), *L'Expansion* (F), *Fortune* (USA) Specialized journals: *Ost–West Journal* (D) National and private TV and radio
Organization of press and TV interviews	One interview every 2–3 months (to coincide with events and visits of VIPs)	To give an opportunity to Russian representatives to communicate 'live' to the public in target countries (the representatives should be chosen carefully for their communication skills and telegenic personality)	Opinion leaders, general public	National and private TV and radio

Box 16.6 Questionnaire used by the Trade and Investment Agency of the State of California to determine the degree of satisfaction among foreign investors, 1997

- Has the FDI project resulted in the opening of a subsidiary (manufacturing/sales) in the State of California? If not, will FDI take place within the next 12 months, 2 years, later, or not at all?
- What was the total amount of FDI invested in the State (in US$)?
- How many new persons were employed in California following the investment?
- Has the company or its international staff acquired private property in California?
- What were the delays for establishing the California subsidiary?
- Was the information material received from the California FDI office informative and useful to expand FDI-related activities?
- Which suggestions could be made for improving framework conditions, FDI approval mechanisms, incentives and promotion measures?
- Is the California FDI office considered an indispensable source of information for foreign operators interested in investing in the State and would the services be recommended further?
- Would the company like to continue cooperating with the Office and remain listed in the database?

the resources to handle large numbers of projects.[45] Moreover, advisory services such as strategy formulation, due diligence of potential partners, executive search and technico–financial feasibility studies require specialists and are best commissioned to external advisory firms and organizations with a track record in such services.

The external advisory network should be established with firms and organizations located both in Russia and selected FDI-source countries (Figure 16.4). In the FDI-source country, corporate investors need pre-investment advice on legalities, formalities and guarantee mechanisms at federal and regional levels. This advice can be provided through Russia's trade commissions and their local partner organizations (chambers of commerce, industry and business associations). The role of the federal agency is to train officials responsible for these services in the various organizations.

In Russia, investors need more specific and detailed advice such as research-based services (market studies, competitor analyses, consumer and brand surveys, due diligence of potential partners) and support for administrative formalities, legal services and financial engineering. Such services

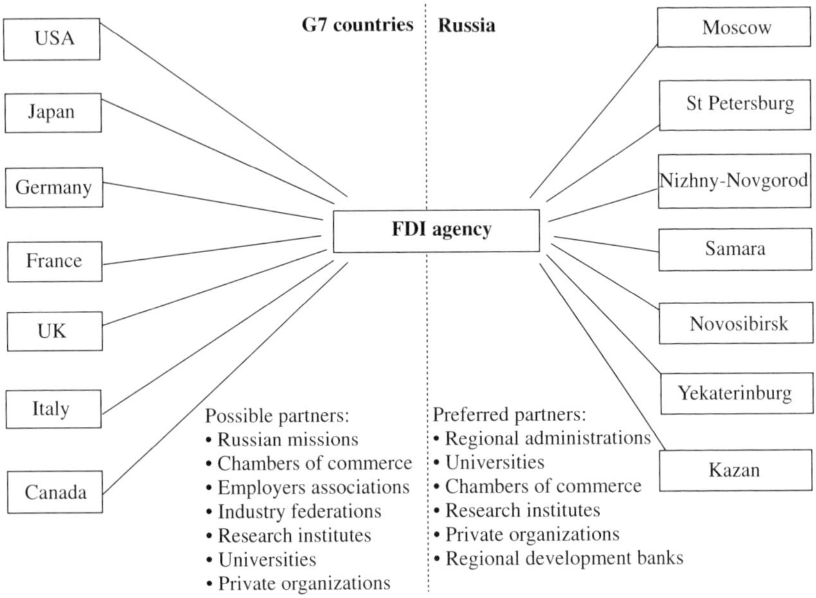

Figure 16.4 External advisory structure

can be provided through local firms or business consulting departments in well-known universities specialized in economics and business.[46] The network in Russia should include organizations in Moscow and important regional capitals (St Petersburg, Nizhny Novgorod, Rostov, Yekaterinburg, Kazan, Samara, Novosibirsk, Vladivostok).

The role of the federal FDI agency is to screen and select suitable members (private advisory firms, and public and semi-public organizations) of the external advisory network. It should check them for their experience, integrity, objectivity, contacts and access to information sources. It should maintain an up-to-date roster so that investors can be rapidly put in contact with the right advisors. The agency should also organize training seminars for officials and advisors involved in this exercise and coaching workshops for corporate executives.

The selected advisory firms and organizations must be capable of – and interested in – representing Russian interests. Top management of each advisory organization participating in the network should show an understanding of Russia's technological and socioeconomic requirements and its cultural specificity (including knowledge of the language). The agency and its network should caution investors against gung-ho tactics that would harm Russia's – and in the long term, their own – interests and its programme of sustainable socioeconomic development.

Such an advisory services system is vital for gaining investor confidence by giving a realistic and reliable view of business prospects in Russia's regions and through the quality standards that it would set for network members.

16.6 Optimizing financial engineering

Innovative financial instruments based on competitive lending terms are essential for enhancing FDI. Finance for FDI needs to be provided through international banks and financial institutions with subsidiaries in Russia, in cooperation with domestic banks.[47] Besides attracting foreign manufacturing technologies, innovative financial engineering will also enable Russian enterprises to actively participate as equal partners in strategic alliances, joint ventures and technical cooperation projects.

Loan generation for FDI-related projects is a complex task in a transition economy. In the long term, it can only function on condition that domestically generated savings and company deposits are tapped by the national capital markets and banking–insurance system, before they are transferred outside the country.[48] Weak financial structures in Russia oblige the Russian investment partners to turn to foreign banks, whose loans are denominated in foreign currency and include 'high risk' provisions in their interest calculations, which raises the cost of the loan. Except for large, export-oriented oil and gas corporations, most borrowers depend on cash flow in roubles to repay the loans.

FDI-oriented financial engineering includes a number of instruments with a specific focus on foreign investors' requirements. The FDI agency and its external advisory network could act as mediators and facilitators between Russian banks, foreign investors and their Russian industrial partners.[49] The type of finance made available for FDI projects varies with the scale and nature of the project as well as the size and financial strength of the TNC:

- consortium-based finance (for large-scale projects);
- bond and share finance through the domestic capital market (for long-term projects);
- leasing finance (mainly for capital equipment);
- venture capital (for SMEs and high-tech companies);
- foreign borrowing instruments (for government-backed projects).

Following the financial crisis of August–September 1998, foreign borrowing instruments have become practically inaccessible to potential investors in Russia. Long-term finance from domestic banks is unavailable because they are compelled to seek short-term gains; besides, state bodies at central and regional levels cannot provide adequate guarantees. The crisis increased risk aversion among domestic and foreign bankers, who are now concerned about liquidity shortages. In this highly critical situation, innovative financial schemes and determined state guidance are even more crucial for supporting FDI projects.

16.6.1 State guidance for generating investment finance

The Russian central bank, Tsentralny Bank, determines the country's monetary policy and sets the overall framework for financial and currency transactions; its policies have a direct impact on money supply, interest rates for domestic savings, the rouble exchange rate and investments, including inward FDI operations.[50] In today's global economy, interest and exchange rates are increasingly conditioned by currency and securities trading on international capital markets. These markets have become extremely volatile with the liberalization of capital transactions around the world despite the widespread use of derivative instruments to hedge risks.[51] Following the series of financial crises worldwide during 1997–98, the central discount rate in Russia shot above 80 per cent compared with 4–7 per cent in the leading OECD countries. It had reached an all time low of 25–30 per cent by mid-1997, which would have been far more stimulating for an emerging economy. In July 1999, the lending rates for 3–6 month loans by the leading banks varied between 40 and 60 per cent, which is still too high for financing industrial projects.

Financial turmoils call for sound crisis management, including a policy of temporary controls of capital inflows (especially on short-term portfolio investments) and outflows (to deter capital flight).[52] A far-sighted FDI policy should be supported by well-functioning capital markets and banking institutions. As in other LEMs, an industrial development bank could provide financial support for Russia's industrial transformation and infrastructure modernization.[53] FDI-related projects cushioned by such a state-backed financial institution could become important at a time when global private-sector capital flows to emerging markets are expected to drop further.[54] Although former Prime Minister Primakov signed a government order to create a Russian development bank (11 March 1999), its equity capital of Rb375 million (US$16.3 million) is too low compared with the magnitude of the projects to be financed.

Multilateral borrowing through the IMF and the World Bank can help bridge short-term payments in the state budget, but cannot finance long-term industrial and infrastructure development. Besides, continuous borrowing without investments in the real economy expose Russian operators to permanent liabilities and foreign exchange risks, which could lead to further liquidity crises in the banking sector. Russian banks should be encouraged to play a more active role in mobilizing domestic savings for long-term investment projects in manufacturing, services and agriculture – just as in China and India.[55] The role of former leading banks such as Sberbank and Oneksimbank will have to be recast so that these institutions can become industrial facilitators in the post-liberalization process.[56]

Already before the crisis, Russia's leading banks had pursued a policy of uniting with industry to form powerful financial–industrial groups (FIGs). These groups were promoted by regional governments (e.g. Tatpromstroybank from Tatarstan, Bashprombank from Bashkortostan) as lenders of last resort. Russian enterprises not belonging to FIGs had difficulties in obtaining domestic bank loans, even if viable projects were presented or foreign partners showed an interest in investing in domestic industry. During 1990–98, few Russian banks pursued an investment-driven strategy. While smaller banks lacked the financial clout to back industrial projects, most large banks concentrated on acquiring controlling stakes in companies rather than providing finance for long-term investments.

The importance of strong national financial structures cannot be overemphasized given that foreign banks will always have limited access to domestic savings in Russia. Although a number of restrictions will be lifted for foreign banks,[57] their regional subsidiary network cannot cover the entire territory. Project evaluations and due diligence of companies, two prerequisites for obtaining bank loans, can therefore be undertaken only in close cooperation with local banks. Access to the domestic banking network and capital markets is therefore crucial to the success of a foreign investment project.

The Russian government should consider providing a more solid legal base for developing long-term financial instruments. It should provide incentives for investment-based loan finance to enterprises and regulate speculative shifts of portfolios. Leasing seems to be one of the few areas of finance which is covered by wide-ranging legislation.[58] The legal base remains weakly developed for most other areas of finance generation including capital markets, foreign borrowing instruments and venture capital.

A firm commitment from the government would send out positive signals to the Russian banking and international investor community. Foreign banks would be more willing to provide the required long-term capital for industry.

16.6.2 Bank consortiums for large-scale project finance

Bank consortiums can, if coordinated at federal level, become an important source of finance for large-scale FDI projects above US$50 million, for which guarantees should be provided by federal and regional bodies. Consortiums are formed by leading financial institutions to spread risks and to offer better rates to borrowers. They can group both foreign and Russian banks.

Most of Russia's large banks are headquartered in Moscow (Table 16.6),[59] although they have expanded their subsidiary network to other cities and towns in recent years. Some of these banks have grown from fledgling

Table 16.6 Top 30 Russian banks, 1997, 1999

1997

Bank	Assets (Rb billion)	Equity (Rb billion)
Sberbank (Moscow)	173.9	9.9
Inkombank (Moscow)	33.2	2.4
Oneksimbank (Moscow)	25.4	5.5
SBS-Agro (Moscow)	22.9	1.6
Menatep (Moscow)	17.9	1.6
Vneshtorgbank (Moscow)	17.4	6.2
Mezhprombank (Moscow)	15.2	2.5
Rossiisky Kredit (Moscow)	14.1	1.4
Gazprombank (Moscow)	11.4	2.1
NRB (Moscow)	8.7	3.2
Most-Bank (Moscow)	8.6	1.0
Toribank (Moscow)	4.9	0.7
Promyshlenno-Stroytelny (St Petersburg)	4.8	0.7
Imperial (Moscow)	9.3	1.1
Avtobank (Moscow)	8.4	1.8
MFK (Moscow)	5.6	1.0
Bashkreditbank (Ufa)	2.9	1.1
Mosnatsbank (Moscow)	2.7	0.6
Inturbank (Moscow)	0.9	0.7
Diamant (Moscow)	2.7	1.1
Sobinbank (Moscow)	2.6	0.5
Tokobank (Moscow)	5.3	1.0
Vozrozhjdenye (Moscow)	6.0	0.7
Guta Bank (Moscow)	4.2	1.2
Unikombank (Moscow)	2.3	0.6
MDM Bank (Moscow)	2.3	0.7
MIB (Moscow)	4.0	0.9
Mosstroyekonombank (Moscow)	2.1	0.5
AK Bars (Kazan)	3.0	2.3
Globeks (Moscow)	1.1	0.5

1999

Bank	Assets (Rb billion)	Equity (Rb billion)
Sberbank (Moscow)	110.4	29
Gazprombank (Moscow)	15.6	6.5
Vneshtorgbank (Moscow)	23.5	5.7
Oneksimbank (Moscow)	3.6	4.3
NRB (Moscow)	3.0	3.6
Sobinbank (Moscow)	1.9	3.5
Alpha-bank (Moscow)	3.6	3.4
AK Bars (Kazan)	0.8	2.5
Menatep (Moscow)	4.2	2.4
Mezhprombank (Moscow)	15.2	2.4
SBS-Agro (Moscow)	19.7	1.9
Bank Moskvy (Moscow)	2.6	1.5
Guta Bank (Moscow)	2.8	1.3
Most-Bank (Moscow)	4.7	1.2
Diamant (Moscow)	1.6	1.2
Rosbank (Moscow)	3.7	1.1
Bashkreditbank (Ufa)	1.0	1.0
Moskovsky Industrialny Bank (Moscow)	0.7	1.0
Doveritelny i Investitsionny Bank (Moscow)	0.7	0.9
Promyshlenno-Stroytelny (St Petersburg)	2.4	0.9
Rossiisky Kredit (Moscow)	3.8	0.9
Mezhdunarodny Moskovsky Bank (Moscow)	13.2	0.8
Avtobank (Moscow)	0.6	0.8
MFK (Moscow)	1.9	0.7
Toribank (Moscow)	0.7	0.7
MDM Bank (Moscow)	1.9	0.7
Inturbank (Moscow)	0.2	0.7
Russky Bank Imuschestvennoi Opeki (Moscow)	0.3	0.7
Vozrozhjdenye (Moscow)	2.2	0.7
Neftekhimbank (Moscow)	1.2	0.6

Sources: Profil, 'The 300 Largest Russian Banks', 6 July 1998; *Kompaniya*, 'The 200 Largest Russian Banks', 8 March 1999.

structures at the beginning of the reform process into big institutions owing mainly to their direct participation in mass privatizations (1991–95). Leading institutions like Sberbank became strong players in Russia's capital markets and have started to open subsidiaries abroad. A number of medium-sized banks (e.g. Sobinbank, AK Bars, Rosbank) have been able to move up in the national ranking through careful asset management. They are also potential candidates for consortiums.

The Russian government plans to reorganize the entire banking system, which will probably comprise only about 300 institutions compared with over 1000 establishments in 1998.[60] Moreover, foreign banks are to be permitted higher stakes in Russia's finance. This will accelerate the formation of consortiums involving solvent domestic and foreign institutions.

FDI projects should also receive the support of leading western banks, most of which are represented by subsidiaries in Moscow and St Petersburg.[61] Many foreign banks had also increased their exposure by purchasing government bonds – the GKOs – and incurred severe losses with the crash. They are now compelled to restructure their operations, shed staff and look for new business and the time is probably appropriate to involve them more actively in FDI-oriented project finance.[62]

Project finance is more flexible than the usual forms of lending. It looks at the viability of a proposed investment project rather the company's size, creditworthiness and overall balance sheet situation. For medium-sized players with strategic interests in economies with higher than average risk ratings such as Russia, this form of finance offers several advantages:

- The investor's financial burden is significantly reduced through 'off balance sheet' financing.
- The investor is required to provide accurate forecasts of expected revenues ('cash flow related' lending); such advance planning increases the chances of success of the project.
- Risks are shared between manufacturers and financial partners in difficult environments.[63]
- Regional authorities can propose projects independently of their budget situation.

For large-scale projects, a separate company – often an independent legal entity – is established to faciltiate planning and ensure control during the investment period. All parties involved in the project (the foreign investor, the local partner, banks and public authorities) are represented on the supervisory and executive boards of the project company.

Project finance has become an important instrument in both industrialized and emerging economies. Originally, it was intended for large-scale projects in energy and infrastructure (e.g. power plants, water treatment and waste disposal systems, airports, telecommunication networks) with stable cash flows based on long-term contracts with state bodies. Banks are using the experience acquired in assessing effectiveness of public sector projects for financing turnkey projects in industry (e.g. cement, glass, paper and chemical production plants). Project finance is also extended to consumer goods industries, if cash flows can be predicted on the

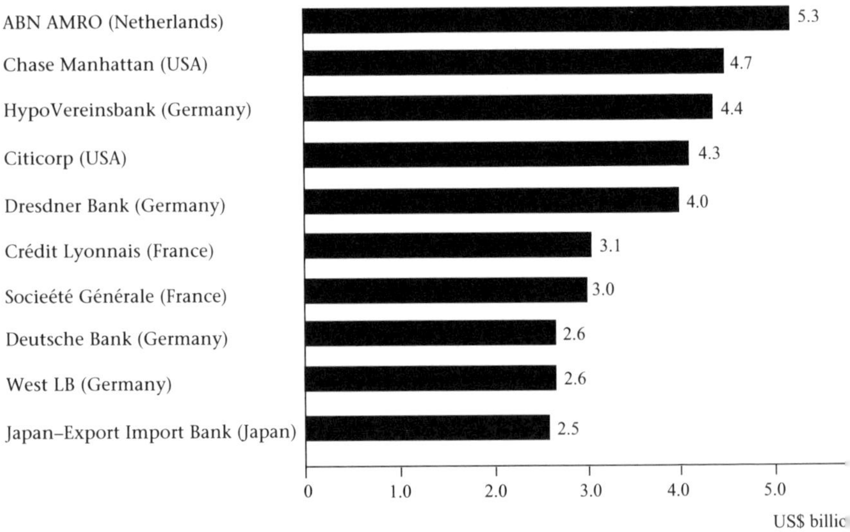

Figure 16.5 Leading western banks offering project finance, loan volume until August 1998

basis of the investor's competitive position (market share, control of distribution).

Project finance is used for investments exceeding US$10–15 million and payoff periods beyond 4 years. In high risk countries, leading banks work with multilateral institutions such as the World Bank and EBRD (Figure 16.5).[64] Banks may also cooperate with state agencies to finance outstanding receivables through 'asset securitization' or 'factoring' arrangements.[65]

For projects in Russia, banks should consider innovative hedging techniques for minimizing risk, including foreign currency, derivatives and mortgage-backed operations.[66] For Russia's regional authorities, project finance could support FDI, provided they

- increase cooperation with experienced western banks,
- improve the local and regional banking network,
- provide clear project definitions (business plans)[67] and guarantee mechanisms to convince investors.

16.6.3 Domestic capital markets and long-term finance

A number of industrialized countries have been able to successfully generate financial resources through domestic capital market instruments for infrastructure and industrial projects. Both the needs of borrowers and lenders could be matched through large-scale issues of bonds, which were supported by coordinated federal and regional guarantee systems.[68] If Russia wants to succeed in modernizing its industries, it must develop the necessary institutions and instruments through which domestic savings can be channelled into long-term FDI projects.

As a first step, numerous stock exchanges and over-the-counter securities markets were formed following the voucher-based mass privatization scheme[69] of 1992–94. The post-voucher reform agenda of 1994 announced new privatization methods based on:

- free transfer or sale of shares to employees through closed subscriptions;
- sale of equity (at least 15–25 per cent of the charter capital) through investment tenders;
- sale of shares at national and regional auctions;
- loan-for-shares schemes, whereby state shareholdings of important enterprises were transferred to selected banks, which held them in trust for several years;[70] they served as guarantees to banks for loans to government bodies;
- convertible bond issues, which could be owned by any legal entity or person.

But these measures were still inadequate for achieving the ultimate objectives of mass privatization: to mobilize private investment from active capital markets and to develop effective ownership and corporate governance schemes for modernizing industrial enterprises. Potential demand (actual savings) has not been transformed into real demand (portfolio investments) because confidence in domestic savings institutions remains low, especially in the regions.

Healthy capital markets depend on reliable institutional investors with refinancing capability, securities markets where shares and bonds can be traded and a consistent legal and regulatory framework. Today, financial markets in Russia are not sufficiently liquid, because the masses of small investors lack confidence. Besides, months of unpaid salaries and job losses have drastically reduced their savings potential. Enterprises cannot issue shares and refinance themselves on the stock exchange.

FDI would help revive portfolio investments and Russia's financial markets.[71] By contributing to job creation in Russian industry, FDI will stabilize contractual savings[72] mechanisms such as pension, insurance and mutual funds, which in return will help generate the long-term capital needed for funding essential FDI-related projects.

16.6.4 Leasing services for industrial equipment

Leasing finance is recommended for projects up to US$10 million usually involving the purchase of new and second-hand equipment for industrial or service applications. Numerous leasing organizations have emerged in Russia since 1993. Most leasing firms are affiliated to larger financial groups, chiefly banks. Some independent leasing organizations also benefit from special refinancing conditions. Like banks, most leasing operators were also affected by the 1998 financial crisis.[73]

In Russia, leasing services are offered by four types of institutions:

- leasing companies created as specialized branches of Russian or foreign banks;
- leasing companies created with participation of state or municipal bodies;
- leasing subsidiaries established by large industrial enterprises or associations;
- subsidiaries of foreign leasing companies.

Leasing companies such as Interesoleasing, Baltic Leasing and Promstroyleasing are backed by their parent banks, who also bring them clients. Leasing companies with municipal participation, like the Moscow Leasing Company and Megaleasing, benefit from extremely advantageous terms, but their statute and mission limit their scope to projects with socioeconomic objectives (e.g. public housing, hospitals, roads). Leasing firms controlled by large industrial enterprises usually specialize in specific branches of industry (e.g. Medleasing in medical equipment, Mashleasing in machinery finance).

In 1990, only two leasing companies existed in Russia, but by the end of 1997 their number had risen to over 300, 80 per cent of which operate in the European part of the Russian Federation. Around 140 leasing companies are based in Moscow. Foreign leasing companies from Austria, Germany, the Netherlands, the United States, the United Kingdom and Finland have created subsidiaries to benefit from the growing market. The total sales volume of leasing operations in Russia in 1997 was estimated at Rb2.5–3.0 trillion or US$400–500 million. In Russia, leasing now accounts for about 5 per cent of total loan provisions and this share is expected to rise to 20 per cent by the turn of the century, which would correspond to the share in industrialized countries (Figure 16.6). Industry and construction are already major users of leased equipment (73 per cent, Figure 16.7 and 16.8), but the tertiary sector (private and public services) is catching up, especially in the larger cities.

The obvious advantage of leasing for the borrower is that it involves a lower risk compared with usual credit financing. Moreover, the bank remains the legal of the equipment until the total amount is paid back, and in case of bankruptcy the equipment returns to the financing organization. Leasing is also a useful option for foreign suppliers as they are immediately paid the full price of the equipment. The Russian customers also gain because they do not incur high initial expenses. The average outlay of a leasing-funded project rose from US$80 000 in 1994 to US$340 000 in 1997. Only large leasing companies are willing to finance projects exceeding US$1 million, which can limit further growth in the procurement of capital equipment

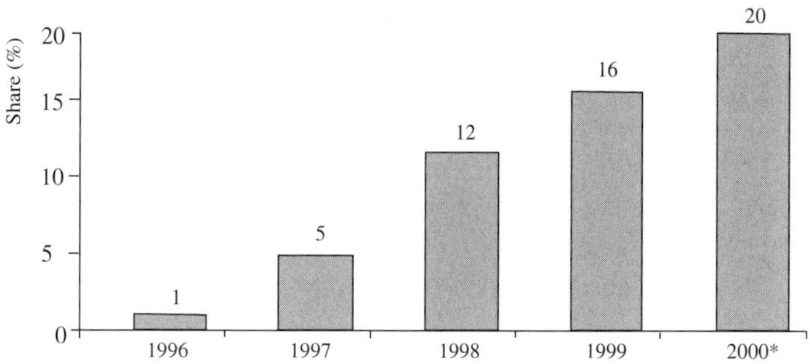

*Estimate.

Figure 16.6 Share of leasing in loan provisions, Russia, 1996–2000

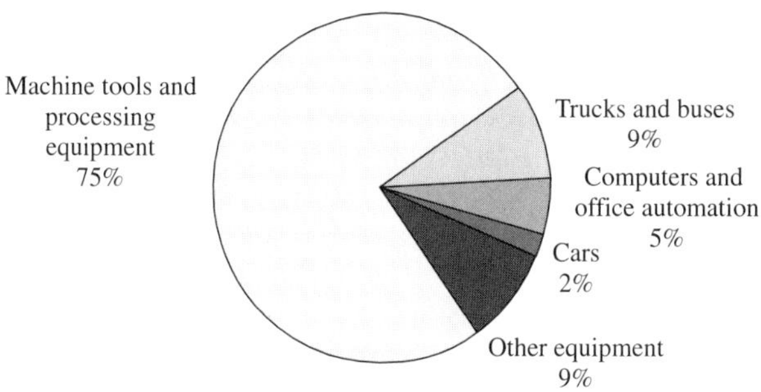

Figure 16.7 Target areas for leasing finance, Russia, 1997

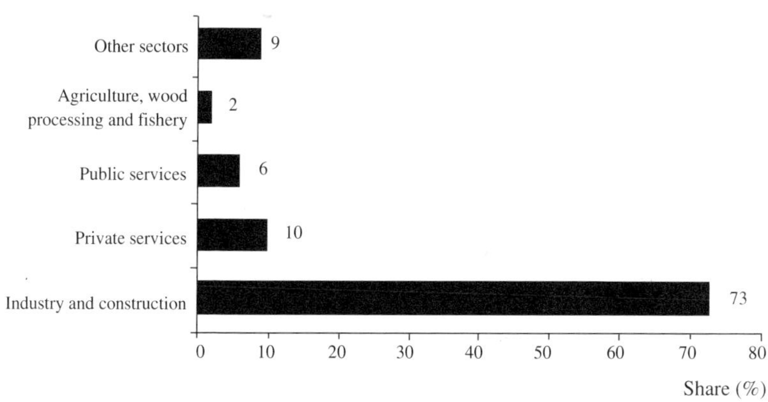

Source: Rosleasing, Russian leasing association.

Figure 16.8 User sectors demanding leased equipment, Russia, 1997

and establishment of large plants. The lifespan of a contract is still quite short: 30 per cent of underwritten contracts have an average duration of up to 1 year, 25 per cent up to 2 years, and 45 per cent up to 3 years.[74]

Leasing could become a key instrument for financing FDI projects. While factory site constructions or modernizations require long-term loans, leasing is a useful medium-term instrument for financing the purchase of essential equipment.

16.6.5 Venture capital finance for knowledge-intensive industries

Venture capital has become an important financial instrument in western economies, particularly for starting new businesses in high-tech areas. The concept aims at high profitability within a short timeframe. The venture capital provider may be a private financial company or a bank. Some industrialized countries created special state banks to provide investment finance, including venture capital, for emerging markets (e.g. Deutsche Entwicklungsgesellschaft, DEG, in Germany). The venture capital organization usually takes part in the new venture and receives a share in the new company's equity. Venture capital firms provide medium-term finance for (mostly small and medium-sized) companies with innovative products and technologies. The venture capital companies become co-owners or partners without collateral as in the case of a bank loan. They thus take the full risk, but are also major beneficiaries if the venture succeeds; this is why target companies are selected very cautiously.[75] The payback period is usually 2–3 years, which allows the venture capital company to sell its equity, for example, by floating the target company's shares on the stock exchange.

The Russian government has started to promote venture capital financing following a decision taken at the 1993 G7 summit in Tokyo.[76] It is supported by the London-based European Bank for Reconstruction and Development (EBRD) and other governments. During the meeting, Russia and its G7 partners decided to allocate US$200 million for venture capital projects, including the conversion of the military–industrial complex. At least 11 venture capital funds have been launched, mostly with the following financial structure:

- US$30 million provided directly by the EBRD;
- US$20 million provided by the participating G7 authority, which may operate through a company specialized in venture capital finance or an investment bank with experience in such loan provisions (e.g. the German company Quadriga for venture capital funding in Greater St Petersburg and in the *oblasts* of Nizhny Novgorod, Vladimir and Yaroslavl);
- equity of Russian company owners, sometimes with foreign partners (usually very low, but sufficient to cover operational expenses).

This type of funding still represents a very small portion of the EBRD's loan facilities for Russia. Funding mostly goes to the banking sector

(€490 million, 35 per cent of the total), and the oil and gas industry (€260 million, 19 per cent).[77] Recently, the EBRD has started investing in industrial ventures. In St Petersburg, for example, venture capital funding was provided to domestic companies in the food (meat processing, brewery), pharmaceuticals and electronics sectors. The success of the scheme has attracted more venture capital providers from OECD countries. European and US venture capital firms[78] have so far focused their activities on OECD countries. They have developed special schemes for certain high-tech industries (information technology, biotechnology, new materials).

More venture capital funds are needed for Russia, considering the advantages and flexibility of this type of finance. Leading industrial companies from the G7 countries should be encouraged to participate as partners in investment projects that are eligible for venture capital funding. The involvement of foreign industrial partners improves the financial base of the new enterprises, reduces risks for the venture capital bank and the foreign partner and ensures continuity of the project after the contracted fund withdrawal period.[79]

16.6.6 Foreign borrowing instruments

Federal and regional governments occasionally issue bonds and debentures in international markets to raise capital. The Moscow city government, for example, financed important infrastructure projects such as the Moscow ring road through euro and dollar bonds. Large companies like Gazprom or Lukoil also use this borrowing facility as they are listed on foreign stock exchanges.

Foreign borrowing involves significant risks and should be utilized with caution, especially during economic transition. Concerned about Russia's rising debt burden, the central government decided to restrict direct borrowing from international capital markets by regional administrations[80] and private enterprises. The government intends to minimize three major risks:

- use of long-term instruments to finance short-term expenditure,
- unpredictable foreign exchange fluctuations, and
- volatility of international capital markets and difficulty of effective hedging.[81]

Foreign borrowing, however, enables governments and companies to access funds from the international financial markets. But the borrower should have a high credit rating.[82] Double- or triple-A ratings enabled western governments and multilateral institutions to tap financial markets at low interest. In 1999, Russia's rating fell from a double-B rating in mid-1997 (BB) to an all-time low of triple-C minus (–CCC).[83] Lack of international confidence makes borrowing expensive, increases risk premiums, and leads to cash flow problems (Figure 16.9).

Other emerging economies like India and China have improved their ratings and now benefit from low risk premiums. During July–August

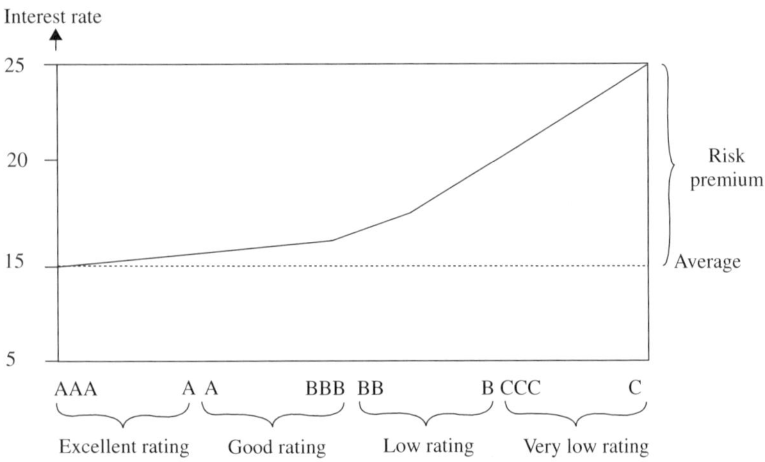

Country ratings (examples)	
Germany, United States, Switzerland	AAA
Italy, Spain	AA
Portugal, Greece, Hungary	A
India, China	BBB
Russia (until December 1997)	BB/B
Russia (after August 1998)	CCC

Figure 16.9 Country ratings and risk premiums

1998, India issued special bonds (India Resurgent Bonds) through the State Bank of India (SBI) to raise funds for urgently needed infrastructure projects in power, telecommunications and road building.[84] The bonds are denominated in dollars, pounds sterling and deutschmarks and directed at foreign investors and expatriate Indians. They are intended to compensate for the shortfall in foreign exchange inflows due to the Asian crisis and economic sanctions imposed by the United States and Japan following the country's nuclear tests. The five-year bonds will be placed on international capital markets at 6.7–8 per cent per annum. The issue has raised almost US$4 billion, twice the initial forecast, owing to the good economic performance and long-term investor confidence in India.

In China, large enterprises such as China Resources and CITIC have borrowed abroad since the beginning of Chairman Deng's open door policy.[85] Funds were raised easily because the country has an excellent international standing and investor rating. The borrowed capital is invested mostly in projects with long-term development potential generating a virtuous economic and financial circle.

Annex 16.1 The MESI experience

A pilot project for developing FDI advisory services, which could serve as an example for national and regional FDI policy-makers, was established at the Moscow State University of Economics, Statistics and Informatics (MESI). The project, which is jointly funded by the German Ministry of Economic Cooperation and Russia's Ministry of Education, resulted in the establishment of an FDI-oriented consulting agency, ICA, through Ministerial Regulation of 31 July 1996.

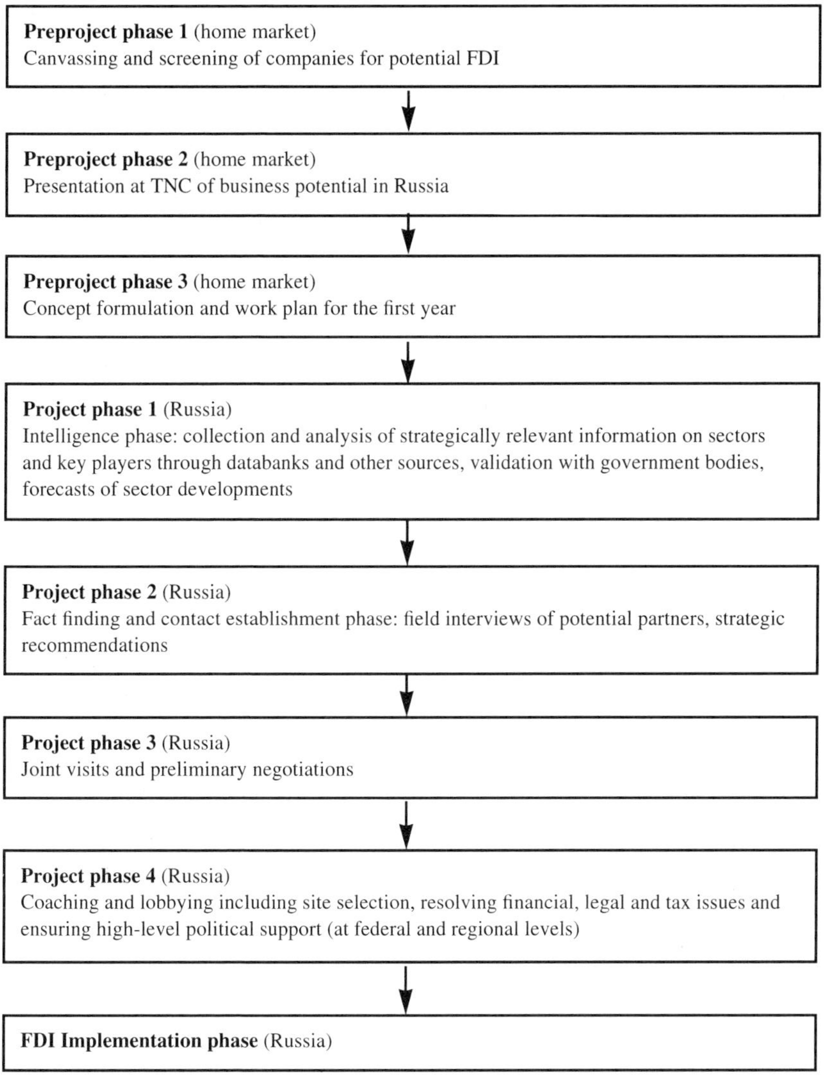

Figure 16.10 Phased programme for FDI projects

ICA integrates all functions for enhancing FDI

- information
- business intelligence
- promotion
- advisory services
- policy research
- training

The first step was to determine priority sectors for FDI. ICA then undertook investment promotion – in Germany and other EU countries. It also surveyed TNCs with offices in Moscow. The objective was to encourage interenterprise alliances with Russian partners in priority sectors for FDI.

During 1996–99, a number of assignments were completed in a number of industries including food processing, wood processing and furniture, building materials and interior components, automotive components, intermediary chemicals, printing equipment, leasing, healthcare and apparel. Special market entry and expansion concepts were designed for each industry. Market leaders in western Europe were then identified and approached with a proposal for transferring technology and know-how. Each project was organized in phases (Figure 16.10). This systematic approach minimizes lead time and risk of error. The investor also has a more transparent view of the business environment and work practices in Russia.

The ICA experience can serve as a model for FDI advisory services in Russia. It has accumulated valuable know-how that could be transferred to other advisory organizations, including educational establishments in the major regions.

Notes

1. Chapter 17.1.
2. Advanced country governments may also promote big projects in recipient countries by subsidizing their domestic companies and lobbying abroad for them (e.g. France's winning of the contract for its rapid train TGV against the German ICE in South Korea in 1996).
3. In France, FDI in 1998 was expected to create almost 30 000 new jobs. *Le Figaro*, 'Ces investissements étrangers qui dopent les emplois hexagonaux' [Stimulating employment in the Hexagon through FDI], 26 April 1999.
4. California attracts most FDI projects among US states. If it were an independent country California would rank seventh in the world in terms of GDP (US$900 billion; population: 30 million). See *Investing in California*, issued by the California Trade and Investment Board, 1997.
5. *The Moscow Times*, 'Daewoo is Wooed by Ukraine', 20 September 1997, p. 7. However, following the financial crash of December 1997 in South Korea, it is not certain whether the investment can be geared up as planned.
6. The European Commission has threatened to close EU borders to cars manufactured under such conditions in the Ukraine.
7. *The Moscow Times*, 'China to Drill Kazakh Oil', 27 September 1997, p. 8.
8. 'Country Report: France', in *Managing 1997*, p. 17.
9. *Auslandskurier*, 'Standort ja, Marketing nein?' [Location yes, marketing no], February 1997, p. 10.
10. UNCTAD, *World Investment Report 1997*, p. 303.
11. 'Country Report: Poland', in *Managing 1997*, p. 19.

12. Especially for FDI in special economic development zones and high-tech parks. See also Chapter 16.2
13. To protect themselves from speculative capital inflows, many governments now allow repatriation only after a minimum of 2–3 years.
14. Sometimes these incentives are communicated only orally without any formal written proposal. A case in point is the failed investment by the leading German paper and stationery manufacturer Herlitz. See *The Moscow Times*, 'The Paper Chase. Who's to Blame for the AO Volga Failure?', 26 August 1997.
15. This could an interesting option for TNCs and their international suppliers; it could help accelerate cluster building in Russia. See also Chapter 12.3.
16. Chapter 17.2.
17. *Ost–West Contact*, June 1996, p. 7.
18. The German development bank KfW has recently become involved in providing funding for bilateral park schemes with German participation abroad. See *Handelsblatt*, 'Industrie- und Gewerbeparks. Vertrautes Umfeld' [Industrial development park, a familiar environment], 8 June 1998, p. B2.
19. M. Quellenec, *L'industrie en France* [Industry in France], 1997, pp. 48–9.
20. There are currently about 180 industrial districts in Italy each consisting of numerous SMEs connected by subcontracting agreements. In 1998, 66 per cent of the districts were located in the northern and 28 per cent in the central part of the country. In certain sectors (e.g. jewellery) they account for up to 60 per cent of Italy's exports. Districts are supported by the local authorities, chambers of commerce and industry associations. The leading districts provide companies with staff training and banking facilities.
21. *Handelsblatt*, 'Industrie- und Gewerbeparks. Grün ist nicht gleich grün' [Industrial and business parks: green is not green], 8 June 1998, B9.
22. This park is part of the Dalian Economic and Technical Development Zone (DETDZ); see Chapter 16.2.3.
23. Information obtained through discussions with zone development authorities in Dalian, northeastern China, August 1997; see also *Dalian Investment Guide* issued by the Dalian Municipal Commission of Foreign Economic Relations and Trade.
24. T. Meng, *Business Opportunities in the Yangtse River Delta*, 1996.
25. *Dalian Investment Guide* issued by the Dalian Municipal Commission of Foreign Economic Relations and Trade, pp. 16–19.
26. By 1997, over 2000 SEZs were recorded worldwide. See also T.G. Morozova *et al*, *Regionalnaya ekonomika* [Regional economics], 1995, p. 294.
27. OECD, *Economic Survey, Russian Federation*, 1997, pp. 192–7.
28. T.G. Morozova *et al*, *Regionalnaya ekonomika* [Regional economics], 1995, p. 301.
29. There are 13 cities with over 1 million inhabitants in Russia: Moscow, St Petersburg, Novosibirsk, Nizhni Novgorod, Kazan, Samara, Yekaterinburg, Volgograd, Rostov, Omsk, Perm, Chelyabinsk, Ufa.
30. M. Porter, *The Competitiveness of Nations*, p. 284.
31. Examples are the regions of Yaroslavl, Kostroma, Orel, Samara, Nizhny Novgorod. Certain districts like Ostrogorsk and Kalatsch (Voronezh region) have also started to disseminate booklets.
32. For example, FDI-related assistance provided by the UK Know-how Fund in Nizhny Novgorod amounts to almost US$5 million. See also *Expert* no. 38, special report on the regions of the Russian Federation, 6 October 1997, p. 10.
33. One possibility would be to produce joint publications, which would be partly covered by regional budgets and then disseminated through the consular services and the international network of the national FDI agency.

34. Most regions tend to draw long lists of investment projects. They should screen, select and group them instead and provide more information on the important projects.
35. For promotional measures, see Chapter 17.
36. The diskette *Doing Business in India* contains major socioeconomic indicators, relevant industrial and regional statistics, and an overview of advantages offered to foreign investors. The diskette is updated annually and disseminated widely.
37. In India, the Ministry of Industry and the Foreign Investment Promotion Board publicize all approved FDI projects through their own website <http://indmin.nic.in>. Foreign investors and analysts can thus study FDI trends on a monthly basis.
38. See also P. Fischer, *System Advice for Russian Statistics, 1994–95. Proposal for the Goskomstat of the Russian Federation. Strategic publications, public relations,* internal report, Eurostat, 1994.
39. Such meetings increasingly receive the sponsorship of chambers of commerce and international bodies such as the European Commission. They may provide an interesting forum for establishing contact but they have so far failed to enhance FDI into LEMs.
40. In 1995, the Russian Ministry of the Economy opened a number of contact bureaus in France, Germany, Italy, the United Kingdom and the United States. So far, these offices have had mixed results. In most cases, companies are not approached systematically and there is significant room for cost reductions. See Chapter 17.
41. There is a strong interdependence between the promotion of FDI and a country's cultural and historical assets, which certain countries intelligently publicize to receive more inbound tourism and corporate investors (e.g. France, India, Italy, Mexico, Spain, Thailand).
42. See also UNCTAD, *World Investment Report 1996.*
43. Based on C. B. M. van Riel, *Principles of Corporate Communication,* 1995.
44. Scenarios are alternative images of possible future realities. Scenario techniques require special skills in lateral thinking that embrace multiple facets of possible future events (political changes, macroeconomic evolution).
45. Because of limited human and technical resources FDI agencies in other countries (e.g. Ireland, Mexico, Singapore, United Kingdom) also use external advisory organizations.
46. See MESI experience, Annex 16.1.
47. As of today, only 18 per cent of bank loans in Russia reach domestic enterprises (industry, trade, services), which is extremely low compared with other industrialized economies. See D. Tscherkasov, 'Banki ustakanivayutsya' [Banks are getting back to normal], *Kompaniya,* 8 March 1998, p. 16.
48. At 31 per cent of GDP, Russia's savings rate is above the average for industrialized countries. Russia's capital base would swell if the large reserves of foreign currency kept outside the domestic banking system are reinvested in the country.
49. Regular round tables should be organized between bankers, Russian companies and foreign TNCs.
50. The central bank sets the national discount or lead rate, which determines refinancing expenses for commercial and investment banks. Sound monetary and financial policies constitute determining framework conditions for a viable FDI policy (Chapter 15.3).

51. *The Economist*, 'Hedge Funds: A Guide', 3 October 1998, p. 94. See also Chapter 2.8.
52. *The Economist*, 'Time to Turn off the Tap?', 12 September 1998, pp. 85–7.
53. The Industrial Development Bank of India (IDBI) plays such a role; it offers preferential loans to foreign companies investing in key industries that are promoted by the national and regional governments; *The Economist*, 'World Trade Survey', 3 October 1998, p. 23.
54. Large institutional investors have withdrawn their funds for fear of a general recession and political instability. Portfolio investments to 29 emerging economies fell to US$160 billion in 1998, down from US$242 billion in 1997 and US$308 billion in the record year 1996. See also *Financial Times*, 'Investors Retreat from Emerging Markets' 1998. This trend will intensify if multilateral donors like the IMF impose 'burden sharing' on private banks in crisis-ridden emerging markets. See the example of Ecuador in *Financial Times*, 'Dilemmas of Default', 20 September 1999.
55. World Bank, *Mobilizing Domestic Capital for Infrastructure Financing*, 1997.
56. Banks are the only recourse for most regional governments as their credit ratings are too low to float their own debentures on international capital markets. See Chapter 16.6.6.
57. Russian banking rules restrict the expansion of foreign banks into the regions and their access to domestic savings.
58. The most important recent legislation on leasing: Resolution of the Government of the Russian Federation of 27 June 1996, no. 752, 'State support for developing leasing activities in the Russian Federation'; Resolution of the State Duma of the Russian Federation of 24 October 1996, no. 735-II, 'Federal law project on leasing'; Resolution of the Government of the Russian Federation of 21 July 1997, no. 915, 'Measures for developing leasing in the Russian Federation during 1997–2000.' See Chapter 16.6.4.
59. Some of the listed banks have ceased operations following the August 1998 crisis. As of May 1999, it is unclear which large banking groups will emerge from total restructuring in the financial sector.
60. George Watzlawek, 'Großbanken suchen ihr Heil in Fusionen' [Large banks strive for mergers], *Handelsblatt*, 30 August 1998; *Kompaniya*, 'Premier Prikamov nashol sebye bankovskii gruppi' [Prime Minister Primakov came across the banking groups], 20 October 1998, pp. 14–18.
61. Bank Austria, Deutsche Bank, Société Générale, ABN Amro, BNP, Dresdner Bank, Citicorp, etc.
62. D. Tytko, *Grundlagen der Projektfinanzierung* [Fundamentals of project finance], 1999; H. Rose, 'Building on the Benefits of Project Financing', in *Mastering Finance*, 1998, pp. 80–5.
63. Although FDI projects are usually 'nonrecourse', in certain cases banks negotiate full or limited recourse contracts that give them the possibility to seize part of the assets if the project fails.
64. HypoVereinsbank, *Project and Asset-based Financing: Tailor-made Solutions for Complex Financing*, November 1998, p. 4.
65. One such example is the Bavaria trust and securitization scheme offered in co-operation with HypoVereinsbank.
66. These techniques should be adapted to the Russian context and based on guarantees (e.g. assets, land or local budgets) obtained from regional authorities.

67. Russia's regional authorities should focus on the most promising projects and provide accurate information on market prospects, value chains, fiscal and financial incentives.
68. Many utility, power and infrastructure projects in the G7 countries were financed on the basis of long-term bonds issued and guaranteed by regional governments; World Bank, *Mobilizing Domestic Capital for Infrastructure Financing*, 1997, pp. 7–11.
69. At the beginning of mass privatization, vouchers were distributed among citizens. By the end of 1994, 40 million Russians held shares in the newly established joint stock companies or voucher investment funds. A. Radygin, *Residual Diverstiture Following Mass Privatization: The Russian Experience. Between State and Market*, 1997, pp. 80–88.
70. Loans-for-share schemes are considered the main vehicle for the formation of large financial–industrial groups (FIGs) in Russia.
71. Following continuously high FDI inflows and good industrial performance over the past 6 years, China recorded a savings rate of 44 per cent in 1997, which the government is now trying to use for domestic capital generation. See World Bank, *Mobilizing Domestic Capital for Infrastructure Financing*, 1997, pp. 41–59.
72. Contractual savings are arrangements under which part of the income of individuals or groups of individuals is put aside and returned at a later stage in form of income, mostly at the time of retirement. They are invested for extended periods in the capital markets and managed by institutional investors, including national provident funds, life insurance companies, private pension funds and funded social pension insurance systems. The importance of such funds for the growth of a national bond market, especially bond financing for large-scale industrial and infrastructure projects, is that they provide long-term investible resources.
73. Some of the leasing companies mentioned in this chapter may have meanwhile faced financial difficulties because of the collapse of the banking and payment system.
74. Source: Rosleasing (Russian leasing association).
75. As a rule, only 3 per cent of requests by start-ups end in a venture capital equity agreement; *Wirtschaftskurier*, 'Sonderbeilage Beteiligungsgesellschaften' [Special report on venture capital], October 1998, pp. 21–22.
76. *Handelsblatt*, 'Die Erfolgsgeschichte beginnt in Sibirien' [The success story starts in Siberia], 4 June 1998, p. 16.
77. *Handelsblatt*, 'Trotz der Krise auch Fortschritte in Rußland' [Despite the crisis, progress in Russia], 9 September 1998.
78. Examples of leading EU venture capital companies are BB Kapitalbeteiligungsgesellschaft mbH and 3i (Germany); NatWest Equity Partners and Electra Fleming (United Kingdom).
79. The payback period for most venture capital schemes is 2–3 years. The main foreign shareholders (mostly financial institutions) seek an early exit option to fund other enterprises in Russia and maximize their overall profits.
80. Three Russian regions encounter difficulties in meeting their obligations for Eurobonds issued before the August crisis: Moscow (US$1.4 billion), St Petersburg (US$300 million), Nizhny Novgorod (US$100 million). See also *The Moscow Times*, 'Nizhny Novgorod Fails to Pay on Eurobond', 15 October 1999.

81. *The Economist*, 'Derivatives. Is there Money in Misfortune?' 18 July 1998, p. 83.
82. International credit rating firms such as Moody's Investor Services and Standard and Poors (S&P) establish annual risk ratings for both countries and large TNCs, usually corporations listed on the stock exchange.
83. *Handelsblatt*, 'Wenig Hoffnung auf IWF Gelder' [Little hope for money from the IMF], 17 September 1998.
84. *China Daily*, 'India Floats Sanction-Busting Bonds', 6 August 1998.
85. L. Brahm, *Red Capital. Hong Kong 1997. China Money Takes Center Stage*, 1997, pp. 44–7.

17
Institution-building and FDI Agenda

17.1 Role of a federal FDI agency

A federal FDI agency holds a central position in FDI promotion and advice, both at enterprise and government levels. A long-term, systematic approach to FDI enhancement demands a powerful institution which is exclusively responsible for policy initiation and implementation, coordination and supervision of all matters concerning FDI. Investment approvals of strategic projects and advisory functions related to them should also be centralized within the agency.[1] Competitor LEMs have instituted such agencies to handle these crucial and sensitive issues.[2] The move has to a large extent gained trust and confidence among investors.

Foreign investors[3] cite various advantages of such a coordinating body that is supported by a network of subagencies in the regions[4] and possibly major FDI source countries:

- direct and effective communication with FDI specialists in the source country and in Russia;
- reliable information on FDI possibilities and opportunities (sectors, regions, technologies, enterprises);
- up-to-date information on policies and procedures;
- a single-window FDI clearing facility in Russia for speedy completion of formalities concerning investment approval;
- less interference from other government bodies and departments because of the technical and administrative autonomy of the agency;
- objective reporting of FDI policies and events in Russia's main regional markets (case studies, success stories);
- possibility to offer consultancy and other strategic services related to FDI to corporate executives.[5]

Institutionalization of FDI issues in the form of an autonomously run entity would send a clear message to the foreign investment community that the Russian government is serious about FDI.

17.1.1 The Russian experience

The Russian government has taken a first step in the direction of promoting FDI by establishing the Foreign Investment Promotion Centre (FIPC) within the Ministry of the Economy on 30 June 1995 (Decree no. 657).[6] The Centre's main function is to inform foreign companies about business opportunities in Russia and to promote inward FDI.[7] During 1995–96, the Ministry opened several promotion offices in major western cities,[8] but although these offices are now operational they have not yet had a significant impact on inward FDI. Opening stand-alone offices is no guarantee of success if their activities are not aligned with the overall FDI policy (target setting, strategic implementation of measures and control).[9]

Promotion and information campaigns cannot be carried out systematically as they are not linked to an integrated national FDI enhancement programme. They do not cover the requirements of Russia's regions, which have to open their own offices. The Centre does not offer advisory services at enterprise level, which would be an additional element of success. These services must be developed and refined through pilot projects with the regions and the major FDI-exporting countries. The Centre also has to improve its internal (Russia) and international research and data-gathering capability so that it can supply strategic information rapidly to potential investors. The Centre focuses on mediation rather than proactive promotion and implementation of investment projects.

Foreign companies find that the present set-up is not conducive to promoting FDI, because the FIPC is not widely recognized as an established, independent, and therefore credible institution. It is not autonomous as it is part of a ministry, and it has not been able to build its identity in international circles. Most TNCs are still unaware of the Centre's existence and the services it offers. The few promotion and public relations activities are not sufficiently coordinated with local industry associations and chambers of commerce; intersectoral and cross-country synergies therefore cannot be exploited to form competitive industrial clusters in Russia's regions.[10] In spite of the Centre's existence, foreign investors still lose time trying to locate the appropriate department among the many existing organizations, agencies and offices involved in resolving FDI issues at federal and regional levels.[11]

The Centre's foreign offices are understaffed and they cannot follow up on projects with potential investors. Furthermore, insufficient budgetary and administrative independence seem to make direct communication (e.g. presentations and workshops at companies, TV interviews, PR conferences) and continuous cooperation with selected regional entities in Russia difficult. As a result, TNCs prefer to be represented at bilateral investment commissions which have been established with a few countries (e.g. US–Russian Investment Commission[12]). The disadvantage of these commissions is that they prefer to lobby on behalf of selected large

TNCs rather than medium-sized players, nor do they have a permanent secretariat.

The role and function of the existing institutional structures should be reassessed given the current budgetary constraints and the need to spread FDI enhancement efforts worldwide. Growing competition from other LEMs necessitates transparent and effective governance and management. Moreover, linkages between the FDI agency and Russian official bodies as well as external advisory organizations will need to be redefined.

Given the lack of significant results, the Russian authorities should seriously consider the imperative need to entrust an independent federal agency with the complex task of attracting FDI and to empower it for carrying out its tasks. The federal FDI agency should be vested with special authority and resources to negotiate directly with foreign enterprises so that its approvals and permits are recognized by law. In Russia, it must interface with all important government departments at federal and regional levels. The agency should be able to carry out independently a number of vital tasks to improve inward FDI, in particular:

- formulate a national FDI policy in cooperation with the regions and ministries;
- propose priority projects in cooperation with regional authorities;
- coordinate FDI-related policies at the highest political level in Russia;
- appear as the main body for FDI issues in foreign countries;
- interact directly with Russian embassies and other official bodies abroad;
- carry out independent information, promotion, public relations and other media-related activities in foreign countries;
- assess objectively the investment potential in Russia (without favouring any city, region or locality)
- hire and train experts, and assign them to important FDI source countries;
- mediate in financial issues related to FDI.

Transparency in all its dealings is important if the agency is to gain the trust and confidence of investors. To avoid conflicts of interest with other ministerial departments or government bodies for resource allocation and managerial talent, the agency should be placed under the governance of the President's Office, the Prime Minister's Office, the Office of the President of the Federation Council or a high-ranking ministerial commission. Its activities and performance should be supervised by the upper (to ensure support from the regions) and lower houses of Parliament.

17.1.2 International practice

FDI agencies in most countries have become increasingly autonomous and powerful since the late 1980s. Western countries have understood that the most democratic model is also the most effective, as it allows the

FDI agency to take quick decisions and concentrate on its main task of increasing FDI. In most LEMs, agencies report directly to the highest levels of the political executive (Prime Minister or a restricted Cabinet of the most important ministers). These single-headed governance models have gradually given way to multi-headed systems which involve more decision-makers.

In India, however, the Foreign Investment Promotion Board (FIPB), which was formerly managed by a joint secretariat consisting of three ministers, has now been placed under one ministry (the Ministry of Industry[13]). The idea was to accelerate decision-making, but it still has to consider the opinion of the ministry for the concerned sector which may not always be the same as that of the FIPB. Moreover, inter-ministerial coordination efforts are being stepped up and more powers granted to state governments (regions) in a move to decentralize approvals and speed up essential infrastructure projects.[14] The idea of creating an FDI ministry has also been put forward to the Indian government. According to the Indian nonresident community, this move would provide India with a more effective and credible institutional framework to compete with other recipient countries for more FDI.[15]

In China, FDI promotion and monitoring is the responsibility of MOFTEC (Ministry of Foreign Trade and Economic Cooperation), which, since the early 1990s, has widened its network of regional offices in China and abroad. Most FDI projects are coordinated locally in collaboration with the respective municipalities. Representatives of important technological development parks working under the jurisdiction of larger cities manage their own promotional budgets and can undertake intelligence missions and public relations campaigns in target countries. Provincial and city governments have the authority to approve most investments and accompany TNCs through projects. Special permissions from MOFTEC in Beijing are required for strategic FDI projects with significant socioeconomic impact (e.g. raw materials extraction, energy or defence-related FDI) for the country as a whole, and where capital transfers exceed US$30 million. As in other emerging economies (e.g. Argentina, Chile, Poland), the maximum limit of investments that can be approved by the regional authorities is being gradually increased.[16] Although overall FDI policy remains centralized in China, approvals and project implementation are increasingly delegated to the corresponding regional and local authorities.

Democratic governance models have emerged in a number of industrialized countries. To demonstrate the shift from interventionism to targeted macroeconomic state guidance, liberal governments have created independent agencies for certain strategic areas of national interest like FDI. This change in approach to FDI began in the Anglo-Saxon countries in the 1980s. Today, Ireland, the United Kingdom and the United States have fairly independent FDI agencies with sizeable budgets for operating foreign antennas, recruiting well-paid professionals and canvassing TNCs directly in their home markets. These agencies have gained an impressive international reputation through results-oriented management and ethical conduct. They regularly publish reports of their activities and advertise in leading international business magazines to promote their services or recruit specialists for their expanding agency networks abroad.[17] Such efforts combined with liberal policies have resulted in higher FDI inflows than in other OECD countries.

The practice in several US states has shown how independence can be combined with minimum control in democratically accountable agencies:[18]

- annual budgets allocated by the highest political office (Congress, President, Governor);
- forecasts and limits on total expenditure mandated by regulation or decree;
- narrowly defined objectives, to facilitate accountability for results;
- reinvestment of earnings in agency expansion and improvement of procedures;[19]
- peer review by a wide spectrum of independent specialists, including university professors, to certify technical quality of projects and objectivity of agency decisions;[20]
- reliance on parliamentary or judicial review to guarantee protection of investors' rights;
- participation of accredited external advisors to enlarge the agency's know-how base and to raise efficiency levels;[21]
- strict transparency stipulations to limit arbitrary decisions and regulatory discretion.

The expansion of FDI and other regulatory agencies in industrialized countries has been guided by these or similar principles. Experience shows that when such a multi-pronged system of controls works efficiently, an independent agency is 'under control' although it is not controlled directly by any single entity. A fundamental advantage is that it can remain committed to a long-term FDI strategy, independently of the government in place. Long-term policy commitment is notoriously difficult to achieve in a democracy, which is a form of government *pro tempore*. The segmentation of the legislative period into relatively short time spans (usually 4–5 years) has serious consequences whenever socioeconomic problems require long-term solutions.

Although each country requires specific solutions, most governments have recognized the advantages of autonomous FDI agencies and the respect of democratic principles to gain the confidence of foreign investors. Greece, for example, which was known for its tight central political control in the past, has recently created a noncommercial, public interest corporation, the Hellenic Centre for Investment (HCI). Its mandate is to seek, inform, encourage, counsel and support prospective investors throughout the investment process, including help in securing the necessary licences and public approvals.

17.1.3 Governance options for Russia's FDI agency

Delegation of policy-making powers to a specialized body in charge of FDI would be welcomed by investors who would finally be able to obtain comprehensive and objective information on legislation, market potential, FDI opportunities and potential Russian partner enterprises. Opinions of FDI specialists should be based on the best available evidence rather than political expediency. An autonomous agency guided by goal-oriented professionals will resist interference from political outsiders and focus on projects with wide socioeconomic impact for the regions. An independent FDI agency would also lower decision-making costs for the federal government and regional administrations by reducing time spent on technical details, implementation and coordination.

The following options can be considered for constituting the Governing Board of the agency (Figure 17.1):

- single-headed (executive): President, Prime Minister, President of the Federation Council,[22] First Deputy Prime Minister;
- multi-headed (executive): cabinet of selected ministers;
- pluri-headed (executive and legislative): Board formed by the highest executive (Prime Minister, selected ministers) supported by the Heads of Duma (main parties) and Federation Council (main regions);
- multifunctional structure, comprising a political governing board and an advisory board of leading scientists and experts.

During the initial period, single-headed governance could be an advantage, provided there is continuity in the country's political leadership. To gain the political support of the regions, the agency could be established under the aegis of the Federation Council. Three- or four-headed governance models involving the highest levels of the executive and legislative powers could also be suitable for Russia. But the Board should be composed in such a way that it does not slow down decision-making. As yet, no large country has adopted a governance model that involves both the executive and the legislative, although there is a general tendency worldwide to include regional authorities. While approval of FDI projects below a certain ceiling are delegated to regional authorities, in most countries the regions cannot participate in policy-making and management of the agency.

Governance	Branch	Advantages	Disadvantages
Single-headed			
	Executive, restricted (President, Prime Minister, President of the Federation Council, First Deputy Prime Minister)	Short line of command, fast implementation of policies	Decisions motivated by election constraints Lack of broad consensus and control in the Parliament
Multi-headed			
	Executive (e.g. President and selected Cabinet members)	Fairly quick decision-making procedure and implementation	'Ideological' compromises in case of coalition governments
Pluri-headed			
	Executive	Consensus-based decision-making supported by all major parties	Longer procedure due to divergent views among the various parties
	Legislative		
Multifunctional			
	Executive	Most objective policy formulation because of wide-ranging expert opinions	Too many experts can dilute political decisions, which must be taken quickly to develop key industries with socioeconomic impact
	Legislative		
	Independent experts		

Figure 17.1 Alternative governance models for Russia's FDI agency

Legislators and the executive in Russia will have to select an agency model that fits into the existing institutional structures and best meets the country's long-term goals:

- Where should Russia stand in terms of inward FDI in the coming years?
- In which ways could confidence levels be restored with foreign governments and among TNCs?
- How could integration in the world market be accelerated through increased FDI and trading activities?
- Which industrial technologies should be developed through capital and know-how exchange by 2015–20?
- In which way will the central authorities cooperate with regional administrations to design an industrial policy for balanced socioeconomic development?

These and other important responses will determine the resource commitments and the final governance structure of Russia's FDI agency.

Inward investment has a chance of attaining a critical mass only if a high degree of autonomy, competence and enforcement powers are delegated to build a strong federal FDI agency, which can thus systematically build international confidence, and Russia's reputation and credibility over time. Whether the emphasis should be placed on democratic legitimacy and openness (pluri-headed or multifunctional governance) or speedy realization and efficiency (single- or multi-headed governance) will need to be examined carefully. A middle path could perhaps be found that combines the advantages of the different alternatives.

17.1.4 Agency organization and management

As in a private corporation, the agency's performance will be the result of three intertlinked dimensions: strategy, structure and leadership. Strategy determines structure in any organization, corporate or governmental. The agency's organization will therefore need to be in line with the policy and overall objectives determined by the Russian government. It must also be sufficiently flexible to adapt to changes in the global FDI scenario. To become an integrated and internationally recognized body, Russia's federal FDI agency should be organized according to seven important functions or departments[23] (Figure 17.2):

- regulation and approvals,
- intelligence,
- communication,
- advisory services,
- networking and cooperation,
- financial engineering,
- administration.

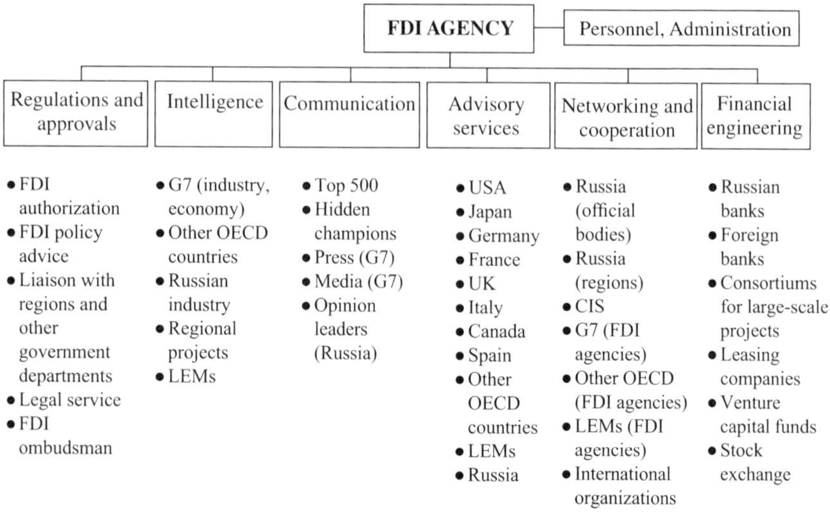

Figure 17.2 Proposed structure of an independent FDI agency

The *regulations and approvals department* performs the core function of the agency (e.g. FIPB in India). In addition to granting authorizations, the department must advise the government on FDI policy, and systemize and simplify procedures for foreign investors. At present, there is no clear system and TNC representatives sometimes do not know which federal or regional authority they should approach for obtaining approvals. To simplify the procedure, the agency could consider decentralizing this function to the regional authorities for investments below a certain level. This implies coordination and information exchange. The department should include a legal service and a business ombudsman, who would hear complaints and suggestions for improvement from TNCs investing in Russia. The feedback from investors could thus be communicated to the policy advisors.

The *intelligence department* provides information support to all the departments of the agency:

- To the regulations department, information on the status of Russian industry so that it can set its sectoral and regional priorities.
- To the communication department, information that is useful for targeting the right TNCs.
- To the advisory services department and its external advisory network, data and statistics on Russian enterprises and sectors, including their current and future business potential.
- To the networking and cooperation department, information on global policy trends and the role of their potential partners.

- To the financial engineering department, information on new sources of finance available for Russian projects.

The *communication department* is responsible for projecting a positive image of Russia and the agency.[24]

The *advisory services department* orients investors on procedures and regulations; it is supported by an external advisory network for consulting on market entry and business development strategies. The network will include nodes in Russia and the leading FDI source countries.[25] In cooperation with other network members (e.g. universities, semi-official regional bodies), the advisory services department will offer the following services:

- strategy advice,
- sector and market analyses (in close cooperation with the intelligence department),
- partner search and evaluation (due diligence),
- location analysis,
- project feasibility studies, and
- coaching and lobbying (legal, administrative and political support).

The *networking and cooperation department* is responsible for coordination and information exchange with the government, the state legislature and the regions. The department should also cooperate with the greater economic areas (GEAs) in their efforts to promote FDI.[26] Within Russia, it should also maintain contacts with chambers of commerce and industry associations. An external relations section will be in charge of strengthening relations with CIS countries (to define common rules and standards[27] and develop triangular FDI projects), 'far abroad' economies and international organizations.

The *financial engineering department* will cooperate closely with the advisory services department to determine viable FDI projects and organize finance. It will maintain close links with selected financial institutions in Russia and abroad.[28]

All these departments should form a cohesive whole based on interaction and exchange. To meet this challenge, the agency's executives should be selected for their:

- readiness to represent the agency's interests in Russia and abroad,
- understanding of different cultures including language and communication skills,
- knowledge of working practices in the private and public sectors,
- dynamism, self-motivation and proactive approach,
- flexibility and creativity,
- team spirit and efforts to mobilize young talent.

Certain management practices of private companies can be usefully adopted by the agency (Figure 17.3).[29] Agency managers should be empowered to use

Strive for differentiation
- Unique selling propositions (USP) in core service areas to compete more effectively with other FDI agencies: imaginative information products, country-specific advisory services, modern financial instruments, etc.

Promote efficiency
- Performance- and results-oriented approach aimed at generating own financial resources
- Cost consciousness while implementing FDI policies so that public budgets are not strained.

Respect timing
- Timely execution of tasks and rapid reactivity to investors' requests

Concentrate forces
- Focus on priority areas
- Consistency in strategy implementation

Build on strengths
- Constant improvement of the agency's strengths while minimizing weaknesses
- Identify industries and assets where Russia has visible competitive advantages

Exploit synergies
- Cooperation between the agency's main departments, but also between the agency and external organizations in Russia, the CIS and other countries
- Networking with specialists in Russia and abroad

React to external opportunities
- Continuous monitoring of global FDI trends
- Alertness in spotting promising investment projects
- Talent spotting

Balance resources and objectives
- Rational use of resources
- Step-by-step approach

Promote corporate identity and culture
- Team spirit
- Flat and open organization

Figure 17.3 Fundamental rules of good agency management

and allocate resources independently so that they can achieve the targets (e.g. annual FDI by sector, technology or region) set before them.

Several issues will need to be addressed during the development phases of the agency, for example:

- What should be Russia's FDI agency's mission? Should it have only a policy and coordinating role or should it be involved mainly in information and advisory services?
- Should it work like a public entity or on a semi-commercial basis?[30] What legal form should it have to work effectively in the Russian context and be accepted by foreign investors?
- Which budget can be allocated for the agency and to what extent can other donors (foreign national and regional governments, international organizations) and private sponsors (TNCs, banks) be mobilized for funding the agency and its foreign offices[31]?
- What is the work plan and the timeframe for the different development phases of the federal agency?
- What are the costs of setting up external advisory structures? Up to what business volume (number of projects per year) should services be carried out internally and when would it be more effective to use external structures?[32]
- Should the federal agency open subagencies in Russia's main economic regions? How many and when? How could it integrate existing and new investment promotion offices set up by the regions?

17.2 Need for an FDI agenda

Foreign investment will play a vital role for Russia's industrial development in the coming decades. To attract more investment, the Russian government will be obliged to maintain a liberal course and, simultaneously, to provide strategic economic guidance. It should emphasize interenterprise and technological cooperation more than public aid projects that are disconnected from the real economy.

The authorities will have to first elaborate and approve a concept adapted to the Russian context, which will then need to be implemented by a strong institution responsible for enhancing inward FDI. Russia needs a consistent FDI strategy that will harmonize the activities already initiated by the government (agency created within the Ministry of the Economy, promotion offices opened in the G7 countries, legislative changes, etc.).

The national FDI agenda or master plan should clearly define the objectives, guidelines and policy instruments to be implemented in the coming years.[33] Russia's FDI agenda should be reviewed by an independent expert commission of specialists drawn from administrative, juridical, economical, industrial, and international business backgrounds. Representatives of the major economic regions, whose support will be needed for policy implementation, should also be invited to send their own proposals for industrial upgrading through FDI. The FDI agenda should address the following issues:

- The importance of promoting FDI as an additional source of capital and investment.
- Priority industries and regions to be developed through FDI.
- FDI targets for 2000–05.
- The role and powers of the federal FDI agency.
- Strategic state guidance for FDI policies.
- Streamlining of procedures and approval mechanisms.
- Incentives and conditions for foreign investors.
- Coordination between ministries and regional authorities.
- Information, promotion and advisory instruments for TNCs and opinion leaders.
- Russia's role in international organizations dealing with FDI issues.

The agenda should have a legal foundation in the form of a presidential decree, regulation or law to ensure broad political support and legitimacy. According to the Russian Constitution, a text becomes law when it is adopted by both houses of legislature (Duma, Federation Council). Although this process is long and requires intensive lobbying, it would confer legitimacy to the FDI policy and agenda. A policy that has wide political consensus would gain the confidence of the international community. It would also encourage the CIS countries to ratify the common Convention for the Protection of Investors' Rights in line with Russia's 1999 Foreign Investment Law.

The FDI agenda would demonstrate the Russian government's intention to distance itself from general aid programmes for developing the market economy. While multilateral aid has focused mainly on large-scale public sector and institution building projects, the FDI agenda attempts to mobilize the private sector in an effort to develop national industries and upgrade their technology.

Continuous benchmarking with other FDI recipients will enable Russian policy-makers to stay in the vanguard and to develop a unique strategy that capitalizes on the country's comparative advantages. Other countries usually include foreign investment in general economic or industrial policies, but they do not specify overall sectoral and regional targets for raising industrial competitiveness through FDI. Very few governments pursue a proactive strategy to approach both large and medium-sized TNCs as potential investors. Among the LEMs, only India has created a powerful institution to screen FDI projects, but even this institution does not undertake any targeted promotion abroad. In industrialized countries, FDI agencies do not have strong advisory and financial engineering functions for developing concrete projects. Russia therefore has a chance to pioneer the concept of an integrated FDI agency supported by an external advisory network.

A proactive FDI policy will eventually help Russia select the TNCs that will contribute most usefully and rapidly to its industrial recovery. This is better than passive acceptance of investors who seek short-term benefits from the market and are not prepared to contribute to socioeconomic development and environment protection.

Notes

1. A ceiling should be established beyond which all FDI projects are supervised directly by the agency, e.g. US$40 million for Greater Moscow, US$20 million for other regions. While the federal agency would supervise all projects originating from the world's top 500 corporations, the regional network could assist in channelling FDI from the 'hidden champions'.
2. A. G. Witt, 'Promoting Transnational Investment: Organizing to Serve Approved Investors', *Transnational Corporations Journal*, 2(1), February 1993, pp. 86–88.
3. Over 60 directors of large and medium-sized companies were interviewed in Germany and Italy for an investor survey conducted for this study during 1996–98.
4. To support the federal agency, regional subagencies could be opened in the leading regions (e.g. Moscow, St. Petersburg, Samara) for investment projects in the greater economic areas. Regional subagencies should be assisted by 'partner' regions in OECD countries in their efforts to attract target companies.
5. See Chapters 16.1 to 16.6.
6. To set up the Centre, the Russian authorities received training and advice from Germany's Ministry of the Economy, the Irish Investment Promotion Office and a number of international organizations.
7. The main tasks and services are presented on the Centre's website <www.fipc.ru/fipc> (Charter, Section III/12 and 13).
8. Offices have so far been opened or are in the process of being started in Frankfurt, Paris, London, Milan, Amsterdam, Stockholm, Singapore, Tokyo and Washington D.C.
9. A. G. Witt, 'Public Marketing of Foreign Investment: Successful International Offices Stand-Alone', *International Journal of Public Sector Management*, 5(5), 1992, pp. 38–39.
10. Chapter 12.3.
11. Investors report of FDI departments which exist simultaneously in the President's office, the Prime Minister's office and in many other national ministries and regional bodies.
12. *US Chamber of Industry News, Moscow*, 1997.
13. Formerly the FIPB reported directly to the Prime Minister. See Chapter 6.3.1.3.
14. Sh. Rangnekar, 'States Given More Latitude to Attract FDI in Core Sectors', *The Economic Times*, 8 May 1998, p. 1.
15. NRI (nonresident Indian) tycoon, S. P. Hinduja, called for the formation of an FDI ministry at a press conference in New Delhi on 8 February 1999. This proposal was included in a memorandum submitted to the Minister of Finance,

Y. Sinha, by the IndusInd Federation, a platform of overseas Indian and resident businessmen.

16. This trend is also observed in Russia, where regional authorities increasingly decide on major FDI projects.
17. The UK and Irish FDI promotion agencies, for example, regularly advertise in Germany's economic journals to search for well-connected investment officers.
18. See also G. Magione, 'The Agency Model: The Growth of Regulation and Regulatory Institutions in the European Union', *Eipascope*, March 1997, pp. 9–14. These control mechanisms in fact refer not only to FDI agencies, but also to other regulatory bodies and 'non-majoritarian' institutions, i.e. institutions that, by design, are not directly accountable to voters or their elected representatives (e.g. central banks, supranational bodies like the European Commission and courts of law).
19. It may be advantageous to consider the legal form of nonprofit organization for the federal agency and its regional affiliates. This would reduce political pressure, and earnings could be reinvested for expansion of the network. The agency network should be results-oriented.
20. The Russian FIPC is assisted by a council of independent experts, whose appointment is 'confirmed by the leadership of the Ministry of Economics at the initiative of the Centre's Director General' (Charter, Section VI/28).
21. See Chapter 16.5.
22. The Federation Council represents both the executive and legislative powers of the regions (88). The Council has 196 members, who are the governors and the heads of regional parliaments.
23. The present organization of the FIPC has only three operational departments: regional programmes and marketing projects, analysis and information, and publishing.
24. Chapter 16.4.
25. Chapter 16.5.
26. *Moscow Times*, 'Yelsin: Time to Halt Battles with Regions', 1 November 1997.
27. An FDI Convention to protect foreign investors' rights across the CIS was approved by the Heads of State and Government of CIS countries. It is expected to be ratified by the respective parliaments (Gosdumas) in the course of 1999–2000. The coordinating work is ensured by the Inter-CIS Economic Committee (MEK). The text of the Convention exists only in Russian. See *Information bulletin*, no. 1(5), MEK, 1997, pp. 5–16.
28. See Chapter 16.6.
29. See also R. Mason *et al*, *Strategic Management*, 1994, p. 482.
30. By statute, the FIPC is entitled to obtain profits from the sale of products, work and services and other entrepreneurial activity (statute IV/16).
31. Part of the bilateral and multilateral funds could be allocated towards the development of the agency. This would demonstrate the commitment of the international community to support Russia's endeavours in reshaping its industries through FDI.
32. A fee-splitting mechanism must be defined for services contracted out to external organizations. But the agency should not forget its socioeconomic mission.
33. According to the medium-term investment plan of the Ministry of the Economy, FDI has to be increased from US$2 billion in 1997 to US$10 billion in 2000. See OECD, *Economic Survey, Russian Federation*, 1997, pp. 123–9.

Appendix: Definitions and Explanatory Notes

In this section, the reader will find definitions and explanations of subject areas related to foreign direct investment (FDI) and covered by the study. The following topics will be explained:

- general characteristics of FDI and its components;
- FDI and portfolio investment;
- FDI stocks and flows;
- types of FDI: greenfield investments, transplants, strategic alliances and joint ventures, acquisitions and mergers;
- motivations to invest abroad: raw materials-seeking FDI, cost-minimizing FDI, market-driven FDI and strategic FDI;
- international practice of industrial classification.

The explanations will help to better understand the implications of FDI, its scope and potential impact on the industrial sector.

1 FDI-related definitions

1.1 General characteristics of FDI and its components

Investment can be defined as expenditure for purposes other than immediate consumption. Different forms of investment can have more or less pronounced effects on overall economic growth depending on the stage of economic development of a country. Basically, three types of investment have an impact on industrial modernization:[1]

- investment in physical capital, especially equipment, machines, buildings and infrastructure;
- investment in human capital, primarily through expenditure on education and training (human resource development);
- investment in technological capital in the form of expenditure on research and development.

Investment operations can be carried out by domestic and foreign operators. FDI is an operation that enables an enterprise to effectively control the management of a legal entity (enterprise) located in a foreign country. It involves the transfer of essential factors of production such as capital, equipment (including second-hand machinery), management and other resources (know-how, patents, etc.) to other manufacturing units or plants. FDI can be characterized as follows:[2]

- It involves a *long-term* relationship and reflects a *lasting* interest and control by an enterprise in the home country (foreign direct investor or parent enterprise) in another enterprise located in the host or recipient country.

- It enables the investor to exert a *significant* degree of influence on the *management* of the enterprise in the host country, which has absorbed the investment in the form of capital and know-how.
- It covers both the initial transaction and all subsequent transactions between the two entities (companies).
- It is undertaken mainly by transnational corporations (TNCs), but also includes direct participation in companies by individuals.
- It can take several forms: sales subsidiary, joint venture, greenfield operation (new plant), full or partial acquisition of a resident firm.
- It is increasingly regulated (and thus protected) by bilateral and international agreements, which promote essential principles of industrial cooperation: 'national treatment' of foreign firms, 'most favoured nation' approach (the same rules apply to all enterprises, independently of the country of origin), nondiscrimination, guarantee not to adopt unexpected coercive measures, adequate compensation in case of expropriation, free transfer of profits, arbitration of legal disputes.

Statistically, FDI comprises four major components, although they are not recorded systematically by every country:

- *Greenfield investment*: creation of a totally new enterprise, including an extension of capacity of a manufacturing unit belonging to the foreign investor.
- *Equity capital*: purchase of a stake by the investor in an enterprise located abroad; depending on the country, the stake has to exceed a ceiling of 10–20 per cent to qualify as FDI.
- *Reinvested earnings*: the direct investor's share in earnings (proportional to the equity participation) that is not distributed as dividends by affiliates or is not remitted to the direct investor. During the first few years of the operation, TNCs usually allow their foreign affiliates to reinvest retained profits for expanding business operations.
- *Intracompany loans*: short- or long-term borrowing and lending of funds between parent enterprises (direct investors) and affiliates (recipients).

1.2 FDI and portfolio investments

FDI implies a long-term relationship and durable control of a business operation by a TNC in a foreign country. This fundamental feature distinguishes FDI from portfolio investments, which are a less permanent participation in enterprises aimed at making speculative financial gains by trading a company's shares on the stock exchange. Both institutional and private portfolio investors pursue mostly short-term strategies of profit maximization. They emphasize the liquidity factor and their ultimate objective is not to control management or any assets of the company.

The distinction between FDI and portfolio investment is not always clear. There is no international consensus on a uniform definition that would be acceptable by all countries. In most countries, equity participation of 10 per cent and above in any foreign company qualifies as FDI. In other cases (e.g. Germany, the United Kingdom) the ceiling is 20 per cent. All capital transactions below the established level are recorded as portfolio operations. Because of these differences, FDI statistics are not always entirely comparable between different countries.

In the case of FDI, actual control of an enterprise may depend less on the equity held by individual investors (minority versus majority stake) than on the overall composition of the shareholder capital, the existence of dominating shareholders, and blocking minority rules. In Germany and a number of other EU countries, for example, a minority stake of 25 per cent of the share capital is sufficient to block major management decisions in limited companies.

1.3 FDI stocks and flows

FDI stock is defined as the value of the share of a parent company's capital and reserves (including retained profits) plus the net indebtedness of its affiliates. FDI stocks are recorded at book value or historical cost, reflecting prices at the time of investment. For most countries, FDI stocks are determined by cumulating FDI flows over a period of time.

FDI flows are recorded as net amounts by deducting debits between TNCs and their foreign affiliates from credits of capital transactions. In the FDI recipient country, net increases in assets or net decreases in liabilities are recorded as credits (positive sign in the balance of payments), whereas net decreases in assets or net increases in liabilities figure as debits (negative sign in the balance of payments). Negative FDI flows are generated by reverse investment or disinvestment, indicating that at least one of the three components of FDI (equity capital, reinvested earnings, or intra-company loans) is negative and not offset by positive values of the remaining two components.

Flows and stocks are closely related. New flows, by definition, add to the FDI stock. At the same time, stocks generate new flows when profits are reinvested, thus increasing the stock. The size of profits depends on the size of FDI stock and general profitability of the investment. Although volumes of inbound and outbound FDI should be equal between countries, significant divergences occur because fiscal years and accounting practices may vary in each country. As outward FDI mainly stems from a small number of countries, whose statistics are generally more reliable than those of many recipient countries, outward flows and stocks serve as a first reference. Inward flows and stocks can then be determined quite accurately from this parameter.

Nevertheless, considerable differences in the calculation of FDI stocks and flows still occur between the two main sources of global FDI: the United Nations Conference on Trade and Development (UNCTAD) and the Organisation for Economic Co-operation and Development (OECD). While UNCTAD has developed its own data collection methodology, OECD statistics are mostly based on FDI data supplied by the central banks of the member countries, which are not usually gathered on the basis of harmonized methodologies.

2 Types of FDI

FDI has developed and diversified considerably over time as it had to adjust to the context of rapidly changing international markets, economic liberalization, worldwide financial deregulation and the introduction of new technologies. The four main forms of FDI are :

- greenfield investments,
- transplants,
- strategic alliances and joint ventures
- mergers and acquisitions

2.1 Greenfield investments

Until the 1980s, greenfield investments represented the main form of FDI. Such investments were customarily undertaken by leading TNCs from industrialized countries interested in establishing production facilities outside their home country. In most cases, such investments were made in other industrialized markets with good growth prospects or in developing countries offering cheap labour and abundance of natural resources. Greenfield FDI is mainly undertaken when the investor intends to retain maximum control of the new manufacturing operation. It is less common in difficult environments, including LEMs, where language, culture, and political and administrative systems can be barriers. Recently the number of greenfield investments has been increasing.

Greenfield operations are highly capital intensive and are usually resource- or market-seeking. New plants are less profitable in small markets, except if they show high stability and offer access to important nearby markets (Singapore as a hub for sales to Malaysia and Indonesia, Belgium as a base for exports to Germany).

Greenfield investments can be found in all industries, but they are undertaken mainly in the raw materials (oil, gas, metallurgy), chemicals, automotive, electronics and food sectors.

2.2 Transplants

The first transplants or 'screwdriver' factories were opened by Japanese and South Korean manufacturers of cars and consumer electronics in the 1980s. They were first established in the United States and later in the United Kingdom. The aim was to circumvent import duties and nontariff trade barriers. Components were imported from the investor's home country and assembled in production units in the host country.

In the United Kingdom, Japanese transplants came under attack by local lobbies for not generating high-skill jobs and for practising price dumping *vis-à-vis* domestic competitors. Investors now have to comply with local content rules.

The *maquiladora*[3] plants in Mexico can be considered as transplants, although they have started producing for the domestic market. For Austrian, German and Italian firms, the Czech Republic, Poland and Hungary have also become important assembly and turnkey locations for reexports to EU markets.

2.3 Strategic alliances and joint ventures

Strategic alliances are formed between two separate legal entities (companies) to exploit synergies and to improve market position. They can cover all business functions (production, R&D, distribution) and are governed by loose or very binding agreements. A joint venture generally constitutes a separate legal entity in which both partners have different (majority and minority) or equal (50 per cent) share of the equity. Joint ventures are designed to optimize mutual strengths of two partners and to overcome weaknesses by pooling essential business functions. They are governed by contracts that specify the aims of the partners as well as the respective shares of the partners in equity, management control and earnings to be reinvested. The success of a joint venture depends on the compatibility of the management philosophies of the promoters. Majority joint ventures often work better than 50:50 joint ventures.

In strategic sectors such as atomic energy, mining of gold and diamonds, railways and air transport, governments only allow minority stakes by foreign investors. In emerging and transition economies, governments permit majority equity in industries that urgently need capital (infrastructure) or technology (biotechnology) infusions.

2.4 Mergers and acquisitions (M&A)

Through an acquisition, a TNC obtains a controlling (majority) stake in an existing operation in the host country. It thus gains rapid market access and benefits from local know-how of the business environment. Generally, large and financially strong TNCs prefer outright purchases of existing firms. Takeovers can also be gradual and start with a majority stake. TNCs consolidate their leadership through M&A. Both hostile and open takeovers are mostly handled by specialized acquisition brokers and investment banks. In the past two decades, numerous new institutions have emerged to help companies identify suitable acquisition candidates and to mastermind investment or divestment projects.

Instead of acquiring a company, a TNC can also choose to merge with another player. Mergers may occur where there is complementarity of production or when the two companies decide to reduce costs and exploit synergies to face increasing competition at home and abroad. Most mergers are between large players. Mergers are not as frequent between medium-sized players, but with increasing competition and the need for global market coverage such deals are expected to rise, especially between companies of the same country of origin.

3 Motivations for investing abroad

The most important motivations for FDI are sourcing of natural resources, efforts to reduce manufacturing costs, access to consumers or users in foreign markets, and strategic positioning. As FDI increases on a global scale leading to further integration of economies and companies, market factors have taken precedence over mere cost-related factors. Well-managed companies will seek opportunities for rationalizing production, but they will not invest significantly in countries that do not offer large domestic markets or access to nearby markets. The size of a country's domestic market is therefore considered a far more important criterion for an investment decision than cost reductions.

3.1 Resource-seeking FDI

For TNCs in extraction (mining, minerals, petroleum) and primary processing (steel) sectors, the critical factor prompting an FDI decision is the availability of raw materials that may be in short supply in the home market. Resources-based FDI reduces the risk of supply shortage and price volatility; it also reduces transport costs.

3.2 Cost-minimizing FDI

TNCs may build plants overseas to take advantage of cheap local inputs, particularly labour, to produce components or assemble products for the parent company. Many western and Japanese investments in the ASEAN countries and Mexico are of this type. As wages rise, such offshore factories are often shifted to other countries where rates are even lower. For example, the production of sports shoes has been shifted from Singapore and Taiwan to China, and recently to Vietnam. High wage countries are compelled to upgrade technical and educational skills to encourage foreign investors to add value to locally produced products. German and other EU companies invested in Central Europe for low-cost considerations. Now that labour costs are increasing in these countries, they have started looking at the most promising CIS countries.

In addition to labour cost, companies analyze a range of other cost and productivity factors:

- social security benefits,
- rents, real estate prices,
- direct and indirect taxes,
- cost of utilities (water, energy),
- transport costs,
- environmental regulations,

- housing facilities,
- educational facilities, and
- cost and quality of living for expatriates.

3.3 Market-driven and strategic FDI

Market-seeking FDI is highly competitive; it aims to drive out competitors from established or new markets; it is thus closely related to strategic FDI. Whereas medium-sized players focus on established markets, large TNCs can afford to establish operations in difficult environments in an effort to position themselves early and to prevent competitors entering the same market. Such investment decisions are considered strategic investments because the idea is to first defend a company's position rather than make profit, although in the long term market-related factors will necessarily have to prevail.

4 International practice of industry classification

Industry comprises all manufacturing activities, including raw materials extraction and mining, the production of intermediary and finished goods for capital-intensive or consumer-oriented manufacturing. The broad definition of industry includes construction activities and operations related to energy.

Industry is divided into branches. Industrialized countries use comparable nomenclatures and definitions, which facilitate intersectoral comparisons between different countries. The Russian industrial classification still differs from that used in the EU or other industrialized countries. The Russian Statistical Office (Goskomstat) still produces data on the basis of a 'classificator', which was in use at the time of the planned economy. This approach lacks focus and is not adjusted to the near reality of a market economy.

The most striking difference at present between Russian and international classifications can be observed in the branches 'light industry' and 'machine building'. Light industry includes only the three categories 'textiles' 'apparel' and 'shoes', whereas the term would include all other consumer items in the western classification. Common consumer durables such as refrigerators, vacuum cleaners, TV sets, or watches and clocks, which would be considered as part of the consumer goods industry in a western context, are classified under the branch 'machine building' in Russia. Here, 'machine building' includes categories such as passenger cars, trucks, buses and tractors, cameras, sewing machines, which would represent separate branches in western European countries. But even in other areas such as food and medical equipment significant differences prevail.

Chapter 8 has reviewed the major industrial branches in Russia. To allow comparison, major industries were regrouped according to western standards. The Russian 'machine building' branch was subdivided into major categories on the basis of internationally familiar divisions: machine tools, automobiles (including trucks and buses), electrical and electronic goods (including household appliances). Chapter 14.3 contains sector targets on the basis of the NACE Rev.1 classification. In Chapter 13, industrial statistics are derived from OECD publications, which are based on the harmonized ISIC classification.

4.1 Classification of Russian industries[4]

I. Electric power industry
II. Fuel industry (oil, gas, coal)

III. Ferrous industry (iron, iron ore, steel)
IV. Nonferrous industry (including precious metals)
V. Chemical and petrochemical industry
VI. Industrial machinery and metal cutting (including defence sector and production of consumer durables such as passenger cars, trucks, combines, refrigerators, TV sets, cameras, etc.)
VII. Wood processing, pulp and paper industry (including forestry)
VIII. Building materials industry
IX. Glass and porcelain industry
X. Light industry (textiles, clothing, leather, furs and footwear)
XI. Food industry (including meat, dairy)
XII. Fertilizer industry
XIII. Pharmaceutical industry
XIV. Medical equipment industry
XV. Printing industry
XVI. Other industries

4.2 International Standard Industrial Classification (ISIC)

Major Division 1: Agriculture, Hunting, Forestry and Fishing
Major Division 2: Mining and Quarrying (including coal, crude petroleum and natural gas production)
Major Division 3: Manufacturing
- Division 31: Manufacture of food, beverages and tobacco
- Division 32: Textile, wearing apparel, and leather industries (including furs, footwear)
- Division 33: Manufacture of wood and wood products, including furniture
- Division 34: Manufacture of paper and paper products; printing and publishing
- Division 35: Manufacture of chemicals and chemical products, petroleum, coal, rubber and plastic products
- Division 36: Manufacture of nonmetallic mineral products, except products of petroleum and coal
- Division 37: Basic metal industries
- Division 38: Manufacture of fabricated metal products, machinery and equipment (including electrical appliances, shipbuilding, motor vehicles and other transport equipment, scientific and measuring equipment, photographic and optical goods, watches and clocks)
- Division 39: Other manufacturing industries (including jewellery, musical instruments, sports goods)

Major Division 4: Electricity, Gas and Water
Major Division 5: Construction
Major Division 6: Wholesale and Retail Trade and Restaurants and Hotels
Major Division 7: Transport, Storage and Communication
Major Division 8: Financing, Insurance, Real Estate and Business Services
Major Division 9: Community, Social and Personal Services

4.3 European Standard Classification NACE Rev. 1

A Agriculture, Hunting and Forestry
B Fishing
C Mining and Quarrying

- D Manufacturing
  - D1 Food products, beverages and tobacco
  - D2 Textiles and textile products (apparel)
  - D3 Leather and leather products
  - D4 Wood products (excluding furniture)
  - D5 Pulp and paper products, publishing and printing
  - D6 Refined petroleum and nuclear fuel
  - D7 Chemicals and man-made fibres (including fertilizers, pesticides, paints, varnishes, glues, print colours)
  - D8 Rubber and plastics (including tubes, packaging materials, floorings, doors, window frames, sanitary wares)
  - D9 Nonmetallic mineral products (including ceramics, glass, tiles, construction materials)
  - D10 Basic metals and fabricated metal products (including iron and steel products, noniron metals, tools, cutlery, locks, tanks, containers, boilers)
  - D11 Machinery and equipment
  - D12 Electrical and optical equipment (including office and telecommunications equipment, cables, medical equipment and instruments, photographic equipment, watches)
  - D13 Transport equipment
  - D14 Manufacturing not elsewhere classified (including furniture, toys, sports goods, musical and writing instruments, jewellery, recycling)
- E Electricity, Gas and Water Supply
- F Construction
- G Wholesaling and Retailing
- H Hotels and Restaurants
- I Transport, Storage and Communication
- J Financial Intermediaries
- K Real Estate, Renting and Business Activities
- L Public Administration and Defence, Social Security (including postal and express services, travel agencies, forwarding and taxi services)
- M Education
- N Health and Social Work
- O Other Community, Social and Personal Services Activities (including trade unions, political organizations).

Notes

1. See UNIDO, *Industrial Development Report 1997*.
2. See IMF, *Balance of Payments Manual*, fifth edition (1993) and OECD, *Benchmark Definition of FDI*, third edition (1996).
3. See chapter 7.5.4.
4. Goskomstat, *Handbook of Statistical Definitions and Methodologies*, 1996.

Bibliography and Selected Reading

1 Books and studies

Adams, C. *et al.*, *Harenberg Länderlexikon 1994–1997*, Dortmund.
Albertini, J.-M., *L'Economie en 200 schémas* [The economy in 200 charts], Paris, 1994.
Archibugi, D. *et al.*, *Economia globale e innovazione – la sfida dell'industria italiana* [Global economy and innovation – the challenge for Italian industry], Rome, 1997.
Astapovich, A., *Foreign Investment in Russia. Salient Features and Trends*, Moscow, 1995.
Azoev, G. L., *Konkurentsyia: analiz, strategiya i praktika* [Competition: analysis, strategy and practice], Moscow, 1996.
Baratta, M., *Der Fischer Weltalmanach* [World Almanach], Frankfurt a. M, 1996, 1997.
Baring, A., *Scheitert Deutschland? Abschied von unseren Wunschwelten* [Will Germany fail? Farewell to wishful thinking], Stuttgart, 1997.
Barker, T. and V. Brailovski, *Oil or Industry? Energy, Industrialisation, and Economic Policy in Canada, Mexico, the Netherlands, Norway and the United Kingdom*, London, 1991.
Bialès, M. *et al.*, *Notions fondamentales d'économie* [Fundamentals of economics}, Paris, 1998.
Bogomolov, O. T., *Reformy v zerkale mezhdunarodnykh sravenenij* [Russian reforms in an international context], Moscow, 1998.
Boguslavski, M. M., *Inostrannyie investitsi: pravovoye regulirovanyie* [Foreign investment: legislation], Moscow, 1996.
Bonder, M., *Wem gehört was in Europa? Die 100 größten Konzerne* [Who owns what in Europe? Profiles of the 100 largest corporations], Düsseldorf, 1998.
Brahm, L., *China as No. 1*, Singapore, 1996.
Brahm, L., *Red Capital. Hong Kong 1997. China Money Takes Center Stage*, Hong Kong, 1997.
Buckley, P. J. and J. Casson, *The Future of the Multinational Enterprise*, London, 1976.
Buckley, P. J. and J. Casson, *The Economic Theory of the Multinational Enterprise*, London, 1985.
Bunkina, M. K., *Nazionalnaya ekonomika* [National economics], Moscow, 1997.
Byars, L., *Strategic Management: Planning and Implementation*, New York, 1987.
Cadot, O. *et al.*, *European Casebook on Industrial and Trade Policy*, London, 1996.
Campbell, A. *et al.*, *Sinergia estrategica* [Strategic synergies], Bilbao, 1994.
Capul, J.-Y., *Les stratégies d'entreprises* [Enterprise strategy], Paris, 1996.
Chan, S. *et al.*, *Foreign Investment in a Changing Global Political Economy*, New York, 1995.
Colombo, D., *El Nafta – en el marco del desafio americano al mercado unico* [NAFTA – against the background of the American challenge toward a single market], Madrid, 1995.
Cragg, C., *The New Maharajas. The Commercial Princes of India, Pakistan and Bangladesh*, London, 1997.
De Mooji, M., *Global Marketing and Advertising – Understanding Cultural Paradoxes*, California, 1998.

Dicken, M., *Global Shift. The Internationalization of Economic Activity*, New York, 1992.
Dickson, T., *Mastering Finance*, London, 1998.
Dolgopiatova, T. *et al.*, *Maly biznes v Rossii* [Small business in Russia], Moscow, 1998.
Droege, W. *et al.*, *Strategie für Investitionsgütermärkte* [Strategies for capital goods industries], Landsberg/Lech, 1993.
Dunning, J. H., *International Production and the Multinational Enterprise*, London, 1981.
Dunning, J. H., *Multinational Enterprises and the Global Economy*, London, 1992.
Dunning, J. H., 'International Investment Pattern', *in* Oxelheim, L., *The Global Race for FDI*, Berlin-Heidelberg, 1993.
Dunning, J. H. and R. Narula (eds.), *Foreign Direct Investment and Governments. Catalysts for Economic Restructuring*, London, 1996.
Duran, J., *Multinacionales espanolas. Vol. I. Algunos casos relevantes* [Spanish multinationals. Vol. I. Selected case studies], Madrid, 1996.
Economist Intelligence Unit. *Country Reports. Brazil, China, India, Mexico, Russia*, London, 1996, 1997.
Ehrmann, H., *Planung. Kompendium der praktischen Betriebswirtschaft* [Planning guide for practitioners], Ludwigshafen, 1995.
Ernst and Young Vneshconsult, *Sostablenyie bisnes-plana* [Preparation of business plans], Moscow, 1995.
Fischer, P., *Enterprise Survey Evaluation and Conclusions for the Strategic Orientations and Launch of an International Consultancy Agency*, MESI internal report, Moscow, 1996.
Fischer, P., *Optimizing Russian Statistics during Transition 1993–1997 – Strategic Orientations for the Russian Government and Statistical Services*, Eurostat internal report, Luxembourg, 1994.
Fischer, P., *System Advice for Russian Statistics, 1994–1995. Proposal for the Goskomstat of the Russian Federation. Strategic Publications, Public Relations*. Eurostat internal report, Luxembourg, 1994.
Foglio, A., *Marketing strategico e competitivo. Le strategie vincenti dell'impresa* [Strategic and competitive marketing. Winning corporate strategies], Milan, 1995.
Fontanel, J., *La conversion économique du secteur militaire* [Conversion of the military sector], Paris, 1994.
Frankfurter Institut, *Schlüsselfrage Innovationsfähigkeit* [Innovative capability as a key issue], Bad Homburg, 1997.
Gamblin, A. *et al.*, *Images économiques du monde 2000* [World economic trends 2000], Paris, 1999.
Garvin, A. P. and H. Bermont, *How to Win with Information or Lose without it*, Washington D. C., 1983.
Gausemeier, J. *et al.*, *Szenario-Management: planen und führen mit Szenarien* [Scenario management: planning and managing with scenarios], Munich, 1996.
Geiss, I., *Europa – Vielfalt und Einheit* [Europe – diversity and unity], Mannheim, 1993.
Glasyev, S., *Genozid: Rossiya i novi mirovoi pariadox* [Genocide: Russia and the new world order], Moscow, 1997.
Gluschtschenko, E. V. *et al.*, *Ocnobyi predmrinimatelstava* [Basics of entrepreneurship], Moscow, 1996.
Golubovich, V. *et al.*, *Ekonomitcheskaya istoria zarubezhnykh stran* [Economic history of foreign countries], Minsk, 1998.
Gorbanyov, V. A., *Ekonomitscheskaya y sozialnaya geografiya Rossiyi y stran SNG* [Economic and social geography of Russia and CIS countries], Moscow, 1996.
Graham, E. M., 'Transatlantic Investment by Multinational Firms: A Rivalistic Phenomenon', *Journal of Post Keynesian Economics*, 1978.

Grewal, S. S., *The Thinking Investor*, New Delhi, 1995.
Groeger, H. *et al.*, *Standort Ausland. Ein Arbeitshandbuch für das international planende Unternehmen* [Foreign locations. A guide book for internationally active corporations], Stuttgart, 1987.
Große-Oetringhaus, W., *Strategische Identität – Orientierung im Wandel* [Strategic identity – changing orientations], Berlin, 1996.
Guerrero, D., *Competitividad: teoria y politica* [Competitiveness: Theory and politics], Barcelona, 1995.
Gouping, G., *International Economic and Technological Cooperation*, Wuhan, 1995.
Gusakov, N. *et al.*, *Natzionalnye interesy i vneshneekonomitcheskaya bezopasnost Rossii* [Russia's national interests and external economic security], Moscow, 1998.
Hauchler, I., *Globale Trends* [Global trends], Bonn, 1996, 1997.
Heribert, D., *Die Asienkrise* [The Asian crisis], Marburg, 1998.
Hickson, D. J. and D. S. Pugh, *Management Worldwide. The Impact of Societal Culture on Organizations around the Globe*, London, 1995.
Hinterhuber, H., *Strategische Unternehmensführung* [Strategic management], Berlin, 1977.
Hornero, A. C., *Integración economica y regionalismo* [Economic integration and regionalism], Madrid, 1994.
Horst, T., 'The Industrial Composition of US Exports and Subsidiary Sales to the Canadian Market', *American Economic Review*, 1972.
Hymer, S. H., *The International Operations of National Firms: A Study of Direct Investment*, Ph.D. thesis, Massachusetts Institute of Technology, Massachusetts, 1976.
Idrisov, A. B. *et al.*, *Strategicheskoye planirovaniye i analiz efektivnosti investitsi* [Strategic planning and analysis of investment], Moscow, 1997.
Johnson, Ch. and S. Briscoe, *Measuring the Economy. A Guide to Understanding Official Statistics*, London, 1995.
Johnson, G. and K. Scholes, *Exploring Corporate Strategy*, Hertfordshire, 1993.
Kimura, Y., 'Firm-specific Strategic Advantages and Foreign Direct Investment Behavior of Firms', *Journal of International Business Studies*, 1989.
Kindleberger, C. P., *American Business Abroad*, New Haven, 1969.
Kirchbaum, J., *Made in Germany, an Overview of 100 Market Leaders*, Cologne, 1997.
Kireyev, A., *Mezhdunarodnaya ekonomika* [International economics], Moscow, 1997.
Knickerbocker, F. T., *Oligopolistic Reaction and the Multinational Enterprise*, Cambridge (USA), 1973.
Kojima, K., *Direct Foreign Investment: A Japanese Model of Multinational Business Operations*, London, 1978.
Kojima, K. and T. Ozawa, 'Micro- and Macro-economic Models of Direct Foreign Investment: Toward a Synthesis', *Hitotsubashi Journal of Economics*, 1984.
Kotler, Ph., *Marketing Management*, New Jersey, 1994.
Kotler, Ph. *et al.*, *The Marketing of Nations*, New York, 1997.
Kryzdal, B. *et al.*, *Mexico – Business Opportunities and Legal Framework*, Mexico City, 1995.
Kumar, N., *Multinational Enterprises in India: Distribution, Characteristics and Performance*, London, 1990.
Lal, D., *India in the World Economy*, New Delhi, 1999.
Lall, S., *Monopolistic Advantages and Foreign Involvement by US Manufacturing Industry*, Oxford Economic Papers, Oxford, 1980.
Lapidus, G. W., *The New Russia. Troubled Transformation*, Boulder, 1995.
Lasserre, Ph. *et al.*, *Business Strategy and Management. Text and Cases for Managers in Asia*, Singapore, 1996.

Li, S. *et al.*, *Sun Wu's Art of War and the Art of Business Management*, Hong Kong, 1994.
Lutz, V., *Horizontale strategische Allianzen* [Horizontal strategic alliances], Hamburg, 1993.
Maisch, Ch., *Beurteiungskriterien für Auslandsinvestitionen deutscher Unternehmen* [Evaluation criteria for foreign investment operations of German companies], Frankfurt a. M., 1996.
Manual for Foreign Collaboration and Investment in India, Nabhi, New Delhi, 1995, 1996.
Meng, T. *et al.*, *Business Opportunities in India*, Singapore, 1996.
Meng, T. *et al.*, *Business Opportunities in the Yangtse River Delta*, Singapore 1996.
Morozova, T. G. *et al.*, *Regionalnaya ekonomika* [Regional economics], Moscow, 1995.
Mort, D., *European Market Information. A Handbook for Managers*, London, 1992.
Mucchielli, R., *Les firmes multinationales: mutations et nouvelles perspectives* [Multinational enterprises: changes and prospects], Paris, 1985.
Munro, D., *Oxford Dictionary of the World*, Oxford, 1996.
Müssig, K., *Die großen 500 auf einen Blick* [Germany's Top 500 at a Glance], Berlin, 1997.
Narula, R., *Multinational Investment and Economic Structure: Globalization and Competitiveness*, Routledge Studies in International Business and the World, 1996.
Nicholas, R. L., *China in the World Economy*, Washington D.C., 1994.
Ninni, A., *et al.*, *La politica industriale – teorie e esperienze* [Industrial policy – theories and experiences], Rome, 1997.
Pauli, K. S., *Leitfaden für die Pressearbeit* [Guidelines for press relations], Munich, 1993.
Peyrard, J., *Gestion financière internationale* [International financial management], Paris, 1999.
Pikulnik, A. V., *Sistema Gosudarstvennova upravleniya* [System of government management], Moscow, 1997.
Piramal, G., *Business Maharajas*, New Delhi, 1996.
Porter, M., *The Competitive Advantage of Nations*, London, 1990.
Quelennec, M., *L'industrie en France* [French industry], Paris, 1997.
Radugin, A. A., *Kulturologyia* [Culturology], Moscow, 1996.
Ramstetter, E., *Export Propensities and Foreign Ownership Shares in Southeast Asian Manufacturing*, Osaka, 1997.
Rao, M. B., *Joint Ventures. International Business with Developing Countries*, New Delhi, 1999.
Robson, W., *Strategic Management and Information Systems*, London, 1997.
Rota, F., *PR und Medienarbeit* [Public and media relations], Munich, 1990.
Rugman, A. M., *Inside the Multinationals, the Economics of Internal Markets*, London, 1981.
Sattler, R., *Unternehmerisch denken lernen. Das Denken in Strategie, Erfolg und Risiko* [Learn to think like an entrepreneur. Thinking in terms of strategy, success and risk], Munich, 1998.
Savona, P., *Geoeconomia – il dominio dello spazio economico* [Geoeconomy – The domination of economic space], Milan, 1995.
Schtscherbanin Y. A. *et al.*, *Mezhdunarodnyie ekonomitscheskyie otnoscheniya* [International economic relations], Moscow, 1997.
Shangquan, G., *New Progress in China's Economic Zones*, Beijing, 1997.
Simon, H., *Hidden Champions. Lessons from the World's Best Unknown Companies*, Boston, 1996.

Simons, J., *Industriepolitik* [Industrial policy], Stuttgart, 1996.
Smith, D., *Eurofutures – Five Scenarios for the Next Millenium*, Oxford, 1997.
Spiridonov, I. A., *Mezhdunarodnaya konkurrentsyia i Rossiya* [International competition and Russia], Moscow, 1997.
Spiridonov, I. A., *Mirovaya ekonomika* [World economics], Moscow, 1997.
Stehn, J., *Determinanten differenzierter Internationalisierungsstrategien* [Determining factors of differentiated internationalization strategies], Kiel, 1989.
Strohbach, J.-U., *Absatzmärkte in Rußland* [Sales prospects in Russia], Cologne, 1995.
Taggart, J. *et al.*, *The Essence of International Business*, New Delhi, 1995.
Tagliacarne, G., *Le piccole e medie imprese dell'industria alimentare italiana* [Small and medium-sized enterprises of the Italian food industry], Milan, 1997.
Tata Services, *Statistical Outline of India*, Mumbai, 1996, 1997, 1998.
Tearle, R., *Managing Transition*, Pretoria, 1992.
Tersen, D. *et al.*, *L'investissement international* [Foreign investment], Paris, 1996.
Turnheim, G., *Chaos Management*, Vienna, 1993.
Tytko, D., *Grundlagen der Projektfinanzierung* [Fundamentals of project finance], Stuttgart, 1998.
Utkin, E. A. and M. A. Eskindarov, *Finansovo-promyschlennye gruppi* [Financial–industrial groups], Moscow, 1998.
Vaitilingam, R., *Guide to Using Economics and Economic Indicators*, London, 1994.
Van Riel, C. B. M., *Principles of Corporate Communication*, Hemel Hempstead, 1995.
Vernon, R., 'International Investment and International Trade in the Product Cycle', *Quarterly Journal of Economics*, London, 1966.
Vernon, R., 'The Location of Economics Activity', in J. H. Dunning, *Economic Analysis and Multinational Enterprise*, London, 1974.
Wolf, J., *Marketing für den Mittlestand* [Marketing for medium-sized enterprises], Munich, 1994.
Yang, J., *Shanghai – Basic Facts 1997*, Shanghai, 1997.
Yergin, D. and Th. Gustafson, *Russia 2010*, New York, 1995.
Yudanov, A. Y., *Konkurrentsyia: teoriya i praktika* [Competition: Theory and practice], Moscow, 1998.
Zorkoczy, P. *et al.*, *Information Technology – An Introduction*, London, 1995.

2 Official publications

All India Association of Chambers of Commerce (ASSOCHAM), New Delhi:
International Workshop on Prospects of FDI in India, 29–30 August 1996, New Delhi, workshop papers.

Austrian Trade Commission, Beijing:
China Nachrichten, quarterly, several issues, 1996, 1997, 1998, 1999.

Bundestelle für Auslandsinformationen (BfAI), Cologne:
Länderreport China. Wirtschaftstrends zur Jahresmitte [Country report. China. Half-yearly economic trends], 1996, 1997, 1998.
Länderreport Indien. Wirtschaftstrends zur Jahresmitte [Country report. India. Half-yearly economic trends], 1996, 1997, 1998.
Länderreport Mexiko. Wirtschaftstrends zur Jahresmitte [Country report. Mexico. Half-yearly economic trends], 1996, 1997, 1998.
Länderreport Rußland. Wirtschaftstrends zur Jahresmitte [Country report. Russia. Half-yearly economic trends], 1996, 1997, 1998.

Mercosur – ein Markt mit Zukurnft [MERCOSUR, a market with future potential], 1995.

Bundesinstitut für ostwissenschaftliche und internationale Studien, Munich:
Zwischen Krise und Konsolidierung. Gefährdeter Systemwechsel im Osten Europas [Between crisis and consolidation. Endangered system change in Eastern Europe], 1995.

Central Statistical Office, New Delhi:
Yearbooks and various publications, 1997, 1998.

Centre d'études prospectives et d'informations internationales (CEPII), Paris:
Compétitivité des nations [Competitiveness of nations], 1998.

Confederation of Indian Industry (CII). New Delhi:
Handbook of Statistics, 1996, 1997, 1998.

Deutsche Industrie- und Handelstag (DIHT), Bonn:
Geschäftserfolg in China [Business success in China], 1994.

European Bank for Reconstruction and Development (EBRD), London:
Transition Report, 1995, 1996, 1997, 1998, 1999.

Eurostat, Luxembourg:
EU Direct Investment Yearbook, 1997.
Europe in Figures, 1995, 1996, 1997, 1998, 1999.
Statistical Yearbook, 1995, 1996, 1997, 1998, 1999.

Goskomstat, Moscow:
Ob investizi v ekonomiki rossiskoi federatsi [About investments in the Russian Federation], 1995, 1996, 1997.
Regioni rossyi [Russia's regions], 1997.
Russia in Figures, 1995, 1996, 1997, 1998, 1999.
Statistical Yearbook, 1995, 1996, 1997, 1998, 1999.

Indira Gandhi Institute of Development Research, Mumbai:
India Development Report 1997, 1998, 1999–2000.

Instituto Nacional de Estadistica, Geografia e Informatica (INEGI), Mexico City:
Yearbooks and various publications, 1997, 1998.

Institut der deutschen Wirtschaft (IdW), Cologne:
Zahlen zur wirtschaftlichen Entwicklung der Bundesrepublik Deutschland [Data on the economic development of the Federal Republic of Germany], 1996, 1997, 1998.

Institut für Wirtschaftsforschung (IFO), Munich:
IFO-Konjunkturbericht [IFO economic trend report], several issues.
IFO Schnellbericht [IFO snap report], several issues.

Institut für Weltwirtschaft Kiel (IfW Kiel), Kiel:
Die wirtschaftliche Lage Rußlands – Investitionsschwäche verhindert Wachstum [Russia's economic situation – low investments hinder growth], discussion paper, 1996.

Institut national de la statistique et des études économiques (INSEE), Paris:
Tableaux de l'économie française [Overview of the French economy], 1995, 1996, 1997, 1998.

International Monetary Fund (IMF), Washington D.C.:

Annual Report, World Economic Outlook, 1996, 1997, 1998, 1999.
'An Overview of Transition: A Decade of Achievements and Challenges', *Finance & Development*, June 1999.
Balance of Payments Manual, 1993.
Directions of Trade Statistics, 1998.
IMF's Response to the Asian crisis, 1998.

Instituto Nazionale della Statistica, Rome:
L'Italia in cifre [Italy in figures], 1996, 1997, 1998.
Profile of Italy, 1997, 1998.
Statistical Yearbook, 1996, 1997, 1998.

Japan External Trade Organization (JETRO), Tokyo
China Newsletter, several issues.

Ministry of Foreign Trade and Economic Cooperation (MOFTEC), Beijing:
China Economic News, several issues.

Mosvneshinform, Moscow:
Bisnes-putevoditel po Rossiyi [Business guide book for Russia], 1997.

Organisation of Economic Co-operation and Development (OECD), Paris:
Benchmark Definition of Foreign Investment, 1995.
Economic Surveys: *France, Germany, Italy*, 1998; *Russian Federation*, 1997.
Industrial Competitiveness, 1996, 1998.
Industrial Competitiveness in the Knowledge–based Economy – The New Role of Governments, conference proceedings, 1997.
Industrial Structure Statistics, 1997.
International Direct Investment Statistics Yearbook, 1996, 1997.
Main Economic Indicators, monthly, several issues, 1997, 1998.
OECD in Figures, 1997, 1998.
Open Markets Matter. The Benefits of Trade and Investment Liberalization, 1998.
Progress Report by the MAI Negotiating Group, 1996.
Regional Development and Structural Policy in Mexico, 1997.
Small Firms as Foreign Investors. Case Studies from Transition Economies, 1996.

State Statistical Bureau of the People's Republic of China, Beijing:
China Statistical Yearbook, 1996, 1997, 1998.
A Statistical Survey of China, 1998, 1999.

Statistisches Bundesamt. Wiesbaden:
Statistisches Jahrbuch [Statistical yearbook], 1996, 1997, 1998, 1999.

Stiftung Entwicklung und Frieden, Bonn:
Globale Trends, 1996, 1997, 1998.

United Nations Commission for Europe, Geneva:
Statistical Survey of Recent Trends in Foreign Investment in East European Countries, 1995.

United Nations Conference for Trade and Development (UNCTAD), Geneva:
World Investment Report, 1995, 1996, 1997, 1998, 1999.

United Nations Industrial Development Organization (UNIDO), Vienna:
Industrial Statistical Yearbook, 1996, 1997.
Industrial Development Report, 1997, 1998, 1999.
UNIDO Manual for the Preparation of Industrial Feasibility Studies, 1995.

World Bank, Washington D.C.:
Between State and Market. Mass Privatization in Transition Economies, 1997.
Clear Water, Blue Skies. China's Environment in the New Century, 1997.
Foreign Direct Investment, [International Finance Corporation], 1997.
Global Development Finance, 1997.
Mobilizing Domestic Capital Markets for Infrastructure Financing, 1997.
World Development Report, 1995, 1996, 1997, 1998, 1999.

World Trade Organization (WTO), Geneva:
Annual Report, 1997, 1998.
Competition-related Provisions in Existing WTO Agreements, 1997.
International Trade Statistics, 1997, 1998.
The Results of the Uruguay Round of Multilateral Trade Negotiations: The Legal Texts, 1995.
Trading into the Future, 1995.

Index